Professional JSP Site Design

Kevin Duffey

Vikram Goyal

Richard Huss

Ted Husted

Meeraj Moidoo Kunnumpurath

Lance Lavandowska

Sathya Narayana Panduranga

Krishnaraj Perrumal

Joe Walnes

Wrox Press Ltd. ®

Professional JSP Site Design

Latest Reprint March 2002

Published by Wrox Press Ltd,
Arden House, 1102 Warwick Road, Acocks Green,
Birmingham, B27 6BH, UK
Printed in the United States

ISBN 1-861005-51-2

Trademark Acknowledgements

Credits

Authors
Kevin Duffey
Vikram Goyal
Richard Huss
Ted Husted
Meeraj Moidoo Kunnumpurath
Lance Lavandowska
Sathya Narayana Panduranga
Krishnaraj Perrumal
Joe Walnes

Technical Reviewers
Kapil Apshankkar
Steve Baker
Michael Boerner
Richard Bonneau
Brian Campbell
Jeff Cunningham
Sam Dalton
Justin Foley
Rahul Kr. Gupta
Phil Hanna
Romin Irani
Dan Jepp
Sachin Khanna
Stephen Kierstead
Lance Lavandowska
Stephen LeClair
Tony Loton
Phil Powers-DeGeorge
David Scultz
Paul Wilt

Proof Reader
Fiver Locker

Category Manager
Emma Batch

Technical Architect
Richard Huss

Technical Editors
Matthew Moodie
Daniel Richardson

Author Agent
Nicola Phillips

Project Manager
Laura Hall

Production Manager
Liz Toy

Production Coordinator
Mark Burdett

Production Assistant
Abbie Forletta
Emma Eato
Natalie O'Donnell

Index
Adrian Axinte

Cover
Dawn Chellingworth
Chris Morris

About the Authors

Kevin Duffey

Kevin started with Java three years ago in a small startup company in the San Francisco Bay Area. His work involved web application development and soon shifted to the J2EE technology as it became available. At the time the company application only used Java in the web tier, so Kevin focused on mastering servlets and JavaServer Pages. While converting the site to JSP, Kevin discovered that MVC and Model 2 development was superior to his present undertaking and soon started on a path to convert the entire site in that direction, using his own MVC framework, Theseus. In his spare time, Kevin continues to further his knowledge of the Java language by reading books like this one. He also enjoys every aspect of music including writing music with his computer music workstation.

Kevin would like to thank his wife, Gerlina, and his two children, Kayla and Andrew for being so patient and understanding while he attempts to further his career. Without their love and support Kevin wouldn't have been able to accomplish what he has. He would also like to acknowledge his father, James, for continuing guidance to do the right thing.

Kevin contributed Chapter 18 to this book.

Vikram Goyal

I have over 5 years of experience in Java, having worked for Ernst and Young LLP, Citibank and Australia's Health Insurance Commission. While programming remains my passion, I love to play PC games (AOE, Close Combat, World Cup 98) and read spy novels (Fredrick Forsyth is the best!!). Some day, I would like to develop a Java-based commercial game and write a book about it!!

My contribution in this book is dedicated to my late father Mr. Navin Chand Goyal, who loved books, and my mother Mrs. Saroj Rani Goyal. The two of you helped me become what I am today. Many heartfelt thanks.

Vikram contributed additional material to Chapter 18.

Richard Huss

Richard Huss is a Technical Architect in the Java team at Wrox Press, creating titles focusing on J2EE web tier technologies, and can never resist downloading new and interesting open source Java stuff. He lives in Solihull, England with his wife Lesley and an excessive number of books. In his spare moments he works as a volunteer on the Talyllyn Railway (http://www.talyllyn.co.uk/), sings in the choir of St. Nicholas Church, Elmdon, and enjoys listening to Elgar, Vaughan Williams, and Anglican chant.

With grateful thanks "for our creation, preservation, and all the blessings of this life;
but above all for thine inestimable love in the redemption of the world by our Lord Jesus Christ;
for the means of grace, and for the hope of glory."

Richard contributed Chapters 3 and 4 to this book.

Ted Husted

Ted Husted is an independent Java developer building web applications with several Jakarta technologies, including Struts, Taglibs, Tomcat, and Lucene. He has been developing business applications since 1983 and building Internet applications since 1995. Ted is an active Committer to the Struts Framework, and a member of the Jakarta Project Management Committee. He also helps out as webmaster for WXXI.ORG, an award-winning web site for his local public broadcating station. Ted lives near the Erie Canal in Western New York, with his wife, two children, an aging cat, and four computers.

Ted contributed Chapters 12-14 to this book.

Meeraj Moidoo Kunnumpurath

Praying for all the suffering innocents in the world. May Allah bless us all!

Thanks Waheeda, for being what you are and showing me the meaning of this life.

Meeraj contributed Chapters 7-9 and 15-17 to this book.

Lance Lavandowska

Lance Lavandowska is a co-founder of Aptura Technologies LLC and has been working with Servlets and JavaServer Pages since 1998. In his spare time he does more of the same. Lance has served as a technical reviewer on various other books, and has contributed to several Apache Jakarta projects and to the Castor project.

Lance would like to thank his family and his co-founders for supporting him while working on this book. Lance would also like to thank the fine people at Wrox for this opportunity. You can visit Lance at http://www.brainopolis.com.

Lance contributed Chapter 6 to this book.

Sathya Narayana Panduranga

I am a Software Design Engineer living in Bangalore, the silicon valley of India. My areas of interest and experience include distributed and component-based application architectures, object-oriented analysis and design, voice over IP, and convergence platforms. I frequently write articles for Codeguru, a web site for developers.

I would like to dedicate my work in this book to Suresh Narasimha, Ravi B Ramarao and Santosh Deshpande for giving me their gift of friendship.

Sathya contributed Chapters 1 and 2 to this book.

Krishnaraj Perrumal

I'm a Sun Certified Java Programmer, founder and director of Adarsh Softech at Salem, a consultancy firm providing web solutions to businesses. I also regularly give presentations on Java and XML, and contribute to magazines. I love to spend most of my time and earnings on books. I've been developing software systems using C, C++, Delphi, and Java for the past 15 years.

I'd like to thank the Wrox team for giving me an opportunity, and to all who have made my work look better. The support and love of my family and friends, especially my son Adarsh and my nieces Sruthi, Preethi, and Vaish keeps me going.

Sathya contributed Chapters 10 and 11 to this book.

Joe Walnes

Joe Walnes currently works at Web-Imps in London, where he floats around with the intention of doing whatever it takes to produce high quality software on low budgets. He is experienced with many forms of application development ranging from small devices to large enterprise systems using a variety of technologies. He takes pride in designing and implementing simple solutions to complicated problems and mentoring others in the approaches. More recently, Joe has become an advocate of J2EE and eXtreme Programming (XP). He is also one of the core developers for the OpenSymphony project.

To mom and dad for doing a great job. Cheers to Dan North for always inspiring me to think differently and to Jaimie for her devoted love, support, and cuteness.

Joe contributed Chapter 5 to this book.

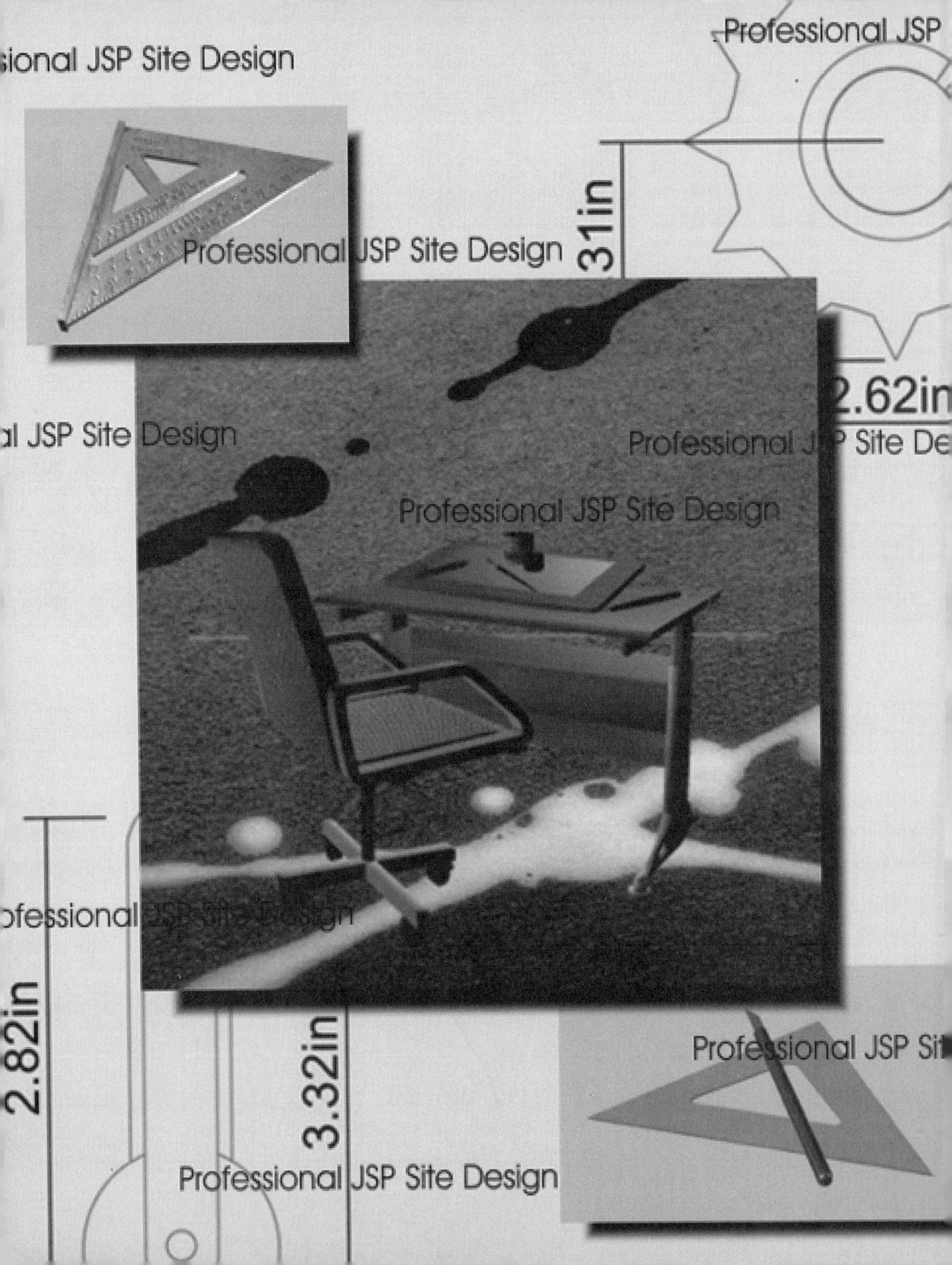

Professional JSP
sional JSP Site Design
Professional JSP Site Design
31in
2.62in
al JSP Site Design
Professional JSP Site De
Professional JSP Site Design
ofessional JSP Site Design
2.82in
3.32in
Professional JSP Sit
Professional JSP Site Design

Table of Contents

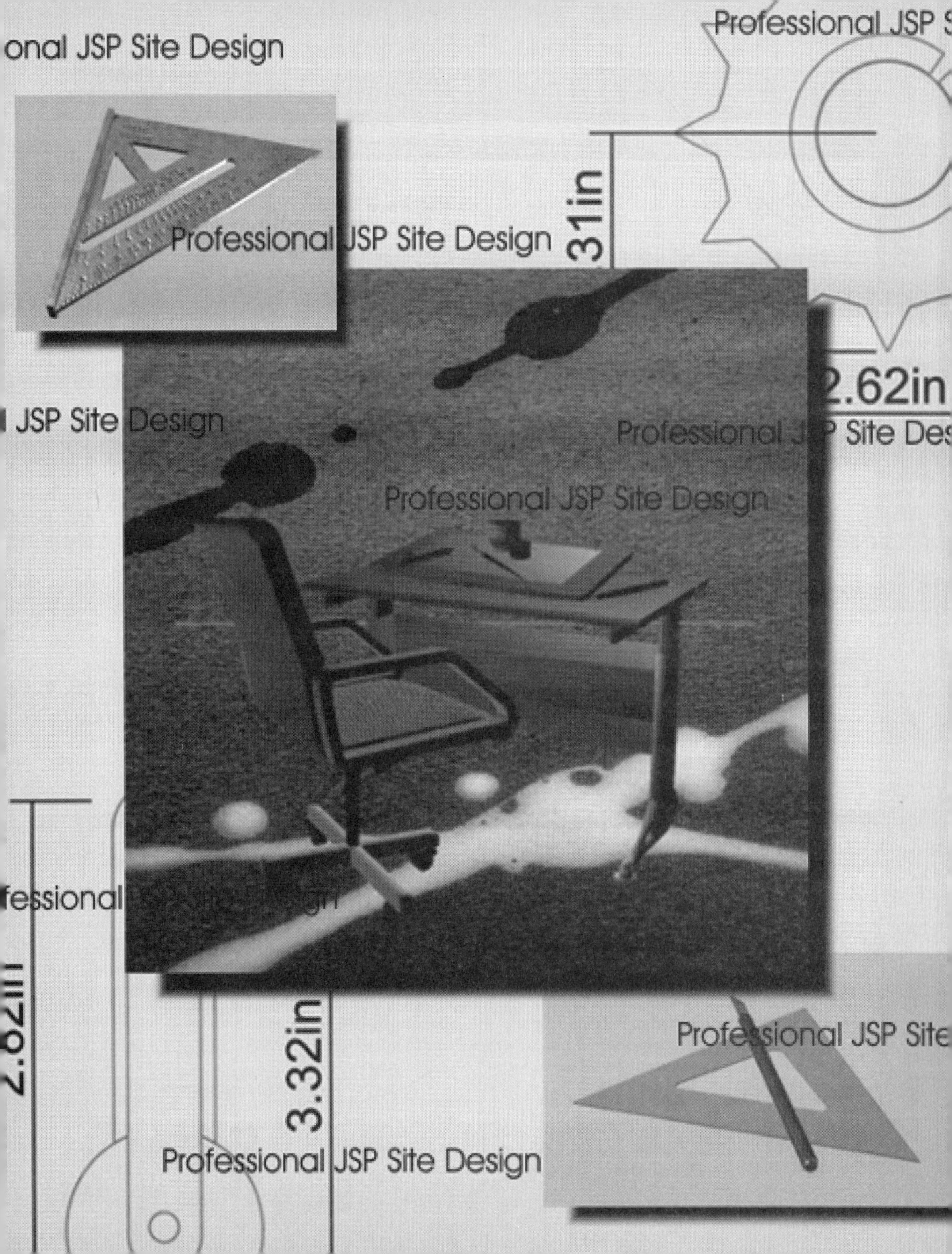
Professional JSP Site Design
31in
Professional JSP Site Design
2.62in
Professional JSP Site Design
3.32in
Professional JSP Site Design

Introduction

Welcome

Welcome to *Professional JSP Site Design*. This book is designed to show you how the **JavaServer Pages** (**JSP**) and **Java Servlet** technologies, together with a wide variety of open source products, can be applied in practice to build powerful, dynamic web sites that provide commonly required functionality such as content management, database integration, and personalization.

This book, unlike many you'll find, is *not* designed to help you learn these technologies. Rather, it helps you to build on your existing knowledge to create more complex, more attractive, and more realistic sites.

JSP pages and servlets together provide the ability to construct an interactive web interface to enterprise-level processing and data, whether within a standalone web container or as part of a full-blown J2EE application. Web programming is in many ways a tricky matter. The HTTP protocol and the HTML markup language weren't really designed with an eye to the uses to which they would be put. As a result, many features that would be straightforward to code in a desktop application can cause real headaches.

In this book we will take you through many of these issues and common applications, looking at how we can best work around the limitations of the platform and deliver users the web site features they want.

Who is this Book For?

This book is aimed at developers who are familiar with the **JavaServer Pages** and **Java Servlet** technologies. We will be using the latest versions of these specifications – versions 1.2 and 2.3 respectively – which have just been finalized by the **Java Community Process** (http://java.sun.com/aboutJava/communityprocess/). It is assumed that readers are familiar at least with JSP 1.1 and Servlet 2.2, along with the Java language and HTML.

The book does not claim to be exhaustive in all areas, particularly in relation to other Java APIs such as Enterprise JavaBeans, JavaMail, and JMS. *Professional Java Server Programming J2EE 1.3 Edition* from *Wrox Press (ISBN 1-861005-37-7)* is an excellent introduction to the whole Java 2 Enterprise Edition platform.

What's Covered in this Book

This book has the following structure:

- We start with an overview of web programming with JSP and servlets, and the various forms of components that can be used to compartmentalize our application.
- In the second chapter we look at the increasingly popular **Struts Framework**, which will be used extensively in the remainder of the book.
- Chapters 3-7 discuss a range of basic techniques for handling the client-side of web site design and creating individual pages. We'll look in turn at **HTTP** and **browser compatibility**, the best ways of tackling the creation of dynamic sites that use **frames** and **popup windows**, **page layout** and decoration, the dynamic construction of **site navigation**, and **error handling** and **logging**.
- An attractive site is one thing, but for any serious application you will need to integrate with the rest of your enterprise. In chapters 8 and 9 we examine techniques for connecting Java web applications to **relational databases**, and for integrating them as part of an overall **J2EE solution**.
- Next we return our attentions to the user by looking at questions of **security** and **user management**, followed by **visitor tracking** and **personalization**.
- Content is what your site's visitors are really after. Chapters 12-14 cover three related topics – **content management**, **indexing and searching**, and creating **portals** – as we develop a Struts-based news application.
- In today's world XML is everywhere, and will be increasingly prevalent as web services gain popularity. In Chapters 15-17 we look at the construction of a web application framework that uses XML document fragments rather than JavaBeans when passing data around, making it much easier to integrate with a web services back end.
- Finally, in Chapter 18 we consider the important topics of web application scalability, performance, and deployment.

What You Need to Use this Book

The code in this book has been tested with the Java 2 Platform, Standard Edition SDK (JDK 1.3.1) and the final release of Tomcat 4.0. JDK 1.3.1 can be obtained from http://java.sun.com/j2se/, and Tomcat from http://jakarta.apache.org/tomcat/. The documentation for Tomcat 4.0, covering basic installation, server configuration, and common administrative tasks, has improved beyond measure since the early beta releases and is your best source for Tomcat setup problems. See http://jakarta.apache.org/tomcat/tomcat-4.0-doc/ for details.

Database

Several of the chapters require access to a database. We have used MySQL, from http://www.mysql.com/ together with the MM.MySQL JDBC driver from http://mmmysql.sourceforge.net/. See Appendix B for more details. However, you should be able to adapt the examples to use any other JDBC-accessible database of your choice.

Struts

A substantial number of chapters leverage the Struts Framework. Struts is an open source project providing a solid basis for developing JSP and servlet-based web applications using the Model-View-Controller architecture. Struts can be downloaded from http://jakarta.apache.org/struts/.

EJB Container

For Chapter 9 you will also need an EJB container supporting 1.1 version of the EJB specification. We used the latest version of jBoss, from http://www.jboss.org/.

Additional Software

Finally, various chapters require additional pieces of software. These are identified in the individual chapters, and wherever possible we have included them in the code download for the book.

Conventions

To help you get the most from the text and keep track of what's happening, we've used a number of conventions throughout the book. For instance:

> **These boxes hold important, not-to-be forgotten information, which is directly relevant to the surrounding text.**

While this background style is used for asides to the current discussion.

As for styles in the text:

- When we introduce them, we **highlight** important words
- We show keyboard strokes like this: *Ctrl-A*
- We show filenames and code within the text like so: `findForward()`
- Text on user interfaces and URLs are shown as: Menu

We present code in three different ways. Definitions of methods and properties are shown as follows:

```
public ActionForward perform(ActionMapping mapping,
                             ActionForm form,
                             HttpServletRequest request,
                             HttpServletResponse response)
        throws IOException, ServletException
```

Example code is shown:

```
In our code examples, the code foreground style shows new, important,
    pertinent code
while code background shows code that is less important in the present
    context, or has been seen before.
```

Customer Support

We always value hearing from our readers, and we want to know what you think about this book: what you liked, what you didn't like, and what you think we can do better next time. You can send us your comments, either by returning the reply card in the back of the book, or by e-mail to feedback@wrox.com. Please be sure to mention the book title in your message.

How to Download the Sample Code for the Book

When you log on to the Wrox site, http://www.wrox.com/, simply locate the title through our search facility or by using one of the title lists. Click on Download in the Code column, or on Download Code on the book's detail page.

The files that are available for download from our site have been archived using WinZip. When you have saved the attachments to a folder on your hard-drive, you need to extract the files using a de-compression program such as WinZip or PKUnzip. When you extract the files, the code is usually extracted into chapter folders. When you start the extraction process, ensure your software (WinZip, PKUnzip, etc.) is set to extract to Use Folder Names.

Errata

We've made every effort to make sure that there are no errors in the text or in the code. However, no one is perfect and mistakes do occur. If you find an error in one of our books, like a spelling mistake or a faulty piece of code, we would be very grateful for feedback. By sending in errata you may save another reader hours of frustration, and of course, you will be helping us provide even higher quality information. Simply e-mail the information to support@wrox.com, your information will be checked and if correct, posted to the errata page for that title, or used in subsequent editions of the book.

To find errata on the web site, log on to http://www.wrox.com/, and simply locate the title through our advanced search or title list. Click on the Book Errata link, which is below the cover graphic on the book's detail page.

E-Mail Support

If you wish to directly query a problem in the book page with an expert who knows the book in detail then e-mail support@wrox.com, with the title of the book and the last four numbers of the ISBN in the subject field of the e-mail. A typical e-mail should include the following things:

- The **name**, **last four digits of the ISBN**, and **page number** of the problem in the Subject field
- Your **name**, **contact information**, and the **problem** in the body of the message

We **won't** send you junk mail. We need the details to save your time and ours. When you send an e-mail message, it will go through the following chain of support:

- Customer Support – Your message is delivered to our customer support staff, who are the first people to read it. They have files on most frequently asked questions and will answer anything general about the book or the web site immediately.
- Editorial – Deeper queries are forwarded to the technical editor responsible for that book. They have experience with the programming language or particular product, and are able to answer detailed technical questions on the subject. Once an issue has been resolved, the editor can post the errata to the web site.
- The Authors – Finally, in the unlikely event that the editor cannot answer your problem, he or she will forward the request to the author. We do try to protect the author from any distractions to their writing; however, we are quite happy to forward specific requests to them. All Wrox authors help with the support on their books. They will e-mail the customer and the editor with their response, and again all readers should benefit.

The Wrox support process can only offer support to issues that are directly pertinent to the content of our published title. Support for questions that fall outside the scope of normal book support, is provided via the community lists of our http://p2p.wrox.com/ forum.

p2p.wrox.com

For author and peer discussion join the P2P mailing lists. Our unique system provides **programmer to programmer™** contact on mailing lists, forums, and newsgroups, all **in addition** to our one-to-one e-mail support system. Be confident that your query is being examined by the many Wrox authors and other industry experts who are present on our mailing lists. At p2p.wrox.com you will find a number of different lists that will help you, not only while you read this book, but also as you develop your own applications.

To subscribe to a mailing list just follow these steps:

- Go to http://p2p.wrox.com/
- Choose the appropriate category from the left menu bar
- Click on the mailing list you wish to join
- Follow the instructions to subscribe and fill in your e-mail address and password
- Reply to the confirmation e-mail you receive
- Use the subscription manager to join more lists and set your e-mail preferences

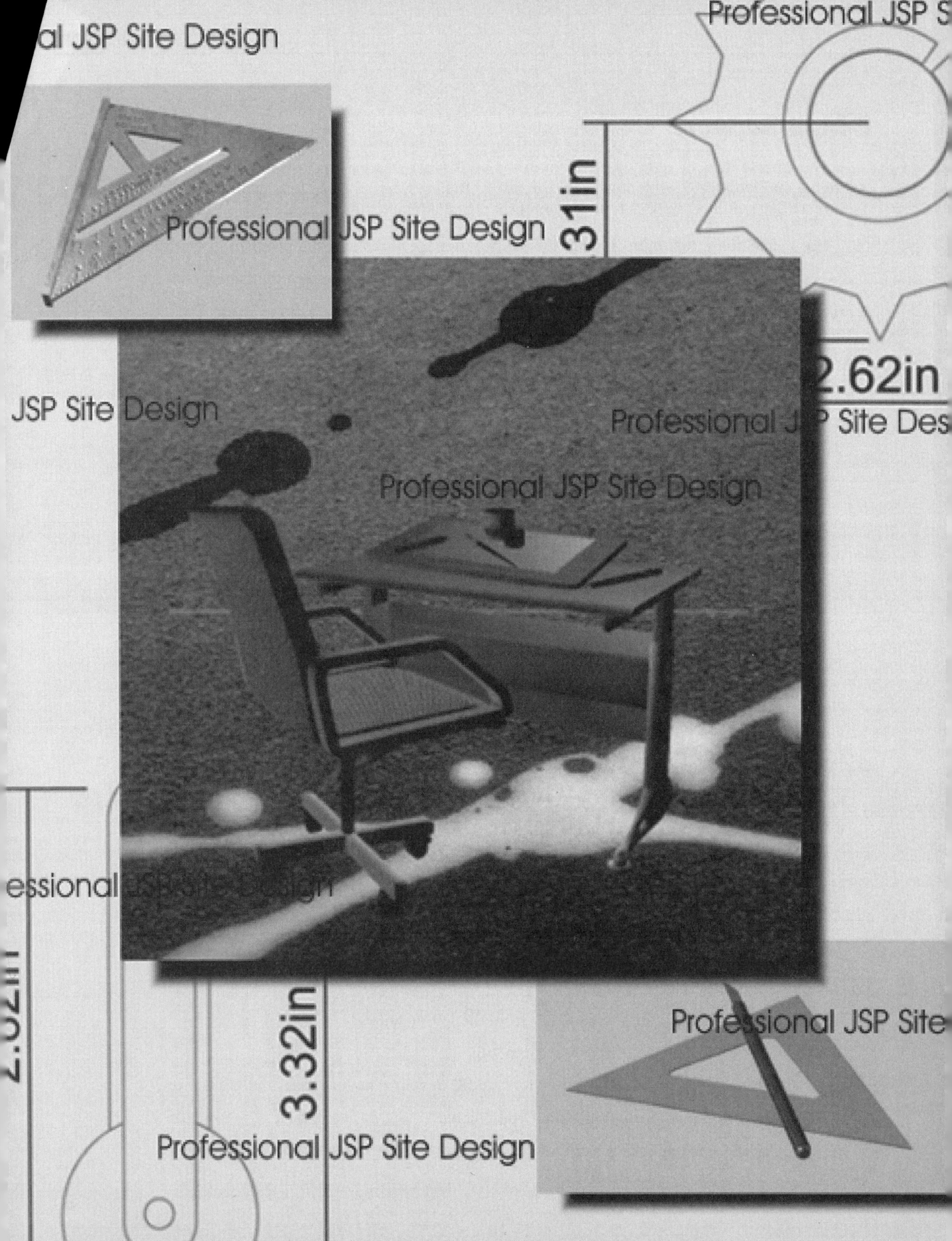

al JSP Site Design
Professional JSP S
31in
Professional JSP Site Design
.62in
JSP Site Design
Professional J
Site Des
Professional JSP Site Design
essional
3.32in
Professional JSP Site
Professional JSP Site Design

1

Component-Driven Web Programming

There are many stages in the development of a web application – from the initial concept, to design, to prototyping, to the actual coding, testing, and deployment. In this book we are going to concentrate on the **design** of these applications. This is a critical stage of the process, as a poor design can lead to problems that only show up when the application is deployed and it is too late to solve them. Alternatively, a good, well thought out design could highlight potential problems early in the process, and lead to the creation of applications that can be easily maintained and changed in the future.

When we are thinking about the design of an application there are two important types of specifications to keep in mind:

- The **functional** specification – what the software will do
- The **non-functional** specification – what qualities the software will possess

A developer comes up with a design by analyzing the different requirements that the customer puts forward, which can be very demanding in terms of both the functional and non-functional requirements. Most web applications have stringent requirements about things like availability, scalability, manageability, and high performance, since commercial web applications are expected to generate revenue through a large number of transactions.

A well-designed web application will be robust, reliable, and easily managed. The requirements of a web application often change and a successful design will allow many of these changes to be made quickly and easily.

In this chapter, we will discuss why it is important that web applications are well designed, and the problems that can arise if this is not the case. We will go on to understand how we can design applications, so that they work well. Specifically, we will look at:

- The problems that can arise if a web application is not well-designed and how it is very easy to create a poorly designed JSP web application
- How we can overcome some of the design problems by using object-orientated concepts, including the use of helper classes and JavaBeans
- The limitations of creating web applications using the object-orientated approach, and how the use of **components** overcomes many of these problems
- The use of components in the design and implementation of a web application, specifically the **Model-View-Controller** (**MVC**) framework
- How **refactoring** can be used to further improve web applications

Common Design Problems

There are three common design strategies: **structured**, **object-oriented**, and **component-based**. We'll begin by looking at some of the problems that can arise when a web application uses a structured design. Also, we will take a look at an example along the way.

Structured Development

Structured development involves functional decomposition of the software problem, and creating functions with the right parameters and return values. The requirements of an application are analyzed and its functionality is identified and modeled as functions, of which there can be many thousands in a single application. These functions can call each other without any defined boundaries, so it can be difficult to ensure that variables are not accessed and modified without other functions also attempting to gain access.

Writing a web application using JSP scriptlets is just like the above scenario. Try to write an application just by using JSP, without using any beans or custom tags. If the application is small, you will not have much of a problem, but if the application grows bigger you will definitely come across the problem mentioned above. This kind of code might satisfy the functional requirements but fails to take care of the non-functional requirements.

For example, it is common to see the data, business logic, and the user interface combined into one module of code in a small JSP application. In addition, the application generally contains the logic that controls the flow of the application. The following example illustrates the single page development approach:

```
<!--purchase.jsp  -->
<html>
  <head><title>Shopping Cart Example</title></head>
```

```
<body>
  <font size="5" color="blue">
  <form type=post action="purchase.jsp">
  <center>
    Shopping Cart Example
    <p>
    <br>
    Please select a Product and add it to your Shopping Cart
    <br>
    <!--Show the products to the user and provide a button to add it to
        the cart-->
    <select name="product">
      <option>Beginning Java 2 by Ivor Horton
      <option>Professional Java Programming by Brett Spell
      <option>Professional Jini by Sing Li
      <option>Professional JSP by Sing Li et al
      <option>Professional XSL by Andrew Watt et al
      <option>XML Applications by Frank Boumphrey et al
      <option>Beginning XML by Nikola Ozu et al
      <option>Instant UML by Pierre-Alain Muller
      <option>Beginning Java Objects by Jacquie Barker
    </select>
    <input type=submit name="submit" value="Add">
  </center>
  <br> <br>

  <!-- The display goes here -->
  <hr>
  <h2 align="center">Your Shopping Cart</h2>
  <p>
  <%
    String submit = request.getParameter("submit");
    String product = request.getParameter("product");
  %>

  <%
    if(submit != null) {
  %>
  <!--Create the ShoppingCart bean in the session scope-->
  <jsp:useBean id="cart" scope="session" type="java.util.Vector"
               class="java.util.Vector" />

  <jsp:setProperty name="cart" property="*" />

  <!--Pass on the request to ShoppingCart bean-->
  <%
    if(submit.equals("Add")) {
      cart.add(product);
    } else {
        cart.remove(product);
    }
  %>
  <table width="75%" align="center" border="1">
    <%
      for(int i=0;i<cart.size();i++) {
    %>
    <!--Provide a way in which the user can remove items from the
        shopping cart-->
    <tr>
      <td><%= cart.get(i) %></td>
      <td><a href="Purchase.jsp?product=<%= cart.get(i)%>
                                    &submit=Remove">Remove</a></td>
    </tr>
    <%
```

```
            }
          %>
          <%
            }
          %>
        </table>
      </body>
    </html>
```

This application is a simple shopping cart, which lets us add and remove items from a `Vector` maintained internally in session scope:

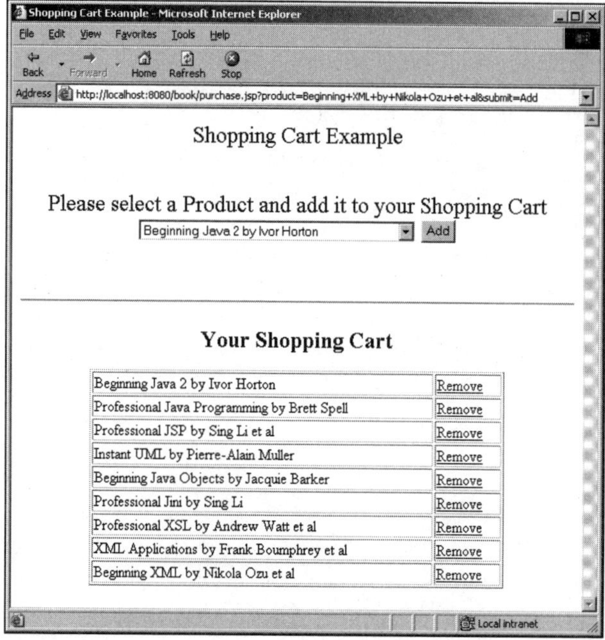

However, if the application gets bigger, it is hard to fix architectural bugs, or to extend functionality. Most of the time no amount of documentation will help us to understand it, and, most importantly, all the parts of the application are tightly coupled. This means that the time needed for development generally increases, and the effort to manage the development definitely increases. The above approach poses the following problems:

- HTML and Java code coupling, which imposes the knowledge of Java on the web developer.
- There can be confusions about the client side JavaScript and JSP code.
- To understand the application logic, we will have to traverse all the pages that are involved in the application. This can be daunting for a big application with hundreds of pages.
- A page, which includes HTML tags, JSP code and Java script is not very pleasant to look at, creates debugging problems and is un-maintainable.

A few of these problems mentioned above can be solved by employing object-oriented development.

Object-Oriented Development

When structured development methodology breaks down, object-oriented analysis, design, and development can solve some of the problems. The goal of an object-oriented methodology is to make the development and maintenance of complex software systems easier. It achieves this by ensuring that the most common mistakes of structured programming are harder to make. A structure is provided that is simultaneously more rigid but just as flexible for average needs.

Object-oriented (oo) analysis and design came into existence with the idea of modeling the domain problems in the real world through objects. An object is an entity that performs a set of related functions. An object interacts with other objects and gets things done. OO development involves modeling the domain and encapsulating the data and functions in a class.

There are four main characteristics to an object-oriented system:

- **Abstraction**
  Abstraction represents the choice of the object modeling parameters (the fields and methods), which are the result of analysis. This means that an analyst chooses a certain set of parameters to represent an object. This is the first step to object modeling. For example, we can analyze a shopping cart and decide that it needs to manage a collection of items. Therefore we should provide a way to manage a collection of items instead of dealing with individual items.

- **Encapsulation**
  Encapsulation represents the hiding of data and methods that have been implemented in a class but for some reason should not be exposed to other objects. This too is a crucial step for object modeling. In this step we decide what is exposed and what is hidden from other objects in the system. This step makes sure that the behavior of an object is provided by simple interfaces and the intricacies are hidden in the implementation. For example, a JavaBean exposes a simple interface for a web page developer.

- **Inheritance**
  Inheritance is a means of defining a new object based on an existing one in such a way that only the differences need to be specified. In addition, changes to the parent class are reflected in all the child classes. Inheritance is used to model generic and specific relationships between classes. Thus a class can extend another class' behavior and state information. For example, a servlet usually derives from `HTTPServlet`. This means that the web server can handle a specific servlet in the same way that it can handle a generic servlet. In other words, inheritance is the single most important feature of an object-oriented system.

- **Modularity**
  Modularity is necessary in software systems to reduce coupling between independently working units. For example, we can define a JavaBean to handle the state of the above mentioned example application. The advantages of this are:

  - The development of both the presentation and data representation can be divided among appropriate personnel
  - Both the modules can be maintained (bug fixes and code changes) independently, thus reducing coupling

Going back to our example, let's abstract the data type used for storing the products and the logic used for adding and removing the items from it:

```
<!--purchase.jsp  -->
<html>
  <head><title>Shopping Cart Example</title></head>
  <body>
    <font size="5" color="blue">
    <form type=post action="purchase.jsp">
    <center>
      Shopping Cart Example
      <p>
      <br>
        Please select a Product and add it to your Shopping Cart
      <br>
      <!--Show the products to the user and provide a button to add it to
          the cart-->
      <select name="product">
        <option>Beginning Java 2 by Ivor Horton
        <option>Professional Java Programming by Brett Spell
        <option>Professional Jini by Sing Li
        <option>Professional JSP by Sing Li et al
        <option>Professional XSL by Andrew Watt et al
        <option>XML Applications by Frank Boumphrey et al
        <option>Beginning XML by Nikola Ozu et al
        <option>Instant UML by Pierre-Alain Muller
        <option>Beginning Java Objects by Jacquie Barker
      </select>
      <input type=submit name="submit" value="Add">
    </center>
    <br> <br>
    <!-- Here goes the display -->
    <hr>
    <h2 align="center">Your Shopping Cart</h2>
    <p>
    <%
      String submit = request.getParameter("submit");
    %>
    <%
      if(submit != null) {
    %>
    <!--Create the ShoppingCart bean in the session scope-->
    <jsp:useBean id="cart" scope="session"
                 type="com.wrox.shop.ShoppingCart"
                 class="com.wrox.shop.ShoppingCart"/>

    <jsp:setProperty name="cart" property="*" />

    <!--Pass on the request to ShoppingCart bean-->
    <%
      cart.processRequest(request);
    %>
    <table width="75%" align="center" border="1">
      <%
```

```
          java.util.Vector products = cart.getProducts();

          for(int i=0;i<products.size();i++) {
        %>
        <!--Provide a way in which the user can remove items from the
            shopping cart-->
        <tr>
          <td><%= products.get(i) %></td>
          <td><a href="purchase.jsp?product=<%= products.get(i) %>
                                     &submit=Remove">Remove</a></td>
        </tr>
        <%
          }
        %>
        <%
          }
        %>
      </table>
    </body>
  </html>
```

The data manipulation is hidden inside a bean called `ShoppingCart` in this case. This example, even though written using JSP, displays object-oriented development by defining an object to store the state information in a transparent way to the presentation tier developer.

Java Servlet technology provides an object-oriented framework for the development of advanced web application development. It gives us a lot of control over logic and flow since we actually write the rendering logic in a Java class and not in the middle of tags. Servlet technology gives a lot of support for advanced web development. However, the code for rendering the HTML page is embedded in Java code. This is not pleasant for web page developers.

On the other hand, bad abstractions create more problems than they solve. Apart from that, the object model needs to span the whole system, which becomes too exhaustive for bigger and complex systems. Therefore, it needs to be supplemented. Several of the problems associated with servlet and JSP-based application development are still not dealt with in the object-oriented domain. So, the search finally leads us to component-based development.

Component-Based Development

Component technology takes abstraction to the next level. Components allow a complex system to be built as an arbitrary number of smaller cohesive systems. Each component is then simple enough to be designed well, and if requirements change greatly, even thrown away and rebuilt.

Each component is built to implement a tight set of responsibilities. Components are considered to be self contained and are not tightly coupled to other components, and have abstracted high-level interfaces to reduce coupling. In other words, a component can be defined as a software unit, which implements a set of interfaces. The key features of components are:

- Components have all the characteristics of objects: their data is encapsulated, they have well defined responsibilities, and they have a well defined interface
- Components can exist in isolation from other components, thus they reduce tight coupling within the system

- Component-based development promotes reuse
- Complexity is managed better, thereby improving the quality of the solution
- Independent design, implementing, and testing allow a high degree of concurrent development
- Loose coupling of components limits the rippling of changes that spread throughout a system when requirements change, or an enhancement is required

JavaBeans are an example of reusable component architecture in Java. JavaBeans component architecture is used in JSP and servlets to encapsulate business functionality. Also, exploiting the power of servlets, JSP, and JavaBean components, we can distribute the functionality (flow, state and presentation) of an application between them and create robust applications.

In the previous example, we used a JavaBean to store the state and JSP for presentation. We can also have a controller, which takes care of the decision or the flow of application logic. It can be either a JSP page or, usually, a servlet. We will learn about this concept in detail in the next section:

```
<%
  if(submit != null) {
%>
<jsp:useBean id="cart" scope="session" type="java.util.Vector"
             class="java.util.Vector "/>
<%
  if(submit.equals("Add")) {
    cart.add(product);
  } else {
      cart.remove(product);
%>
<jsp:forward page="PurchaseView.jsp"/>
<%
  }
%>
```

The Role of Frameworks

Components are often designed to be a part of a framework. The framework is the glue that binds the individual components into an application that can be deployed. Frameworks are designed to solve a specific set of problems, or to make solving problems easier. Most often frameworks contain generic sets of components, which provide generic solutions for the problem domain. They might contain a set of generic classes or interfaces, which can be extended or implemented in order to provide specific functionality. There are several kinds of frameworks in use:

- **Application Frameworks**
  Used across wide variety of applications.
- **Domain Frameworks**
  Built for solving problems for a specific domain.
- **Support Frameworks**
  Provide system level services.

An example of a simple application framework is the Java Servlet API. The Servlet API provides:

- A set of utility classes, the objects of which are created by the framework and passed around. For example, `Session` and `Request`.
- A set of high-level classes, which implement generic functionality. For example, `GenericServlet` and `HttpServlet`.
- A set of interfaces that your classes can extend to derive additional functionality. For example, `SingleThreadModel`.

All this functionality is implemented by the servlet container components internally.

In summary, the advantages of framework-based development are:

- Development of solutions for the problem domain is easy
- The quality of the product increases
- The time to market is reduced
- Changes can be responded to comfortably
- The cost of development is reduced
- A high degree of reuse is possible

The MVC Framework

The **Model-View-Controller** (**MVC**) framework is the most popular framework for web application development. It has been tried, tested, and accepted as the most appropriate pattern in client-server and web application development. This framework was first applied in applications developed using SmallTalk. Later many tools like the Microsoft Foundation Class Library supported it as the de-facto standard for client-server application development. This pattern is useful when the user of an application is expected to interact with it frequently. It makes the development of web applications easier as the problem is divided into three categories:

- **Model**
  The model contains the core of the application's functionality. It encapsulates the data structures and business logic that collectively represent the state of the application. Sometimes the only functionality it contains is state, as the model knows nothing about the view or the controller. A JavaBean fits into this role since it is designed to hold most of the business logic and data structures. It can interact with a database or file system, assuming responsibility for maintaining the application data.

- **View**
  The view provides the presentation of the model. It is the look of the application. The view can access the model getters, but it has no knowledge of the setters. In addition, it knows nothing about the controller. The view may be notified when changes to the model occur. The view can access the model's data, but it may not change the data. A web interface developer need not know or care about what happens in the database or what goes on in the business logic component. The developer is expected to have knowledge of HTML but may not have an in-depth knowledge of Java. A JSP page fits into this role since it is designed to have a small amount of non-HTML code.

- **Controller**
  The controller reacts to the user input and ties the view and model components together. It creates and sets the model. A servlet can take the HTTP requests from the client, make decisions on creating necessary JavaBeans, and notify the view about the changes to the model.

If the MVC framework were applied to our web application, the design of our application would be:

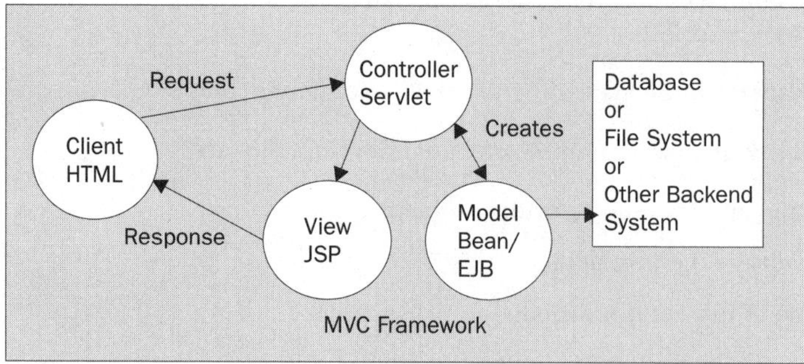

Here the servlet is used as a controller, which invokes JavaBeans, and also takes care of choosing the right JSP page to create and render the dynamic content. The clients will have only one point of contact, whereas the responsibilities are delegated intelligently in the system to make the application stable, easy to maintain and more resilient to change. Servlets make good controllers because they are designed for request and response processing.

If we look at the web scenario of MVC architecture, because of the stateless nature of HTTP, we can see that the client has to re-query the server to get the changes to the state of the application made by its input to the server. In this case, the controller cannot notify the view of the changes made to the application state. If we relate it to our sample application, which represents a simple shopping cart, the requests are repeatedly submitted to the controller upon user's interaction with the view. Depending on the request it will add or remove an item from the shopping cart.

In an ordinary scenario (if we didn't have the `<jsp:forward>` block) the clients would have to re-query the view to get the updated picture of the shopping cart:

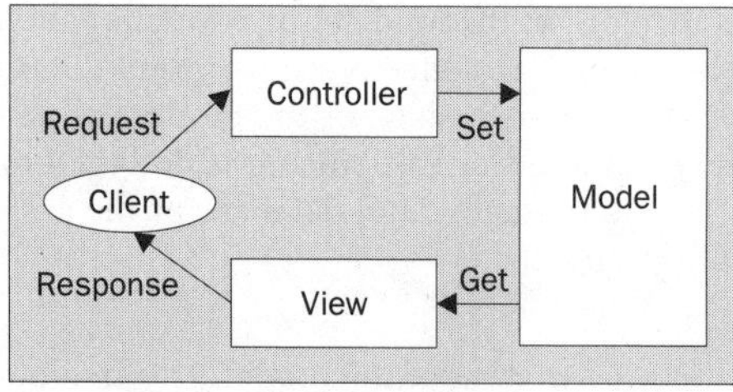

This model is called MVC **Model 2** architecture. As Model 2 follows the MVC structure closely the terms Model 2 and MVC are often used interchangeably. This architecture has become so popular with developers that now there are open source efforts to improve this model and make it available to the developers as a framework. It is called the **Struts** Framework, which we will be introduced to fully in Chapter 2.

MVC/Model 2 Web Application Components

An application implementing the Model 2 framework requires a controller component, which manages the application flow. Programmers most often use a servlet to build this component. The dynamic presentation logic is usually written with the support of JSP technology. JavaBeans can be used to encapsulate application state, and persistence of data. Tag libraries are used to increase the re-use of code, by encapsulating most frequently used operations. We can also use include files to reduce the inclusion of static code in our JSP pages. We will discuss all these components further in this chapter.

Servlets

A servlet is a web component that is managed by a container. Servlets generate dynamic content, and are small, platform independent Java classes compiled to an architecture neutral byte-code that can be loaded dynamically into and run by a web server. Servlets interact with web clients via a request response paradigm implemented by the servlet container.

Servlet technology was a great improvement over CGI scripts for the development of web applications based on dynamic web content. It brought the advantages of object-oriented development in to the development community. Due to this attribute, servlets are used to build the controller components of Model 2 web applications.

The controller in the previous example can be re-written using the Servlet API as shown in the listing below:

```
public class ShoppingCartController extends HttpServlet {

  public void doGet(HttpServletRequest request,
                    HttpServletResponse response)
                    throws ServletException, IOException {
    Vector cart;
    synchronized(session) {
      cart = (Vector)session.getValue("shoppingCart");

      if (cart == null) {
        cart = new Vector();
        session.putValue("shoppingCart", cart);
      }

      if(submit != null) {
        if(submit.equals("Add")) {
          cart.add(product);
        } else {
            cart.remove(product);
        }
        RequestDispatcher dispatcher =
        req.getRequestDispatcher("/("PurchaseView.jsp"");
        dispatcher.forward(req, res);
      }
    }
  }
}
```

Some of the useful attributes of servlets are:

- They have all the advantages of the Java programming language, including ease of development and platform independence
- They can access the large set of APIs available for the Java platform
- The special servlet framework, with extensible classes that the programmer is free to make use of means that classes can be extended to provide application specific functionality
- They run within a servlet container and provide HTTP specific functionality
- They provide facilities for session tracking and storing session related information and application specific data
- They provide facilities for request forwarding, and security

We use servlets mainly to implement controller functionality when developing a Model 2 based web application. They should contain the code to handle all the user requests and co-ordinate responses. The presentation logic is left to JSP pages and the business logic to beans.

JavaServer Pages

In its basic form, a JSP page is simply a text file that contains markup similar to HTML, and that contains additional bits of code that execute application logic to generate dynamic content. This application logic may involve JavaBeans, JDBC objects, Enterprise JavaBeans (EJB), and Remote Method Invocation (RMI) objects, all of which can be easily accessed from a JSP page. JSP gives web authors what they need: liberation from complex Java code. It provides for encapsulation of business logic in beans and tag libraries, which are written by developers and can be used by web authors. The important features of JSP pages are:

- **JSP supports the separation of developer and web page author roles**
  Developers write components that encapsulate application functionality and interact with server-side objects. Authors can put data and dynamic content together to create presentations suited for their intended audiences.

- **Reuse of components and tag libraries**
  JSP emphasizes the use of reusable components such as JavaBeans, Enterprise JavaBeans, and tag libraries. These components can be used for component development and page composition, resulting in considerable savings in development time.

- **Separation of dynamic and static content**
  JSP enables the separation of static content in a template from dynamic content that is inserted into the static template. This greatly simplifies the creation of content.

- **Support for scripting and actions**
  JSP supports scripting elements as well as actions. Actions encapsulate useful functionality in a convenient form that can be manipulated by tools. Scripts provide a mechanism to glue together this functionality in a per-page manner.

To take the maximum advantage of JSP pages for creating high performance, reliable applications we should use JSP pages predominantly to implement presentation logic. When we need to include data access logic, we separate the code from presentation logic. We should write code for minimal user input validation and keep the actual Java code to the minimum. When including other files, we should use static and dynamic include directives wisely. Static includes increase the page size whereas dynamic includes increase the processing overhead.

Tag Libraries

A **tag library** is a collection of custom actions described by a tag library descriptor (TLD) and Java classes. In addition to the standard actions, JSP supports the development of reusable modules called custom actions. A custom action is invoked by using a custom tag in a JSP page. A tag library is a collection of custom tags, and has many useful features:

- They can be customized via attributes passed from the calling page.
- They have access to all the objects available to JSP pages.
- They can modify the response generated by the calling page.
- They can communicate with each other. We can create and initialize a JavaBeans component, create a variable that refers to that bean in one tag, and then use the bean in another tag.
- They can be nested within one another, allowing for complex interactions within a JSP page.
- They allow web designers to use custom tags in HTML tools as part of their normal toolset.

We can encapsulate common functionalities in a custom tag library. Once a tag library is developed, it can be reused in several applications. It makes the life of a web designer easier, by encapsulating functionality in easy to understand tags, so that they can focus on the presentation issues. This is the obvious way to package add-ons for web page developers – as tag libraries on top of whatever Java code we wish to create.

Make sure you have a clear distinction between beans and custom tags. Beans are used to encapsulate a complex application specific functionality, whereas a tag library is used to encapsulate generic functionality.

JavaBeans

The JavaBeans API makes it possible to write component-based software in Java. JavaBeans typically form the implementation of the model in the MVC architecture and contain the core of the application's functionality. They encapsulate the state of the application, and have support for:

- **Introspection**
  So that a builder tool can analyze how a bean works
- **Customization**
  So that when using an application builder a user can customize the appearance and behavior of a bean
- **Events**
  Used as a simple communication metaphor than can connect beans
- **Properties**
  Both for customization and for programmatic use
- **Persistence**
  So that a bean can be customized in an application builder and then have its customized state saved and reloaded later

JavaBeans also provide a mechanism for the encapsulation of application specific functionality in a reusable component, which allows beans to be used to encapsulate both application specific behavior and application specific state.

During the lifecycle of an application (design, development, testing, maintenance), the code has to go through several changes. The changes may be related to the structure or the behavior of the application. Alternatively, the changes may be driven by the need to extend the existing functionality, by the need to make the application more readable, or by an iterative design process. In the next section we will learn when and how to make these changes efficiently.

Analyzing and Refactoring Application Code

As we all know, software development goes through several iterations throughout its development cycle. Also, when developing component-based applications, we need to make the code reusable. The high cost of developing software motivates the reuse and evolution of existing software. Closely related to reuse is software maintenance, where knowledge about a software system is used for bug fixing and feature addition. In short, programs need to be resilient to change and reusable. They should be maintainable and extensible.

Let us assume that we have developed an application, which works, but when we try to add more features, we discover that the code is not reusable or extensible. On the other hand we don't want to touch the code because it works and because we believe in the saying "if it ain't broke, don't fix it". The only option we can see is re-writing that part of the application as required. In this section, we will discuss the tools and techniques for analyzing and refactoring such applications and we will take a look at an example where we will apply various forms of refactoring.

Refactoring

Refactoring is a method of re-structuring existing working code. It is a technique employed to change the structure of the code without changing its behavior. This method is used to increase the maintainability and extensibility of the program. Refactorings do not change the behavior of a program; that is, if the program is called before and after a refactoring with the same set of inputs, the resulting set of output values will be the same.

Advantages of Refactoring

Traditional software design methodologies emphasize that it is important that the design of an application is well thought out before any coding begins, in the hope that the more time and effort that is spent on the design, the less time will have to be spent on coding, and the maintenance of the application will be easier.

On the other hand, a philosophy called extreme programming calls for writing a working piece of code by not concentrating on overall design. Applications can be tuned later by re-organizing the code depending on the requirements for change in the design (it is also called late-design). Refactoring can support software design and evolution by restructuring a program in the way that allows other changes to be made more easily.

Refactoring is used to:

- **Extract reusable components from existing code**
  We can use refactoring to extract reusable components from the existing code. Reusable components reduce the entropy (disorder) in the code by reducing the length of code, thus making it more maintainable.

- **Improve consistency among components**
  Let's assume that we have a system which has multiple working components. We discover that some of the components share some common functionality. Hence, to make the design of the system easier to understand, and to reduce future maintenance costs, it is desirable to refactor the system and make the commonality explicit by declaring a single inheritance hierarchy between those components.

- **Support iterative design of an application**
  Most software systems go through several design iterations. Sometimes the design might change in such a way that it is necessary to change the structure of the system in some way.

Refactoring occurs at all levels. There are high-level refactorings that are major design changes, and there are low-level refactorings such as renaming a variable. Most of the refactorings are focused on:

- Organizing data
- Making method calls simpler
- Changing inheritance relationships
- Converting from procedural design to object-oriented design
- Moving functions between classes

Analyzing a Design for Refactoring

Refactoring depends on our requirements for maintainability, extensibility, and reusability. However, if we start with a prototype of the application in a simple way and start adding functionality without emphasizing design, we might find a problem when the prototype becomes a fully-fledged application, and our code might lack the critical qualities that needs to make it extendable and reusable. At this point of time, instead of rewriting the application, we can refactor it in such a way as to satisfy our application's design requirements. We can think about refactoring our application code when we find a few of these problems with our code:

- **Duplicated Code**
  This problem occurs in big projects where there are several modules sharing some amount of common functionality. This increases the ambiguity and future maintenance cost of the software.

- **Long Method Definitions**
  Some developers still have a habit of writing long methods instead of breaking the functionality into different function calls. This problem makes it difficult to understand and, fix bugs, and extend the function. In other words it increases maintenance costs and decreases reusability.

- **Large Classes**
  Large classes that encapsulate huge amount of data and functionality are quite common. These kinds of classes usually don't have proper abstractions and are thus difficult to understand.

- **Long Parameter List**
  It is not a rare sight to see functions with big parameter lists in a procedure-oriented (structured) program. This can be reduced in an object-oriented program by way of proper encapsulation and abstraction.

- **Feature Rigidity**
  Adding a new feature to a badly designed application can cause it to break down.

Refactoring Patterns

In this section we will take a look at a number of refactoring techniques.

Defining an Interface for One or More Existing Classes

In a mature software system, classes are implemented as a specific case of a general abstraction. For example, let's take a system which implements two classes for extracting text from a postscript file and a PDF document. Both of the classes are built to provide single functionality, extracting text from the document. In this case, if we define an interface that defines this general functionality, and both these classes derive from it, then in future it is possible to add a class to the system, which extracts text from a word document:

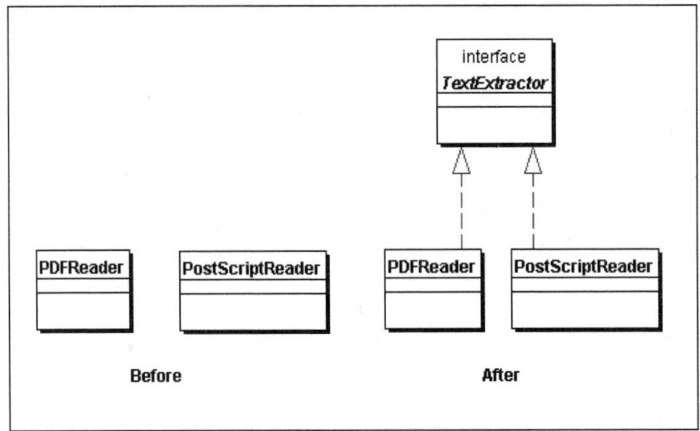

Using Sub-Classing to Eliminate Conditional Tests

Some classes might contain some general functions and some specific functions, which are conditionally called. This kind of a class contains the implementation of both generic and case specific functionality. Here we can improve the design by migrating the specific functionality to subclasses. This is done by defining subclasses corresponding to cases and migrating the case specific behavior down to subclasses.

Let's take an example where a class called `UserAccount` manages a normal user's account as well as an administrator's account. We can restructure this class by sub-classing the administrator's account:

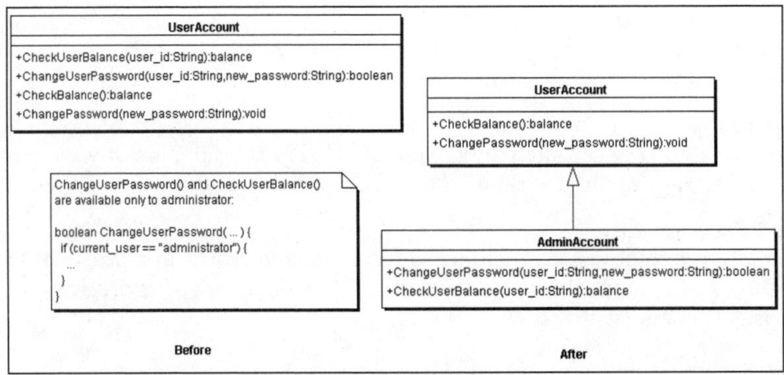

Changing Aggregation and Inheritance Relationships

There are two kinds of whole-part relationships between classes. They are "is kind of" and "is part of" relationships. If class X is a kind of class Y, we can represent class X as a subclass of class Y. However, if class X is a part of class Y, then it represents an aggregation relationship. In the second case, class Y is called as a composite or an aggregate and X is called as a component. In the first kind of relationship, X needs to know about Y, whereas in the second type of relationship, Y needs to know about X.

Refactoring: An Example

Till now we have discussed several refactoring methods. However, there are a huge number of methods in use. Some are trivial and others are complex. We cannot discuss them all in this chapter. For in-depth understanding of Refactoring refer to *Refactoring: Improving the Design of Existing Code* from *Addison-Wesley (ISBN 0-201-48567-2)*, or visit http://www.refactory.org/.

However, other forms of refactoring involve:

- Moving member variables and functions
- Replacing a piece of code with a method call
- Changing names of classes, variables and functions
- Changing inheritance hierarchies
- Converting from procedural design to object oriented design

We have learnt a few needs and techniques of refactoring. Now let us go through a small example. Let's take a look at the `ShoppingCart` bean code from the above example:

```
package com.wrox.shop;

import java.util.Vector;
import javax.servlet.http.HttpServletRequest;

//The shopping cart bean
public class ShoppingCart extends Object {

  //Shopping cart will be a vector
  private Vector cart = null;
  //Currently product is referred by a string
  String product = null;
  //To store the value of submit
  String submit = null;

  public ShoppingCart() {
    cart = new Vector();
  }

  public void setProduct(String product) {
    this.product = product;
  }
```

```
  public void setSubmit(String submit) {
    this.submit = submit;
  }

  public Vector getProducts() {
    //products are stored in the cart
    return cart;
  }

  public void addProduct(String product) {
    cart.add(product);
  }

  public void removeProduct(String product) {
    cart.remove(product);
  }

  public void processRequest(HttpServletRequest req) {
    if(submit != null) {
      //add or remove the product from cart
      if(submit.equals("Add")) {
        addProduct(product);
      } else {
          removeProduct(product);
      }
      //cleanup the values of product and submit
     reset();
    }
  }

  public void reset() {
    submit = null;
    product = null;
  }
}
```

As we can see in this bean, all we know about the product is the name. We need to do better than this. Real shopping carts need to store a lot of information about the product, like product type, price, and running discounts. This requires that we define a separate class called `Product` and define attributes and methods:

```
package com.wrox.shop;

class Product {
  private String name;
  private double price;
  private int type;

  //public get and set methods for all
}
```

Now we will store Product objects in the cart instead of strings. That means we need to change the type of variable product from a String to a Product class. This too is a kind of refactoring.

We will also provide a method to get the current total for all the products called currentTotal():

```
public double currentTotal() {
  double totalAmount = 0;
  for(int i=0;i<cart.size();i++) {
    Product each = (Product) cart.get(i);
    totalAmount += each.getPrice();

    double discount = 0;
    //determine amounts for each line
    switch (each.getType()) {
      case TYPE_A:
        //calculate discount based on hour of day
        break;
      case TYPE_B:
        //calculate discount based on quantity in store
        break;
      case TYPE_C:
        //calculate discount based on expiry date
        break;
    }
    totalAmount -= discount;
  }
  return totalAmount;
}
```

This method is the next step in refactoring our shopping cart. We will have to change our presentation and controller code to take advantage of these additional features. In the code above, we can see that the function is cluttered with a switch statement. In this case, the function is small due to the limited classification of objects, but we can expect it to grow over time. So, we can introduce another function, which is a breakaway from this one:

```
public double getDiscount(Integer productType) {
  double discount = 0;
  //determine amounts for each line
  switch (each.getType()) {
    case TYPE_A:
      //calculate discount based on hour of day
      break;
    case TYPE_B:
      //calculate discount based on Quantity in store
      break;
    case TYPE_C:
      //calculate discount based on expiry date
      break;
  }
  return discount;
}
```

So, extracting the method `getDiscount()` out of the function `currentTotal()` makes it much easier to manage:

```
public String currentTotal() {
  double totalAmount = 0;
  for(int i=0;i<products.size();i++) {
    Product each = (Product) cart.get(i);
    totalAmount += (each.getPrice() - getDiscount(each.getType()));
  }
  return totalAmount;
}
```

The method `getDiscount()` is actually using information from the `Product`. We are simply passing the `Product` type on to `getDiscount()`. Thus it makes more sense if we embed the logic for getting the discount information in the `Product` itself, thus protecting the encapsulation of the object:

```
class Product {
  ...
  public Double getCurrentPrice() {
    double discount =  someBean.calculateDiscount(type /*Product Type*/);
    //apply additional logic
    return (price - discount);
  }
  ...
}
```

So, our method `currentTotal()` becomes:

```
public String currentTotal() {
  double totalAmount = 0;
  for(int i=0;i<products.size();i++) {
    Product each = (Product) cart.get(i);
    totalAmount += each.getCurrentPrice();
  }
  return totalAmount;
}
```

Now let us look at how we can dynamically manage discounts. As there can be several types of objects, there can be several types of discounts. Regular discounts, off-season discounts, limited discounts, and so on. We are going to follow the "state" pattern to dynamically decide the discounts:

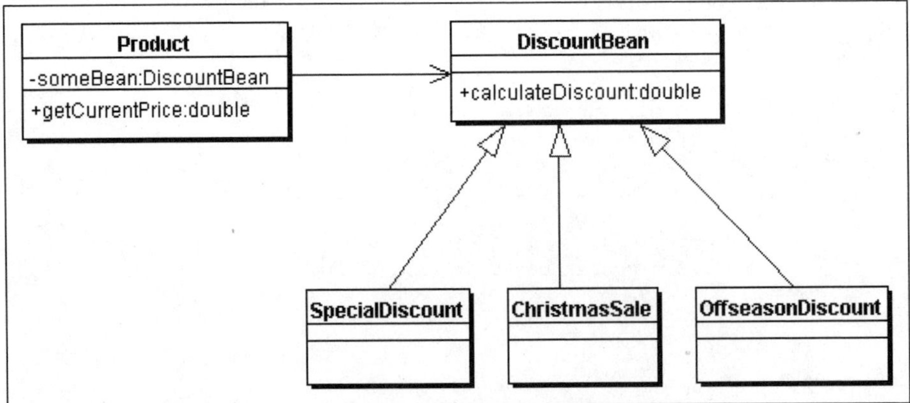

Here we have defined an abstract base class called `DiscountBean`, which is sub-classed by discounting logics for off-season, or Christmas, discounts. At run time, the appropriate discount bean is configured. `Product` calculates its current price using this bean. We will have to add the `setDiscountBean()` method and a variable of type `DiscountBean` to our `ShoppingCart`.

The above example is simple enough to make us feel that refactoring is easy. However, if we explored all the above-mentioned methods of refactoring, we might come across the difficulties of renaming variables, moving data around, creating new hierarchies, and so on. It is strongly suggested that at every stage of refactoring, appropriate test cases be applied to make sure that the code doesn't break down. To make this process easy, we can make use of several refactoring tools available on the market.

Refactoring Tools

There are several tools available for refactoring Java code. An example is **JRefactory** (http://JRefactory.sourceforge.net/). It supports several forms of refactoring, like moving a class, renaming a class, adding an abstract parent class, adding a child class, extracting an interface, and renaming parameters. It is a pretty useful tool to start with.

Summary

In this chapter we covered:

- Different paradigms of software development: procedure-oriented, object-oriented, and component-based
- How component based frameworks reduce design/development time and promote reuse
- What problems the Model 2 framework solves
- What should go into each component of a Model 2 framework based application
- The different techniques and tools for analyzing and refactoring

In the next chapter, we will look in detail at the Struts Framework from the Apache group.

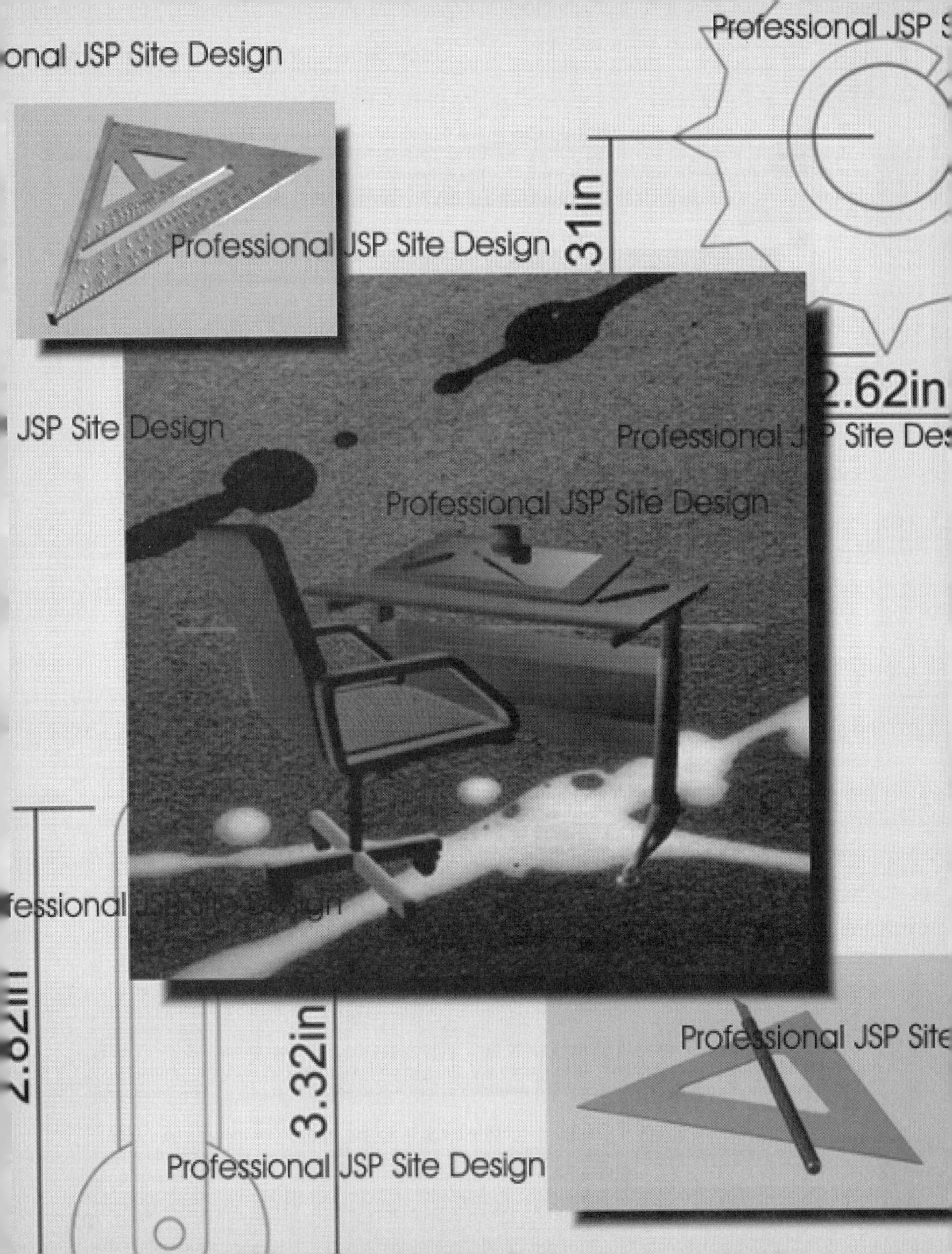

Professional JSP Site Design
31in
Professional JSP Site Design
3.32in
Professional JSP Site Design

2

The Struts Framework

Java servlets provide web developers with a technology that is more powerful and extensible than CGI scripts. They are a great way to provide the functionality of a web application, such as decision-making and the handling of resources like databases; however, trying to provide the presentation of a web application using servlets can be a tedious and difficult to maintain process. When servlets are used to provide the presentation of a web application, they can easily become full of `println()` statements. Then, if we decide to change the look and feel of a web application, we might have to change many lines of code in many different servlets.

The problem is that much of the code ends up related to the production of HTML – but this isn't what servlets are designed to do easily. What we need is a technology that makes it easy to produce HTML: enter JavaServer Pages (JSP). JSP allows developers to create servlets in a way that is similar to the creation of HTML pages. However, using JSP pages alone leads to a new set of problems: those of difficult flow control and spaghetti code.

So, we have two great technologies – servlets and JSP – each with strengths and weaknesses. In fact, where servlets is strong, JSP is weak, and vice versa. The solution is obvious: we need to use the two technologies together, using servlets to provide the functionality of the web application, and JSP pages to present HTML to clients.

The next thing to consider is how exactly we should use servlets and JSP pages together. The roles we assign to the different components within an application determine the architecture of the application. The type of architecture we have mind – one that uses servlets to control the program flow, and JSP pages to provide presentation of data – is **Model 2** architecture, which is similar in concept to the Model-View-Controller (MVC) design pattern introduced in Chapter 1. Recall that MVC architecture has the following beneficial features:

- It brings modularity to the application
- It reduces the coupling of HTML and Java code
- It allows developers to provide multiple views of the same data

- It simplifies application flow
- It makes an application easier to maintain
- It is a tried and tested model for web application development

In an effort to bring the advantages of MVC to J2EE web application development, this model has been implemented in a framework called **Struts**, available for download from http://jakarta.apache.org/struts/. Version 1.0 of Struts was released under the Apache Software License in July 2001 and has many benefits, including:

- It provides all the features and benefits of an MVC model
- It simplifies MVC-based application development
- It provides a number of objects that implement the fundamental aspects of MVC (and which can be extended to implement specific requirements)
- It allows developers to configure a great deal of the default framework using XML files
- It provides a flexible mechanism to handle errors and exceptions
- It provides an easy mechanism for internationalizing application messages

> **The Struts Framework provides the benefits of modularity, flexibility, reusability of components, combined with the easy development associated with MVC based web applications.**

Struts is an ongoing project and is updated almost daily. Despite this rapid pace of change, it is already used by a worldwide developer community, which means that the framework is continuously tested.

In this chapter, we will discuss the Struts framework in detail. We'll look at how Struts makes it easy to develop applications that cleanly separate control, business logic, and presentation. We'll go on to look at the classes that Struts provides that make this development so much easier, including:

- Classes to control the flow of the application
- Classes that implement and execute the business logic of the application
- Custom tag libraries that make it easy to create and validate HTML forms

Once we've understood how Struts works we'll demonstrate how it can be used by building an example web application powered by Struts. Of course, before we can start using Struts we need to download and install it.

Installing Struts

Installing Struts is an easy process and it can be used with any web container that supports the Servlet 2.2 and JSP 1.1 specifications (or later), although we'll be using it with Apache Tomcat 4.0 (available for download from http://jakarta.apache.org/tomcat/).

The latest version of Struts is available for download from http://jakarta.apache.org/struts/, and will be in the form of a compressed file that you will need to expand to a convenient location. The expanded folder will be named `jakarta-struts-1.0` and will contain two directories named `lib` and `webapps`. The files we need to create applications using Struts are found in the `lib` directory, and include:

File	Description
`jdbc2_0-stdext.jar`	Contains the JDBC 2.0 Optional Package API classes. This will need to be placed in the `WEB-INF\lib\` directory of a web application if we wish to utilize the data sources support provided by Struts.
`struts.jar`	Contains all of the Java classes included in Struts. This needs to be copied into the `WEB INF\lib\` directory of any web application that uses Struts.
`struts*.tld`	The tag library descriptor files that describe the custom tags in the various Struts tag libraries. This also needs to be copied into the `WEB-INF\` directory of any web application that uses Struts.

The `webapps` directory contains some useful web applications:

Web Application	Description
`struts-blank.war`	A simple web application that provides a starting point for building Struts-based applications.
`struts-documentation.war`	Contains all of the Struts documentation found on the Struts web site.
`struts-example.war`	Demonstrates many of features of Struts.
`struts exercise-taglib.war`	Contains test pages for the custom tags supported by Struts. It is primarily of use to developers who are enhancing the Struts custom tag libraries, but also serves as an example of how to use the Struts tags.
`struts-template.war`	This web application both introduces and demonstrates the Struts template tags.
`struts-upload.war`	A quick example of how to upload files using the Struts framework.

Struts Architecture

The Struts Framework consists of a set of cooperating classes, servlets, and JSP tags that together make up a reusable Model 2 pattern.

For more information about the MVC and Model 2 architecture you should refer back to Chapter 1.

Let's take a look at various components of the Struts Framework from an MVC perspective:

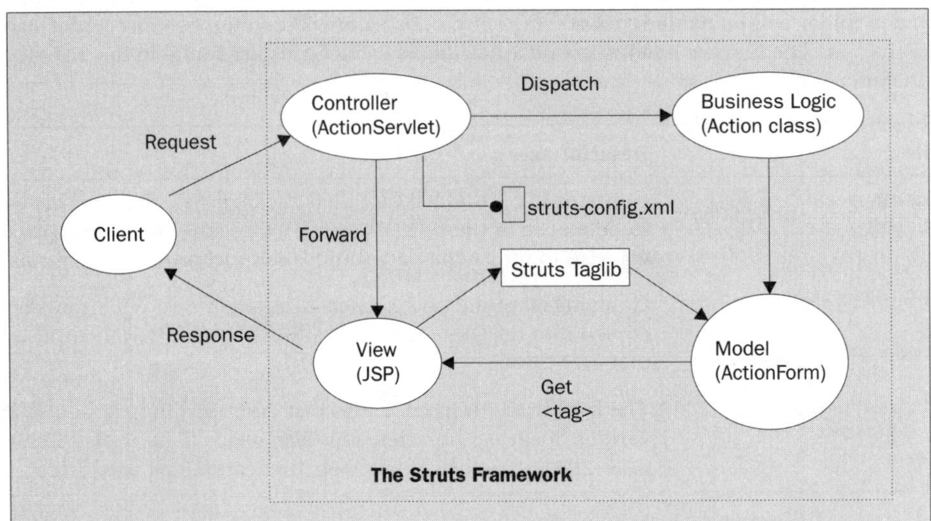

The framework has three parts that we will look at in turn: the model, the view, and the controller.

The Model

The **Model** of a Struts-based system can be divided into:

- The internal state of the system
- The actions that can be taken to change that state (in other words, the business logic)

An application will usually represent the internal state of the system as a set of JavaBeans. These beans will have properties that represent the details of the system's state. Depending on the design and complexity of the application, these beans can be self-contained and have persistent state, or they may retrieve information only when necessary (say from a database).

> **In the Struts Framework, the application state is usually stored in a set of `ActionForm` JavaBeans.**

Large-scale applications will often encapsulate business logic (actions) within methods that can be called on beans that maintain state information. For example, a shopping cart bean, stored in session scope for each current user, would have properties to represent the items that the user has decided to purchase. Such a bean might also have a `checkOut()` method that first authorizes the user's credit card, and then sends the order information to a warehouse so that it can be picked and shipped. Other systems might represent the available actions separately, perhaps as session Enterprise JavaBeans.

In smaller scale applications, actions might be embedded within the `Action` classes that are part of the Controller role in the Struts Framework. This approach is appropriate when the logic is very simple. The Struts Framework supports both these approaches. However, I would recommend that you always separate the business logic ("what to do") from the role that `Action` classes play ("deciding what to do"), as doing so gives you the flexibility to change one without affecting the other.

The View

The **View** portion of a Struts-based application is usually constructed using JSP. Struts includes an extensive custom tag library that facilitates the creation of user interfaces that are fully internationalized, and that can interact with the `ActionForm` beans that are part of the Model.

The Controller

The **Controller** is focused on receiving requests from the client, deciding what business logic function should be performed in order to fulfill that request, and then delegating responsibility for producing the next phase of the user interface to an appropriate View component.

In Struts, the primary component of the Controller is a servlet of class `ActionServlet`. The actual servlet to be used is defined in a set of mappings (described by the class `ActionMapping`) in a configuration file. Each mapping defines a path and the fully qualified class name of an `Action` class. If the path is matched against the URI of the incoming request, the specified `Action` class is given responsibility for performing the desired business logic, and then dispatching control to the appropriate View component.

We can also use `ActionMapping` classes that have additional properties beyond those required to operate the Struts Framework. This allows us to store additional information specific to an application. Struts also allows us to define logical names to which control should be forwarded. For example, an action method can ask for the `Main Menu` page, without having to know the actual name of the corresponding JSP page. This feature greatly assists in the separation of control logic from view logic.

Architectural Overview

Let's take a quick tour of some of the major features of the architecture of a Struts application.

The `ActionServlet` is responsible for routing HTTP requests to other objects in the framework, including JSP pages. When it is initialized it parses a configuration file (named by default `struts-config.xml`), and uses the mappings defined in it to route the HTTP request accordingly.

A mapping must specify a **request path** and an **object type**. The `Action` object handles the request and then responds to the client, or indicates where the control should be forwarded. For example, if a login succeeds in a mail application, a `LoginAction` object may wish to forward control to an `inboxMenu` action, this `inboxMenu` action could then send the response to the client.

`Action` objects are linked to the application's `ActionServlet`, and so have access to its methods. When forwarding control, an object can indirectly forward one or more shared objects, including JavaBeans, by placing them in request, session, or application scope. For example, an `Action` object can create a shopping cart bean, add an item to the cart, place the bean in the session collection, and then forward control to another action. This action might in turn use a JSP page to display the contents of the user's cart. Since each client has its own session, they will also have their own shopping cart.

A common problem in the design of web applications is deciding how to retain and validate what a user has entered between requests. In an application built using Struts, JavaBeans can be used to manage input forms. The data from a form can be easily stored in an `ActionForm` bean, which is then saved in either request, session or application scope. This allows it to be used by other objects, particularly the `Action` object.

The stored `ActionForm` bean can be used by:

- A JSP page to collect data from the user
- An `Action` object to validate the user entries

To deal with errors that occur during validation, Struts has a shared mechanism for raising and displaying error messages through `ActionError` objects. The Struts Framework includes custom tags that can automatically populate fields from an `ActionForm` bean, which means that the only thing most JSP pages need to know about the rest of the framework is the proper field names and where to submit the form. Components such as the messages set by the `Action` object can be displayed using a single custom tag, and other application-specific tags can also be defined to hide implementation details from the JSP pages.

Components of the Struts Framework

We're ready to take a closer view at the Struts Framework, exploring the main components and the relationships between them. The following UML component diagram gives us an overview of the Struts architecture:

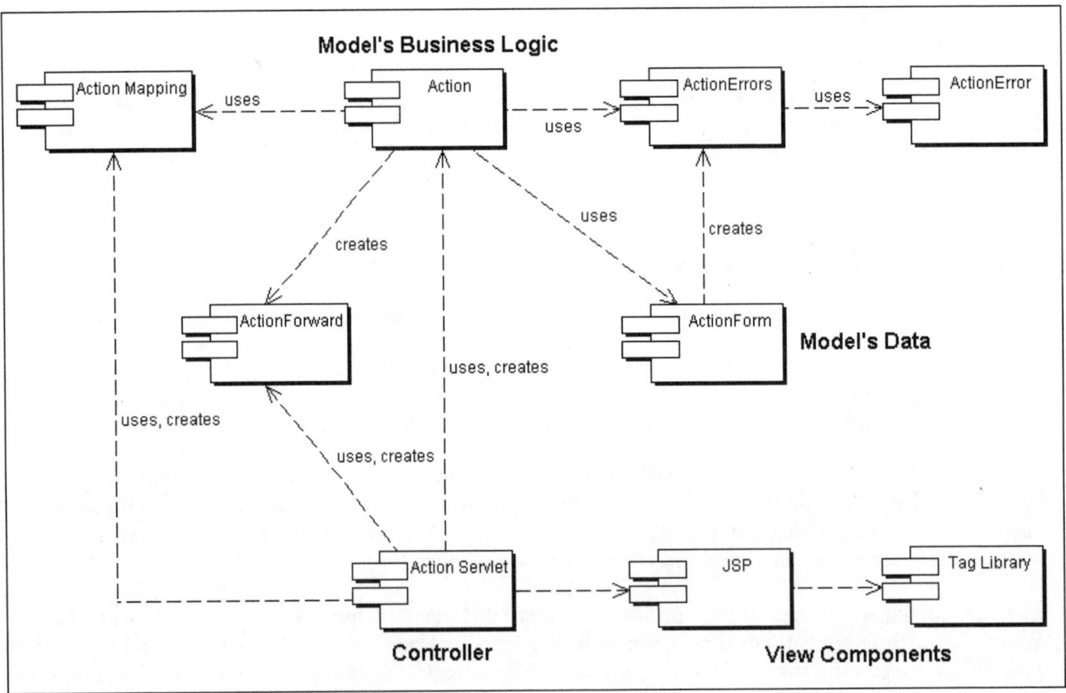

There are a number of components that are used by the framework:

Component	Role
`ActionServlet`	Acts as the controller
`ActionClass`	Contains business logic
`ActionForm`	Represents model data
`ActionMapping`	Helps controller in mapping requests to actions
`ActionForward`	Used to indicate forwarding of actions to other objects
`ActionError`	Used to store and retrieve errors
The Struts Tag Library	Used to make presentation tier developers breathe freely

Next, let's examine their roles and responsibilities as parts of the framework.

The Struts Configuration File

First of all, let's discuss the glue that makes various Struts components work together: the `struts-config.xml` file (an XML file with a root element of `<struts-config>`). The name and the location of the configuration file can be defined as an initialization parameter to the `ActionServlet`; if it's not specified, it defaults to `\WEB-INF\struts-config.xml`.

The configuration file is used to define:

- Global forwards
- `ActionMapping` classes
- `ActionForm` beans
- JDBC data sources

Configuring Global Forwards

Global forwards are used to create logical name mappings between commonly used JSP pages in a web application. It offers a solution to the inconvenience of hard-coding the names of JSP pages in our application. They are defined using the `<global-forwards>` element, which contains `<forward>` elements for each global forward.

Each of these forwards is available through a call to the action mapping instance, for example:

```
actionMappingInstace.findForward("logicalName");
```

This is an example of a global forwards declaration:

```
<global-forwards>
  <forward name="cart" path="/shoppingcart.jsp"/>
</global-forwards>
```

The name attribute simply defines the name of the global forward, and the path attribute gives the relative path to the target URL.

Configuring ActionMappings

ActionMapping objects help the flow control within the framework. They are used for mapping incoming request URIs to Action classes, and to associate Action classes to ActionForm beans. The ActionServlet uses these mappings internally and transfers the control to an instance of the specific Action class. All Action classes implement the application-specific code in the perform() method, which returns an ActionForward object that contains the name of the target resource to which the response has to be forwarded.

ActionMapping objects are defined using the <action-mappings> element, which includes one or more <action> elements. The <action> element has a number of attributes:

Attribute	Description
path	The relative path to the Action class.
name	The name of the Action bean associated with this action. This is the same name used to define the form bean element.
type	The fully qualified name of the Action class that is linked to this mapping.
scope	The scope (either request or session) of the ActionForm bean.
prefix	The prefix used to match request parameters to bean properties.
suffix	The suffix used to match request parameters to bean properties.
attribute	The name of the request or session scope attribute under which the ActionForm bean is stored (if different from the name attribute).
className	The fully qualified name of the class used by Struts to create the ActionMapping object. The default class is org.apache.struts.action.ActionMapping.
input	The path to the input form, to which the control must be returned if a bean validation error is encountered.
unknown	If the value of this attribute is set to true, then this action will be used as the default for any URIs for which the ActionMappings are not defined.
validate	If this attribute value is set to true, the ActionServlet will call the validate() method on the ActionForm bean to perform input validation, before it can call perform() method on the Action object.

The first three of these are the most important and commonly used attributes. A typical `<action-mappings>` element would look like:

```
<action-mappings>
  <action path="/saveRegistration"
          type="diagnosis.action.SaveRegistrationAction"
          name="registrationForm"
          scope="request"
          input="/registration.jsp"
          validate="true">
    <forward name="failure" path="/registration.jsp"/>
    <forward name="cancel"  path="/index.jsp"/>
  </action>
</action-mappings>
```

This mapping matches a path `/saveRegistration` and uses an `Action` class of type `diagnosis.action.SaveRegistrationAction`. A session-scoped form bean with the logical name of `registrationForm` is associated with this mapping.

Using the `<forward>` element we can define logical names to resources to which responses from the `Action` class are to be forwarded. By doing this we can ensure that the `Action` classes are independent of the actual names of the JSP pages that are used by the page designers. Then, the JSP pages can be renamed with no impact on the `Action` classes themselves.

This `<forward>` element has the following attributes:

Attribute	Description
`id`	ID.
`className`	The fully qualified class name of the `ActionForward` class. If a value is not specified the value defaults to `org.apache.struts.action.ActionForward`.
`name`	The logical name by which an action class can access `ActionForward`.
`path`	The path to the resource to which the response should be forwarded.
`redirect`	If this value is set to true, the `ActionServlet` uses the `sendRedirect()` method to forward the resource.

In our example snippet from `config-struts.xml`, the relative path to the form page that originated the request is `/registration.jsp`, and a local forward is defined called `failure`. This forwards responses from the `Action` class to `/registration.jsp`.

Configuring ActionForm Beans

`ActionForm` beans are used by an `ActionServlet` to hold request parameters. These beans have attribute names that correspond to the names of the HTTP request parameters. The controller populates the `ActionForm` bean instances from the request parameters, and then passes the instances to `Action` classes.

ActionForm beans are declared globally within the configuration file using <form-bean> elements. The attributes of this element are as follows:

Attribute	Description
id	ID
className	The fully qualified class name of the ActionForm bean. If not specified the value defaults to org.apache.struts.action.ActionFormBean.
name	The name of the form bean in its associated scope. This attribute is used to associate the bean to an ActionMapping.
type	The fully qualified name of the class.

A typical <form-bean> element that declares a Form bean would look like:

```
<form-beans>
  <form-bean name="registrationForm"
             type="diagnosis.form.RegistrationForm"/>
</form-beans>
```

This declares a bean of type diagnosis.form.RegistrationForm that uses the name registrationForm in its associated scope.

Configuring JDBC Data Sources

JDBC data sources can be defined in the configuration file under the element <data-sources>. Multiple data sources can be defined within the <data-sources> element using the <data-source> element. The <data-source> element defines different attributes for specifying the data source properties:

Attribute	Description
id	ID
key	Name used by Action classes for looking up this connection
type	Name of the class which implements the JDBC interface

The following attributes have been deprecated in version 1.1 of the framework. Although they can still be used in version 1.0, you should use the <set-property> element to define them, as shown in the example file:

Attribute	Description
description	Description of the data source
autoCommit	Default auto commit mode for connections created using this data source

Attribute	Description
driverClass	A class used by the data source that exposes the JDBC driver interface
loginTimeout	Value of the database login timeout in seconds
maxCount	Maximum number of connections that can be made
minCount	Minimum number of connections to be created
password	Password for accessing database
readOnly	Read only state for connections created
user	User name for accessing database
url	JDBC URL

The following listing shows how to define a data source in the struts-config.xml:

```
<data-sources>
  <data-source id="DS1"
               key="conPool"
               type="org.apache.struts.util.GenericDataSource"
               autoCommit="true"
               description="Example Data Source Configuration"
               driverClass="org.gjt.mm.mysql.Driver"
               maxCount="4"
               minCount="2"
               password="wrox"
               url="jdbc:mysql://localhost/diagnosis"/>
               user="struts"
  </data-source>
</data-sources>
```

The data source can be accessed from an Action class (using a method defined in ActionServlet) by specifying the key name. For example:

```
javax.sql.DataSource ds = servlet.findDataSource("conPool");
javax.sql.Connection con = ds.getConnection();
```

Where servlet is an instance of ActionServlet that is passed to the Action class after the ActionServlet creates the Action class. The database connection is taken from a connection pool, for which the string "conPool" is the key name.

The ActionServlet Class

The Controller component of the framework is implemented by the Struts class org.apache.struts.action.ActionServlet (which extends the javax.servlet.http.HttpServlet class). In a Struts-based application, forms and hyperlinks that require business logic to be executed will be submitted to a request URI, which is mapped to this servlet. There will be a single instance of this servlet class, which receives and processes all requests that change the state of a user's interaction with the application.

The Controller performs the following tasks when handling a request:

- It matches a request URI to the appropriate `ActionMapping`.
- It maps this request to the Java class name of the corresponding `Action` class (an implementation of the `Action` interface). It instantiates and caches this instance if this is the first request for that particular `Action` class.
- It creates or finds an `ActionForm` bean instance (if one is declared in the mapping), and populates the properties of the bean from the request parameter.
- It calls the `perform()` method on the appropriate `Action` class instance (declared in the `ActionMapping`), and passes it the `ActionForm` bean (if declared in the mapping), the `ActionMapping` object, and the `request` and `response` objects.
- It forwards the response to the resource specified by the `ActionForward` object, which was returned by the `perform()` method.

ActionServlet Configuration

We need to declare the `ActionServlet` in the web application's deployment descriptor (`web.xml`), and configure it to load on startup. This servlet also has a host of configurable initialization parameters:

Parameter	Default Value	Description
`application`	`null`	The application resource bundle class (provides tools for supporting locale-specific resources)
`bufferSize`	`4096`	Buffer size for file upload
`config`	`/WEB_INF/struts-config.xml`	The location and name of the configuration file
`content`	`text/html`	The default content type
`debug`	`0`	The debug level
`detail`	`0`	The debug detail level
`factory`	`null`	Message resource factory. Message resources are explained in the section on internationalization
`FormBean`	`org.apache.struts.action.ActionFormBean`	The name of the class that encapsulates information on `ActionForm` beans
`forward`	`org.apache.struts.action.ActionForward`	The name of the class that encapsulates information on `ActionForward` objects
`locale`	`true`	If set to `true` this stores a locale object in the user's session

Parameter	Default Value	Description
mapping	org.apache.struts.action.ActionMapping	The name of the class that encapsulates information on ActionMappings
maxFileSize	250M	Maximum size for file upload
multipartClass	org.apache.struts.upload.DiskMultipartRequestHandler	The name of the class for handling multipart requests
noCache	False	Determines whether the required HTTP headers are to be set to disable caching
null	True	If set to true, a null is returned for an invalid message key
tempDir	The working directory provided to this web application as a servlet attribute	Temporary working directory to use when processing file downloads
validate	True	Determines whether the new form of configuration file is used (old versions of Struts used a different form of configuration file)
validating	True	Determines whether to use a validating parser for the configuration file

Specialized subclasses of ActionServlet *may take additional configuration parameters, although for most cases the standard servlet will be sufficient to meet all your requirements.*

The ActionServlet instantiates the appropriate Action class when a particular request URI is received for the first time. The ActionServlet then stores a reference to itself in the Action class instance in a variable named servlet. After it has been instantiated, the Action class is cached for reuse.

The ActionServlet also provides methods that can be used by Action classes for accessing resources such as data sources and global forwards.

ActionServlet Methods

ActionServlet provides a set of methods that can be used by Action objects.

Complete information about the Struts API can be found in the Struts documentation web application, struts-documentation.war.

ActionServlet has methods that allow us to dynamically add or remove ActionForm beans, ActionForwards, and ActionMappings. These methods affect the current instance of the application only:

```
public void addFormBean (ActionFormBean formBean)
public void removeFormBean (ActionFormBean formBean)
public void addForward (ActionForward actionForward)
public void removeForward (ActionForward actionForward)
public void addMapping (ActionMapping actionMapping)
public void removeMapping (ActionMapping actionMapping)
```

The following methods find objects by name:

```
public ActionFormBean findFormBean (String name)
public ActionForward findForward (String name)
public ActionMapping findMapping (String name)
```

The next two methods are used to handle data sources:

```
public void addDataSource (String key, DataSource ds)
public DataSource findDataSource (String key)
```

Finally, we can use:

- The destroy() method to gracefully shut down the ActionServlet
- The reload() method to reload the information from the Struts configuration file into the ActionServlet

The ActionMapping Class

An ActionMapping represents the information about the mapping of a particular request to a particular Action. The ActionServlet passes the ActionMapping to the perform() method of an Action class. The specific Action class is determined by the information in the <action> element of the configuration file (which we discussed earlier), for example:

```
<action-mappings>
  <action path="/logon"
      type="diagnosis.action.LogonAction"
      name="logonForm"
      scope="request"
      input="/logon.jsp">
    <forward name="failure" path="/registration.jsp"/>
    <forward name="doctor"  path="/doctorMenu.jsp"/>
    <forward name="patient" path="/patientMenu.jsp"/>
  </action>
</action-mappings>
```

Once it has processed the request, an Action can use the findForward() method of the ActionMapping to find local forwards, which returns the ActionForward with the specified name. If there is no ActionForward with the specified name it returns null:

```
public ActionForward findForward(String name)
```

The `findForwards()` method returns the logical names of all locally defined forwards for a mapping. Then we can pass these values to `findForward()` to get the corresponding `ActionForward` object:

```
public String[] findForwards()
```

We also have a method that dynamically adds an `ActionForward` to the mapping:

```
public void addForward(ActionForward forward)
```

a method that returns the name of the form bean associated with this mapping:

```
public String getName()
```

and a method that returns the attribute scope (either session or request) for this mapping:

```
public String getScope()
```

The Action Class

An `Action` class is where the actual business logic of an application is implemented; they are responsible for processing requests. When a request is received, the `ActionServlet` will:

- Select an appropriate `Action` for the request
- If necessary, create an instance of the `Action`
- Call the `perform()` method on the `Action`

If the `ActionServlet` can't find a valid mapping it will invoke the default `Action` class (if there is one defined in the configuration file). If it has a mapping, the `ActionServlet` passes the appropriate `ActionMapping` class to the `Action`. The `Action` can use the `ActionMapping` to find local forwards, and to get and set `ActionMapping` attributes. The `ActionServlet` also passes the `ServletRequest` or `HttpServletRequest` object. Which one is passed depends on the servlet environment and the signature of the `perform()` method that is overridden.

All `Action` classes are required to extend the Struts class `org.apache.struts.action.Action` and override one of the `perform()` methods defined in the class. There are two defined, one handles non-HTTP (generic) requests:

```
public ActionForward perform(ActionMapping action,
                             ActionForm form,
                             ServletRequest request,
                             ServletResponse response)
                     throws IOException, ServletException
```

and the other handles HTTP requests:

```
public ActionForward perform(ActionMapping action,
                             ActionForm form,
                             HttpServletRequest request,
                             HttpServletResponse response)
                     throws IOException, ServletException
```

The `Action` classes implement the business logic required to process requests in the `perform()` method. This method returns an `ActionForward` object to the `ActionServlet`. This `ActionForward` contains a path that points to the resource to which the response should be forwarded.

`Action` classes must be programmed in a thread-safe manner, because the controller will share the same instance for multiple simultaneous requests. Accordingly, there are some guidelines to bear in mind when designing `Action` classes:

- Instance and static variables must not be used to store information related to the state of a particular request. They may be used to share global resources across requests for the same action.
- Access to other resources (such as JavaBeans and session variables) must be synchronized if those resources require protection from concurrent access.

Action Class Methods

In addition to the `perform()` method the Action class has a number of other useful methods. The following methods get or set the locale associated with a request:

```
public Locale getLocale(HttpServletReguest request)
public void setLocale(HttpServletRequest request, Locale locale)
```

The following method gets the message resources for the application. `MessageResources` is a general-purpose abstract class of the Struts Framework that defines an API for retrieving locale-specific messages from underlying resource locations:

```
public MessageResources getResources()
```

`PropertyMessageResources` is a concrete subclass of `MessageResources` that reads message keys and corresponding strings from named property resources. `Action` also has a method that checks if the cancel button on the form associated with the action was pressed, it returns `true` if it was pressed:

```
public boolean isCancelled(HttpServletRequest request)
```

`Action` classes can use the following method to store error messages when application errors occur:

```
public void saveErrors (HttpServletRequest request, ActionErrors errors)
```

The `ActionErrors` instance is used to store error messages. This method stores the `ActionErrors` object in the request attribute list under an error key. JSP pages can display these error messages using custom tags defined in the Struts HTML tag library, which we will cover later.

The ActionForm Class

The framework assumes that you have created an `ActionForm` bean for each input form required in your application. For every bean defined in the `struts-config.xml` file, the framework does the following before calling the `perform()` method of the `Action` class:

- It checks in the user's session for an instance of a bean of the appropriate class, under the appropriate key. If there is no such bean available under the session, a new one is automatically created and added to the user's session.

- For every request parameter whose name corresponds to the name of a property in the bean, the corresponding setter method is called.
- The updated ActionForm bean is passed to the Action perform() method when it is called, which makes these values immediately available.

The ActionForm classes extend the Struts class org.apache.struts.action.ActionForm. Beans created by application developers can contain extra properties and are accessed by the ActionServlet using reflection (which allows the retrieval of information about loaded objects).

The ActionForm class provides an alternative way to handle errors. It provides two methods:

```
public ActionErrors validate(ActionMapping mapping,
                             ServletRequest request)

public ActionErrors validate(ActionMapping mapping,
                             HttpServletRequest request)
```

Application developers should override the validate() method in their bean, and set the validate attribute to true in the <action> element in the configuration file. Then, the ActionServlet will call the validate() method *before* it invokes an Action class. If the validate() method returns an ActionErrors that is not null, the ActionForm will save the ActionErrors in the request attribute list by the error key name.

If the returned ActionErrors instance is not null and the size is greater than zero, it will save the instance in the request attribute list by the error key name. The ActionServlet then forwards the response to the input attribute value specified for the <action> element in the configuration file. For example:

```
public class MyForm extends ActionForm {
  private double number;

  ...

  public ActionErrors validate(ActionMapping map, HttpServletRequest req) {

    ActionErrors errors = new ActionErrors();

    ...

    if(condition) {
      ActionError error = new ActionError("error.newError", reason);
      errors.add (ActionErrors.GLOBAL_ERROR, error);
    }
  return errors;
}
```

If we need to perform validation of data that is specific to an application, it is better to do it in the Action class, rather than in the ActionForm class.

The ActionForm class also has methods that reset the properties of a bean to their default values:

```
public void reset(ActionMapping mapping, HttpServletRequest request)
public void reset(ActionMapping mapping, ServletRequest request)
```

While developing a class that extends the ActionForm interface, we should keep some key points in mind. An ActionForm bean will typically have only property getter and setter methods; it will not have methods that implement business logic. We should define a property for each field that is present in the form. The field and property names must match according to the JavaBeans specification; for example, a field named username will match getter and setter methods named getUserName() and setUsername().

There will be very little input validation logic in an ActionForm bean. The primary reason such beans exist is to save the most recent values entered by the user for the associated form, so that the same page can be reproduced, along with a set of error messages. This allows the user to correct the fields that have incorrect values. The actual validation of user input should be performed within Action classes or appropriate business logic beans.

The ActionForward Class

The ActionForward class represents a destination to which a Controller servlet can forward the result of an Action class' processing activities.

An Action class creates a response to a user's request, and then uses an ActionForward class to forward the response to another resource. The logical name of the ActionForward class is defined in the <forward> element of the configuration file.

Action classes can get a handle to an ActionForward instance and then return them back to the ActionServlet in three ways. We can use findForward() on:

- The ActionServlet to get a global forward by name
- The ActionMapping instance passed to the perform() method, to find a local forward by name

Another way is to create an instance themselves by calling one of the three constructors provided:

```
public ActionForward()
public ActionForward(String path)
public ActionForward(String path, boolean redirect)
```

Error Handling

The Struts Framework provides two classes to handle errors: ActionErrors and ActionError, both of which are part of the org.apache.struts.action package. ActionErrors holds a collection of ActionError objects, each of which represent individual error messages. Each ActionError contains key values that can be mapped to error messages stored in a resources file, which is specified as an initialization parameter to the ActionServlet.

The ActionError Class

The ActionError class defines a set of overloaded constructors for creating error messages. The first constructor method takes a string as an argument, for example:

```
ActionError error = new ActionError("error.Invalid");
```

In this case, the instance error maps to an error message in the application resources file:

```
error.invalid=<b>Invalid Number</b>
```

Using the <html:error> custom tag in the JSP page would result in the following message being displayed in bold: **Invalid Number.**

Another form of the constructor can be used for specifying replacement strings within messages using the java.text.MessageFormat class. Say, for example, the following line is present in the resources file:

```
error.invalid=<b>lnvalid Number{0})</b>
```

Then if we created an error message as follows:

```
ActionError error = new ActionError('error.invalid',new Double(-1));
```

The message displayed by the JSP page using the <html:error> tag would be: **Invalid Number -1**. We could also specify more than one replacement string in the constructor, for example:

```
ActionError (String key.Object value0, Object valuel.Object value2)
```

The ActionError class also provides a method for getting the error key for a particular message:

```
public String getKey()
```

And a method to get a string array of replacement values for the error message:

```
public String[] getValues()
```

The ActionErrors Class

ActionError classes are never used on their own to error handling, they are always stored in a ActionErrors object. The ActionErrors object holds a collection of ActionError class instances and their specified property values. We can either use our own property values, or ActionErrors.GLOBAL_ERROR.

The following code illustrates a typical error-handling scenario in the `perform()` method of an `Action` class:

```
MyForm form = (MyForm) form;

if (number == -1) {
  ActionErrors errors = new ActionErrors ();
  ActionError error = new ActionError("error.bellowLimit", new Double(-1));
  errors.add(ActionErrors.GLOBAL_ERROR, error)
  saveErrors(req, errors);
  String input = mapping.getInput()
  return new ActionForward(input);
}
```

The `add()` method takes two arguments: a string representing a property, and an `ActionError` object. The `ActionError` passes a replacement string as a `Double` object containing the number entered by the user. Finally the `input` JSP page that instigated the `Action` class is retrieved from the `ActionMapping` object, and an `ActionForward` is returned back to the `ActionServlet`, which is asked to display the `input` JSP page.

`ActionErrors` has a number of useful methods:

Method	Description
`clear()`	Clears all error messages.
`empty()`	Returns true if `ActionErrors` object is empty.
`get()`	Returns error messages. If no argument is supplied, all messages will be returned as an `Iterator` object.
`properties()`	Returns an `Iterator` containing the property names which have at least one error.
`size()`	Returns the (integer) number of errors. If no argument is supplied the total number of errors for all properties is returned. If a string property name is supplied as the argument, the number of errors for this property is returned.

The Struts Tag Library

The Struts Tag Library, used by JSP View components, is comprised of four sets of tags:

- **Bean tags**
  For managing beans within the JSP page
- **Logic tags**
  For flow control within the JSP page
- **HTML tags**
  For generating HTML tags, displaying values in forms, and encoding URLs with the session ID
- **Template tags**
  For constructing pages that use a common format, using dynamic templates

Bean Tags

This tag library contains useful tags for accessing beans and their properties, as well as defining new beans. The Struts Framework provides a variety of custom tags for handling JavaBeans within JSP pages. These tags are packaged into a common tag library, whose tag library descriptor is defined in the file `struts-bean.tld`. The bean tag library defines tags that fall into four subcategories:

- Bean creation and copying tags
- Scripting variable definition tags
- Bean rendering tags
- Message internationalization tags

Bean Copying Tags

The bean tag library defines a powerful tag for performing actions such as defining new beans, copying existing beans, and copying properties from existing beans.

The `<bean:define>` tag is used to:

- Define new String constants
- Copy existing bean objects to newly defined bean objects
- Copy properties of existing bean objects in order to create new beans

Here are the attributes for the `<bean:define>` tag:

Attribute	**Description**
`id`	The name of the scripting variable by which the newly defined bean will be available. This attribute is required.
`type`	Defines the class for the scripting variable introduced.
`value`	Assigns a new object to the scripting variable defined by the id attribute.
`name`	The name of the target bean. This is a required attribute if the value attribute is not specified.
`property`	The property name of the bean defined by the name attribute that is used to define the new bean.
`scope`	The scope of the source bean. If not defined it is searched for from page scope to application scope.
`toScope`	The scope of the target bean. If not specified this defaults to page scope.

For example, the tag below defines a bean:

```
<bean:define id="example" value="This is an Example" />
```

In the example below, the bean is in the page scope, and is copied to another bean in the request scope:

```
<bean:define id="targetBean" name="sourceBean"
             scope="page" toScope="request" />
```

Tags for Defining Scripting Variables

The bean tag library defines various tags for defining and populating scripting variables from a variety of sources like cookies, request parameters, HTTP headers, and so on. The attributes of these tags are:

Attribute	Description
`id`	The name of the scripting variable and page scope attribute to be defined.
`name`	The name of the cookie/header/parameter.
`multiple`	If any arbitrary value for this attribute is specified, causes all matching cookies to be accumulated and stored into a bean of type `Cookie[]` (an array). If not specified, the first value for the specified cookie will be retrieved as a value of type `Cookie`.
`value`	A default cookie or value to return if not match is found.

An example for the `<bean:cookie>` tag is shown below:

```
<bean:cookie id="myCookie" name="userName" />
```

Here the name of the scripting variable is `myCookie`, and the name of the cookie used to create this attribute is `userName` (see Chapter 10 for information about setting cookies). Here's an example of the `<bean:header>` tag:

```
<bean:header id="myHeader" name="Accept-Language" />
```

In this case the name of the scripting variable is `myHeader`, and the name of the request header is `Accept-Language`. Finally, an example for the `<bean:parameter>` tag is:

```
<bean:parameter id="myParameter" name="myParameter" />
```

Here the scripting variable is called `myParameter`, and it holds the value of a request parameter also called `myParameter`.

The `<bean:include>` tag will retrieve the response of a resource and introduce a scripting variable and page scope attribute of type `String`. The resource can be a page, a Struts `ActionForward`, or an external URL. This is very similar to the `<jsp:include>` action, but the response of the resource stored in a page scope bean instead of being written to the output stream. Here are some of the attributes for this tag:

Attribute	Description
id	The name of the scripting variable and page scope attribute to be defined
page	An internal resource
forward	A Struts ActionForward
href	Fully qualified URL of the resource to be included

For example:

```
<bean:include id="mylnclude" page="MyJsp?x=l" />
```

Here the name of the scripting variable is `mylnclude`, and the response to retrieve is from the resource `MyJsp?x=l`.

The `<bean:resource>` tag will retrieve a web application resource, and introduce a scripting variable and page scope attribute of type `InputStream` or string. If there is a problem retrieving the resource a request time exception is thrown. The attributes of this tag are explained below. All of the attributes can take runtime expressions:

Attribute	Description
id	The name of the scripting variable and page-scope attribute to be defined
name	Relative path to the resource
input	If this attribute is not present the resource is made available as a string

An example for the `<bean:resource>` tag is shown below:

```
<bean:resource id="myResource" name="/WEB-INF/images/myResource.xml" />
```

Here the name of the scripting variable is `myResource`, and the name of the resource to retrieve is `myResource-xml`.

Rendering Bean Properties

The bean tag library defines the `<bean:write>` tag for writing bean properties to the enclosing JSP page writer. This tag is similar to the standard `<jsp:getProperty>` tag. The attributes of this tag are:

Attribute	Description
name	The name of the bean whose properties are to be rendered.
property	The name of the property to be rendered. If the property class has a `java.beans.PropertyEditor` the `getAsText()` method will be called or the `toString ()` method will be called.

Table continued on following page

Attribute	Description
scope	The scope of the bean. If not specified the bean will be searched for from page to application scope.
filter	If set to true any HTML special characters in the property values will be changed to their corresponding entity references.
ignore	If set to false a request time exception is thrown if the property is not found, otherwise a null value is returned.

Here's an example of using the <bean:write> tag:

```
<bean:write name="myBean" property="myProperty" scope="request"
                                                filter="true" />
```

Here we see that the property myProperty of the bean myBean should be rendered. The bean has request scope, and if any HTML special characters are found they should be changed to their corresponding entity references.

Message Tag and Internationalization

The Struts Framework supports internationalization and localization. The user defines their locale on their machine, and then when the web application needs to print a message, it refers to a resources file containing all of the messages written in the correct language. An application may provide many resource files, each of which provides messages written in a different language. If the resource is not found for the selected culture or language the default locale is used.

Struts supports internationalization using the <bean:message> tag, along with the Java 2 platform's inbuilt support for these tasks using the Locale and ResourceBundle classes defined in the java.util package. Message formatting is also supported using the techniques defined by the java.text.MessageFormat class. The power of Struts is such that the application developers need not know about the intricacies of these classes in order to use internationalized and formatted messages. In this section we will have a look at how internationalization and localization can be achieved using Struts.

The first step is to define a name for the application resources file that will contain all the messages for the application in the default language for the server. The messages need to be stored as key-value pairs as shown below:

```
error.validation.location=The entered location is invalid
```

Here error.validation.location is the key, while "The entered location is invalid" is the value.

This file needs to be stored in the class path, and its location needs to be passed to the ActionServlet as the value of the initialization parameter application. The value passed should follow the standard naming scheme for fully qualified Java classes. For example, if the resources file is stored in the directory WEB-INF\classes\ and the file is called Resources.properties, the value that needs to be passed is simply Resources. If the file is stored in the directory WEB-INF\classes\com\example then it should be com.example.Resources.

To enable internationalization, all resource files must be stored in the same directory as the one in which the base resources file (the resources file which contains messages written in the default locale – the local language) is stored. If the base resource file is called `Resources.properties` then the resources files containing messages in other specific languages are called `Resources_xx.properties`, where `xx` is the ISO code for the particular language (for instance, English is `en`, while Spanish is `es`). These files should therefore contain the same keys, but values in the specific languages.

The locale initialization parameter for the `ActionServlet` needs to be passed with a value `true`. This will enable the `ActionServlet` to store a locale object specific to the user's client machine in the user session under the key `Action.LOCALE_KEY`. Now everything is set up to run a truly internationalized web site which will automatically serve web pages in the language set for the locale on the user's client machine.

If we need to replace portions of our messages with specific strings we can define placeholders in the messages in the same way as we use `java.text.MessageFormat`:

```
error.invalid.number = The number {0} is invalid
```

We can use the Struts `<bean:message>` tag to replace the string `{0}` in the above message with any number we want. This tag allows us to write internationalized messages, labels, and prompts in our JSP application. The attributes for the `<bean:message>` tag can all take runtime expressions:

Attribute	Description
`key`	The key of the message as defined in the resource file.
`locale`	The name of the attribute under which the locale object is stored in the user's session. If not specified, the value of `Action.LOCALE_KEY` is used.
`bundle`	The name of the attribute under which the resources object is stored in the application context. If not specified, the value of `Action.MESSAGES_KEY` is used.
`arg0`	First parametric replacement value.
`arg1`	Second parametric replacement value.
`arg2`	Third parametric replacement value.
`arg3`	Fourth parametric replacement value.

The following example illustrates the use of the `<bean:message>` tag. Suppose there is a message defined in the resources file as follows:

```
info.myKey = The numbers entered are {0}, {1}, {2}, {3}
```

Then, if we use the following message tag:

```
<bean:message key="info.myKey" arg0="5" arg1="6" arg2="7" arg3="8" />
```

The output written to the JSP page by the message tag will be: The numbers entered are 5,6,7,8.

Logic Tags

The Logic library supplies tags that are useful for manipulating presentation logic without the use of scriptlets. The Struts logic tag library contains tags that are useful in managing conditional generation of output text, looping over object collections for repetitive generation of output text, and application flow management. It also provides a set of tags for handling flow control within a JSP page, for instance, iteration or conditional evaluation of the tag body. These tags are packaged into a common tag library with a TLD file `struts-logic.tld`. The logic tag library defines tags that perform three functions:

- Conditional logic
- Iteration
- Forwarding/redirecting response

Conditional Tags

There are three categories of Struts conditional tags. The first category of tags compares the value of one of the following entities to a specified constant:

- A cookie
- A request parameter
- A bean or a bean property
- A request header

The tags defined in this category are the following:

Tag	Functionality
`<equal>`	Returns `true` if the constant value is equal to that of the defined entity
`<notEqual>`	Returns `true` if the constant value is not equal to that of the defined entity
`<greaterEqual>`	Returns `true` if the constant value is equal to or greater than that of the defined entity
`<lessEqual>`	Returns `true` if the constant value is equal to or less than that of the defined entity
`<lessThan>`	Returns `true` if the constant value is less than that of the defined entity
`<greaterThan>`	Returns `true` if the constant value is greater than that of the defined entity

All of the tags belonging to this category have the same attributes (note that all of these attributes can take runtime expressions):

Attribute	Description
`Value`	The constant value that is to be compared.
`Cookie`	The name of the HTTP cookie to be compared against.
`Header`	The name of the HTTP request header to be compared against.
`Parameter`	The name of the HTTP request parameter to be compared against.
`Name`	The name of the bean if the value is to be compared against a bean or a bean property.
`Property`	The bean property that is to be compared against.
`Scope`	The scope of the bean. If the scope is not specified it is searched for from page to application scope.

Now let's have a look at a few examples using these logic tags. Here's the first, that uses the `<logic:equal>` tag:

```
<logic:equal parameter="name" value="Some Name">
  The entered name is Some Name
</logic:equal>
```

This tag evaluates the body if there is a request parameter called `name` and the value equals `Some Name`. Here is another example, which uses the `<logic:greaterThan>` tag:

```
<logic:greaterThan name="bean" property="prop" scope="page" value="7">
  The value of bean.Prop is greater than 7
</logic: greaterThan>
```

This tag evaluates the body if there is a bean named bean in the page scope, which has a property named `prop`, but only if the value of the property is greater than `7`. If the property can be converted to a numeric value a numeric comparison is performed, otherwise a string comparison is made.

The second category of conditional tags defines two tags:

- `<logic:present>`
- `<logic:notPresent>`

As their name suggests, these tags check whether a particular item is present or not before evaluating the tag body. The `<logic:present>` tag evaluates the body if a particular item is present, while the `<logic:notPresent>` tag only evaluates the body if the item is not present. The item checked for is governed by the attributes of the tag, and the values of these attributes:

Attribute	Description
cookie	The presence of the cookie specified by the attribute is checked.
header	The presence of the request header specified by the attribute is checked.
parameter	The presence of the request parameter specified by the attribute is checked.
name	The presence of the bean specified by the attribute is checked, if the property attribute is not specified. If the property attribute is specified, the existence of the bean as well as that of the property within the bean is checked.
property	The presence of the bean property specified by the attribute is checked for the bean specified by the attribute name
scope	If the bean name is specified, this is the scope of the bean. If the scope is not specified it is searched from page to application scope.
role	Checks whether the currently authenticated user belongs to the specified role.
user	Checks whether the currently authenticated user has the specified name.

Now let's have a look at a few examples using these tags. First, we have an example of how to use the `<logic:notPresent>` tag:

```
<logic:notPresent parameter="name">
  Parameter name is not present
</logic:notPresent>
```

This tag evaluates the body if the request parameter called `name` is not present. Next, here's an example of how you would use the `<logic:present>` tag:

```
<logic:present name="bean" property="prop" scope="page">
  The bean property bean.prop is present
</logic:present>
```

In this case, the tag evaluates the body if there is a bean named `bean` in the page scope, and this bean has a property named `prop`.

A third type of conditional tag is a bit more complicated to understand than those before. These tags evaluate the body content based on the result of pattern matching; in other words, the tags evaluate whether the value of a particular item is a sub-string of a specified constant:

- `<logic:match>`
- `<logic:notMatch>`

The tags allow the JSP engine to evaluate the body of the tag if a match is found (for `<logic:match>`) or not found (for `<logic:notMatch>`). Both of the tags belonging to this category have the same set attributes:

Attribute	Description
`cookie`	The name of the HTTP cookie to be compared against.
`header`	The name of the HTTP request header to be compared against.
`parameter`	The name of the HTTP request parameter compared against.
`location`	If a value for this attribute is specified, the match should occur at this specified location (index value).
`name`	The name of the bean if the value is to be compared against a bean or a bean property.
`property`	The bean property that is compared against the value.
`scope`	If the bean name is specified, the bean scope. If the scope is not specified it is searches from page to application scope.
`value`	The constant value that is to be compared.

Now we will have a look at a few examples that use the tags explained above:

```
<logic:notMatch parameter="name" value="xyz">
  The parameter name is not a substring of the string xyz
</logic:notMatch>
```

This `<logic:notMatch>` tag above only evaluates the body if there is a request parameter called name whose value is not a sub-string of the string xyz. Here's another example:

```
<logic:match parameter="name" value="xyz" location="1">
  The parameter name is a sub-string of the string xyz from the index 1
</logic:match>
```

This tag only evaluates the body if there is a request parameter called name whose value is a sub-string of the string `"xyz"`, but this sub-string must start from the index `1` of `"xyz"` (in other words the sub-string must be `"y"` or `"yz"`).

The Iterate Tag

The logic tag library defines the `<logic:iterate>` tag, which evaluates the body content of the tag multiple times, depending on the number of elements in a particular collection. The collection can be of type `java.util.Iterator`, `java.util.Collection`, `java.util.Map`, or an array. There are three ways of defining the collection:

- Use a runtime expression that returns a collection for the attribute collection
- Define the collection as a bean, and specify the name under which the attribute is stored using the name attribute
- Use the name attribute to define a bean, and the property attribute to define a bean property that would return a collection

The current element of the collection will be defined as a page scope bean. The attributes of the tag are explained below. All the attributes can take runtime expressions:

Attribute	Description
`collection`	The collection to be iterated if the name attribute is not specified.
`id`	The name of the page scope bean and the scripting variable that holds the handle to the current element in the collection.
`indexId`	The name of a page scope JSP bean that will contain the current index of the collection after each iteration.
`length`	The maximum number of iterations.
`name`	The name of the bean that is the collection, or the name of the bean whose property defined by the property attribute is a collection.
`offset`	An index from where the iteration has to be started.
`property`	The name of the bean property that is a collection.
`scope`	If the bean name is specified, the bean scope. If the scope is not specified it searched from page to application scope.
`type`	The type of the page scope bean defined for the current element.

An example for the `<logic:iterate>` tag is:

```
<logic:iterate id="currentlnt"
               collection="<%= myList %>"
               type="java.lang.Integer"
               offset="1"
               length="2">
<%= currentint %>
</logic:iterate>
```

This code will iterate two elements from the list starting from the second element, and it can make the current element available as a page scope bean and scripting variable of type `java.lang.Integer`. In other words, if the array `myList` contains elements 1, 2, 3, 4, and so on, the code will print 1 and 2.

Forwarding and Redirecting Tags

The Struts logic tag library defines a tag for forwarding the response, and another for redirecting to a URL.

Forward Tag

The `<logic:forward>` tag will either forward or redirect the response to the specified global `ActionForward`. The type of the global `ActionForward` decides whether the response is forwarded using the `PageContext` or redirected using `sendRedirect`. The only attribute defined for the tag is the name attribute that contains the name of the global `ActionForward`, for example:

```
<logic:forward name="MyGlobalForward" />
```

Redirect Tag

The `<logic:redirect>` tag is a powerful mechanism for performing an HTTP redirect. The redirect can be achieved in different ways, depending on the attributes specified. It also lets the developers specify query arguments for the redirected URL. The attributes for the tag are explained below. All of these attributes can take runtime expressions:

Attribute	Description
`forward`	The logical name of the global `ActionForward` that maps to the relative path of the resource
`href`	The fully qualified URL of the resource
`page`	The relative path of the resource
`name`	Either the name of a page, request, session, or application attribute of type `Map` that contains the name-value pairs of the query arguments to be attached to the redirected URL (if the property attribute is not specified); or the name of a bean which has a property of type `Map` that contains the same information (if the property attribute is specified)
`property`	The name of the bean property that is a `Map`. The bean's name is given by the name attribute above
`scope`	If the bean name is specified, this is the scope in which the bean is searched for. If the scope is not specified it is searched for from page to application scope
`paramID`	Defines the name of a particular query argument
`paramName`	Either: the name of bean of type String that contains the value of the query argument (if the attribute `paramProperty` is not specified), or a bean that has a property (specified by the name `paramProperty`) that contains the query argument value
`paramProperty`	The name of the string bean property that contains the query argument value
`paramScope`	The scope in which the bean defined by the `paramName` attribute is searched for

The tag should specify either one of the `forward`, `href` or `page` attributes to identify the resource to which the response should be redirected.

HTML Tags

The struts HTML tag library contains JSP custom tags useful for creating dynamic HTML user interfaces, including input forms. The tags in the Struts HTML library form a bridge between a JSP view and the other components of a web application. Since a dynamic web application often depends on gathering data from a user, input forms play an important role in the Struts framework. Consequently, the majority of the HTML tags involve HTML forms. Other important issues addressed by the Struts HTML tags are error messages, hyperlinking and internationalization. These tags can be broadly classified into the following functionalities:

- Rendering form elements and input controls
- Displaying error messages
- Rendering other HTML elements

Let's start by looking at tags that render forms and form controls.

Tags for Rendering Form and Input Elements

Struts tightly couples an HTML form to the corresponding `ActionForm` bean defined for the action of the form. The name of the form input fields should correspond to the property names defined in the `ActionForm` bean. The first time the form is rendered, the form input fields are populated from the `ActionForm` bean, and when the form is submitted the `ActionForm` bean instance is populated from the request parameters.

All of the nested tags for rendering HTML input elements that can be used within the `<form>` tag have the following attributes for defining JavaScript event handlers:

Attribute	Description
`onblur`	For when the field loses focus
`onchange`	For when the field loses focus and its value has changed
`onclick`	For when the field receives a mouse click
`ondblclick`	For when the field receive a mouse double-click
`onfocus`	For when the field receives input focus
`onkeydown`	For when the field has focus and a key is pressed
`onkeypress`	For when the field has focus and a key is pressed and released
`onkeyup`	For when the field has focus and a key is released
`onmousedown`	For when the field is under the mouse pointer and a mouse button is pressed
`onmousemove`	For when the field is under the mouse pointer and a mouse button is pressed

Attribute	Description
`onmouseout`	For when the control was under the mouse pointer, but the pointer is moved outside the element
`onmouseover`	For when the field was not under the mouse pointer, but the pointer is moved inside the element
`onmouseup`	For when the field is under the mouse pointer, and a mouse button is released

The other common attributes that can be defined against the `<form>` elements are:

Attribute	Description
`accesskey`	Defines the shortcut key for accessing the input field
`style`	Defines the styles for the input field
`styleClass`	Defines the style sheet class for the input field
`tabindex`	The tab order for the input field

Form Tag

The `<html:form>` tag is used for rendering an HTML tag. The name and class name of the `ActionForm` bean can be specified with the tag. If these attributes are not specified, the configuration file is queried for the `ActionMapping` for which the current JSP page is the input, and the bean name and class are retrieved from this mapping. If a bean of the specified name is not found in the scope specified in the `ActionMapping`, a new bean is created and stored, or if one is found it will be used.

The `<form>` tag may contain other child tags corresponding to the different HTML input fields; these tags are explained later in this section. The attributes for the `<html:form>` tag are:

Attribute	Description
`action`	The action associated with the form. This action will also be used to identify the `ActionForm` bean associated with the form, from the configuration.
`enctype`	The encoding type used for the form HTTP method.
`focus`	The field within the form that needs initial focus.
`method`	The HTTP method used for the form.
`name`	The name of the `ActionForm` bean associated with the form. If not specified the name is retrieved from the configuration information.
`onreset`	JavaScript event handler when the form is reset.
`onsubmit`	JavaScript event handler when the form is submitted.

Attribute	Description
scope	The scope within which the ActionForm bean has to be searched. If not specified the name is retrieved from the configuration information.
style	The styles to be applied.
styleClass	The style sheet class for this element.
type	The fully qualified name of the ActionForm bean. If not specified the name is retrieved from the configuration information.

A simple example for the <html:form> tag is:

```
<html:form action="validateEmployee.do" method="post">
  <!-- Rest of document goes here -->
</html:form>
```

We see that the action path associated with the form is validateEmployee, and the form data is passed via POST. For this form, all the ActionForm bean information like the bean name type, and scope are retrieved from the ActionMapping for the action specified for the form:

```
<form-beans>
  <form-bean name="empForm" type="com.example.EmployeeForm" />
</form-beans>

<action-mappings>
  <action path="/validateEmployee"
          type="com.example.ValidateEmployeeAction"
          name="empForm"
          scope="request"
          input="/employeelnput. jsp">
    <forward name="success" path="/employeeOutput.jsp" />
  </action>
</action-mappings>
```

If the configuration file containing the information listed above and the request URIs *.do are mapped to the Struts ActionServlet, the name, type, and scope of the ActionForm bean associated with the form will be empForm, com.example.EmployeeForm and request respectively. These properties can also be explicitly defined using the <html:form> tag attributes.

Button and Cancel Tags

The <html:button> is used for rendering an HTML button control, while the <html:cancel> tag is used for rendering an HTML cancel button. These tags must be nested within an <html:form> tag. The attributes of the tags, both of which can take runtime expressions, are:

Attribute	Description
`property`	Defines the request parameter name sent back to the server when the form is submitted
`value`	The value of the label to be placed on the button

Reset and Submit Tags

The `<html:reset>` and `<html:submit>` tags can be used for rendering HTML reset and submit buttons respectively. These tags must be nested within a `<html:form>` tag.

Text and Textarea Tags

The `<html:text>` and `<html:textarea>` tags are nested inside an `<html:form>` tag, and are used for rendering HTML textboxes and textareas respectively. Here are the attributes of these tags:

Attribute	Description
`Name`	The name of the bean whose property is queried to decide the current value of the textbox or textarea. If this attribute is not specified, the name of the `ActionForm` bean associated with the enclosing form is used.
`Property`	Defines the request parameter name sent back to the server when the form is submitted, and the bean property name that is queried to decide the current value of the text element.

The `<html:text>` tag also has the following attributes:

Attribute	Description
`maxlength`	The maximum number of characters that can be entered
`Size`	The size of the textbox (in characters)

An example of its use is:

```
<html:text property="username" size="16" maxlength="16"/>
```

The attributes below are specific to the `<html:textarea>` tag:

Attribute	Description
`Rows`	The number of rows in the textarea
`Cols`	The number of columns in the textarea

An example is shown below:

```
<html:textarea property="description" rows="6" cols="25"/>
```

Checkbox and Multibox Tags

The <html:checkbox> tag can be used for rendering a checkbox control. This tag must be nested within an <html:form> tag.

The <html:multibox> tag nested in an <html:form> tag can be used for rendering an HTML checkbox control. This tag is preferred to the <html:checkbox> tag if we wish to render multiple checkboxes with the same name, so that a `getParameterValues()` call on the request object passing the checkbox name would give back an array of strings.

All of the attributes of these tags can take runtime expressions:

Attribute	Description
`name`	The name of the bean whose property is queried to decide whether the checkbox is rendered as checked or not. If this attribute is not specified the name of the `ActionForm` bean associated with the enclosing form is used.
`property`	The name of the checkbox, as well as the name of the bean property that decides whether the checkbox is rendered as checked or not. In the case of a multibox, the property needs to be an indexed property defined as an array.
`value`	The value of the request parameter that will be sent back to the server if the checkbox is checked.

An example use of <html:checkbox> is:

```
<html:checkbox property="married" value="Y" />
```

Here we have a checkbox called `married` that will send a value of `Y` back to the server on submission of the form.

File Tag

The <html:file> tag can be used for rendering an HTML file control. This tag must be nested within an <html:form> tag. The attributes of this tag are explained below. All the attributes can take runtime expressions:

Attribute	Description
`Name`	The name of the bean whose property is queried to decide the contents to be rendered in the file control. If this attribute is not specified, the name of the `ActionForm` bean associated with the enclosing form is used.
`property`	This attribute defines the request parameter name sent back to the server when the form is submitted, as well as the bean property name that is queried to decide the contents to be rendered in the file control.

Attribute	Description
`Accept`	Set of content types that the server can process. This also filters the file types available for selection in the dialog box on the client browser.
`Value`	Value of the label to be placed on the button for browsing the file on the local file system.

Radio Tag

We can use the `<html:radio>` tag nested within an `<html:form>` tag for rendering an HTML radio button control. The attributes of this tag are explained below:

Attribute	Description
`Name`	The name of the bean whose property is queried to decide whether the radio button should be rendered as checked or not. If this attribute is not specified the name of the action form bean associated with the enclosing form is used.
`property`	The request parameter name sent back to the server when the form is submitted, as well as the bean property name that is queried to decide whether the radio button should be rendered as checked or not.
`value`	The value sent back to the server if the radio button is checked.

An example is shown below, which is taken from the sample application described in this chapter. This example specifies a group of two radio buttons for selection:

```
<td align="left">
  <html:radio property="userType" value="doctor"/>
  <bean:message key="prompt.type1"/>
   
  <html:radio property="userType" value="patient"/>
  <bean:message key="prompt.type2"/>
</td>
```

Hidden Tag

The `<html:hidden>` tag, when nested within a `<form>` tag, can be used for rendering an HTML hidden input element. The attributes of this tag are:

Attribute	Description
`name`	The name of the bean whose property is queried to decide the current value of the hidden element. If this attribute is not specified the name of the action form bean associated with the enclosing form is used.
`property`	Defines the request parameter name sent back to the server when the form is submitted, as well as the bean property name that is queried to decide the current value of the hidden element.
`Value`	The value that needs to be initialized for the hidden input element.

Table continued on following page

This example defines a hidden property called action:

```
<html:hidden property="action"/>
```

Password Tag

The <html:password> tag can be used for rendering an HTML password control. This tag has to be nested within an <html:form> tag. The attributes of this tag are:

Attributes	Description
maxlength	The maximum number of characters that can be entered.
name	The name of the bean whose property is queried to decide the current value of the password element. If this attribute is not specified the name of the ActionForm bean associated with the enclosing form is used.
property	This attribute defines the request parameter name sent back to the server when the form is submitted, as well as the bean property name that is queried to decide the current value of the password element.
redisplay	Whether to display the password contents if the corresponding bean property is already populated when the field is rendered.
size	The size of the field.

The following example prompts user for password and provides a password field for input.

```
<tr>
  <th align="center" width="50%">
    <bean:message key="prompt.password"/>
  </th>
  <td align="left" width="50%">
    <html:password property="password" size="16" maxlength="16"
                   redisplay="false"/>
  </td>
</tr>
```

Select Tag

The <html:select> tag, when nested inside an <html:form> control, can be used for rendering an HTML select control. The attributes of this tag are:

Attribute	Description
multiple	Indicates whether the select control allows multiple selections.
name	The name of the bean whose property is queried to decide which one of the options needs to be selected. If this attribute is not specified the name of the ActionForm bean associated with the enclosing form is used.

Attribute	Description
property	Defines the request parameter name sent back to the server when the form is submitted, as well as the bean property name that is queried as to which one of the options needs to be selected.
size	The number of options that can be displayed at one time.
value	Can be used to indicate the option that needs to be selected.

Options Tag

The `<html:options>` tag can be used for rendering a collection of HTML option elements. This element should be nested within the `<html:select>` tag. The attributes of this tag can all take runtime expressions:

Attribute	Description
collection	The name of a collection that is stored as an attribute in some scope that contains a collection of beans. The number of options is the same as the number of elements in the collection. The property attribute can be used to define the bean property used for the option's value and the `labelProperty` attribute can be used to define the bean property used for the option's label.
labelName	Used to specify a bean stored in some scope, which is a collection of strings that can be used to define the labels for the `<html:option>` elements if they are different from the values.
labelProperty	Defines the bean property used to write the option's label when used with the collection attribute.
Name	If this is the only attribute specified, this identifies a bean stored in some scope, which would return a collection of strings used to write the value attribute for `<html:option>` elements.
property	The property attribute, when used with the collection attribute, defines the name of the property in each individual bean that will render the value of the option. If used without the collection attribute, this defines the property of the bean defined by the `name` attribute (if the `name` attribute is present) or the `ActionForm` bean that would return a collection to write the values for the options.

Now we will see a few examples for this tag. Here's the first:

```
<html:options collection="optionCollection" property="optionValue"
                                            labelProperty="optionLabel" />
```

This tag assumes that there is a collection called `optionCollection` stored in some scope that contains individual beans each with a property called `optionValue` that is used as the value of an option. Each option's label is defined by a bean's `optionLabel` property:

```
<html:options name="optionValues" labelName="optionLabels" />
```

In this case optionValues represents a bean stored in some scope, which is a collection of strings that can be used to write the values of the option, and optionLabels represents a bean stored in some scope, which is a collection of strings that can be used to write the option labels:

```
<html:options name="optionValues" />
```

In this case optionValues represents a bean stored in some scope that is a collection of strings that can be used to write the values of the options, and the option labels are left empty.

Finally, here is an example that demonstrates the use of <html:select> and <html:options> together:

```
<html:select property="parentId">
  <html:options collection="parentIds" property="value"
                labelProperty="label"/>
</html:select>
```

Tags for Rendering Error Messages

The <html:errors> tag can be used in conjunction with ActionErrors to display error messages. The tag first reads the message key error.header from the resources file for the current locale, and then renders the message text. Next, it loops through the ActionErrors object (generally stored as a request attribute under the key Action.ERROR_KEY), reads the message key for individual ActionError objects, reads and formats the corresponding messages from the resources file for the current locale, and renders them. Then it reads the message corresponding to the key error.footer and renders it too.

Defining the property attribute can filter the error messages that are displayed. The value of this attribute should correspond to the key under which the ActionError object was stored in the ActionErrors object. The attributes of this tag are explained below. All of the attributes can take runtime expressions:

Attribute	Description
bundle	The name of the application scope attribute that contains the message resources. The default value is Action.MESSAGE_KEY.
locale	The name of the session scope attribute that stores the locale for the user currently logged on. The default value is Action.LOCALE_KEY.
name	The name of the request attribute that stores the ActionErrors object. The default value is Action.ERROR_KEY.
property	This can be used for specifying the keys under which individual ActionError objects are stored within the ActionErrors object, for filtering messages.

Two examples follow:

```
<html:errors/>
```

This will display all the errors from the collection.

```
<html:errors property="missing.name" />
```

This code will display only those errors stored against the `missing.name` key.

Other HTML Tags

The Struts HTML tags also define the following tags for rendering other HTML elements:

- `<html:html>`
  Renders the HTML element
- `<html:img>`
  Renders the HTML image tag
- `<html:link>`
  Renders an HTML link or an anchor
- `<html:rewrite>`
  Generates a URI without the anchor tag

You should refer to the Struts documentation for more information on these tags.

Template Tags

Dynamic templates are a powerful way of modularizing web page layout. Let's assume we have a web application that has hundreds of web pages that all use the same layout: a header section, a footer section and a main content section. A simplistic way of implementing a common layout is to use HTML tables and JSP includes as shown below.

```
<html>
  <head>
    <title></title>
  </head>
  <body>
    <table width=100% height=100%>
      <tr height="10%">
        <td>
          <jsp:include page="header.html"/>
        </td>
      </tr>
      <tr height="80%">
        <td>
          <jsp:include page="employeeList.jsp"/>
        </td>
      </tr>
<tr height="10%">
        <td>
          <jsp:include page="employeeFooter.jsp"/>
        </td>
```

```
        </tr>
      </table>
    </body>
  </html>
```

The problem with the code shown above is that the template is hard-coded into the JSP code. If we decide to change the height of the header to 15% and we have hundreds of JSP pages it will become a time-consuming and error prone process to change the code. This is where dynamic templates come into their own. Dynamic templates encapsulate the layout, and the template page is included in all our JSP pages rather than hard-coding the details. So if we decide to change the template, the only place we need to make changes is in the template JSP page.

The Struts template tag library defines custom tags for implementing dynamic templates.

Insert Tag

The `<template:insert>` tag can be used within an application's JSP pages to insert a dynamic template. The tag only takes the `template` attribute, which is used to define the template JSP page. The pages to be inserted into the template are specified using multiple `<template:put>` tags defined as the body content for the `<template:insert>` tag.

Put Tag

The `<template:put>` tags are used within the `<template:insert>` tag for specifying the resources to be inserted in to the template. The attributes for the tag are:

Attribute	Description
`content`	Defines the content to be inserted, like a JSP file or an HTML file
`direct`	If set to `true` the string specified by the content attribute is printed directly rather than being included in the JSP page
`name`	The name of the content to be inserted
`role`	If this attribute is specified, the content is inserted only if the currently authenticated user has the specified role

Get Tag

The `<template:get>` tag is used within the template JSP page to retrieve the resources inserted by the `<template:put>` tags into the content JSP pages. The attributes of the tag are the following:

Attribute	Description
`name`	The name of the content that was inserted by the `<template:put>` tag
`role`	If this attribute is specified, the content is inserted only if the currently authenticated user has the specified role

Using Template Tags

Next, we'll see how the Struts template tags can be used to create dynamic templates. First we will write a template JSP page that will be used by all our web pages:

```
<html>
  <%@ taglib uri="/template" prefix="template" %>
  <head>
    <title></title>
  </head>
  <body>
    <table width=100% height=100%>
      <tr height="10%">
        <td>
          <template:get name="header" />
        </td>
      </tr>
      <tr height="80%">
        <td>
          <template:get name="content" />
        </td>
      </tr>
      <tr height="10%">
        <td>
          <template:get name="footer" />
        </td>
      </tr>
    </table>
  </body>
</html>
```

Let's call this file `template.jsp`. This file uses the `<template:get>` tag to get the contents supplied by our content JSP pages using the `<template:put>` tag, and lays out the contents in an HTML table. The three content types expected are `header`, `content`, and `footer`. A typical content JSP might look like:

```
<%@ taglib uri="/template" prefix="/template" %>
<template:insert template="template.jsp">
  <template:put name="header" content="header.html" />
  <template:put name="content" content="employeeList.jsp" />
  <template:put name="footer" content="footer.html" />
</template:insert>
```

This application JSP page uses the `<template:insert>` tag to define the template, and then uses the `<template:put>` tag to push three resources identified by unique content names to the template JSP page. If we have hundreds of JSP pages using the same scheme, and we suddenly decide to change the template, the only place we will have to make a change now is the `template.jsp` file.

So far, we have gone through various components of the framework. Now we're ready to put it all together and develop an application using Struts.

An Example Web Application Based on Struts

The Struts Framework has become an increasingly popular platform for constructing web applications based on a MVC type design pattern. It has achieved this popularity due to:

- The simplicity of structuring and developing web applications
- The feature of **logical naming** to assist in isolating the View layer and the Model layer, so that changes in one do not have to impact the other
- A rich set of tools to assist in creating pages with dynamic content exposed by the Model layer through JavaBeans

In order to demonstrate the features of the Struts Framework, we will create an application that serves as a tool for practicing doctors. It assists patients in securing an appointment with a doctor by answering an online pre-diagnostic test. It helps doctors to understand the seriousness of the patient's condition before their appointment.

We want to concentrate more on the analysis and design part of the application development; so many details of implementation will be left out. Please download the full application from the Wrox web site (http://www.wrox.com/).

Problem Analysis

A doctor registers with the application and creates an online diagnostic test. The test will be of a multiple-choice type and can be logically presented in the form of a tree. Patients register with the application and take the online diagnostic test administered by a doctor. After the test, the application sends an e-mail informing the doctor of the test results and patient's preferred date for appointment. The doctor assesses the seriousness of the illness depending upon the test results, and replies to the patient about the appointment for consultation.

There is room for improvement in this application, and we urge you to add more features and experiment with it.

A doctor or patient must register with the system. A doctor can create a pre-diagnostic test, and a patient can take the test and request an appointment for consultation with the doctor. The request will be sent to the doctor by e-mail after which the doctor is expected to get back to the patient with the date of consultation.

A new user can register either as a doctor or as a patient. After registering, the user will be taken to either the doctor or patient main menu page. From here, a user will be able to edit their registration information, or log off. A doctor will have an option to create a topic and create a questionnaire under that topic.

A questionnaire will consist of multiple-choice questions and every unique answer will lead to a particular question:

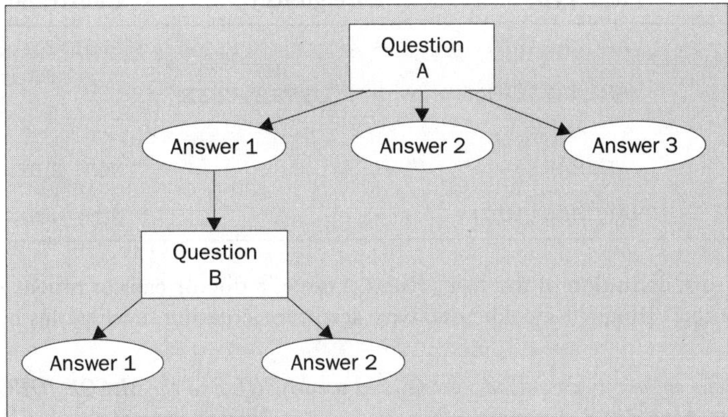

Choosing Answer 1 for Question A will lead to Question B. This sequence will continue until the patient reaches a leaf node, i.e. one that does not point to any other question. For example Answer 1 of Question B doesn't have a child node. If we consider the following example sequence, the final answers of this test can either be, Answer 1 or Answer 2 of Question B or Answers 2 or 3 of question A:

A doctor can save this test in XML for later use and an individual doctor can administer several tests. A patient, after logging in, can: select a doctor, select a test administered by the doctor, and start answering the questions. Once the patient reaches the end node, they will be given an option to input a convenient date and time for consultation. If the patient submits the test, the application constructs a mail and sends it to the doctor. This mail contains the test result and details of the patient, including the preferred choice of date and time for consultation. The doctor is expected to take notice of these things, and allocate time for the patient based on appointment availability and the severity of the illness, and then reply to the patient regarding these details.

Application Design

It's time to decide how we are going to fulfill all the requirements. First of all, we will have to store the user and topic details in a database. The following tables show the structure of these database tables: `APP_USERS` and `APP_TOPICS`.

APP_USERS

Field Name	Field Type	Foreign Key	Constraint
USERNAME	VARCHAR(20)	-	PRIMARY KEY
PASSWORD	VARCHAR(10)	-	NOT NULL
USERTYPE	VARCHAR(10)	-	NOT NULL
FULL_NAME	VARCHAR(40)	-	NOT NULL
ADDRESS	VARCHAR(50)	-	NOT NULL
EMAIL	VARCHAR(50)	-	NOT NULL

APP_TOPICS

Field Name	Field Type	Foreign Key	Constraint
TOPICNAME	VARCHAR(30)	-	PRIMARY KEY
USERNAME	VARCHAR(20)	APP_USERS.USER NAME	
FILENAME	VARCHAR(30)	-	NOT NULL
DESCRIPTION	VARCHAR(150)	-	NOT NULL

As can be seen from definition of the APP_TOPICS table, a doctor cannot repeat a topic name. Hence, we have a combined Primary Key. The database script for creating these tables in MySQL is provided.

> *For instructions on how to download, install, and use MySQL and the MySQL JDBC driver you should refer to Appendix B. For more information on databases in general you should refer to Chapter 8.*

If you change the user and password created in this script you will need to update their values in the source code as well:

```
CREATE DATABASE diagnosis;

USE diagnosis;

CREATE TABLE APP_USERS (
       USERNAME VARCHAR(20) PRIMARY KEY,
       PASSWORD VARCHAR(10) NOT NULL,
       USERTYPE VARCHAR(20) NOT NULL,
       FULL_NAME VARCHAR(40) NOT NULL,
       ADDRESS VARCHAR(50) NOT NULL,
       EMAIL VARCHAR(50) NOT NULL);

CREATE TABLE APP_TOPICS (
       TOPIC_NAME VARCHAR(30) NOT NULL,
       USERNAME VARCHAR(20) NOT NULL,
       FILE_NAME VARCHAR(30) NOT NULL,
       DESCRIPTION VARCHAR(150) NOT NULL);

ALTER TABLE APP_TOPICS ADD (
      CONSTRAINT C1 PRIMARY KEY (TOPIC_NAME, USERNAME),
      CONSTRAINT C2 FOREIGN KEY (USERNAME) REFERENCES APP_USERS);

GRANT ALL PRIVILEGES
      ON diagnosis.*
      TO struts@localhost IDENTIFIED BY 'wrox';
```

We will have a generic SQL helper class, which is going help us in constructing and executing queries, which we will look at later on.

The tests are stored in XML files. The name of the file for a given topic is stored in `APP_TOPICS` table under the column `FILE_NAME`. A generic example of such a file is:

```
<TOPIC NAME="Some Topic" OWNER="Some User">
  <NODE ID="1">
    <QUESTION>Question #1</QUESTION>
    <ANSWER ID="1" END="false" NEXTQ="2">Answer #1</ANSWER>
    <ANSWER ID="2" END="false" NEXTQ="3">Answer #2</ANSWER>
    <ANSWER ID="3" END="false" NEXTQ="4">Answer #3</ANSWER>
  </NODE>
  <NODE ID="N"> <!-- Where N is some number -->
    <QUESTION>Question #N </QUESTION> <!--Test ends here -->
    <ANSWER ID="1" END="true">Answer #1</ANSWER>
    <ANSWER ID="2" END="true">Answer #2</ANSWER>
    <ANSWER ID="3" END="true"></ANSWER> <!--No answer here-->
  </NODE>
</TOPIC>
```

We need to store and retrieve XML files on the server. So we will have an XML serializing helper class. We will also have an e-mail helper class that will be used to send e-mails. You should refer to the code download for details of these classes.

Implementation

We are going to apply most of the concepts we have learnt in this chapter so far including:

- Struts configuration file
- `ActionForm` beans and `Action` classes
- `ActionMappings`, `ActionForwards`, and `ActionErrors`
- Struts tag libraries (including an application specific tag library)

We will also discuss various implementation details of this application. We will start with user registration. The user can be a doctor or a patient. Once they register their details (username, password, e-mail address, mailing address, full name), and have them validated, they can access the services of the application. If there is any missing information, the user is presented with a "missing information" error and the input form retaining all the data they entered. The registration information will be stored in a JavaBean, `RegistrationForm`, which extends `org.apache.struts.action.ActionForm`.

The RegistrationForm Class

This form is declared in the `struts-config.xml` file under the `<form-beans>` element.

This example application is based on the example web application that ships with Struts 1.0. You should refer to Appendix C for the details of the license under which this code is distributed.

```
<?xml version="1.0" encoding="ISO-8859-1" ?>

<!DOCTYPE struts-config PUBLIC
          "-//Apache Software Foundation//DTD Struts Configuration 1.0//EN"
          "http://jakarta.apache.org/struts/dtds/struts-config_1_0.dtd">

<struts-config>

  ...

  <form-beans>
    <form-bean name="registrationForm"
               type="diagnosis.form.RegistrationForm"/>
  </form-beans>

  ...

</struts-config>
```

Let's take a look at the source code of the JavaBean:

```
package diagnosis.form;

import javax.servlet.http.HttpServletRequest;
import org.apache.struts.action.ActionError;
import org.apache.struts.action.ActionErrors;
import org.apache.struts.action.ActionForm;
import org.apache.struts.action.ActionMapping;
import diagnosis.action.*;
import diagnosis.form.*;
import diagnosis.util.*;
import diagnosis.servlets.*;
import diagnosis.tag.*;

public final class RegistrationForm extends ActionForm  {

  private String action = "Create";

  public String getAction() {
    return (this.action);
  }

  public void setAction(String action) {
    this.action = action;
  }
```

We create similar properties for `emailId`, `address`, `fullName`, `userType`, `password`, `password2`, and `username`, before creating methods named `reset()` and `validate()`:

```
  public void reset(ActionMapping mapping, HttpServletRequest request) {
    this.action = "Create";
    this.emailId = null;
    this.address = null;
```

```
    this.fullName = null;
    this.password = null;
    this.password2 = null;
    this.username = null;
  }

  public ActionErrors validate(ActionMapping mapping,
                               HttpServletRequest request) {
    ActionErrors errors = new ActionErrors();
    if ((username == null) || (username.length() < 1)) {
      errors.add("username", new ActionError("error.username.required"));
    }
    if (userType == null) {
      errors.add("userType", new ActionError("error.userType.required"));
    }
    if (address == null) {
      errors.add("address", new ActionError("error.address.required"));
    }
    if ((password == null) || (password.length() <1)) {
      errors.add("password", new ActionError("error.password.required"));
    }
    if ((password2 == null) || (password2.length() < 1)) {
      errors.add("password2", new ActionError("error.password2.required"));
    }
    if (!password.equals(password2)) {
      errors.add("password2", new ActionError("error.password.match"));
    }
    if ((emailId == null) || (emailId.length() < 1)) {
      errors.add("emailId", new ActionError("error.emailId.required"));
    } else {
      int atSign = emailId.indexOf("@");
      if ((atSign < 1) || (atSign >= (emailId.length() - 1))) {
        errors.add("emailId",
                   new ActionError("error.emailId.format",emailId));
      }
    }
    if ((fullName == null) || (fullName.length() < 1)) {
      errors.add("fullName", new ActionError("error.fullName.required"));
    }
    return errors;
  }
}
```

There are variables to store the state and a minimal set of validations covering the required fields and the checking of the e-mail address format.

The SaveRegistrationAction Class

The `Action` class validates, creates, and updates the user's registration information. The class name is `SaveRegistrationAction` and it uses the form `registrationForm` as declared in the `struts-config.xml` under the `<action-mappings>` element. The action `saveRegistration` is mapped to this `Action` class:

```
<action-mappings>
  ...
  <!-- Save user registration -->
  <action path="/saveRegistration"
          type="diagnosis.action.SaveRegistrationAction"
          name="registrationForm"
          scope="request"
          input="/registration.jsp"
          validate="true">
    <forward name="failure" path="/registration.jsp" />
  </action>
  ...
</action-mappings>
```

This class will inherit from the class `org.apache.struts.action.Action` and override the `perform()` method:

```
package diagnosis.action;

import java.io.IOException;
import java.lang.reflect.InvocationTargetException;
import java.util.*;
import javax.servlet.ServletException;
import javax.servlet.http.*;
import org.apache.struts.action.*;
import org.apache.struts.util.*;
import diagnosis.action.*;
import diagnosis.form.*;
import diagnosis.util.*;
import diagnosis.servlets.*;
import diagnosis.tag.*;

public final class SaveRegistrationAction extends Action {

  public ActionForward perform(ActionMapping mapping,
                                               ActionForm form,
                                               HttpServletRequest request,
                                               HttpServletResponse response)
                       throws IOException, ServletException {
```

We extract the attributes and parameters we are going to need:

```
    Locale locale = getLocale(request);
    MessageResources messages = getResources();
    HttpSession session = request.getSession();
    RegistrationForm regform = (RegistrationForm) form;
    String action = request.getParameter("action");
    if (action == null) {
        action = "Create";
    }
    Object obj =
           servlet.getServletContext().getAttribute(Constants.DATABASE_KEY);
```

```
Hashtable database = null;
if(obj == null) {
  database = new Hashtable();
} else {
  database = (Hashtable)obj;
}
```

Check if there a logged-on user (unless we're creating one):

```
User user = (User) session.getAttribute(Constants.USER_KEY);

if ((!"Create".equals(action)) && (user == null)) {
  return (servlet.findForward("logon"));
}
```

Check if this transaction was cancelled:

```
if (isCancelled(request)) {
  if (mapping.getAttribute() != null) {
    session.removeAttribute(mapping.getAttribute());
  }
  if(action.equals("Create")) {
    return (mapping.findForward("cancel"));
  } else {
    return (mapping.findForward(user.getUserType()));
  }
}
```

Validate the transactional control token:

```
if (!isTokenValid(request)) {
  errors.add(ActionErrors.GLOBAL_ERROR,
             new ActionError("error.transaction.token"));
}
resetToken(request);
```

Validate the request parameters specified by the user:

```
String username = regform.getUsername();
String password = regform.getPassword();
String password2 = regform.getPassword2();
String userType = regform.getUserType();
String fullName = regform.getFullName();
String address = regform.getAddress();
String emailId = regform.getEmailId();

if (("Create".equals(action)) && (database.get(username) != null)) {
  errors.add("username",
             new ActionError("error.username.unique",
                             regform.getUsername()));
}
```

Report any errors we have discovered back to the original form:

```
    if (!errors.empty()) {
      saveErrors(request, errors);
      saveToken(request);
      return (new ActionForward(mapping.getInput()));
    }
```

Update the user's persistent profile information:

```
    if ("Create".equals(action)) {
      user = new User();
      user.setUsername(username);
      user.setPassword(password);
      user.setUserType(userType);
      user.setFullName(fullName);
      user.setAddress(address);
      user.setEmailId(emailId);

      int result = 0;
      try {
        result = User.addUser(user);
      } catch(Exception e) {
        e.printStackTrace();
      }
```

If appropriate, log the user in:

```
      if (result == 1) {
        database.put(user.getUsername(), user);
        servlet.getServletContext().setAttribute(Constants.DATABASE_KEY,
                                                 database);
        session.setAttribute(Constants.USER_KEY, user);
      }
    }
```

This class can handle two different operations, "create" or "edit". Let's take a look at the "create" action first. The variable by `database` is a `Hashtable`. We are caching the user information in the cache table at runtime. The validation involves checking the desired user id with the existing user id. If such a user id is found, an error is thrown to the user asking them to select another id. After validation, the user information is added to the `APP_USERS` table. This means that user has been successfully registered with the system. Then the user is logged in to the application by setting the appropriate session properties.

Now let us look at the "edit" section:

```
    if("Edit".equals(action)) {
      user.setFullName(fullName);
      user.setAddress(address);
      user.setEmailId(emailId);

      int result = 0;
```

```
        try {
          result = User.modifyUser(user);
        } catch(Exception e) {
          e.printStackTrace();
        }
```

If appropriate, log the user in:

```
        if (result == 1) {
          database.put(user.getUsername(), user);
          servlet.getServletContext().setAttribute(Constants.DATABASE_KEY,
                                                   database);
          session.setAttribute(Constants.USER_KEY, user);
        }
      }
```

Remove the obsolete form bean:

```
      if (mapping.getAttribute() != null) {
        if ("request".equals(mapping.getScope())) {
          request.removeAttribute(mapping.getAttribute());
        } else {
            session.removeAttribute(mapping.getAttribute());
        }
      }
```

First the user information is modified and stored in the database. At this stage, the user is automatically logged in and is forwarded to the appropriate main menu page:

```
      if(user.getUserType().equals(Constants.DOCTOR)) {
        return (mapping.findForward("doctor"));
      } else {
          return (mapping.findForward("patient"));
      }
    }
  }
```

The `findForward()` function finds the appropriate resource to forward using the `<global-forwards>` setting in `struts-config.xml` file as shown below:

```
  <global-forwards>
    ...
    <forward name="doctor" path="/doctorMenu.jsp"/>
    <forward name="patient" path="/patientMenu.jsp"/>
    ...
  </global-forwards>
```

`saveRegistration` is mapped to `SaveRegistrationAction` class. It uses `RegistrationForm` bean and takes input from `SaveRegistration.jsp`:

```
<action path="/saveRegistration"
        type="diagnosis.action.SaveRegistrationAction"
        name="registrationForm"
        scope="request"
        input="/registration.jsp"
        validate="true">
  <forward name="failure" path="/registration.jsp" />
</action>
```

Let's take a look at registration.jsp. This JSP page handles both register and edit registration info options in the application. These actions are dubbed as "create" and "edit" internally:

```
<logic:equal name="registrationForm" property="action"
             scope="request" value="Edit">
  <app:checkLogon/>
</logic:equal>
```

As you can see, if the action is "edit", this file checks whether the user has already logged in. Here <app:checkLogon> is an application specific custom tag. We will discuss this tag later in this section. This tag is used to check whether the user information is available for us to edit:

```
<head>
  <logic:equal name="registrationForm" property="action"
               scope="request" value="Create">
    <title><bean:message key="registration.title.create" /></title>
  </logic:equal>
  <logic:equal name="registrationForm" property="action"
               scope="request" value="Edit">
    <title><bean:message key="registration.title.edit" /></title>
  </logic:equal>
  <html:base/>
</head>
```

This piece of code sets the header according to the action requested (create/edit). This page uses logic tags extensively to support both of these functionalities. The rest of the page displays a form to input user profile details for registration. If the profile is being edited, then the form elements are selectively filled:

```
<logic:equal name="registrationForm" property="action"
             scope="request" value="Create">
  <html:text property="username" size="16" maxlength="16" />
</logic:equal>

<logic:equal name="registrationForm" property="action"
             scope="request" value="Edit">
  <bean:write name="registrationForm" property="username"
              scope="request" filter="true" />
  <html:hidden property="username" />
</logic:equal>
```

If the action is "edit", the user name is printed and cannot be changed, otherwise the user name will appear in an input text box.

The Custom Tag: CheckLogonTag

The usage of this tag is an excellent example of the usage of custom tags in Struts application. This tag looks to see if the user is logged in by checking for an object named "User" in the session context. If it is not found, control is forwarded to `login.jsp`. So, to make sure that the user is logged in before accessing a page, `<app:checkLogon/>` is used as we saw earlier.

The functionality of this tag is defined in the class `CheckLogonTag`, which extends `javax.servlet.jsp.tagext.TagSupport`:

```
package diagnosis.tag;

import java.io.IOException;
import javax.servlet.http.HttpSession;
import javax.servlet.jsp.JspException;
import javax.servlet.jsp.JspWriter;
import javax.servlet.jsp.PageContext;
import javax.servlet.jsp.tagext.TagSupport;
import org.apache.struts.action.Action;
import org.apache.struts.util.BeanUtils;
import org.apache.struts.util.MessageResources;
import diagnosis.action.*;
import diagnosis.form.*;
import diagnosis.util.*;
import diagnosis.servlets.*;
import diagnosis.tag.*;

public final class CheckLogonTag extends TagSupport {

  private String name = Constants.USER_KEY;
  private String page = "/logon.jsp";

  public String getName() {
      return (this.name);
  }

  public void setName(String name) {
      this.name = name;
  }

  public String getPage() {
      return (this.page);
  }

  public void setPage(String page) {
      this.page = page;
  }

  public int doStartTag() throws JspException {
      return (SKIP_BODY);
  }

  public int doEndTag() throws JspException {
```

Check if there is a valid user logged on:

```
    boolean valid = false;
    HttpSession session = pageContext.getSession();
    if ((session != null) && (session.getAttribute(name) != null)) {
        valid = true;
    }
```

Forward control based on the results:

```
    if (valid) {
        return (EVAL_PAGE);
    } else {
      try {
        pageContext.forward(page);
      } catch (Exception e) {
        throw new JspException(e.toString());
      }
      return (SKIP_PAGE);
    }
  }

  public void release() {
    super.release();
    this.name = Constants.USER_KEY;
    this.page = "/logon.jsp";
  }
}
```

Application Overview

We have dealt in detail with the user registration part of the application (with the core Struts features in mind). We'll just walk through rest of the application, examining the functionality of each component as we go.

As we can see from the use case diagram for the application, we have just covered one generic use case. Now let's get into specifics. The doctor can create and delete online diagnostic tests. The patient can login, choose a doctor, choose a topic, and take a test. These two use cases are so tightly coupled that we will use the same set of core components to deal with both of them.

There are four classes that deal directly with the management of diagnostic tests. They handle creation, collection, and deletion of diagnostic test sequences in the application:

- `TopicForm` bean
  This bean stores the intermediate state of the application when the topic is created. It holds the information about a single node in session. It knows the topic name, description, topic id, and current set of question and answers (limited to three).

- `Topic`
  This holds the information about a topic as stored in the database, such as the topic name, file name, user who owns the topic, and the topic description.

- `TopicCollection`
  This represents a set of topics for a specific doctor.

- `SaveTopicAction`
  This class helps in creating or deleting diagnostic tests by doctors. It takes care of creating each node in the test XML file and writing it to the appropriate XML file.

- `topics.jsp`
  This JSP page is responsible for presenting the current set of question and answers to the client. It raises appropriate actions to save or delete a test topic. If you go through the code you can see that, if the finish check box is selected, the creation of the test ends. The test is saved in the `topic-topicname.xml` format we saw earlier.

Now let's take a look at the set of components that deal with the test part of the application. They are responsible for the administration tests created by doctors:

- `test.jsp`
  This JSP page handles the presentation part of the administration of tests. A patient can select a doctor, then select a test administered by that doctor and take the online test. It uses the following components.

- `TestForm` bean
  This bean stores the session state of the test, which is being answered by a patient. It stores the test details such as topic name, doctor name, appointment date, the action being performed on the test data (creation, for example), and the current question ID.

- `SaveTestAction`
  This class handles the patient part of the test. If the patient is in the process of selecting a doctor, it creates a list of available doctors. Once the patient selects a doctor, it creates a list of topics by that doctor. Once the patient chooses a test, it reads the appropriate XML file and presents the patient with the appropriate test sequence. Once the test is completed, it helps in sending a mail to the physician, including the additional comments entered by the patient and preferred date and time for consultation.

Helper classes

- `XMLSerializer`
  This class helps to read and write the tests created by doctors from XML files.

- `SQLHelper`
  This is a generic class from which we can interact with the database without writing SQL statements, for example:

```
public int insert(String tableName, HashMap namesValues) throws SQLException
```

  This code inserts the given values into the specified table

- `TableInfo`
  Using this class, we can get all the information about a given table, like number of columns, their names, widths, and data types

- `ConnectionPool`
  This class is used to get database connections from the connection pool

- `MailClient`
  This class is used to send e-mails to a doctor

This pretty much completes the description of the example application. We wanted to concentrate more on the analysis and design part of the application development. We suggest you to take a look at the source code, which is available for download at the Wrox web site (http://www.wrox.com/).

Running the Application

Let's take a look at how the application works in practice. It will provide an introductory page, `index.jsp`, which offers two links, one to register with the application and one to login (if you have already registered). To access this application after deployment, you will have to start Tomcat and navigate to http://localhost:8080/diagnosis/:

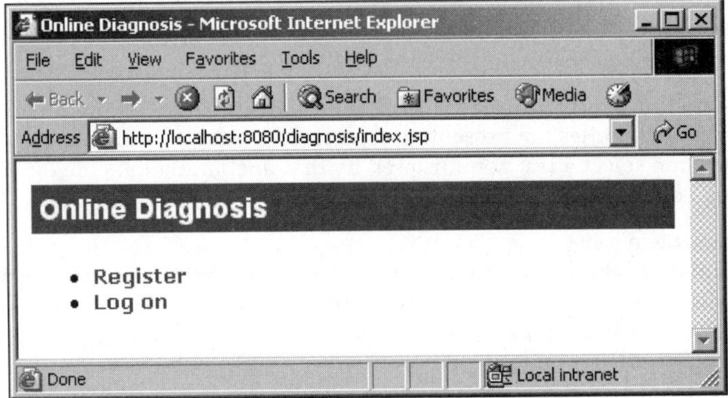

A user can either register as a patient or doctor. Depending on the type, they will be able to access relevant services. All the fields in the form must be completed:

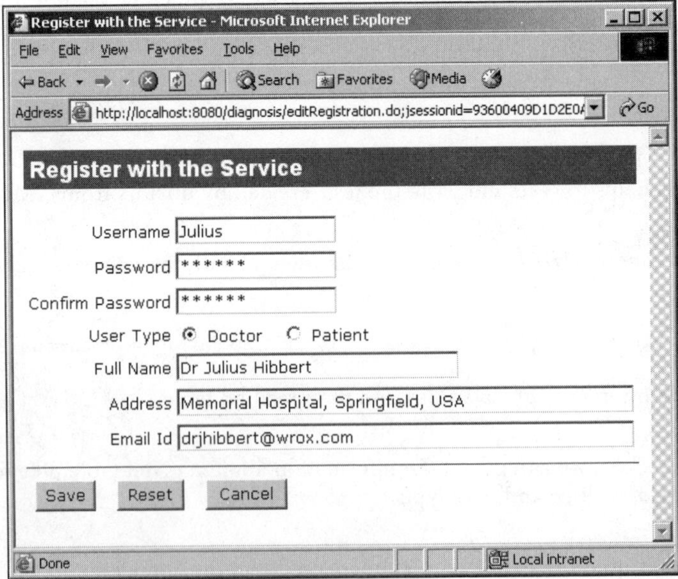

If the user has already registered, they can use the logon hyperlink to access the logon page of the application:

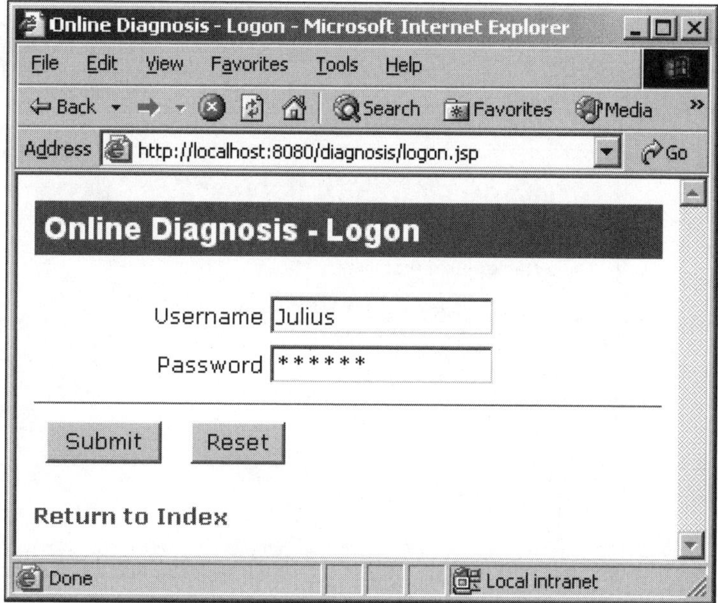

Both of the above actions lead the user to the page shown below. Since the user has registered as a doctor, they will be able to create a new diagnostic test or delete an existing one. Apart from these services, the user also can edit their profile and log off from this page:

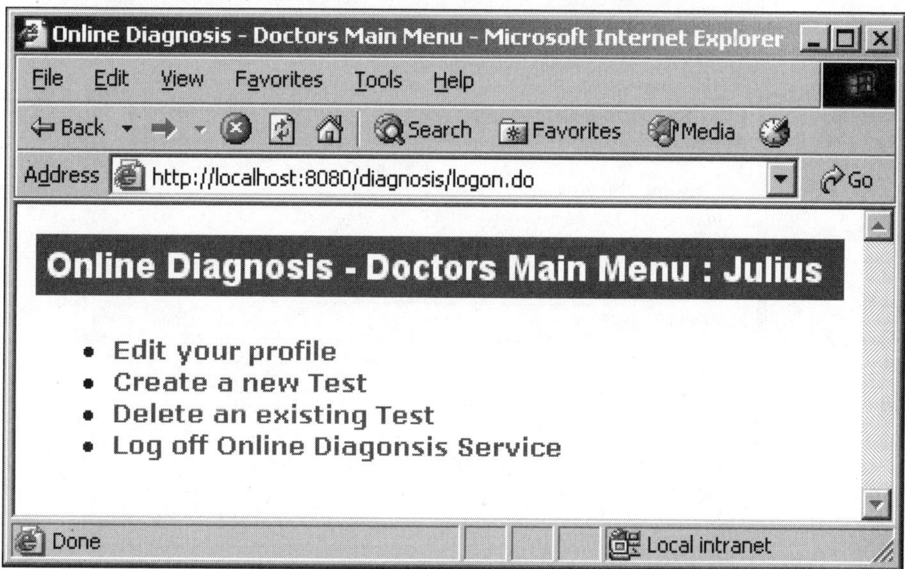

Now, we will go through various steps of a doctor creating an online diagnostic test. This page has topic name and description fields:

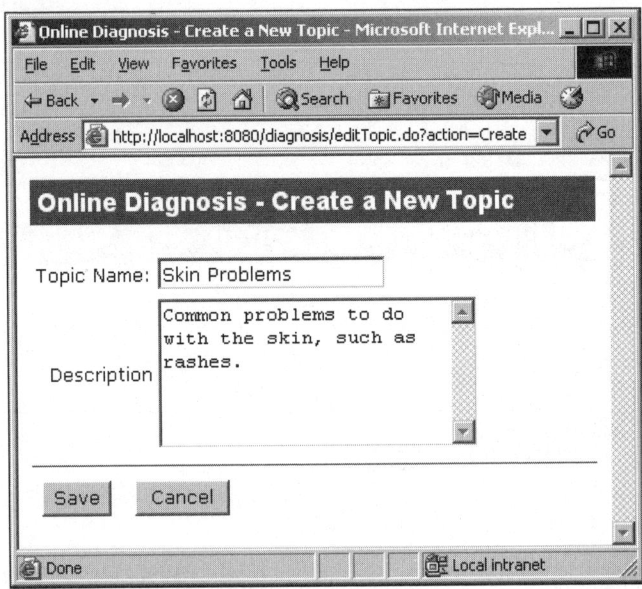

The `save action` will lead the user to the page where questions and answers can be created. A question has a maximum of three answers:

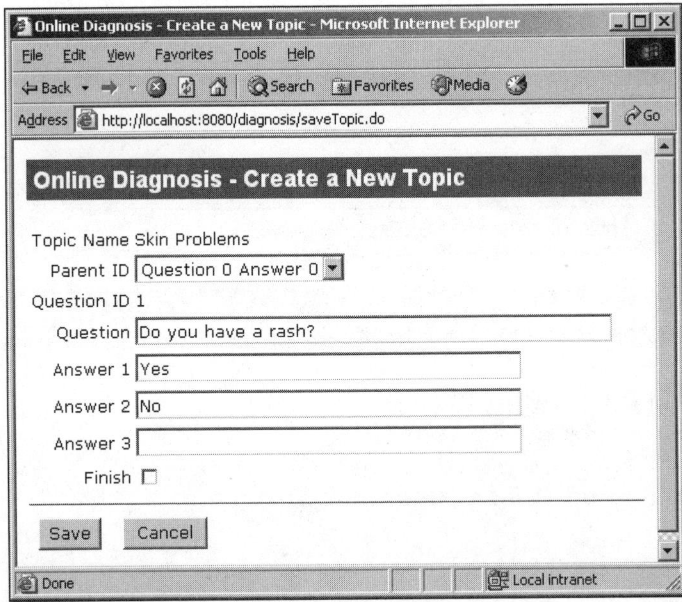

Each question has a parent question and a parent answer. The first question has its parent question and parent answer as Question 0 Answer 0. The following question is the last question of the test and has Question 2 and Answer 1 as a parent element. It has only two possible answers. As we can see, the finish check box has been selected to end the creation of the test:

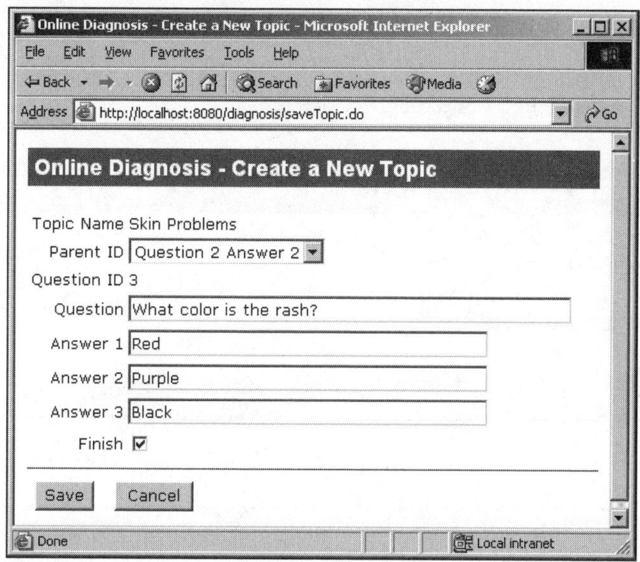

The above process of creating the test results in the following XML file `topic-skin-diagnosis.xml`:

```
<?xml version="1.0" encoding="UTF-8"?>
<TOPIC NAME="Skin Problems" OWNER="Julius">
      <NODE ID="1">
            <QUESTION>Do you have a rash?</QUESTION>
            <ANSWER ID="1" END="false" NEXTQ="2">Yes</ANSWER>
            <ANSWER ID="2" END="true">No</ANSWER>
            <ANSWER ID="3" END="true"></ANSWER>
      </NODE>
      <NODE ID="2">
            <QUESTION>Where is the rash located?</QUESTION>
            <ANSWER ID="1" END="true">Arms</ANSWER>
            <ANSWER ID="2" END="false" NEXTQ="3">Legs</ANSWER>
            <ANSWER ID="3" END="true">Torso</ANSWER>
      </NODE>
      <NODE ID="3">
            <QUESTION>What color is the rash?</QUESTION>
            <ANSWER ID="1" END="true">Red</ANSWER>
            <ANSWER ID="2" END="true">Purple</ANSWER>
            <ANSWER ID="3" END="true">Black</ANSWER>
      </NODE>
</TOPIC>
```

If the user has registered as a patient, they will be able to reach the page shown below. A patient can take a test, edit their profile, and log off:

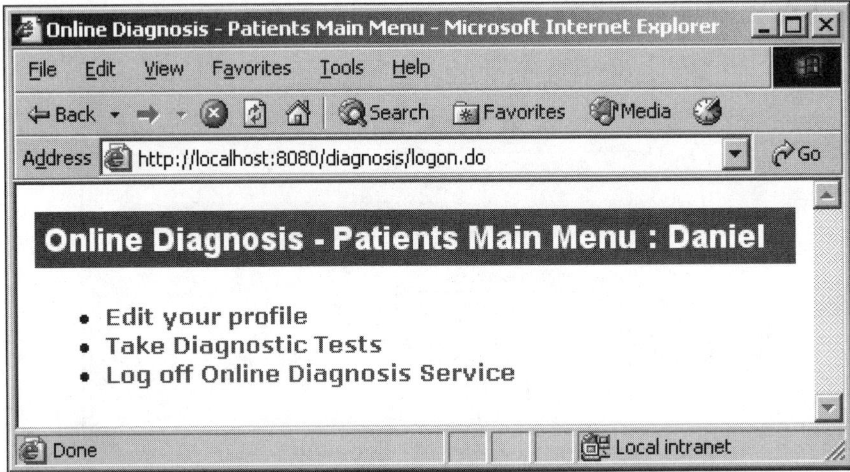

Selecting the second link gives the user an option to choose a doctor for consultation:

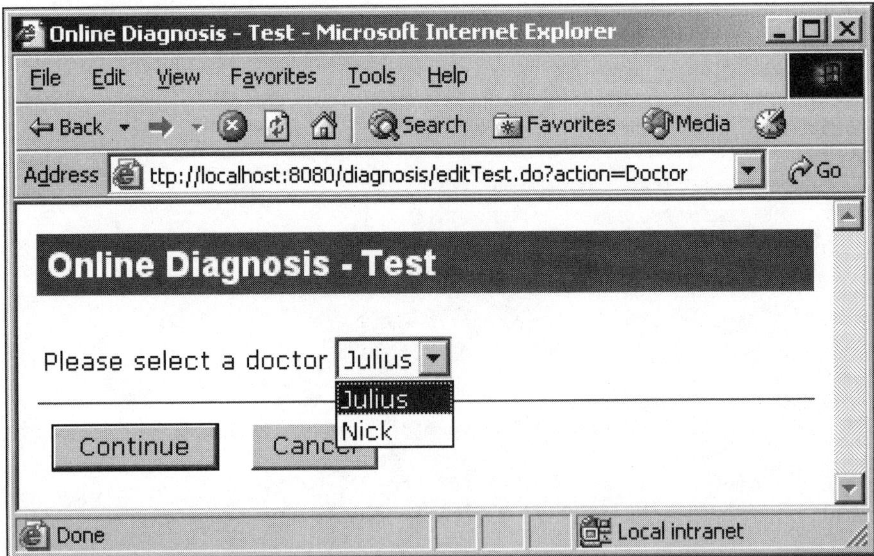

Upon selecting the doctor, we can see the tests they administer:

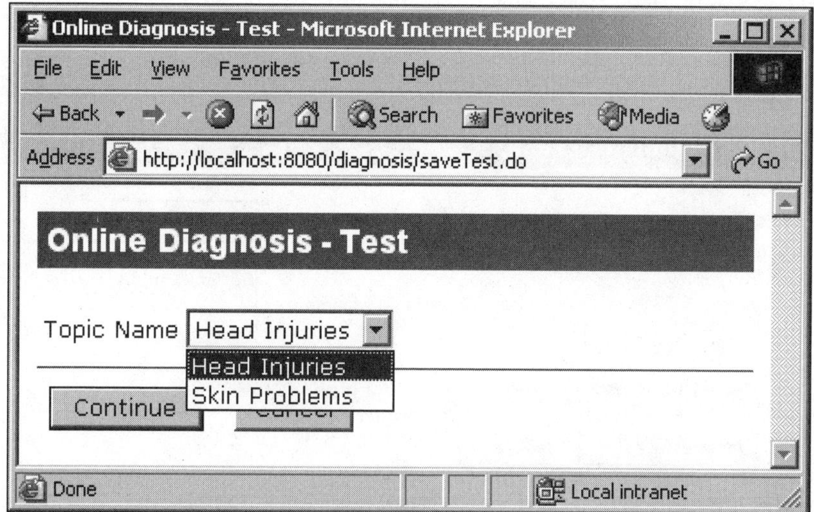

Once the user decides to take the test, they will be asked a series of questions like those shown below:

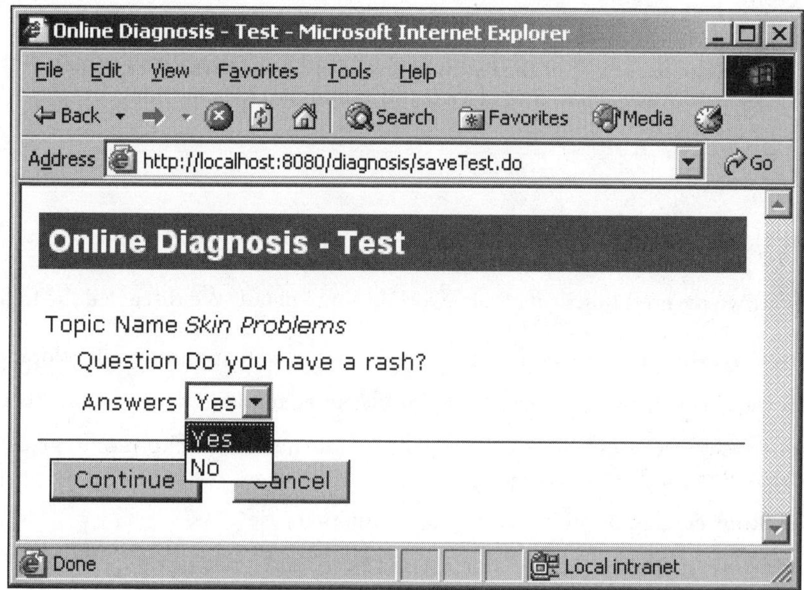

All the sequences of questions are expected to end in a logical conclusion about the nature of illness. We are assuming that the problems associated with each skin type vary. So, it is up to doctors to design the right sequence of questions. However, at the end, there is a provision for the patients to enter their own comments and give out a preferred date and time for consultation:

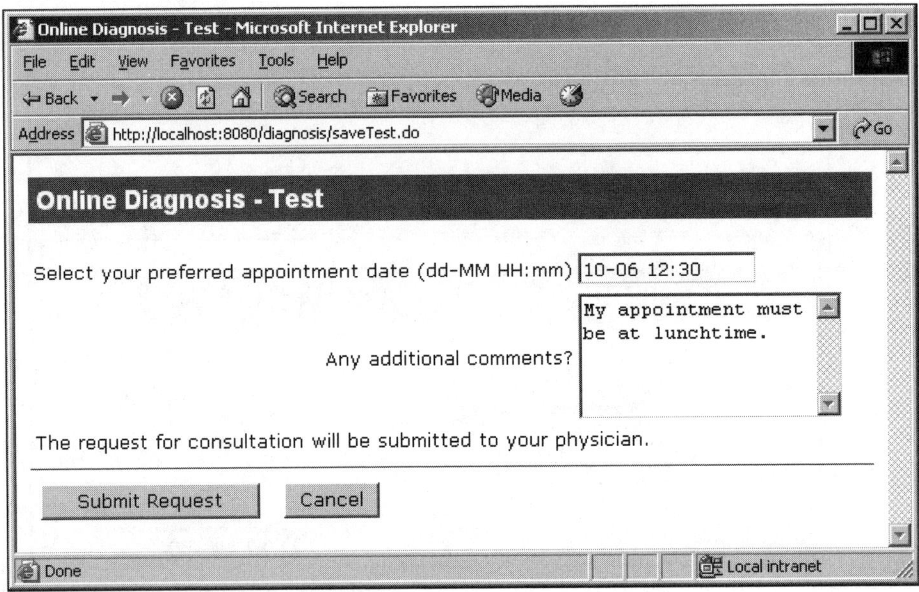

This way the physician gets an initial indication of the patient's complaint.

This application uses most of the features provided by the Struts Framework. However I encourage you to add more features and make some changes to get a hands-on feel for developing applications with Struts.

Summary

In this chapter, we covered the Struts Framework in some detail. We discussed the following aspects:

- Advantages and relevance of using MVC model in web application development
- Advantages of using a framework like Struts, an example to demonstrate this point
- Struts architecture and roles of different components like `ActionServlet`, `ActionMapping`, `ActionForward`, `ActionForm`, and `ActionClass`
- The Struts configuration file, its elements and their use
- The Struts tag library (`logic`, `bean`, `template`, and `html` tags)

Then we looked at an example web application, built using Struts. This example demonstrates many of the features of Struts. Although we didn't go into the details of all the implementation of the application, we examined how Struts could be used to solve common problems of application development.

In the next chapter, we're going to look at how we can manage the browser from the client side. This will include caching content, and discovering the capabilities of the browsers that access our applications – so that we can better manage the content we deliver them.

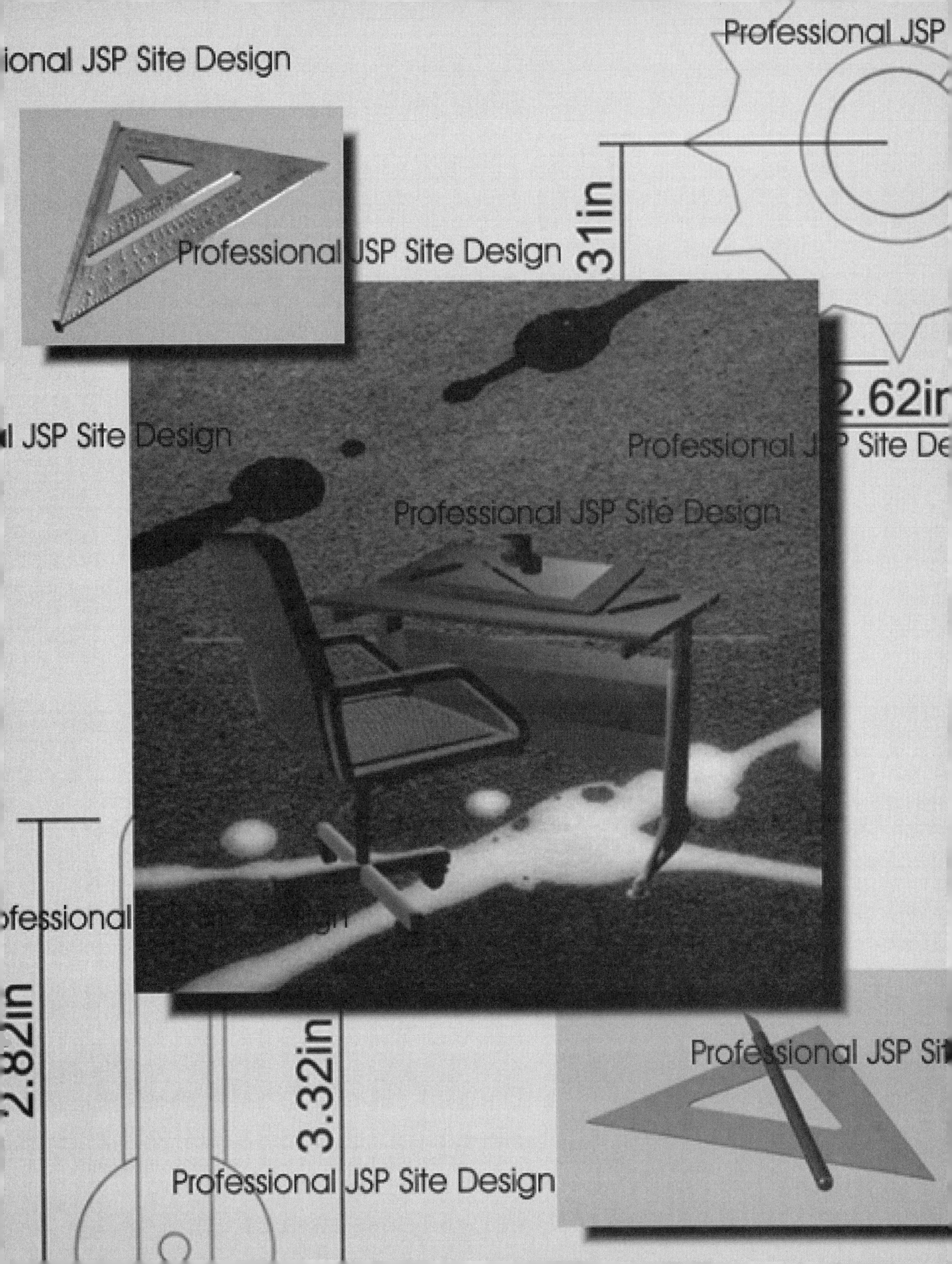
Professional JSP Site Design
31in
Professional JSP Site Design
3.32in
Professional JSP Site Design

3

Caches and Browsers

When it comes to creating web applications, we can't avoid the browser. We can write all the JSP pages, servlets, filters, and tag libraries we like but their output still has to be understandable to the browser, and a lot can happen between the web container and the end user. In this chapter we'll look at a couple of the particular issues that arise with this:

- Managing the browser cache, and any proxy caches that content may pass through on the way to the user. We'll also see how we can implement caching within the web container.
- Finding out about the browser that is being used and its capabilities, to allow us to make use of features supported by advanced browsers (such as JavaScript or XML) whilst retaining compatibility with older ones.

Along the way we'll make quite a lot of use of filters and tag libraries, as these make it much easier to provide advanced features whilst keeping life easy for the page designer.

Managing Caches

Often, when an operation is expensive, we choose to **cache** its result to avoid incurring the expense repeatedly. For example, if a calculation is computationally expensive but its result remains valid for a significant period of time we may choose to recalculate only infrequently. Similarly, if a network operation is costly (for example, if we are aggregating and sorting stock quotes from a different site), we could cache the results so that they are recalculated only every 10 minutes.

There are three situations where content from our web sites might be cached:

- By the client (the browser)
- By the server (by the server-side code within our web application)
- By something in between (such as a proxy server)

The only one of these three we can *reliably* control is the caching on the server. HTTP headers can indicate to the client and to proxies whether the content should be cached, but precisely how this works varies between implementations. Browsers such as Internet Explorer also provide a variety of possible users settings to control this (under Tools | Internet Options | General | Temporary Internet Files | Settings):

Sometimes we don't want our content to be cached – for example, if it is frequently changing or if it depends on the user's session state. In the next chapter, for instance, we will be creating a photo gallery site where the result presented by the view pages will depend on the user's session data, without any difference in the URL to indicate this. We will therefore want to disable browser caching to ensure that the view seen by the user is always accurate.

It's instructive to explore the different ways we can implement this functionality in a Java-based web application, and to do this we'll look at:

- A simple page that can be cached freely by the client or any proxy
- How to prevent the caching of the page, by using a ready-made tag library
- How to prevent the caching of the page, using a custom-build tag library
- How to create a servlet filter that can manage the caching of a page, without any change to the page itself

A Simple Cached Page

As a baseline case, let's write a very simple JSP page, `cache.jsp`, that makes no special provision regarding caching and displays the current date and time. We arrange for it to make an entry in the server log file each time it is accessed:

```
<% application.log("This is cache.jsp"); %>

<html>
  <head>
    <title>Caching allowed!</title>
  </head>
  <body>
    <h1>Caching allowed!</h1>

    <p>The current date and time: <%= new java.util.Date() %></p>
  </body>
</html>
```

On Tomcat 4, by default this log message will end up in `%CATALINA_HOME%/logs/`, in a file whose name incorporates the current date, for example, `localhost_log.2001-09-17.txt`.

This JSP page is extremely simple, but is sufficient to demonstrate whether or not a particular page is cached. We'll see some more concrete examples of the techniques shown here in the next chapter.

As we can see from the log, `cache.jsp` is only accessed once, even when we create a number of browser windows pointing to it. Each window shows the same date and time:

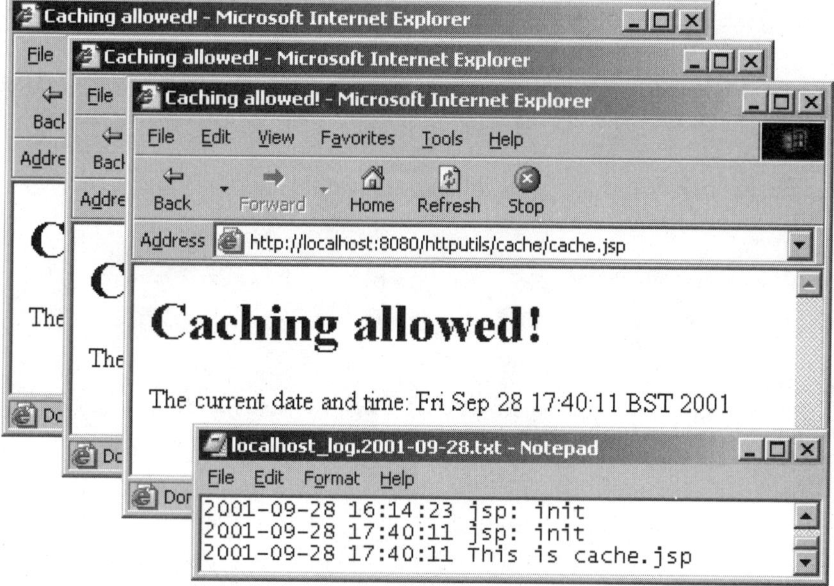

That's often a good thing, but we may want to turn this functionality off.

Using the Jakarta Response Tag Library

So, how do we go about turning off caching of our pages? Essentially, by setting various HTTP response headers. Whilst browsers and caches vary in their interpretation of the headers, in general almost all browsers and proxies will respond to setting the following three headers:

- `Cache-Control: no-cache`
- `Expires:` *<a date in the past>*
- `Pragma: No-cache`

The `Pragma: No-cache` header is part of the HTTP 1.0 specification, while the `Cache-Control: no-cache` is part of the HTTP 1.1 protocol. HTTP 1.1 clients *ought* to interpret `Pragma: No-cache` as being equivalent to `Cache-Control: no-cache`; unfortunately, IE5 doesn't do this. The `Expires:` header is used to give a time after which the content should be discarded. Any one of these headers ought to do the trick. However, for maximum compatibility all three should be set.

So, how to set the headers? The most obvious way is to use the response object's `setHeader()` and `setDateHeader()` methods, but perhaps a more JSP-friendly approach is to use a tag library. The Jakarta Response Tag Library (freely available from http://jakarta.apache.org/taglibs/) does just that, and so we can put together a simple JSP fragment, `nocache.jspf`, that does this:

```
<%@ taglib uri="http://jakarta.apache.org/taglibs/response-1.0"
           prefix="response" %>

<response:setHeader name="Cache-Control">no-cache</response:setHeader>
<response:setDateHeader name="Expires">0</response:setDateHeader>
<response:setHeader name="Pragma">No-cache</response:setHeader>
```

The `.jspf` file extension is recommended in the JSP 1.2 specification for fragments of JSP code that will be incorporated using a static include.

We can simple use include this fragment within our main JSP page, `nocache-jakartatags.jsp`, to prevent caching of the page:

```
<%@ include file="nocache.jspf" %>

<% application.log("This is nocache-jakartatags.jsp"); %>

<html>
  <head>
    <title>Caching not allowed! (Using Jakarta tags)</title>
  </head>
  <body>
    <h1>No caching! (Using Jakarta tags)</h1>

    <p>The current date and time: <%= new java.util.Date() %></p>
  </body>
</html>
```

Finally, we need to make the web container aware of the Response Tag Library:

```
<?xml version="1.0" encoding="ISO-8859-1"?>

<!DOCTYPE web-app
    PUBLIC "-//Sun Microsystems, Inc.//DTD Web Application 2.3//EN"
    "http://java.sun.com/j2ee/dtds/web-app_2_3.dtd">

<web-app>

  <taglib>
    <taglib-uri>http://jakarta.apache.org/taglibs/response-1.0</taglib-uri>
    <taglib-location>/WEB-INF/response.tld</taglib-location>
  </taglib>

</web-app>
```

As the log file shown below indicates, Internet Explorer does not cache this version of the page but requests a fresh copy each time. The time when the page was fetched from the server is now different in each window:

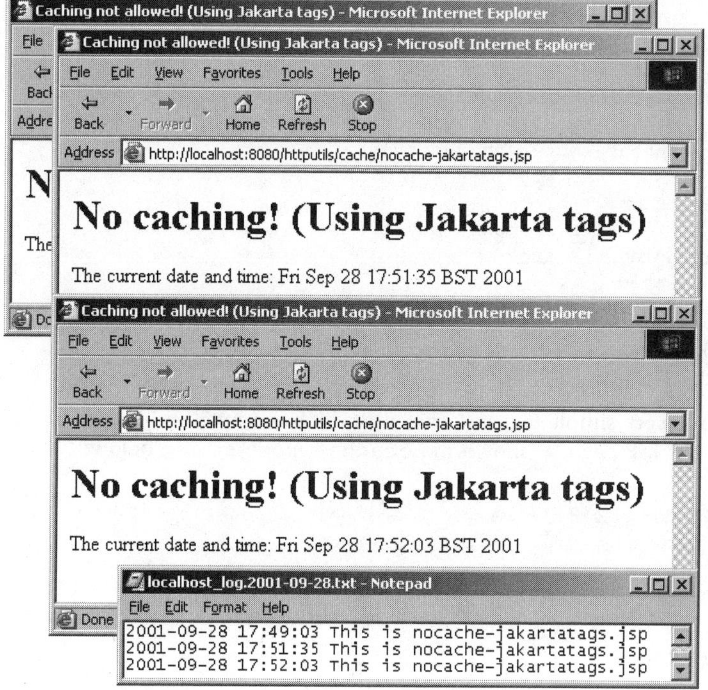

Creating a Caching Tag Library

So we've managed to prevent our page from being cached, but the solution still isn't especially elegant. The Jakarta Response Tag Library provides a general way to set response headers, but with three headers to set (and the header values unchanging) we could easily write our own custom tag that sets all three response headers in one fell swoop.

Let's start with the tag library descriptor, `cache.tld`:

```
<?xml version="1.0" encoding="ISO-8859-1" ?>
<!DOCTYPE taglib
  PUBLIC "-//Sun Microsystems, Inc.//DTD JSP Tag Library 1.2//EN"
  "http://java.sun.com/dtd/web-jsptaglibrary_1_2.dtd">

<taglib>
  <tlib-version>1.0</tlib-version>
  <jsp-version>1.2</jsp-version>
  <short-name>cache</short-name>
  <uri>http://www.wrox.com/taglib/cache</uri>
  <display-name>Cache Control Tags</display-name>

  <description>Wrox Cache Control Tag Library.</description>

  <tag>
    <name>noCaching</name>
    <tag-class>com.wrox.http.NoCachingTag</tag-class>
    <body-content>empty</body-content>

    <description>
      Generates HTTP response headers to prohibit caching of the
      page using the tag.
    </description>
  </tag>

</taglib>
```

This declares one very simple tag, `noCaching`, which is empty and has no attributes. We can simply add this tag to our JSP page, as shown in `nocache-wroxtag.jsp` below:

```
<%@ taglib uri="http://www.wrox.com/taglib/cache" prefix="cache" %>
<cache:noCaching/>

<% application.log("This is nocache-wroxtag.jsp"); %>

<html>
  <head>
    <Title>Caching not allowed! (Using Wrox tag)</title>
  </head>
  <body>
    <h1>No caching! (Using Wrox tag)</h1>
  </body>
</html>
```

Finally, here's the Java class `NoCachingTag`. This is nice and simple as there are no tag attributes and the tag's body content is empty. All we need do is extend `TagSupport` and override `doEndTag()` to add the response headers:

```
package com.wrox.http;

import javax.servlet.http.HttpServletResponse;
import javax.servlet.jsp.tagext.TagSupport;

public class NoCachingTag extends TagSupport {

  public int doEndTag() {
    HttpServletResponse response =
            (HttpServletResponse) pageContext.getResponse();
    response.setHeader("Cache-Control", "no-cache");
    response.setDateHeader("Expires", 0);
    response.setHeader("Pragma", "No-cache");
    return SKIP_BODY;
  }
}
```

It works just the same as our static include version, but packaged as a single custom tag. That's all very well, but our page authors still need to include the `<cache:noCaching/>` tag in each page we want to protect from caching.

J2EE is built on a declarative, rather than a programmatic, approach. For example, to require users to log into your application you don't code the login routines, you just declare that users need to have logged in to access certain parts of the site. In the same way, Servlet 2.3 filters allow us to use the `web.xml` file to map a filter to a particular resource, to a whole directory or web application, to a particular filename extension, or to a specific servlet. The resource itself need not know anything about the filter. So our final example in this section will be of a filter for disabling caches.

Creating a Caching Filter

The filtering API has been added to the latest version (2.3) of the Servlet specification. Filters provide an additional type of web component, in addition to JSP pages and servlets. In fact, filters sit between the browser and the end resource (a JSP page or servlet) requested by the user. They form a pipeline along which requests flow to the resource:

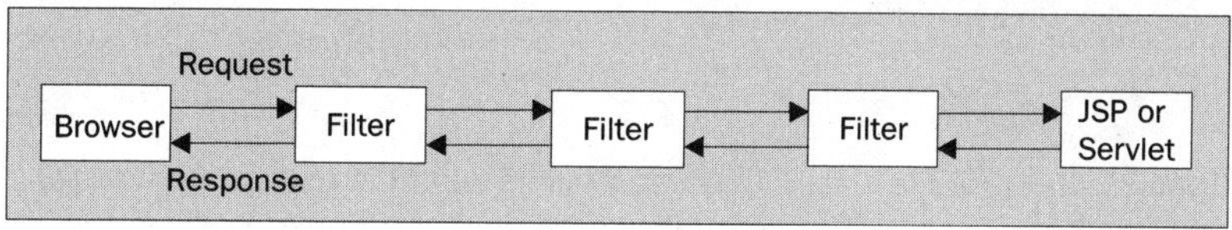

Filters are able to:

- Examine the request before it is sent to the resource
- Examine the response after it is created by the resource
- Modify the request or response objects

- ❑ Provide custom request and response objects that wrap the original ones and modify their functionality
- ❑ Capture and modify the output from the resource
- ❑ Create the response itself and prevent the request from reaching the resource

Filters are defined in the deployment descriptor for the web application (the `web.xml` file), and may be mapped to a specific URI pattern or to a particular servlet.

The filtering API is covered in detail in *Professional JSP, 2nd Edition* from *Wrox Press (ISBN 1-861004-95-8)*; here we will introduce the interfaces briefly. The Servlet 2.3 API provides three interfaces for implementing filters. These interfaces are `Filter`, `FilterConfig`, and `FilterChain`, and belong to the `javax.servlet` package.

The Filter Interface

`Filter` is implemented by the application developer, to provide the filter class. This interface defines the callback methods invoked by the J2EE web container when a request configured with the filter is processed. The methods defined by the interface are:

```
public void init(FilterConfig config)
```

The container calls this method when the filter is initialized. The `FilterConfig` object contains context information related to the web application:

```
public void destroy()
```

The container calls the `destroy()` method just before the filter is destroyed. Filter providers can use this method for cleaning up resources:

```
public void doFilter(ServletRequest request, ServletResponse response,
                     FilterChain chain)
```

The container calls `doFilter()` each time it receives a request that is configured to use the filter, and this is where the filtering logic should be implemented. The `doFilter()` method should first do any pre-processing logic, then use the `FilterChain.doChain()` method to forward the request to the next filter in the chain (or to its ultimate destination, if this is the last filter). Once the `doChain()` method returns, the filter may implement any post-processing logic.

The FilterConfig Interface

The web container will provide a class that implements the `FilterConfig` interface, and pass it to the filter's `init()` method. `FilterConfig` defines methods that provide access to configuration information for the filter:

```
public String getFilterName()
```

getFilterName() returns the name of the filter, as defined in the deployment descriptor file:

```
public ServletContext getServletContext()
```

getServletContext() returns a handle to the web application:

```
public Enumeration getInitParameterNames()
```

getInitParameterNames() returns an Enumeration of the names of the initialization parameter declared for the filter in the deployment descriptor file:

```
public String getInitParameter(String name)
```

getInitParameter() returns the value (specified in the deployment descriptor) of the named initialization parameter.

The FilterChain Interface

FilterChain is another interface implemented by the container provider. An instance of FilterChain is passed to the filter's doFilter() method, which should then use it for forwarding the request to the next filter in the chain (or to the servlet that is mapped to the request if the filter is the last filter in the chain).

FilterChain defines only one method, which forwards the request to the next filter in the chain:

```
Public void doChain(ServletRequest request, ServletResponse response)
```

The NoCachingFilter Class

So let's see how to go about writing a basic filter. NoCachingFilter is nice and simple; it just wants to set some response headers (as we have seen already) to prevent caching of the response. Our filter class has to implement the Filter interface, so let's start there:

```
package com.wrox.http;

import java.io.IOException;
import javax.servlet.ServletException;
import javax.servlet.ServletResponse;
import javax.servlet.ServletRequest;
import javax.servlet.Filter;
import javax.servlet.FilterConfig;
import javax.servlet.FilterChain;
import javax.servlet.http.HttpServletResponse;

public class NoCachingFilter implements Filter {
```

Filter declares three methods: init(), destroy(), and doFilter(). We have to implement all of these since we're not given a convenient base class to use. We're not really interested in the FilterConfig object but, for the sake of completeness, we'll take the trouble to store it safely away:

```
  private FilterConfig filterConfig = null;

  public void init(FilterConfig filterConfig) {
    this.filterConfig = filterConfig;
  }

  public void destroy() {
    this.filterConfig = null;
  }
```

The real work happens in `doFilter()`. The reference to the response object is of type `ServletResponse`, so we need to cast it to `HttpServletResponse`:

```
  public void doFilter(ServletRequest request, ServletResponse response,
                       FilterChain chain)
           throws IOException, ServletException {

    HttpServletResponse httpResponse = (HttpServletResponse) response;
```

Then we just set the appropriate headers, and invoke the next filter in the chain:

```
    httpResponse.setHeader("Cache-Control", "no-cache");
    httpResponse.setDateHeader("Expires", 0);
    httpResponse.setHeader("Pragma", "No-cache");
    chain.doFilter(request, response);
  }
}
```

Configuring Filters

Filters need to be specified in `web.xml`. This is a two-stage process; first we need to declare the filter itself, give it a name, and specify any initialization parameters (none in this case):

```
<filter>
  <filter-name>No Caching Filter</filter-name>
  <filter-class>com.wrox.http.NoCachingFilter</filter-class>
</filter>
```

Secondly, we need to map it to the relevant resources, so the container knows which filters to apply to which resources. A filter can be mapped either to a URL pattern (as here) or to a particular named servlet:

```
<filter-mapping>
  <filter-name>No Caching Filter</filter-name>
  <url-pattern>/cache/nocache-filter.jsp</url-pattern>
</filter-mapping>
```

If more than one filter applies to a resource, then they are called in the order specified in the `web.xml` file.

Here's nocache-filter.jsp, our simple page that the filter prevents from being cached:

```
<% application.log("This is nocache-filter.jsp"); %>

<html>
  <head>
    <title>Caching not allowed! (Using filter)</title>
  </head>
  <body>
    <h1>No caching! (Using filter)</h1>

    <p>The current date and time: <%= new java.util.Date() %></p>
  </body>
</html>
```

Pause for a moment and read that code again: there's nothing in the JSP page that has anything to do with caching. That's the power of filters; they provide a convenient place where we can place code that is independent of the particular page or resource in question.

Let's review the different approaches we've seen for controlling client-side caching. They all produce the same end result. However, we can draw some interesting inferences about the merits of the different approaches:

- There is very little difference between the two tag-based approaches. Both require us to add code to each page for which we want to disable caching. Arguably the home-made tag is more directly suited to the task but writing a short include file to do the job with the ready-made tag meant there was little practical difference.
- The filter approach makes things much cleaner. The actual content of a page is separated from any notion of whether it is to be cached or not, which is configured in the web.xml file. Filters are particularly useful when you want to incorporate some functionality into a site that is not directly related to generating the content of an individual page. If the functionality is related to the page's content it belongs in that page, probably in the form of a custom tag.

Server-Side Caching

So we know how to turn off client-side caching of our content. The other time we may be interested in caches is when we have some content of our own that is expensive to generate but which remains valid for a period of time, and which we therefore want to cache within the server. For instance, we might have a page that requires a complicated series of database queries, and want to cache the resulting content so that the queries are performed only every 10 minutes.

As it happens, this is a sufficiently common requirement that an open source product is available. **OSCache**, part of the OpenSymphony project (http://www.opensymphony.com/) is a tag library for caching generated content within a JSP page. The latest version (1.6.1) also contains a filter that can cache entire pages.

OSCache can store cached data in memory or on disk, and offers good control of how the content is cached. Cached items can be shared globally or be specific to a single user (by storing them in the HttpSession); each item is also stored with a unique key, allowing cached content to be optionally shared between JSP pages.

We'll see how we can use OSCache by building a small news portal site. We'll see the portal again in Chapter 5 when we discuss page layout techniques. It's not the actual application that's of interest so much as the way it makes use of OSCache, so we'll skip quickly over some parts of the code.

The News Data

The data for our little portal all comes from an XML file, `news.xml`. A short section from the file is shown below. The news consists of a series of numbered stories, and each story is part of a numbered section:

```
<?xml version="1.0" encoding="ISO-8859-1" ?>
<!DOCTYPE news [
<!ELEMENT news          (section+,story+)>
<!ELEMENT section       (#PCDATA)>
<!ELEMENT story         (headline, date, correspondent, text)>
<!ELEMENT headline      (#PCDATA)>
<!ELEMENT date          (#PCDATA)>
<!ELEMENT correspondent (#PCDATA)>
<!ELEMENT text          (#PCDATA)>
<!ATTLIST section id      ID    #REQUIRED>
<!ATTLIST story   id      ID    #REQUIRED
                  section IDREF #REQUIRED>
]>

<news>
  <section id="1">Traffic News</section>
  <section id="2">Engineering News</section>
  <section id="3">General News</section>

  <story id="1" section="1">
    <headline>Jubilee Festival Week a Huge Success</headline>
    <date>31 July 2001</date>
    <correspondent>Roger Whitehouse</correspondent>
    <text>
      The Jubilee Festival Week is now over, having finished with 50
      hours of continuous public service. The final train of the
      weekend, the 7.30pm departure from Wharf on Sunday 29th, was
      hauled as far as Pendre by all five working steam locos (Nos.
      1, 2, 3, 6, and 7) following an hour of extensive interest
      from many photographers, both members and visitors.
    </text>
  </story>

  <story id="2" section="2">
    <headline>No. 7 Back in Service</headline>
    <date>19 July 2001</date>
    <correspondent>MRFS</correspondent>
    <text>
      Loco No. 7 made a test run yesterday, Wednesday 18th, following
      its repaint.  It worked light engine from Pendre to Wharf, up to
      Bryngla, before returning to Pendre. Today (Thursday) it was
      expected to put in some further running-in workings,
      double-heading one of the service trains.
    </text>
  </story>

  ...

</news>
```

Accessing the News Data

To access the data we'll make use of the XTags Tag Library from Jakarta (see http://jakarta.apache.org/taglibs/ for further details) which provides a very convenient and flexible set of tags that give us XSLT-type functionality within a JSP page. For example, we can parse the `news.xml` file and create a list of news headlines like this:

```
<%@ taglib uri="http://jakarta.apache.org/taglibs/xtags-1.0"
    prefix="xtags" %>

<xtags:parse uri="/news/data/news.xml"/>

<html>
  <head>
    <title>News Headlines</title>
  </head>

  <body>

    <h1>News Headlines</h1>

    <ul>
      <xtags:forEach select="/news/story">
        <li>
          <b><xtags:valueOf select="headline/text()"/></b>
             (<xtags:valueOf select="correspondent/text()"/>,
             <xtags:valueOf select="date/text()"/>)
        </li>
      </xtags:forEach>
    </ul>

  </body>
</html>
```

Here, the `<xtags:parse/>` tag reads in the specified XML file and parses it. The `<xtags:forEach>` and `<xtags:valueOf>` tags then behave just like `<xsl:forEach>` and `<xsl:value-of>` do in XSLT, allowing the use of XPath expressions to select portions of the XML document.

> *The difference in name between `<xtags:valueOf>` and `<xsl:value-of>` is because of a bug in Tomcat (now fixed in Tomcat 4.0) which prevented the use of custom tags whose name contained a hyphen.*

The result looks like this:

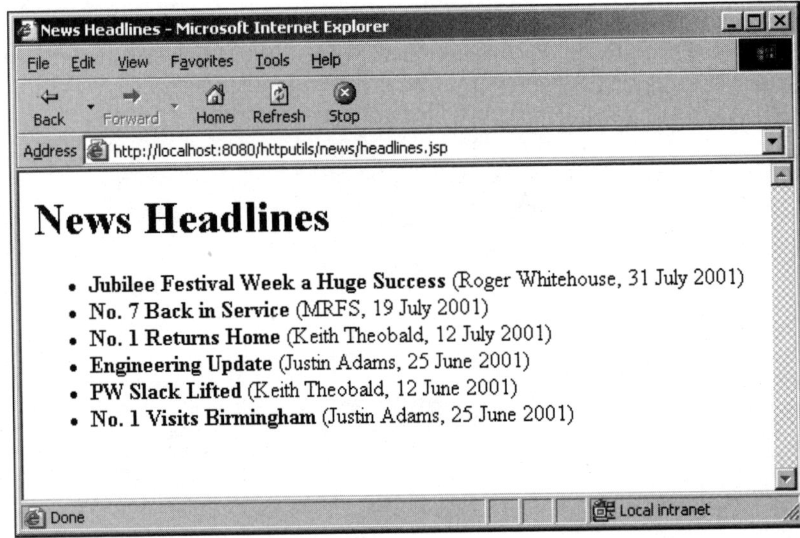

Caching in on the News

That's all very well, but what if the `news.xml` file comes from a different server, perhaps half-way around the globe? In that case we would want to cache the contents of the XML file; fortunately the `<xtags:parse>` tag allows us to specify the XML content as its body content rather than via the `uri` attribute, for example:

```
<xtags:parse>
  <-- XML content here -->
</xtags:parse>
```

As we expand our news application a bit we'll need more pages – pages to view an individual article, list the articles within a section, or list the sections. Each of these will need the read and parse functionality, so we can factor that out into a static include file, `parsenews.jspf`:

```
<%@ taglib uri="http://jakarta.apache.org/taglibs/xtags-1.0"
           prefix="xtags" %>
<%@ taglib uri="http://jakarta.apache.org/taglibs/io-1.0" prefix="io" %>
<%@ taglib uri="oscache" prefix="oscache" %>

<xtags:parse>
  <oscache:cache key="news.xml" time="1800">
    <% try { %>
         <io:request url="/news/data/news.xml"/>
    <% } catch (Exception e) { %>
         <oscache:usecached/>
    <% } %>
  </oscache:cache>
</xtags:parse>
```

Let's unpick this code a little. There are now three tag libraries in use:

- **XTags**
  Which we've already seen.
- **IO**
  Another tag library from Jakarta. Here we use it to send an HTTP GET request for the `news.xml` file and returns its contents. We're not using its full potential here by any means. The library contains tags for performing much more complex requests over HTTP, SOAP, and XML-RPC.
- **OSCache**
  As we've already discussed, this is the caching tag library whose use we're exploring.

Reading the code from the inside out, we find:

- The `<io:request>` tag retrieves the `news.xml` file and passes its contents to the `<oscache:cache>` tag.
- The `<io:request>` tag may not be evaluated if there is a cached copy. The name `"news.xml"` is used to identify the cached fragment of content, so that multiple JSP pages can access the same item in the cache. The cached content will be retained for up to 30 minutes (1800 seconds).
- The XML data, whether cached or freshly retrieved, is passed to the `<xtags:parse>` tag which will parse it as before.

The final point of note is the `try-catch` block in the code. If the `<io:request>` tag throws an exception (perhaps because the server holding the `news.xml` file is down), the `<oscache:usecached/>` tag will be called. This essentially says "Just use the cached version for this". In this way, our application gains resilience against the unavailability of this resource.

`viewStory.jsp`, below, is a typical page that uses `parsenews.jspf` to display a single news story. The id of the story to be displayed is specified by the `story` request parameter. We start by including `parsenews.jspf`:

```
<%@ taglib uri="http://jakarta.apache.org/taglibs/xtags-1.0" prefix="xtags" %>

<%@ include file="parsenews.jspf"%>
```

Next we use a short scriptlet to construct an XPath expression that will select the correct `<story>` node from the XML file, and use the `<xtags:variable>` tag to declare a scripting variable (also called `story`) to hold that node:

```
<% String storyXPath = "/news/story[@id=" +
                       request.getParameter("story") +
                       "]"; %>
<xtags:variable id="story" type="node" select="<%= storyXPath %>" />
```

The remainder of the page simply uses the `<xtags:valueOf>` tag to select the relevant data. The tag's `context` attribute is used to tell it that the XPath expressions are relative to the `story` node:

```
<html>
  <head>
    <title>
      News From the Talyllyn Railway:
      <xtags:valueOf select="headline/text()" context="<%= story %>"/>
    </title>
  </head>

  <body>

    <h1>News from the Talyllyn Railway</h1>

    <h2><xtags:valueOf select="headline/text()"
                       context="<%= story %>"/></h2>

    <p><i>From <xtags:valueOf select="correspondent/text()"
                              context="<%= story %>"/>,
               <xtags:valueOf select="date/text()"
                              context="<%= story %>"/></i></p>

    <p><xtags:valueOf select="text/text()"
                      context="<%= story %>"/></p>

  </body>
</html>
```

The output from this page will typically look like the following:

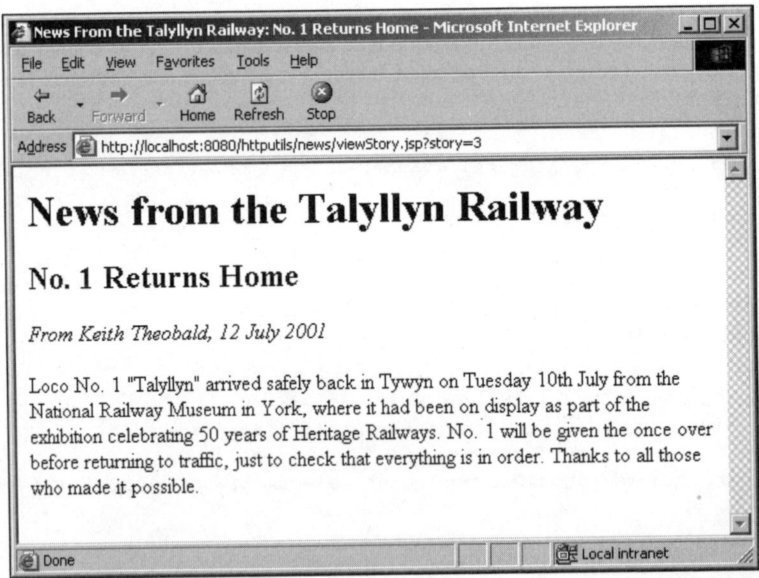

If we examine the server access logs as we access this page a number of times, you'll see that `news.xml` is only requested once, the first time a page using `parsenews.jspf` is requested. On subsequent requests, a cached copy of the file is used:

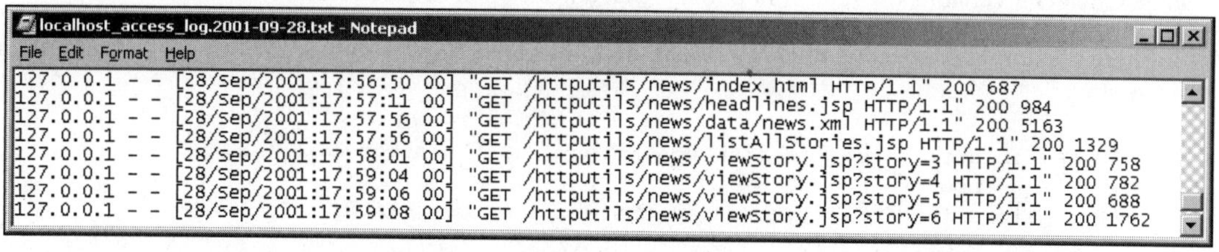

```
localhost_access_log.2001-09-28.txt - Notepad
File Edit Format Help
127.0.0.1 - - [28/Sep/2001:17:56:50 00] "GET /httputils/news/index.html HTTP/1.1" 200 687
127.0.0.1 - - [28/Sep/2001:17:57:11 00] "GET /httputils/news/headlines.jsp HTTP/1.1" 200 984
127.0.0.1 - - [28/Sep/2001:17:57:56 00] "GET /httputils/news/data/news.xml HTTP/1.1" 200 5163
127.0.0.1 - - [28/Sep/2001:17:57:56 00] "GET /httputils/news/listAllStories.jsp HTTP/1.1" 200 1329
127.0.0.1 - - [28/Sep/2001:17:58:01 00] "GET /httputils/news/viewStory.jsp?story=3 HTTP/1.1" 200 758
127.0.0.1 - - [28/Sep/2001:17:59:04 00] "GET /httputils/news/viewStory.jsp?story=4 HTTP/1.1" 200 782
127.0.0.1 - - [28/Sep/2001:17:59:06 00] "GET /httputils/news/viewStory.jsp?story=5 HTTP/1.1" 200 688
127.0.0.1 - - [28/Sep/2001:17:59:08 00] "GET /httputils/news/viewStory.jsp?story=6 HTTP/1.1" 200 1762
```

Note that we *are* still incurring the expense of parsing the XML file each time – it's simply the fetching of the data itself that is optimized. The OSCache Tag Library caches textual data, such as the output from the `<io:request/>` tag, rather than Java objects such as the parsed representation of the XML data.

OSCache Odds and Ends

There are a few bits of OSCache we haven't seen yet. Notably, it requires a configuration file by the name of `oscache.properties`, which needs to be saved in the `WEB-INF\classes\` directory. This is used to configure the cache, notably whether data is to be saved to disk (and if so, where it should be kept), or stored in memory, or both. In our case we simply use the default settings, which results in cached data being saved to disk (in the `C:\cachetagscache\` folder) and in memory:

```
cache.path=c:\\cachetagscache
cache.debug=false
```

There is a third OSCache tag that we haven't seen yet, `<oscache:flush/>`,which causes some or all of the cached data to be discarded. For example, `flush.jsp` disposes of our cached `news.xml` data without affecting anything else in the cache:

```
<%@ taglib uri="oscache" prefix="oscache" %>

<oscache:flush scope="application" key="news.xml"/>

<html>
  <head>
    <title>Cache flushed!</title>
  </head>
  <body>
    <h1>Cache flushed!</h1>
  </body>
</html>
```

For full details of the OSCache tags and their attributes, see the documentation at http://www.opensymphony.com/oscache/tags.html.

Finally, OSCache also comes with a Servlet 2.3 filter that implements similar functionality to the tags, but simply caches the whole page. At present it is less configurable than the tags (notably, it is not possible to specify the time for which the content should be cached) but expect further enhancements in later OSCache versions (or send in a patch – that's what open source is all about).

So, here's a simple page using our `news.xml` data, `filter.jsp`, which prints out the full text of each news story:

```
<%@ taglib uri="http://jakarta.apache.org/taglibs/xtags-1.0"
           prefix="xtags" %>
<%@ taglib uri="http://jakarta.apache.org/taglibs/io-1.0"
           prefix="io" %>

<xtags:parse>
  <io:request url="/news/data/news.xml"/>
</xtags:parse>

<html>
  <head>
    <title>All News Stories (Full Text)</title>
  </head>

  <body>

    <h1>All News Stories (Full Text)</h1>

    <p>It is now <%= new java.util.Date() %>.</p>

    <xtags:forEach select="/news/story">
      <h3><xtags:valueOf select="headline/text()"/></h3>
      <p><i>From <xtags:valueOf select="correspondent/text()"/>,
            <xtags:valueOf select="date/text()"/></i></p>
      <p><xtags:valueOf select="text/text()"/></p>
    </xtags:forEach>

  </body>
</html>
```

Nothing about caching there – each time the page is executed, the `news.xml` file will be retrieved – which of course is the point. The caching is configured by a couple of entries in `web.xml`:

```
<filter>
  <filter-name>OSCache filter</filter-name>
  <filter-class>
    com.opensymphony.module.oscache.filter.CacheFilter
  </filter-class>
</filter>
```

```
<filter-mapping>
  <filter-name>OSCache filter</filter-name>
  <url-pattern>/news/filter.jsp</url-pattern>
</filter-mapping>
```

If we then access this page and reload it several times, the filter intercepts the second and subsequent requests and returns the cached content rather than letting the request reach `filter.jsp`. In the screenshot below we see both the Internet Explorer window and Tomcat's access log file:

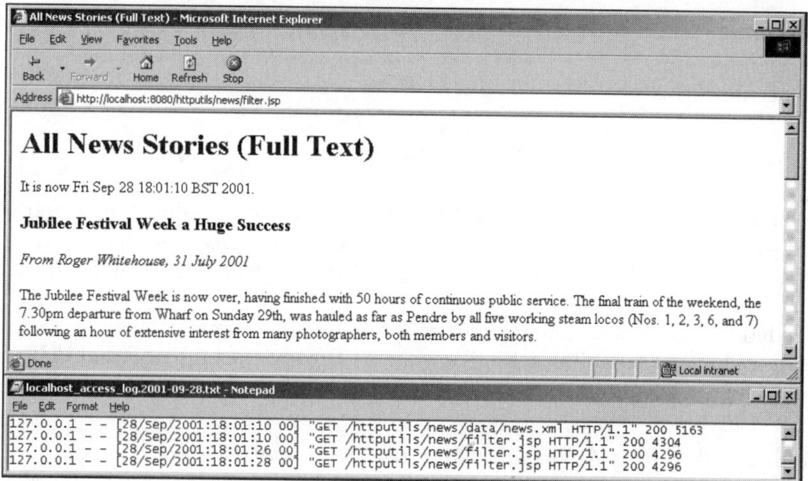

The multiple requests to `filter.jsp` show up in the access log (which only records the URL requested, not which bit of code actually served the response) but there are two give-away signs that the content is being cached:

- `news.xml` is not being re-requested with each request to `filter.jsp`
- The timestamp in the page that is returned is not being updated – it is sticking with the time when the page was first requested

Managing Browser Compatibility

One of the more difficult features of web site design is trying to make sure that our site works well in all target browsers, particularly if we want to make use of less common browser features whilst retaining compatibility with other, older browsers. In the early years of the web the differences between browsers were fairly obvious – for example, Netscape and IE support frames while Lynx doesn't – but often the differences are subtler. Particular problems are the different levels of support for JavaScript and DHTML features.

There are essentially two ways round these problems:

- Simply code for the lowest common denominator target browser, or use only those advanced features that will degrade gracefully on browsers that do not support them
- Detect which browser a particular visitor has, and customize the response to make best use of the facilities supported by that browser

The HTTP specification provides for web clients to send a self-describing request header, USER-AGENT. The header is not required, but the HTTP specification recommends that clients send it. For example, on the author's machine, Internet Explorer sends this header:

```
USER-AGENT=Mozilla/4.0 (compatible, MSIE 5.01; Windows NT 5.0; DigExt)
```

While Lynx sends this:

```
USER-AGENT=Lynx/2.8.3rel1.1 libwww-FM/2.14FM
```

There are many, many web browsers and other clients available, sending a huge variety of USER-AGENT strings, and sometimes even trying to pretend to be each other. Users of Opera can even configure which browser it should identify itself as, to ensure that they get access to all features of a site.

What is needed is some mechanism for identifying the browser, and associating it with a set of properties describing its capabilities. Similar systems already exist for ASP and PHP; these rely on a file called `browscap.ini` to describe the many browsers available.

There are also third-party (but non-free) Java components available – see http://www.cyscape.com/ – but here we will examine how we might develop our own solution. Also, see Chapter 5 to see how the SiteMesh filter tackles this problem.

Browser Properties

Stage one of our browser compatibility component is to know about the various types of web browser out there and their features or properties; from this we can construct a database of the browser types we want to recognize.

Let's take a look at the format of the `browscap.ini` file. It is divided into sections, each representing a particular browser and containing a pattern to compare against the USER-AGENT header and property name-value pairs for each recognized browser.

When attempting to recognize a browser, the steps for matching a `browscap.ini` entry are:

- First, check the USER-AGENT header to see if one of the ones specified in `browscap.ini` matches exactly.
- If there is no exact match, compare using wildcards. The wildcard characters recognized are `*`, which matches zero or more characters, and `?`, which matches any single character. If more than one pattern matches when using wildcards, the best fit is the one for which the smallest number of characters matched the wildcard characters. Fortunately we can make use of an open source regular expression package, ORO (http://jakarta.apache.org/oro/) to do the wildcard matching for us.
- If no pattern matches, the default browser is used.
- The pattern that fits best may have a parent specified, allowing us to inherit browser properties if we have a set of similar browsers.

There are some disadvantages to this approach:

- The `browscap.ini` file needs to be updated regularly if new versions of browsers are to be detected correctly.
- As we are only looking at the information given to us in the `USER-AGENT` header, we can only determine the *capabilities* of a browser, rather than how it is actually configured on the user's machine. For example, the user might have disabled cookies.

The browscap.ini File

Let's take a closer look at `browscap.ini`. It can be downloaded from http://bilmuh.ege.edu.tr/~sorubank/download/php-mysql/browscap.zip. Another good source is http://www.cyscape.com/browscap/.

Each section is introduced by a line enclosed by square brackets, inside which is the name for this browser section. Comment lines start with a '`;`', and properties are specified by name-value pairs separated by an equals sign. The property names are case-insensitive and numeric property values are properly preceded by a hash sign (#), but this is commonly ignored:

```
;;;;;;;;;;;;;;;
;;;  Opera  ;;;
;;;;;;;;;;;;;;;

[Opera 5.0]
browser=Opera
version=5.01
majorver=5
minorver=0
frames=True
tables=True
cookies=True
backgroundsounds=False
vbscript=False
javascript=True
javaapplets=True
activexcontrols=False
beta=False
```

As you can see, Opera 5.01 supports frames, tables, and cookies, but does not support background sounds or ActiveX controls. Next, we find a pair of rather shorter sections, containing specific `USER-AGENT` strings with wildcards. These sections inherit the properties of the `[Opera 5.0]` section above. In fact, the name of the above section was only a placeholder to allow us to specify it as a parent rather than being the actual `USER-AGENT` string for Opera:

```
[Mozilla/4.0 (compatible; MSIE 5.0; Windows NT 5.0) Opera 5.0  *]
parent=Opera 5.0
platform=Win2000

[Opera/5.01 (Windows NT 5.0; *)  *]
parent=Opera 5.0
platform=Win2000
```

Similarly, for the Lynx browser we have a generic entry followed by several more specific patterns that invoke the parent section and then set some more specific properties:

```
;;;;;;;;;;;;;;
;;;  Lynx  ;;;
;;;;;;;;;;;;;;

[Lynx]
browser=Lynx
frames=False
tables=True
cookies=False
backgroundsounds=FALSE
vbscript=FALSE
javascript=FALSE
javaapplets=FALSE
platform=UNIX

[Lynx/2.6*]
parent=Lynx
browser=Lynx
version=2
majorver=2
minorver=6
```

Finally, the `[Default Browser Capability Settings]` section gives the properties to use if no pattern matches:

```
;;;;;;;;;;;
; Default ;
;;;;;;;;;;;

[Default Browser Capability Settings]
browser=Default
Version=0.0
majorver=0
minorver=0
frames=False
tables=True
cookies=False
backgroundsounds=False
vbscript=False
javascript=False
javaapplets=False
activexcontrols=False
AK=False
SK=False
AOL=False
beta=False
Win16=False
Crawler=False
CDF=False
```

Overall Architecture

Ideally we would like to make the browser detection into a nice, reusable component, which can then expose information about the particular browser to the servlet or JSP page that processes the request. This sort of pre-processing of requests is an ideal task for a filter, so we will create a filter that intercepts requests, determines the browser's properties, and makes them available in the form of a request or session bean. This bean can then be used in any JSP page or servlet that is interested in the browser's properties. The overall architecture of our solution will therefore be as follows:

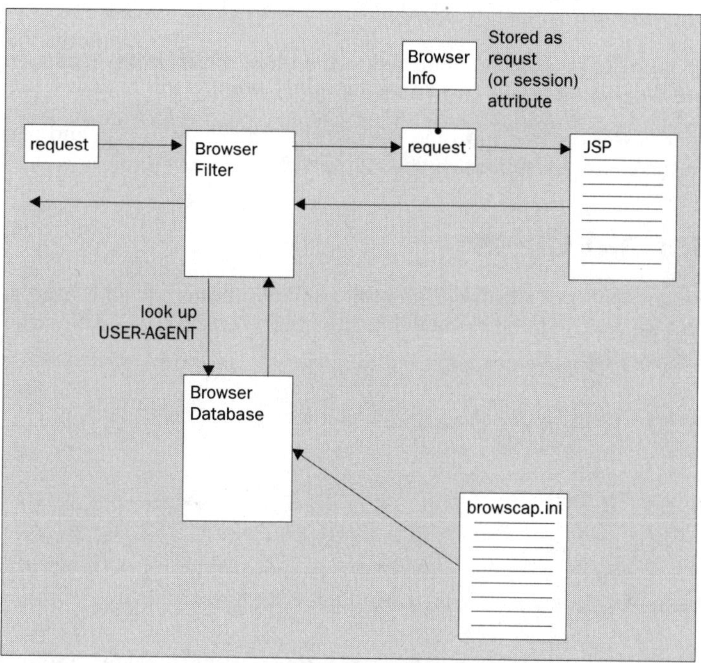

So how does this translate into a set of classes to implement? The four main classes we'll write are:

- `BrowserFilter` is the Servlet 2.3 filter that intercepts requests, and arranges for a bean exposing the properties of the user's browser to be made available to the end resource.
- `BrowserInfo` is the class used to represent the browser – the results of the attempt to match an incoming `USER-AGENT` header against the data we have amassed from the `browscap.ini` file. It will expose a variety of property getter methods that can be used to retrieve that data.
- `BrowserDatabase` encapsulates the parsing of `browscap.ini` and the process of searching for the closest match browser.
- `BrowserPattern` is a class used by `BrowserDatabase` to encapsulate a section of data read from the `browscap.ini` file. The reason for using a separate class for this purpose, rather than simply reusing the `BrowserInfo` class, is related to the format used for the `browscap.ini` file. With the use of `parent=` entries in this file, there is not a simple one-to-one mapping between sections of the file and the possible `BrowserInfo` objects that may need to be created.

A BrowserDatabase is constructed when the filter is initialized. Then, when a request comes in, the sequence of operations is:

- The BrowserFilter's doFilter() method is called by the container. The filter examines the USER-AGENT header and passes it to the BrowserDatabase's lookup() method.
- lookup() iterates through the known BrowserPattern objects representing entries in the browscap.ini file and identifies the best match.
- lookup() creates a BrowserInfo object to encapsulate the results, making sure to include the properties of any 'parent' entry.
- The BrowserInfo object is returned to the filter, which stores it as a request or session attribute depending on the browser's configuration.
- The filter passes control on to the next filter in the chain (or the end resource, if this is the last filter in the chain) by calling FilterChain.doFilter().

The BrowserInfo Class

The most important aspect of a browser identification component from a page designer's point of view will be the object we expose to describe the browser. Accordingly, we'll describe this, the BrowserInfo class, first:

```
package com.wrox.browser;

import java.io.Serializable;
import java.util.HashMap;
import java.util.Iterator;
import java.util.Map;

public class BrowserInfo implements Serializable {
```

The browser properties are of three types – pure strings, boolean values, and integer values – and each needs to be treated differently. However, for simplicity we will store all the properties as String values, within a HashMap:

```
  private HashMap properties;
```

We will be able to retrieve property values using either generic getProperty(), getBooleanProperty(), and getIntProperty() methods, or using specific getXXX() methods provided for common properties.

The first question is: how do the properties get into the BrowserInfo object? Firstly, we can pass a HashMap into the BrowserInfo constructor:

```
  protected BrowserInfo(HashMap properties) {
    this.properties = (HashMap) properties.clone();
  }
```

Note that we take care to clone this HashMap rather than just use it directly, so that we can add further properties to this BrowserInfo object without affecting the original data from which it was created.

It turns out that we need to be able to add new properties to a BrowserInfo object after it has been created, because of the format of the browscap.ini file with its parent references. Two methods provide for this: addProperty(), which takes a simple name-value pair, and addProperties(), which takes a HashMap as a parameter and adds its contents to the HashMap already maintained by the BrowserInfo object:

```
protected void addProperty(String name, String value) {
  properties.put(name, value);
}

protected void addProperties(HashMap newProperties) {
  properties.putAll(newProperties);
}
```

So much for getting properties *into* the BrowserInfo object, but what's of most interest in the end is getting them *out* again. We define a helper method for each type of property the component supports, starting with the easiest: string properties. The only slightly unintuitive thing here is the folding of property names to lower case. Later, when we see the code that reads browscap.ini, we'll see that all the property names are stored as lower case:

```
public String getProperty(String propertyName) {
  return (String) properties.get(propertyName.toLowerCase());
}
```

Boolean properties aren't much different, though we do need to convert the String value stored in the HashMap into a boolean. The behaviour of the Boolean.valueOf() method means that this method will return false unless the String value is "true" (the comparison being case-insensitive):

```
public boolean getBooleanProperty(String propertyName) {
  String stringValue =
                    (String) properties.get(propertyName.toLowerCase());
  return Boolean.valueOf(stringValue).booleanValue();
}
```

Integer properties are treated in a similar way. However, it's possible that converting the String to an int might throw a NumberFormatException, in which case we throw a BrowserException to highlight the problem:

```
public int getIntProperty(String propertyName)
          throws BrowserException {
  String stringValue = (String) properties.get
                                        (propertyName.toLowerCase());
  try {
    return Integer.parseInt(stringValue);
  } catch (NumberFormatException e) {
     throw new BrowserException ("Error converting browser property " +
                             propertyName + " to an integer");
  }
}
```

Lastly, we define proper getter methods for common browser properties. These are all rather similar, so we'll only show a selection here. `getUserAgent()` returns the original `USER-AGENT` HTTP header value. Remember that the keys used to store the properties in the `HashMap` are all lower case:

```
  public String getUserAgent() {
    return (String) properties.get("useragent");
  }
```

The `getBrowser()`, `getBrand()`, `getPlatform()`, and `getVersion()` methods are similar.

`getMajorVer()` returns the value of the `majorver` property (the browser major version number). This method, like the equivalent `getMinorVer()` method, will throw a `BrowserException` if the property value could not be converted to an `int`:

```
  public int getMajorVer() throws BrowserException {
    return getIntProperty("majorver");
  }
```

`getActiveXControls()` returns the value of the `activexcontrols` property (whether the browser supports ActiveX controls):

```
  public boolean getActiveXControls() {
    return getBooleanProperty("activexcontrols");
  }
}
```

The `getAK()`, `getAOL()`, `getAuthenticodeUpdate()`, `getBackgroundSounds()`, `getBeta()`, `getCDF()`, `getCookies()`, `getCrawler()`, `getDHTML()`, `getFrames()`, `getJavaApplets()`, `getJavaScript()`, `getKit()`, `getMSN()`, `getSK()`, `getTables()`, `getVBScipt()`, `getWin16()`, and `getXML()` methods work the same way.

`BrowserException` is a very simple exception that is thrown by the various classes in our browser detection component in the event of an error condition. Its sole constructor simply creates a new `BrowserException` object with the specified message:

```
package com.wrox.browser;

public class BrowserException extends Exception {

  public BrowserException(String message) {
    super(message);
  }

}
```

The Browser Database

We've seen how the browser information comes to us, in the form of browscap.ini, and how we plan to expose it to web applications. However, the real work lies in reading the file, building an internal representation of it, and using it to translate a USER-AGENT string into a BrowserInfo object. This task splits into two classes:

- BrowserPattern
  Represents a single section of the browscap.ini file
- BrowserDatabase
  Models the entire database of browser entries and can perform the necessary searching

The BrowserPattern Class

A BrowserPattern represents a section of the browscap.ini file. There are two major pieces of information encapsulated here: the USER-AGENT string to match, and the properties of a browser that matches that pattern. The USER-AGENT may also contain wildcard characters. To deal with these, we will use the open-source ORO regular expression engine from the Jakarta project (http://jakarta.apache.org/oro/):

```
package com.wrox.browser;

import java.util.HashMap;
import org.apache.oro.text.regex.Perl5Compiler;
import org.apache.oro.text.regex.Pattern;
import org.apache.oro.text.regex.MatchResult;
import org.apache.oro.text.regex.MalformedPatternException;
import org.apache.oro.text.regex.Perl5Matcher;

class BrowserPattern {
```

Let's start with the constructor, which takes only one parameter, the USER-AGENT pattern:

```
  protected BrowserPattern(String pattern) throws BrowserException {
    this.pattern = pattern;
```

After storing the pattern itself, we check whether any wildcard characters occur in it. This allows us to avoid doing expensive regular-expression matching operations in cases where a simple string comparison will suffice. We call the makeRegExp() method to convert the simple wildcard characters used in browscap.ini into a regular expression string of a form understood by ORO (a Perl 5 regular expression). The various ORO classes used here are:

- Perl5Compiler
  Used to compile a regular expression
- Pattern
  Representing a compiled regular expression
- Perl5Matcher
  Used to compare a Pattern to a particular string

```
    if ((pattern.indexOf('*') != -1) || (pattern.indexOf('?') != -1)) {
      usingRE = true;
```

Next, we compile the regular expression into a `Pattern`. We use the `READ_ONLY_MASK` compiler flag to ensure that the resulting pattern can be used safely from multiple concurrent threads (for example, when several clients are accessing the server simultaneously):

```
      Perl5Compiler compiler = new Perl5Compiler();
      matcher = new Perl5Matcher();
      try {
        oroPattern = compiler.compile(makeRegExp(pattern),
                                      Perl5Compiler.READ_ONLY_MASK);
      } catch (MalformedPatternException e) {
          throw new BrowserException("Invalid browser pattern: " +
                                     pattern + ":" + e.getMessage());
      }
    }
  }
```

So much for the constructor. We also require various properties and accessor methods in connection with the code we've just seen, including the `USER-AGENT` string or pattern to match:

```
  private String pattern;
```

We also need to remember whether this pattern uses regular expression matching for the `USER-AGENT`:

```
  private boolean usingRE = false;
```

We also provide a couple of methods to retrieve the values of these properties:

```
  protected String getPattern() {
    return pattern;
  }

  protected boolean usesRE() {
    return usingRE;
  }
```

If we are using regular expressions, we will also need to remember the `org.apache.oro.text.regex.Pattern` to match, and an `org.apache.oro.text.regex.Perl5Matcher` to use when comparing strings against the pattern. The purpose of these variables will become apparent shortly:

```
  private Pattern oroPattern = null;
  private Perl5Matcher matcher = null;
```

As we saw earlier, the `USER-AGENT` patterns use `*` to match zero or more characters, and `?` to match a single character. These patterns closely resemble those used with the Unix shell and Windows command prompt, commonly called **glob** patterns. ORO, on the other hand, requires regular expressions in the syntax used by Perl 5. To convert the patterns we need to do several things:

- Where a `*` occurs, replace it with `.*`
- Where a `?` occurs, replace it with `.`
- Make sure any characters that are special to ORO are escaped appropriately
- Make sure that any `*` or `?` characters that are escaped in the original are preserved correctly

These next three methods are based closely on code from the `GlobCompiler` class in the `org.apache.oro.text` package, distributed under the Apache Software License. Unfortunately we can't use `GlobCompiler` directly as the glob syntax it supports isn't quite the same as that used in `browscap.ini`.

`makeRegExp()` does this work of converting a glob-like pattern into an equivalent Perl 5 regular expression:

```
  private String makeRegExp(String thePattern) {
    char[] pattern = thePattern.toCharArray();
    int ch;
    StringBuffer buffer;
    buffer = new StringBuffer(2*pattern.length);

    for(ch=0; ch < pattern.length; ch++) {
      switch(pattern[ch]) {
      case '*':
        buffer.append("(.*)");
        break;
      case '?':
        buffer.append("(.)");
        break;
      case '\\':
        buffer.append('\\');
        if(ch == pattern.length - 1) {
          buffer.append('\\');
        } else if(isGlobMetaCharacter(pattern[ch + 1])) {
          buffer.append(pattern[++ch]);
        } else {
          buffer.append('\\');
        }
        break;
      default:
        if(isPerl5MetaCharacter(pattern[ch])) {
          buffer.append('\\');
        }
        buffer.append(pattern[ch]);
        break;
      }
    }
    return buffer.toString();
  }
```

`makeRegExp()` uses two short helper methods. First, `isPerl5MetaCharacter()` returns `true` if the specified character is a metacharacter in a Perl 5 regular expression:

```
private boolean isPerl5MetaCharacter(char ch) {
  return (ch == '*' || ch == '?' || ch == '+' || ch == '[' ||
          ch == ']' || ch == '(' || ch == ')' || ch == '|' ||
          ch == '^' || ch == '$' || ch == '.' || ch == '{' ||
          ch == '}' || ch == '\\');
}
```

Secondly, `isGlobMetaCharacter()` returns `true` if the specified character is a metacharacter in a `browscap.ini` browser definition:

```
private boolean isGlobMetaCharacter(char ch) {
  return (ch == '*' || ch == '?');
}
```

All this is of little use without the ability to take a particular `USER-AGENT` header and see whether a particular `BrowserPattern` matches it. There are two cases to consider here, depending on whether we are using regular expression matching. The simple case is to see whether we have an exact match:

```
protected boolean matchExact(String userAgent) {
  return (pattern.equals(userAgent));
}
```

The regular expression case is more complex. Recall that if there is no exact match for a particular `USER-AGENT` we need to compare `BrowserPatterns` to see which matches most closely; that is, with the least number of characters matching wildcards. We start by looking to see whether there is any match at all, and if not we return the constant `NO_MATCH`:

```
protected static final int NO_MATCH = 9999999;

protected int matchRE(String userAgent) {
  if (!usingRE) {
    return NO_MATCH;
  }

  if (!matcher.matches(userAgent, oroPattern)) {
    return NO_MATCH;
  }
```

If we did get a match, we ask our `Perl5Matcher` object for a `MatchResult` object containing information about the matching process. `MatchResult` has two methods of interest to us:

- `groups()`
  Returns the number of groups of characters that matched wildcards
- `group()`
  Returns the string of characters that matched a particular wildcard

We loop through the matches and count up how many characters were matched in total. Note that `group(0)` returns the whole matched string, which we're not interested in, so we start counting from 1. First we figure out how many characters matched:

```
      MatchResult result = matcher.getMatch();
      int groups = result.groups();
      int charsMatched = 0;
      for (int count=1; count<groups; count++) {
        charsMatched += result.group(count).length();
      }
      return charsMatched;
    }
```

Finally, our `BrowserPattern` naturally needs to encapsulate the properties of this particular browser. We store these in a `HashMap`, and provide methods for adding and retrieving properties, and returning the entire `HashMap`:

```
    private HashMap properties = new HashMap();
```

`addProperty()` adds a single browser property to this `BrowserPattern` object:

```
    protected void addProperty(String property, String value) {
      properties.put(property, value);
    }
```

Next, we create a method to return a property of this `BrowserPattern`, as a `String`, taking as an argument the name of the property to retrieve:

```
    protected String getProperty(String name) {
      return (String) properties.get(name);
    }
```

The last method returns all the properties of this `BrowserPattern` object:

```
    protected HashMap getProperties() {
      return properties;
    }
  }
```

The BrowserDatabase Class

So far we can represent a section of the `browscap.ini` file. Our next need is to read and parse the file itself, construct a number of `BrowserPattern` objects as necessary, and search and weigh them to match a particular browser's `USER-AGENT` string. This is the task of our `BrowserDatabase` class, which represents the database of web clients loaded from the file:

```
package com.wrox.browser;

import java.io.IOException;
import java.io.BufferedReader;
import java.io.InputStream;
import java.io.InputStreamReader;
import java.util.HashMap;
import java.util.ArrayList;
import java.util.Iterator;

class BrowserDatabase {
```

We naturally need to store our BrowserPatterns. Often we just need to be able to iterate through them, but when we have a pattern with a parent property we will need to be able to look up a BrowserPattern by name. In this case we will store them in a HashMap, with the USER-AGENT pattern as the key. We can easily obtain a Collection containing just the BrowserPatterns by calling HashMap's values() method. We also keep a reference to the default browser, since we will often require access to it:

```
private HashMap browserMap = new HashMap();
private BrowserPattern defaultBrowserPattern;
```

The BrowserDatabase constructor is where the fun begins. In an effort to reduce coupling between BrowserDatabase and the servlet environment, the constructor takes as a parameter an InputStream that must point to the browscap.ini data. This means that the BrowserDatabase class itself is agnostic as to where the browser data comes from. It may well be loaded from a file, but could also be loaded across the network, or even generated dynamically:

```
protected BrowserDatabase(InputStream is) throws BrowserException {
```

We read the data one line at a time, constructing BrowserPattern instances as required. When we read a line there are three possibilities:

- It is a comment or blank line
- It starts a new section, being enclosed within [and] characters
- It specifies a property name-value pair for the current browser

To keep track of this, we keep a reference to the current BrowserPattern as we go through the file:

```
  BrowserPattern currentBrowser = null;
```

We start by opening the browscap.ini file for reading:

```
  BufferedReader reader =
          new BufferedReader(new InputStreamReader(is));

  try {
    String line, trimLine;
    while ((line = reader.readLine()) != null) {
      trimLine = line.trim();
      if ((trimLine.equals("")) || (trimLine.startsWith(";"))) {
        continue;
      }
```

If we are starting a new section, we create a new BrowserPattern and keep it as the current pattern:

```
      if ((trimLine.startsWith("[")) && (trimLine.endsWith("]"))) {
        String browserLine =
                trimLine.substring(1, trimLine.length()-1);

        currentBrowser = new BrowserPattern(browserLine);
```

The new BrowserPattern can then be stashed away in our HashMap. We use the USER-AGENT string (browserLine) as the key since that is the term we want to be able to use to look BrowserPatterns up:

```
          browserMap.put(browserLine, currentBrowser);
          continue;
        }
```

A browser property line is treated by separating it into the name and value parts, and storing that in the current BrowserPattern. We take care to convert all property names to lower case, and to check for property values starting with a # character (denoting an integer value):

```
        if (currentBrowser != null) {
          int equalsSign = trimLine.indexOf('=');
          if (equalsSign != -1) {

            String name = trimLine.substring(0,equalsSign)
                                  .toLowerCase();
            String value = trimLine.substring(equalsSign+1,
                                              trimLine.length());

            if (value.charAt(0) == '#') {
              value = value.substring(1);
            }
            currentBrowser.addProperty(name, value);
          }
        }
      }
```

Finally, we must remember to close the input data:

```
      reader.close();
      is.close();
    } catch (IOException e) {
      throw new BrowserException
           ("Problem reading browser capabilities file");
    }
```

and retrieve our reference to the default browser settings:

```
    defaultBrowserPattern = (BrowserPattern)
            browserMap.get("Default Browser Capability Settings");
    if (defaultBrowserPattern == null) {
      throw new BrowserException("No default browser settings found");
    }
  }
```

With our database constructed, we can search it. This functionality is split into two methods:

- `performSearch()`
  Takes a `USER-AGENT` string and performs the actual search through the database, returning the `BrowserPattern` that best matches it.
- `lookup()`
  Returns a `BrowserInfo` object representing that browser, suitable for being made available to the rest of a web application. If a `parent` property is specified, its properties will be copied into the `BrowserInfo` object.

`performSearch()` implements the rules for matching a browser `USER-AGENT` string against the patterns specified in `browscap.ini`: first check for an exact match; if there is none, return the pattern that has the smallest number of characters matching wildcards:

```
  private BrowserPattern performSearch(String userAgent) {
```

We start by iterating through the `BrowserPatterns`, checking for an exact match. If we find one, we simply return it:

```
    Iterator entries = browserMap.values().iterator();
    while (entries.hasNext()) {
      BrowserPattern currentEntry = (BrowserPattern) entries.next();
      if (currentEntry.matchExact(userAgent)) {

        return currentEntry;
      }
    }
```

If there was no exact match, we must instead look for the best match involving wildcards:

```
    entries = browserMap.values().iterator();
    BrowserPattern bestPattern = null;
    int bestScore = BrowserPattern.NO_MATCH;

    while (entries.hasNext()) {
      BrowserPattern currentEntry = (BrowserPattern) entries.next();
```

If a particular `BrowserPattern` doesn't have any wildcards, there's obviously no need to try:

```
      if (!currentEntry.usesRE()) {
        continue;
      }
```

Otherwise, we check how good a match it was and compare with the previous known best match:

```
      int currentScore = currentEntry.matchRE(userAgent);
      if (currentScore < bestScore) {
        bestScore = currentScore;
        bestPattern = currentEntry;
      }
    }
    return bestPattern;
  }
```

Finally, the `lookup()` method is used to convert an `USER-AGENT` into a `BrowserInfo` object. This is the method that our filter will call when a request comes in. Starting with the default browser properties, we first check to see whether it has a `parent` property and if so add the parent's properties, then add the properties of the `BrowserPattern` that matches best:

```
  protected BrowserInfo lookup(String userAgent) {
```

Load the default browser properties:

```
    BrowserInfo theBrowser =
            new BrowserInfo(defaultBrowserPattern.getProperties());
```

We need to check just in case someone fails to give us a `USER-AGENT` at all – in that case, we simply return the default settings:

```
    if (userAgent == null) {
      return theBrowser;
    }
```

For completeness, we store the `USER-AGENT` string in the `BrowserInfo` object:

```
    theBrowser.addProperty("useragent", userAgent);
```

Next, we invoke `performSearch()` to try to match the `USER-AGENT`:

```
    BrowserPattern thePattern = performSearch(userAgent);
```

If we didn't find anything we just return the defaults:

```
    if (thePattern == null) {
      return theBrowser;
    }
```

If we have a `parent` entry, add its properties:

```
    String parentName = thePattern.getProperty("parent");
    if (parentName != null) {
      BrowserPattern parentEntry =
              (BrowserPattern) browserMap.get(parentName);
      theBrowser.addProperties(parentEntry.getProperties());
    }
```

Finally, we add our specific properties to the `BrowserInfo` object and return it:

```
    theBrowser.addProperties(thePattern.getProperties());
    return theBrowser;
  }
}
```

Building the Filter

We've now constructed our database of browser settings and can search it, returning a `BrowserInfo` object encapsulating everything we know about a particular browser. The last step is to make this functionality available to our web applications. As we discussed earlier, we do this with a filter that intercepts requests and parses the `USER-AGENT` request header, exposing a `BrowserInfo` object as an attribute of either the request or the session.

Defining Constants

First we need to define some constants that the filter (and the custom tags we will build shortly) will need: the default name of the request or session attribute, and the default location of the `browscap.ini` file. We will allow both to be overridden by specifying initialization parameters for the filter:

```
package com.wrox.browser;

public class Constants {

  public final static String BROWSER_INFO = "com.wrox.browser";

  public final static String DEFAULT_BROWSCAP_LOCATION =
          "/WEB-INF/browscap.ini";
}
```

The BrowserFilter Class

The filter itself is the next component to be written. Three initialization parameters can be specified:

Parameter	Meaning	Defaut Value
`scope`	The scope under which the `BrowserInfo` object should be stored: `request` or `session`	`session`
`name`	The name of the request or session attribute containing the `BrowserInfo` object	`com.wrox.browser`
`browscap`	The location within the web application of the `browscap.ini` file	`/WEB-INF/browscap.ini`

`BrowserFilter` starts simply enough: it holds instance variables that will contain the scope and name information from the initialization parameters, along with our `BrowserDatabase` instance. These are set in the `init()` method. Here we also use the `ServletContext` method `getResourceAsStream()` to open an `InputStream` on the `browscap.ini` file, which we then pass to the `BrowserDatabase` constructor:

```
package com.wrox.browser;

import java.io.IOException;
import java.io.InputStream;
import javax.servlet.ServletException;
```

```
import javax.servlet.ServletRequest;
import javax.servlet.ServletResponse;
import javax.servlet.Filter;
import javax.servlet.FilterChain;
import javax.servlet.FilterConfig;
import javax.servlet.http.HttpServletRequest;
import javax.servlet.http.HttpSession;

public class BrowserFilter implements Filter {
```

We need a number of instance variables. Here is our `FilterConfig` instance:

```
  private FilterConfig filterConfig = null;
```

A `boolean` to remember whether we want to store the `BrowserInfo` bean under request scope, rather than the default session scope:

```
  private boolean requestScope = false;
```

Our `BrowserDatabase` instance:

```
  private BrowserDatabase data = null;
```

The name to use when stashing the bean away in request or session:

```
  private String name = null;
```

The `init()` method initializes the `BrowserFilter`. If the browser information database could not be opened or read it will throw a `ServletException`:

```
  public void init(FilterConfig filterConfig) throws ServletException {
    this.filterConfig = filterConfig;
```

After storing away the `FilterConfig` we need to check the values of the various initialization parameters:

```
    String sessionParam =
            filterConfig.getInitParameter("scope");
    if ((sessionParam != null) &&
        (sessionParam.equalsIgnoreCase("request"))) {
      requestScope = true;
    }

    String browscapLocation =
            filterConfig.getInitParameter("browscap");
    if (browscapLocation == null) {
      browscapLocation = Constants.DEFAULT_BROWSCAP_LOCATION;
    }

    name = filterConfig.getInitParameter("name");
    if (name == null) {
      name = Constants.BROWSER_INFO;
    }
```

The location of the browscap.ini file was as a path within the web application, so we use the ServletContext method getResourceAsStream() to open an InputStream to it:

```
    try {
      InputStream in = filterConfig.getServletContext()
                            .getResourceAsStream(browscapLocation);
      if (in == null) {
        throw new ServletException
                ("Could not open browser settings file " +
                 browscapLocation);
      }
      data = new BrowserDatabase(in);
    } catch (BrowserException e) {
        throw new ServletException(
                            "Browser filter initialization failed", e);
    }
  }
```

No special work is required in the destroy() method to take the filter out of service:

```
  public void destroy() {
    this.filterConfig = null;
  }
```

As with all filters, the real work happens in doFilter(). Before invoking the next filter in the chain we look up the USER-AGENT request header and ask the database for the best-match BrowserInfo to represent it. This is then stored as a request or session attribute, depending on the filter configuration. Note that if we are storing it in the session we only need to do the database lookup once, since we can assume that all requests in the same session will be coming from the same actual browser instance:

```
  public void doFilter(ServletRequest request, ServletResponse response,
                       FilterChain chain)
          throws IOException, ServletException {

    HttpServletRequest httpRequest = (HttpServletRequest) request;
    if (filterConfig == null) {
      return;
    }
```

If the BrowserInfo bean is to be stored in request scope, then we just obtain the USER-AGENT header and ask the BrowserDatabase to look it up:

```
    if (requestScope) {
      String userAgent = httpRequest.getHeader("USER-AGENT");
      BrowserInfo info = data.lookup(userAgent);
      request.setAttribute(name, info);
```

If, on the other hand, it is to be stored in the session, we first check whether there is already a session attribute of the correct name. If there is, then this user session has already had its browser detected and there is no need to repeat the operation:

```
      } else {
          HttpSession session = httpRequest.getSession();
          if (session.getAttribute(name) == null) {
            String userAgent = httpRequest.getHeader("USER-AGENT");
            BrowserInfo info = data.lookup(userAgent);
            session.setAttribute(name, info);
          }
      }
      chain.doFilter(request, response);
    }
  }
```

Building the Tag Library

A `BrowserInfo` object is now available to our pages, and it's up to the authors of the JSP page to make use of its properties. However, we can try to make things easier for the page designer by designing a set of custom tags that conditionally include their body content depending on the `BrowserInfo` data.

We will construct two pairs of tags:

- Tags that check for a particular boolean browser property, allowing us to conditionally include content depending on whether a feature (for example, frames) is supported or not.
- Tags that check for a particular browser, or a particular browser version. For example, a tag could be made to include its body content if the browser is Internet Explorer 5.5 or higher.

The browser.tld File

When designing a tag library it is often easiest to start with the Tag Library Descriptor (TLD) file, which lets you sketch out quickly how the tags will function. It starts ordinarily enough:

```
<?xml version="1.0" encoding="ISO-8859-1" ?>
<!DOCTYPE taglib
  PUBLIC "-//Sun Microsystems, Inc.//DTD JSP Tag Library 1.2//EN"
  "http://java.sun.com/j2ee/dtds/web-jsptaglibrary_1_2.dtd">

<taglib>
  <tlib-version>1.0</tlib-version>
  <jsp-version>1.2</jsp-version>
  <short-name>browser</short-name>
  <uri>http://www.wrox.com/taglib/browser</uri>
  <display-name>Browser Compatibility Tags</display-name>

  <description>
    Wrox Browser Compatibility Tag Library. Use in conjunction with
    a filter of type com.wrox.browser.BrowserFilter - see JavaDoc
    for details of configuring the filter.
  </description>
```

Our first two tags are very similar. We start with the <browser:supportFor> tag, which will typically be used as follows:

```
<browser:supportFor feature="frames">
  <%-- Body evaluated only if browser supports frames --%>
</browser:supportFor>
```

There is also an optional attribute name, which is used to specify the bean name to search for if the filter is using a value other than the default of "com.wrox.browser":

```
<tag>
  <name>supportFor</name>
  <tag-class>com.wrox.browser.SupportForTag</tag-class>
  <body-content>JSP</body-content>

  <description>
    Includes its body content if the detected web browser supports
    the specified feature.
  </description>

  <attribute>
    <name>feature</name>
    <required>true</required>
    <description>
      The name of the browser feature to check for.
    </description>
  </attribute>

  <attribute>
    <name>name</name>
    <required>false</required>
    <description>
      The name used by BrowserFilter to store the browser information.
      If this was not customized in web.xml, there is no need to
      set this tag attribute.
    </description>
  </attribute>
</tag>
```

The second tag is an exact mirror image, only it includes its body if a feature is *not* supported, for example:

```
<browser:noSupportFor feature="frames">
  <%-- Body evaluated only if browser supports frames --%>
</browser:noSupportFor>
```

```
<tag>
  <name>noSupportFor</name>
  <tag-class>com.wrox.browser.NoSupportForTag</tag-class>
  <body-content>JSP</body-content>

  <description>
    Includes its body content if the detected web browser does not
```

```
      support the specified feature.
    </description>

    <attribute>
      <name>feature</name>
      <required>true</required>
      <description>
        The name of the browser feature to check for.
      </description>
    </attribute>

    <attribute>
      <name>name</name>
      <required>false</required>
      <description>
        The name used by BrowserFilter to store the browser information.
        If this was not customized in web.xml, there is no need to
        set this tag attribute.
      </description>
    </attribute>
  </tag>
```

The other two tags are slightly more complex. Let's start with the `<browser:is>` tag, which includes its body content if the browser matches the requirements set out in its attributes. Some typical usage examples might be:

```
<browser:is browser="IE">
  <%-- Body evaluated only if browser is Internet Explorer --%>
</browser:is>

<browser:is browser="IE" majorVer="4" minorVer="0">
  <%-- Body evaluated only if browser is Internet Explorer 4.0
       or higher --%>
</browser:is>

<browser:is browser="IE" majorVer="4" minorVer="0" exact="true">
  <%-- Body evaluated only if browser is Internet Explorer 4.0 --%>
</browser:is>
```

There is also a `name` attribute to specify the name to use when searching for the `BrowserInfo` bean:

```
  <tag>
    <name>is</name>
    <tag-class>com.wrox.browser.IsTag</tag-class>
    <body-content>JSP</body-content>

    <description>
      Includes its body content if the current browser matches that
      specified in the tag attributes.
    </description>

    <attribute>
```

```
      <name>browser</name>
      <required>false</required>
      <description>
        The name of the browser.
      </description>
    </attribute>

    <attribute>
      <name>name</name>
      <required>false</required>
      <description>
        The name used by BrowserFilter to store the browser information.
        If this was not customized in web.xml, there is no need to
        set this tag attribute.
      </description>
    </attribute>

    <attribute>
      <name>majorVer</name>
      <required>false</required>
      <description>
        The name of the major version to check for
      </description>
    </attribute>

    <attribute>
      <name>minorVer</name>
      <required>false</required>
      <description>
        The name of the minor version to check for
      </description>
    </attribute>

    <attribute>
      <name>exact</name>
      <required>false</required>
      <description>
        Should the version-number check be exact? If false (the
        default), any higher version number also matches.
      </description>
    </attribute>
  </tag>
```

Lastly the `<browser:isNot>` tag is, as its name suggests, the opposite of `<browser:is>`, for example:

```
<browser:isNot browser="lynx">
  <%-- Body evaluated only if browser is not Lynx --%>
</browser:isNot>
```

```
  <tag>
    <name>isNot</name>
    <tag-class>com.wrox.browser.IsNotTag</tag-class>
```

```
    <body-content>JSP</body-content>

    <description>
      Includes its body content if the current browser does not match
      that specified in the tag attributes.
    </description>

    <attribute>
      <name>browser</name>
      <required>false</required>
      <description>
        The name of the browser.
      </description>
    </attribute>

    <attribute>
      <name>name</name>
      <required>false</required>
      <description>
        The name used by BrowserFilter to store the browser information.
        If this was not customized in web.xml, there is no need to
        set this tag attribute.
      </description>
    </attribute>

    <attribute>
      <name>majorVer</name>
      <required>false</required>
      <description>
        The name of the major version to check for
      </description>
    </attribute>

    <attribute>
      <name>minorVer</name>
      <required>false</required>
      <description>
        The name of the minor version to check for
      </description>
    </attribute>

    <attribute>
      <name>exact</name>
      <required>false</required>
      <description>
        Should the version-number check be exact? If false (the
        default), any higher version number also matches. Default
        is false.
      </description>
    </attribute>
  </tag>
</taglib>
```

One could ask whether there is there a need for these tags at all, given that the browser properties are made available as a bean and could be accessed by any generic flow-control tags. They are useful, for two reasons:

- The syntax chosen will make the tags' function quite clear and easy to read.
- The <browser:is> and <browser:isNot> tags in particular hide a lot of boolean logic. Expressing this by combining tags would be painful. XML is poorly adapted to expressing boolean expressions.

The SupportForTag Class

These tags are nice and simple, and as they only need to be able to decide whether or not to include their body the tag handlers can just extend TagSupport. SupportForTag is the handler for the <browser:supportFor> tag:

```
package com.wrox.browser;

import javax.servlet.jsp.PageContext;
import javax.servlet.jsp.JspException;
import javax.servlet.jsp.JspTagException;
import javax.servlet.jsp.tagext.TagSupport;

public class SupportForTag extends TagSupport {
```

We need to take care to ensure correct behavior if the container is using tag pooling (reusing instances of our tag handler class), by making sure that attribute values are initialized correctly both on initial construction of the tag handler instance and when release() is called. The feature and name instance variables hold the current values of the attributes:

```
  protected String feature;
  protected String name;
```

The constructor and the release() method both call init():

```
  public SupportForTag() {
    super();
    init();
  }

  public void release() {
    super.release();
    init();
  }
```

init() is where we initialize the tag attributes to their default values. The feature attribute is mandatory, so setFeature() will always be called before doStartTag() and we can simply initialize the value to null at this stage. The name attribute, on the other hand, is optional so we make sure that the default value, Constants.BROWSER_INFO, is set. Recall that the feature attribute specifies the name of the browser feature to check for, and the name attribute can be used to specify the name that was used to store the BrowserInfo bean in the request or session:

```
    private void init() {
      feature = null;
      name = Constants.BROWSER_INFO;
    }
```

The property getter and setter methods are standard fare:

```
    public void setFeature(String feature) {
      this.feature = feature;
    }

    public String getFeature() {
      return feature;
    }

    public void setName(String name) {
      this.name = name;
    }

    public String getName() {
      return name;
    }
```

Lastly, in `doStartTag()` we simply search for the `BrowserInfo` object in the standard JSP scopes (using the `PageContext.findAttribute()` method) and look up the specified property to see whether or not to include the tag body. Following the normal rules for writing tag handlers, we return `EVAL_BODY_INCLUDE` if the tag body should be evaluated or `SKIP_BODY` if it should not:

```
    public int doStartTag() throws JspException {

      BrowserInfo browser = (BrowserInfo) pageContext.findAttribute(name);

      if (browser == null) {
        throw new JspTagException ("Could not find BrowserInfo object - " +
                                   "is BrowserFilter configured?");
      }

      if (browser.getBooleanProperty(feature)) {
        return EVAL_BODY_INCLUDE;
      } else {
          return SKIP_BODY;
      }
    }
  }
```

The NoSupportForTag Class

The `NoSupportForTag` class takes a shortcut by extending `SupportForTag` and just overriding its `doStartTag()` method to provide the correct functionality in this case:

```
  package com.wrox.browser;
```

```
import javax.servlet.jsp.PageContext;
import javax.servlet.jsp.JspException;
import javax.servlet.jsp.JspTagException;

public class NoSupportForTag extends SupportForTag {
```

Process the start tag: include the body if the browser supports the specified feature, otherwise skip it. This throws a `JspException` if an error occurs during processing of the tag:

```
  public int doStartTag() throws JspException {

    BrowserInfo browser = (BrowserInfo) pageContext.findAttribute(name);

    if (browser == null) {
      throw new JspTagException ("Could not find BrowserInfo object - " +
                                 "is BrowserFilter configured?");
    }

    if (!(browser.getBooleanProperty(feature))) {
      return EVAL_BODY_INCLUDE;
    } else {
      return SKIP_BODY;
    }
  }
}
```

The IsTag Class

Like the previous two tags, `IsTag` simply needs to decide whether or not to evaluate its body. The logic, however, is much more complex. As we saw earlier, there are various possible usage patterns, for example:

```
<browser:is browser="Netscape">
  <%-- Body evaluated only if browser is Netscape --%>
</browser:is>

<browser:is browser="IE" majorVer="5" minorVer="5">
  <%-- Body evaluated only if browser is Internet Explorer 5.5
       or higher --%>
</browser:is>

<browser:is browser="Netscape" majorVer="4">
  <%-- Body evaluated only if browser is Netscape 4.x or higher --%>
</browser:is>

<browser:is browser="IE" majorVer="6" minorVer="0" exact="true">
  <%-- Body evaluated only if browser is Internet Explorer 6.0 --%>
</browser:is>
```

```
package com.wrox.browser;
```

```
import javax.servlet.jsp.PageContext;
import javax.servlet.jsp.JspException;
import javax.servlet.jsp.JspTagException;
import javax.servlet.jsp.tagext.TagSupport;

public class IsTag extends TagSupport {
```

Our first task is to deal with the tag attributes:

- `browser`
  An optional `String` containing the name of the browser we want to match.
- name
  The `String` to use when looking up the `BrowserInfo` bean.
- `majorVer`
  The optional major version number we want to match. This is an `int` property.
- `minorVer`
  The optional minor version number to match. This too is an `int`.
- `exact`
  An optional boolean specifying whether the version number must match exactly. The default is `false`.

The current values of these attributes are stored in instance variables. We also use two `boolean` variables, `majorVerSpecfied` and `minorVerSpecified`, to remember whether the `majorVer` and `minorVer` attributes were specified:

```
  protected String browser;
  protected String name;
  protected int majorVer;
  protected boolean majorVerSpecified;
  protected int minorVer;
  protected boolean minorVerSpecified;
  protected boolean exact;
```

These values are initialized in the `init()` method, which is called from both the constructor and the `release()` method:

```
  private void init() {
    browser = null;
    name = Constants.BROWSER_INFO;
    majorVer = 0;
    majorVerSpecified = false;
    minorVer = 0;
    minorVerSpecified = false;
    exact = false;
  }

  public IsTag() {
    super();
    init();
```

```
  }

  public void release() {
    super.release();
    init();
  }
```

The property setter and getter methods are much as one would expect, but note that `setMajorVer()` and `setMinorVer()` record not just the property value but also the fact that it has been specified:

```
  public void setBrowser(String browser) {
    this.browser = browser;
  }

  public String getBrowser() {
    return browser;
  }

  public void setName(String name) {
    this.name = name;
  }

  public String getName() {
    return name;
  }

  public void setMajorVer(int majorVer) {
    this.majorVer = majorVer;
    this.majorVerSpecified = true;
  }

  public int getMajorVer() {
    return majorVer;
  }

  public void setMinorVer(int minorVer) {
    this.minorVer = minorVer;
    this.minorVerSpecified = true;
  }

  public int getMinorVer() {
    return minorVer;
  }

  public void setExact(boolean exact) {
    this.exact = exact;
  }

  public boolean getExact() {
    return exact;
  }
```

doStartTag() has to decide whether the browser matches the page author's requirements, in which case it returns EVAL_BODY_INCLUDE and the tag's body is evaluated, or whether it fails to meet them, in which case it returns SKIP_BODY. It devolves this decision to the browserMatches() method, which we will examine shortly:

```
public int doStartTag() throws JspException {

  BrowserInfo userBrowser = (BrowserInfo) pageContext.findAttribute(name);

  if (userBrowser == null) {
    throw new JspTagException("Could not find BrowserInfo object - " +
                              "is BrowserFilter configured?");
  }

  try {
    if (browserMatches(userBrowser.getBrowser(),
                       userBrowser.getMajorVer(),
                       userBrowser.getMinorVer())) {
      return EVAL_BODY_INCLUDE;
    } else {
      return SKIP_BODY;
    }
  } catch (BrowserException e) {
    throw new JspTagException("Error retrieving browser properties");
  }
}
```

browserMatches() receives as parameters the name, and major and minor version numbers, of the user's browser. It starts by checking whether the page author specified a particular browser name. If so, we check whether it matches and if not return false:

```
protected boolean browserMatches(String userBrowser,
                                 int userMajorVer,
                                 int userMinorVer) {

  if (browser != null) {
    // The "browser" attribute was specified, so we need to check
    // whether that matches.
    if (!(browser.equalsIgnoreCase(userBrowser))) {
      // Definite non-match
      return false;
    }
    // Otherwise go on to check other attributes
  }
```

Even if the browser name does match we are not home and dry – we may well still need to compare version numbers. Comparison of the versions is deferred to two further methods, versionMatchesExact() and versionMatches(). The method called depends on the value of the tag's exact attribute:

```
  if (majorVerSpecified) {
    if (exact) {
```

```
        return versionMatchesExact(userMajorVer, userMinorVer);
      } else {
        return versionMatches(userMajorVer, userMinorVer);
      }
    } else {
      return true;
    }
  }
```

An exact comparison is easy:

```
  public boolean versionMatchesExact(int userMajorVer, int userMinorVer) {
    if (minorVerSpecified) {
      return ((userMajorVer == majorVer) && (userMinorVer == minorVer));
    } else {
      return (userMajorVer == majorVer);
    }
  }
```

In the inexact version there are a number of possibilities:

- The page author specified only the major version number. The version matches if the user's major version number is greater than or equal to that specified in the page.
- If the minor version is specified, the version matches if the major version matches and the minor version is at least as high as specified in the page, *or* if the major version is higher than specified.

```
  public boolean versionMatches(int userMajorVer, int userMinorVer) {
    if (minorVerSpecified) {
      if (userMajorVer > majorVer) {
        return true;
      } else if ((userMajorVer == majorVer) && (userMinorVer >= minorVer)) {
        return true;
      } else {
        return false;
      }
    } else {
      return (userMajorVer >= majorVer);
    }
  }
}
```

The IsNotTag Class

The `IsNotTag` class, our final tag handler, can take advantage of nearly all the code we've seen in the previous section. It extends `IsTag` and simply overrides its `doStartTag()` method, negating the result of the `browserMatches()` method:

```
package com.wrox.browser;

import javax.servlet.jsp.JspException;
import javax.servlet.jsp.JspTagException;
```

```
public class IsNotTag extends IsTag {

  public int doStartTag() throws JspException {

    BrowserInfo userBrowser = (BrowserInfo) pageContext.findAttribute(name);

    if (userBrowser == null) {
      throw new JspTagException("Could not find BrowserInfo object - " +
                                "is BrowserFilter configured?");
    }

    try {
      if (!(browserMatches(userBrowser.getBrowser(),
                           userBrowser.getMajorVer(),
                           userBrowser.getMinorVer()))) {
        return EVAL_BODY_INCLUDE;
      } else {
          return SKIP_BODY;
      }
    } catch (BrowserException e) {
        throw new JspTagException("Error retrieving browser properties");
    }
  }
}
```

Using the Filter

Everything is now ready for us to configure and deploy our filter and tags. We'll do this fairly briefly, as we'll see further examples in the next chapter. The relevant extracts of the `web.xml` file are shown below. All the initialization parameters are specified explicitly, though the default values for `scope` and `browscap` are used.

First we configure the filter and specify its initialization parameters. Choosing the value of the `name` parameter was interesting. The default, `com.wrox.browser`, fits in with the suggestion in the Servlet specification that attribute names should follow package-naming conventions to avoid name clashes. Unfortunately, `com.wrox.browser` isn't a valid Java identifier (although `com_wrox_browser`, for example, would be), and so if we follow the conventions we can't use the `<jsp:useBean>` tag to access our `BrowserInfo` instance.

If we're just interested in using the tags that's not a problem, but for the first example we want to list all the browser properties and `<jsp:useBean>` and `<jsp:getProperty>` provide an obvious way of doing this. To get around this, plain old `browser` is used as the attribute name in this instance:

```
<filter>
  <filter-name>Browser Detection Filter</filter-name>
  <filter-class>com.wrox.browser.BrowserFilter</filter-class>
  <init-param>
    <param-name>scope</param-name>
    <param-value>session</param-value>
  </init-param>
  <init-param>
```

```
      <param-name>name</param-name>
      <param-value>browser</param-value>
    </init-param>
    <init-param>
      <param-name>browscap</param-name>
      <param-value>/WEB-INF/browscap.ini</param-value>
    </init-param>
  </filter>
```

The second step is to map the filter to the relevant resources (everything in the application):

```
  <filter-mapping>
    <filter-name>Browser Detection Filter</filter-name>
    <url-pattern>/*</url-pattern>
  </filter-mapping>
```

We don't need a `<taglib>` element for the Browser Tag Library if we package the tags into a JAR file with the `.tld` file in its `META-INF\` directory. Don't forget to put the `browscap.ini` files in the `WEB-INF\` directory.

Displaying Browser Properties – browsercapabilities.jsp

The first example, as promised, uses the `<jsp:useBean>` and `<jsp:getProperty>` tags to display your browser's properties. Everything is very simple, if a bit repetitive:

```
<html>
  <head>
    <title>Your Browser's Capabilities</title>
  </head>

  <body>

    <h1>Your Browser's Capabilities</h1>

    <jsp:useBean id="browser" class="com.wrox.browser.BrowserInfo"
                 scope="session" />

    <table border="1">
      <tr>
        <th>Property</th>
        <th>Value</th>
      </tr>
      <tr>
        <td>userAgent</td>
        <td><jsp:getProperty name="browser" property="userAgent" /></td>
      </tr>
      <tr>
        <td>browser</td>
        <td><jsp:getProperty name="browser" property="browser" /></td>
      </tr>
      ...
```

And so on for `brand`, `platform`, `version`, `majorVer`, `minorVer`, `AK`, `activeXControls`, `AOL`, `authenticodeUpdate`, `backgroundSounds`, `beta`, `CDF`, `cookies`, `crawler`, `DHTML`, `frames`, `javaApplets`, `javaScript`, `kit`, `MSN`, `SK`, `tables`, `VBScript`, `win16`, and `xml`:

```
        ...
      </table>
    </body>
  </html>
```

Here's the result, first with Internet Explorer 6.0:

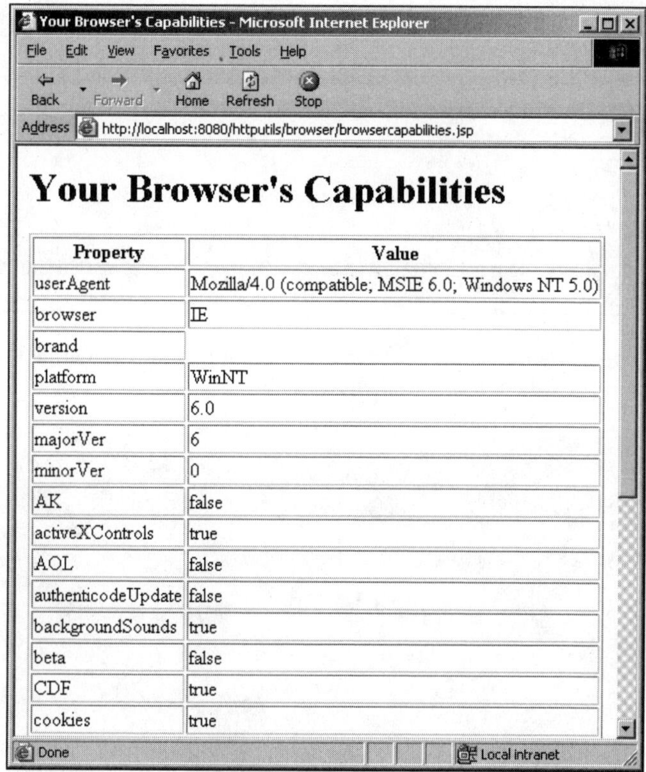

Then with the doyen of text-only browsers, Lynx:

```
http://localhost/httputils/browser/browsercapabilities.jsp
                                                  Your Browser's Capabilities

                         Your Browser's Capabilities

      Property                          Value
   userAgent            Lynx/2.8.3rel.1 libwww-FM/2.14FM
   browser              Lynx
   brand
   platform             UNIX
   version              2.8
   majorVer             2
   minorVer             8
   AK                   false
   activeXControls      false
   AOL                  false
   authenticodeUpdate   false
   backgroundSounds     false
   beta                 false
   CDF                  false
   cookies              false
   crawler              false
   DHTML                false
   frames               false
   javaApplets          false
   javaScript           false
   kit                  false
   MSN                  false
   SK                   false
   tables               true
   VBScript             false
   win16                false
   XML                  false

Commands: Use arrow keys to move, '?' for help, 'q' to quit, '<-' to go back.
  Arrow keys: Up and Down to move.  Right to follow a link; Left to go back.
 H)elp O)ptions P)rint G)o M)ain screen Q)uit /=search [delete]=history list
```

As one final check, we can ensure that it works even in the event of someone telnetting directly to the server and omitting to provide a USER-AGENT header:

```
richardh@RICHARDH ~
$ telnet localhost 80
Trying 127.0.0.1...
Connected to richardh.
Escape character is '^]'.
GET /httputils/browser/browsercapabilities.jsp HTTP/1.0

HTTP/1.1 200 OK
Content-Type: text/html;charset=ISO-8859-1
Date: Fri, 17 Aug 2001 10:14:19 GMT
Server: Apache Tomcat/4.0-b7 (HTTP/1.1 Connector)
Connection: close
Set-Cookie: JSESSIONID=8394A3C038358702B8B140B6203313D0;Path=/httputils

<html>
<head>
  <title>Your Browser's Capabilities</title>
</head>

<body>

<h1>Your Browser's Capabilities</h1>



<table border="1">
  <tr>
    <th>Property</th>
    <th>Value</th>
  </tr>
  <tr>
    <td>userAgent</td>
    <td>

    </td>
  </tr>
  <tr>
    <td>browser</td>
    <td>
      Default
    </td>
  </tr>
```

The filter has correctly given us the default settings, which it also does should we send it an unknown USER-AGENT:

```
richardh@RICHARDH ~
$ telnet localhost 80
Trying 127.0.0.1...
Connected to richardh.
Escape character is '^]'.
GET /httputils/browser/browsercapabilities.jsp HTTP/1.0
USER-AGENT: wibble

HTTP/1.1 200 OK
Content-Type: text/html;charset=ISO-8859-1
Date: Fri, 17 Aug 2001 10:13:44 GMT
Server: Apache Tomcat/4.0-b7 (HTTP/1.1 Connector)
Connection: close
Set-Cookie: JSESSIONID=F960A995A331A802F2A3054262F681D3;Path=/httputils

<html>
<head>
  <title>Your Browser's Capabilities</title>
</head>

<body>

<h1>Your Browser's Capabilities</h1>



<table border="1">
  <tr>
    <th>Property</th>
    <th>Value</th>
  </tr>
  <tr>
    <td>userAgent</td>
    <td>
      wibble
    </td>
  </tr>
  <tr>
    <td>browser</td>
    <td>
      Default
    </td>
  </tr>
```

Using the Tags – browsertags.jsp

Our second example makes use of the tags we designed, in a variety of ways. As you can see, whilst the tags allow a lot of flexibility the syntax is nice and simple, just right for the page designer:

```
<%@ taglib uri="http://www.wrox.com/taglib/browser" prefix="browser" %>

<html>
  <head>
    <title>Browser Capabilities Filter and Tags</title>
  </head>
  <body>
    <h1>Browser Support Tags!</h1>

    <p>Your browser...</p>

    <ul>
      <browser:supportFor feature="frames" name="browser">
        <li>supports frames</li>
      </browser:supportFor>

      <browser:noSupportFor feature="frames" name="browser">
        <li>does not support frames</li>
      </browser:noSupportFor>

      <browser:is name="browser" browser="ie">
        <li>is IE</li>
      </browser:is>
```

```
      <browser:isNot name="browser" browser="ie">
        <li>is not IE</li>
      </browser:isNot>

      <browser:is name="browser" browser="lynx">
        <li>is Lynx</li>
      </browser:is>

      <browser:isNot name="browser" browser="lynx">
        <li>is not Lynx</li>
      </browser:isNot>

      <browser:is name="browser" browser="IE" majorVer="4" minorVer="0">
        <li>is IE 4.0 or greater</li>
      </browser:is>

      <browser:isNot name="browser" browser="IE" majorVer="4" minorVer="0">
        <li>is not IE 4.0 or greater</li>
      </browser:isNot>

      <browser:is name="browser" browser="IE" majorVer="6" minorVer="0"
                  exact="true">
        <li>is IE 6.0</li>
      </browser:is>

      <browser:isNot name="browser" browser="IE" majorVer="6" minorVer="0"
                     exact="true">
        <li>is not IE 6.0</li>
      </browser:isNot>

      <browser:is name="browser" majorVer="2">
        <li>is version 2.x or higher</li>
      </browser:is>

      <browser:isNot name="browser" majorVer="2">
        <li>is not version 2.x or higher</li>
      </browser:isNot>

      <browser:is name="browser" majorVer="2" exact="true">
        <li>is version 2.x</li>
      </browser:is>

      <browser:isNot name="browser" majorVer="2" exact="true">
        <li>is not version 2.x</li>
      </browser:isNot>
    </ul>

  </body>
</html>
```

In Internet Explorer the result is as we would expect:

With Lynx we again get the right answer:

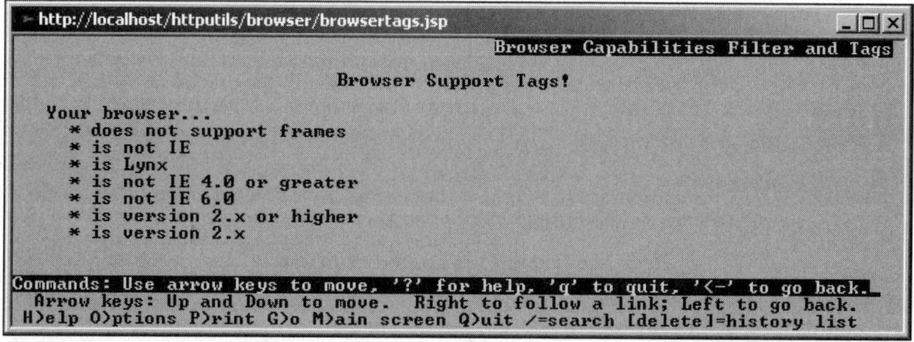

Creating Cascading Style Sheets – styles.jsp

Let's try one final, more realistic example. JSP pages are good for generating much more than just HTML, and some of the trickiest browser-specific problems relate to Cascading Style Sheets (CSS). Our last example looks at using the browser tags to generate browser-specific style sheets. Although the changes we'll make to the style sheet are fairly minor, the principles can be extended much more broadly as the style sheet requirements become more complex.

We'll start with the style sheet itself, which is generated by `styles.jsp`. We start by overriding the default content-type for the page (by default, a JSP page generates the content-type `text/html`) and importing the Browser Tag Library:

```
<%@ page contentType="text/css" %>
<%@ taglib uri="http://www.wrox.com/taglib/browser" prefix="browser" %>
```

The first block of styles is uncontroversial and common to all browsers:

```
BODY {
  background-color: #FFFFCC;
}

P {
  color: black;
  font: 12pt sans-serif;
}

PRE {
  font: 8pt monospace;
  border: double #CC0000;
}
```

For the `<H1>` tag, we will change the text color and the font depending on the user's browser. Users with IE 6.0 or higher will get maroon headings in a 36 point serif font, while those without will have blue headings in a 24 point cursive font:

```
H1 {
  <browser:is name="browser" browser="ie" majorVer="6" minorVer="0">
    color: maroon;
    font: bold 36pt serif;
  </browser:is>
  <browser:isNot name="browser" browser="ie" majorVer="6" minorVer="0">
    color: blue;
    font: bold italic 24pt cursive;
  </browser:isNot>
}
```

Similarly, people using Opera will have the default style for the `<EM>` tag overridden so that white text is used, on a black background:

```
<browser:is name="browser" browser="opera">
  EM {
    font-style: normal;
    font-weight: normal;
    background-color: black;
    color: white;
  }
</browser:is>
```

The page that references the stylesheet is `stylesheet.jsp`, which is a conventional HTML-producing JSP page:

```
<html>
  <head>
    <title>Dynamic Stylesheet</title>
  </head>
  <link rel="stylesheet" type="text/css" href="styles.jsp">
  <body>
    <h1>Dynamic Stylesheet</h1>

    <p>This page uses a stylesheet that is generated
    <em>dynamically</em> depending on which browser you
    are using.</p>
```

To help us see what's going on, we also display the stylesheet within `<pre>` tags, invoking it using the `<jsp:include>` action:

```
    <p>Here is the stylesheet:</p>

    <pre>
      <jsp:include page="styles.jsp"/>
    </pre>

  </body>
</html>
```

So, here's the resulting page – first in Internet Explorer 6.0:

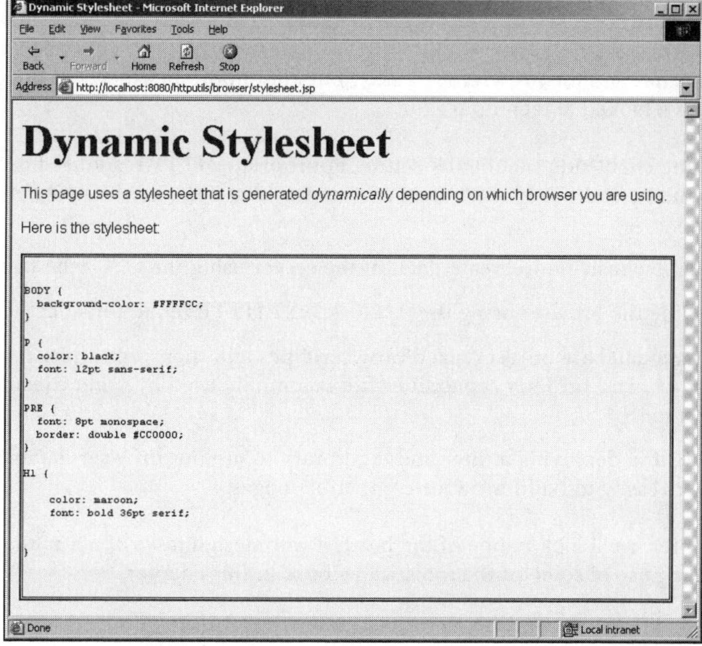

Then in Opera 5.0:

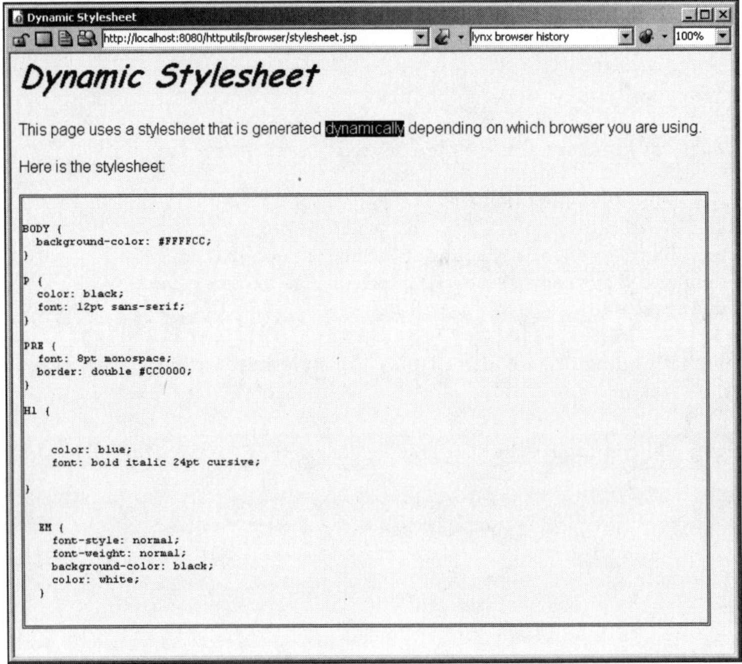

Summary

Managing the caches and the browser isn't easy, but are important aspects of designing a web application. We've looked at techniques for:

- Managing client-side caching by setting appropriate HTTP response headers, both manually and by using both ready-made and custom tag libraries, and the new Servlet 2.3 filter capability
- Caching expensive-to-recreate data on the server using the OSCache tags and filter
- Identifying the browser using the `USER-AGENT` HTTP request header
- Building a database of recognized browser types and their properties, leveraging the `browscap.ini` browser capabilities file commonly used by other dynamic web content creation tools
- Creating and deploying a filter and tag library to use our browser database, allowing page designers easily to build browser-compatible pages.

In the next chapter, we'll look at one of the hardest web design tasks of all, managing frames. In doing so we'll be making use of some of the tools we've built in this chapter.

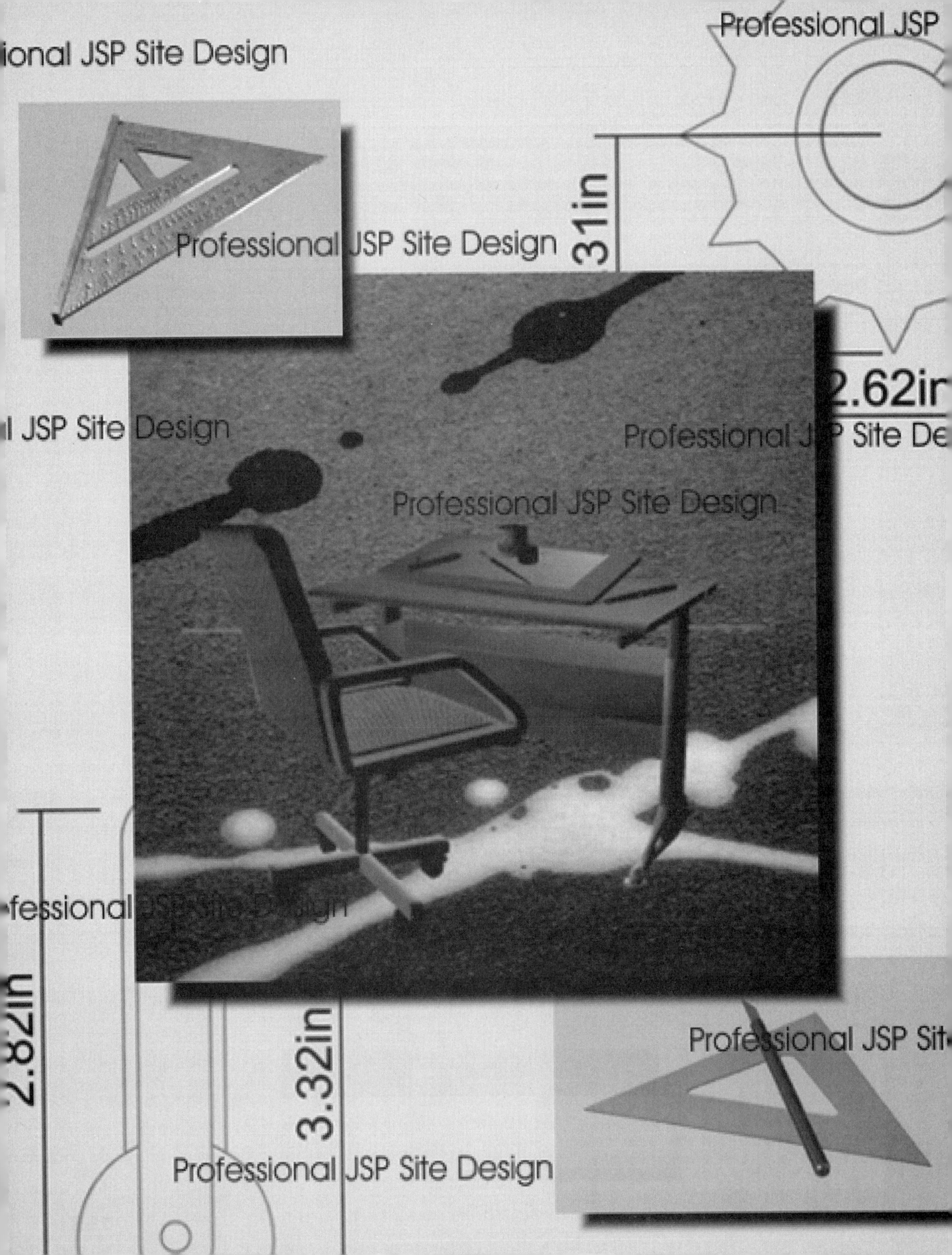

Professional JSP
Professional JSP Site Design
31in
2.62in
Professional JSP Site Design
3.32in
Professional JSP Site Design

Coping with Frames

Frames have been a controversial aspect of HTML ever since they were first invented. However, they do serve a useful purpose: freeing pages from the "one scrollbar fits all" of non-framed pages. Take, for example, Microsoft's Outlook Web Access application:

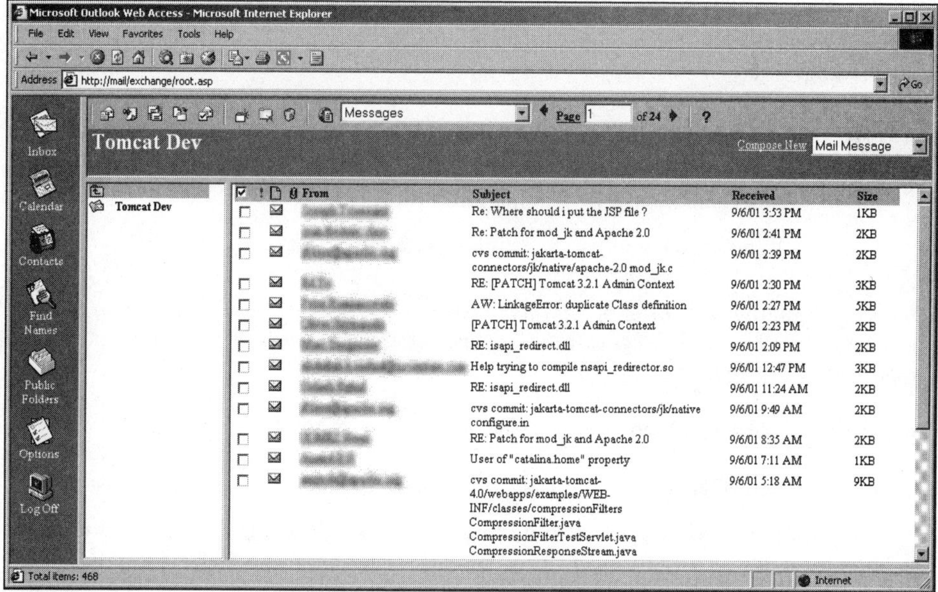

Here, frames are used in an intelligent way to make the application easier to use. The message listing can be scrolled independently of the folder list (the column headed Tomcat Dev). The toolbars at the top and left stay put wherever we scroll.

Frames have their downside too. Both for users and for those of us who get to code the applications. In this chapter we'll be looking at the issues that arise when we try to marry frames with server-side coding. Our itinerary for the chapter is as follows:

- We'll start by looking at the problem with frames in general terms – why is integrating frames with server-side code a particular headache?
- Next, we'll take a preliminary look at our case study for this chapter – an online photograph gallery application.
- Then we will make a first attempt at "framing" our site. This turns out to be fairly straightforward, until we want to update more than one frame at a time.
- Model-View-Controller (MVC) architectures are now widely adopted for Java web application design. We'll look at how we can use an MVC approach in designing a frame-based site.
- Lastly, we'll explore the issue of adding popup windows to the site. Popups are relevant to us here since, though they are created differently to frames, we link them together using the same `<a target="x">` HTML syntax. This will cause some further headaches, and we'll see how rigorously adhering to MVC architecture makes things easier.

The Problem with Frames

I'll be honest about this: I don't like frames. They make my head hurt. I'd not be at all surprised if they made your head hurt too – the frame tags are just badly designed. If you're just after a nice page layout, go with tables (or CSS if you're feeling brave). Jakob Nielsen's seminal Alertbox column at http://www.useit.com/alertbox/9612.html gives a good summary of the arguments from the user's point of view.

What about the server-side programmer? For server-side programmers the real issue is the model used for page loading:

- Each frameset, and each frame, requires a separate HTTP request from the browser
- Due to the stateless nature of the HTTP protocol, these requests may well be coming in simultaneously, and not in any defined order
- The only thing we have to tie the requests together is the `HttpSession`

Interestingly, during the writing of this chapter we found a nasty race condition in Tomcat 4.0's web application class loader that only came to light once you were using frames in earnest and the requests were pounding in on the server.

Compare this free-for-all with how things work in a Model 2 (MVC) architecture:

- A single controller servlet acts as a central point of contact for every request
- Unless we're generating images on the fly, there is only a single request per user action
- The controller servlet can therefore easily keep track of the system state: a request arrives, we perform the command, save any state information, prepare the data for the view, and forward to it

This makes for a nice, simple (and easily understood) dataflow: it's obvious what happens, in what order, and what the result will be. One might hypothesize that what we need is a way of tying an MVC architecture into even a frame-based site. As we progress through ever more complex examples, we'll see in more detail why this is indeed vital, and explore techniques for doing it. Employing an MVC architecture turns out to be even more important in a frame-based site than it is normally.

Setting the Scene

In my spare moments, I run a web site for a tourist railway in the middle of Wales, UK (the Talyllyn Railway, pronounced Tal-ith-lin – see http://www.talyllyn.co.uk/ for more information). Part of the site is a gallery of photographs, which over the years has come to be quite extensive. Maintaining this part of the site used to be very tedious, until I wrote a little script in Perl that generated the galleries from data stored in a flat text file. Over time this has been rewritten in Java, and the raw data from which the pages are generated is now in an XML format.

Until now, however, all that my program has done is generate static HTML pages, which I can then upload onto the server. That's a lot better than maintaining all those pages by hand but I couldn't help feeling that it was worth exploring a dynamic server-side approach, possibly using frames to enhance the presentation. That's what we're going to be exploring in this chapter.

First, let's take a tour of the current, static version. There's a page for each photograph, showing the photo itself, a caption, and details of who took it:

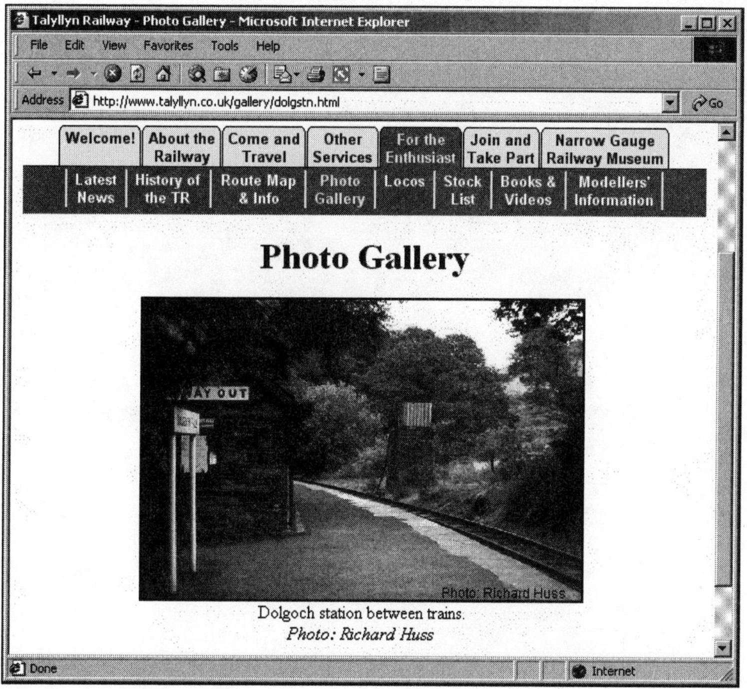

The photos are also categorized into sections – for example, here's the page listing the photographs taken at or near Dolgoch Falls station:

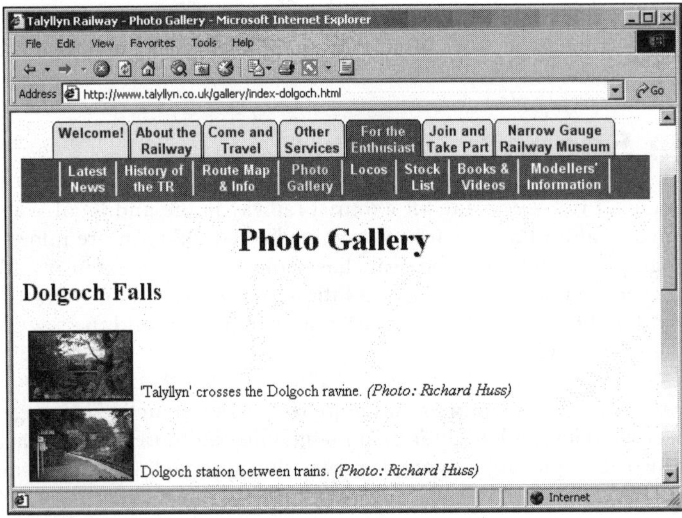

The thumbnail pictures are resized automatically as part of the page generation process (but that's another story). The sections within the gallery are of various types: some list photographs taken at a particular location, others list photographs of a particular locomotive, others have some other special purpose. An implication of this is that certain photographs appear in more than one section.

The final page (which is the first page visitors view on entering the gallery) lists all these sections, suitably categorized:

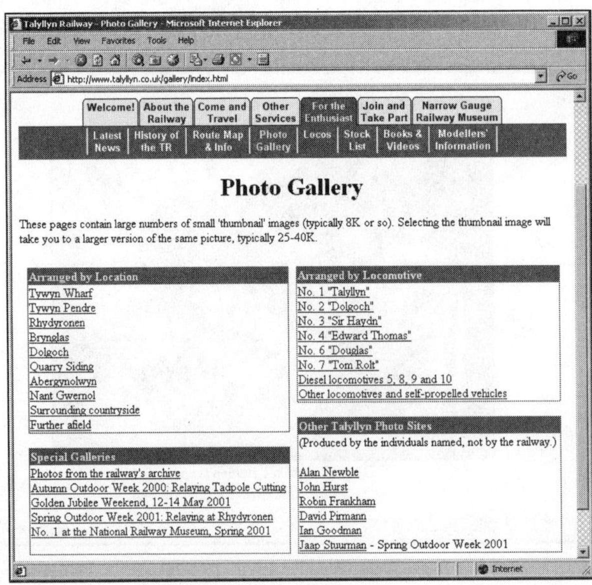

So that's the existing setup – but a dynamic and frame-based approach would have a number of advantages:

- **Much easier updating of the site**
  Only the XML data file and the photos themselves would require updating. At present it is necessary to upload the hundred-plus generated HTML files, a tedious and error-prone operation.
- **Richer user interface possible**
  In the existing interface, a user is constrained to work at only one "level" of the gallery at a time – to navigate around the gallery it is necessary to move from the individual photo level up to the section page or the list of sections. Providing additional context information would make life easier for the user.
- **Opportunity for exploration**
  Server-side generation of the gallery pages makes an ideal case study in the use of frames with JSP pages. There is plenty of data to be presented, but relatively little in the way of business logic to get in the way.

We'll use this data as a springboard for exploring issues related to using frames within dynamic web sites, creating a number of different versions of the site that use different techniques and create ever more complex interactions between user and server.

The Gallery Data

First, we ought to start by sorting out the data and how it's going to be represented internally. I was fortunate in having some code handy from my previous static page generation system. This is driven by XML data using a simple DTD, `photos.dtd`:

```
<?xml version="1.0" encoding="ISO-8859-1" ?>

<!ELEMENT gallery (section+, photo+, spotlight+)>
<!ATTLIST gallery
  largeDirectory  CDATA  #REQUIRED
  smallDirectory  CDATA  #REQUIRED
>

<!ELEMENT section (name, description)>
<!ELEMENT photo (name, description, photographer?, section-ref*)>
<!ELEMENT spotlight (#PCDATA)>

<!ELEMENT name (#PCDATA)>
<!ELEMENT description (#PCDATA)>
<!ELEMENT photographer (#PCDATA)>
<!ELEMENT section-ref (#PCDATA)>
```

The data itself, `photos.xml`, is pretty simple, being divided into three sections. First, we define the different sections of the gallery:

```
<?xml version="1.0" encoding="ISO-8859-1" ?>

<!DOCTYPE gallery PUBLIC
 "-//Talyllyn Railway Company//DTD Photo Gallery 1.0//EN"
```

```
  "http://www.talyllyn.co.uk/gallery/photos.dtd">

<gallery
  largeDirectory="http://www.talyllyn.demon.co.uk/jpeg/"
  smallDirectory="http://www.talyllyn.co.uk/images/thumbnail/">

  <section>
    <name>wharf</name>
    <description>Tywyn Wharf</description>
  </section>

  <section>
    <name>pendre</name>
    <description>Tywyn Pendre</description>
  </section>

  <section>
    <name>loco-1</name>
    <description>Loco No. 1 'Talyllyn'</description>
  </section>

  <section>
    <name>loco-2</name>
    <description>Loco No. 2 'Dolgoch'</description>
  </section>

  <section>
    <name>loco-4</name>
    <description>Loco No. 4 'Edward Thomas'</description>
  </section>
```

Next, we list the individual photographs, with their descriptions and so on, and assign them to the appropriate sections of the gallery:

```
  <photo>
    <name>wharfgf1</name>
    <description>
      'Talyllyn' running round its train at Tywyn Wharf.
    </description>
    <photographer>Richard Huss</photographer>
    <section-ref>wharf</section-ref>
    <section-ref>loco-1</section-ref>
  </photo>

  <photo>
    <name>wharfgf2</name>
    <description>
      'Dolgoch' backs onto a special train at Wharf.
    </description>
    <photographer>Richard Huss</photographer>
    <section-ref>wharf</section-ref>
    <section-ref>loco-2</section-ref>
```

```
  </photo>

  <photo>
    <name>wharfgf4</name>
    <description>
      'Peter Sam' ready to depart from Tywyn Wharf.
    </description>
    <photographer>Richard Huss</photographer>
    <section-ref>wharf</section-ref>
    <section-ref>loco-4</section-ref>
  </photo>
```

Finally, we can select some photos for highlighting in a special today's choice area, which allows us to create a brief list of especially interesting photographs:

```
  <spotlight>pendre_7</spotlight>
  <spotlight>parly1</spotlight>
  <spotlight>brynstn</spotlight>
  <spotlight>bryn_7_toolvan</spotlight>

</gallery>
```

The Photo, Section, and Gallery Classes

The `Gallery` class, which we'll see shortly, converts this data into a set of Java objects. However, we do need an exception type, `GalleryException`, that we can use to flag up any gallery-specific errors that occur:

```
package uk.co.talyllyn.gallery;

public class GalleryException extends Exception {
  public GalleryException(String message) {
    super(message);
  }
}
```

The three key classes are `Photo`, `Section`, and `Gallery`. We'll not go into the full details of how they work – this chapter is about frames, not photograph galleries – but the code is of course available as part of the download at http://www.wrox.com/. The `uk.co.talyllyn.gallery.Photo` class is used to represent a single photograph. Its public methods are:

```
public String getName()
public String getDescription()
public String getPhotographer()
public String getLargeURL()
public String getSmallURL()
public List getSections()
public int getNumSections()
public Section getFirstSection() throws GalleryException
```

These methods are all pretty straightforward. `getName()` returns the name of the photograph – a unique string identifying that photo. `getDescription()` and `getPhotographer()` are self-explanatory. `getLargeURL()` and `getSmallURL()` return the locations respectively of the full size and thumbnail versions of the photo. `getSections()` returns a `Collection` containing all the sections that this photo appears in, and `getNumSections()` returns the number of such sections. Lastly, `getFirstSection()` returns the first section that is listed for this photo.

A section within the gallery is represented by an instance of the `uk.co.talyllyn.gallery.Section` class. The public methods of `Section` are:

```
public String getName()
public String getDescription()
public List getPhotos()
public int getNumPhotos()
public Photo getFirstPhoto() throws GalleryException
```

Again, these are straightforward to understand. The `uk.co.talyllyn.gallery.Gallery` class encapsulates the whole gallery, with its photos and sections. Its public methods allow us to retrieve the full sets of photos or sections, any photos that are "spotlighted", and the first section. We can also look up a particular photo or section by name:

```
public List getPhotos()
public List getSections()
public List getSpotlight()
public Section getFirstSection() throws GalleryException
public Photo getPhoto(String name) throws GalleryException
public Section getSection(String name) throws GalleryException
```

A `Gallery` is constructed by passing it an `InputStream` pointing to the `photos.xml` file:

```
protected Gallery(InputStream input) throws GalleryException
```

The class diagram below shows the relationships between `Gallery`, `Section`, and `Photo`:

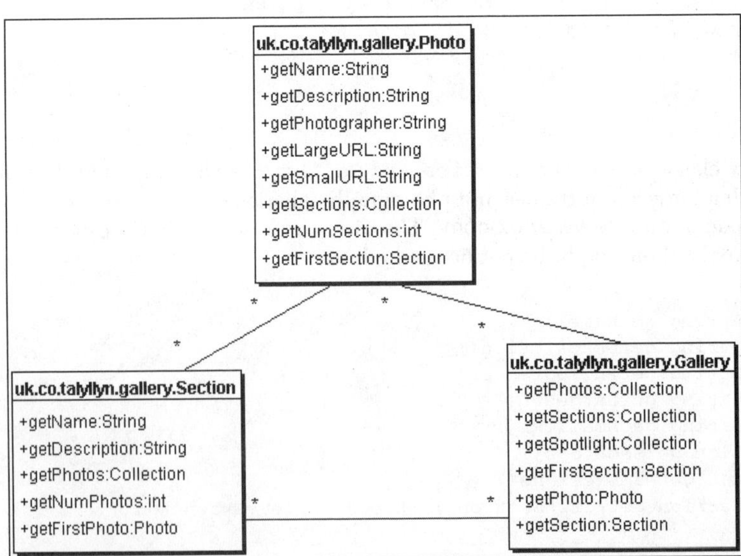

Initializing the Gallery

The gallery is initialized by an event listener named `GalleryListener`. (Event listeners are a feature of the new Servlet 2.3 specification.) When the web application starts up, it creates a `Gallery` object and stores it in the `ServletContext`. First, we need some constants, kept in `Constants.java`:

```
package uk.co.talyllyn.gallery;

public class Constants {
```

The constants we need are:

- The default name of the `ServletContext` attribute to expose; we will store a `uk.co.talyllyn.gallery.Gallery` bean in the context under this name:

```
  public static final String GALLERY = "uk.co.talyllyn.gallery";
```

- The name of a `ServletContext` attribute that we will use to trigger reloading of the gallery data; `GalleryListener` will reload the data if a `ServletContext` attribute with this name is stored:

```
  public static final String RELOAD = "uk.co.talyllyn.gallery.reload";
```

- The default location of the `photos.xml` file within the web application:

```
  public static final String CONFIG = "/WEB-INF/photos.xml";
```

- The public id for our DTD (this is needed by the `Gallery` class when parsing the XML file):

```
  public static final String DTDPublicId =
          "-//Talyllyn Railway Company//DTD Photo Gallery 1.0//EN";
```

- Finally, the location of a local copy of DTD. Again, this is needed by the `Gallery` class for parsing the `photos.xml` file. The DTD will be stored within the JAR file containing the `uk.co.talyllyn.gallery` classes, and this constant references the location within the JAR file:

```
  public static final String DTDLocation =
          "/uk/co/talyllyn/gallery/photos.dtd";
}
```

The behavior of our `GalleryListener` class may be customized by means of two context initialization parameters:

Parameter	Meaning	Default Value
gallery.name	The name used to store the Gallery object in the ServletContext	uk.co.talyllyn.gallery
gallery.config	The location within the web application of the photos.xml file	/WEB-INF/photos.xml

The code for GalleryListener is nice and simple. Its task is to load the data from the XML file in two different sets of circumstances:

- **When the application is first started up**
  GalleryListener implements ServletContextListener, and so its contextInitialized() method will be called at the appropriate time, being passed a ServletContextEvent object.
- **When the user wants to force a reload of the data**
  JSP pages can force this by setting a ServletContext attribute with the appropriate name (Constants.RELOAD). Since GalleryListener implements ServletContextAttributeListener, this will result in either the attributeAdded() or the attributeReplaced() method being called. In either case, the method is passed a ServletContextAttributeEvent object.

In either case, the loadGallery() method is used to read the photos.xml file:

```
package uk.co.talyllyn.gallery;

import java.io.InputStream;
import javax.servlet.ServletContext;
import javax.servlet.ServletContextEvent;
import javax.servlet.ServletContextAttributeEvent;
import javax.servlet.ServletContextListener;
import javax.servlet.ServletContextAttributeListener;

public class GalleryListener
        implements ServletContextListener, ServletContextAttributeListener {
```

We'll start by implementing the methods of ServletContextListener. The contextInitialized() method is called when the application starts up, so we need to load the photos.xml file, create a Gallery object encapsulating its contents, and store it in the ServletContext:

```
  public void contextInitialized(ServletContextEvent event) {
    loadGallery(event.getServletContext());
  }
```

contextDestroyed() is called when the application is shut down. In our case no special action is needed:

```
public void contextDestroyed(ServletContextEvent event) {
  // Nothing special required
}
```

Next, we'll consider the `ServletContextAttributeListener` methods. `attributeAdded()` is called when a new `ServletContext` attribute is added – if the attribute name is `Constants.RELOAD`, we reload `photos.xml`:

```
public void attributeAdded(ServletContextAttributeEvent event) {
  if (event.getName().equalsIgnoreCase(Constants.RELOAD)) {
    loadGallery(event.getServletContext());
  }
}
```

Similarly, `attributeReplaced()` is called if an existing `ServletContext` attribute is replaced. Again, we reload `photos.xml` if the attribute name is `Constants.RELOAD`:

```
public void attributeReplaced(ServletContextAttributeEvent event) {
  if (event.getName().equalsIgnoreCase(Constants.RELOAD)) {
    loadGallery(event.getServletContext());
  }
}
```

The last `ServletContextAttributeListener` method is `attributeRemoved()`, which we're not interested in:

```
public void attributeRemoved(ServletContextAttributeEvent event) {
  // Nothing special required
}
```

The last method in `GalleryListener` is `loadGallery()`, which does the real work when called upon to do so by the event handling methods. It checks to see whether any context initialization parameters have been used to override the defaults, then opens an `InputStream` to the `photos.xml` file, uses it to construct a `Gallery` object, and stores it in the `ServletContext`. It requires as a parameter the `ServletContext` in which we are running:

```
public void loadGallery(ServletContext context) {

  // Decide what attribute name to store the Gallery object under
  String name = context.getInitParameter("gallery.name");
  if (name == null) {
    name = Constants.GALLERY;
  }

  // Decide where to look for the photos.xml file
  String config = context.getInitParameter("gallery.config");
  if (config == null) {
    config = Constants.CONFIG;
  }

  // Open an InputStream on the photos.xml file
```

```
      InputStream in = context.getResourceAsStream(config);
      if (in == null) {
        context.log("Could not open gallery data file " + config);
        return;
      }

      try {

        // Create a Gallery object from the photos.xml file
        Gallery data = new Gallery(in);

        // Store it in the ServletContext
        context.setAttribute(name, data);

      } catch (GalleryException e) {
        context.log("Error initializing photo gallery bean", e);
        return;
      }
    }
  }
```

Lastly, we need a way of triggering a reload of the gallery. The `reload.jsp` page below forces a reload when it is accessed by the administrator. We use the Cache Tag Library, introduced in the previous chapter, to make sure that the page is always executed when the administrator accesses it rather than being cached:

```
<%@ taglib uri="http://www.wrox.com/taglib/cache" prefix="cache" %>
<cache:noCaching/>

<% application.setAttribute("uk.co.talyllyn.gallery.reload", "reload"); %>

<html>
  <head>
    <title>Gallery Reload</title>
  </head>

  <body>
    <h1>Gallery Reload</h1>

    <p>The gallery file should have been reloaded.</p>
  </body>
</html>
```

As we'll see later, in `web.xml` we'll protect this with a security constraint so that only administrators can trigger a reload of the data.

Introducing JSPTL

Just to add to the fun, we'll be taking the opportunity in this chapter to explore some of the facilities provided by the current early access version (1.1) of the **JSP Standard Tag Library (JSPTL)**. This version is far from finished, and far from final, but provides an indication of the sorts of features we can expect to see in the release version. The aim is to supply a common set of tags that will eliminate most uses of scriptlet elements in JSP, and provide a standard that will be widely accepted and available.

This will inevitably be a *very* quick tour of the tags in the current early access version – download the current release from http://jakarta.apache.org/taglibs/doc/jsptl-doc/intro.html for more information, including the full documentation for the tags themselves. Future versions should include tags for I/O operations, XML manipulation and transformation, JDBC database access, internationalization, and page composition.

> *Remember that we are discussing an early access release of JSPTL, which is still under development in the Java Community Process. The expert group has released this version to give us an idea of what they're planning, and to let us give them feedback on their deliberations so far. The address for feedback is jsr052-comments@sun.com. The tags and APIs presently available are not a standard, and will definitely change before the first formal release of JSPTL.*

Expression Language Support

Expression Language Support is how JSPTL manages to abolish the dreaded scriptlets. In fact, there are two expression languages supplied with the current release, the simpler **Simplest Possible Expression Language (SPEL)** and the rather more complex **JPath**, though the intention is to reduce this to a single language by the final release. JSPTL is actually two main tag libraries: one, known as `jx`, using this expression language support, and the `jr` library that uses conventional JSP runtime expressions instead (in other words, normal Java expressions embedded in JSP pages).

The examples we'll see in this chapter are in the SPEL expression language. JPath isn't yet documented in the current early access download and SPEL is designed to be very simple and accessible to page designers. SPEL allows you to:

- Access beans in any of the standard JSP scopes (page, request, session, and application), together with the values of request parameters and HTTP headers
- Access bean properties, recursively
- Perform simple comparison operations

For example, `<jx:expr/>` is used to evaluate an expression and print it out. The following will print out the value of the request parameter `section`:

```
<jx:expr value="$param:section"/>
```

While the following will print out the value of the `photo` object's `description` property:

```
<jx:expr value="$photo.description"/>
```

There is also a `<jx:set/>` tag that evaluates an expression and stores its result. For instance the following will store the value of the `section` request parameter as a session-scoped bean named `currentSection`:

```
<jx:set var="currentSection" scope="session"
        value="$param:section"/>
```

Here, the `scope` attribute is used to specify which of the standard JSP scopes the object should be stored in. It can have the values `page` (the default), `request`, `session`, or `application`.

There is also a `<jx:declare/>` tag used to bridge the gap between the old (scripting) and new (expression language) worlds, and as we'll see later, it's also possible to integrate the expression language into your own custom tags.

Iteration Tags

These are superficially simple, allowing us to specify a set of items to iterate over and the name of the variable used to make the current item available within the loop:

```
<jx:forEach var="photo" items="$currentSection.photos">
  <jx:expr value="$photo.description"/><br>
</jx:forEach>
```

If we were to eschew the expression language support of the `jx` library in favor of the `jr` library and its old-style JSP runtime expressions, this loop could instead be written in this form:

```
<jr:forEach var="photo" items="<%= currentSection.getPhotos() %>">
  <%-- Code to be executed for each photo --%>
</jr:forEach>
```

Within this simplicity is a lot of power. The items expression can be a Java array, a `Collection`, an `Iterator` or `Enumeration`, a `Map`, a `ResultSet`, or even a set of comma-separated values. That provides a lot of flexibility, and you can also specify range parameters to indicate which subset of the items should be selected in turn.

An optional `status` attribute tells the tag to create an `IteratorTagStatus` object that contains information about the current state of the iteration, such as the index of the current item. There's also a more advanced `<jx:forTokens/>` tag that allows you to perform more complex string tokenization.

Conditional Tags

The conditional tags are interesting in the way they mirror XSLT syntax:

```
<jx:if test="$param:section != currentSection">
  <%-- Code to change sections --%>
</jx:if>
```

```
<jx:choose>

  <jx:when test="$category == 'photos'>
    <jsp:include page="photos.jsp"/>
  </jx:when>

  <jx:when test="$category == 'books'>
    <jsp:include page="books.jsp"/>
  </jx:when>

  <jx:otherwise>
    <jsp:include page="overview.jsp"/>
  </jx:otherwise>

</jx:choose>
```

The Gallery Tag Library

The `Gallery`, `Section`, and `Photo` classes have been designed to be as bean-like as possible, and this makes it nice and easy to use them with the JSPTL early access 1.1 release. For example, the `Photo` object has `name`, `description`, `photographer`, `largeURL`, and `smallURL` properties (among others), which we can utilize using JSP snippets such as the following:

```
<p align="center">
  <img src="<jx:expr value="$thePhoto.largeURL"/>" border="2">
  <br>
  <jx:expr value="$thePhoto.description"/><br>
  <i><font size="-1">
    Photo: <jx:expr value="$thePhoto.photographer"/>
  </font></i>
</p>
```

However, there is one omission from the functionality of JSPTL's SPEL expression language that affects us here (and remember that we're working with a very early access release here). It is not currently possible to write an expression that looks items up in a `Map` – and consequently we cannot use JSPTL expressions to look up photos and sections in the gallery by name, even though these `Maps` are exposed as properties of the `Gallery` class.

We overcome this by using one of the most powerful features of JSPTL: the ability to create our own tags that leverage its expression-language functionality. We will create a couple of custom tags to assist us. The first is `<gallery:lookupPhoto>`, which in typical usage might look like this:

```
<gallery:lookupPhoto id="thephoto" photo="$param:name"
                     gallery="gallery" scope="session" />
```

This creates a session-scoped bean called `thephoto`, referencing the section whose name is specified by the expression `$param:name`, in other words the request parameter `name`. The `gallery` attribute specifies the `ServletContext` attribute containing the `Gallery` object.

The bean thephoto can then be used with the standard JSPTL tags, for example:

```
<jx:expr value="$thephoto.description"/>
```

The other tag, <gallery:lookupSection>, is very similar:

```
<gallery:lookupSection id="thesection" photo="$param:whichsection"
 gallery="gallery" scope="request" />
```

Let's take a look at the TLD file, gallery.tld:

```
<?xml version="1.0" encoding="ISO-8859-1" ?>
<!DOCTYPE taglib
  PUBLIC "-//Sun Microsystems, Inc.//DTD JSP Tag Library 1.2//EN"
  "http://java.sun.com/dtd/web-jsptaglibrary_1_2.dtd">

<taglib>
  <tlib-version>1.0</tlib-version>
  <jsp-version>1.2</jsp-version>
  <short-name>gallery</short-name>
  <uri>http://www.talyllyn.co.uk/tags/gallery</uri>
  <display-name>Photo Gallery Tags</display-name>
```

After the usual preamble, we digress slightly to take advantage of the JSP 1.2 ability to specify event listeners within tag libraries. We could declare our listener, GalleryListener, in the web.xml file, but since any web application using the gallery code will be using the tag library, we can declare the listener in the tag library instead. This avoids the possibility of the person writing the web application forgetting to declare the listener – he can simply drop our gallery.jar file into the WEB-INF\lib\ directory and forget about it:

```
  <listener>
    <listener-class>
      uk.co.talyllyn.gallery.GalleryListener
    </listener-class>
  </listener>
```

<gallery:lookupPhoto> is declared next. Note that the photo attribute (like the others) is declared as <rtexprvalue>false</rtexprvalue>. This is the first step to integrating JSPTL's expression language support:

```
  <tag>
    <name>lookupPhoto</name>
    <tag-class>uk.co.talyllyn.gallery.LookupPhotoTag</tag-class>
    <body-content>empty</body-content>

    <variable>
      <name-from-attribute>id</name-from-attribute>
      <variable-class>uk.co.talyllyn.gallery.Photo</variable-class>
      <declare>true</declare>
      <scope>AT_END</scope>
    </variable>
```

```
    <attribute>
      <name>id</name>
      <required>true</required>
      <rtexprvalue>false</rtexprvalue>
    </attribute>

    <attribute>
      <name>photo</name>
      <required>true</required>
      <rtexprvalue>false</rtexprvalue>
    </attribute>

    <attribute>
      <name>gallery</name>
      <required>false</required>
      <rtexprvalue>false</rtexprvalue>
    </attribute>

    <attribute>
      <name>scope</name>
      <required>false</required>
      <rtexprvalue>false</rtexprvalue>
    </attribute>
  </tag>
```

The final section of `gallery.tld` declares the `<gallery:lookupSection>` tag. It is almost identical to the previous section:

```
  <tag>
    <name>lookupSection</name>
    <tag-class>uk.co.talyllyn.gallery.LookupSectionTag</tag-class>
    <body-content>empty</body-content>

    <variable>
      <name-from-attribute>id</name-from-attribute>
      <variable-class>uk.co.talyllyn.gallery.Section</variable-class>
      <declare>true</declare>
      <scope>AT_END</scope>
    </variable>

    <attribute>
      <name>id</name>
      <required>true</required>
      <rtexprvalue>false</rtexprvalue>
    </attribute>

    <attribute>
      <name>section</name>
      <required>true</required>
      <rtexprvalue>false</rtexprvalue>
    </attribute>

    <attribute>
```

```
      <name>gallery</name>
      <required>false</required>
      <rtexprvalue>false</rtexprvalue>
    </attribute>

    <attribute>
      <name>scope</name>
      <required>false</required>
      <rtexprvalue>false</rtexprvalue>
    </attribute>
  </tag>

</taglib>
```

On to the tag handlers. `LookupSectionTag` is the handler for the `<gallery:lookupSection>` tag. Since the tag always has an empty body, we simply need to extend `TagSupport`. Note that we import `ExpressionEvaluationManager` (we'll see why when we come to the `doEndTag()` method):

```
package uk.co.talyllyn.gallery;

import javax.servlet.jsp.PageContext;
import javax.servlet.jsp.JspException;
import javax.servlet.jsp.JspTagException;
import javax.servlet.jsp.tagext.TagSupport;
import org.apache.taglibs.jsptl.lang.support.ExpressionEvaluatorManager;

public class LookupSectionTag extends TagSupport {
```

Most of the tag handler code is very simple, though we do need to be careful how we implement the constructor and the `release()` method to ensure that the tag attributes are correctly set. We start with constants and the instance variables used to store the attribute values:

```
  private final String APPLICATION = "application";
  private final String SESSION = "session";
  private final String REQUEST = "request";
  private final String PAGE = "page";

  protected String id;
  protected String sectionExpr;
  protected String gallery;
  protected String scope;
```

> **The `sectionExpr` variable stores the JSPTL expression supplied for the `section` tag attribute; as such, it is a `String` variable. We will evaluate the expression itself later, in the `doEndTag()` method.**

Both the constructor and the release() methods call init() to ensure that the tag attribute values are correctly initialized:

```
public LookupSectionTag() {
  super();
  init();
}

public void release() {
  super.release();
  init();
}
```

Within init() itself we initialize the instance variables. The id, section, and scope attributes are mandatory, but the gallery attribute defaults to the value Constants.GALLERY:

```
private void init() {
  id = sectionExpr = scope = null;
  gallery = Constants.GALLERY;
}
```

The getter and setter methods for the id, gallery, and scope properties all are of type String and completely standard, so are not shown here. As we said earlier, the section property's value is the *JSPTL expression*, rather than the *result* of evaluating the expression, and is stored in the String variable sectionExpr. (The variable name was chosen to ensure a clear distinction between the expression and its result.) Other than this, the setter and getter methods for the section property are also standard.

doEndTag() is where we get down to business, and is where the JSPTL expression evaluation occurs. Note that we *don't* evaluate the expression inside setSection(). Whilst we're guaranteed that it *will* be called before doStartTag(), we shouldn't make any assumptions about *when* that might happen, since JSP allows servers to pool tag handler instances. It may not even happen for each use of a tag if the attribute values don't change.

For example, consider this snippet of (rather contrived) code:

```
<jx:set var="name" scope="page" value="$param:hello"/>
<mytags:useExpression expr="$page:name"/>

<jx:set var="name" scope="page" value="$request:wibble"/>
<mytags:useExpression expr="$page:name"/>
```

If the <mytags:useExpression> tag evaluated the expression in its setExpr() method the results would be unpredictable. We would expect the second invocation of <mytags:useExpression> to use the updated name variable, but to the JSP page compiler the value of expr has not changed, and so the existing tag handler instance might be reused, without setExpr() being called a second time. Therefore we must make sure that any such evaluations occur in the doStart() method, which *is* guaranteed to be called once each time the tag is executed.

The overall task of doEndTag() is to determine which section is sought, search for it in the gallery, and expose it as a bean in the specified scope. By the time this is called, we will have the expression that will evaluate to the name of a section in the photo gallery. As we have seen, this is held in the variable sectionExpr. To evaluate the expression we use the ExpressionEvaluatorManager class's evaluate() method:

```
  public int doEndTag() throws JspException {
    Object section = ExpressionEvaluatorManager.evaluate
            ("section", sectionExpr, String.class, this, pageContext);
```

The parameters here are:

- The name of the tag attribute whose value we are evaluating
- The expression itself (the value of the tag attribute)
- A Class object indicating the expected type of the result
- The tag handler instance itself
- The PageContext for the JSP page in which we are operating

In return we get a reference to an Object that contains the result of evaluating the expression, which we can cast to the appropriate type for the result we're expecting (String, in our case).

As of this writing the JSP Standard Tag Library is only available as an early access release. It is highly likely that the syntax for invoking expression evaluation will change in future releases.

With that done, we check that we got a real result (rather than null), look up the Gallery itself in the ServletContext, and then the desired Section within the Gallery:

```
    if (section == null) {
      throw new JspTagException("The section attribute evaluated to null");
    }
    Gallery theGallery = (Gallery) pageContext.getAttribute(gallery,
                                       PageContext.APPLICATION_SCOPE);
    if (theGallery == null) {
      throw new JspTagException("Could not locate gallery bean " + gallery
                              + " - is GalleryListener configured?");
    }

    Section theSection;
    try {
      theSection = theGallery.getSection((String) section);
    } catch (GalleryException e) {
      throw new JspTagException("Could not locate section " + section);
    }
```

Finally, we store the `Section` object in the specified scope (as determined by the `scope` tag attribute), and retire:

```
    if (scope == null || scope.equals(PAGE)) {
      pageContext.setAttribute(id, theSection,
                               pageContext.PAGE_SCOPE);
    } else if (scope.equals(APPLICATION)) {
      pageContext.setAttribute(id, theSection,
                               pageContext.APPLICATION_SCOPE);
    } else if (scope.equals(SESSION)) {
      pageContext.setAttribute(id, theSection,
                               pageContext.SESSION_SCOPE);
    } else if (scope.equals(REQUEST)) {
      pageContext.setAttribute(id, theSection,
                               pageContext.REQUEST_SCOPE);
    } else {
      throw new JspTagException("Invalid 'scope' attribute value");
    }

    return EVAL_PAGE;
  }
}
```

`LookupPhotoTag` is very similar to `LookupSectionTag`. Consult the code download for details.

Our First Frameset

With the infrastructure in place, let's put together an initial version of our frame-based, JSP photo gallery site. We'll need three frames:

- Top left, the list of sections within the gallery
- Bottom left, the thumbnail photos within the current section
- On the right, the currently-selected photograph

The screenshot below illustrates this:

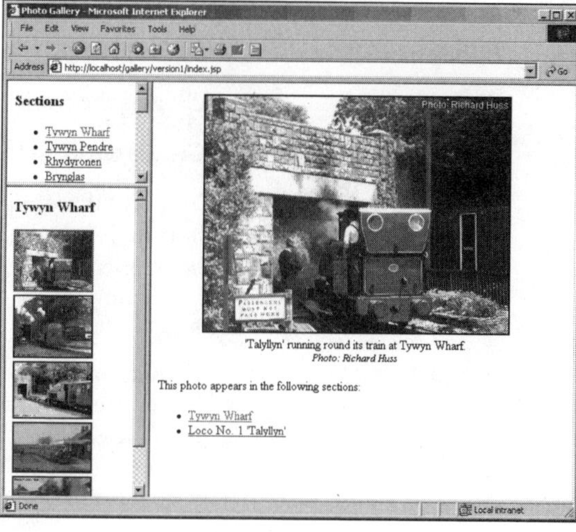

Scrolling down through the list of sections, we can click on Loco No. 1 'Talyllyn'. This brings up the thumbnails for that section in the bottom-left frame. Clicking on one of the thumbnails causes that photograph to occupy the right-hand frame:

Note that an innovation in this version is the section in the lower part of the right-hand frame, listing the sections that this photo appears in. Clicking on one of these links brings up the thumbnails for that section in the bottom-left frame.

In fact, this isn't terribly dynamic at all – we could perfectly well have generated this as a static site, though we do gain the advantage of easy updating simply by changing the `photos.xml` file and recreating the `Gallery` object. Later versions of the site will have more dynamic behavior. To create this we need a frameset page, together with one page for each frame. In this initial version of the system, the JSP pages we will create are:

Page	Frame name	Description
`index.jsp`	`_top`	Creates the frameset.
`sectionList.jsp`	`sectionListFrame`	Creates the list of sections, for the top left frame.
`section.jsp`	`sectionFrame`	Displays thumbnails for one section, for the bottom left frame. Request parameter `section` specifies name of section to list. For example: `section.jsp?section=loco-1`
`photo.jsp`	`photoFrame`	Displays a single photo, for the right hand frame. Request parameter `photo` specifies the name of the photo to display. For example: `photo.jsp?photo=wharfgf1`

Schematically, our frameset looks like this:

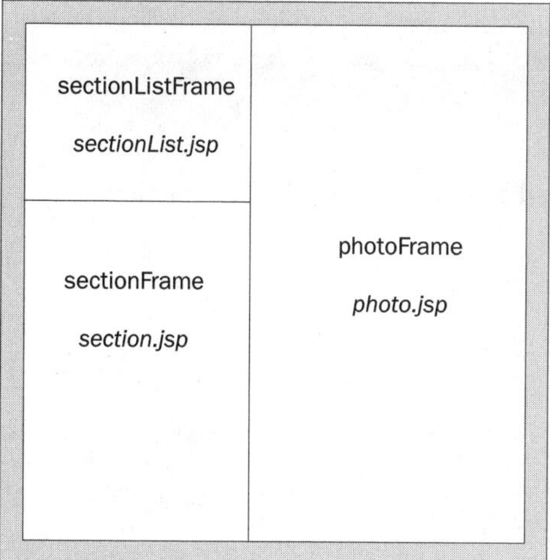

Let's consider each of these pages in turn.

The index.jsp Page

index.jsp starts by using the <jx:set> tag to look up the names of the first section in the gallery and the first photo in that first section:

```
<%@ taglib uri="http://java.sun.com/jsptl/ea/jx" prefix="jx" %>

<jx:set var="section" value="$gallery.firstSection.name"/>
<jx:set var="photo" value="$gallery.firstSection.firstPhoto.name"/>
```

Here we have made the assumption that our event listener, GalleryListener, has stored a Gallery object in the ServletContext under the name gallery.

We'll see the full web.xml *file, where this is configured, at the end of the chapter along with other useful deployment information.*

We can then use the <jx:expr> tag to retrieve these values when constructing the URLs for the initial pages to occupy each frame:

```
<html>
  <head>
    <title>Photo Gallery</title>
  </head>
  <frameset cols="25%,*">
    <frameset rows="25%,*">
      <frame name="sectionListFrame" src="sectionList.jsp">
      <frame name="sectionFrame"
```

```
            src="section.jsp?section=<jx:expr value="$section"/>">
    </frameset>
    <frame name="photoFrame"
           src="photo.jsp?photo=<jx:expr value="$photo"/>">
  </frameset>
</html>
```

The actual HTML generated by `index.jsp` will be something like:

```
<html>
  <head>
    <title>Photo Gallery</title>
  </head>
  <frameset cols="25%,*">
    <frameset rows="25%,*">
      <frame name="sectionListFrame" src="sectionList.jsp">
      <frame name="sectionFrame"
             src="section.jsp?section=wharf">
    </frameset>
    <frame name="photoFrame"
           src="photo.jsp?photo=wharfgf1">
  </frameset>
</html>
```

Note how the URLs we have generated to the `section.jsp` and `photo.jsp` pages include request parameters that specify the names of the initial section and photo.

The sectionList.jsp Page

The `sectionList.jsp` page creates a bulleted list of the sections within the gallery, using the `<jx:forEach>` tag to iterate over the `List` retrieved from the gallery's `sections` property:

```
<%@ taglib uri="http://java.sun.com/jsptl/ea/jx" prefix="jx" %>

<html>
  <body>
    <h3>Sections</h3>
    <ul>
      <jx:forEach var="section" items="$gallery.sections">
```

For each section, we then need to construct a link that the user can click on to switch to a different section. So we link to `section.jsp`, targeting the bottom left frame (`sectionFrame`), and passing the correct section name as a request parameter:

```
        <li>
          <a href="section.jsp?section=<jx:expr value="$section.name"/>"
             target="sectionFrame">
            <jx:expr value="$section.description"/>
          </a>
        </li>
```

```
      </jx:forEach>
    </ul>
  </body>
</html>
```

The output generated by this will be along the lines of:

```
<html>
  <body>
    <h3>Sections</h3>
    <ul>
      <li>
        <a href="section.jsp?section=wharf" target="sectionFrame">
          Tywyn Wharf
        </a>
      </li>
      <li>
        <a href="section.jsp?section=pendre" target="sectionFrame">
          Tywyn Pendre
        </a>
      </li>
      <!-- ... -->
    </ul>
  </body>
</html>
```

The section.jsp Page

The role of `section.jsp` is to display the thumbnails for a particular section of the gallery, selected by the `section` request parameter. Our first step is to use our `<gallery:lookupSection>` tag to locate the desired section within the gallery:

```
<%@ taglib uri="http://java.sun.com/jsptl/ea/jx" prefix="jx" %>
<%@ taglib uri="http://www.talyllyn.co.uk/tags/gallery" prefix="gallery" %>

<html>
  <body>

    <gallery:lookupSection gallery="gallery" section="$param:section"
                           id="theSection"/>
```

Note how our own tag, `<gallery:lookupSection>`, uses the JSPTL expression language syntax. With that done, we can display the section's properties and iterate over the photos within the section:

```
    <h3><jx:expr value="$theSection.description"/></h3>
    <p>
      <jx:forEach var="photo" items="$theSection.photos">
```

For each photo, we construct a link to display that photo in the main, right hand frame. The page we link to is `photo.jsp`, the link target is `photoFrame`, and we pass the name of the photo as a request parameter. The content of the link is an `<img>` tag displaying the thumbnail version of the image:

```
          <a href="photo.jsp?photo=<jx:expr value="$photo.name"/>"
             target="photoFrame">
            <img src="<jx:expr value="$photo.smallURL"/>"
                 alt="<jx:expr value="$photo.description"/>">
          </a>
          <br>
        </jx:forEach>
      </p>
    </body>
  </html>
```

The output from this JSP page will typically be along the lines of:

```
<html>
  <body>
   <h3>Tywyn Wharf</h3>
   <p>
     <a href="photo.jsp?photo=wharfgf1" target="photoFrame">
       <img
           src="http://www.talyllyn.co.uk/images/thumbnail/wharfgf1_sml.jpg"
           alt="'Talyllyn' running round its train at Tywyn Wharf.">
     </a>
     <br>
     <a href="photo.jsp?photo=wharfgf2" target="photoFrame">
       <img
          src="http://www.talyllyn.co.uk/images/thumbnail/wharfgf2_sml.jpg"
          alt="'Dolgoch' backs onto a special train at Wharf.">
     </a>
     <br>
     <!-- ... -->
    </p>
  </body>
</html>
```

photo.jsp

Finally, `photo.jsp` is used to display a single photograph, specified by the request parameter `photo`. We start by looking up the photograph by name in the gallery:

```
<%@ taglib uri="http://java.sun.com/jsptl/ea/jx" prefix="jx" %>
<%@ taglib uri="http://www.talyllyn.co.uk/tags/gallery" prefix="gallery" %>

<html>
  <body>

    <gallery:lookupPhoto gallery="gallery" photo="$param:photo"
                         id="thePhoto"/>
```

Displaying the photograph is a simple case of looking up the relevant properties of the `Photo` object:

```
<%-- Display the photo, caption, etc. --%>
<p align="center">
  <img src="<jx:expr value="$thePhoto.largeURL"/>" border="2">
  <br>
  <jx:expr value="$thePhoto.description"/><br>
  <i><font size="-1">
    Photo: <jx:expr value="$thePhoto.photographer"/>
  </font></i>
</p>
```

The final step is to produce the list of the sections that this photo appears in, by iterating over the collection we obtain from the `Photo`'s `sections` property:

```
<p>This photo appears in the following sections:</p>
<%-- Iterate over all the sections this photo appears in --%>
<ul>
  <jx:forEach var="theSection" items="$thePhoto.sections">
```

For each such section we construct a link pointing back to the bottom-left frame:

```
        <li>
          <%-- Construct a link to each section --%>
          <a href="section.jsp?section=<jx:expr value="$theSection.name"/>"
             target="sectionFrame">
            <jx:expr value="$theSection.description"/>
          </a>
        </li>
      </jx:forEach>
    </ul>
  </body>
</html>
```

The output of this page will resemble the following:

```
<html>
  <body>
    <p align="center">
      <img src="http://www.talyllyn.demon.co.uk/jpeg/wharfgf1.jpg"
          border="2">
      <br>'Talyllyn' running round its train at Tywyn Wharf.<br>
      <i><font size="-1">Photo: Richard Huss</font></i>
    </p>
    <p>This photo appears in the following sections:</p>
    <ul>
      <li>
        <a href="section.jsp?section=wharf" target="sectionFrame">
          Tywyn Wharf
        </a>
      </li>
```

```
        <li>
          <a href="section.jsp?section=loco-1" target="sectionFrame">
            Loco No. 1 'Talyllyn'
          </a>
        </li>
      </ul>
    </body>
  </html>
```

Refreshing Several Frames

Our gallery is nice (particularly if you enjoy looking at photographs of small steam trains...) and is an improvement over the static version, but it's still a bit dull. A definite improvement would be to highlight the current section within the section list, and the current photo within the thumbnail list.

However, this would require us to refresh several frames at once. For example, when clicking on a section name in the section list frame, we would ideally want to:

- Reload the top-left frame with the newly-selected frame highlighted
- Display the thumbnails for the new section, with the first photo in that section highlighted
- Display the first photo in that section in the right-hand frame

For example, the result might look like this:

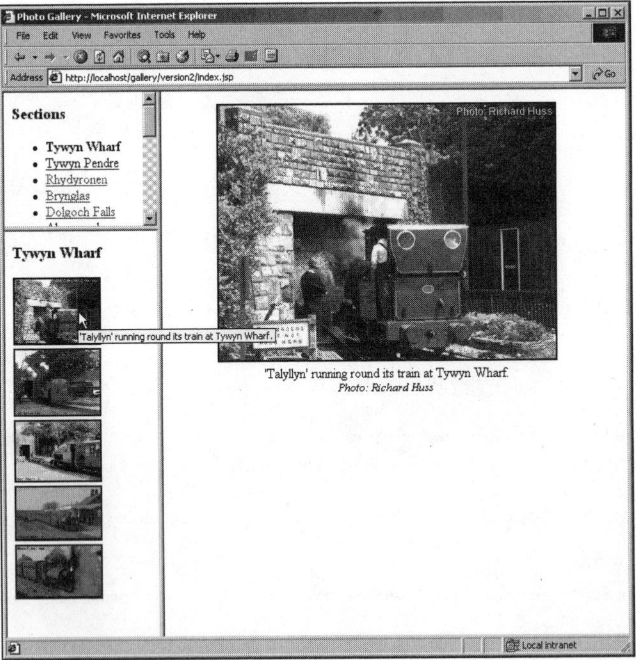

Note that in this screenshot neither the text Tywyn Wharf nor the first thumbnail photograph are clickable.

The way to achieve this seems obvious – we need to add some extra request parameters to `sectionList.jsp` (`section`, so that it knows which section to highlight) and `section.jsp` (`photo`, so that it knows which photo to highlight). We also need some JavaScript magic to make several frames load in response to a single click.

The updated `index.jsp` looks just a little more complex than before, to make sure that these pages get the extra parameters, `section` and `photo`:

```
<%@ taglib uri="http://java.sun.com/jsptl/ea/jx" prefix="jx" %>

<jx:set var="section" value="$gallery.firstSection.name"/>
<jx:set var="photo" value="$gallery.firstSection.firstPhoto.name"/>

<html>
  <head>
    <title>Photo Gallery</title>
  </head>
  <frameset cols="25%,*">
    <frameset rows="25%,*">
      <frame src="sectionList.jsp?section=<jx:expr value="$section"/>"
             name="sectionListFrame">
      <frame src="section.jsp?section=<jx:expr value="$section"/>
                  &photo=<jx:expr value="$photo"/>" name="sectionFrame">
    </frameset>
    <frame src="photo.jsp?photo=<jx:expr value="$photo"/>"
           name="photoFrame">
  </frameset>
</html>
```

Those URLs are getting a bit long, but let's not worry about that for now. The `sectionList.jsp` page also gets more complex. Firstly, within our `<jx:forEach>` tag we check whether each section in turn is the current section, so that we can generate different markup in each case:

```
<%@ taglib uri="http://java.sun.com/jsptl/ea/jx" prefix="jx" %>

<html>
  <body>
    <h3>Sections</h3>
    <ul>
      <%-- Iterate over all the sections in the gallery --%>
      <jx:forEach var="section" items="$gallery.sections">
        <li>
        <jx:choose>
```

If this *is* the current section, we choose not to create a link but just to display the section's name in bold (there's no need for a link – we're there already):

```
            <jx:when test="$section.name == param:section">
              <b><jx:expr value="$section.description"/></b>
            </jx:when>
```

In all other cases we do need to create a link, and in this case that includes creating the relevant JavaScript. Here it really begins to get horrid:

```
            <jx:otherwise>
              <%-- Construct a link to each section --%>
              <a href="section.jsp?section=<jx:expr
                 value="$section.name"/>
                 &photo=<jx:expr value="$section.firstPhoto.name"/>"
                 target="sectionFrame"
                 onclick="parent.frames['photoFrame'].location.href=
'photo.jsp?photo=<jx:expr value="$section.firstPhoto.name"/>'
;parent.frames['sectionListFrame'].location.href='sectionList.jsp?section=
<jx:expr value="$section.name"/>';return true;">
                <jx:expr value="$section.description"/>
              </a>
            </jx:otherwise>
          </jx:choose>
        </li>
      </jx:forEach>
    </ul>
  </body>
</html>
```

The actual code generated for the link, cleaned up a little, looks like this:

```
<a href="section.jsp?section=rhydyronen&photo=rhydstna"
   target="sectionFrame"
   onclick="parent.frames['photoFrame'].location.href='photo.jsp?photo=rhyds
tna';parent.frames['sectionListFrame'].location.href='sectionList.jsp?secti
on=rhydyronen';return true;">
    Rhydyronen
</a>
```

Similar changes need to be made to `section.jsp`. In this case we need to load two pages when a user clicks on a thumbnail image: we reload the thumbnail page with the correct photo highlighted, and of course we display the large version of that photograph in the right-hand frame:

```
<%@ taglib uri="http://java.sun.com/jsptl/ea/jx" prefix="jx" %>
<%@ taglib uri="http://www.talyllyn.co.uk/tags/gallery" prefix="gallery" %>

<html>
  <body>
```

The first step is to locate the section we're interested in, using the request parameter `section`, and iterate over the photos within it:

```
    <gallery:lookupSection gallery="gallery" section="$param:section"
                           id="theSection"/>

    <h3><jx:expr value="$theSection.description"/></h3>
    <p>
      <jx:forEach var="photo" items="$theSection.photos">
```

Like in `sectionList.jsp`, we need to decide whether we have reached the current photo, and adjust the display accordingly:

```
        <jx:choose>
          <jx:when test="$photo.name == param:photo">
          <%-- Display the thumbnail --%>
            <img src="<jx:expr value="$photo.smallURL"/>"
                 alt="<jx:expr value="$photo.description"/>"
                 border="2">
            <br>
          </jx:when>
```

If we're not on the current photo we need to link to the photo as well as displaying the thumbnail:

```
          <jx:otherwise>
            <a href="photo.jsp?photo=<jx:expr value="$photo.name"/>"
               target="photoFrame"
               onclick="parent.frames['sectionFrame'].location.href=
'section.jsp?photo=<jx:expr value="$photo.name"/>'&section=<jx:expr
value="$theSection.name"/>';return true;">
              <img src="<jx:expr value="$photo.smallURL"/>"
                   alt="<jx:expr value="$photo.description"/>">
            </a>
            <br>
          </jx:otherwise>
        </jx:choose>
      </jx:forEach>
    </p>
  </body>
</html>
```

We'll remove the This photo appears in ... portion of `photo.jsp` for the moment, to save you from having to see more of that awkward JavaScript:

```
<%@ taglib uri="http://java.sun.com/jsptl/ea/jx" prefix="jx" %>
<%@ taglib uri="http://www.talyllyn.co.uk/tags/gallery" prefix="gallery" %>

<html>
  <body>
    <gallery:lookupPhoto gallery="gallery" photo="$param:photo"
                         id="thePhoto"/>
```

```
    <p align="center">
      <img src="<jx:expr value="$thePhoto.largeURL"/>" border="2">
      <br>
      <jx:expr value="$thePhoto.description"/><br>
      <i><font size="-1">
        Photo: <jx:expr value="$thePhoto.photographer"/>
      </font></i>
    </p>
  </body>
</html>
```

Problems with this Approach

This much works, but the code is getting stringy and hard to follow. One possible avenue of exploration would be to simplify the JavaScript code by generating it using a tag library. For example, we might consider writing a set of cooperating tags that would allow us to write something like this:

```
<frames:multiLink>
  <frames:mainLink target="sectionFrame">
    section.jsp?section=rhydyronen&photo=rhydstna
  </frames:mainLink>
  <frames:link target="parent.frames['photoFrame']">
    photo.jsp?photo=rhydstna
  </frames:link>
  <frames:link target="parent.frames['sectionListFrame']">
    sectionList.jsp?section=rhydyronen
  </frames:link>
  <frames:linkContent>
    Rhydyronen
  </frames:linkContent>
</frames:multiLink>
```

That would definitely be better, with a much clearer logical structure. The `<frames:mainLink>` tag specifies the normal HTML link, which will still work if the user has disabled JavaScript; its body content gives the URL to jump to. The `<frames:link>` tags allow us to specify other frames we want to target, though still using the (confusing) JavaScript syntax to nominate the target frames. The actual HTML content is given using a separate tag, `<frames:linkContent>`.

Such a tag library might well be of use (and in fact we shall return to this tag library later), but the application is still getting out of hand. Looking at the URLs that are being used, it is apparent that we are passing around lots of request parameters. Oftentimes, we are passing the same parameter and value to several frames at once, which points to the root of the problem, and to its solution.

> **We are trying to make a stateful application stateless.**

In the current implementation, clicking on a section name in the section list causes three distinct actions to be performed. Translating these into user actions, these would be:

- "Show me the list of sections, with this one highlighted"
- "Show me the list of thumbnails for that section, with the first one selected"
- "Show me the first photo in the section"

What the user actually wants to do is just to switch sections; it is incidental to them that this affects several frames in different ways. An alternative way of looking at this is that the user is requesting a change in their current session state, and a consequent redrawing of the display.

An MVC Approach

This suggests that we should try exploring MVC-type architecture for the application, and maintain the user's session state on the server rather than passing request parameters round from page to page. We'll also take the opportunity to enhance the appearance of the pages somewhat, to integrate them better with the main web site for the railway:

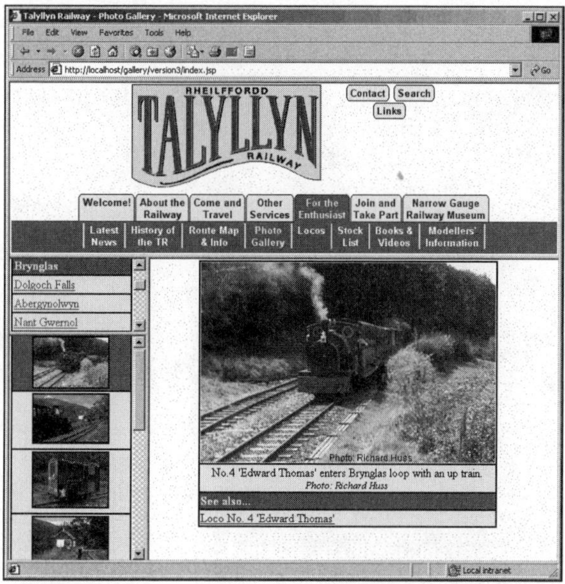

Note how the currently selected section and photograph are highlighted. If we click on the link under See also... in the photo frame, the system jumps to that section:

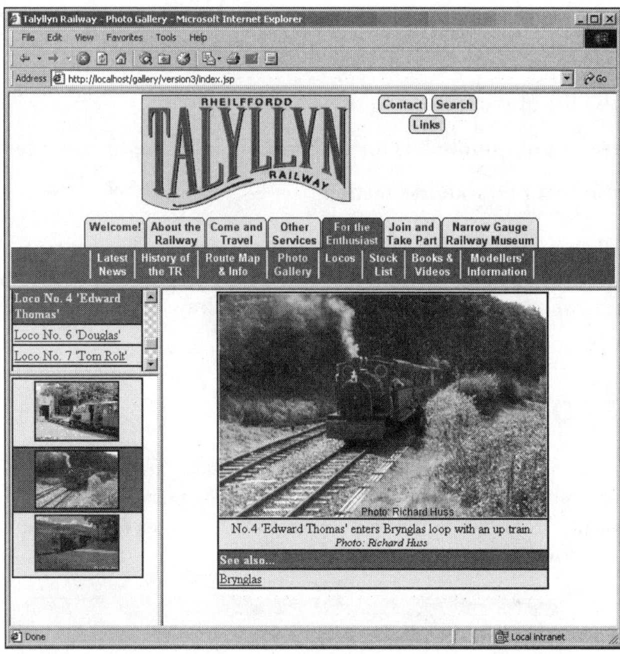

This view actually consists of two framesets, nested one inside the other. The outer frameset contains the top header frame and a main frame, inside which is a frameset containing the section list, section details, and the photo itself:

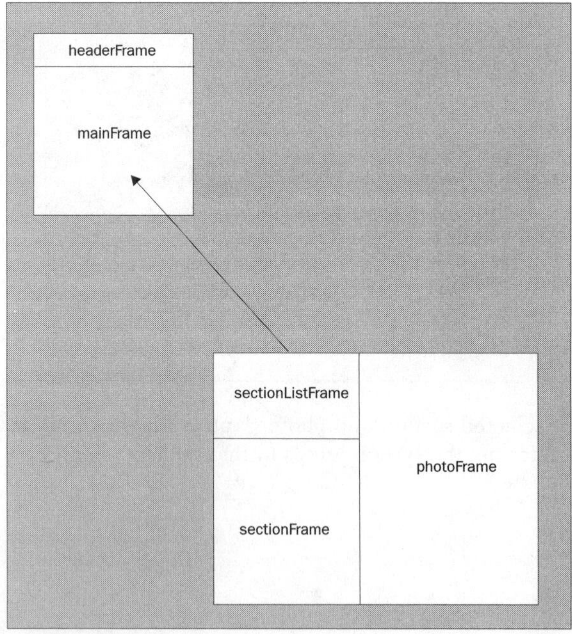

Each user has two associated pieces of information, the currently selected section and the currently selected photograph, which we will store in the user's session under the names `currentSection` and `currentPhoto` respectively. Note that these session attributes will hold the actual `Section` and `Photo` objects themselves, rather than their names.

Our process for updating the user interface when the user clicks on a link is as follows:

- The links for selecting gallery sections, photographs, and so on, are of the form `<a target="mainFrame" href="whatever.jsp">` so that they refresh the whole of the main content frame, along with its three subframes
- These links point to JSP pages that act as controllers in a simple MVC-type architecture, and update the user's session state as appropriate so that it contains the newly selected section and photo
- The controller JSP page then forwards to the page that constructs the "inner" frameset, forcing a reload of the section list, section, and photo frames
- These pages (which use the no-caching tag library from Chapter 3) then regenerate the appropriate views based on the values stored in the session

This keeps the query strings simple: only the controller JSP pages need query strings at all. Enough of the theory – let's look at some code.

The index.jsp Page

`index.jsp` has the task of creating the outer frameset for our application. We start by declaring the tag libraries and turning off caching:

```
<%@ taglib uri="http://www.wrox.com/taglib/cache" prefix="cache" %>
<%@ taglib uri="http://www.wrox.com/taglib/browser" prefix="browser" %>
<%@ taglib uri="http://jakarta.apache.org/taglibs/response-1.0"
           prefix="response" %>

<cache:noCaching/>
```

Next, we'll make use of our browser compatibility component from Chapter 3. If the user's browser doesn't support frames, we redirect them to the static HTML version of the site using the Jakarta Response Tag Library:

```
<browser:noSupportFor feature="frames">
  <response:sendRedirect>
    http://www.talyllyn.co.uk/gallery/index.html
  </response:sendRedirect>
</browser:noSupportFor>
```

Otherwise, we build the outer frameset. The top frame contains `header.html` (which we'll not show here – it's just static HTML):

```
<browser:supportFor feature="frames">
  <html>
    <head>
      <title>Talyllyn Railway - Photo Gallery</title>
    </head>

    <frameset rows="232,*">
      <frame src="header.html" name="headerFrame" scrolling="no"
             marginheight="2" marginwidth="2">
```

In the lower frame (`mainFrame`) we load `initialize.jsp` to initialize the session state before creating the nested, inner frameset:

```
      <frame src="initialize.jsp" name="mainFrame" scrolling="no"
             marginheight="2" marginwidth="2">
    </frameset>

  </html>
</browser:supportFor>
```

The Controller JSP Pages

With the outer frameset constructed, let's look in turn at the controller JSP pages, before moving on to look at the inner frameset. Since this is a very simple application we can make our point by using a series of simple JSP pages as our controller component, but the principles are clearly applicable to any controller architecture. The essential features are the centralization of control and the separation of logic and view.

Each of these controller pages forwards control to `main.jsp` after manipulating the session state appropriately.

The initialize.jsp Controller

`initialize.jsp` is responsible for setting things up when the user first visits the gallery. It looks up the `Gallery` object's `firstSection` property and stores it as a session attribute named `currentSection`, then looks up that section's `firstPhoto` property and stores it as the `currentPhoto` session attribute:

```
<%@ taglib uri="http://java.sun.com/jsptl/ea/jx" prefix="jx" %>

<jx:set var="currentSection" scope="session"
        value="$gallery.firstSection"/>
<jx:set var="currentPhoto" scope="session"
        value="$currentSection.firstPhoto"/>
```

With the user's session state thus initialized, it forwards to `main.jsp`, which will construct the inner frameset:

```
<jsp:forward page="main.jsp"/>
```

The chooseSection.jsp Controller

`chooseSection.jsp` is called when the user selects a section in the section list frame, with a URL of the form `chooseSection.jsp?section=newSection`. It looks in the gallery for a section with the specified name, using the `<gallery:lookupSection>` tag:

```
<%@ taglib uri="http://java.sun.com/jsptl/ea/jx" prefix="jx" %>
<%@ taglib uri="http://www.talyllyn.co.uk/tags/gallery" prefix="gallery" %>

<gallery:lookupSection gallery="gallery" section="$param:section"
 id="currentSection" scope="session"/>
```

It then looks for the first photo within it using the `Section` object's `firstPhoto` property:

```
<jx:set var="currentPhoto" scope="session"
        value="$currentSection.firstPhoto"/>
```

Finally, it forwards to `main.jsp` to construct the inner frameset:

```
<jsp:forward page="main.jsp"/>
```

The choosePhoto.jsp Controller

`choosePhoto.jsp` is used when the user selects a photo in the section frame; a typical URL fragment would be `choosePhoto.jsp?photo=newPhoto`. It selects the named photo using the `<gallery:lookupPhoto>` tag, but keeps the currently-selected section:

```
<%@ taglib uri="http://www.talyllyn.co.uk/tags/gallery" prefix="gallery" %>

<gallery:lookupPhoto gallery="gallery" photo="$param:photo"
 id="currentPhoto" scope="session"/>

<jsp:forward page="main.jsp"/>
```

The switchSections.jsp Controller

The last controller is `switchSections.jsp`, called when the user wants to switch to a different section in which the current photo occurs, by clicking on one of the links displayed below the photo itself. When called (with a URL fragment such as `switchSections.jsp?section=newSection`), it selects the new section (looking it up with the `<gallery:lookupSection>` tag), but keeps the currently selected photo:

```
<%@ taglib uri="http://java.sun.com/jsptl/ea/jx" prefix="jx" %>
<%@ taglib uri="http://www.talyllyn.co.uk/tags/gallery" prefix="gallery" %>
```

```
<gallery:lookupSection gallery="gallery" section="$param:section"
 id="currentSection" scope="session" />

<jsp:forward page="main.jsp"/>
```

Note the difference compared to the behavior of chooseSection.jsp.

The main.jsp Page

All four controllers forward control to main.jsp once they have updated the session state appropriately. We start by referencing the tag libraries we need, and requesting that the resulting page should not be cached:

```
<%@ taglib uri="http://java.sun.com/jsptl/ea/jx" prefix="jx" %>
<%@ taglib uri="http://www.wrox.com/taglib/cache" prefix="cache" %>
<cache:noCaching/>
```

All that remains is to build the main frameset for the application, referencing the sectionList.jsp, section.jsp, and photo.jsp pages that will supply the frame content. The one complication is that, to make the application easier to use, we will make the section list and section frames scroll automatically to the selected section or photograph. To do this, these pages will contain embedded anchors containing the name of each section or photo, for example:

```
<a name="pendre"></a>
<!-- Code for the "pendre" section -->
```

The main frame code can then reference these named anchors:

```
<html>

  <frameset cols="25%,*">
    <frameset rows="25%,*">
      <frame src="sectionList.jsp#<jx:expr value="$currentSection.name"/>"
             name="sectionListFrame" marginwidth="2" marginheight="2">
      <frame src="section.jsp#<jx:expr value="$currentPhoto.name"/>"
             name="sectionFrame" marginwidth="2" marginheight="2">
    </frameset>
    <frame src="photo.jsp#top" name="photoFrame"
           marginwidth="2" marginheight="2">
  </frameset>

</html>
```

A typical example frameset generated by main.jsp is shown below. Note how we link to sectionList.jsp#wharf to scroll to the entry for the wharf section, and to section.jsp#wharfgf1 to scroll to that photograph in the collection of thumbnails:

```
<html>

  <frameset cols="25%,*">
    <frameset rows="25%,*">
      <frame src="sectionList.jsp#wharf"
             name="sectionListFrame" marginwidth="2" marginheight="2">
      <frame src="section.jsp#wharfgf1"
             name="sectionFrame" marginwidth="2" marginheight="2">
    </frameset>
    <frame src="photo.jsp#top" name="photoFrame"
           marginwidth="2" marginheight="2">
  </frameset>

</html>
```

The Content Pages

The last three pages we need are those for the three content frames. These are now nice and simple, since they need only use the `Gallery` object stored in the `ServletContext`, along with the session attributes `currentSection` and `currentPhoto`. The template text is a little more complex, though, as we've migrated to using tables to highlight the selected section and photo.

The sectionList.jsp Page

`sectionList.jsp` does what it has always done – it lists the sections in the gallery. We start with the normal preamble and cache-disabling code:

```
<%@ taglib uri="http://java.sun.com/jsptl/ea/jx" prefix="jx" %>
<%@ taglib uri="http://www.wrox.com/taglib/cache" prefix="cache" %>
<cache:noCaching/>

<html>
  <body>

    <table width="100%" border="1" bordercolor="#000000"
           cellspacing="0" cellpadding="2">
```

Then we iterate through each section in the gallery in turn:

```
      <jx:forEach var="section" items="$gallery.sections">
```

For each section, we check to see whether it is the current section, and if so we highlight it. Note that the expression "`$section == currentSection`" is comparing the `Section` objects themselves, rather than the section names as was the case previously:

```
        <jx:choose>
          <jx:when test="$section == currentSection">
```

If this is the current section, we simply display its name and build an anchor (so we can scroll to this point in the page, as discussed earlier):

```
          <tr><td bgcolor="#339900"><font color="#ffff99">
            <a name="<jx:expr value="$section.name"/>"></a>
            <b><jx:expr value="$section.description"/></b>
          </font></td></tr>
        </jx:when>
```

If it's not the current one, on the other hand, we use different colors, and additionally link to the chooseSection.jsp controller:

```
        <jx:otherwise>
          <tr><td bgcolor="#ffff99">
            <a name="<jx:expr value="$section.name"/>"></a>
            <a href="chooseSection.jsp?section=<%--
                    --%><jx:expr value="$section.name"/>"
               target="mainFrame">
              <jx:expr value="$section.description"/>
            </a>
          </td></tr>
        </jx:otherwise>
      </jx:choose>
    </jx:forEach>
  </table>
 </body>
</html>
```

> **Note that the target of this link is the `mainFrame` frame. We are linking to the appropriate controller JSP, which in turn will forward to `main.jsp` and rebuild the entire inner frameset from scratch.**

The section.jsp Page

The logic in section.jsp is almost identical. For each photo in the current section we insert the thumbnail. If it's the current photo we highlight it, otherwise we build an appropriate link to choosePhoto.jsp, again targeting the mainFrame frame:

```
<%@ taglib uri="http://java.sun.com/jsptl/ea/jx" prefix="jx" %>
<%@ taglib uri="http://www.wrox.com/taglib/cache" prefix="cache" %>
<cache:noCaching/>

<html>
 <body>

  <table width="100%" border="1" bordercolor="#000000"
         cellspacing="0" cellpadding="2">

    <jx:forEach var="photo" items="$currentSection.photos">

      <jx:choose>
```

If it's the currently selected photo, highlight it and don't insert a link (but do insert an anchor, to enable the scrolling functionality):

```
          <jx:when test="$photo == currentPhoto">
            <tr><td bgcolor="#339900" align="center" valign="center">
              <a name="<jx:expr value="$photo.name"/>"></a>
              <img src="<jx:expr value="$photo.smallURL"/>"
                   alt="<jx:expr value="$photo.description"/>"
                   border="2"></td></tr>
          </jx:when>
```

But otherwise we don't highlight it, and do insert a link:

```
          <jx:otherwise>
            <tr><td bgcolor="#ffff99" align="center" valign="center">
              <a name="<jx:expr value="$photo.name"/>"></a>
              <a href="choosePhoto.jsp?photo=<jx:expr value="$photo.name"/>"
                 target="mainFrame">
                <img src="<jx:expr value="$photo.smallURL"/>"
                     alt="<jx:expr value="$photo.description"/>"
                     border="2">
              </a>
            </td></tr>
          </jx:otherwise>
        </jx:choose>
      </jx:forEach>
    </table>
  </body>
</html>
```

The photo.jsp Page

The final page for this version of the gallery application is `photo.jsp`. The first section is very straightforward, simply displaying the photo and its metadata:

```
<%@ taglib uri="http://java.sun.com/jsptl/ea/jx" prefix="jx" %>
<%@ taglib uri="http://www.wrox.com/taglib/cache" prefix="cache" %>
<cache:noCaching/>

<html>
  <body><a name="top"></a>

    <table align="center" border="1" bordercolor="#000000"
           cellspacing="0">
      <tr><td>
        <img src="<jx:expr value="$currentPhoto.largeURL"/>"></td></tr>
      <tr><td bgcolor="#ffff99" align="center">
        <jx:expr value="$currentPhoto.description"/><br>
        <i><font size="-1">
          Photo: <jx:expr value="$currentPhoto.photographer"/>
        </font></i>
      </td></tr>
```

The second half creates the links to other sections that the photo appears in. A refinement here over previous versions is that we only insert links to sections other than the current one, and so our See also... heading should only appear if the photo appears in more than one section:

```
      <jx:if test="$currentPhoto.numSections > 1">
        <tr><td bgcolor="#339900"><font color="#ffff99">
          <b>See also...</b>
        </font></td></tr>
```

We can then iterate over those sections, taking care to skip the one we're currently in, and construct appropriate links to the `switchSections.jsp` controller:

```
        <jx:forEach var="theSection" items="$currentPhoto.sections">
          <jx:if test="$theSection != currentSection">
            <tr><td bgcolor="#ffff99">
              <a href="switchSections.jsp?section=<%--
                       --%><jx:expr value="$theSection.name"/>"
                 target="mainFrame">
                <jx:expr value="$theSection.description"/>
              </a>
            </td></tr>
          </jx:if>
        </jx:forEach>
      </jx:if>

    </table>

  </body>
</html>
```

MVC Retrospect

We've ended up with rather more JSP pages than we had before, but this version of our application is actually a lot more manageable and understandable than the previous version with the JavaScript links. The main advantages of this approach are:

- The view state is centralized in the user's `HttpSession`, so it is no longer necessary to pass complex query strings around from frame to frame.
- Control of the view itself is centralized in the `mainFrame` frameset, which can then rebuild the nested frames as necessary. As a side effect, this allows us to control the scrolling position of the section list and section pages.
- We eliminated the complex, hard to understand JavaScript code that was previously necessary.

This is in many ways a very simple application, with little in the way of state. More complex applications have even more to gain from this approach, and many frame-based web applications take this "dump the frameset and start again" approach, for example Microsoft's (ASP-based) Outlook Web Access:

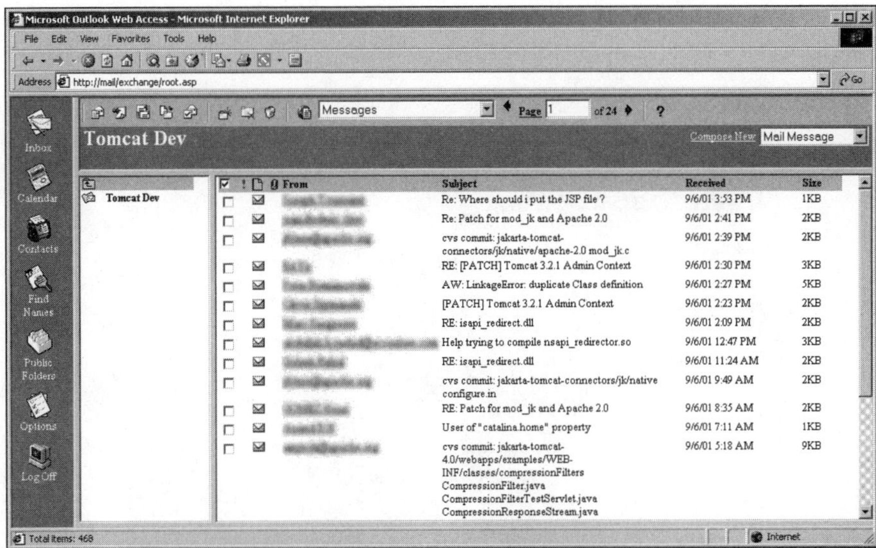

Here, any operation that changes which is our current folder causes the system to reloading everything except the column of icons on the left – in other words, the whole of the nested frameset is reloaded, with the attendant advantages outlined above. The frame hierarchy is as follows:

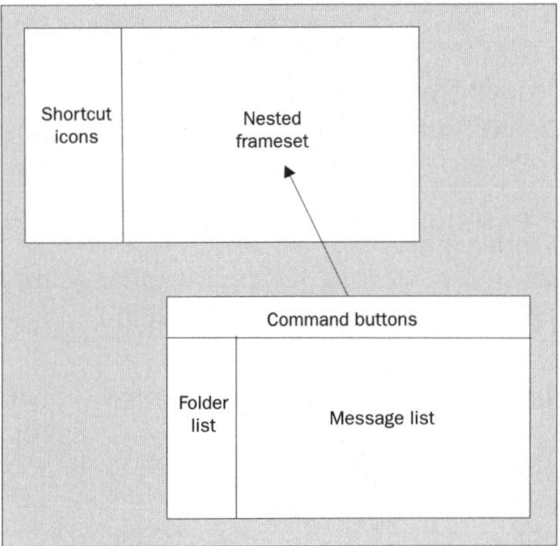

Adding Popup Windows

Let's make one final enhancement to the gallery application: a popup window listing today's specially picked highlights from the gallery. Recall that these are specified in `<spotlight>` elements within the `photos.xml` file. A `Collection` containing them is available via the `Gallery` object's `getSpotlight()` method.

To make the implementation more interesting, when one of the today's choice photos is selected from the popup we'll make it reflect the choice in the popup window:

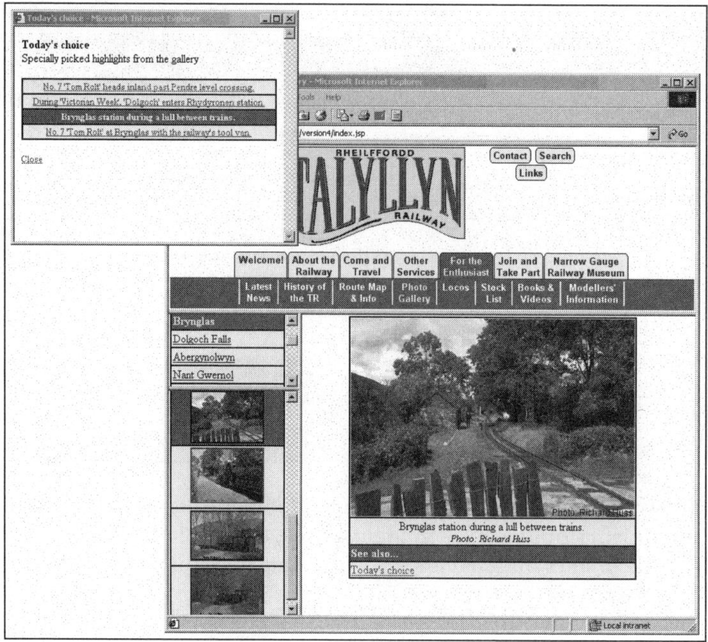

To assist in building this, we'll build the tag library we mentioned earlier that will help us to construct links that load more than one frame. We'll also add a tag to help us construct the JavaScript code to create popup windows.

> *Note that these tags are simply helping us to build complex constructs in the resulting page. Everything that the tag library does could be done using plain HTML and JavaScript code but at the expense of being rather less readable.*

The tag library descriptor file, `frames.tld`, starts in conventional style:

```
<?xml version="1.0" encoding="ISO-8859-1" ?>
<!DOCTYPE taglib
  PUBLIC "-//Sun Microsystems, Inc.//DTD JSP Tag Library 1.2//EN"
  "http://java.sun.com/dtd/web-jsptaglibrary_1_2.dtd">

<taglib>
  <tlib-version>1.0</tlib-version>
  <jsp-version>1.2</jsp-version>
  <short-name>frames</short-name>
  <uri>http://www.wrox.com/taglib/frames</uri>
  <display-name>Browser Frame Tags</display-name>
```

Multi-Frame Linking Tags

Four tags are involved in creating the multi-frame links:

- `<frames:multiLink>` is the top level tag. The generated code is configured by specifying an optional nested `<frames:mainLink>` tag, any number of nested `<frames:link>` tags, and a single nested `<frames:linkContent>` tag.
- `<frames:linkContent>` specifies the content of the link – the material that will appear between the generated `<a>` and `</a>` tags.
- `<frames:mainLink>` specifies the main page to be loaded when the link is followed, via the `<a>` tag's `href` attribute. This link will therefore be followed even if JavaScript has been disabled in the browser. The optional `target` attribute specifies the name of the frame that this page is to be loaded into. The tag's body content specifies the URL.
- `<frames:link>` specifies an additional page to be loaded. The enclosing `<frames:multiLink>` tag will use this information to create the `onclick` event handler. The frame to be targeted is specified using the `target` attribute, but for this tag we must specify the frame using a JavaScript expression. For example, `target="self"` would cause this page to be loaded into the current frame, while using `target="parent.frames['sectionList']"` specifies the sibling frame named `sectionList`.

As we saw earlier, typical usage of these tags might be:

```
<frames:multiLink>
  <frames:mainLink target="sectionFrame">
    section.jsp?section=rhydyronen&photo=rhydstna
  </frames:mainLink>
  <frames:link target="parent.frames['photoFrame']">
    photo.jsp?photo=rhydstna
  </frames:link>
  <frames:link target="parent.frames['sectionListFrame']">
    sectionList.jsp?section=rhydyronen
  </frames:link>
  <frames:linkContent>
    Rhydyronen
  </frames:linkContent>
</frames:multiLink>
```

This would generate the following HTML/JavaScript code:

```
<a href="section.jsp?section=rhydyronen&photo=rhydstna"
   target="sectionFrame"
   onclick="parent.frames['photoFrame'].location.href=
'photo.jsp?photo=rhydstna';parent.frames['sectionListFrame'].location.href='sectio
nList.jsp?section=rhydyronen';return true;">Rhydyronen</a>
```

The relevant portions of `frames.tld` for these tags read as follows:

```
<tag>
  <name>multiLink</name>
  <tag-class>com.wrox.frames.MultiLinkTag</tag-class>
  <body-content>JSP</body-content>
</tag>

<tag>
  <name>mainLink</name>
  <tag-class>com.wrox.frames.MainLinkTag</tag-class>
  <body-content>JSP</body-content>

  <attribute>
    <name>target</name>
    <required>false</required>
  </attribute>
</tag>

<tag>
  <name>link</name>
  <tag-class>com.wrox.frames.LinkTag</tag-class>
  <body-content>JSP</body-content>

  <attribute>
    <name>target</name>
    <required>true</required>
  </attribute>
</tag>

<tag>
  <name>linkContent</name>
  <tag-class>com.wrox.frames.LinkContentTag</tag-class>
  <body-content>JSP</body-content>
</tag>
```

Popup Window Tag

Our final tag is intended to simplify the creation of code for popup windows. Typical usage of this tag might be:

```
<a href="#"
   onclick="<frames:openWindow name="popup"
                 width="400" height="300" top="50" left="25"
                 scrollbars="true">
               popup.jsp
             </frames:openWindow>">Open popup!</a>
```

We've designed the tag only to create the actual JavaScript code, rather than the enclosing HTML code. This allows us to use it within any event handler, rather than being restricted to (say) being activated by the user clicking on a link.

The tag has many attributes, corresponding to the desired properties of the new window. The supported attributes are:

Attribute	Default value	Meaning
`name`	Required attribute	The name for the new window
`toolbar`	`false`	Should new window display toolbars?
`location`	`false`	Should new window display location bar?
`directories`	`false`	Should new window display directory buttons (IE "Links Toolbar", Netscape "Personal Toolbar")?
`status`	`false`	Should new window display status bar?
`menubar`	`false`	Should new window display menubar?
`scrollbars`	`false`	Should new window display scrollbar?
`resizable`	`false`	Should new window be resizable?
`replace`	`false`	Should new window history replace the existing history?
`width`	Browser default	How wide should the new window be?
`height`	Browser default	How high should the new window be?
`top`	Browser default	How far should the new window be positioned from the top of the screen?
`left`	Browser default	How far should the new window be positioned from the left hand side of the screen?

The URL for the new window's content is specified using the tag's body content, so the TLD extract looks like this:

```
<tag>
  <name>openWindow</name>
  <tag-class>com.wrox.frames.OpenWindowTag</tag-class>
  <body-content>JSP</body-content>

  <attribute>
    <name>name</name>
    <required>true</required>
  </attribute>

  <attribute>
    <name>toolbar</name>
    <required>false</required>
  </attribute>
```

```
    <!-- And similarly for the location, directories, status, menubar,
         scrollbars, resizable, replace, width, height, top, and left
         properties. -->

  </tag>

</taglib>
```

To save space we'll not look at the tag handlers themselves here. The source code is of course in the download available from http://www.wrox.com/.

Implementing the Gallery Popup

With our trusty Frames Tag Library in hand, let's see how we can implement the popup window in our photo gallery application. The obvious first step is to generate the link to open the popup; to do this we need to change photo.jsp a little.

Modifications to photo.jsp

The changes to photo.jsp are threefold. First, we need to reference the new Frames Tag Library:

```
<%@ taglib uri="http://java.sun.com/jsptl/ea/jx" prefix="jx" %>
<%@ taglib uri="http://www.wrox.com/taglib/cache" prefix="cache" %>
<%@ taglib uri="http://www.wrox.com/taglib/frames" prefix="frames" %>
<cache:noCaching/>

<html>
  <body><a name="top"></a>

    <table align="center" border="1" bordercolor="#000000"
           cellspacing="0">

      <%-- Display the photo itself --%>
      <tr><td>
        <img src="<jx:expr value="$currentPhoto.largeURL"/>"></td></tr>

      <%-- Display the caption and other metadata --%>
      <tr><td bgcolor="#ffff99" align="center">
        <jx:expr value="$currentPhoto.description"/><br>
        <i><font size="-1">
          Photo: <jx:expr value="$currentPhoto.photographer"/>
        </font></i>
      </td></tr>
```

Secondly, the conditional code around the See also... heading is removed, as there will always be, at a minimum, the link for the Today's choice section, and so this heading is always required:

```
      <tr><td bgcolor="#339900"><font color="#ffff99">
        <b>See also...</b>
      </font></td></tr>
```

Below this, we create a link to pop up `spotlight.jsp`. We'll see the reason for the `highlight=none` request string shortly:

```
        <tr><td bgcolor="#ffff99">
          <a href="#"
             onclick="<frames:openWindow name="popup"
             width="400" height="300" top="50" left="25"
             scrollbars="true">
             spotlight.jsp?highlight=none
             </frames:openWindow>">Today's choice</a>
        </td></tr>
```

The rest of `photo.jsp` is the same as we saw before:

```
        <%-- ... iterate over each of those sections ... --%>
        <jx:forEach var="theSection" items="$currentPhoto.sections">

          <%-- ... (but not the one we're currently in) ... --%>
          <jx:if test="$theSection != currentSection">
            <tr><td bgcolor="#ffff99">

              <%-- ... and construct a link to switchSections.jsp to
                     change to that section --%>
              <a href="switchSections.jsp?section=<%--
                       --%><jx:expr value="$theSection.name"/>"
                 target="mainFrame">
                <jx:expr value="$theSection.description"/>
              </a>
            </td></tr>
          </jx:if>
        </jx:forEach>

      </table>

    </body>
  </html>
```

The chooseHighlightPhoto.jsp Controller

We need an additional controller for the main window, which will be called when the user clicks on one of the links in the popup – the URL will be of the form `chooseHighlightPhoto.jsp?photo=wharfgf1`.

The newly selected photo could be *any* photograph, from *any* section of the gallery; it's likely that it won't appear in the user's current section, so we need to make sure that the main window display jumps to a section that the photo does appear in. We do this using the `Photo` object's `firstSection` property to locate the first-named section for that photo:

```
<%@ taglib uri="http://www.talyllyn.co.uk/tags/gallery" prefix="gallery" %>
<%@ taglib uri="http://java.sun.com/jsptl/ea/jx" prefix="jx" %>

<gallery:lookupPhoto gallery="gallery" photo="$param:photo"
```

```
    var="currentPhoto" scope="session"/>

  <jx:set var="currentSection" scope="session"
          value="$currentPhoto.firstSection"/>

  <jsp:forward page="main.jsp"/>
```

The spotlight.jsp Page

`spotlight.jsp` caused some headaches. On the face of it, the task is simple:

- List the descriptions of the today's choice photographs
- If a particular photo is the current photo in the main window, highlight it
- For the other photos, create a multi-frame link that will update both main and popup windows

Sounds easy? Unfortunately, it quickly becomes clear that our hopes of protecting page designers from having to delve into JavaScript are, if not doomed, at least somewhat over-optimistic. There are a couple of problems:

- We find our tidy MVC architecture starting to creak a bit when we can't simply point to a controller JSP page that updates an entire frameset. If we use our `<frames:multiLink>` tag to update both the main and the popup window, we can't control the order in which these two requests will be processed. The controller page will be updating the session state, but there's no guarantee that it will complete this before the request for the popup page comes in. So `spotlight.jsp` can't just use the session attributes to look up the current state of the user's session; they may not yet have been updated.

  There seem to be two possible solutions to this. We'll come to the second, more satisfactory solution in the *An MVC Compliant Popup* section. The first is for the popup page simply to ignore the MVC side of the application. The only things we need within this page are the `Gallery` object and the currently-selected photo (so that we can highlight it if necessary). This is the reason for the `highlight` request parameter we saw earlier. We can duck out of the issue by passing the name of the photo to be highlighted to `spotlight.jsp` directly.

- Actually referencing both windows is itself tricky, and there's simply no alternative to being sure of your JavaScript. I started out trying to use the JavaScript variable `opener` to refer back to the main window. And it worked, at first, but unfortunately after reloading `spotlight.jsp` the opener variable no longer exists. The simple answer is just to transpose the "main" and "additional" links in the `<frames:multiLink>` so we don't need to use JavaScript to refer back to the main window. The alternative would be to employ the old trick of using an invisible frame to hold session data – at the risk of some further code obfuscation.

So here's the first version of `spotlight.jsp`, warts and all:

```
<%@ taglib uri="http://java.sun.com/jsptl/ea/jx" prefix="jx" %>
<%@ taglib uri="http://www.wrox.com/taglib/cache" prefix="cache" %>
<%@ taglib uri="http://www.wrox.com/taglib/frames" prefix="frames" %>
<cache:noCaching/>

<html>
```

```
<head>
  <title>Today's choice</title>
</head>
<body>

  <p><b>Today's choice</b><br>
  Specially picked highlights from the gallery</p>

  <table width="100%" border="1" bordercolor="#000000"
         cellspacing="0" cellpadding="2">
```

Unsurprisingly, we find ourselves iterating again, this time over the items in the `Collection` we find in the `Gallery`'s `spotlight` property:

```
    <jx:forEach var="photo" items="$gallery.spotlight">
```

Checking whether we ought to be highlighting this photo is simple too, but we do need to make sure that the `highlight` request parameter is present otherwise we'll get an exception from JSPTL – hence the dummy `highlight=none` query string used when the popup is first opened. (Hope there isn't a photo called none.)

```
      <jx:choose>
```

If it's the currently selected photo, we highlight it and don't bother inserting a link:

```
        <jx:when test="$photo.name == param:highlight">
          <tr><td bgcolor="#339900" align="center" valign="center">
            <font color="#ffff99" size="-1">
              <b><jx:expr value="$photo.description"/></b>
            </font>
          </td></tr>
        </jx:when>
```

Otherwise, we don't highlight it and do insert a link:

```
        <jx:otherwise>
          <tr><td bgcolor="#ffff99" align="center" valign="center">
            <font size="-1">
```

Next we need to build the multi-frame link itself, pointing both our controller in the main window *and* back to ourselves to highlight the newly selected photo. As we've seen, we reference the controller through a normal, HTML link (targeting the `mainFrame` frame) rather than in the JavaScript `onclick` event handler:

```
              <frames:multiLink>
                <frames:link target="self">
                  spotlight.jsp?highlight=<jx:expr value="$photo.name"/>
                </frames:link>
                <frames:mainLink target="mainFrame">
```

```
                    chooseHighlightPhoto.jsp?photo=<%--
                                          --%><jx:expr value="$photo.name"/>
                  </frames:mainLink>
                  <frames:linkContent>
                    <jx:expr value="$photo.description"/>
                  </frames:linkContent>
                </frames:multiLink>
              </font>
            </td></tr>
          </jx:otherwise>
        </jx:choose>
      </jx:forEach>
    </table>

    <p><font size="-1"><a href="#" onclick="self.close();">Close</a></font>
  </p>

  </body>
</html>
```

An MVC-Compliant Popup

We have one final trick up our sleeves to tidy things up. On the one hand it does involve some more JavaScript, but on the other hand it leaves the user's session state where it belongs (in the session), and keeps the MVC architecture clean. Essentially, we allow our popup window *only* to reference the controller, which as before creates the nested frameset in the main window. The popup doesn't attempt to reload itself. The trick is that the frameset page uses a little dollop of JavaScript to force the popup to reload.

To get this to work, we need to get the main window to keep a reference to the popup. Fortunately, our controller is already embedded in a frameset that provides an ideal place to store the reference. So, our popup-creation code in `photo.jsp` becomes:

```
    <tr><td bgcolor="#ffff99">
      <a href="#"
         onclick="parent.parent.popup=<frames:openWindow name="popup"
                                         width="400" height="300" top="50"
                                         left="25" scrollbars="true">
                                         spotlight.jsp
                                       </frames:openWindow>">Today's
                                       choice</a>
    </td></tr>
```

In the main frameset page (`main.jsp`), we can now add some clever JavaScript that will force the popup (if it exists) to be updated. We'll see in a moment where this gets called:

```
<%@ taglib uri="http://java.sun.com/jsptl/ea/jx" prefix="jx" %>
<%@ taglib uri="http://www.wrox.com/taglib/cache" prefix="cache" %>
<cache:noCaching/>

<html>
```

```
    <script language="JavaScript">
      function updatePopup() {
        if ((parent.popup != null) && (!(parent.popup.closed))) {
          parent.popup.location.reload(true);
        }
      }
    </script>
```

The last section of `main.jsp` builds the main frameset for the application. The change here is that we use the `onLoad()` event handler to trigger a reload of the popup window once the main frameset has finished loading:

```
    <frameset onLoad="updatePopup(); return true;" cols="25%,*">
      <frameset rows="25%,*">
        <frame src="sectionList.jsp#<jx:expr value="$currentSection.name"/>"
               name="sectionListFrame" marginwidth="2" marginheight="2">
        <frame src="section.jsp#<jx:expr value="$currentPhoto.name"/>"
               name="sectionFrame" marginwidth="2" marginheight="2">
      </frameset>
      <frame src="photo.jsp#top" name="photoFrame"
             marginwidth="2" marginheight="2">
    </frameset>

  </html>
```

Finally, `spotlight.jsp` itself no longer requires the request parameter to tell it the current photograph:

```
  <%@ taglib uri="http://java.sun.com/jsptl/ea/jx" prefix="jx" %>
  <%@ taglib uri="http://www.wrox.com/taglib/cache" prefix="cache" %>
  <%@ taglib uri="http://www.wrox.com/taglib/frames" prefix="frames" %>
  <cache:noCaching/>

  <html>
    <head>
      <title>Today's choice</title>
    </head>
    <body>

      <p><b>Today's choice</b><br>
        Specially picked highlights from the gallery</p>

      <table width="100%" border="1" bordercolor="#000000"
             cellspacing="0" cellpadding="2">

        <%-- Iterate through the photos that are spotlighted --%>
        <jx:forEach var="photo" items="$gallery.spotlight">
          <jx:choose>
            <%-- If it's the currently selected photo, highlight it and
                 don't insert a link ... --%>
            <jx:when test="$photo == currentPhoto">
              <tr><td bgcolor="#339900" align="center" valign="center">
```

```
              <font color="#ffff99" size="-1">
                <b><jx:expr value="$photo.description"/></b>
              </font>
            </td></tr>
          </jx:when>

          <%-- ... otherwise don't highlight it and do insert a link --%>
          <jx:otherwise>
            <tr><td bgcolor="#ffff99" align="center" valign="center">
              <font size="-1">
                <a href="chooseHighlightPhoto.jsp?photo=<jx:expr
                                                  value="$photo.name"/>"
                   target="mainFrame">
                  <jx:expr value="$photo.description"/></a>
                </a>
              </font>
            </td></tr>
          </jx:otherwise>
        </jx:choose>
      </jx:forEach>
    </table>

    <p>
      <font size="-1"><a href="#" onclick="self.close();">Close</a></font>
    </p>

  </body>
</html>
```

This works just the same as our previous version, but with one added bonus. Before, if the user opened the popup, then started using the main window navigation again, the popup would not be updated to reflect the current state of the application. With this version, the popup (if it is open) is updated on every user interaction with the system, whichever window the user clicked in.

Deployment

Lastly, let's run quickly through the deployment considerations for our application. The directory structure for the application is shown below:

```
gallery/
        index.html
        admin/
              reload.jsp
        version1/
                 index.jsp
                 photo.jsp
                 section.jsp
                 sectionList.jsp
        version2/
                 index.jsp
                 photo.jsp
```

```
            section.jsp
            sectionList.jsp
      version3/
            choosePhoto.jsp
            chooseSection.jsp
            header.html
            index.jsp
            initialize.jsp
            main.jsp
            photo.jsp
            section.jsp
            sectionList.jsp
            switchSections.jsp
      version4/
            chooseHighlightPhoto.jsp
            choosePhoto.jsp
            chooseSection.jsp
            header.html
            index.jsp
            initialize.jsp
            main.jsp
            photo.jsp
            section.jsp
            sectionList.jsp
            spotlight.jsp
            switchSections.jsp
      version5/
            chooseHighlightPhoto.jsp
            choosePhoto.jsp
            chooseSection.jsp
            header.html
            index.jsp
            initialize.jsp
            main.jsp
            photo.jsp
            section.jsp
            sectionList.jsp
            spotlight.jsp
            switchSections.jsp
      WEB-INF/
           browscap.ini
           browser.tld
           cache.tld
           frames.tld
           gallery.tld
           jx.tld
           photos.dtd
           photos.xml
           response.tld
           web.xml
           lib/
               crimson.jar
               frames.jar
               gallery.jar
```

```
                    httputils.jar
                    jakarta-oro-2.0.4.jar
                    jaxp.jar
                    jsptl.jar
                    response.jar
```

Of these JAR files, three are our own work:

- `gallery.jar`
  Contains the photo gallery classes (the `uk.co.talyllyn.gallery` package)
- `httputils.jar`
  Contains the code from the previous chapter – the caching tags and browser filter
- `frames.jar`
  Contains the Frame Tag Library we developed towards the end of this chapter

The `web.xml` file contains quite a lot of deployment information:

```
<?xml version="1.0" encoding="ISO-8859-1"?>

<!DOCTYPE web-app
    PUBLIC "-//Sun Microsystems, Inc.//DTD Web Application 2.3//EN"
    "http://java.sun.com/dtd/web-app_2_3.dtd">

<web-app>
```

First of all, we set some application initialization parameters to configure the gallery listener:

```
  <context-param>
    <param-name>gallery.name</param-name>
    <param-value>gallery</param-value>
  </context-param>

  <!-- Specify the location of the photos.xml file -->
  <context-param>
    <param-name>gallery.config</param-name>
    <param-value>/WEB-INF/photos.xml</param-value>
  </context-param>
```

The current JSPTL early access release also requires an initialization parameter to configure its expression language support:

```
  <context-param>
    <param-name>
      javax.servlet.jsptl.ExpressionEvaluatorClass
    </param-name>
    <param-value>
      org.apache.taglibs.jsptl.lang.spel.Evaluator
    </param-value>
  </context-param>
```

We also need to set up our browser detection filter:

```
<filter>
  <filter-name>Browser Detection Filter</filter-name>
  <filter-class>com.wrox.browser.BrowserFilter</filter-class>
  <init-param>
    <param-name>scope</param-name>
    <param-value>session</param-value>
  </init-param>
  <init-param>
    <param-name>browscap</param-name>
    <param-value>/WEB-INF/browscap.ini</param-value>
  </init-param>
</filter>
```

Apply it to the whole application:

```
<filter-mapping>
  <filter-name>Browser Detection Filter</filter-name>
  <url-pattern>/*</url-pattern>
</filter-mapping>
```

We've ended up using no fewer than six tag libraries:

```
  <taglib>
    <taglib-uri>http://www.wrox.com/taglib/cache</taglib-uri>
    <taglib-location>/WEB-INF/cache.tld</taglib-location>
  </taglib>

  <taglib>
    <taglib-uri>http://www.wrox.com/taglib/browser</taglib-uri>
    <taglib-location>/WEB-INF/browser.tld</taglib-location>
  </taglib>

  <taglib>
    <taglib-uri>http://www.wrox.com/taglib/frames</taglib-uri>
    <taglib-location>/WEB-INF/frames.tld</taglib-location>
  </taglib>

  <taglib>
    <taglib-uri>http://www.talyllyn.co.uk/tags/gallery</taglib-uri>
    <taglib-location>/WEB-INF/gallery.tld</taglib-location>
  </taglib>

  <taglib>
    <taglib-uri>http://java.sun.com/jsptl/ea/jx</taglib-uri>
    <taglib-location>/WEB-INF/jx.tld</taglib-location>
  </taglib>

  <taglib>
    <taglib-uri>http://jakarta.apache.org/taglibs/response-1.0</taglib-uri>
    <taglib-location>/WEB-INF/response.tld</taglib-location>
</taglib>
```

Lastly, we want to protect our administration page (`reload.jsp`, which reloads the gallery as we saw near the start of the chapter) by requiring users to log in if they want to administer the application:

```
    <security-constraint>
      <web-resource-collection>
        <web-resource-name>
          Admin Pages
        </web-resource-name>
        <url-pattern>
          /admin/*
        </url-pattern>
      </web-resource-collection>
      <auth-constraint>
        <role-name>
          manager
        </role-name>
      </auth-constraint>
    </security-constraint>

    <login-config>
      <auth-method>
        BASIC
      </auth-method>
      <realm-name>
        Talyllyn Railway Photo Gallery Administration
      </realm-name>
    </login-config>
  </web-app>
```

Summary

Working with HTML frames is hard work – but they can sometimes give a richer user experience that warrants the heartache they cause. In this chapter we've:

- Looked at some of the problems that frames cause and why they occur – essentially, the issue is the lack of a central point of reference compared to conventional MVC architectures.
- Seen techniques for regaining control by force-fitting MVC architecture onto the frameset, reloading the whole frameset for each command rather than trying to address individual frames for updating.
- Seen how the problem recurs with popup windows, owing to the lack of a common parent frameset to reload, and examined a technique for overcoming this at the expense of requiring some extra JavaScript code.
- Looked at lots of nice photographs of small trains. It's got to be worth it for that alone.

In the next chapter, we will move on to look at techniques for page layout and composition of information from different sources.

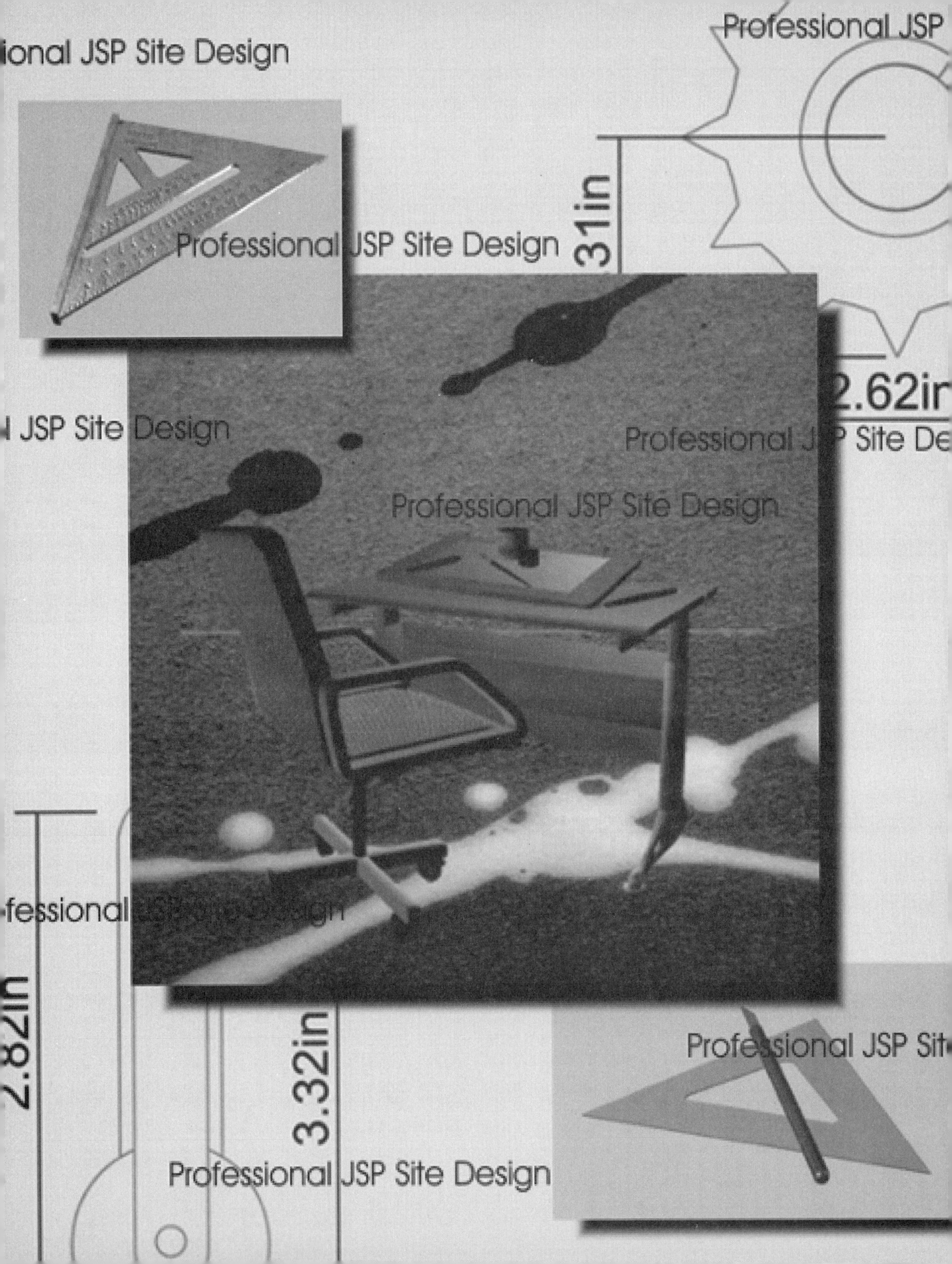

5

Page Layout

We've built our web application and it has all the functionality we want – but the boss looks at it and the first thing he asks is why it looks so plain. It's probably because we're developers, not graphic designers. So, a graphic designer works some design magic, and we have to work our way through our elegant code – inserting the HTML and JavaScript that's required to make the application look good.

At some point, we're probably going to want to modify some of our code that supplies functionality in the application. Of course, it's not as easy to read as we remember it being when we wrote it – the JSP pages have tripled in size and it's hard to pick out the code and JSP tags from the HTML and JavaScript. Next, we want all the pages to display a dynamic navigation bar down the side – but it's been written as a standalone web application and wasn't designed to be integrated with the entire site. Now someone else has written a servlet that outputs all the most recently added news articles in a database – and that needs to be integrated with every page too.

By this stage, all these changes are getting to be quite a handful to manage. The code from various web applications and the HTML to make the site look good are intermingled. Then of course, the inevitable happens – it's decided that the graphic design just doesn't suit the company and it needs to be redesigned. We have to trawl through all our code (of which there is a great deal by now) amending the design, while being careful not to break the functionality. The graphic designer mumbles something about how easily he could change the design in his favorite WYSIWYG HTML package, so we have to explain how his editor can't deal with our inline custom tags, code, and backend MVC framework.

A WYSIWYG HTML package stands for What You See Is What You Get. A good WYSIWYG HTML package can make producing web pages as easy as creating standard office documents, but web developers who write code for dynamic sites generally fear these packages as they can wreak havoc on the code.

OK, not every web application is going to go through all these changes and a well-planned application will have everything well documented. Nonetheless, laying out web applications to make them look great can cause headaches. This chapter will help make layout one less thing for you to worry about, in particular we'll look at:

- Separating the front end's functionality from the graphic design of the web application. This allows the graphic designer and developer to do what they are best at without getting in each other's way.
- Assembling pages from smaller components. This allows each component to be developed in isolation from the overall page layout and graphic design.

Separating Functionality from Graphic Design

Separating the functionality and presentation of an application is important. When we develop a web application, we shouldn't have to put too much thought into the fonts, colors, and images to be used when the application is placed into production. To avoid this we need to abstract the presentation from the data.

Java Swing developers generally don't need to worry about such things – they write code that creates and interacts with graphical widgets. Characteristics such as fonts used, colors, and even how the widgets look, can be altered in isolation from the code that provides the functionality. This was one of the greatest advantages of Layout Managers, as the responsibility of how the components look was delegated from the components to the Layout Managers. Visual components can also be layered on top of existing components without modifications to the underlying component code. For example, one developer can create a widget for entering a date, another developer can add a fancy border that allows the component to be dragged around the screen and docked to the edge. Both of these components can be developed in isolation, with very little known about the other components it's going to be used with.

In the GUI world, the **Decorator Design Pattern** is commonly used to make this easy.

> *Patterns are used describe recurring concepts. 'Design Patterns' are a collection of patterns used to solve common problems with simple solutions for how code is designed. We'll learn more about patterns in Chapter 15.*

The Decorator Design Pattern allows the application of a **decorator** to a component. The decorator alters the appearance of the component. In a traditional GUI application, a component could be a text-field or directory-tree, and a decorator could refer to a border or scroll-bar. Each of these could be developed in isolation and then combined as developers see fit. New decorators can be developed without the knowledge of how the component to which it is to be applied works, and vice versa.

The Decorator Design Pattern is an elegant solution for separating the functionality of an application from the graphical-design. However, the pattern is usually used with object-oriented visual widgets, and our components are created using HTML. It doesn't matter though, as a pattern is just a concept that helps us to get started. Now that we understand how easy it should be, we can apply the concepts to our web applications.

Our components are plain HTML pages (which can of course contain dynamically generated data like forms or client-side scripts), for example, a welcome page, search form, search results, or the latest news items.

Decorators are HTML templates that contain graphic elements to make our pages look more impressive. The HTML contains placeholders to insert the body of the components and any extra information that may be necessary (such as a title or preferred color). Decorators may be used to enhance the entire page or just a fragment of a page in different ways.

Assembling Pages from Components

As well as decorating pages, we want to make it easy to assemble pages from smaller components. Then, once we have developed all our components and decorators, we will be able to use them to easily and quickly build pages. Pages are often crammed full of windows containing news, search forms, logins, navigation bars, mailing list signups, advertisements, top ten items, product lists, and so on.

> **A window is a section of a page. It usually has some characteristics that separate it from other windows on the same page, such as a border or a title.**

The following screenshot shows four windows from http://www.wrox.com/ surrounded by a thick black border:

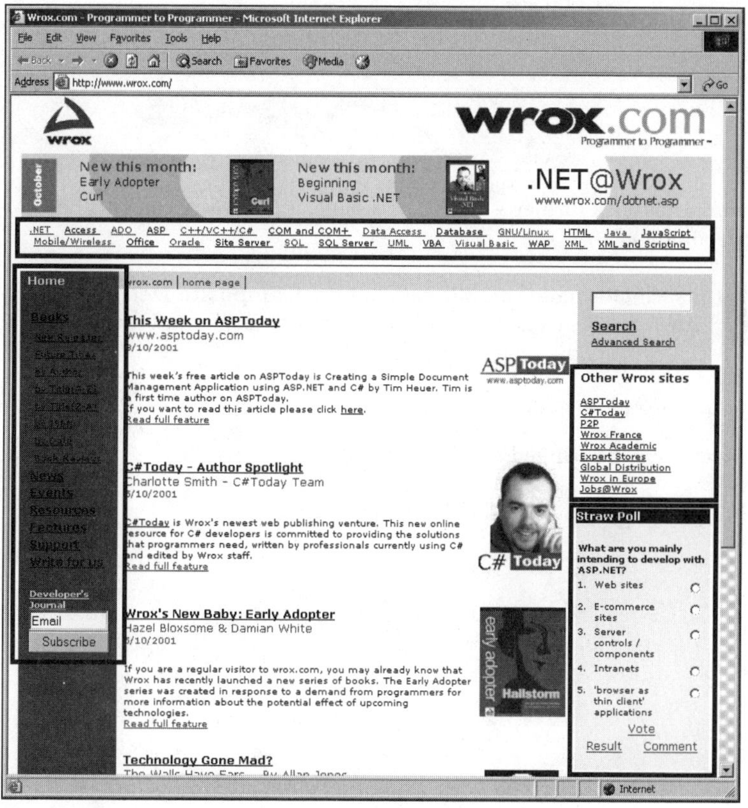

At first sight, we might imagine that such a page could be difficult to construct. Information must be gathered from all types of resources – different databases, a content management system, JavaBeans, or even XML feeds from third party sites. However, it can be easily managed by treating each window as an individual component. These components can be developed in isolation and then simply arranged on a page to create a suitable layout. Finally, we can apply some decorators to the components to give the page a finishing touch.

The overall page can contain **includes**. Includes can also contain other includes (which in turn can contain more includes, and so on). A decorator can be applied to a page, and a decorator can also include includes. The following diagram shows how a page can be constructed from a decorator and includes:

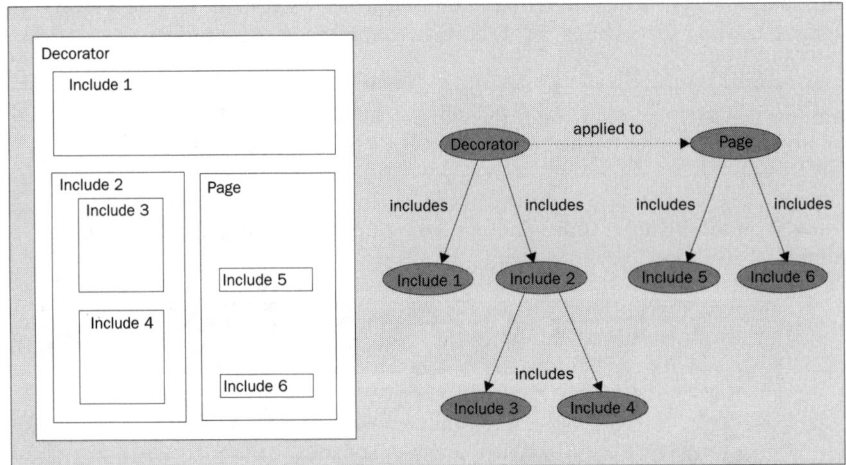

We can expand on this a bit further – as well as a page, a decorator can also be applied to an include, or even another decorator.

This structure at first sounds quite complicated, but the **Composite Design Pattern** offers a simple solution. If we create a generalization, such that decorators, pages and includes are all types of components, we can express the relationships clearly:

- A component can include an include
- A decorator can be applied to a component

These relationships are illustrated in the following model:

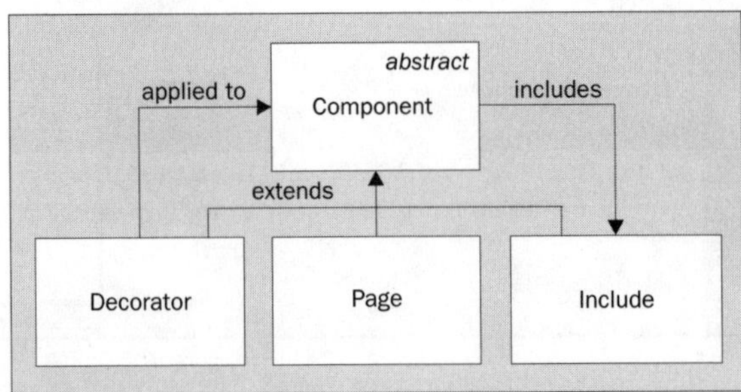

Using the Composite Design Pattern, we can build complicated page layouts from simple trees of components.

Factors To Take Into Account

When we decide how to handle layout in our web applications, we must take into account some key factors. Some of these are more important than others, some may not even be applicable to our particular web application. However, it's important to discuss them before we begin work – otherwise they could cause us problems later.

Consistency

Do all the pages need to conform to a standard look? For example, perhaps we need to use the corporate colors and fonts. This is often the case, so we need to make it easy to apply a consistent look throughout the application.

This also applies to individual components. For example, should the titles of each component appear in the same font and with the same border around the contents?

Flexible Page Layout

Different sections of the site may require content to be structured in different ways. For example, all news features could present a consistent look for the navigation-bar, title, date, author, together with large areas for body content. However, a discussion forum will most likely require a completely different layout.

Easy Maintenance and Evolution

Is the look likely to change? How about the layout, or content, or functionality? We need to be prepared for this. And when we do need to change something, it needs to be simple to do. If we are changing the layout, we shouldn't have to modify (or even see) any code related to our dynamically generated content. The same applies for the opposite situation – we shouldn't need to deal with layout or style when modifying our dynamic content code.

If our site has expanded in size, a style or layout change should not mean we have to modify lots of sections of our code – it should be as simple as if our site contained only a few pages.

Graphic Design Decoupled from Content and Functionality

Sites that look great are not an uncommon sight. Neither are sites that prove really useful with their functionality. But sites that combine visual and functional elegance seem somewhat of a rarity. Sure, we do see them, but not nearly as much as we should. The reason for this is that development strategies for a site are usually driven by one of two mindsets, that of a programmer or a graphic designer. It's tricky work trying to think about functionality and graphic design at the same time as developing an application. The programmer should focus on functionality and the graphic designer on graphic design. If the layout has been decoupled from functionality, it is easy for this to happen without treading on each other's feet.

The Right Tools for the Right Job

We need to use the right tools (and the right skills) for the right job – we need the best of both worlds. The programmers should use their favorite tools, as should the graphic designers. After all, how can a WYSIWYG tool be used to design a page when the contents of the page are being dynamically generated from custom code? We can't expect the editor to generate all of our database-code and logic for us. Likewise, our JSP IDE isn't usually an effective tool for creating HTML tables containing buttons with fancy image rollover effects.

It is essential that the graphic designer and the programmer can both use the tools that make them most productive without hindering each other's work.

Performance

Sites need to be fast. If a page takes more than a few seconds to load, your visitor is going to get frustrated and impatient; we don't want that. Performance is dependent on how much processing is required to generate the page with all its components and decorators. The amount of processing will be dependent on the technique used to combine them together.

Remember that our layout strategies are going to be used on virtually every single page of the site and the site may be getting hundreds of concurrent hits. However we handle the layout, we must make sure it does not cause a bottleneck in the site's performance. For example, suppose each component in a page needs to be converted to XHTML, and then transformed using an XSL transformation, and then perhaps transformed again. As a one-off request, the overhead of this isn't too great, but if every request requires this to be done for each component, the time and processing taken might become unacceptable. Simple techniques such as caching can drastically improve performance in this sort of situation.

On the other hand, we must not become obsessed with squeezing every last millisecond of performance out of our application. Doing so might mean that we end up sacrificing simplicity and manageability, which are much more likely to cause us problems in the future. When our code is kept clean and simple, it also allows us to easily find and fix the crucial bottlenecks in our system.

Specific Page Tweaks

It's likely that most of the pages of our site will stick to a generic layout, but sometimes the rules need to be bent slightly. If we create a system for laying out pages, we must be prepared for those freak situations we weren't expecting. That doesn't mean we need to build a system that can cater for all the possible things that could ever happen, rather we should keep things simple so any changes at a later date are painless and not likely to break half the site.

Assembling Component-Based Pages

We've already touched on how we should be able to assemble pages from smaller components. This might not be needed for some sites – perhaps the site only ever contains a single element of functionality per page. However, more often than not, pages are built up from smaller components, many of which are reused across different pages. The front page of a site is a common place for this to happen.

If assembling component-based pages is needed there are other factors to consider, such as how we control which components are displayed. Once a user enters the forum section of the site, they are probably no longer interested in seeing the component displaying the latest weather forecast. Do we need to control this; where do we control this; how do we control this?

Retaining Flexibility Inside Components

Our components are likely to have more than simple paragraphs of text in them. Do we still need to be able to use complicated table layouts, images, JavaScript, forms, applets and whatever else we can use in HTML these days? Will the decorators affect these when they are applied? How about other components on the same page?

Integration With Existing Code

Do we need to start building a site from scratch or can we integrate old with new? Sometimes starting over from scratch seems like the only option, because the old stuff will not fit into our new architecture, but this should only ever be a last resort. Although old code will rarely work with the new without some modification, the time taken to perform the modifications will usually be a lot less than writing the code from scratch.

On the other hand, it may be that rewriting really is the only option; but we should think long and hard before going down that route, looking closely at the existing code. Where possible, we should try to reuse what already exists. After all, we'd much rather go forward and build our exciting new add-ons than redo last year's work.

Some techniques can make it very hard to integrate new code with old code. Although it's highly unlikely that we can just copy the old system into the new and it will work without modification, we should be able to migrate parts of the old system without causing ourselves too much work.

Content From Disparate Sources

Do we need to integrate content from sources outside of our control? These could be from third party sites or web applications that we cannot modify (perhaps the original source code is no longer available).

For example, suppose we already have an online shopping-cart solution that needs to be used on our existing site, but it has not been written in JSP rather than Perl. How is that going to deal with our page layout system? Are we going to have to modify the source for this application so it uses a system similar to ours? What if we don't have access to the source code? How can we combine content from JSP and a Perl CGI script on the same page? What if extra details (such as variables about the user currently logged in or the state of the component) need to be transferred between the components?

The last thing we want to have to do is rewrite some of our old applications just because they were written in a different programming language.

Programmatic Control

Do the developers of a web application need to be able to control aspects of the presentation from their code? Suppose we built a custom content management system that stores and retrieves news articles in a backend database. We may wish to use different page layouts or styles depending on a flag stored in the database, such as a user's preferred color scheme or location. Our application will not know which layout to use until the code to generate the news page is actually executed. How do we let our code select the appropriate layouts to be displayed?

Techniques

Now that we have an idea of some of the crucial factors that need to be considered we can look at techniques to actually solve the problems. We'll take a look over some different strategies. For each technique we'll list the main advantages and disadvantages. In fact, some of the techniques we cover can cause more harm than good – they have been listed so we can recognize them and understand how to avoid them.

Copy and Paste

Generally, the graphic design for the website is done up front, and the necessary HTML to produce it is simply copied and pasted into every single page of the site, including the dynamically generated ones. To include additional components, the code for these is simply copied into the page where they are required.

Copying and pasting is perhaps the easiest short-term solution to laying out pages and the worst long-term solution. Because of its ease, it is also one of the most widely used solutions.

Advantages

- It's really, really easy to do up front
- No special tools or code are required
- It's fast because there are no overheads or additional processing involved in generating the layout
- Specific page tweaks are easy – the code on one page can easily be modified without affecting other pages

Disadvantages

- The HTML for the layout and style of the site is heavily intermixed with the code that provides the site's functionality. This can make it hard to modify one without affecting the other.
- Code is heavily duplicated. If the style or functionality of the site needs to change it can involve a lot of work, as every page needs the same modification to be performed. This can often result in differences between pages caused by human error. Search and replace tools can help to avoid this to an extent, but sometimes these aren't flexible enough to perform the necessary modifications.
- Technologies cannot be mixed, for example a fragment of Perl code cannot be copied into a JSP page and be expected to work.

Although the advantages look tempting, the disadvantages are too great. The cost of maintaining a site using a copy and paste strategy is very high. If at all possible, avoid this technique – it will only cause you suffering in the long term (and by long term I mean next week, not next year).

Code Generation Tools

This is a similar method to the copy and paste technique, except that a tool can automate the method of inserting the code. Typically, some files or templates are created that contain the code we want to copy, and then placeholders are inserted into all the files where we want the code inserted. This makes it much faster, less tedious, and greatly reduces the chance of human-error. It is important to note that the code is generated **before** the site is deployed.

There are many tools available that can scan files for placeholders and insert the right code. These include mail-merge tools, simple Perl scripts, the C language pre-processor, and most HTML development packages (the exact techniques used vary depending on the particular tool). A very simple approach is to use a tool such as Ant (http://jakarta.apache.org/ant/) and the `<filter>` task to replace tokens such as `@header@` and `@footer@` with predefined HTML fragments.

If we are using a pure JSP site, we could use the JSP include directive to insert common code when the JSP page is compiled.

Advantages

- Like copy and paste it's fast, as there is no overhead of additional processing to generate the layout at run time.
- It can be used on sites where dynamic page generation isn't possible. This could include basic web-servers or CD-ROM based distributions.
- Style and functionality can be easily decoupled from each other as the functionality of components can be developed with placeholders inserted where elements of style will be applied. The style can then be developed without the developer needing to know the details of the underlying component to which it shall be applied. The code generation stage is where the two elements are merged.
- Maintenance is quite easy as the code for the functionality or layout can easily be modified before regenerating and redeploying the site.
- As with layout, code can also be automatically generated.

Disadvantages

- If we're using the features built into a chosen HTML development package, there could be problems in using any other development tools on the same site. This often ends with an application locked to a proprietary tool.
- Like copy and paste, different technologies cannot be mixed. A code generator cannot insert Perl into a JSP page and expect it to work at run time.
- Programmatic control of layout (such as displaying different content for different scenarios such as time of day or the logged in user's details) is not possible as pages are generated at build rather than run time. Although it is possible to tweak the generated code after it has been built these tweaks have to be applied every time the pages are rebuilt.
- Specific page tweaks can be impossible unless templates are duplicated, or some flexible macros are allowed in the template system. A macro could contain conditional code, such as an IF/ELSE to allow the same template to be applied with slight differences depending on certain conditions. For example, if the current page is the front page, then we might display the usual template, but without the usual 'home' link.
- Auto-generated code is often unreadable to humans called upon to maintain it. Although, as a rule, developers should never touch auto-generated code, there are certain cases where it is necessary, particularly when sites start out as auto-generated and later move to a state where they are entirely maintained by hand.

Code generation is certainly a lot more desirable than copy and paste, but it still lacks flexibility. A better solution is to use server-side includes (which we will cover later).

XML and XSL Transformations

XSL Transformations (XSLT) allow a range of different approaches. The most common approach is to have the content of your site produce a simple XML representation of each component, which is then transformed into a suitable style for the site. Going into the details of how to achieve this is beyond the scope of this book.

Advantages

- It's very flexible as XSL allows much finer grain control than basic HTML decorators. For example, an XSL template could convert all `<h1>` tags into a chunk of HTML that includes a title laid out in a table with some images. But of course, all modern browsers support CSS, which provides similar functionality without having to modify any of the HTML tags.
- XSL is a standardized technology that is being increasingly adopted by developers.
- There are many tools and accompanying technologies available that can assist XML and XSL development.

Disadvantages

- The upfront infrastructure must be rolled out to bind aspects of XML together and perform automatic transformations. This could be a custom solution or based on existing third party products. Some Servlet engines provide out-of-the box XSL solutions, but these vary from vendor to vendor and most do not. Just placing an XSL page alongside an XML page is no guarantee that the XML will actually be transformed. Usually a tool such as a JSP tag library, servlet or filter is required to actually perform the transformation.
- Whoever implements the style and layout needs to understand XSLT. This can often end up with the bulk of the style being placed back in the hands of the developer.
- The developer and person responsible for layout must agree on the XML tags to be used.
- All dynamic content must be generated in XML, which can make integrating with existing web applications difficult unless they already output XML. XSL transformations typically cannot be applied to standard HTML unless it is in the form of well-formed XHTML or undergoes some cleaning at runtime.
- There is a general lack of tools for developing style and layout.
- Unless some form of caching is used, XSL transformations can have a negative impact on performance.

XML and XSLT are a very powerful combination, but restrict you to using XML based content and require a fair amount of upfront infrastructure preparation. Having said that, there are some excellent third party tools already existing to help you get started.

Server-Side Includes

Server-side includes (SSI) have been around nearly as long as web servers. They come in many different forms across various technologies, but the concept behind them is the same. Special directives are inserted into files that contain a reference to another file. When these are encountered by the web-server at run time, the referenced file is inserted in the place of the directive.

The following JSP pages for a sample site contain fragments of common page components that are to appear on each page: a page header, a footer, and a search form that points to the site's search engine. Each of these is very straightforward.

Here is `header.jsp`:

```
<table class="header">
  <tr>
    <td class="header">Welcome!</td>
  </tr>
</table>
```

Here is `searchform.jsp`:

```
<form action="searchresults.jsp">
  <b>Search for things:</b>
  <input type="text" name="query" />
  <input type="submit" value="Search!" />
</form>
```

Finally, here is `footer.jsp`:

```
<%@ page import="java.util.Date, java.text.DateFormat" %>

<%
  DateFormat df = DateFormat.getDateInstance(DateFormat.MEDIUM,
                                              request.getLocale());
%>
<table class="disclaimer">
  <tr>
    <td class="disclaimer">
        <b>Disclaimer:</b>
         All content on this site is mine.
         Today is <%= df.format(new Date()) %>
    </td>
  </tr>
</table>
```

The next page is the default entry page for the site, and it uses JSP server-side includes to assemble the previous three page components into a single page. The `<jsp:include>` tag tells the JSP processor to execute the contents of the referenced page, include them on the current page, and then return control to the current page

There is a subtle difference between the `<jsp:include>` tag and `<jsp:forward>` tag in that the latter does not return control to the current page. If `<jsp:forward>` is used, no content or code after it on the same page shall be executed.

Another tag similar to `<jsp:include>` is `<%@ include %>`. This tag will include the contents from the included file directly in the class built by the JSP engine. An advantage of this is that variables already defined in the page and declarations such as imports of packages and taglibs are automatically available to the included page. This can also be a disadvantage as it violates encapsulation and can lead to errors that are hard to trace. The `<%@ include %>` tag should therefore be used sparingly.

```
<html>
  <head>
    <title>Welcome</title>
    <link rel="stylesheet" type="text/css" href="style/global.css" />
  </head>
  <body>
    <jsp:include page="header.jsp" />
    <jsp:include page="searchform.jsp" />
    <h1>Welcome to my site!</h1>
    <p>This is my humble site. Thank you for dropping by.</p>
    <jsp:include page="footer.jsp" />
  </body>
</html>
```

The result is shown below:

A second page can then easily be constructed that has a similar look (by including the header and footer) and includes the same components (the search form):

```
<html>
  <head>
    <title>Search Results</title>
    <link rel="stylesheet" type="text/css" href="style/global.css" />
  </head>
  <body>
    <jsp:include page="header.jsp" />
    <jsp:include page="searchform.jsp" />
    <h2>Search Results for <%= request.getParameter( "query" ) %></h2>
    <ul>
      <% for ( int i = 0; i < 5; i++ ) { %>
      <li>A dummy result</li>
      <% } %>
```

```
    </ul>
      <jsp:include page="footer.jsp" />
    </body>
  </html>
```

This time, we don't need to worry about building the included components because we can just reuse them:

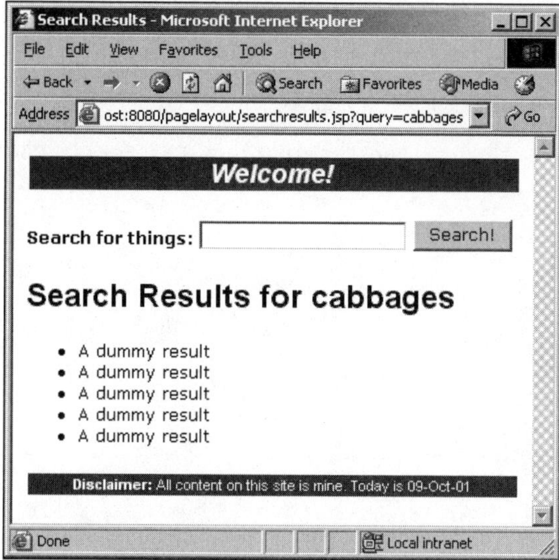

Now let's suppose we want to change the page layout to be used across the site. All we need to do is to modify the header and footer files that have been included, as we know that they are included by the other pages.

Here's the new header.jsp:

```
<table class="header">
  <tr>
    <td class="header">Welcome!</td>
  </tr>
</table>
```

```
<table class="main">
  <tr>
    <td class="menu"><jsp:include page="menu.jsp" /></td>
    <td>
```

We can also introduce a new component (referenced from the include above) that generates a little menu for our site (menu.jsp):

```
<p>
  <b>News</b><br />
  <a href="latestnews.jsp" class="menu">Latest</a><br />
  <a href="oldnews.jsp" class="menu">Old</a><br />
  <a href="searchnews.jsp" class="menu">Search</a><br />
```

```
  </p>
  <p>
    <b>Stuff</b><br />
    <a href="links.jsp" class="menu">Links</a><br />
    <a href="help.jsp" class="menu">Help</a><br />
    <a href="about.jsp" class="menu">About Us</a><br />
  </p>
```

The new footer.jsp:

```
<%@ page import="java.util.Date, java.text.DateFormat" %>

<% DateFormat df = DateFormat.getDateInstance(DateFormat.MEDIUM,
request.getLocale()); %>

    </td>
  </tr>
</table>

<table class="disclaimer">
  <tr>
    <td class="disclaimer">
       <b>Disclaimer:</b>
        All content on this site is mine.
        Today is <%= df.format(new Date()) %>
    </td>
  </tr>
</table>
```

All of our included files act as components. New components can be added in isolation. As illustrated in header.jsp, components can contain components (as per the Composite Design Pattern).

What may not have been obvious is that the combination of header.jsp and footer.jsp results in a decorator (as per the Decorator Design Pattern). These two files create HTML that surrounds the standard body of the page with layout and style information.

Now let's modify the decorator so we can change the title it displays in the page header, depending on the page that's calling it. We can do this by passing a parameter to the included page using the `<jsp:param>` tag. The parameter passed can be retrieved from the included page using `request.getParameter(String parameterName)`.

Here's `default.jsp`:

```
<html>
  <head>
    <title>Welcome</title>
    <link rel="stylesheet" type="text/css" href="style/global.css" />
  </head>
  <body>
    <jsp:include page="header.jsp">
      <jsp:param name="title" value="Welcome!" />
    </jsp:include>
    <jsp:include page="searchform.jsp" />
    <h1>Welcome to my site!</h1>
    <p>This is my humble site. Thank you for dropping by.</p>
    <jsp:include page="footer.jsp" />
  </body>
</html>
```

Here's the new `searchresults.jsp`:

```
<html>
  <head>
    <title>Search Results</title>
    <link rel="stylesheet" type="text/css" href="style/global.css" />
  </head>
  <body>
    <jsp:include page="header.jsp">
      <jsp:param name="title" value="Search Results" />
    </jsp:include>
    <jsp:include page="searchform.jsp" />
    <h2>Search Results for <%= request.getParameter( "query" ) %></h2>
    <ul>
      <% for ( int i = 0; i < 5; i++ ) { %>
      <li>A dummy result</li>
      <% } %>
    </ul>
    <jsp:include page="footer.jsp" />
  </body>
</html>
```

Finally, we change `header.jsp` to retrieve the `title` parameter that is passed to it:

```
<table class="header">
  <tr>
    <td class="header"><%= request.getParameter("title") %></td>
  </tr>
</table>

<table class="main">
  <tr>
    <td class="menu"><jsp:include page="menu.jsp" /></td>
    <td>
```

The results should be the same as the last two screenshots.

We've seen how to create decorators that can be applied to an entire page, how to pass parameters to them, and how to include components from other pages. We can combine these techniques to create a simple solution for including components in a page and decorating them.

First, we create a decorator for making components look nice by decorating them in a little box with a title. It is going to be called as an include and expects three parameters to be passed to it:

- `title`
  The title to display (e.g. Latest News)
- `width`
  The width of the box (e.g. 250)
- `page`
  The page of the actual component to use (e.g. `latestnews.jsp`)

Here is the code for `component-decorator.jsp`:

```
<table style="width:<%= request.getParameter("width") %>"
       class="searchBox">
  <tr>
    <td class="searchBoxTitle">
        <%= request.getParameter("title") %>
    </td>
  </tr>
  <tr>
    <td class="searchBoxBody">
        <% pageContext.include( request.getParameter( "page" ) ); %>
    </td>
  </tr>
</table>
```

Notice how the included decorator includes the page specified by the `page` parameter.

We're using `pageContext.include()` here, instead of `<jsp:include>`. These provide the same functionality, except one provides us with an interface, which we can access through Java, allowing us the control to pass custom variables across instead of hard-coded strings.

Now we replace our earlier include that called `searchform.jsp` with one to our new include, passing `searchform.jsp` as one of the parameters (in `default.jsp`):

```
<html>
  <head>
    <title>Welcome</title>
    <link rel="stylesheet" type="text/css" href="style/global.css" />
  </head>
  <body>
    <jsp:include page="header.jsp">
      <jsp:param name="title" value="Welcome!" />
    </jsp:include>
```

```
      <jsp:include page="component-decorator.jsp">
        <jsp:param name="title" value="Search Box" />
        <jsp:param name="width" value="150" />
        <jsp:param name="page" value="searchform.jsp" />
      </jsp:include>
      <h1>Welcome to my site!</h1>
      <p>This is my humble site. Thank you for dropping by.</p>
      <jsp:include page="footer.jsp" />
    </body>
  </html>
```

Here is the result:

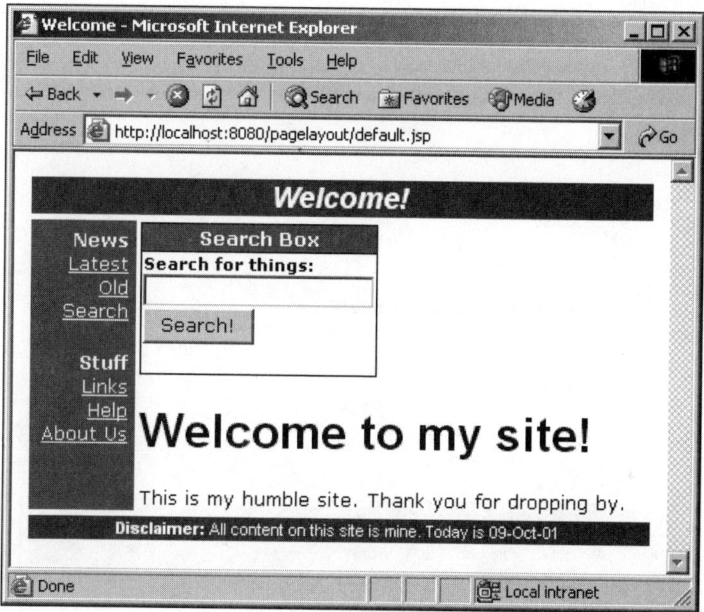

However, our search box should appear on every page, not just the front page. In that case we should move it out of `default.jsp` and into our page decorator. Let's create a right hand column using the table we defined in `header.jsp` and `footer.jsp` and place the component there. This will remove some of the clutter in `default.jsp` and stop us from having to duplicate the includes in the other pages of the site:

```
<html>
  <head>
    <title>Welcome</title>
    <link rel="stylesheet" type="text/css" href="style/global.css" />
  </head>
  <body>
    <jsp:include page="header.jsp">
      <jsp:param name="title" value="Welcome!" />
    </jsp:include>
    <%-- jsp:include was here, but has now been moved to footer.jsp --%>
    <h1>Welcome to my site!</h1>
```

```
<p>This is my humble site. Thank you for dropping by.</p>

    <jsp:include page="footer.jsp" />
  </body>
</html>
```

Now we have the includes as part of `footer.jsp`:

```
<%@ page import="java.util.Date, java.text.DateFormat" %>

<% DateFormat df = DateFormat.getDateInstance(DateFormat.MEDIUM,
request.getLocale()); %>

    </td>
    <td class="search">
      <jsp:include page="component-decorator.jsp">
        <jsp:param name="title" value="Search Box" />
        <jsp:param name="width" value="165" />
        <jsp:param name="page" value="searchform.jsp" />
      </jsp:include>
    </td>
  </tr>
</table>

<table class="disclaimer">
  <tr>
    <td class="disclaimer">
       <b>Disclaimer:</b>
        All content on this site is mine.
        Today is <%= df.format(new Date()) %>
    </td>
  </tr>
</table>
```

Here's the result:

Let's just add another component to our site to show how easy it is. We will create `latestnews.jsp` to display any breaking news:

```
<%-- This should be generated from a database --%>
<p>
  <span class="big">Tuesday</span><br />
  Got out of bed
</p>
<p>
  <span class="big">Wednesday</span><br />
  Had some food
</p>
<p>
  <span class="big">Thursday</span><br />
  Went back to bed
</p>
```

And then add it to our page `footer.jsp` decorator using our component decorator:

```
<%@ page import="java.util.Date, java.text.DateFormat" %>

<% DateFormat df = DateFormat.getDateInstance(DateFormat.MEDIUM,
request.getLocale()); %>

    </td>
    <td class="search">
      <jsp:include page="component-decorator.jsp">
        <jsp:param name="title" value="Search Box" />
        <jsp:param name="width" value="165" />

        <jsp:param name="page" value="searchform.jsp" />
      </jsp:include>
      <br />
      <jsp:include page="component-decorator.jsp">
        <jsp:param name="title" value="Latest News" />
        <jsp:param name="width" value="165" />
        <jsp:param name="page" value="latestnews.jsp" />
      </jsp:include>
    </td>
  </tr>
</table>

<table class="disclaimer">
  <tr>
    <td class="disclaimer">
       <b>Disclaimer:</b>
        All content on this site is mine.
        Today is <%= df.format(new Date()) %>
    </td>
  </tr>
</table>
```

That was easy:

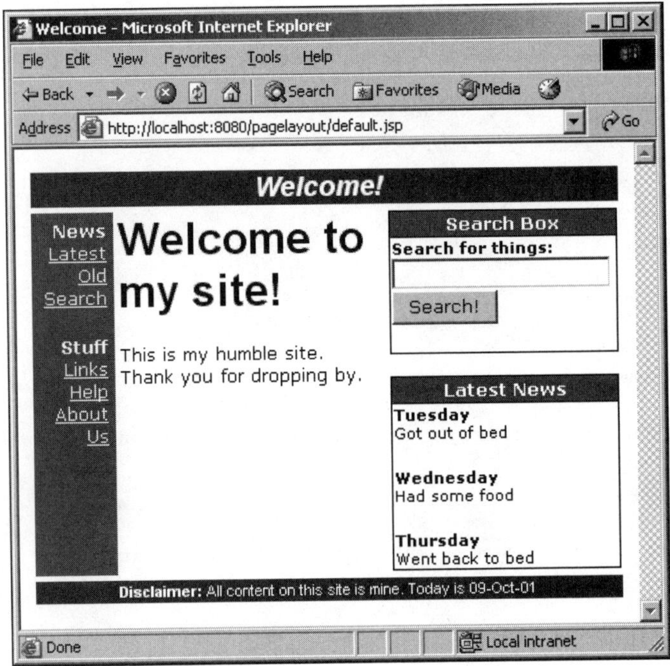

Advantages

- The design can easily be decoupled from content and functionality allowing each to be developed in isolation.
- No third-party tools are needed. JSP server-side includes are supported by all standard JSP containers.
- Allowing dynamic parameters to be passed around retains a degree of programmatic control.
- Easy to get started with.
- Easy to maintain the site as it grows and changes.
- Extra flexibility can be added by using inline JSP scriptlets to deal with special circumstances. For example, dynamic code can easily be inserted into both the decorators and components to provide conditional functionality.

Disadvantages

- Too many includes can get confusing, although this can easily be remedied by sorting using suitable naming conventions, dividing pages into directories, and documenting the component hierarchy.
- Decorators are executed **before** the component they are decorating. This means that it's too late for the component to alter the behavior of the decorator. For example, a component may wish to be responsible for choosing the title of the decorator.

- There is a distinct separation between pages that are requested directly by the browser (for example, `default.jsp` and `searchresults.jsp`) and included components (for example, `searchform.jsp` and `latestnews.jsp`), making it hard to use a page in both contexts. This is because we have to explicitly call the includes to the page decorator (`header.jsp` and `footer.jsp`) in pages requested by the browser.
- The page decorators have to be split into two files. This can make them awkward to work with and neither of them contains well-formed HTML (for example table start and end tags). HTML tools probably will not be able to work with these.
- Pages requested by the browser must be JSP pages (or at least something built on top of the Servlets framework) as you need to call the include method. This makes it hard to use existing systems developed using other technologies such as Perl or PHP.
- JSP scriptlets are interspersed in the presentation decorators, making it harder for people with little JSP knowledge to maintain.

Server-side includes are a step in the right direction. They bring a lot of power, however there are still some shortcomings, which we've seen. They're a good solution for applying decorators to components, but fall a bit short when it comes to decorating entire pages.

JSP Tags

Using custom JSP tags, we can build on the techniques we were using with server-side includes, however we can also encapsulate any additional functionality inside the tag, hiding it from the front-end code to the application. Although tags require more upfront development work, once written they are very easy to understand and use.

As an example, let's create a simple tag-library to allow us to apply a decorator to a chunk of HTML on an existing JSP page. We could create a simple tag that wraps around the body of the HTML that the decorator needs to apply – extra attributes such as the title could be passed to the tag:

```
<%@ taglib uri="layout" prefix="layout" %>
<html>
  <head>
    <title>Welcome</title>
    <link rel="stylesheet" type="text/css" href="style/global.css" />
  </head>
  <body>
    <h1>Welcome to my site.</h1>
    <layout:decorate title="Search Engine">
      <form action="search.jsp">
        Please type search term below<br />
        <input type="text" name="query" />
        <input type="submit" />
      </form>
    </layout:decorate>
    <p>Blah blah blah</p>
  </body>
</html
```

At run time, the contents of the tag body would be evaluated as a normal JSP page, except the tag would not display it directly. Instead it would include the contents of a decorator file, inserting the relevant data into the decorator's placeholders.

The decorator could also contain simple tags for marking placeholders for the data:

```
<%@ taglib uri="layout" prefix="layout" %>

<table class="searchBox">
  <tr>
    <td class="searchBoxTitle">
        <layout:title />
    </td>
  </tr>
  <tr>
    <td class="searchBoxBody">
        <layout:body />
    </td>
  </tr>
</table>
```

These tags will simply insert the data extracted by the previous tag. Constructing a set of tags like this is easy. Firstly we define a tag (`DecorateTag`) that shall apply the inline decorator.

```
package com.wrox.layout.taglib;

import javax.servlet.jsp.*;
import javax.servlet.jsp.tagext.*;
```

Our tag has body content (data between the opening and closing tags) that needs to be evaluated, so we extend `BodyTagSupport`. This class implements the `BodyTag` interface required by JSP tags that need to access the data inside the tag with some default implementation and utility methods:

```
public class DecorateTag extends BodyTagSupport {
```

As our tag has an attribute passed to allow the title to be set, we need to allow the JSP container to set this attribute:

```
  private String title;

  public void setTitle(String title) {
    this.title = title;
  }
```

The JSP container calls the `doAfterBody()` method when it has evaluated the body to determine whether it should write it back to the browser or not. The default is to write it out, however we don't want it written out yet, because we want the body to be stored in a temporary variable so the decorator can execute and insert the body in the correct place (in the HTML template). To prevent the body being written out immediately, we override this method to return the code that avoids this:

```
public int doAfterBody() {
  return SKIP_BODY;
}
```

This method is called just after the previous method, signifying that the JSP container has reached the closing tag. Not until we reach the closing tag do we want to actually apply the decorator, so we can be sure we have all the required data. If anything bad happens inside this method, we throw a `JspException`, which is caught by the container and handled appropriately (in the form of an error-page):

```
public int doEndTag() throws JspException {
  try {
```

We need our decorator to be able to access the title of the component, so we set it as an attribute in the JSP `PageContext` with the name `title`. When manipulating attributes, the default behavior is to store them in a scope only available to the current JSP page. This is not suitable because we need to access the attribute from the decorator page. Instead we have to store it in the scope of the request, which will keep the attribute until the HTTP request is complete. The JSP specification also allows attributes to be stored in the session scope, which lasts for a single user's entire session and the application scope, which is shared between all users and lasts until the entire web application is shutdown. The third parameter to the method signifies this:

```
    pageContext.setAttribute("title", title,
                             PageContext.REQUEST_SCOPE);
```

In the same way we stored the title, we also need to store the body of the tag. The `BodyTagSupport` class makes this easy for us by providing a `BodyContent` object, which encapsulates the data inside the tag:

```
    pageContext.setAttribute("body", bodyContent.getString(),
                             PageContext.REQUEST_SCOPE);
```

Now that we've extracted the data necessary and stored it in the request scope, we include the contents of our decorator JSP page. The actual decorator that is included contains the HTML template and will retrieve the values we previously set. This works in exactly the same manner as the `<jsp:include>` tag we used previously:

```
    pageContext.include("/component-decorator.jsp");
```

After our decorator has been included, we want the JSP engine to carry on processing the rest of the page as normal. Returning the `EVAL_PAGE` status signifies this:

```
      return EVAL_PAGE;
    } catch (Exception e) {
      throw new JspException(e.getMessage());
    }
  }
}
```

This class needs to be compiled and placed in `WEB-INF\classes\`. If it's to be reused it could be bundled into a JAR file and put in `WEB-INF\lib\` instead. Now we need to create our Tag Library Descriptor (TLD) so the JSP container understands what to do with the tag. We will call the following `layout.tld`.

We start with our standard headers for a TLD: XML and DTD declarations, tag implementation version, and a short name to identify our tags (`layout` seems an appropriate name):

```
<?xml version="1.0"?>
<!DOCTYPE taglib PUBLIC
        "-//Sun Microsystems, Inc.//DTD JSP Tag Library 1.1//EN"
        "http://java.sun.com/j2ee/dtds/web-jsptaglibrary_1_1.dtd">
<taglib>
  <tlibversion>1.0</tlibversion>
  <jspversion>1.1</jspversion>
  <shortname>layout</shortname>
```

Define our tag named `decorate` and associate it with our class:

```
  <tag>
    <name>decorate</name>
    <tagclass>com.wrox.layout.taglib.DecorateTag</tagclass>
```

Our tag contains some body content, which is to be interpreted as standard JSP:

```
    <bodycontent>JSP</bodycontent>
```

Finally, our tag has an attribute called `title`. This attribute is not necessarily required, and can be a runtime expression value (e.g. generated on the fly using a JSP `<%= xxxx %>` expression). This is mapped by the JSP engine to our `setTitle()` method in the class:

```
    <attribute>
    <name>title</name>
    <required>false</required>
    <rtexprvalue>true</rtexprvalue>
  </attribute>
  </tag>
</taglib>
```

To deploy our tag we firstly need to place this file in the `WEB-INF\` directory and then insert a declaration in `web.xml` so our tag is available to use in the web application:

```
...
<taglib>
  <taglib-uri>layout</taglib-uri>
  <taglib-location>/WEB-INF/layout.tld</taglib-location>
</taglib>
...
```

Now we create the tags that act as placeholders in the decorator JSP page. We require two tags, one to insert the title and the other to insert the body. Instead of creating two very similar classes that only differ in the actual attribute they request, we can make one abstract tag class and two simple subclasses that simply override the name of the attribute to retrieve. This results in less code and makes changes easier (particularly when we end up with a lot more tags). Here is the `WriteAttributeTag` (the abstract superclass to the other two tags) class:

```
package com.wrox.layout.taglib;

import javax.servlet.jsp.*;
import javax.servlet.jsp.tagext.*;
```

As our tags do not contain a body, we shall extend the much simpler `TagSupport` class (that lacks the methods required for body tags):

```
public abstract class WriteAttributeTag extends TagSupport {
```

The only thing our abstract class shall not do is to determine the name of the attribute (`title` or `body`). The `getAttributeName()` method is implemented by the subclasses:

```
  protected abstract String getAttributeName();
```

We will write the actual value out when we reach the end of the tag. This is the typical place for body-less tags to perform their work:

```
  public int doEndTag() throws JspException {
```

We now need to retrieve the data stored earlier from the page context in the request scope. The result is cast to a `String`. The first argument to this method is the name of attribute to retrieve – this of course is determined by the subclasses implementations of `getAttributeName()`:

```
    try {
      String value = (String)pageContext.getAttribute(
                                           getAttributeName(),
                                           PageContext.REQUEST_SCOPE );
```

Write the retrieved value to the page:

```
      pageContext.getOut().write(value);
```

And carry on with the rest of the page:

```
      return EVAL_PAGE;
    } catch (Exception e) {
      throw new JspException(e.getMessage());
    }
  }
}
```

We then create our two subclasses for the individual tags. First we have `WriteTitleTag`:

```
package com.wrox.layout.taglib;

public class WriteTitleTag extends WriteAttributeTag {
```

```
    protected String getAttributeName() {
      return "title";
    }
  }
```

Then we have WriteBodyTag:

```
  package com.wrox.layout.taglib;

  public class WriteBodyTag extends WriteAttributeTag {

    protected String getAttributeName() {
      return "body";
    }
  }
```

These subclasses simply define the name of the attribute to be retrieved by the parent class. Compile them and add them to WEB-INF\classes\ as before.

We can now add these new tags to our TLD:

```
    <tag>
      <name>title</name>
      <tagclass>com.wrox.layout.taglib.WriteTitleTag</tagclass>
      <bodycontent>empty</bodycontent>
    </tag>
    <tag>
      <name>body</name>
      <tagclass>com.wrox.layout.taglib.WriteBodyTag</tagclass>
      <bodycontent>empty</bodycontent>
    </tag>
```

These tags are pretty simple – no attributes and no body content.

Now we can put it all together and actually use them. Here's a new default.jsp. In our simple page, we first of all import the tag using a JSP taglib declaration, and then we actually use it to apply a decorator to an inline search form:

```
  <%@ taglib uri="layout" prefix="layout" %>
  <html>
    <head>
      <title>Welcome</title>
      <link rel="stylesheet" type="text/css" href="style/global.css" />
    </head>
    <body>
      <h1>Welcome to my site.</h1>
      <layout:decorate title="Search Engine">
      <form action="search.jsp">
        Please type search term below<br />
        <input type="text" name="query" />
        <input type="submit" />
      </form>
```

```
    </layout:decorate>
    <p>Blah blah blah</p>
  </body>
</html
```

Now we create our decorator (component-decorator.jsp) – similar to before except now we can use our tags:

```
<%@ taglib uri="layout" prefix="layout" %>

<table class="searchBox">
  <tr>
    <td class="searchBoxTitle">
        <layout:title />
    </td>
  </tr>
  <tr>
    <td class="searchBoxBody">
        <layout:body />
    </td>
  </tr>
</table>
```

Again, we declare our tags and then we insert the placeholders. All we need to do now is look at the result:

That was a simple example of how tags can be used to make decorator applying and building easier. The trickiest part of the tag building has already been done. From here the tags could be easily reused and further expanded to be more flexible and generic.

Advantages

- JSP tags are very clean and simple to use. Somebody with HTML experience but no Java experience could easily understand how to use them.
- The Java for JSP tags is relatively simple to develop and to expand as needs evolve.

Disadvantages

- The tags work very well for decorating included components in a page. However, they do not offer an elegant solution to decorating entire pages. It is possible to use the tags to build a system for laying out entire sites, but the complexity of this may defeat its purpose.
- When using JSP tags, you tightly couple the system with JSP. Integrating other components that are not JSP based may be problematic.

Overall, JSP tags are a nice solution that's simple and easy to develop. Tags can easily be extended so we can get customized functionality without cluttering up our HTML and JSP code. The downside we still have is that components cannot easily control decorators and that they still do not provide an elegant solution for decorating entire pages.

> *We've touched on creating our own tags here, but it's worth mentioning that Apache's Struts Framework (see Chapter 2 for details) contains a library called Template Tags and there is also a product called Tiles, both of which are out-of-the box versions of what we've developed here.*

Content Filtering

The final technique we are going to explore takes a slightly different approach. One of the great new features of the Servlet 2.3 API is the ability to define filters, and also to be able to pass around our own versions of the `HttpServletRequest` and `HttpServletResponse` objects in our pages.

> *For more information on Filters and how to use them you should refer to Chapter 3.*

Previously we've been calling a decorator, which in turn includes the content. The problem with this is that our content may need to control aspects of the decorator but it's already too late in the request's lifecycle. Instead, we will generate our content first and then apply the decorator afterwards. Conceptually, this is simple:

- The request is received
- The servlet engine invokes the filter before anything else
- The filter sets up its own `HttpServletResponse`, which stores details about the output page to a temporary buffer instead of sending it to the browser immediately
- The filter allows the original request to be processed as normal using the custom response object
- After the request has been processed, the filter extracts any necessary content from the buffered response
- The filter then forwards the request to an appropriate decorator, passing the extracted content
- The decorator outputs itself to the browser, inserting any parsed content

Pages (or decorators) can contain links to other components that are processed in a similar way, in that a buffer is set up before the vanilla component is included and then the result is sent to a decorator.

Advantages

- The content of the page or component does not necessarily need to be a JSP page (or even Java based). It could be plain HTML, or content produced by legacy code such as CGI.
- As the content is generated before the decorator it has the option to pass information to the decorator (such as style of navigation bar, author of document, or document category). This is particularly useful for dynamically generated content such as that produced by a content management system.
- Based on the results of the content, different decorators could be applied (if any at all).
- Very quick and simple to use if utilizing an existing filtering tool.

Disadvantages

- Storing the contents of the page or component to a buffer means that the whole thing is temporarily stored in memory (usually, content is sent back to the browser as it is generated and then forgotten about). Although this buffer does not last for long, enough memory needs to be made available to store it (and any other pages also being requested at the same time).
- Extracting content from the page can require overhead as some form of parsing needs to occur.
- For each page requested, an additional internal request is made to generate the decorator, which is extra load for the servlet engine.
- It's generally tricky to write and debug content filtering tools that are flexible and fast.

Although there are significant advantages to using content-filtering, the complexity of building the tool can be a large burden – developing this from scratch could take more time than the rest of the site.

SiteMesh is an out-of-the-box content filtering tool that can be dropped into any new or existing web-application. It's an open-source product released by the OpenSymphony project (http://www.opensymphony.com/sitemesh/). It's fast, easy to use, and addresses every one of the factors we considered at the beginning of the chapter.

To demonstrate how it's used we're going to use it with an example application.

Example Application

Now we are familiar with some basic techniques, we can put most of them together to create an application. For the remainder of this chapter we shall take an existing application that consists of a collection of small components and assemble them into an application that looks impressive. We shall not go into depth how the functionality is implemented but explain how it is all assembled into the final look. For example, we're not going to show the CSS stylesheets we use, but as usual all the code is available for download from http://www.wrox.com/.

We'll mainly be taking advantage of server-side includes and SiteMesh, but to run the full application you will need `dom4j.jar` in Tomcat's classpath and the XTags tag library. You can download them from http://dom4j.org/download.html and http://jakarta.apache.org/taglibs/doc/xtags-doc/intro.html respectively.

Getting Started

Starting from scratch, we configure the web-application to use SiteMesh. First of all we need to download SiteMesh (from http://www.opensymphony.com/sitemesh/) and create a new web application directory structure containing the following files:

```
/WEB-INF/lib/sitemesh.jar
/WEB-INF/sitemesh-decorator.tld
/WEB-INF/sitemesh-page.tld
/WEB-INF/web.xml
/WEB-INF/sitemesh.xml
/WEB-INF/decorators.xml
```

Configuration of SiteMesh consists of placing four entries in `web.xml`:

```
<?xml version="1.0" encoding="ISO-8859-1"?>

<!DOCTYPE web-app
    PUBLIC "-//Sun Microsystems, Inc.//DTD Web Application 2.3//EN"
    " http://java.sun.com/dtd/web-app_2_3.dtd">

<web-app>
```

The core of SiteMesh is a Servlet 2.3 filter that will extract the relevant contents of each request and will apply the appropriate decorator (if any at all) before sending the result back to the browser. Here we define the filter:

```
  <filter>
    <filter-name>sitemesh</filter-name>
    <filter-class>com.sitemesh.filter.PageFilter</filter-class>
  </filter>
```

Here we setup the URL pattern that the filter applies to. We have used `/*` because we want all requests in all directories of the web application to be processed by SiteMesh:

```
  <filter-mapping>
    <filter-name>sitemesh</filter-name>
    <url-pattern>/*</url-pattern>
  </filter-mapping>
```

A convenience tag library is used to make building our decorators easier. We shall refer to these as **decorator tags** for the remainder of this example. When a decorator is built, decorator tags are inserted as placeholders for the actual content from the component:

```
  <taglib>
    <taglib-uri>sitemesh-decorator</taglib-uri>
    <taglib-location>/WEB-INF/sitemesh-decorator.tld</taglib-location>
  </taglib>
```

Finally a second tag library is used to allow us to apply decorators to included and inline components in any other JSP page. We shall refer to these as **page tags**:

```
    <taglib>
      <taglib-uri>sitemesh-page</taglib-uri>
      <taglib-location>/WEB-INF/sitemesh-page.tld</taglib-location>
    </taglib>

  </web-app>
```

Now we need to create our SiteMesh configuration file (`sitemesh.xml`) in the `WEB-INF\` directory. It defines the configuration for two main components of SiteMesh:

- `page-parsers`
  The classes responsible for extracting information from a page
- `decorator-mappers`
  The classes responsible for determining the correct decorators to use for a request

We shall keep the file minimal and use the default classes bundled with SiteMesh:

```
  <sitemesh>
    <page-parsers>
```

To extract the content from any items with a MIME-type of `text/html` we'll use the `FastPageParser`. This extracts HTML content from the page or component **fast**:

```
      <parser content-type="text/html"
              class="com.sitemesh.parser.FastPageParser" />
```

For all other MIME-types (images, downloadable files, plain text, and so on) we shall use the `DefaultPageParser`. This simply doesn't parse the page at all, so the page is written directly back to the browser and not processed by SiteMesh, causing no extra overhead to be generated:

```
      <parser default="true"
              class="com.sitemesh.parser.DefaultPageParser" />
    </page-parsers>
```

When a response is generated from a component, it is first parsed by the suitable parser for the MIME-type (defined above), and then each configured decorator-mapper is supplied details about the request and the parsed page until one of them can suggest a suitable decorator to use. As soon as one decorator-mapper suggests a parser, no more are considered. If no decorator-mappers respond, no decorator is applied to the page or component.

For now, we shall only use one decorator-mapper. The `ConfigDecoratorMapper` will read a configuration file that defines decorators and maps them to URL patterns. Decorator-mappers shall be described in more detail later in the chapter. The `config` parameter states the file to use (relative to the web application context root):

```
  <decorator-mappers>
    <mapper class="com.sitemesh.mapper.ConfigDecoratorMapper">
      <param name="config" value="/WEB-INF/decorators.xml" />
    </mapper>
  </decorator-mappers>
</sitemesh>
```

For the last part of the initial configuration we create a file containing the decorator-mappings (`decorators.xml`). This file can contain many `<decorator>` and `<decorator-mapping>` elements. The convention of the file is similar to that used for servlets and filters in `web.xml` (named definitions and URL pattern matching).

Next, we create our main decorator to use on the pages of the site, called `main`. The actual look of the decorator is specified in a file called `main.jsp` in the `decorators\` directory at the root of the web application. We've put the file in this directory so we don't confuse it with other content:

```
<decorators>
  <decorator>
    <decorator-name>main</decorator-name>
    <jsp-file>/decorators/main.jsp</jsp-file>
  </decorator>
```

This mapping says that for any URL-pattern requested, the main decorator shall be applied:

```
  <decorator-mapping>
    <decorator-name>main</decorator-name>
    <url-pattern>*</url-pattern>
  </decorator-mapping>
</decorators>
```

Building our First Page and Decorator

To start our application off, we'll create a simple front page placed in the root directory called `index.html`:

```
<html>
  <head>
    <title>My News!</title>
  </head>
  <body>
    <h3>Welcome!</h3>
    <p>Inside you'll find all the latest news...</p>
  </body>
</html>
```

Notice the lack of presentation in this file. It's just a plain HTML file. It's not even a JSP page. SiteMesh doesn't care if the page is static or dynamic, and if it is dynamic, it doesn't care how it's generated (it could be a JSP page, a servlet, or even a CGI).

Now we create our main decorator (main.jsp) that we configured in decorators.xml. We create a basic HTML template for our decorator that consists of a simple table containing a common header and footer, plus the placeholders to insert the content parsed out of our pages. The page parser we are using extracts three chunks of content from the page:

```
<%@ taglib uri="sitemesh-decorator" prefix="decorator" %>

<html>
  <head>
```

This is where the title of the page obtained from the text inside the <title> tag in the <head> section of the original HTML page is inserted:

```
    <title><decorator:title /></title>
```

This is where the entire contents of the <head> section of the original page excluding the title are inserted. This includes things like <script>, <link>, or <meta> tags that have been specified on the undecorated page, so they still exist in the decorated version:

```
    <decorator:head />
    <link rel="stylesheet" type="text/css" href="style/global.css" />
  </head>

  <body>
    <table class="main">
      <tr>
        <td class="title">
```

We also want a title to be inserted at the top of the page:

```
          <decorator:title />
        </td>
      </tr>
      <tr>
        <td class="body">
```

This is where the entire contents of the <body> section of the original page are inserted:

```
          <decorator:body />
        </td>
      </tr>
      <tr>
        <td class="footer">
          footer
        </td>
      </tr>
    </table>
  </body>
</html>
```

Now, for the magic, we access our plain `index.html` file using our webbrowser through our servlet engine:

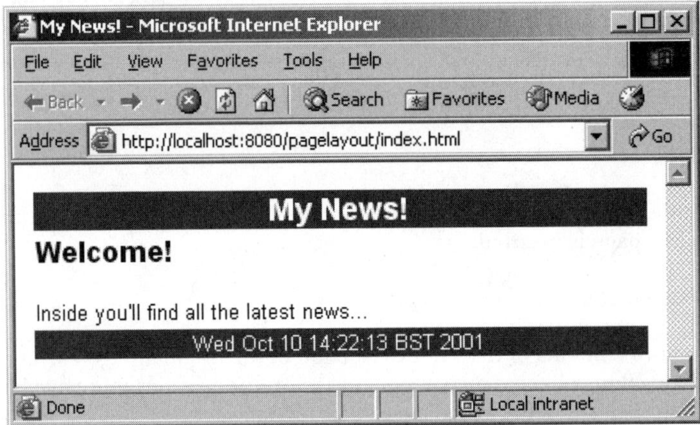

What happened?

- The HTTP request was made to the servlet engine
- The servlet engine invoked the SiteMesh filter
- The SiteMesh filter invoked the original page (`index.html`)
- The original page was stored in a temporary buffer instead of being written directly back to the browser.
- The buffer is then parsed to extract content to be used by the decorator such as the contents of the `<head>`, `<title>` and `<body>` tags
- The SiteMesh filter asked the configured decorator-mapper if a decorator is to be applied
- The decorator-mapper replied saying that `decorators/main.jsp` should be used
- The SiteMesh filter then forwarded the request to the decorator
- The decorator inserted the content parsed from the page where the placeholder tags were
- The final page was returned to the browser

Although it sounds like a lot of processing, optimizations occur behind the scenes that make the process very fast, such as a parser optimized for extracting only the relevant parts from the HTML (instead of building a generic parse-tree) and caching techniques.

The actual page containing the content could just as easily be a JSP page or any other dynamically generated page.

At this point we can add more pages into our web application. If you want to add your own pages here or code from an existing web application, go ahead. We will make use of the sample news application we developed in Chapter 3. By default, any new pages we add shall also have our main decorator applied.

Composite Components

Now we need some simple components that make up the site. Below are screenshots of some simple HTML pages before and after they have the main decorator applied:

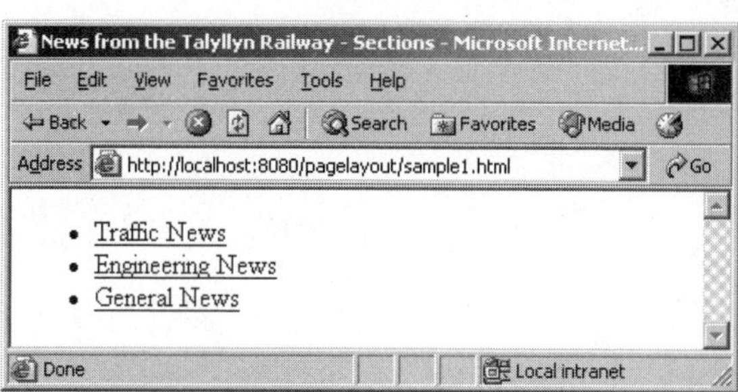

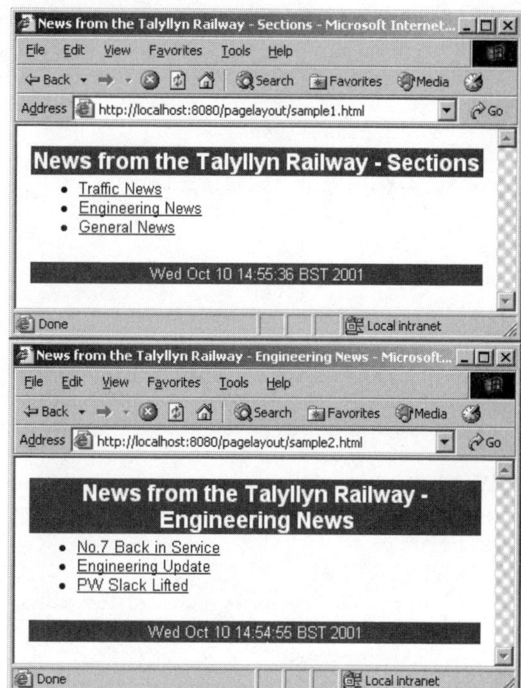

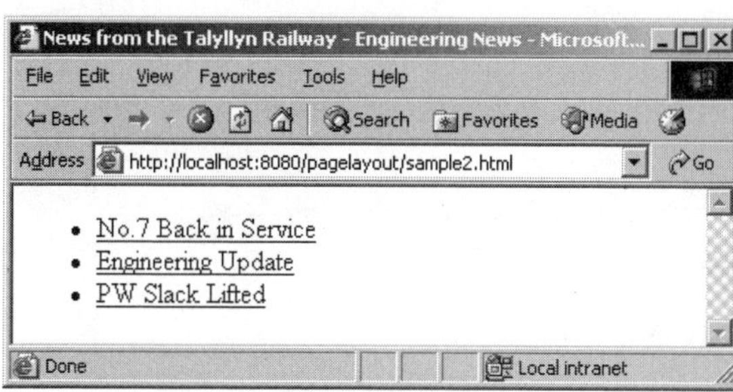

Note that the main title on the page is obtained from the `<title>` tag in the original HTML page. Now, suppose we want every page on the site to include one of our components above (for example, the list of news sections), it would make sense to add a server-side include to that JSP in our main decorator.

However, the page we're including is a full HTML page. It contains `<html>`, `<head>`, `<title>`, and `<body>` tags. It also does not contain any information about how it is to be presented (other than the content inside it). We need to treat this like the other pages on the site – SiteMesh should parse the contents out and then apply a decorator.

Although the page contains a complete HTML document, we can run it through SiteMesh to extract only the relevant information (the title and the body). This means a complete HTML page can be used as an included component without any modification. Of course, we would use a decorator to define how the title and the body are to be presented by our inline component.

We will reuse the JSP pages from the application we developed in Chapter 3. Copy the `WEB-INF` directory and all its contents from this application and remove the following lines from `listAllSections.jsp`:

```
    <h1>News from the Talyllyn Railway</h1>
    <h2>News Sections</h2>
```

Next, we need to create a new decorator for our component. This is done the same way as our main decorator. We create a decorator (`panel.jsp`) in the `decorators` directory:

```
<%@ taglib uri="sitemesh-decorator" prefix="decorator" %>

<table class="panel">
  <tr>
    <td class="panelTitle">
        <decorator:title />
    </td>
  </tr>
  <tr>
    <td class="panelBody">
        <decorator:body />
    </td>
  </tr>
</table>
```

We also need to define our decorator in the `decorators.xml` mapping file. This allows us to refer to our decorator as `panel`:

```
  <decorator>
    <decorator-name>panel</decorator-name>
    <jsp-file>/decorators/panel.jsp</jsp-file>
  </decorator>
```

Next we modify our main decorator to include this component:

```
<%@ taglib uri="sitemesh-decorator" prefix="decorator" %>
<%@ taglib uri="sitemesh-page" prefix="page" %>

<html>
  <head>
    <title><decorator:title /></title>
    <decorator:head />
    <link rel="stylesheet" type="text/css" href="style/global.css" />
  </head>

  <body>
    <table class="main">
      <tr>
        <td class="title" colspan="2">
          <decorator:title />
        </td>
      </tr>
      <tr>
        <td>
          <decorator:body />
        </td>
```

The tag below takes two arguments: one defines the page containing the content of the component and the other the name of the decorator to apply to it:

```
          <td>
            <page:applyDecorator  name="panel"
                                  page="/news/listAllSections.jsp" />
          </td>
        </tr>
        <tr>
          <td class="footer" colspan="2">
            <%= (new java.util.Date()).toString() %>
          </td>
        </tr>
      </table>
    </body>
</html>
```

And there it is. Our component (which was designed as it was a standalone page, with vanilla HTML) is included, parsed, and has a decorator applied to it so it appears as a component of another page:

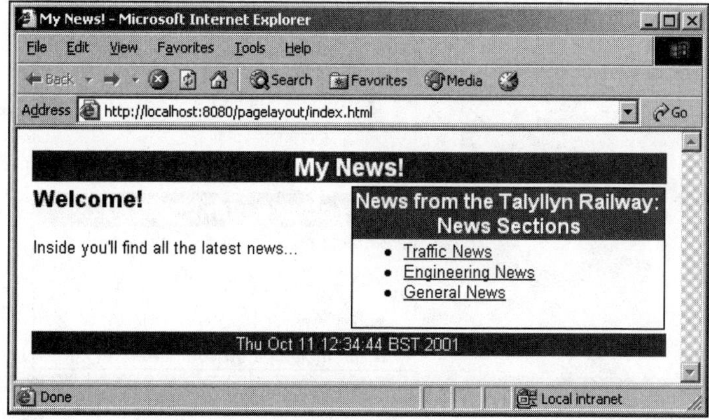

We can easily add a new component to the web application. Let's add a simple random number generator, called `random-number.jsp`:

```
<% int rnd = (int) (Math.random() * 100L); %>

<html>
  <head>
    <title>Today's number is <%= rnd %></title>
  </head>

  <body>
    <p>Our magic number today is the wonderful:</p>
    <p class="number"><%= rnd %></p>
    <p>Why not include it on your lottery ticket?</p>
  </body>
</html>
```

We can use this component in other pages by adding it to our main decorator, main.jsp:

```
...
<td>
  <page:applyDecorator name="panel"
                       page="/news/list-all-sections.jsp" />
  <br />
  <page:applyDecorator name="panel"
                       page="/random-number.jsp" />
</td>
...
```

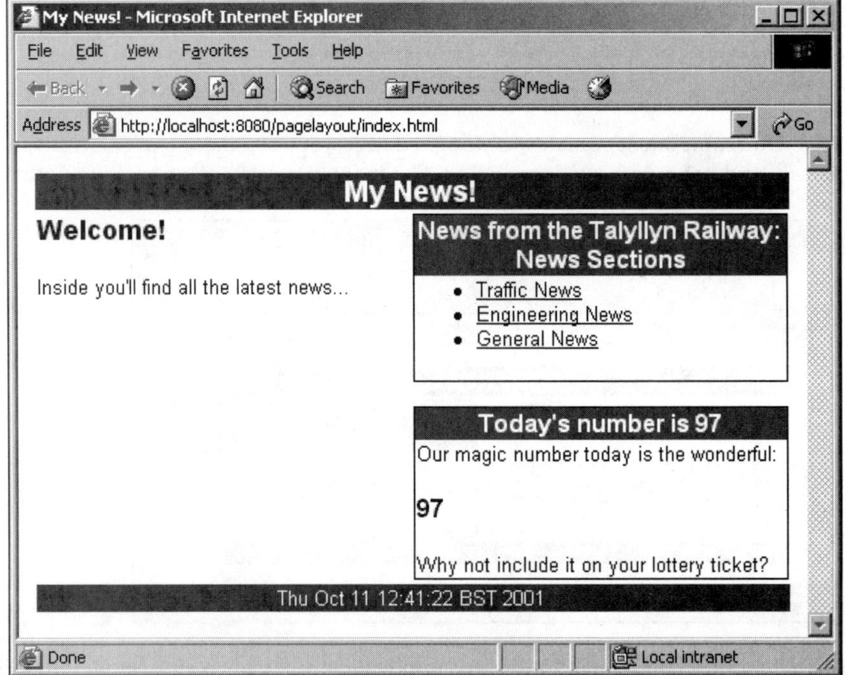

Remember that decorators can contain other components and also that components can contain other components.

Enhancing the Look

Now we have a web application starting to take shape, we probably want it to look a bit better. Remember that just by modifying the two decorators (main.jsp and panel.jsp) we can apply a new style to the entire site.

The nice thing about all our decorators is that they contain well-formed HTML – we don't have to worry about having half the HTML in a header and half in the footer. Because of this, it's easy to edit the files independently of the site. We can even use a WYSIWYG editor to make changes to the decorators, as the decorator tags are the only non-standard HTML elements in the page. If an editing package doesn't like these tags, it's easy to remove them during development of the HTML and add them back in afterwards.

It's good practice to use decorators that are scriptlet free (or at least contain very minimal code). If code does need to be added, consider placing it in an external file and including it with a server-side include, or even better, encapsulate it inside a custom tag. This keeps JSP code and HTML from interfering with each other.

Our friend the graphic designer can redesign the look of the whole site by editing a single HTML file (or maybe a few files if there are different types of decorators).

Passing Parameters Around

What happens if we want to pass information generated by the component to the decorator? For example, suppose we have a JSP page that dynamically generates content from a database and we need the author and category for the document (that are stored in the database) to be available to the decorator.

This is easy. We've already done this for the title of the page – when a page is displayed, the text in the `<title>` tag is extracted and then inserted into the decorator using the `<decorator:title>` tag. We can also pass other values in a similar way.

As we already know, when a page is parsed, three main elements are extracted. These are the contents of the `<title>`, `<head>`, and `<body>` tags. However, the `<meta>` tags are also parsed, which allows extra information to be passed across.

For example, consider the following HTML:

```
<html>
  <head>
    <title>My Page</title>
    <meta name="author" content="Myself">
    <meta name="email" content="me@example.com">
    <meta name="category" content="news">
  </head>
  <body>
    <p>Hi</p>
    ...
  </body>
</html>
```

After the page has been parsed, the `<decorator:body>` tag will insert the body into the decorator and the `<decorator:title>` tag will insert `My Page`. Likewise we can use the `<decorator:getProperty>` tag to get additional parameters passed across from the page:

```
<html>
  <head>
    <title><decorator:title /></title>
    <decorator:head />
  </head>
  <body bgcolor="yellow">
    <h1><decorator:title /></h1>
    <decorator:body />
    <div align="right">
      <i>Contact the author:</i>
```

The following tag will insert the content of the <META> tag named `author` into the decorator, and the following two insert the e-mail address:

```
        <decorator:getProperty property="meta.author" />
        <a href="mailto:<decorator:getProperty property="meta.email" />">
          <decorator:getProperty property="meta.email" />
        </a>
      </div>
    </body>
</html>
```

> **The reason the `meta.xxx` prefix is used when accessing the property is that properties can also come from other locations in the document. This also allows for further flexibility if custom extensions are to be made to SiteMesh.**

In some cases, it's desirable to do more than simply print out the value of a property. We may wish to alter the value beforehand or perform some conditional logic based on the result. If that's the case, we can expose the representation of the parsed page as a Java object, which allows us more control. For example, a property from the page (such as the `<title>`, or a `<meta name="author">` tag) may need to be cross-referenced with a database so the decorator can include a suitable disclaimer. This requires programmatic access to the data in the page.

The following tag will expose the Java object that contains the information extracted from the page so it is available to JSP scriptlets. The `id` parameter specifies the name of the variable that the object will be available under. The object exposed is of type `com.sitemesh.HTMLPage`:

```
...
<decorator:useHtmlPage id="html" />
<%
```

The tag below gets the value of the `meta.category` tag as a `String`. If the property is not set, `null` is returned:

```
    String category = html.getProperty("meta.category");
    if (category != null) {
        %>
      <jsp:include page="<%= "/navigation/" + category + ".jsp" %>" />
        <%
    } else {
        %>
      <jsp:include page="/navigation/default.jsp" />
        <%
    }
%>
...
```

These are the most commonly used methods of `HTMLPage`:

Method	Description
`String getTitle();`	Returns the title of the HTML page (from the `<TITLE>` tag).
`String getProperty(String name);`	Returns the value of the property in a page as a string. If the property does not exist, `null` is returned. To access `<META>` tags, the `meta.xxx` prefix must be used. (Example: `meta.category`)

`int getIntProperty(String name);`
`long getLongProperty(String name);`
`boolean getBooleanProperty(String name);`
	These are convenience methods to get a property and convert it to a suitable primitive. If property is not found or cannot be converted, 0 (or `false` for Boolean) is returned.

`boolean isPropertySet(String name);`	A convenience method to detect if a property has been set in the page.
`String[] getPropertyKeys();`	List the names of all the properties available.
`HttpServletRequest getRequest();`	Returns the `Request` object in the state it was while the page was being generated. This could be used to obtain details about the original page such as request parameters or the URI. Accessing these methods through the implicit JSP request object in the decorator shall return details about the decorator itself, whereas using the `Page.getRequest()` object provides details about the page that the decorator is being applied to.

Switching Decorators

At the moment, when a page is requested, an appropriate decorator is chosen from the `decorators.xml` file. If we want to change the decorator used for a particular request we can add another decorator and a mapping to the file:

```
<decorators>

  <decorator>
    <decorator-name>main</decorator-name>
    <jsp-file>/decorators/main.jsp</jsp-file>
  </decorator>
```

```
    <decorator>
        <decorator-name>panel</decorator-name>
        <jsp-file>/decorators/panel.jsp</jsp-file>
      </decorator>

      <decorator>
        <decorator-name>news</decorator-name>
        <jsp-file>/decorators/news.jsp</jsp-file>
      </decorator>

      <decorator-mapping>
        <decorator-name>main</decorator-name>
        <url-pattern>*</url-pattern>

      </decorator-mapping>

      <decorator-mapping>
        <decorator-name>news</decorator-name>
        <url-pattern>/news/</url-pattern>
      </decorator-mapping>

    </decorators>
```

Now, whenever a request is made to anything in the /news/ directory of the web-app, the news decorator will be used instead of main. The pattern in the <url-pattern> tag uses the same matching syntax as the standard web.xml <servlet-mapping> and <filter-mapping> tags.

If we do not want any decorator to be used for a particular request, we can define a mapping that refers to the special none decorator:

```
<decorator-mapping>
  <decorator-name>none</decorator-name>
  <url-pattern>/somedir/</url-pattern>
</decorator-mapping>
```

This is simple enough to use, but unfortunately isn't flexible enough for many applications. Here are some scenarios where we may require more control:

- Some pages could be dynamically generated. If this is the case, they should also get a say in which decorator is applied to them. For example, the name of the decorator to use on a news article may be stored in a database along with the article.
- Depending on the browser requesting the page, a slightly different decorator may be used. For example, there could be a decorator containing some features only available to some browsers (such as dynamic HTML, client-side XML, Active-X, Applets), or a decorator that shows a much slimmer version of the site for text-only browsers.
- We may wish to have a printable version of every page on the site. For that, we can use the same page with different decorators applied depending on whether a flag is set to display the printable version or not.

- and includes things like extra keywords and navigation enabling it to find its way around the site quickly. This could be detected by the IP address or user-agent requesting the page.
- If a page contains definitions of HTML framesets, we may wish to not apply any decorator to that page (only the pages actually inside the frames).

SiteMesh easily caters for this by allowing a different **mapper** to be plugged in. A mapper is a Java class that is responsible for determining which decorator to use for a particular request. SiteMesh is bundled with a collection of commonly used mappers, but it's also possible to implement our own by creating a class that implements the `com.sitemesh.DecoratorMapper` interface. A mapper is passed the `Page` object representing the parsed page and the `HttpServletRequest` – from this it can decide whether a particular decorator should be applied – and if so, which one.

Multiple mappers can be configured for a single web application and for each request the mappers will be queried in order until one of them can determine the decorator to use – this is known as the **Chain of Responsibility** design pattern.

Recall our configuration file called `sitemesh.xml` that contained the following entry:

```
<mapper class="com.sitemesh.mapper.ConfigDecoratorMapper">
  <param name="config" value="/WEB-INF/decorators.xml" />
</mapper>
```

This defines our default mapper, `ConfigDecoratorMapper`, which will determine the decorator to use by reading our `decorators.xml` file. What's important here is the order that they are defined. The order the `<mapper>` elements appear in the file is the same order they are queried when attempting to match a decorator. Obviously we want our custom mappers to override the default behavior of `ConfigDecoratorMapper` so we place them before it:

```
<sitemesh>

  <page-parsers>
    <parser content-type="text/html"
            class="com.sitemesh.parser.FastPageParser" />
    <parser default="true"
            class="com.sitemesh.parser.DefaultPageParser" />
  </page-parsers>

  <decorator-mappers>
```

The `PageDecoratorMapper` allows a page itself to determine the decorator to be applied to it. It does this by setting one of its properties to the name of the decorator to use. In this case, the property of the page that contains the decorator name is `meta.decorator`. So, if a page contains a `<META>` tag named `decorator`, the content of that tag shall contain the name of the decorator to use. This could be dynamically generated by the page from an entry in the database, for example.

If there is no <meta> tag with this name, the next mapper in the chain is queried:

```
<mapper class="com.sitemesh.mapper.PageDecoratorMapper">
  <param name="property" value="meta.decorator" />
</mapper>
```

The next mapper simply determines whether the page requested contains an HTML frameset definition. If it does, then it tells SiteMesh **not** to use any decorator on this page at all. If it doesn't, the next mapper is queried:

```
<mapper class="com.sitemesh.mapper.FrameSetDecoratorMapper">
</mapper>
```

The `AgentDecoratorMapper` can switch decorators depending on the user-agent (web browser) requesting the page. This mapper will actually allow mappers after it in the chain to reply first. Suppose a page is requested that maps to our main decorator (as defined in `decorators.xml` by the `ConfigDecoratorMapper` later in the chain). This decorator is actually the file `/decorators/main.jsp`.

The `AgentDecoratorMapper` then checks whether a match has been configured that matches the `User-Agent` HTTP header of the request. If the user-agent is Internet Explorer, the header contains the string `MSIE` somewhere in it, which is associated (by the <param> tags) with the value `ie`. The `AgentDecoratorMapper` then checks whether a file named `/decorators/main-ie.jsp` exists, and if so it uses that as the decorator.

So, all you need to do to use this mapper is to add the <mapper> to the `sitemesh.xml` file (as below) and then for any decorators that you want to use a browser specific version for, create a separate file next to `main.jsp` called `main-XXXX.jsp` (where `XXXX` is `ie`, `ns`, `opera`, or `lynx`). To configure more browsers, add more matches using the <param> tags.

If the `User-Agent` HTTP header is not matched, or the browser specific decorator file does not exist, the next mapper is queried:

```
<mapper class="com.sitemesh.mapper.AgentDecoratorMapper">
  <param name="match.MSIE"       value="ie" />
  <param name="match.Mozilla/"   value="ns" />
  <param name="match.Opera"      value="opera" />
  <param name="match.Lynx"       value="lynx" />
</mapper>
```

The next mapper checks whether the URI requested contains `printable=true` as a parameter, and if so, uses the decorator named `printable` instead of the default. It's important that we define a decorator named `printable` in our `decorators.xml` pointing to the correct file for this to work. If this parameter is not present, the next mapper in the chain is queried:

```
<mapper class="com.sitemesh.mapper.PrintableDecoratorMapper">
  <param name="decorator"       value="printable" />
  <param name="parameter.name"  value="printable" />
  <param name="parameter.value" value="true" />
</mapper>
```

`ConfigDecoratorMapper` is our default mapper that uses our `decorator.xml` file. This is the last mapper in the chain. Therefore, no decorator is to be applied and the page should be returned in its original form:

```
      <mapper class="com.sitemesh.mapper.ConfigDecoratorMapper">
        <param name="config" value="/WEB-INF/decorators.xml" />
      </mapper>

    </decorator-mappers>

  </sitemesh>
```

Let's make use of some of these.

First, let's create a decorator for the printable version of this site (`printable.jsp`). As usual, we'll put it in the `decorators\` directory:

```
<%@ taglib uri="sitemesh-decorator" prefix="decorator" %>

<html>
  <head>
    <title><decorator:title /> (Printable version)</title>
    <decorator:head />
  </head>
  <body>

    <h2 align="center"><decorator:title /></h2>
    <hr>
    <decorator:body />
    <hr>
    <p align="center"><i><small>Printable version

  </body>
</html>
```

We also need to add our decorator to the `decorators.xml` file with the name `printable` (the same name we used when defining the `PrintableDecoratorMapper` in `sitemesh.xml`).

```
<decorators>

  <decorator>
    <decorator-name>main</decorator-name>
    <jsp-file>/decorators/main.jsp</jsp-file>
  </decorator>

  <decorator>
    <decorator-name>printable</decorator-name>
    <jsp-file>/decorators/printable.jsp</jsp-file>
  </decorator>
    ...
```

If we append ?printable=true (or &printable=true if there are already request URI parameters) to the URL, we get the printable version:

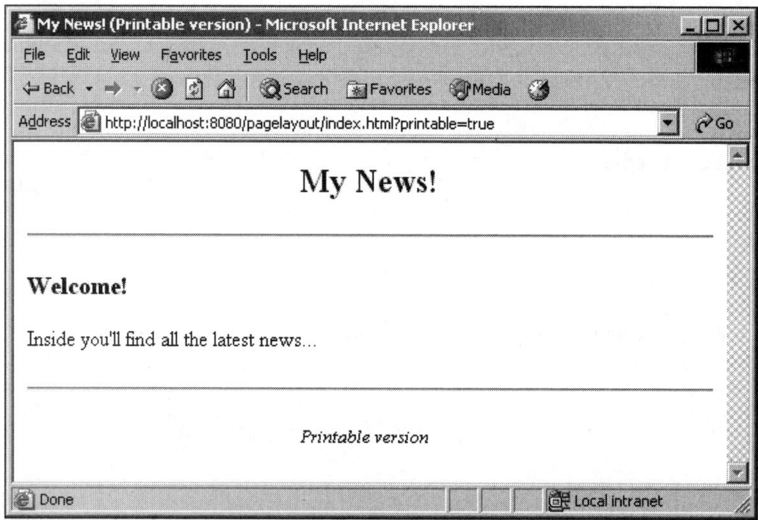

Now to use the AgentDecoratorMapper, we simply create some decorators alongside \decorators\main.jsp called \decorators\main-ie.jsp and \decorators\main-ns.jsp that contain browser specific features:

Here's main-ie.jsp:

```
<%@ taglib uri="sitemesh-decorator" prefix="decorator" %>
<%@ taglib uri="sitemesh-page" prefix="page" %>
<html>
  <head>
    <title><decorator:title /></title>
    <decorator:head />
  </head>
  <body>
    <table width="100%">
      <tr>
        <td bgcolor="#dddddd" align="center"
            style="font-family: arial; font-size: 20pt;" colspan="2">
          <decorator:title /><br>
          <font color="blue">
            Internet Explorer Enhanced Version
          </font>
        </td>
      </tr>
      <tr>
        <td style="font-family: arial;" valign="top" width="100%">
          <decorator:body />
        </td>
      </tr>
    </table>
  </body>
</html>
```

Here's main-ns.jsp:

```
<%@ taglib uri="sitemesh-decorator" prefix="decorator" %>
<%@ taglib uri="sitemesh-page" prefix="page" %>
<html>
  <head>
    <title><decorator:title /></title>
    <decorator:head />
  </head>
  <body>
    <table width="100%">
      <tr>
        <td bgcolor="#dddddd" align="center"
            style="font-family: arial; font-size: 20pt;" colspan="2">
          <decorator:title /><br>
          <font color="red">
            Opera Enhanced Version
          </font>
        </td>
      </tr>
      <tr>
        <td style="font-family: arial;" valign="top" width="100%">
          <decorator:body />
        </td>
      </tr>
    </table>
  </body>
</html>
```

And that's it. Requesting a page that uses the main decorator will now use different decorators depending on the browser (main-opera.jsp/main-ie.jsp). If no browser specific decorator is found, the default decorator is used (main.jsp):

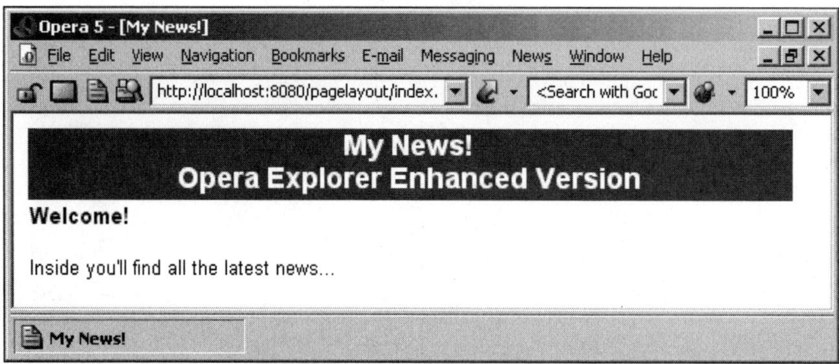

Finally, let's make use of `PageDecoratorMapper`. This allows us to choose a decorator based on the `<META NAME="decorator">` tag in the actual content page. For the sake of an example, we'll use the existing `main` and `printable` decorators we've already defined. Let's create a JSP page with some content that dynamically chooses the decorator based on whether the current minute is an odd or even one. We'll call it `chooser.jsp`:

```
<%@ page import="java.util.*, java.text.*" %>
<%
    Date now = new Date();
    DateFormat format = DateFormat.getTimeInstance();
    Calendar cal = Calendar.getInstance( request.getLocale() );
    cal.setTime( now );
    int minute = cal.get( Calendar.MINUTE );
    boolean even = minute % 2 == 0;
%>
<html>
  <head>
    <title>Silly Page</title>
    <meta name="decorator" content="<%= even ? "main" : "printable" %>">
  </head>
  <body>
    <p>The current time is <%= format.format( now ) %></p>
    <p>That's an <i><%= even ? "even" : "odd" %></i> minute</p>
  </body>
</html>
```

This results in the following for an odd minute:

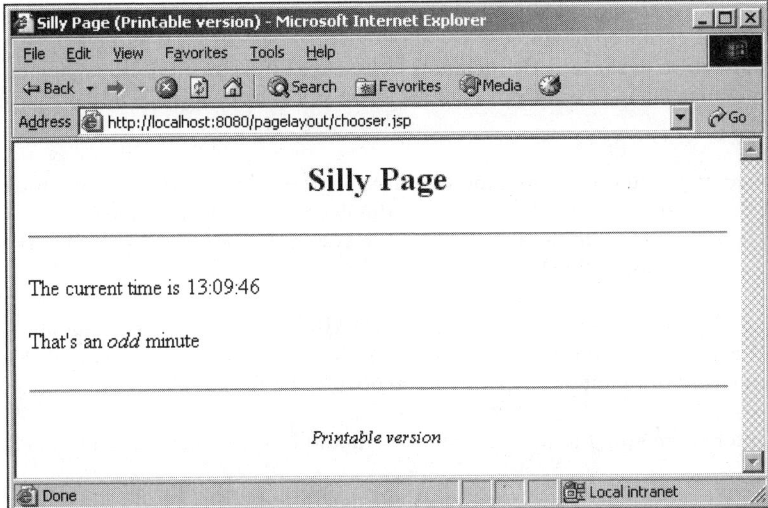

And this for an even minute:

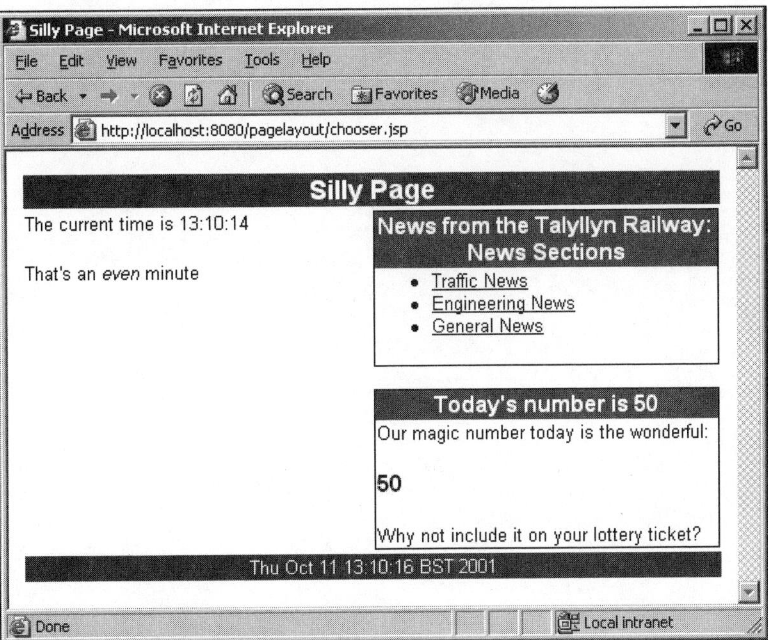

These examples illustrate how easy it is to let the content of the page (not just JSP content) choose the decorator to us. In a real application, the `<meta>` tag would probably be generated based on the contents of a backend data-store.

Summary

In this chapter we've explored techniques for applying a consistent look and feel to a web application based on the foundation of server-side includes. In essence all we need to do is include a decorator file, which in turn includes the necessary presentation. This is a simple approach that can be tweaked to fit many situations.

We've also looked at an alternative method that uses content filtering. This allows the content to be generated *first*, then parsed and finally applied to the decorator. This approach solves the problem of some common techniques resulting in a very flexible system that's easy to use. Finally we developed a comprehensive example using SiteMesh.

The most crucial thing to remember is to keep the HTML that drives the functionality of your applications lightweight – the decorators can beef up the presentation. Following this rule can make your code much easier to maintain, expand and evolve in the future.

In the next chapter we're going to look at how we can add effective navigation to our web applications.

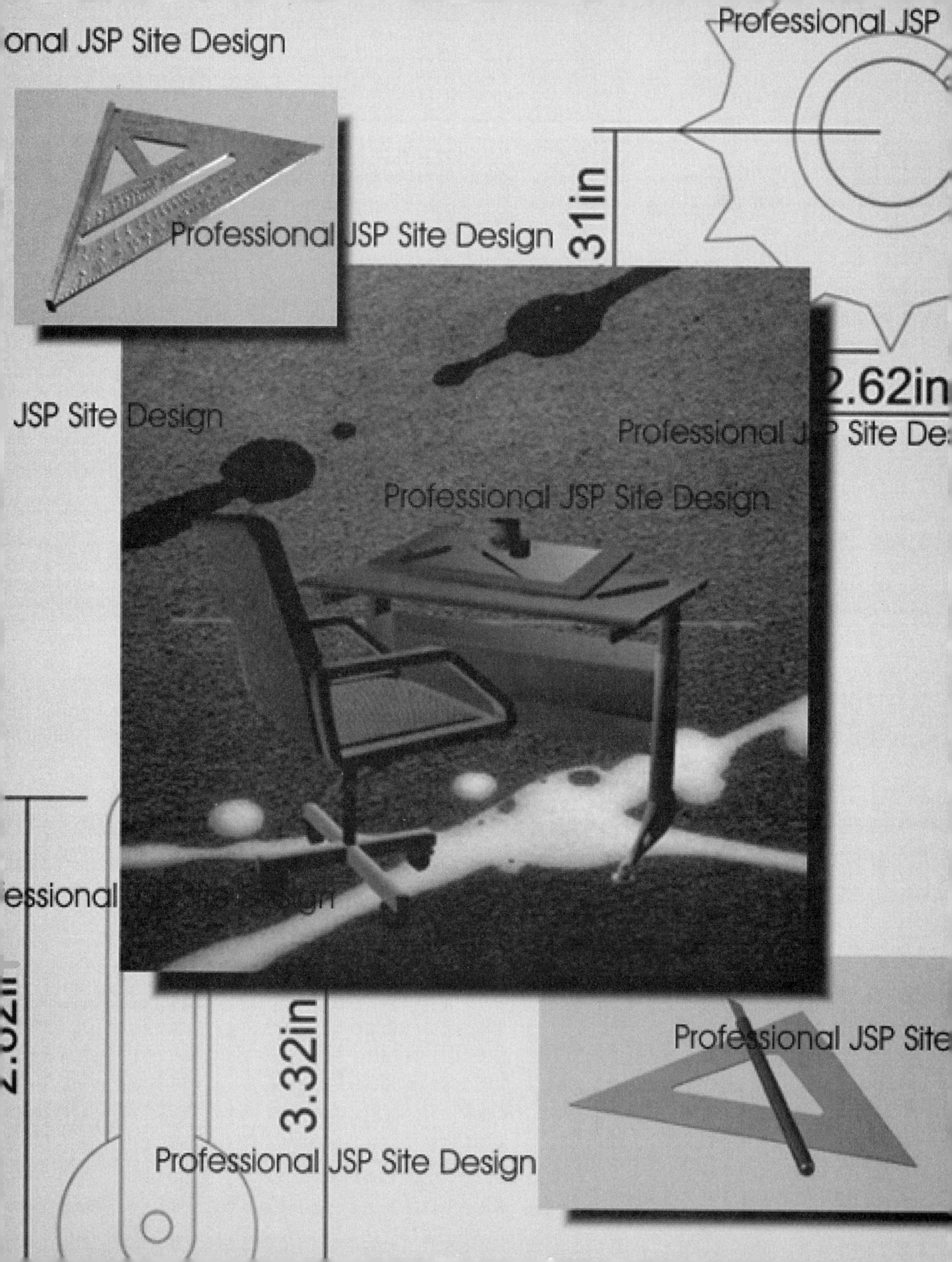

onal JSP Site Design
Professional JSP
Professional JSP Site Design
31in
JSP Site Design
2.62in
Professional J P Site De
Professional JSP Site Design
essional
3.32in
Professional JSP Site
Professional JSP Site Design

6

Navigation

We often find ourselves wanting to build site navigation dynamically from a database, rather than it being predetermined at design time. For example, we might have an e-commerce catalog where product categories can be added, removed, or otherwise altered. Or we might want to create a website directory such that it has pages added frequently. This chapter will examine strategies for building a dynamic navigation system and offer an example of such a system.

Creating any application presents us with challenges and opportunities. Of primary importance is properly designing the data structure that holds the information about our site. If we don't do this it can easily become unusable as the application acquires more functionality. Likewise, the web tier of an application should be suitably thought out. A valuable exercise is the creation of a prototype or demo application, as this can raise issues and solutions not originally foreseen.

Our prototype will consist solely of JSP pages, which will utilize tag libraries from the Jakarta Taglibs project and JavaBeans for our data. Once our prototype has provided a proof-of-concept, we will use it as a stepping-stone to a more solid architecture. In doing so we'll again take advantage of the Jakarta Struts Framework we were introduced to in Chapter 2.

Once our architecture is complete, any database-driven web application should provide an easy to use interface for the management of the data.

Building our catalog will allow us to discuss how to:

- Model the data
- Use Model 1 architecture for rapid prototyping
- Convert our prototype to the Struts Model View Controller (MVC) model
- Create a workable data management application

Data Modeling

A **Data Model** can be thought of as a subset of the **Object Model**. An object model represents the components of an application, and how the components interact. These components represent data and behavior. Object models are typically created when designing a large application, where it is vital to understand and plan every facet of object interaction.

The data model part of an object model represents the concrete objects that will be represented by the application. As such, it is important that we have a clear understanding of what the data needs of the application are, and how they relate to each other. The most obvious representation of a data model is the database. A database table represents a class of objects, and the foreign keys (linking one table to another) are the data representation of how they relate.

While not an object model, modeling our data and its relationships will infer the interactions and behavior of our application. One particular challenge to data modeling lies with the database chosen to contain our data: some databases are better suited to modeling complex relationships between objects (tables). This presents us with a dilemma: either we choose our database based on our needs or we alter our model based on our database's capabilities.

In this application, we'll make use of MySql (http://www.mysql.com/, and see Appendix B for setup details). The documentation recommends against using foreign-key constraints, but we will make use of them. The use of constraints aids in enforcing the data structure, and can protect against unwanted consequences. Just as a unique-key constraint ensures that there will only be one row with a given id, foreign-key constraints ensure that the relationships they signify will not be broken by the deletion of the foreign table data.

If problems arise while running the examples provided in this chapter the constraints can be removed. While not as readily available, Microsoft's SQL Server product provides excellent support for foreign-key constraints, as does the Oracle database.

Our example application will have a diverse collection of products, and we need a category structure to classify them. The range of products may increase over time and so the category structure must be scalable and easily modified.

We will need to provide at least two levels to the directory: one broad categorization and sub-categories (possibly containing increasing levels of specificity) to which the products are assigned.

Categories could be placed into a hierarchy, for example:

```
Books > Programming > Java > JavaServer Pages
```

Categories could even occur multiple times within the hierarchy. For example, in addition to its position above the category `JavaServer Pages` could also occur in:

```
Books > Web Development > JavaServer Pages
```

However, this adds considerable complexity to the SQL that must be written and creates challenges in the business logic such as:

- How many levels of sub-categories are allowed?
- Should we allow products to be listed at any level?
- Or should products be attached only to the lowest level categories?
- How does the system decide which is the lowest level category?

To simplify things, we'll place categories within a single section, which will act as our top-level category. If we later decide to add more levels of categories, the section can remain as the high-level abstraction of a category. We will assign various properties to section, category, and product such as an id and a name:

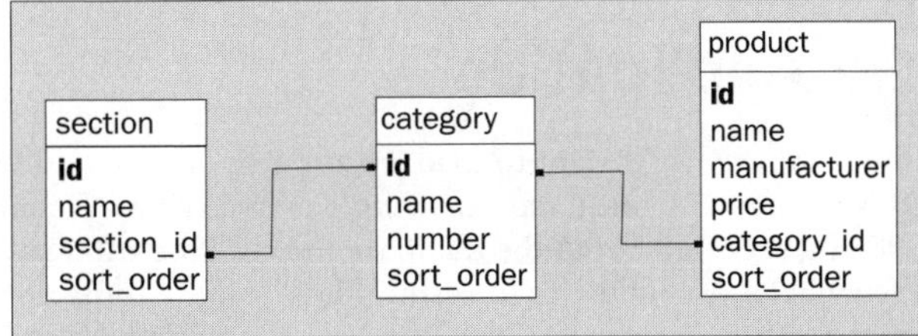

As you can see, the data model is quite simple and straightforward. Each table is linked by a sensibly named column title:

- `section_id` links `category` to `section`
- `category_id` links `product` to `category`

To support any number of category levels, we could have created `category` with a `parent_id` property that linked it back on itself, that is, to the `id` of another instance of a `category`. In this way, each category could have a set of child categories, much as how `section` has its children. However, this is complicated and could lead to trouble enforcing data integrity constraints and orphaned categories (a category with no parent) and the questions enumerated earlier.

Included with the code for this chapter is a SQL script to create this data model. Another gross simplification we've taken is to express the products' price as an integer. This is for the sake of our example, leaving out any complications of properly formatting a float value:

```
CREATE DATABASE navigation;
USE navigation;

CREATE TABLE category (id INT NOT NULL PRIMARY KEY,
                       name VARCHAR(30) NOT NULL,
                       section_id INT NOT NULL,
                       sort_order INT NOT NULL);

CREATE TABLE product (id INT NOT NULL PRIMARY KEY,
                      name VARCHAR(30) NOT NULL,
                      manufacturer VARCHAR(30) NULL,
                      price INT NOT NULL,
                      category_id INT NOT NULL,
                      sort_order INT NOT NULL);

CREATE TABLE section (id INT NOT NULL PRIMARY KEY,
                      name VARCHAR(20) NOT NULL,
                      sort_order INT NOT NULL);
```

This script will create the `navigation` database, and create the tables we'll be using in our example application. Depending on the database used, it may or may not be necessary to set up a database user with the proper permissions to insert, delete, and modify the tables defined in our `CREATE` statements above.

Setting Up the Application

Once we've created the database, we'll want to load it with data. This could be done by tediously entering multiple SQL statements to our database using our favorite SQL tool. Or we could write a helper application to load a set of data into the database for us. This will allow us to populate the database with only a few clicks, and allow us to restore the database to its initial values if we decide to start from fresh or if our database is ever lost.

In our example we'll be using a variety of pre-built components, graciously supplied by the Apache Foundation's Jakarta Project. The Jakarta Project is found at http://jakarta.apache.org/, and there we'll find Struts and the Taglibs project. Download and install Struts and the DBTags, Input, and JSPTL Tag Libraries. In addition, we'll be using a code library from the Jakarta Commons project. This library is named `util`, and, as of the time of writing, has not been released as a package. You can get the `commons.util` package from the cvs server at anoncvs@cvs.apache.org and compile it yourself, or download a prebuilt JAR from http://www.wrox.com/.

To make use of the various taglibs include the following in the file `web.xml` for the navigation web-application:

```
<!-- JAKARTA DBTAGS TAGLIB -->
<taglib>
  <taglib-uri>http://jakarta.apache.org/taglibs/dbtags</taglib-uri>
  <taglib-location>/WEB-INF/dbtags.tld</taglib-location>
</taglib>
```

```
<!-- JSPTL JR TAGLIB -->
<taglib>
  <taglib-uri>http://jakarta.apache.org/taglibs/jsptl-jr</taglib-uri>
  <taglib-location>/WEB-INF/jsptl-jr.tld</taglib-location>
</taglib>

<!-- STRUTS LOGIC TAGLIBS -->
<taglib>
  <taglib-uri>http://jakarta.apache.org/struts/tags-logic-1.0</taglib-uri>
  <taglib-location>/WEB-INF/struts-logic.tld</taglib-location>
</taglib>

<!-- JAKARTA INPUT TAGLIB -->
<taglib>
  <taglib-uri>http://jakarta.apache.org/taglibs/input</taglib-uri>
  <taglib-location>/WEB-INF/input.tld</taglib-location>
</taglib>
```

An Index Page

First, let's introduce a starting point for all the examples to follow. We'll create `index.html` to provide convenient links into the application. We'll want a link to the page were we will populate the database, a link to our prototype, a link to our final architecture, and a link to each of the management pages. The result would look like this:

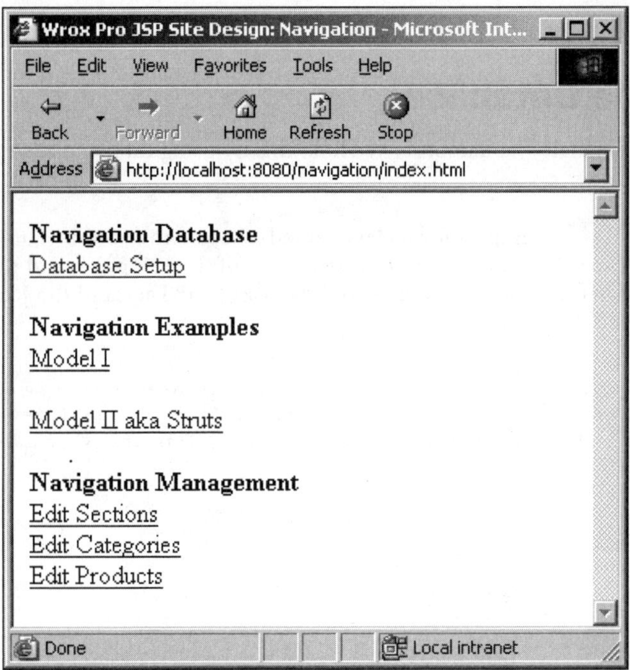

The HTML to create this page is simple:

```
<html>
  <head>
    <title>Wrox Pro JSP Site Design: Navigation</title>
  </head>

  <body>
    <b>Navigation Database</b><br/>
    <a href="buildDatabase.jsp">Database Setup</a>
    <br/>
    <br/>

    <b>Navigation Examples</b><br/>
    <a href="model1/displaySections.jsp">Model I</a>
    <br/>
    <br/>
    <a href="displaySections.do">Model II aka Struts</a>
    <br/>
    <br/>

    <b>Navigation Management</b><br/>
    <a href="editSections.do">Edit Sections</a><br/>
    <a href="editCategories.do">Edit Categories</a><br/>
    <a href="editProducts.do">Edit Products</a><br/>
  </body>
</html>
```

Populating the Database

Our next step is to populate the database. We'll do this by using the **Database Setup** link. This will take us to `buildDatabase.jsp`.

In the first line you'll see an import for a class named `DatabaseLoader`. This class will allow us to take a great deal of work (constructing insert statements) out of the JSP page, and put the work in a more appropriate place. Then we state the taglibs we'll be using, DBTags and the JSPTL, and name them `sql` and `jr` respectively:

```
<%@ page import = "prowebdesign.navigation.DatabaseLoader" %>
<%@ taglib uri='http://jakarta.apache.org/taglibs/dbtags' prefix='sql' %>
<%@ taglib uri='http://java.sun.com/jsptl/ea/jr' prefix='jr' %>

<html>
  <head>
    <title>Database Setup</title>
  </head>
  <body>
```

Here we see that despicable scriptlet tag. We'll check if the user has submitted a request to fill the database. If so, we create a connection to our database using the DBTag `<sql:connection>`. The first two sub-tags read plainly enough: we need to supply our JDBC URL and driver information. Then we need to (optionally) provide our user credentials. Why optional? If no user has been configured for our MySql database the credentials don't need to be presented. DBTags won't accept empty `<sql:userId>` or `<sql:password>` tags, so we'll need to remove them if our database doesn't require user credentials:

```
<%
if (request.getParameter("fillDatabase") != null) {
%>
    <sql:connection id="conn1">
      <sql:url>jdbc:mysql://localhost/navigation</sql:url>
      <sql:driver>org.gjt.mm.mysql.Driver</sql:driver>

      <!-- remove the next two fields if using MySql
           and no user has been created. -->
      <sql:userId>wrox</sql:userId>
      <sql:password>wrox</sql:password>
    </sql:connection>
```

We'll intialize our `insertQuery` variable and prepare the generated page for the user. We'll reflect the `INSERT` queries back to the user, and we'll wrap them all in a `<pre>` tag for readability. Any SQL operation has the potential to throw a `SQLException`, but rather than letting control forward to an error page and halt execution we'll catch the exception and print it to the page. If we've configured our connection properly in the `<sql:connection>` tag we should have nothing to worry about.

Now we get to the part where we instantiate a `DatabaseLoader`. We'll see this class in a moment, so let's continue. We'll use the `DatabaseLoader` to fetch an `INSERT` query. So long as this query is not null we'll print it to the page and execute the query using DBTag's `<sql:statement>` and `<sql:query>` tags. Once the query is null, we set a session attribute marking that we successfully inserted all of our queries.

```
<%
  String insertQuery = "";
  out.print("<pre>");
  try {
    DatabaseLoader loader = new DatabaseLoader();

    // while loader.getNextQuery() does not return a null...
    while ((insertQuery = loader.getNextQuery()) != null) {
      out.println(insertQuery);
%>
    <sql:statement id="stmt1" conn="conn1">

      <sql:query>
        <%= insertQuery %>
      </sql:query>

      <sql:execute/>
    </sql:statement>
<%
```

```
    }
    session.setAttribute("databaseFilled", Boolean.TRUE);
  } catch (Exception e) {
      out.println("<font color='red'>
                       Error filling the Navigation database:<br /><pre>");
      out.println(org.apache.commons.util.StringUtils.stackTrace(e));
      out.println("</pre></font>");
  }
```

After we've completed inserting all of our sections, categories, and products, we'll close the database connection we opened earlier (via `<jsp:closeConnection />`) and close our `<pre>` tag. Lastly, we'll use a set of JSPTL tags to determine if we should display the link to **Populate Navigation Database** or a bold **Navigation Database has been populated**. We do this to prevent the user from attempting to insert the same values into the database more than once, as this would cause a Primary Key Unique Constraint violation (only one row can have any particular key value):

```
%>
    <sql:closeConnection conn="conn1" />
<%
    out.print("</pre>");
  }
%>

    <%-- check to see if databaseCreated flag has been set.
          If so, create link to populate database.
          If database already populated, do not create link --%>
    <jr:choose>
      <jr:when test='<%= session.getAttribute("databaseFilled") == null %>'>
        <a href="buildDatabase.jsp?fillDatabase=1">
                                        Populate Navigation Database</a>
        <br/>
        <br/>
        <a href="index.html"> Back to Index</a>
      </jr:when>
      <jr:otherwise>
        <b>Navigation Database has been populated</b>
      </jr:otherwise>
    </jr:choose>

  </body>
</html>
```

More information on the usage of the JSPTL conditional tags can be found at http://jakarta.apache.org/taglibs/doc/jsptl-doc/jsptl-ea1/Conditionals_FunctionalDescription_1_EA1.html, but it isn't hard to see that we are using the session attribute `databaseFilled` to determine the behavior we want.

Just to be nice we'll include a link back to our index page:

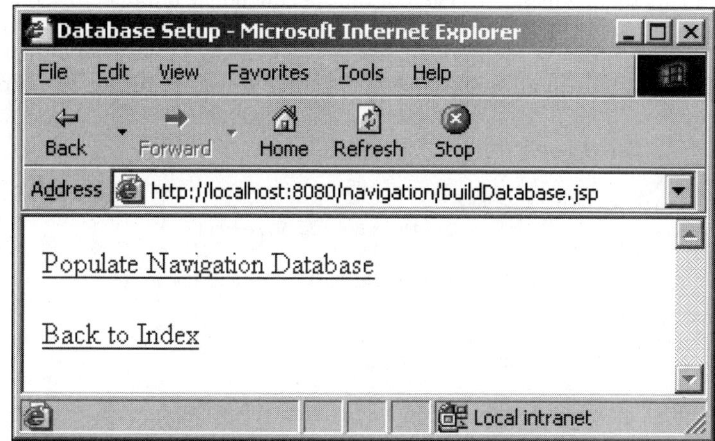

The DatabaseLoader Class

The `DatabaseLoader` class aids us in pre-populating the database. The actual data to be loaded is found in static arrays at the bottom of this class:

```
package com.wrox.navigation;

import java.util.Hashtable;

public class DatabaseLoader {
```

`DatabaseLoader` requires several variables to track our information as we proceed. The `sectionHash` and `categoryHash` are used to store each entry for use by their children in assigning the foreign key `category.section_id` or `product.category_id`, respectively:

```
  // These hashtables will track the global id's
  private Hashtable sectionHash = new Hashtable();
  private Hashtable categoryHash = new Hashtable();
```

The `globalCounter` will allow us to set a **globally unique identifier** to each row, regardless of the table, while the following three counters will aid us as we loop over the insert query building process. Finally, we set String fragments that represent the basic building blocks of each insert query:

```
  // These counters help the methods return the right values
  private int globalCounter = 1;
  private int sectionCounter = 0;
  private int categoryCounter = 0;
  private int productCounter = 0;

  // We build the queries from these strings
  private String insertSection = "INSERT section (id, name, sort_order)
                                                              VALUES (";
  private String insertCategory = "INSERT category (id, name, sort_order,
                                                    section_id) VALUES (";
  private String insertProduct = "INSERT product (id, name, manufacturer,
                                  price, sort_order, category_id) VALUES (";
```

We've made a blank constructor, since there is no initialization work to be done. Next is the `getNextQuery()` method, which calls each of the specific query builders in sequence (due to data constraints we need to insert the sections before the categories before the products). As each specific query builder exhausts its data it returns null, which is our signal to proceed to the next one. Finally, when we've gone through them all we'll return null to signal `buildDatabase.jsp` that we've finished:

```
public DatabaseLoader() {}

public String getNextQuery() {
  String insertQuery = this.getNextSectionQuery();

  // if getNextSectionQuery returned null, try Category
  if (insertQuery == null) {
    insertQuery = this.getNextCategoryQuery();
  }

  // if getNextCategoryQuery returned null, try Product
  if (insertQuery == null) {
    insertQuery = this.getNextProductQuery();
  }
  return insertQuery;
}
```

The methods `getNextSectionQuery()`, `getNextCategoryQuery()`, and `getNextProductQuery()` all operate the same, using different datasets. Each method checks first to see if it has processed all of its data and returns null if it has. This is the contract that `getNextQuery()` counts on.

If data exists, and it is a section or category, the name of the row is `put()` into the proper `Hashtable` along with the current value of `globalCounter`. Then a `StringBuffer` is built from the query fragments that we saw earlier and the unique data for this row. The counter for section, category, or product is incremented, `globalCounter` is incremented, and we return the `StringBuffer`'s value as a string:

```
/** load the Sections **/
private String getNextSectionQuery() {
  // when we run out of sections, return null
  if (sectionCounter >= sections.length) {
    return null;
  }

  // put section information into hash for later use
  sectionHash.put(sections[sectionCounter][0],
                                        String.valueOf(globalCounter));

  // build insert section statement
  StringBuffer buf = new StringBuffer(insertSection);
  buf.append(globalCounter).append(", '");
  buf.append(sections[sectionCounter][0]).append("', ");
  buf.append(sections[sectionCounter][1]).append(")");

  sectionCounter++;
  globalCounter++;

  return buf.toString();
}
```

To this general process, getNextCategoryQuery() and getNextProductQuery() add a check. If no value can be found in the parent Hashtable, the row is skipped. Again, this shouldn't happen, but is a safety measure we've added to be extra certain to avoid NullPointerExceptions and bad data:

```
/** load the Categories **/
private String getNextCategoryQuery() {
  // when we run out of categories, return null
  if (categoryCounter >= categories.length) {
    return null;
  }

  // make sure we have a section entry for this category
  if (sectionHash.get(categories[categoryCounter][2]) != null) {
    // store category information for later use
    categoryHash.put(categories[categoryCounter][0],
                                       String.valueOf(globalCounter));

    // build insert category statement
    StringBuffer buf = new StringBuffer(insertCategory);
    buf.append(globalCounter).append(", '");
    buf.append(categories[categoryCounter][0]).append("', ");
    buf.append(categories[categoryCounter][1]).append(", ");
    buf.append(sectionHash.get(categories[categoryCounter][2]));
    buf.append(")");

    categoryCounter++;
    globalCounter++;

    return buf.toString();
  }

  // otherwise return null
  return null;
}

/** load the Products **/
private String getNextProductQuery() {
  // when we run out of products, return empty string
  if (productCounter >= products.length) {
    return null;
  }

  // make sure we have a category entry for this product
  if (categoryHash.get(products[productCounter][4]) != null) {
    // build insert product statement
    StringBuffer buf = new StringBuffer(insertProduct);
    buf.append(globalCounter).append(", '");
    buf.append(products[productCounter][0]).append("', '");
    buf.append(products[productCounter][1]).append("', ");
    buf.append(products[productCounter][2]).append(", ");
    buf.append(products[productCounter][3]).append(", ");

    buf.append(categoryHash.get(products[productCounter][4]));
    buf.append(")");

    productCounter++;
    globalCounter++;

    return buf.toString();
  }

  // otherwise return null
  return null;
}
```

The last part of DatabaseLoader sets our data into string arrays for use by the getNextXXXQuery() methods. Our sections consist of a name and sort_order. The array for categories contains a name, sort_order, and section-name for each row. The section-name should match one of the section names from the sections array.

One further assumption is that each section name will be unique. This isn't unreasonable since it would provide our end-users with quite a challenge if we presented them with a list of identically named sections. The products array likewise contains a parent category-name for each row, in addition to a name, manufacturer, price, and sort_order:

```
    // load section information: name, sort_order, section-id
    private static String[][] sections = new String[][]{
                                         {"Books", "1"},
                                         {"Cameras", "2"},
                                         {"Games", "3"},
                                         {"Phones", "4"}};

    // load section information: name, sort_order, section-name
    private static String[][] categories = new String[][]{
                                         {"Art", "1", "Books"},
                                         {"Horror", "2", "Books"},
                                         {"Programming", "4", "Books"},
                                         {"Children", "1", "Books"},
                                         {"Accessories", "1", "Cameras"},
                                         {"Camcorders", "3", "Cameras"},
                                         {"Digital", "4", "Cameras"},
                                         {"Batteries", "2", "Cameras"},
                                         {"Cellular", "1", "Phones"},
                                         {"Accessories", "2", "Phones"},
                                         {"Home", "3", "Phones"},
                                         {"Computer", "1", "Games"},
                                         {"Console", "2", "Games"},
                                         {"Boardgames", "3", "Games"}};

    // load section information:
    // name, manufacturer, price, sort_order, category-name
    private static String[][] products = new String[][]{
      {"Max Payne", "Gathering of Developers", "45", "1", "Computer"},
      {"Mech Commander 2", "Microsoft", "40",  "2", "Computer"},
      {"Diablo 2", "Blizzard", "35",  "3", "Computer"},
      {"The Sims", "Electronic Arts", "40",  "4", "Computer"},
      {"Nokia 3390", "Nokia", "100", "1", "Cellular"},
      {"Samsung Ear Bud", "Samsung", "15", "1", "Accessories"},
      {"Pro JSP", "Wrox", "42", "1", "Programming"}};

  }
```

So long as we follow the rule of matching section.name to section-name, and category.name to category-name in these arrays, we could change our initial values to anything we like. If care is taken to set globalCounter properly (to avoid the PrimaryKey violation) we could also use this class to populate the database with more information later. If we wanted to do this, it would be best to rewrite it such that it loads the arrays from an external source (thus avoiding recompiles every time we wanted to use this approach).

Prototyping Using Model 1 Architecture

We'll begin our application by creating a rapid prototype using Model 1 architecture. Not only will building a prototype allow us to identify any issues in our design, we'll have created much of the process and code necessary to finish the application later. When we are done, we will be able to re-use our queries and our data beans should carry over into the Struts Framework as `ActionForm` beans.

When we use the term "Model 1 Architecture" we refer to the practice of putting any necessary code (for conditionals or iterations) directly into the JSP page, and where the URL requested is directly mapped to a file on the server. This is opposed to Model 2, where a predominance of code (if not all code) is placed within an object acted on before the server proceeds to executing a display template. In Model 2, there is not necessarily a correlation between the URL and the file containing the display template. The display template **may** be a JSP file, an XML file, or some other templating system.

A JSP Fragment – dbTag_include.jspf

Let's begin by looking at a JSP fragment, for centrally locating our database connection information, in `\model1\dbTag_include.jspf`:

```
<%-- open a database connection --%>
<sql:connection id="conn1">
  <sql:url>jdbc:mysql://localhost/navigation</sql:url>
  <sql:driver>org.gjt.mm.mysql.Driver</sql:driver>

  <!-- remove the next two fields if using MySql
       and no user has been created. -->
  <sql:userId>wrox</sql:userId>
  <sql:password>wrox</sql:password>
</sql:connection>
```

We may need to change these values depending on the setup of our database, as was discussed earlier (in `buildDatabase.jsp`). What we didn't discuss earlier is that this fragment instantiates a JDBC connection, named `conn1` and places it into the `Page` context. Each page in our Model 1 application will use this fragment, so let's look at them.

Displaying the Sections – displaySections.jsp

We'll start out at the top, displaying the sections, by covering the code from `displaySections.jsp`.

Here we've imported the necessary taglibs for the operations we'll be performing on the page, and entered the template HTML for the page's header. Next we use the include directive to include the contents of `dbTag_include.jspf` when the JSP page is compiled into a servlet. In the `<jsp:useBean>` we've declared the data bean that we'll be using:

```
<%@ taglib uri='http://jakarta.apache.org/taglibs/dbtags' prefix='sql' %>
<%@ taglib uri='http://java.sun.com/jsptl/ea/jr' prefix='jr' %>

<html>
  <head>
    <title>Display Sections</title>
  </head>
  <body>
    <%@ include file="dbTag_include.jspf" %>

    <jsp:useBean id="sectionsBean"
              class="com.wrox.navigation.model1.DisplaySectionsBean" />
```

As was done earlier, we've used the <sql:statement> tag to instantiate and load a JDBC statement. Then we set up the basic query to fetch the sections from our database, ordered by their sort_order. Next we get to the heart of the operation, where we iterate over the ResultSet. We've taken advantage of <sql:getColumns> ability to set the result into a variable rather than just printing it to the page. We've put the variables (sectionId and sectionName) into the request, but we could have just as easily chosen the page context or the session:

```
<sql:statement id="stmt1" conn="conn1">

  <sql:query>
    SELECT id, name, sort_order
    FROM section
    ORDER BY sort_order
  </sql:query>

  <sql:resultSet id="rset1" loop="true">
    <sql:getColumn position="1" to="sectionId" scope="request" />
    <sql:getColumn position="2" to="sectionName" scope="request" />
```

The next step is to take advantage of the built in <jsp:setProperty> tag, and its reflection capabilities. We use this to set the sectionId and sectionName into our data bean. We'll show how the data is handled by our DisplaySectionsBean later. So far, we've collected names and ids of our sections. We close our <sql:resultSet> and <sql:statement> before proceeding. In order to present more information to our visitors, we want to capture the number of products within each section. This will allow them to see the amount of relevant items within each section, but will take another round of queries:

```
    <jsp:setProperty name="sectionsBean"
                     property="sectionId"
                     value='<%= request.getAttribute("sectionId") %>' />
    <jsp:setProperty name="sectionsBean"
                     property="sectionName"
                     value='
                         <%= request.getAttribute("sectionName") %>' />
  </sql:resultSet>

</sql:statement>
```

The new JSPTL taglib provides an iteration tag forEach which will accept any Java 2 Collection for the items attribute, and return each member as a page scoped variable named in the var attribute. Again we create a JDBC statement and a query. Notice that in this query, we are using the pageContext.getAttribute("sectionId") value since we are looping over the Collection of ids from all of our sections.

The result of each query is printed to the page inside the <sql:resultSet>. Again we use each value of sectionId to create our link to the displayCategories.jsp page. We use the <jsp:getProperty> tag to return the value of the section name as the label of our link. We use the actual results of the query to provide the count of products held by the categories for this section:

```
    <jr:forEach var="sectionId" items="<%= sectionsBean.getIds() %>" >

      <sql:statement id="stmt2" conn="conn1">

        <sql:query>
          SELECT count(*)
          FROM product p, category c, section s
          WHERE s.id = <%= pageContext.getAttribute("sectionId") %>
          AND s.id = c.section_id
          AND c.id = p.category_id
        </sql:query>

        <sql:resultSet id="rset2">
          <a href="displayCategories.jsp?section=
                          <%= pageContext.getAttribute("sectionId") %>">
          <jsp:getProperty name="sectionsBean" property="sectionName" />
                                    </a> (<sql:getColumn position="1"/>)
          <br/><br/>
        </sql:resultSet>

      </sql:statement>

    </jr:forEach>
```

Finally, we close the connection we opened at the top (and close our HTML). This is an important cleanup step as we don't want our database littered with open and unused connections:

```
    <sql:closeConnection conn="conn1" />
  </body>
</html>
```

The DisplaySectionsBean Class

How did `<jsp:getProperty name="sectionsBean" property="sectionName" />` know which section name to return? We'll need to look at `DisplaySectionsBean` to see how this is done:

```
package com.wrox.navigation.model1;

import java.util.ArrayList;

public class DisplaySectionsBean {
  protected ArrayList ids;
  protected ArrayList names;

  protected int namesCounter;
```

At first, `DisplaySectionsBean` appears to be a straight-forward application of the JavaBeans specification. We have three members, instantiated in the constructor, each with associated getters and setters. Looking at the `setSectionId()` and `setSectionName()` methods we see that they add the string value to their respective `ArrayLists`. These are the methods called, using reflection, by the `<jsp:setProperty>` tags that we saw in the first query section of `displaySections.jsp`:

```
public DisplaySectionsBean() {
  ids = new ArrayList();
  names = new ArrayList();
  namesCounter = 0;
}

public void setIds(ArrayList ids) {
  this.ids = ids;
}

public ArrayList getIds() {
  return ids;
}

public void setNames(ArrayList names) {
  this.names = names;
}

public ArrayList getNames() {
  return names;
}

// Add a sectionId to the ids array.
public void setSectionId(String sectionId) {
  ids.add(sectionId);
}

// Add a sectionName to the _names array.
public void setSectionName(String sectionName) {
  names.add(sectionName);
}
```

The `getSectionName()` method is called by the `<jsp:getProperty name="displayBean" property="sectionName" />` tag that we saw near the end of `displaySections.jsp`. It takes advantage of the `namesCounter` that we instantiated in the constructor to track how many times the method has been called.

If the `names ArrayList` is empty it returns our default value for `sectionName`. If `namesCounter` is less than the size of the `names` list, we'll use `namesCounter` as the index to get a value from `names`, and increment `namesCounter`. If `namesCounter` does match or exceed the size of `names` we'll reset `namesCounter` to 0, set `sectionName` to the value of the first element in `names`, and then increment `namesCounter`.

Lastly, we return `sectionName` to our caller. All of this allows us to automatically iterate over our `names` collection using the simple `<jsp:getProperty>` tag:

```
public String getSectionName() {
  String sectionName = ""; //"No Section Names"
  if (names.size() == 0) {
    return sectionName;
  } else if (namesCounter < names.size()) {
      // increment counter *after* doing fetch operation
      sectionName = (String) names.get(namesCounter);
```

```
            namesCounter++;
        } else {
            namesCounter = 0;
            sectionName = (String) names.get(namesCounter);
            namesCounter++;
        }

        return sectionName;
    }
}
```

When we navigate to this JSP page we see something like:

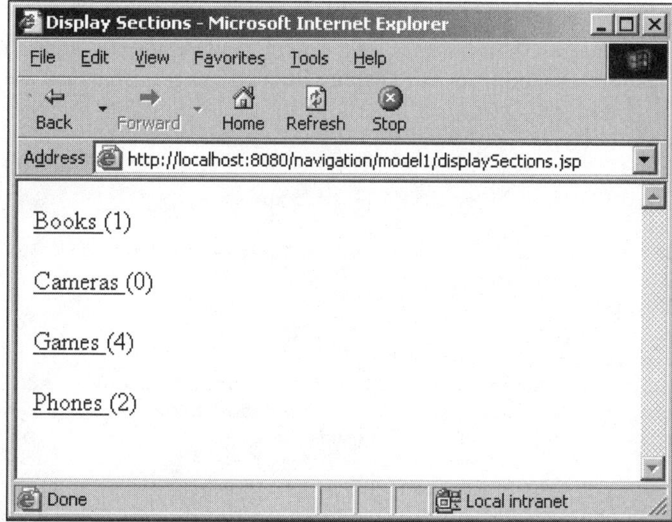

Displaying the Categories – displayCategories.jsp

Similarly, displayCategories.jsp lists the categories for the selected section, and the count of products within each category. The code for displayCategories.jsp follows the same pattern as displaySections.jsp, and includes another bean (DisplayCategoriesBean) that behaves the same as DisplaySectionsBean:

```
<%@ taglib uri='http://jakarta.apache.org/taglibs/dbtags' prefix='sql' %>
<%@ taglib uri='http://java.sun.com/jsptl/ea/jr' prefix='jr' %>

<html>
  <head>
    <title>Display Categories</title>
  </head>
  <body>
    <%@ include file="dbTag_include.jspf" %>
```

The first differences we see is that we've provided a link back up to `displaySections.jsp`, and though we've again used `<jsp:useBean>`, this time we've added a `<jsp:setProperty>` to set the value of a `sectionId` member within our `DisplayCategoriesBean`:

```
<a href="displaySections.jsp">Up to Sections</a><br/><br/>

<jsp:useBean id="categoriesBean"
             class="com.wrox.navigation.model1.DisplayCategoriesBean">
  <jsp:setProperty name="categoriesBean" property="sectionId"
                                         param="section" />
</jsp:useBean>

<sql:statement id="stmt1" conn="conn1">
```

The next difference is that we then use that `sectionId` in our query to fetch only those categories belonging to the section selected from our Display Sections page. After that, we follow the same pattern:

```
  <sql:query>
    SELECT id, name, section_id, sort_order
    FROM category
    WHERE section_id = <%= categoriesBean.getSectionId() %>
    ORDER BY sort_order
  </sql:query>

  <sql:resultSet id="rset1" loop="true">
    <sql:getColumn position="1" to="categoryId" scope="request" />
    <sql:getColumn position="2" to="categoryName" scope="request" />
    <jsp:setProperty name="categoriesBean"
                     property="categoryId"
                     value='
                         <%= request.getAttribute("categoryId") %>' />
    <jsp:setProperty name="categoriesBean"
                     property="categoryName"
                     value='
                       <%= request.getAttribute("categoryName") %>' />
  </sql:resultSet>

</sql:statement>

<jr:forEach var="categoryId" items="<%= categoriesBean.getIds() %>" >

  <sql:statement id="stmt1" conn="conn1">

    <sql:query>
      SELECT count(*)
      FROM category c, product p
      WHERE c.id = p.category_id
      AND c.id = <%= pageContext.getAttribute("categoryId") %>
    </sql:query>

    <%-- loop through the rows of your query --%>
    <sql:resultSet id="rset2">
      <a href='displayProducts.jsp?category=
```

```
                                   <%= pageContext.getAttribute("categoryId") %>
                                   &section=<jsp:getProperty
                                   name="categoriesBean"
                                   property="sectionId" />'>

                 <jsp:getProperty name="categoriesBean"
                                  property="categoryName" />
               </a> (<sql:getColumn position="1"/>)
               <br/><br/>
             </sql:resultSet>

           </sql:statement>

         </jr:forEach>

         <sql:closeConnection conn="conn1" />
       </body>
     </html>
```

The DisplayCategoriesBean Class

`DisplayCategoriesBean` significantly differs from the `DisplaySectionsBean` class only in the following ways:

```
protected String sectionId;

public void setSectionId(String sectionId) {
  this.sectionId = sectionId;
}

public String getSectionId() {
  return sectionId;
}
```

This allows our `<jsp:useBean><jsp:setProperty></jsp:useBean>` section to operate properly. The only other differences entail changing section to category.

The result of following the **Games** link is:

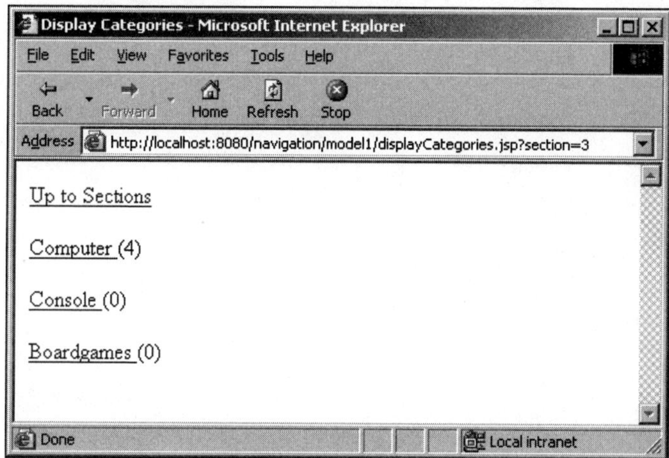

Displaying the Products – displayProducts.jsp

We continue to pass the section's id along from `displayCategories.jsp` to `displayProducts.jsp`. This allows us to provide upward navigation so that it isn't necessary for the user to use their browser's Back button. The code for `displayProducts.jsp` begins (after taglib declarations and template HTML) by retrieving the section and category parameters from the request and setting them into our `DisplayProductsBean`:

```
<jsp:useBean id="productsBean"
             class="com.wrox.navigation.model1.DisplayProductsBean">
  <jsp:setProperty name="productsBean" property="sectionId"
                                       param="section" />
  <jsp:setProperty name="productsBean" property="categoryId"
                                       param="category" />
</jsp:useBean>
```

Once we have these values, we can put them to use. Due to quirks in the way some containers implement taglib caching, the DBTags used in a page must return the same number of columns in their `ResultSets` if used more than once. Since we'll be returning four values later (a product's id, name, manufacturer, and price) we need to have our first query return four values as well:

```
<sql:statement id="stmt1" conn="conn1">
  <sql:query>
    SELECT name, name, name, name
    FROM section
    WHERE id = <%= productsBean.getSectionId() %>
  </sql:query>
```

This isn't necessary running under Tomcat 4, but it is required to successfully run with OrionServer 1.5.2. While we could have just passed in the section's name on the query string (making the first query unnecessary), we've left it as an illustration of how you cannot be certain of a tag library's behavior given differences in servlet containers. At the time of writing, OrionServer does not have full JSP 1.2 support, but such support may exist by the time of publication. Perhaps then OrionServer won't require this workaround:

```
  <sql:resultSet id="rset1">
    <a href="displayCategories.jsp?
                          section=<%= productsBean.getSectionId() %>">
      Return to <sql:getColumn position="1"/> Categories
    </a>
  </sql:resultSet>
</sql:statement>

<sql:statement id="stmt1" conn="conn1">
  <sql:query>
    SELECT id, name, manufacturer, price
    FROM product
    WHERE category_id = <%= productsBean.getCategoryId() %>
    ORDER BY sort_order
  </sql:query>
```

```
      <%-- loop through the rows of your query --%>
      <table border="1">
        <sql:resultSet id="rset2">
          <tr>
            <td>
              <b>Name:</b> <sql:getColumn position="2"/><br/>
              <b>Manufacturer:</B> <sql:getColumn position="3"/><br/>
              <b>Price:</B> $<sql:getColumn position="4"/>
            </td>
          </tr>
        </sql:resultSet>
      </table>

    </sql:statement>

  </body>
</html>
```

The first query lets us build the upward navigation back to our Display Categories page, the second selects the products for the chosen category and displays them in a HTML table.

The DisplayProductsBean Class

Since we don't need to take the extra counting step we used for sections and categories, we won't need such a fancy data bean:

```
package com.wrox.navigation.model1;

public class DisplayProductsBean {
  protected String categoryId;
  protected String sectionId;

  public DisplayProductsBean() {
    sectionId = "1";
    categoryId = "1";
  }

  public void setCategoryId(String categoryId) {
    this.categoryId = categoryId;
  }

  public String getCategoryId() {
    return categoryId;
  }

  public void setSectionId(String sectionId) {
    this.sectionId = sectionId;
  }

  public String getSectionId() {
    return sectionId;
  }
}
```

If we followed the Computer link from the previous screen we see:

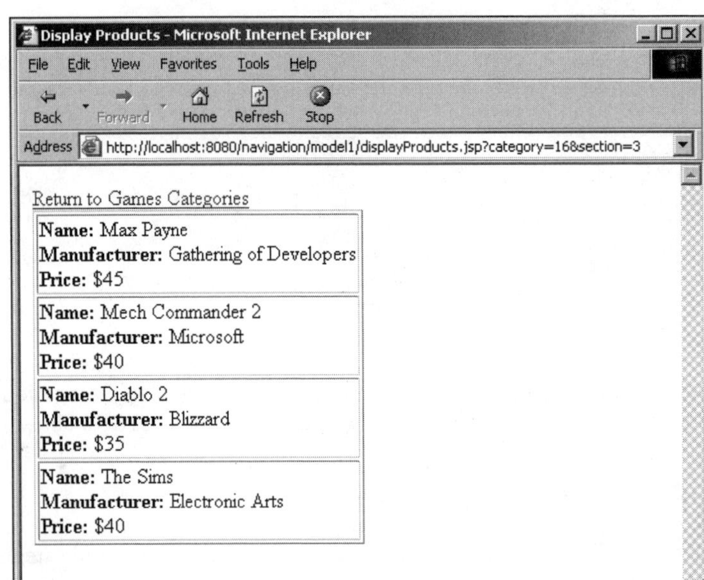

So far we've developed all the display pages for the navigation of our directory structure. On our list of features is the ability to add, remove, and edit any one of the sections, categories, or products. Since each page will need to track which action we are performing we can expect that the pages will require a lot of code, in the form of scriptlets or JSPTL tags, to traverse the decision tree and to actually do the work.

The more code we place into a page, the greater the maintenance burden becomes. This is why we've already identified the target of moving our application to the Struts Framework. This will allow us to better separate the application logic from the display templates. In particular, our management pages won't suffer from all the code being found within each JSP page, but located in an `Action` class. Since we've already created data beans for our Model 1 application, let's look first at migrating our prototype to Struts.

Model 2 Architecture Using Struts

Now we'll rewrite our navigation application with Jakarta Struts to use the Model 2 architecture. This will also demonstrate how we can migrate an application to good design practices. The benefit we receive from first writing the display pages using scriptlets is that we can clearly see which parameters and attributes are used in creating the desired HTML.

We won't cover here how Struts is installed or configured, or how it works, as this is discussed in Chapter 2.

As with any Struts application, we'll be sub-classing the `ActionForm` and `Action` classes but rather than using the `xxxForm` designation common to Struts, our `ActionForm` classes will end in `Bean`, since they are in reality simple JavaBeans. Conforming to Struts naming conventions, our `Action` classes will end in `Action`. For example, our `ActionForm` class for the category display page will be named `DisplayCategoriesBean`, and the `Action` class will be `DisplayCategoriesAction`. With this naming strategy in mind, let's create the mappings we'll need in our `struts-config.xml` file:

```
<?xml version="1.0" encoding="ISO-8859-1" ?>

<!DOCTYPE struts-config PUBLIC
          "-//Apache Software Foundation//DTD Struts Configuration 1.0//EN"
          "http://jakarta.apache.org/struts/dtds/struts-config_1_0.dtd">

<struts-config>
```

First we configure the datasources:

```
  <data-sources>
    <data-source>
      <set-property property="autoCommit"
                    value="true"/>
      <set-property property="description"
                    value="WROX Chapter 10 Data Source Configuration"/>
      <set-property property="driverClass"
                    value="org.gjt.mm.mysql.Driver"/>
      <set-property property="maxCount"
                    value="5"/>
      <set-property property="minCount"
                    value="1"/>
      <set-property property="password"
                    value="wrox"/>
      <set-property property="url"
                       value="jdbc:mysql://localhost/navigation"/>
      <set-property property="user"
                    value="wrox"/>
    </data-source>
  </data-sources>
```

Next we define the form beans:

```
  <form-beans>

    <!-- Section display bean -->
    <form-bean name="displaySections"
               type="com.wrox.navigation.struts.DisplaySectionsBean"/>

    <!-- Category display bean -->
    <form-bean name="displayCategories"
               type="com.wrox.navigation.struts.DisplayCategoriesBean"/>

    <!-- Product display bean -->
```

```
    <form-bean name="displayProducts"
               type="com.wrox.navigation.struts.DisplayProductsBean"/>

    <!-- Section edit bean -->
    <form-bean name="editSections"
               type="com.wrox.navigation.struts.EditSectionsBean"/>

    <!-- Category edit bean -->
    <form-bean name="editCategories"
               type="com.wrox.navigation.struts.EditCategoriesBean"/>

    <!-- Product edit bean -->
    <form-bean name="editProducts"
               type="com.wrox.navigation.struts.EditProductsBean"/>

  </form-beans>
```

Finally, we define the action mappings:

```
  <action-mappings>

    <!-- display Sections -->
    <action path="/displaySections"
            type="com.wrox.navigation.struts.DisplaySectionsAction"
            name="displaySections"
            scope="request"
            validate="false">
      <forward name="success" path="/struts/displaySections.jsp"/>
    </action>

    <!-- display Categories -->
    <action path="/displayCategories"
            type="com.wrox.navigation.struts.DisplayCategoriesAction"
            name="displayCategories"
            scope="request"
            validate="false">
      <forward name="success" path="/struts/displayCategories.jsp"/>
    </action>

    <!-- display Products -->
    <action path="/displayProducts"
            type="com.wrox.navigation.struts.DisplayProductsAction"
            name="displayProducts"
            scope="request"
            validate="false">
      <forward name="success" path="/struts/displayProducts.jsp"/>
    </action>

    <!-- edits Sections -->
    <action path="/editSections"
            type="com.wrox.navigation.struts.EditSectionsAction"
            name="editSections"
```

```
              scope="request"
              validate="false">
        <forward name="success" path="/struts/editSections.jsp"/>
      </action>

      <!-- edit Categories -->
      <action path="/editCategories"
              type="com.wrox.navigation.struts.EditCategoriesAction"
              name="editCategories"
              scope="request"
              validate="false">
        <forward name="success" path="/struts/editCategories.jsp"/>
      </action>

      <!-- edits Products -->
      <action path="/editProducts"
              type="com.wrox.navigation.struts.EditProductsAction"
              name="editProducts"
              scope="request"
              validate="false">
        <forward name="success" path="/struts/editProducts.jsp"/>
      </action>

    </action-mappings>

  </struts-config>
```

The first benefit we'll see is in truly centralizing our database connection information. Not only is it centralized (we did that using `dbTag_include.jspf`) but more secure. Using the `dbTag_include.jspf` left the possibility that someone could read our filesystem's structure and access that file. If so, that person would have free access to our database using the connection information listed there. By placing this information into the `struts-config.xml` we've made this inaccessible, as JSP/servlet containers are not allowed to permit direct web access to anything inside the `WEB-INF\` directory.

Following the `DataSource` configuration, we've listed out our form beans and given each type a name, or alias. After that, we've mapped a URL path to each `Action` class. We've correlated them to the form beans by name, and specified where Struts should forward the user in case of success.

The first step in building our application is to identify the data that will be held by the `ActionForm` classes. Any parameters passed on the request (as query string parameters or post parameters) will be set on the bean by Struts via standard JavaBean setter methods and we'll need to support those. Since we've already constructed data beans, let's look at how they might change.

The DisplaySectionsBean class

The Struts version of the `DisplaySectionsBean` hasn't changed significantly.

We've changed the package to reflect the change in usage, and to avoid potential naming conflicts. Likewise, we've added an import of `org.apache.struts.action.ActionForm` as we're extending that class. As we'll be fetching and storing all of our data separately from the template page, we've added members: the `counts ArrayList` and a counter for each list. In accordance, we've initialized each of these properties in our constructor:

```
package com.wrox.navigation.struts;

import java.util.ArrayList;
```

```
import org.apache.struts.action.ActionForm;

public class DisplaySectionsBean extends ActionForm {
  protected ArrayList counts;
  protected ArrayList ids;
  protected ArrayList names;

  protected Integer countsCounter;
  protected Integer idsCounter;
  protected Integer namesCounter;

  public DisplaySectionsBean() {
    counts = new ArrayList();
    ids = new ArrayList();
    names = new ArrayList();

    countsCounter = new Integer(0);
    idsCounter = new Integer(0);
    namesCounter = new Integer(0);
  }
```

The basic JavaBean getters and setters are present, and we've added support for our new members. We've dropped the `setSectionId()` and `setSectionName()` methods, and in place of `getSectionName()` we now have the `getName()`, `getId()`, and `getCount()` methods. These new methods follow the same pattern as `getSectionName()` except that our counter for each method is no longer incremented within the method but set externally:

```
  // Basic getter and setter methods for the bean's attributes
  ...

  public String getName() {
    if (namesCounter.intValue() < names.size()) {
      return (String)names.get(namesCounter.intValue());
    }

    return "No Section Name";

  }

  public String getId() {
    if (idsCounter.intValue() < ids.size()) {
      return (String)ids.get(idsCounter.intValue());
    }

    return "-1";
  }

  public String getCount() {
    if (_countsCounter.intValue() < _counts.size()) {
      return (String)_counts.get(_countsCounter.intValue());
    }

    return "0";
  }
}
```

We'll see why this change is necessary when we look at the display template \struts\displaySections.jsp next.

Displaying the Sections – displaySections.jsp

displaySections.jsp is considerably shorter than our original displaySections.jsp, and we've more or less started from scratch, though we've kept our header HTML intact. Obviously we won't need the DBTags tag library anymore; we'll replace any iteration with the tags readily available to us from Struts itself.

By the time the container is executing our template file, all our data should have been loaded into our DisplaySectionsBean data class. In fact, as we've seen in previous Struts examples, the user won't access displaySections.jsp directly, but rather the template will be loaded by going to the URL displaySections.do:

```
<%@ taglib uri='http://jakarta.apache.org/struts/tags-logic-1.0' prefix='logic' %>

<html>
  <head>
    <title>Display Sections</title>
  </head>
  <body>
```

We're using a Struts Logic tag to iterate over the section names, placing each one into the variable sectionName. We've also instructed <logic:iterate> to keep track of our current index in the variable named counter, and this is what we'll use to control the counters in DisplaySectionsBean. This is accomplished using <jsp:setProperty> by properly naming the property within each <jsp:setProperty> we set idsCounter and countsCounter to the current index value. With this done, we can use <jsp:getProperty> to fetch the corresponding id and count values:

```
    <%-- iterate over the names ArrayList from the DisplaySectionsBean --%>
    <logic:iterate id="sectionName"
                   name="displaySections"
                   property="names"
                   scope="request"
                   type="java.lang.String"
                   indexId="counter" >

      <jsp:setProperty name="displaySections"
                       property="idsCounter" value="<%=counter%>" />

      <jsp:setProperty name="displaySections"
                       property="countsCounter" value="<%=counter%>" />
```

One last trick we've employed comes as a lesson learned from our prototype: remember that we were forced to write a second query to get the section name when we reached the Display Products page? This time, we're going to pass the section name as a parameter in each link. This will let each subsequent template in our directory get the name directly rather than making another database request.

To make this parameter safe for all browsers (because we cannot count on Netscape, in particular, passing it along properly) we've passed the section name through `java.net.URLEncoder.encode()`. This will replace any spaces with a plus (+), as well as encoding any other values that might interfere with the proper operation of a query string:

```
        <a href='displayCategories.do?sectionId=<jsp:getProperty
                name="displaySections" property="id"/>
                &sectionName=<%= java.net.URLEncoder.encode(sectionName) %>'>
                <%= sectionName %></a>

        (<jsp:getProperty name="displaySections" property="count" />)
        <br/><br/>

      </logic:iterate>
    </body>
  </html>
```

The DisplaySectionsAction Class

We've seen how we store the data, and how we access it, so let's look now at how that information got into our data bean.

The first order of business is to properly package our class, and import the required classes and interfaces:

```
package com.wrox.navigation.struts;

import java.sql.Connection;
import java.sql.ResultSet;
import java.sql.SQLException;
import java.sql.Statement;
import java.util.ArrayList;
import javax.servlet.http.HttpServletRequest;
import javax.servlet.http.HttpServletResponse;
import org.apache.commons.util.StringUtils;
import org.apache.struts.action.Action;
import org.apache.struts.action.ActionForm;
import org.apache.struts.action.ActionForward;
import org.apache.struts.action.ActionMapping;

public class DisplaySectionsAction extends Action {
```

Here we've implemented the `perform()` method in agreement with our contract to implement a Struts `Action`. Our first action (pardon the pun) is to take advantage of the datasource we configured in `struts-config.xml` to get a JDBC connection:

```
    public ActionForward perform(ActionMapping mapping,
                                 ActionForm form,
                                 HttpServletRequest request,
                                 HttpServletResponse response) {
      Connection myConnection = null;
      try {
        javax.sql.DataSource dataSource =
                          servlet.findDataSource(Action.DATA_SOURCE_KEY);
        myConnection = dataSource.getConnection();
```

We need to cast the standard `ActionForm` (that Struts passes into the `perform()` method on the `Action` class) into a `DisplaySectionsBean` object. This will allow us to call our `get()` methods later. We then pass this into each of the methods `fillSections()` and `getCounts()` along with our JDBC connection:

```
      // cast ActionForm to DisplaySectionsBean
      DisplaySectionsBean sForm = (DisplaySectionsBean)form;

      // get the sections and fill the ids & names
      this.fillSections(myConnection, sForm);

      // iterate over the ids and fill the counts list
      this.getCounts(myConnection, sForm);
```

Of course, we want to catch any exceptions thrown. Here we've just printed it to the system's `stdout`, but we could have logged it otherwise, or returned a mapping to a failure page:

```
    } catch (SQLException sqle) {
        System.out.print("DisplaySectionsAction threw an Exception");
        System.out.println(StringUtils.stackTrace(sqle));
        //getServlet().log("Connection.process", sqle);
```

As usual, once we're done using the connection, we must be sure to close it lest we leave a nasty memory leak or lock up our database with unused connections:

```
    } finally {
        //enclose this in a finally block to make
        //sure the connection is closed
        try {
          myConnection.close();
        } catch (SQLException e) {
            getServlet().log("Connection.close", e);
        }
    }
```

After we've completed our `perform()` operation we return the value that represents our display template. This corresponds to the value we set in our `struts-config.xml` previously:

```
    return mapping.findForward("success");
  }
```

As we did in our Model 1 application, we fetch all the sections from the database and load them into our data bean. Since we have direct access to our `ArrayLists` we can add the values directly rather than using reflection and the `<jsp:setProperty>` tags as we did previously. We `get()` each list from the bean and then add each new value as we loop over the `ResultSet`:

```
  private void fillSections(Connection myConnection,
                            DisplaySectionsBean bean) throws SQLException {
    ArrayList ids = bean.getIds();
    ArrayList names = bean.getNames();
```

```
    String query = "SELECT id, name " +
                   "FROM section " +
                   "ORDER BY sort_order";

    Statement myStatement = myConnection.createStatement();
    ResultSet rset = myStatement.executeQuery(query);
    while (rset.next()){
      ids.add(rset.getString(1));
      names.add(rset.getString(2));
    }
    rset.close();
    myStatement.close();
  }
```

Likewise, we then iterate over the `ids` list (requested from the bean, along with the `counts` list) and fetch the number of products for each section. This time, rather than displaying the counts directly, we store them in our `counts` list for later retrieval as we've seen in our `\struts\displaySections.jsp` above:

```
  private void getCounts(Connection myConnection,
                         DisplaySectionsBean bean) throws SQLException {
    ArrayList ids = bean.getIds();
    ArrayList counts = bean.getCounts();

    String query = "SELECT count(*) " +
                   "FROM product p, category c, section s " +
                   "WHERE s.id = c.section_id " +
                   "AND c.id = p.category_id " +
                   "AND s.id = ";

    Statement myStatement = myConnection.createStatement();
    ResultSet rset = null;
    for (int counter=0; counter < ids.size(); counter++) {
      rset = myStatement.executeQuery(query + (String)ids.get(counter));
      while (rset.next()) {
        counts.add(rset.getString(1));
      }
    }

    if (rset != null) rset.close(); {
      myStatement.close();
    }
  }
}
```

The results look quite familiar:

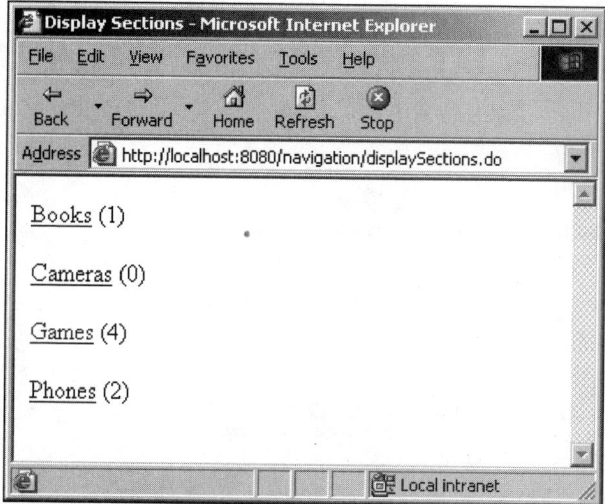

The display pages for sections and products use the same strategy for converting from a Model 1 approach to using Struts and the MVC model:

- Modify data JavaBean by adding `counts` variable and adding a counter for each `ArrayList`
- Extend `ActionForm` in each bean
- Create an `Action` class to properly load the desired values
- Then the JSP page can be modified to take advantage of Struts infrastructure and tag libraries

We mentioned earlier the lesson learned regarding section names. Let's look quickly at how this is accomplished using the Struts framework. Rather than review all the code, we'll examine only those bits related to the section name.

The DisplayCategoriesBean Class

In `DisplayCategoriesBean` we've added support that allows Struts to reflectively set our values directly from the request:

```
package com.wrox.navigation.struts;

import java.util.ArrayList;
import org.apache.struts.action.ActionForm;

public class DisplayCategoriesBean extends ActionForm {
  protected ArrayList counts;
  protected ArrayList ids;
  protected ArrayList names;
  protected String sectionId;
```

```
  protected String sectionName;

  // Basic getter and setter methods for the bean's attributes
  ...

  public void setSectionId(String sectionId) {
    this.sectionId = sectionId;
  }

  public String getSectionId() {
    return sectionId;
  }

  public void setSectionName(String sectionName) {
    this.sectionName = sectionName;
  }

  public String getSectionName() {
    return sectionName;
  }

  public String getSectionNameUrl() {
    return java.net.URLEncoder.encode(sectionName);
  }
```

The last method relieves us from having to use the URLEncoder in our template.

Displaying the Categories – displayCategories.jsp

Here's the Struts version:

```
<%@ taglib uri='http://jakarta.apache.org/struts/tags-logic-1.0' prefix='logic' %>

<html>
  <head>
    <title>Display Categories</title>
  </head>
  <body>
    <a href="displaySections.do">Up to Sections</a><br/><br/>

    <%-- iterate over the ids ArrayList from the DisplayCategoriesBean --%>
    <logic:iterate id="categoryName"
                   name="displayCategories"
                   property="names"
                   scope="request"
                   type="java.lang.String"
                   indexId="counter" >

      <jsp:setProperty name="displayCategories" property="idsCounter"
                                                value="<%=counter%>" />
      <jsp:setProperty name="displayCategories" property="countsCounter"
                                                value="<%=counter%>" />
```

Building links can get ugly, as we don't want to introduce spaces into the query string. We've once again taken advantage of the <jsp:getProperty> tag, where we can thank Struts for setting the value for us:

```
        <a href='displayProducts.do?categoryId=
             <jsp:getProperty name="displayCategories" property="id"/>
                                  &sectionId=
             <jsp:getProperty name="displayCategories" property="sectionId" />
                                  &sectionName=
             <jsp:getProperty name="displayCategories"
                         property="sectionNameUrl"/>'>

        <%= categoryName %></a>
        (<jsp:getProperty name="displayCategories" property="count"/>)
        <br/><br/>
      </logic:iterate>
    </body>
  </html>
```

As these frameworks (Struts and the JSP container) provide us with useful functionality we had minimal work to do to support passing the section name from one page to another:

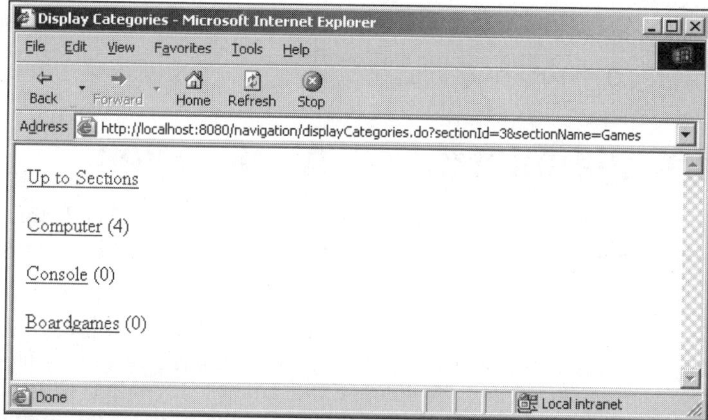

Displaying the Products – displayProducts.jsp

The `displayProducts.jsp` page repeats this process in order to build the upwards navigation link:

```
  <a href='displayCategories.do?sectionId=
             <jsp:getProperty name="displayProducts" property="sectionId" />
                         &sectionName=
             <jsp:getProperty name="displayProducts"
                         property="sectionNameUrl" />'>
    Return to <jsp:getProperty name="displayProducts"
                         property="sectionName" /> Categories</a>
```

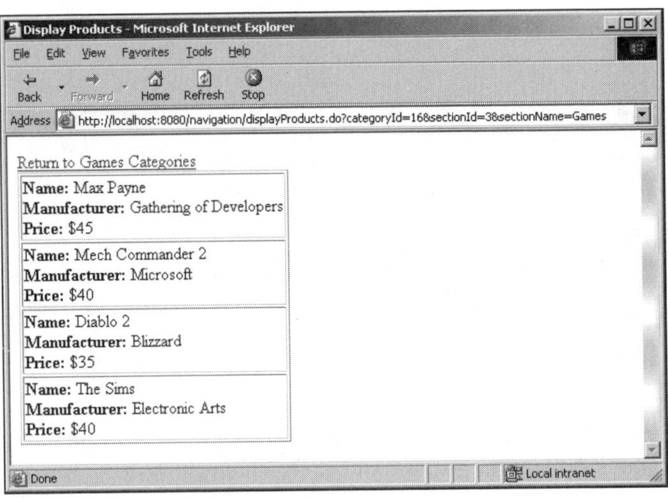

Now that we've made use of our prototype code, and gotten some practical experience using Struts, let's create an application for managing our navigation directory.

Building an Administration Application

We'll want to be able to edit, create, and delete items in our directory. While this could be done with raw SQL, it's considerably more convenient to have a web interface for these tasks. Building these pages will require forethought.

Before a section or category can be deleted, we'll have to know whether it has any children, or items with a foreign key to it. Trying to delete a database entry that has foreign key dependencies can cause error messages, or worse, cause a cascade delete if the database is configured to allow them. This would cause not only the deletion of the desired section, but all its categories and products as well. More likely the database would return a foreign-key constraint error, for example:

```
DELETE statement conflicted with COLUMN REFERENCE constraint 'FK_category_section'
```

Outside of not having foreign-key constraints, the easiest way to prevent an error in this instance is to disallow the deletion of items with children. If we remove foreign-key constraints, we introduce the potential for another problem: orphans. That is, child categories and products without a parent. So we won't present a delete option if a section or category has any children. Likewise, we'll want our application to present a simple interface for the directory's administrator to specify an item's parent.

Our items, and their relationships, are rather simple. For a section we'll build an `ActionForm` bean that holds its `id`, `name`, `sort_order`, a count of its child categories, and a collection of all sections. Similarly, the category bean will contain its `id`, `name`, `section_id`, `sort_order`, a count of its child products, and a collection of all categories.

For the ease of constructing our category administration interface, we'll also build a collection of sections to aid the administrator in selecting a `sectionId` for each category. The product bean will contain its constituent attributes, a collection of all products, and a collection of categories for the selection of a `categoryId`. We'll present these parent collections as an HTML select list, creating an easy, intuitive interface.

The `Action` classes for our administration pages will be considerably more complex than our `DisplayXXXAction` classes. The administration pages do more than simply display information, they allow the user to edit values, as well as create and delete items.

Editing Sections

We will cover editing sections in detail here, and apply these techniques to categories and products in a later section.

The EditSectionsBean Class

Let us begin with administering sections. The `ActionForm` bean is a straightforward JavaBean.

As stated above, each instance of the bean will contain the `id`, `name`, `sortOrder`, and `number` of child categories. Additionally, we'll populate a `TreeMap` of all sections for use in selecting which section the administrator wishes to edit:

```
package com.wrox.navigation.struts;

import java.util.TreeMap;
import org.apache.struts.action.ActionForm;

public class EditSectionsBean extends ActionForm {
  protected String id = "";
  protected String name = "";
  protected String sortOrder = "";
  protected int numChildren = 0;

  protected TreeMap allSections = new TreeMap();

  // Basic getter and setter methods for the bean's attributes
  ...
}
```

The EditSectionsAction Class

Our `Action` class will need to distinguish between a section being loaded, a section being updated, and a section being created:

```
package com.wrox.navigation.struts;

import java.sql.Connection;
import java.sql.ResultSet;
import java.sql.SQLException;
import java.sql.Statement;
```

```
import java.util.TreeMap;
import javax.servlet.http.HttpServletRequest;
import javax.servlet.http.HttpServletResponse;
import org.apache.commons.util.StringUtils;
import org.apache.struts.action.Action;
import org.apache.struts.action.ActionForm;
import org.apache.struts.action.ActionForward;
import org.apache.struts.action.ActionMapping;

public class EditSectionsAction extends Action {

  public ActionForward perform(ActionMapping mapping,
                               ActionForm form,
                               HttpServletRequest request,
                               HttpServletResponse response) {
    Connection myConnection = null;
```

We've been explicit with our import statements, we've retrieved our database connection, and cast the `ActionForm` to our specific subclass:

```
    try {
      javax.sql.DataSource dataSource =
                      servlet.findDataSource(Action.DATA_SOURCE_KEY);
      myConnection = dataSource.getConnection();

      EditSectionsBean sForm = (EditSectionsBean)form;
```

Following this, we begin our decision tree. If the **Delete** button was clicked, we delete this section:

```
      if (request.getParameter("deleteButton") != null) {
        this.deleteSection(myConnection, sForm);
```

Otherwise we check if the **Save** button was clicked:

```
      } else if (request.getParameter("saveButton") != null) {
```

If it is a new section, we'll call the `insertSection()` method and set a request attribute with the new value of `sForm.getId()`. Otherwise, the user is editing a pre-existing section, in which case we'll call the `updateSection()` method:

```
          if (("").equals(sForm.getId()) || ("-1").equals(sForm.getId())) {
            this.insertSection(myConnection, sForm);
            request.setAttribute("id", sForm.getId());
          } else {
              /* else its pre-existing and just needs its values updated */
              this.updateSection(myConnection, sForm);
          }
      }
```

Our interface will contain two submit buttons: **Save** and **Delete**, which we name `saveButton` and `deleteButton`. We can use these names to distinguish which behavior is being requested. Since a new section won't have an `id` yet, we'll identify them by submitting a value not valid as an id. In our application, we'll use the value `-1` or an empty string to denote a new item.

The `perform()` method is closed with the following code:

```
        // make sure all the Bean values are set
        this.fillBeanValues(myConnection, sForm);

        // now that all the work is done, fetch all Sections
        this.fillAllSections(myConnection, sForm);
      } catch (SQLException sqle) {
        System.out.print("EditSectionsAction threw an Exception:");
        System.out.println(StringUtils.stackTrace(sqle));
        getServlet().log("Connection.process", sqle);
      } finally {
        //enclose this in a finally block to make
        //sure the connection is closed
        try {
          myConnection.close();
        } catch (SQLException e) {
            getServlet().log("Connection.close", e);
        }
      }

      return mapping.findForward("success");
    }
```

This consists of two worker methods, `fillBeanValues()` and `fillAllSections()`, in addition to the now familiar cleanup code.

We'll examine the work methods in the order they appear in the code above. A common technique used is to pass a reference to the `EditSectionsBean` itself (in fact, we used this in the display `Action` classes). This allows us to act directly upon the bean and its properties, and aids us especially in the cases where multiple return values would be needed otherwise.

In our `deleteSection()` method it is important to ensure that we have a non-empty id. If the id were null or any empty string, we'd be guaranteed to throw a `SQLException`. Once the query has been executed, it's important that we set the bean's properties back to their default state so that our edit template can respond appropriately:

```
    private void deleteSection(Connection myConnection,
                               EditSectionsBean sForm)
                               throws SQLException {
      if (sForm.getId() != null && !sForm.getId().trim().equals("")) {
        Statement myStatement =
        myConnection.createStatement();
        int rows = myStatement.executeUpdate("DELETE section WHERE id = " +
                                             sForm.getId());
        sForm.setId("");
        sForm.setName("");
        sForm.setSortOrder("");
        sForm.setNumChildren(0);
        myStatement.close();
      }
    }
```

If the user clicked the **Save** button, and the value of `id` was empty or −1, we'll insert a new section:

```
private synchronized void insertSection (Connection myConnection,
                                         EditSectionsBean sForm)
                                         throws SQLException {
  String nextId = "-1";
  Statement myStatement = myConnection.createStatement();
  ResultSet rset =
            myStatement.executeQuery("SELECT max(id)+1 FROM section");
  while (rset.next()) {
    nextId = rset.getString(1);
  }
```

Once we've obtained a new id from the database, we build the insert query by pulling the values from our bean, as populated by Struts upon submission of the JSP form to the controller servlet. We make use of a `StringBuffer` to build our query from these values, and call `executeUpdate()` on the statement we created from the JDBC connection:

```
  sForm.setId(nextId);
  StringBuffer query =
     new StringBuffer("INSERT section (id, name, sort_order) VALUES (");
  query.append(nextId).append(", '");
  query.append(sForm.getName()).append("',");
  query.append(sForm.getSortOrder()).append(")");
  int rows = myStatement.executeUpdate(query.toString());
  myStatement.close();
}
```

Note, our `insertSection()` method isn't thread-safe, and this is a deliberate decision. We've decided that only one administrator will be using the application at any given time. Perhaps this is a naïve assumption, but in all likelihood true. The reason it isn't thread safe is the manner in which the id of the new section is obtained:

```
SELECT max(id)+1 FROM section
```

This value won't be inserted until the next query is run, and if another thread were to run `insertSection()` before the `INSERT` query finished it would be possible for both new sections to have the same id, creating a unique index constraint error. For this reason we've made the method synchronized. Since Struts creates only one instance of an `Action` class and passes multiple threads through the `perform()` method, this will prevent two threads from executing the `insertSection()` method at the same time.

If the administrator clicked the **Save** button, and the `id` is not empty or -1, the `updateSection()` method is called:

```
private void updateSection(Connection myConnection,
                           EditSectionsBean sForm)
                           throws SQLException {
  StringBuffer query = new StringBuffer("update section ");
  query.append("set name = '").append(sForm.getName()).append("', ");
```

```
    query.append("sort_order = ").append(sForm.getSortOrder()).append(" ");
    query.append("where id = ").append(sForm.getId());

    Statement myStatement = myConnection.createStatement();
    int rows = myStatement.executeUpdate(query.toString());
    myStatement.close();
  }
```

Since our decision tree earlier eliminated the possibility of `sForm.getId()` being empty, we won't have to make that check here. Again, we use the values of the `EditSectionsBean` to build our query.

Returning to our `perform()` method, we see that after any deletions, inserts, and updates, more work is performed. Next, the `fillBeanValues()` method is called. This method will perform two functions: populate the `name` and `sort_order` properties (necessary if this is not a save or delete action), and to populate the `numChildren` property:

```
  private void fillBeanValues(Connection myConnection,
                              EditSectionsBean sForm)
                              throws SQLException {
```

As before, we first must check that we have an id that is not null or empty. Again, if the id were null or empty, our database would throw a `SQLException`. As long as we have an id from `sForm`, run the queries. First we'll fetch the `name` and `sort_order` and set them into our bean:

```
    if (sForm.getId() != null && !sForm.getId().trim().equals("")) {
      Statement myStatement = myConnection.createStatement();
      ResultSet rset = myStatement.executeQuery(
              "SELECT name, sort_order FROM section WHERE id = " +
              sForm.getId());
      while (rset.next()) {
        sForm.setName(rset.getString(1));
        sForm.setSortOrder(rset.getString(2));
      }
```

After which we'll fill the `numChildren` value:

```
      rset = myStatement.executeQuery("SELECT count(*) FROM category " +
            "WHERE section_id = " + sForm.getId());
      while (rset.next()) {
        sForm.setNumChildren(rset.getInt(1));
      }
      myStatement.close();
    }
  }
```

The last thing we need to do before forwarding control onto our display is to load a collection of sections. This will allow our administrator to select from a list of sections, rather than having to enter an id or use some other search technique (we'll see this in practice shortly).

We've used a TreeMap to provide a semblance of ordering (which we would not get from a Hashtable or a HashMap). The TreeMap will sort according to 'natural order', in this case the strings representing the names of our sections, rather than the order in which we've fetched them from the database. We could write a Map that guarantees FIFO access, but that is well beyond this exercise (perhaps one will appear in the Jakarta Commons Collections project). In any case, alphabetical ordering by name will be more easily understood than the usual jumble that a HashMap is likely to produce:

```
    private void fillAllSections(Connection myConnection,
                                 EditSectionsBean sForm)
                                 throws SQLException {
      TreeMap allSections = sForm.getAllSections();
      Statement myStatement = myConnection.createStatement();
      ResultSet rset = myStatement.executeQuery(
        "SELECT id, name FROM section ORDER BY sort_order");
      while (rset.next()) {
        allSections.put(rset.getString(2), rset.getString(1));
      }
    }
  }
```

JDK 1.4 will contain a Map that maintains insertion order of the keys. For more information, read http://www-106.ibm.com/developerworks/library/j-mer0821/?n-j-8231/.

The editSections JSP page

Finally, we'll construct our template, editSections.jsp.

Our first order of business is to declare the tag libraries that we will be using. We could have used the Struts HTML package rather than the Jakarta Taglibs Input tags, but the latter are a bit more easily understood and straightforward in their implementation. Conversely, at this time the Struts Logic tags provide functionality that would be difficult to reproduce with the Jakarta Taglibs JSPTL project.

Next we've used the standard jsp:useBean tag to get our EditSectionsBean out of the request, and placed into the page attribute editSections, and we produce our header HTML:

```
<%@ taglib uri='http://jakarta.apache.org/struts/tags-logic-1.0' prefix='logic' %>
<%@ taglib uri='http://jakarta.apache.org/taglibs/input' prefix='input' %>

<jsp:useBean id="editSections" scope="request"
             type="com.wrox.navigation.struts.EditSectionsBean" />

<html>
  <head>
    <title>Edit Sections</title>
  </head>

  <body>
```

Here we've retrieved the `allSections` and `id` values from our `EditSectionsBean`, and used them to build a select list. The `allSections TreeMap` that we just obtained above is used to fill the options in the `input:select` tag. Finally, we create a link that will instruct our Struts components that we are preparing to create a new section object:

```
<!-- The Edit Sections Select List -->
<form action="editSections.do" >
  <input:select options="<%= editSections.getAllSections() %>"
                name="id" /><br/>
  <input type=submit value="Edit Section" />
</form>
<a href="editSections.do?id=-1">New Section</a><br/>
<br/>
```

The one drawback of using the `input:select` tag here is that it won't detect the id of a newly inserted section:

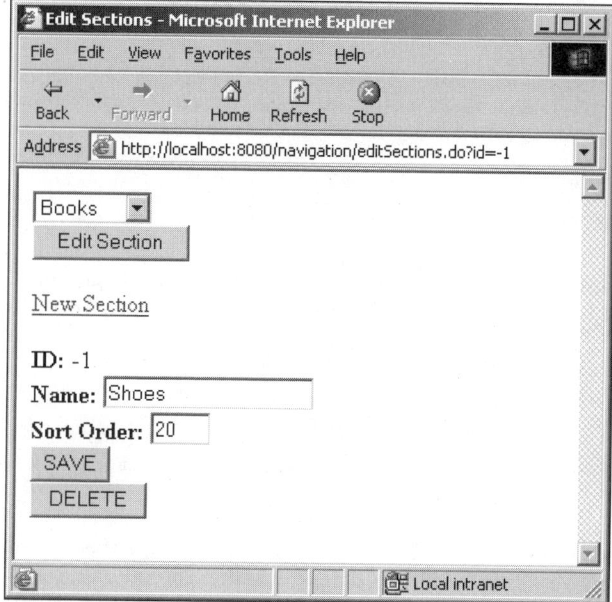

It is hoped that this deficiency can be corrected in a future release of the Input taglib. In anticipation of this, we've inserted the new `id` into a request attribute (as we saw earlier). Once corrected, `input:select` should automatically detect the request attribute and use it as the selected value.

When `editSections.jsp` is loaded, it determines if a section has been requested by checking whether `id` is an empty string or not. If not, the page will display a form for editing the section:

The presentation of the form is a straightforward use of regular HTML and the Input Tag Libraries. First we give the administrator feedback by displaying the id of the section being edited by use of the `jsp:getProperty` tag. For this value to be auto-populated when we save, a normal hidden form tag is used:

```
<form action="editSections.do" method="post">
  <input type="hidden" name="id"
         value='
         <jsp:getProperty name="editSections" property="id" />' />

  <b>ID:</b> <jsp:getProperty name="editSections" property="id" />
  <br/>
```

The name and sort_order values are displayed using the standard input tag, and the TreeMaps that we created at the beginning of this page are put to use. We've used the maxlength attribute on the name field to prevent the administrator from entering overly long values (name is restricted to 20 characters in the database). And we must give the administrator a button with which to save this information:

```
<b>Name:</b>
<input type="text" name="name" maxlength="20"
       value='
       <jsp:getProperty name="editSections" property="name" />' />
<br/>

<b>Sort Order:</b>
<input type="text" name="sortOrder" size="3"
       value='
      <jsp:getProperty name="editSections"
                       property="sortOrder" />' />
<br/>

<input type="submit" name="saveButton" value="SAVE" />
```

How will the administrator delete sections? We want to prevent the administrator from attempting to delete a section that has categories, so we'll need to add some logic. Fortunately, we provided for this in our ActionForm:

```
<logic:lessThan name="editSections"
                property="numChildren"
                value="1" >
  <br/> <input type="submit" name="deleteButton" value="DELETE">
</logic:lessThan>
```

If numChildren is less than 1 (i.e. is 0) then we can safely delete this section, so we add the deleteButton. Our Struts Action class detects whether the save or delete button has been clicked, so we've now completed that contract by supplying one or both buttons. Additionally, we've provided feedback to the administrator, allowing her to see why the delete button is not displayed:

```
<logic:greaterThan name="editSections"
                   property="numChildren"
                   value="0" >
  <p><FONT size="1"><i>
    You must delete all of this section's child categories
    before it can be deleted
  </i></font></p>
</logic:greaterThan>
```

The logic here is directly inverse to the `logic:lessThan` tag above. We've used the Struts Logic `greaterThan` tag and set the threshold to 0. If the number of child categories is greater than zero we provide the administrator with instructions on what must be done before we will allow the section to be deleted:

```
    </form>
  </logic:notEqual>
```

To finish things off we must close the `form` tag, and close the `logic:notEqual` tag that we used in displaying the edit form (or not).

Editing Categories and Products

The category and product edit pages follow the same procedure, adding a section or category select list, respectively, to the form. These lists then allow the administrator to pick the parent from a list rather than having to enter the parent's id or using some other approach to identify the parent. Since this is the only significant deviation from our Edit Sections page, let's look at how it's done. We'll add an appropriately named `TreeMap` to our `EditCategoriesBean`:

```
protected TreeMap sectionOptions = new TreeMap();

public void setSectionOptions(TreeMap sectionOptions) {
  sectionOptions = sectionOptions;
}

public TreeMap getSectionOptions() {
  return sectionOptions;
}
```

Likewise, we'll add code to our `EditCategoriesAction` to fill this `Map`. The `fillSectionOptions()` method is called during the `perform()` method of our `Action` class. It replicates the behavior from `EditSectionsAction`: executing a "get all sections by `sort_order`" query and putting them into the `TreeMap`. Much like we did in `editSections.jsp`, this `Map` is then used to populate a select list:

```
private void fillSectionOptions(Connection myConnection,
                                EditCategoriesBean cForm)
                                throws SQLException {
  TreeMap allSections = cForm.getSectionOptions();
  Statement myStatement = myConnection.createStatement();
  ResultSet rset = myStatement.executeQuery(
                   "SELECT id, name FROM section ORDER BY sort_order");
  while (rset.next()) {
    allSections.put(rset.getString(2), rset.getString(1));
  }
}
```

The difference being that this select list is a part of the form conditionally displayed if there is a valid category id. Since one of the members of our `EditCategoriesBean` is `sectionId`, we can use that to set the value of our category's select list:

```
<B>Section:</B>
<input:select name="sectionId"
              options="<%= editCategories.getSectionOptions() %>"
              default="<%= editCategories.getSectionId() %>" />
<BR/>
```

One other point of note is that our EditCategoriesAction's fillAllCategories() method goes to a little more effort to provide useful information to our administrator:

```
private void fillAllCategories(Connection myConnection,
                               EditCategoriesBean cForm)
                               throws SQLException {
  TreeMap allCategories = cForm.getAllCategories();
  Statement myStatement = myConnection.createStatement();
  ResultSet rset = myStatement.executeQuery(
                                    "SELECT c.id, s.name, c.name " +
                                    "FROM category c, section s " +
                                    "WHERE c.section_id = s.id " +
                                    "ORDER BY c.sort_order");

  while (rset.next()) {
    allCategories.put(rset.getString(2) + "-" + rset.getString(3),
                                               rset.getString(1));
  }
}
```

This results in a select list that includes the parental section name as well as the category name:

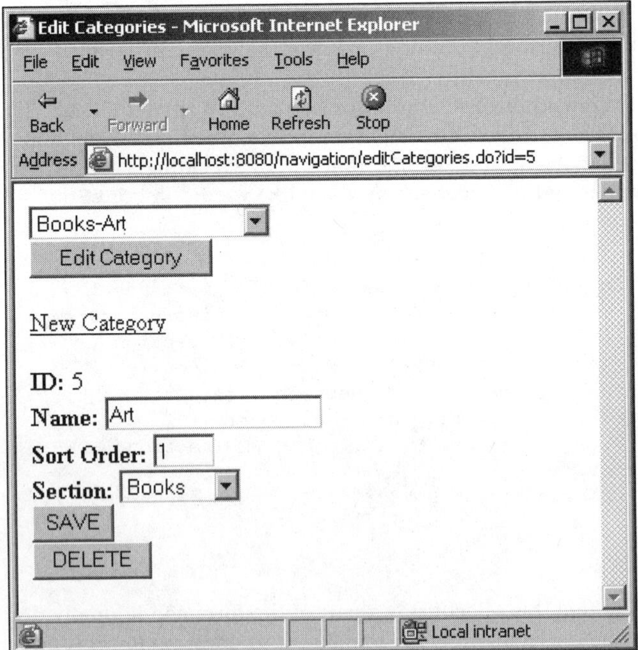

The select lists for the **Edit Products** page use the same approach in building both the list of products and the list of parental categories:

```
private void fillAllProducts(Connection myConnection,
                             EditProductsBean pForm)
                             throws SQLException {
  TreeMap allProducts = pForm.getAllProducts();
  Statement myStatement = myConnection.createStatement();
  ResultSet rset = myStatement.executeQuery(
                                 "SELECT p.id, c.name, p.name " +
                                 "FROM product p, category c " +
                                 "WHERE p.category_id = c.id " +
                                 "ORDER BY p.sort_order");
  while (rset.next()) {
    allProducts.put(rset.getString(2) + "-" + rset.getString(3),
                    rset.getString(1));
  }
}

private void fillCategoryOptions(Connection myConnection,
                                 EditProductsBean pForm)
                                 throws SQLException {
  TreeMap allCategories = pForm.getCategoryOptions();
  Statement myStatement = myConnection.createStatement();
  ResultSet rset = myStatement.executeQuery(
                                 "SELECT c.id, s.name, c.name " +
                                 "FROM category c, section s " +
                                 "WHERE c.section_id = s.id " +
                                 "ORDER BY c.sort_order");
  while (rset.next()) {
    allCategories.put(rset.getString(2) + "-" + rset.getString(3),
                      rset.getString(1));
  }
}
```

All of this work results in a lovely and intuitive interface:

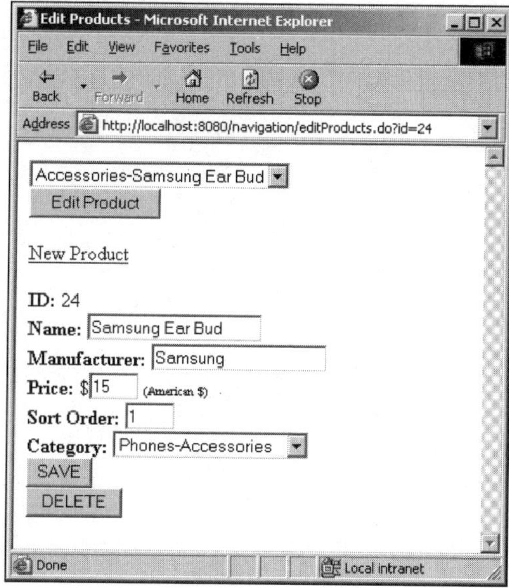

Summary

In this chapter we've covered several strategies used in designing a web application. We've seen how a well thought-out data design can aid us in designing the structure of the pages, and dictates certain rules that should be implemented (don't allow the user to delete database elements that have a foreignkey dependency).

We've also examined how the Model 1 approach can be useful both as a rapid development aid, and as a prototype to building in the MVC paradigm. The Struts framework has been used as an example of an able MVC framework.

In addition, we've made extensive and thoughtful use of tag libraries. We've taken advantage of the tags that come with Struts, as well as using those from the Jakarta Taglibs Project. When the JSPTL (JSR-052) project is completed it may be possible to replace all of the Struts tag libraries with JSPTL equivalents. At this time, however, the Struts Logic tags provide considerable power. Substitution of the Struts tag libraries with JSPTL would allow the developer to easily move from one MVC framework to another. A number of other frameworks can be found at http://husted.com/struts/links.htm#mvc/frameworks/.

In the next chapter we will take a look at a very important aspect of designing web applications – how we can effectively and usefully deal with errors that occur.

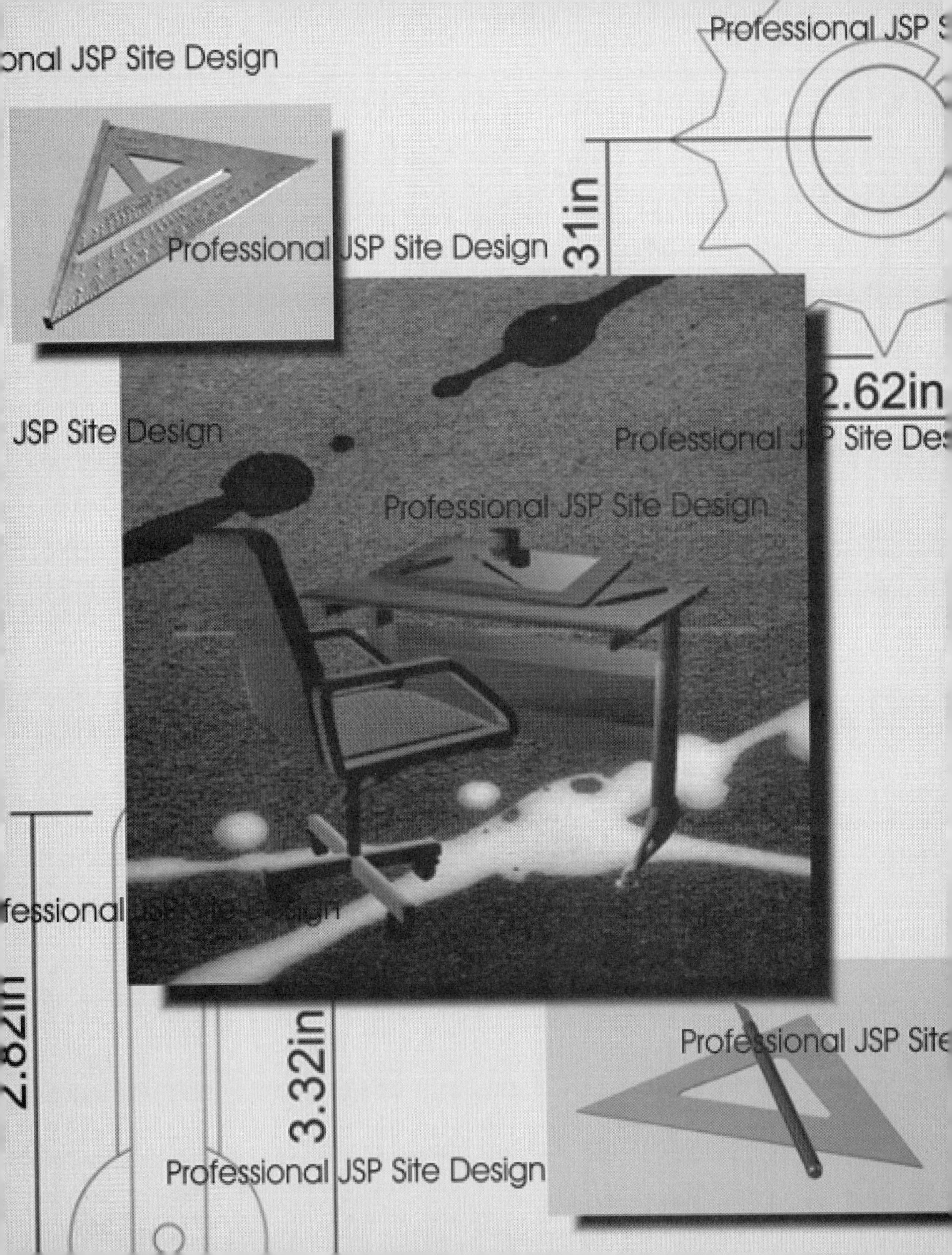
Professional JSP Site Design
31in
.62in
Professional JSP Site Design
3.32in
Professional JSP Site Design

7

Error Handling, Logging, and Notification

Handling errors gracefully and notifying the end users properly is an essential feature of a well-designed application. An application can encounter both expected and unexpected error conditions. Expected error conditions are in most of the cases caused by the end users entering invalid data, while unexpected error conditions might be caused by bugs in the code or communication failure with other applications or resources. This means that the handling for these two types of error will differ.

The proper logging and tracing of information can make error handling more efficient in your applications. This information can be used track the error's source and fix it. Logging is also immensely useful in debugging in a multi-tiered and multi-threaded application environment. It is also helpful in tracking down problems that occur once the application has been deployed, as these problems may not have arisen during development.

When a fatal error occurs in an application, it is always desirable to notify the system administrator about the error condition. Sophisticated logging mechanisms can send messages to remote server sockets, SMTP servers, operating system event logs, or remote message queues.

In this chapter, we will cover:

- The basics of error handling in the Java language
- Error handling in code, including expected and unexpected errors

- Error handling in J2EE web applications, including:
  - The use of JSP error pages
  - Mapping exceptions and HTTP error codes in the web application deployment descriptor
  - Using the `TryCatchFinally` interface for resource management
- The fundamentals of logging and tracing including priorities, filters, formatters, and destinations
- The Log4J API from the Apache Foundation
- The logging features in J2SE version 1.4
- Error notification, and how to send them by e-mail using custom tags

Error Handling

Error handling is very important in a multi-tiered J2EE application and as a vital part of the application, designing the error handling should be considered from the very start of the design. Errors can happen at various tiers of the application for many different reasons, therefore a well-designed system should:

- Where possible, recover from the error condition
- Notify the end user about the error condition in a graceful manner, if it was unable to work around, or recover from, the error
- If necessary, log information about the error
- Where appropriate, notify the administrator about the error

Of course, not all errors should be logged or notified. Errors may occur because of invalid data provided by the user that causes a violation of the business logic. In such cases, the system should provide the end users with appropriate error messages informing them of the correct form of data to provide. In this case, it would be inappropriate for the system to log the error or inform an administrator of its occurrence.

The logging and tracing of the error information should support:

- **Filtering log messages**
  The application administrator should be able to decide what messages should be logged, and from which parts of the application
- **Setting priority**
  The application administrator should be able to assign different priority levels to the information that is logged
- **Formatting the information**
  The application administrator should be able to format the information that is logged as required
- **Multiple destinations**
  The logging system should be able to send the information to multiple destinations, such as the console, files, operating system event logs, remote message queues, or even by e-mail to the administrator

Java Exceptions

The Java language provides us with a framework based on throwing and catching errors for handling the error conditions in code. These error conditions are handled by a specialized set of classes that have `java.lang.Throwable` at the root of their inheritance hierarchy. J2SE provides a set of classes that inherit, directly or indirectly, from this class that can be used to handle many different error conditions. Third party class libraries usually come with their own set of subclasses of `Throwable` and we may define our own set of classes to handle error conditions specific to the code we write.

All these classes may broadly be classified into **errors** and **exceptions** and exceptions may be further classified into **checked exceptions** and **runtime exceptions**. The following class diagram depicts the important subclasses of the class `Throwable`:

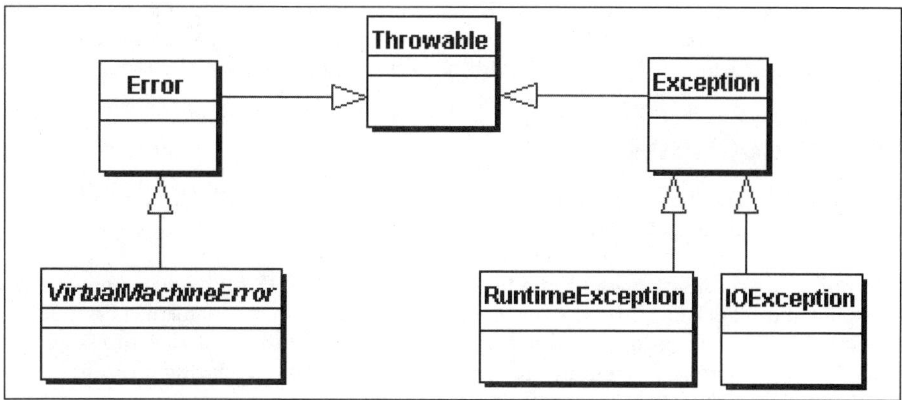

Checked Exceptions

Checked exceptions are classes that (directly or indirectly) extend `java.lang.Exception` but are not (direct or indirect) subclasses of `java.lang.RuntimeException`.

If we call a method that is declared to throw a checked exception, it is mandatory to catch any exceptions that are thrown, or to declare that the calling method throws the same exception. J2SE specifies a set of checked exceptions that are specific to different types of error conditions. For example:

- `SQLException`
  This is thrown by the methods defined in the interfaces belonging to the `java.sql` package when errors occur involving SQL operations

- `IOException`
  This is thrown by the methods defined in the classes and interfaces belonging to the `java.io` package and is thrown when error conditions occur involving I/O operations

We may extend the `Exception` class and define our own exceptions representing error conditions in our application. We should use checked exceptions to handle business logic violations. The code below defines a checked exception for handling a business rule violation:

```
public class InsufficientFundsException extends Exception {
  public InsufficientFundsException(String message) {
    super(message);
  }
}
```

The following code shows how this exception could be used in a business method:

```
public void debit(double amount) throws InsufficientFundsException {
  if(amount > funds) {
    throw new InsufficientFundsException("Insufficient funds");
  }
```

These exceptions are seldom bubbled beyond the request delegate tier. In a properly partitioned application, business exceptions will be thrown only from the business tier and will be handled by the request delegate tier, which will in turn provide a meaningful message to the user.

Runtime Exceptions

Runtime exceptions are classes that are extended directly or indirectly from `RuntimeException` and are normally caused by bugs in code.

Such exceptions are mostly thrown by the Java Virtual Machine (JVM) when it encounters errors that are not expected or checked for by the normal checked exception mechanism – essentially they are bugs in code. Runtime exceptions need not be declared in a method signature or caught within calling methods. However, there is no language feature that stops us from declaring a runtime exception in our `throws` clause or catching them in a method.

J2SE provides a variety of runtime exceptions that represent different types of error conditions. For example:

- `NullPointerException`
  This exception is thrown by the JVM if we try to invoke a method on a null object reference
- `IndexOutOfBoundException`
  This exception is thrown by the JVM if we try to access an index of some sort (which could be to an array, a string, or a vector) that is out of range

If we are writing class libraries or service classes such as business or data access objects, we may define our own runtime exceptions by extending `RuntimeException`. These exceptions are thrown by the service methods which are incorrectly called by client classes. However, J2SE provides a set of classes for handling some of the more common scenarios.

IllegalArgumentException

We may throw this exception in a method if a calling method passes an invalid value for one of the arguments. For example, in a properly partitioned web application, business objects may create value objects and pass them to create/update/delete methods on the data access objects that perform database operations. The data access objects might expect non-null references for the value objects. Nevertheless, they can throw an instance of `IllegalArgumentException` if a null object reference is passed by the business object:

```
public class EmployeeDAO {
  public void createEmployee(Employee employee) {
    if(employee == null)
     throw new IllegalArgumentException("Employee must not be null");
    }
}
```

This exception doesn't need to be declared in the `throws` *clause of the method.*

IllegalStateException

We may throw this exception in a method if the method is called at an illegal or inappropriate time. For example, suppose we have a generic utility class for writing data to a remote server socket. We initialize the connection in the constructor of the class. As a check, we throw an instance of `IlleagalStateException` in the method for writing the data if the client side socket is invalid:

```
public class SocketUtil {
  private java.net.Socket sock;

  public void write(byte[] data) {
    if(sock == null)
      throw new IllegalStateException("Socket not open");
    }
}
```

In the Servlet API, if we use a request dispatcher to forward a resource when data has been committed to the current output stream, it throws an `IllegalStateException`.

UnsupportedOperationException

We may throw this exception if an unsupported method is called. There are many potential uses for this exception. For example, we could notify a client class if it calls a method that is to be implemented in a later version of the class:

```
public class MyService {
  public void myUnsupportedOperation(byte[] data) {
    throw new UnsupportedOperationException("Operation not supported");
  }
}
```

Another important use of this exception is if we define an abstract interface for a group of classes and only a subset of the concrete subclasses provides implementations for some of the methods. For example, the W3C DOM interface `org.w3c.dom.Node` defines a method called `appendChild(org.w3c.dom.Node)` for adding a child node to the current node. However, if we try to pass an object of type `org.w3c.dom.Attribute` to this method, an `UnsupportedOperationException` will be thrown, even though `Attribute` is a subinterface of `Node`. To set an attribute we need to call the `setAttribute(org.w3c.dom.Attribute)` method on the `org.w3c.dom.Element` interface that is a subinterface of `Node`.

Errors

Errors indicate serious problems that normal applications don't bother to catch, like JVM out of memory errors and unsatisfied link errors. Errors are not generally thrown in normal conditions and methods don't need to declare errors in their `throws` clause or catch them within their body. The direct subclasses of `Error` are:

- `AWTError`
  This is thrown when the abstract window toolkit encounters a serious error.
- `LinkageError`
  Subclasses of this are thrown when dependencies between classes are violated. For example, if we define two classes and the first class calls a method in the second class. After we have compiled the classes, we remove the method from the second class and recompile it. Now if we try to run the first class and it tries to invoke the nonexistent method on the second class, the JVM will throw a `NoSuchMethodError`. This is a subclass of `IncompatibleClassChangeError`, which in turn subclasses `LinkageError`.
- `ThreadDeath`
  This is thrown when a thread is stopped by a call to the stop method. However, it is not recommended to call the stop method on threads. Threads should be allowed to return normally from the `run()` method. Also it is better to use the wait and notify mechanisms for relinquishing control over monitor locks.
- `VirtualMachineError`
  This error is thrown when there is a serious problem with the JVM. One of the familiar subclasses of this is `OutOfMemoryError`, which is thrown when the system runs out of resources.

In an application server environment, all the instances of `Throwable` are caught in order to stop the JVM from crashing.

Error Handling Patterns

Most modern J2EE web applications use some variation of the Model 2 architecture. Although the architecture may have a wide variety of flavors, the basic concept will remain the same. A group of requests will be sent to a controller object that will use some sort of configuration information to route these requests to a delegate object capable of handling them.

The delegate object will in turn use business objects to access enterprise data and to communicate with other disconnected applications. The business objects will delegate the actual data access tasks to data access objects. The request delegates will then pass some sort of information to the view dispatcher module of the front controller that can be used to select the request responsible for rendering the view.

For more information on Model 2 architecture, see Chapter 1.

From an error handling perspective, the advantage of the above model is that the exceptions thrown by the various components in the different tiers may be allowed to bubble up to the front controller, which allows us to have a centralized decision point that decides what to do with the exception. This means exceptions are either not caught or caught and re-thrown to the calling method. The calling method will also throw it to the method that called it in a similar way, until the exceptions reach the front controller.

The front controller could be implemented as a servlet or a JSP page with an embedded JavaBean. This choice greatly influences the error handling mechanisms the system will use. With a servlet controller, the only exceptions we can throw are `ServletException` and `IOException`. However, with a JavaBean controller, we can throw any exception to the enclosing JSP page so long as the request processing method of the bean declares that it throws the exception. The controller JSP page can then use the `errorPage` attribute of the `page` directive to handle the errors.

Exception Types

In multi-tiered enterprise applications, components belonging to various tiers in the applications may throw exceptions that can be broadly classified into:

- **Runtime exceptions**
  These can be thrown because of bugs in the code or by service methods when they are called incorrectly by a client.
- **Unexpected checked exceptions**
  These should either be caught in our methods or declared in `throws` clauses. They include:
  - SQL exceptions thrown when we invoke methods on data access objects
  - Remote exceptions thrown when we invoke remote methods
  - IO exceptions thrown during local and remote communication
  - Unexpected finder exceptions in the EJB home interface for multi-object finders
  - JMS and naming exceptions
- **Expected checked exceptions**
  These are in most cases the business exceptions that are thrown from the methods in business objects. These exceptions are normally caused by users entering invalid data and are normally thrown by the business objects to the request delegate objects.

Next, we'll cover the different strategies used to handle these different types of exception.

Expected Checked Exceptions

Expected checked exceptions are usually thrown by business objects to the request delegate objects. The request delegate objects can either throw these exceptions back to the front controller or handle them. When users enter invalid data, the application should present the original form to the users, retaining the original data entered, along with a relevant error message.

A popular pattern of handling expected checked exceptions is where the request delegate will store the error information present in the business exception thrown by the business object. The request delegate will then notify the view dispatcher module of the front controller, which will forward the request to the page that generated the current request. This page can use JSP custom tags to render the error message.

In the next section we will design a framework that can handle expected exceptions. The framework could be used for handling other exceptions, such as unexpected checked exceptions and runtime exceptions. However, those exceptions would normally be handled differently. For example, we may need to perform extra tasks like notification, logging, resource cleanup, or session invalidation.

An Error Handling Framework

In this section, we will cover the expected functionality of the error-handling framework. Specifically, the framework should:

- Enable the web application to use the same resource for gathering information from the users and representing the form back to the users on validation errors and business rule violations. For example, suppose the resource `input.jsp` is used to gather the information. If a validation error occurs, the controller should be able to use the same resource for sending the response back to the user. This is quite important, as the response will be identical to the original input screen. However, the response will also be displaying the relevant error messages.
- Store the error messages in a centralized repository so that messages may be amended easily.
- Handle internationalized error messages.
- Support parameterized error messages so that application developers can specify replacement values when the error is created. This means the application developers should be able to insert relevant values within the error messages predefined in the central repository. For example, in the error repository we may store the string "`Invalid amount {0}`". However, when the message is sent back to the users, the system should be able to replace `{0}` with a real value.
- Support cumulative error handling so that application developers perform all the business checks and send all the error messages back to the end users rather than sending only the first error that is encountered. For example, suppose there is an input form containing two fields for entering rate and quantity, both of which should be positive numbers. If the user enters invalid data for both the fields, the system should be able to do both the validations and provide both the error messages back to the users, rather than providing them with the first error message.
- Group multiple error messages so that the messages may be filtered in the JSP page that renders the error message. This will be quite useful in the above example, if we want to display the error message related to quantity next to the quantity field and that related to the rate next to the rate field.

Now we're ready to design the framework.

Designing the Framework

The most appropriate component for rendering the error message is a JSP custom tag because they can query the various HTTP collections like request, session, page, and applications for attributes defined by a key specified as a tag attribute. The tags may decide to do nothing if the specified error attribute is not found. Therefore, we can use the same JSP page for rendering the view the first time and after each time an error occurs. This is also useful in retaining the original information entered by the user along with specific error messages if the page is sent back due to validation errors.

A tag can be used that will render the error message if it is available in the requirement parameter list. Therefore, when the JSP page is rendered the first time, the tag won't display any error message but when it is sent back to the user by the controller because of validation errors, it will display the error messages stored by the request delegate.

The second and third requirements can be implemented using a Java resource bundle. Resource bundles can store locale-specific messages. When a program needs a locale-specific message, it can load one from the resource bundle that is appropriate for the current user's locale. In this way, we can write program code that is largely independent of the user's locale. We will store the error messages against error keys in a resource bundle. The custom tag will extract the end user's locale from the incoming request and read the error message from the appropriate resource bundle.

> **The code assumes that the base resource bundle is called `errors.properties` and it is available to the class loader. The more specific resource bundles should be called `error_XX.properties` where `XX` correspond to the ISO code for that locale. All the properties files should be stored in the `WEB-INF\classes\` directory of the web application.**

The fourth requirement can be solved by using placeholders in the error messages that can be replaced using the `java.util.MessageFormat` class. When an error is created by the request delegate object, it will specify an error key in the resource bundle and an optional list of replacement values. The custom tag will read the error message from the appropriate resource bundle and replace the placeholders with specified list of values. We'll represent an error by an instance of the class `CustomError` which contains two attributes representing the error key and a list of replacement values.

The fifth and sixth requirements can be fulfilled by defining an aggregation class called `CustomErrors` that will hold a list of `CustomError` objects. The container will maintain the aggregation as a map of error categories so that the custom tag can filter the group of errors for those it is interested in. For this the custom tag will define an optional attribute called `errorCategory`. If this attribute is not specified, the tag will render all the errors belonging to the `GLOBAL_ERROR` category. The `CustomErrors` class will provide two overloaded methods for adding `CustomError` objects. The first will take an error category and the `CustomError` object. The second one takes only the `CustomError` object and adds it against the `GLOBAL_ERROR` category.

The CustomError Class

Let's look at the source code for the `CustomError` class, which will model a single error message:

```
package errors;

import java.util.List;

public class CustomError {
```

The `paramList` variable stores the list of values that may be used to replace the placeholders, as defined in the actual error message stored in the resource bundle:

```
  private List paramList;
```

The `errorKey` variable represents the key against which the actual error message is stored in the resource bundle:

```
    private String errorKey;

    public CustomError(String errorKey) {
      this.errorKey = errorKey;
    }

    public CustomError(String errorKey, List paramList) {
      this.errorKey = errorKey;
      this.paramList = paramList;
    }

    public String getErrorKey() {
      return errorKey;
    }

    public List getParamList() {
      return paramList;
    }
  }
```

The CustomErrors Class

Now we will have a look at the `CustomErrors` class. This class will function as an aggregation of `CustomError` class objects:

```
  package errors;

  import java.util.HashMap;
  import java.util.List;
  import java.util.ArrayList;

  public class CustomErrors {
```

`DEFAULT_CATEGORY` stores the value for the key that `CustomError` objects without a category are stored against:

```
    public static final String DEFAULT_CATEGORY = "";
```

`ERROR_MESSAGE_KEY` holds the name of the HTTP request attribute that stores the `CustomErrors` object:

```
    public static final String ERROR_MESSAGE_KEY = "errors";
```

This map stores the list of the error objects against the required categories:

```
    HashMap errorMap = new HashMap();
```

The addError() method stores the passed CustomError object against the default error category:

```
    public void addError(CustomError error) {
      addError(DEFAULT_CATEGORY, error);
    }
```

This version of the addError() method stores the passed CustomError object in the requested error category:

```
    public void addError(String errorCategory, CustomError error) {
      List errorList = (List)errorMap.get(errorCategory);
      if(errorList == null) {
        errorList = new ArrayList();
      }
      errorList.add(error);
      errorMap.put(errorCategory, errorList);
    }
```

Access the list of error objects for the specified error category:

```
    public List getErrorList(String errorCategory) {
      return (List)errorMap.get(errorCategory);
    }
  }
```

The ErrorMessageTag Class

This class implements the tag handler for the custom tag that can be used in the input JSP pages for displaying the error messages. The sequence of events that occur when the tag is processed by the container is:

- Get a reference to the current request from the page context object
- Retrieve the CustomErrors object stored as a request attribute
- Get the list of errors stored against the error category specified as a tag attribute (if this optional attribute is not specified, the list stored against the default category is used)
- Iterate through the list of error objects and get the message stored in the resource bundle for the preferred locale object retrieved from the incoming request
- If the error object has an associated list of replacement values, use the MessageFormat object to replace the placeholders in the message
- Write the messages back to the enclosing writer

Place the source for this class in a file called ErrorMessageTag.java:

```
package errors;

import javax.servlet.jsp.tagext.TagSupport;
import javax.servlet.jsp.JspWriter;
import javax.servlet.jsp.JspException;
```

```
import javax.servlet.ServletContext;
import javax.servlet.ServletRequest;

import java.util.ResourceBundle;
import java.util.List;
import java.util.Iterator;

import java.text.MessageFormat;

import java.io.IOException;

public class ErrorMessageTag extends TagSupport {
```

First we define the default error category:

```
  private String errorCategory = CustomErrors.DEFAULT_CATEGORY;
```

These are the methods for getting and setting the error category. This will be set by the container if the `errorCategory` attribute is not specified:

```
  public String getErrorCategory() {
    return errorCategory;
  }

  public void setErrorCategory(String errorCategory) {
    this.errorCategory = errorCategory;
  }

  public int doStartTag() throws JspException {
```

Get a reference to the request from the page context:

```
    ServletRequest req = pageContext.getRequest();
```

Retrieve the resource bundle for the locale associated with the request. Instead of hard coding the base resource bundle name as `errors` we may store it as a servlet context attribute:

```
    ResourceBundle rb = ResourceBundle.getBundle("errors", req.getLocale());
```

Retrieve the `CustomErrors` object stored as a request attribute. Here we may also define the name under which the `CustomErrors` object is stored as a tag attribute instead of hard coding it as public static final variable in the `CustomErrors` class:

```
    CustomErrors errors =
            (CustomErrors)req.getAttribute(CustomErrors.ERROR_MESSAGE_KEY);
```

If there is no CustomErrors object associated with the current request, return from the method. The request will contain CustomErrors object only when the pages are returned back to the users because of validation errors:

```
    if(errors == null) {
      return EVAL_BODY_INCLUDE;
    }
```

Retrieve the list of CustomError objects for the defined category:

```
    List errorList = errors.getErrorList(errorCategory);
```

If there are no CustomError objects available for the defined category, return from the method:

```
    if(errorList == null) {
      return EVAL_BODY_INCLUDE;
    }

    Iterator it = errorList.iterator();
    CustomError error = null;
    String message;
    StringBuffer out = new StringBuffer();
```

Iterate through the list of CustomError objects:

```
    while(it.hasNext()) {
       error = (CustomError)it.next();
```

Get the message defined in the resource bundle corresponding to the key stored in the CustomError object:

```
      message = rb.getString(error.getErrorKey());
      if(message == null) {
        continue;
      }
```

Get the list of replacement values stored in the CustomError object. If the list is not null, replace the placeholders defined in the error message:

```
      if(error.getParamList() != null) {
          out.append(MessageFormat.format(message,
                                                 error.getParamList().toArray()));
      } else {
          out.append(message);
      }
    }
```

Write all the messages back to the enclosing writer:

```
      try {
        JspWriter writer = pageContext.getOut();
        writer.println(out);
      } catch(IOException ex) {
          throw new JspException(ex.getMessage());
      }
      return EVAL_BODY_INCLUDE;
    }
  }
```

Tag Library Descriptor

Name this `errors.tld`:

```
<?xml version="1.0" encoding="ISO-8859-1" ?>
<!DOCTYPE taglib
          PUBLIC "-//Sun Microsystems, Inc.//DTD JSP Tag Library 1.1//EN"
          "http://java.sun.com/dtd/web-jsptaglibrary_1_2.dtd">

<taglib>
  <tlibversion>1.0</tlibversion>
  <jspversion>1.1</jspversion>
  <shortname>simple</shortname>
  <uri></uri>
  <info>A simple tab library for the examples</info>

  <tag>
    <name>errorMessage</name>
    <tagclass>errors.ErrorMessageTag</tagclass>
    <info> Displays info from a XML node </info>
    <attribute>
       <name>errorCategory</name>
       <required>false</required>
       <rtexprvalue>true</rtexprvalue>
    </attribute>
  </tag>
</taglib>
```

Using the Framework

Next, we'll write a small application to test the framework. It will have two JSP pages. `input.jsp` will have a field within an HTML form for entering the amount to be withdrawn. When the form is submitted, a servlet will perform a business check to verify the entered amount is less than 1000. If not, it will store an appropriate `CustomError` object and send the request back to `input.jsp`. Otherwise, it will send the response to `output.jsp`. `input.jsp` will have the custom tag for displaying the error message that displays nothing the first time the JSP is downloaded.

In a real Model 2 scenario, the request will be sent to a controller and the controller will delegate the request to an appropriate request delegate. The request delegate will call a business object that will perform the business logic checks. If the business rules are violated, the business object will create a business exception that encapsulates the `CustomErrors` object and throws it back to the request delegate. The request delegate will store the `CustomErrors` object as a request attribute and ask the view dispatcher module of the controller to forward the request to the page that initiated the current request. This page will use custom tags to render the error messages as well as the original data entered by the users.

The input JSP Page

This page displays the input form for entering the data. This will also have the custom tag for rendering the error message:

```
<%@ taglib uri="/WEB-INF/errors.tld" prefix="errors" %>

<html>
  <head>
    <title></title>
  </head>

  <body>
```

Use the custom tag to render the error messages if present. The tag is used without the optional error category attribute. This will render the error messages belonging to the default category:

```
    <errors:errorMessage/>
```

The form's action is mapped to the request processing servlet:

```
    <form action="DebitServlet" method="post">
```

Extract the original value entered by the user in case this page is sent back because of a validation error:

```
      <%
        String amt = request.getParameter("amt");
        amt = amt==null?"":amt;
      %>
```

Define the input controls for entering the data and submitting the form:

```
      <input name="amt" type="text" size="10" value="<%= amt %>" />
      <input type="submit" value="debit" />
    </form>
  </body>
</html>
```

The output JSP Page

This page just prints a confirmation message once the debit process has completed successfully:

```
<html>
  <head>
    <title></title>
  </head>
  <body>
    <h2>Debit Complete</h2>
  </body>
</html>
```

The DebitServlet Class

This is the request processing servlet that validates the business rules and dispatches the next view:

```
package errors;

import java.io.IOException;
import javax.servlet.http.HttpServlet;
import javax.servlet.http.HttpServletRequest;
import javax.servlet.http.HttpServletResponse;
import javax.servlet.ServletException;
import java.util.List;
import java.util.ArrayList;

public class DebitServlet extends HttpServlet {

  public void doPost(HttpServletRequest req, HttpServletResponse res)
    throws IOException, ServletException {
```

Get the amount entered by the user:

```
    double amt = Double.parseDouble(req.getParameter("amt"));
```

If the amount is greater than 1000, create an instance of the `CustomErrors` class and add a `CustomError` object to it. The `CustomError` object is created by specifying the message key and a list of replacement values that contain the original value entered by the user. The response is forwarded to the page that initiated the current request:

```
    if(amt > 1000) {
      CustomErrors errors = new CustomErrors();
      List paramList = new ArrayList();
      paramList.add(new Double(amt));
      errors.addError(new CustomError("error.invalidFund", paramList));
      req.setAttribute(CustomErrors.ERROR_MESSAGE_KEY, errors);
      req.getRequestDispatcher("/input.jsp").forward(req, res);
    } else {
        req.getRequestDispatcher("/output.jsp").forward(req, res);
    }
  }
}
```

The errors.properties File

This file acts as the resource bundle for the locale on the server. This file should be made available to the class loader. A convenient location to store this file is WEB-INF\classes\ directory. The string {0} will be replaced by the value specified by the request processing servlet:

```
error.invalidFund=The entered amount {0} exceeds the funds in the account<br/>
```

The resource file for the German locale should be named as errors_de.properties and may contain markup defined in the German language. Similarly a locale for the English language spoken in Great Britain may be named as errors_en_GB.properties.

We can include HTML markup in the message, so we have a line break at the end of our message.

Deployment Descriptor

The deployment descriptor contains the declaration and mapping for our request processing servlet and our Errors Tag Library:

```
<?xml version="1.0" encoding="ISO-8859-1"?>

<!DOCTYPE web-app
          PUBLIC "-//Sun Microsystems, Inc.//DTD Web Application 2.3//EN"
          "http://java.sun.com/dtd/web-app_2_3.dtd">

<web-app>
  <taglib>
    <taglib-uri>errors</taglib-uri>
    <taglib-location>/WEB-INF/errors.tld</taglib-location>
  </taglib>

  <servlet>
    <servlet-name>DebitServlet</servlet-name>
    <servlet-class>errors.DebitServlet</servlet-class>
  </servlet>

  <servlet-mapping>
    <servlet-name>DebitServlet</servlet-name>
    <url-pattern>/DebitServlet</url-pattern>
  </servlet-mapping>
</web-app>
```

Running the Application

To run the application we must perform the usual steps:

- Create a web application directory structure
- Copy all the compiled classes and the resource bundle files to WEB-INF\classes\ directory
- Copy the JSP pages to the root directory
- Copy the tag library and deployment descriptors to the WEB-INF\ directory

Start Tomcat, navigate to http://localhost:8080/errors/input.jsp, then enter a value greater than 1000:

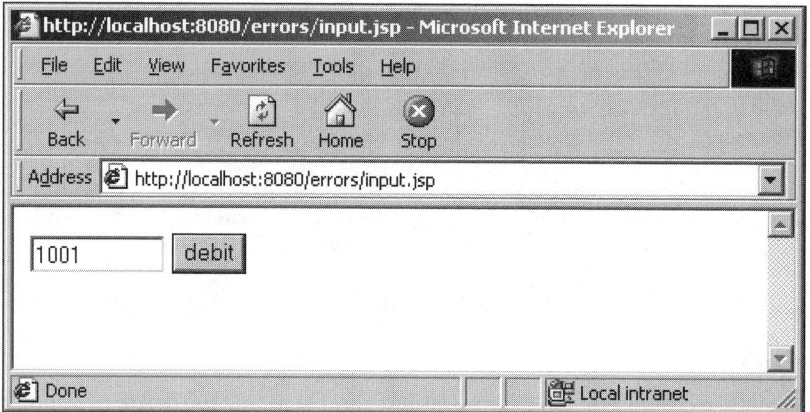

Submit the form and you should see something like:

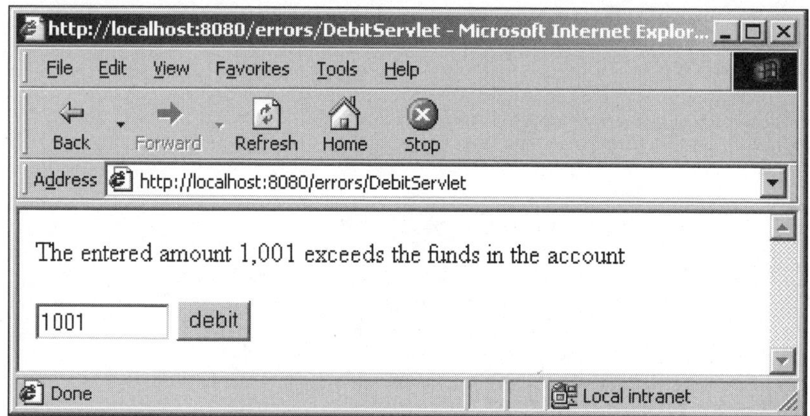

The actual placeholder in the error message will be replaced by the value that you entered.

Unexpected Checked and Runtime Exceptions

In the previous section, we saw how expected checked exceptions are in most cases business exceptions thrown from business objects. However, we will need to handle various unexpected instances of checked exceptions and runtime exceptions in different tiers of an application. Suppose we have a business method that looks up a database connection from a JNDI tree, executes some SQL, sends some JMS messages, and then writes some local files. This method may also throw a business exception when business rules are violated. This signature of such a method might be:

```
public void businessMethod( ... )
            throws NamingException, SQLException, JMSException,
                   IOException, BusinessException
```

If this business method is called from a request delegate and we decide to bubble all the exceptions up to the front controller the signature of the request delegate method will be:

```
public Resource handleRequest(ServletRequest req, ServletResponse res)
                throws NamingException, SQLException, JMSException,
                       IOException, BusinessException
```

An issue that arises from the above scenario is that the signature of the business method looks untidy. With Model 2 architecture, the request delegates may need to expose a common interface. In this case, they may not be able to declare the exceptions that are not defined in the common interface in their `throws` clause.

A solution to this problem is to have the business methods catch all the unexpected checked exceptions and throw a single exception that represents an unexpected checked exception. It may also throw the business exception. Now the business method will be:

```
public void businessMethod(args …) throws SystemException,
                                          BusinesException {
  try {
    // Perform the business logic
  } catch(Exception e) {
     if(e instanceof BusinessException) {
       throw new BusinessException (e.getMessage());
     } else {
        throw new SystemException(e.getMessage());
     }
  }
}
```

The request delegate will let the `SystemException` bubble up to the front controller. However, the business exception will be caught by the delegate and the `CustomErrors` object stored in the exception will be stored as a request attribute. The request delegate will then ask the front controller to forward the request to the page that initiated the current request. The request delegate may also catch an instance of `RuntimeException` at the end and re-throw it as a `SystemException` to handle all the runtime exceptions. The implementation of the request delegate method will be something like:

```
public Resource handleRequest(ServletRequest req, ServletResponse res)
                throws SystemException {
  try {
    //Call business methods
  } catch(BusinessException ex) {
     request.setAttribute(CustomErrors.ERROR_MESSAGE_KEY, ex.getErrors());
     return new Resource("input.jsp");
  } catch(RuntimeException ex) {
     throw new SystemException(ex.getMessage());
  }
}
```

In the above example, the class `BusinessException` will have a method that returns a `CustomErrors` object. Therefore, we can abstract this functionality to a common class that serves as an ancestor for all the business exceptions in our system – the `Resource` class models a resource capable of rendering a response.

Severity and Chaining

In the last section, we caught the unexpected checked exceptions and re-threw them as instances of the class `SystemException`. There are two potential flaws in this approach:

- We are treating all the unexpected checked exceptions and runtime exceptions in a similar way. It will be very useful to set severity levels for the exceptions as we may need to handle these exceptions differently depending on the severity level. For example, an `SQLException` thrown from a database connection pool when there is no connection available in the pool is often of lesser severity than a `NamingException` thrown due to an unsuccessful JNDI lookup.
- In the previous examples we were catching the unexpected checked and runtime exceptions and re-throwing them as instances of the class `SystemException` specifying the message retrieved from the source exception. However, to debug unexpected exceptions what we need foremost is the stack trace, which we no longer have.

The first problem can be solved by creating an interface that defines constants to represent the various levels of severity and a method to get the current severity level. The `SystemException` class can implement this interface and provide an implementation for the method to get the severity. For this, it can define an instance variable that represents the severity and initialize it by an argument passed in the constructor.

The second problem may be solved by defining an instance variable of type `Throwable` in the exception class and initializing it using an argument passed in the constructor. The client classes can pass the source exception to the constructor of the `SystemException` class. The `SystemException` class also will override the various methods for printing the stack trace defined in the `Throwable` class. These methods will first print the stack trace of the source exception before they print the stack trace of the current exception.

The Severity Interface

```
package errors;

public interface Severity {
```

Define the various levels of severity:

```
  public static final int WARNING = 0;
  public static final int ERROR = 1;
  public static final int FATAL_ERROR = 2;
```

Define a method to get the current severity. Exceptions that can have severity levels should implement this interface:

```
  public int getSeverity();
}
```

The SystemException Class

```
package errors;

import java.io.PrintStream;
import java.io.PrintWriter;

public class SystemException extends Exception implements Severity {
```

Define the instance variable that holds the severity level. The default severity level is set to `WARNING`:

```
  private int severity = WARNING;
  private Throwable parent;
```

This constructor takes a message, the root exception, and the severity level:

```
  public SystemException(String message, Throwable parent, int severity) {
    super(message);
    this.parent = parent;
    this.severity = severity;
  }
```

This constructor takes a message and the root exception. The severity level is set to `WARNING`:

```
  public SystemException(String message, Throwable parent) {
    this(message, parent, WARNING);
  }
```

This constructor takes a message and the severity level. This is useful when a root exception is not available:

```
  public SystemException(String message, int severity) {
    this(message, null, severity);
  }
```

This constructor takes the root exception and the severity level:

```
  public SystemException(Throwable parent, int severity) {
    this(parent.getMessage(), parent, severity);
  }
```

This constructor takes just a message. The severity level is set to `WARNING`:

```
  public SystemException(String message) {
    this(message, null, WARNING);
  }
```

This constructor takes just the root exception. The severity level is set to WARNING:

```
    public SystemException(Throwable parent) {
      this(parent.getMessage(), parent, WARNING);
    }
```

Here we implement the method for getting the severity level:

```
    public int getSeverity() {
      return severity;
    }
```

Override the methods for printing the stack trace. These methods will now print the root exception's stack trace if the root exception is not null, before printing the current stack trace:

```
    public void printStackTrace() {
      if(parent != null) {
        parent.printStackTrace();
      }
      super.printStackTrace();
    }

    public void printStackTrace(PrintStream ps) {
      if(parent != null) {
        parent.printStackTrace(ps);
      }
      super.printStackTrace(ps);
    }

    public void printStackTrace(PrintWriter pw) {
      if(parent != null) {
        parent.printStackTrace(pw);
      }
      super.printStackTrace(pw);
    }
  }
```

Using JSP Error Pages

Errors that occur during request processing in JSP pages may be forwarded to the resource defined in the errorPage attribute of the page directive. Both expected and unexpected exceptions may occur in our view JSP pages while handling custom tags and model beans. However, in this section we will be continuing our discussion on handling unexpected checked exceptions. In the previous sections, we saw that the request delegates can bubble the instances of SystemException back to the front controller. What would the controller do with this exception? The answer is that it depends on the type of the controller.

If the controller is a servlet controller, the servlet can only throw instances of ServletException and IOException back to the container. This is because of the signature of the service method defined in the Servlet interface. ServletException can wrap any Throwable object so we can wrap the SystemException in an instance of ServletException and throw it to the container:

```
try {
  // Delegate the request to the relevant request delegate
} catch(SystemException e) {
    throw new ServletException(e);
}
```

We'll look at how the container would handle this exception in the next section.

If the controller is a JSP page with an embedded JavaBean, the error handling can be more flexible. Now we are not constrained by the Servlet API and hence we can define the controller bean's request processing method to throw a `SystemException`. We will also define a value for the `errorPage` attribute in the page directive of the controller JSP page in which the controller bean is embedded. The error page will have the exception object available and may do what ever it wishes depending on the severity level of the exception. This is the code for the controller bean:

```
public class Controller {
  public Resource processRequest(javax.servlet.PageContext ctx)
                  throws SystemException {
```

Pick a request delegate:

```
    return delegate.handleRequest(ctx.getRequest(), ctx.getResponse());
  }
}
```

The code below is for the controller JSP page. The `errorPage` attribute is set to the resource to which the container will forward the request if an error occurs in the JSP page:

```
<%@ page errorPage="error.jsp" import="Resource"%>
```

Declare the session scope controller bean:

```
<jsp:useBean id="controller" scope="session" class="Controller" />
```

Process the request:

```
<% Resource res = controller.processRequest(pageContext); %>
```

And forward to the next page:

```
<jsp:forward page="<%= res.getPage() %>" />
```

In the page directive for `error.jsp`, we should set the `isErrorPage` attribute to `true`. In the JSP page, we can implement the logic for handling the error depending on the severity level. The code below simply prints the stack trace back to the user:

```
<%@ page isErrorPage="true" %>
<html>
  <head><title>Error</title></head>
  <body>
    <p>Unexpected error. Please inform application support.</p>
    <p><b><%= exception.getMessage() %></b></p>
    <p><% exception.printStackTrace(new java.io.PrintWriter(out)); %></p>
  </body>
</html>
```

Mapping Errors in the Deployment Descriptor

We have seen that if we use a servlet as the controller, we can nest an unexpected exception inside an instance of `ServletException` and throw it back to the container. By default, this will send a container-specific error page back to the end users. However, we can control the look and feel of the error pages by mapping the exceptions to resources in the web deployment descriptor. When an exception (or any of its ancestors) occurs the container will scan the deployment descriptor for any resource to which the response should be forwarded.

If the resource defined is a servlet or a JSP page, the container will make the following request attributes available for the resource:

- `javax.servlet.error.status_code`
  An integer representing the status code
- `javax.servlet.error.exception_type`
  A class representing the type of exception
- `javax.servlet.error.message`
  A string representing the exception message
- `javax.servlet.error.exception`
  An object representing the exception
- `javax.servlet.error.request_uri`
  A string representing the request URI that caused the exception

The J2EE web deployment descriptor allows us to map both exception types and HTTP error codes to resources responsible for handling the error. The excerpt below shows how an exception is mapped to an error resource. When an instance of `ServletException` is thrown, the response will be forwarded to `error.jsp`:

```
<error-page>
  <exception-type>javax.servlet.ServletException</exception-type>
  <location>/error.jsp</location>
</error-page>
```

In the following excerpt, when a non-existent resource is requested the response will be forwarded to `notFound.jsp`:

```
<error-page>
  <error-code>400</error-code>
  <location>/notFound.jsp</location>
</error-page>
```

The TryCatchFinally Interface

The JSP 1.2 specification introduced a new interface called `TryCatchFinally` that can be used for performing resource cleanup in JSP custom tags. This interface may be implemented by the `Tag`, `BodyTag`, and `IterationTag` handler classes, and defines two methods:

- `doCatch(Throwable th)`
  This method is called by the container if an exception occurs while evaluating the body of the tag or in the methods `doStartTag()`, `doEndTag` (), `doAfterBody()`, and `doInitBody()`. This method is not called if an exception occurs in the methods for setting the attribute values. The container will pass the root exception to this method. Code for resource cleanup can be added to this method.

- `doFinally()`
  This method is always called after the `doEndTag` method is called.

We will write a small custom tag to illustrate the functionality of the `TryCatchFinally` interface:

```
package errors;

import javax.servlet.jsp.tagext.TagSupport;
import javax.servlet.jsp.tagext.TryCatchFinally;
import javax.servlet.jsp.JspException;

public class TryCatchFinallyTag extends TagSupport
                                implements TryCatchFinally {
```

Throw an exception in the `doStart()` method:

```
  public int doStartTag() throws JspException {
    throw new JspException("Testing try catch finally.");
  }
```

Print the exception message in the `doCatch()` method:

```
  public void doCatch(Throwable th) throws Throwable {
    System.out.println(th.getMessage());
    System.out.println("doCatch called");
  }
```

Print a message in the `doFinally()` method:

```
  public void doFinally() {
    System.out.println("doFinally called");
  }
}
```

The excerpt below shows the tag library descriptor for the above tag:

```
<tag>
  <name>tryCatchFinally</name>
  <tagclass>errors.TryCatchFinallyTag</tagclass>
  <info></info>
</tag>
```

Now we will call this tag in a very simple JSP page:

```
<%@page contentType="text/html"%>
<%@ taglib uri="/WEB-INF/errors.tld" prefix="errors" %>

<errors:tryCatchFinally/>

<P>TryCatchFinallyTag called. See the command console for results.</P>
```

The screenshot below shows the Tomcat command window when this JSP page is accessed. The messages from the `doCatch()` and `doFinally()` methods have been printed:

```
Start Tomcat
Starting service Tomcat-Standalone
Apache Tomcat/4.0
Starting service Tomcat-Apache
Apache Tomcat/4.0
Testing try catch finally.
doCatch called
doFinally called
```

Logging and Tracing

Logging and tracing information is an important aspect of any enterprise application and it is particularly important in distributed multi-threaded and multi-tiered application environments. Proper logging of error messages and information can help us in tracing error conditions, matrix generation for auditing purposes, performance tuning, and tracking access patterns. Logging and tracing is closely associated with error handling.

In this section, we will be covering the various aspects of efficient logging in enterprise application development. We will also be covering the popular Log4J API from the Apache Software Foundation and the new JDK 1.4 logging and error handling features.

Logging Fundamentals

The development of a large-scale enterprise application requires an efficient logging framework and development teams often come up with their own logging frameworks. The basic functionalities expected of a properly designed logging framework are:

- **Prioritization**
  Most applications need the priorities set for different levels like debug, information, warning, error, or fatal error. We may want to log a failed JNDI lookup as an error, whereas failed JDBC connection retrieval from a data source implementation counts as a warning. A good logging framework should provide the facility for logging the messages at the aforementioned priority levels. More than five priority levels may make our logging schema rather convoluted. Logging debug and information messages are very useful for tracking various bugs during the development phase.

- **Filters**
  We may want to selectively switch logging on and off for individual entities in our applications. These entities may be packages, classes, or methods. This is where filtering comes in. Filters let us specify the log messages that should be logged from specific entities within our application.

- **Multiple Channels**
  A properly designed logging framework should let us log our messages to multiple channels. These may include console screens, file system, JMS queues, remote sockets, or operating system event logs. Multi-channel logging is very important in a multi-threaded distributed environment. For example, if we are emitting log messages from our EJBs to files on the local file system and if the EJBs are running in a clustered environment, the information will be difficult to trace. In such cases, we may find it useful to write the messages to a centralized channel like a JMS destination. In a multi-threaded environment, we may find it difficult to get multiple threads to write to a single operating system file. In such cases, it may be useful to write the messages to a remote server socket and get the remote process to write it to a file.

- **Formatting**
  We should be able to set automatic formatting for our log messages without explicitly specifying it in our code. At the basic level, the formatting could prefix the messages with date and time stamps. There can be other information like the name of the host in a clustered environment or the security principal of the current thread.

- **Hierarchy**
  We should be able to define a hierarchy of entities similar to a tree structure and define priorities, channels, and formatting at node level in such a way that a child node inherits the parent's properties unless explicitly overridden at the child level. In such a scenario, we can set all the default properties at the root level and override them for special cases at the relevant nodes.

- **Declarative Configuration**
  All the above properties should be mentioned in a declarative manner in a configuration file rather than hard coding them in the code.

- **Dynamic Configuration**
  Once the logging scheme is configured and the application is started, we should be able to change the configuration settings and apply them to the application at run time without disturbing the application.

If we look at the above requirements it is quite evident that writing an efficient logging framework is not a simple task – this is where logging frameworks like Log4J come into the picture. J2SE 1.4 (currently in beta) also provides a framework for logging and assertions. There is discussion going on about whether Log4J should be adopted as the logging framework for J2SE. A simple argument is that the J2SE 1.4 logging features can only be used with that version of J2SE, whereas Log4J can be used even with JDK 1.1. Anyway, we will be covering both J2SE 1.4 and Log4J.

Log4J API

Log4J is a tried and tested logging framework from the Apache Software Foundation and can be freely downloaded from http://jakarta.apache.org/log4j/. The Log4J API provides most of the features desired of a logging framework explained in the last section. The framework uses three main components:

- **Categories**
  These are similar to filters as explained in the last section. They allow us to selectively set logging properties to entities within our application. These entities may be arbitrarily selected and can be packages, classes, or methods.

- **Appenders**
  These send log statements to multiple channels.

- **Layouts**
  These define formats for log messages.

The JAR files required to use Log4J are `log4j.jar` and `log4j-core.jar`, which can be found in the expanded distribution of Log4J.

Categories

Categories allow us to filter and prioritize log messages. Categories are similar to hierarchical namespaces in programming languages. We can set our logging preferences at the root of the namespace and override them as we wish in the lower levels. Categories are defined as a list of named entities separated by periods:

```
level1.level2.level3
```

`level2` is the parent of `level3` and a child of `level1`. The logging preferences set at `level1` are applicable to `level2` and `level3` unless they are explicitly overridden at `level2` or `level3`. The root category is always implicitly available and doesn't have a name associated with it.

The class `org.apache.log4j.Category` represents a category in Log4J. This class provides a variety of methods for setting logging preferences and logging messages at different priorities. This class provides methods for performing the following tasks:

- Setting the priority level for the current category. Priority levels are defined by the class `org.apache.log4j.Priority`.

- Logging messages at various priorities like debug, information, warning, and error. Only those messages with a priority level greater than or equal to the priority level for the current category are emitted to the registered appenders.

- Adding and removing the appenders to which the messages are sent. A category can have one or more appenders.

These are the methods provided by `Category`:

Method	Purpose
`void addAppender(Appender appender)`	Adds an appender to the category
`void assert(boolean condition, String message)`	Asserts the condition and sends the message with error priority to all the registered appenders if the condition is asserted as `false`
`void debug(Object message)` `void debug(Object message, Throwable th)`	Sends the message and the `throwable` instance to all the registered appenders at debug priority
`void error(Object message)` `void error(Object message, Throwable th)`	Sends the message and the `throwable` instance to all the registered appenders at error priority
`void fatal(Object message)` `void fatal(Object message, Throwable th)`	Sends the message and the `throwable` instance to all the registered appenders at fatal error priority
`void info(Object message)` `void info(Object message, Throwable th)`	Sends the message and the `throwable` instance to all the registered appenders at information priority
`void warn(Object message)` `void warn(Object message, Throwable th)`	Sends the message and the `throwable` instance to all the registered appenders at warning priority
`void log(Priority priority, Object message)` `void log(Priority priority, Object message, Throwable th)`	General purpose logging method
`void removeAppender(Appender appender)` `void removeAllAppenders()`	Removes the specified appenders or all the appenders
`void setPriority(Priority priority)`	Sets the priority for the current category
`Category getRoot()`	Gets the root category
`Category getInstance(String name)`	Gets a category defined by the specified name

Let's take look at a simple example for logging messages using categories:

```
package logging;

import org.apache.log4j.Category;
import org.apache.log4j.WriterAppender;
```

```
import org.apache.log4j.Priority;
import org.apache.log4j.SimpleLayout;

public class TestLogging {

  public static void main(String args[]) {
```

Create a category with the name `logging.TestLogging`:

```
    Category cat = Category.getInstance("logging.TestLogging");
```

Set the priority to warning:

```
    cat.setPriority(Priority.WARN);
```

Add an appender to the category. The class `WriterAppender` can be used for writing the error messages to the specified writer or output stream. Use the `FileAppender` class to write to a log file. When we create the appender we need to specify the layout that will be used by the appender (see the *Layout* section for more details):

```
    cat.addAppender(new WriterAppender(new SimpleLayout(), System.out));
```

Write a debug message to the appender:

```
    cat.debug("Debug Message");
```

Write a warning message to the appender:

```
    cat.warn("Warning Message");
    }
}
```

In this example, only the warning message will be appear in the console as the priority level for the category is set as warning and debug has got a lower priority than warning. Priority levels are covered in the next section. First, a category is created and the logging preferences and the appenders are set on the category. Instead of doing this we can define the logging preferences and appenders for categories in a configuration file (this is explained in a later section).

An efficient naming convention for categories is to give them the fully qualified names of the classes within which they are used, for example:

```
Category myCategory = Category.getInstance(getClass().getName());
```

Priority

Log4J defines a class called `Priority` that stores enumerated constants for different priority levels. The table below shows the different priority levels in descending order of priority:

Priority	Purpose
`FATAL`	Fatal error messages
`ERROR`	Error messages
`WARN`	Warning messages
`INFO`	Information messages
`DEBUG`	Debug messages

We will see later how we can use priorities in conjunction with the `SystemException` class for sending e-mail messages to the system administrator when a fatal error occurs.

Appenders

Appenders define the destination to which the log messages are routed. The Log4J API defines an interface called `org.apache.log4j.Appender` that defines the methods that need to be implemented by the appender classes. In most of the cases we won't have to implement our own appenders as Log4J provides the following ready to use appenders. The Log4J API notifies the appenders about logging messages using logging events:

Appender	Purpose
`AsyncAppender`	This appender can have other appenders attached to it. This appender buffers all the logging events and dispatches them to all the attached appenders when the buffer limit is reached. This appender can be quite useful in a multi-threaded environment where multiple threads that are logging to a physical file should not get involved in lock contention. Instead all the messages can be sent to an asynchronous appender, which will take care of the actual task of writing the log messages to a file.
`JMSAppender`	This appender is used for sending messages to JMS destinations. These appenders are quite useful in a distributed environment where the various tiers of the applications are hosted by different machines and we need to send all the log messages to a centralized location. They are also very useful in a clustered environment where components are deployed across multiple servers to balance the load.

Table continued on following page

Appender	Purpose
`NTEventLogAppender`	This appender is used for sending messages to NT event logs. This works only with Microsoft Windows NT/2000 (`NTEventLogAppender.dll` that comes with the Log4J API should be in the path). The messages sent to the event log can be viewed using the Windows NT administrative tools.
`SMTPAppender`	This appender can be used for sending e-mail messages. This is quite useful if we want to send an e-mail message to the system administrator when a fatal error occurs.
`SocketAppender`	This appender can be used for sending the messages to a remote socket. Appenders to remote sockets are also quite useful for logging in a multithreaded distributed environment.
`SyslogAppender`	This appender sends the messages to the UNIX `syslog` daemon.
`WriterAppender`	This appender sends the messages to the specified writer.
`ConsoleAppender`	This appender sends the messages to the standard output. This appender is very useful for observing the console on which the application server is running and viewing the various log messages.
`FileAppender`	This appender sends the messages to a file. This appender may be difficult to use in a multithreaded environment, but can be used in conjunction with an asynchronous appender or some other appender that can take care of the issues regarding multiple threads, tiers, clustering, and distributed environments.
`DailyRollingFileAppender`	This appender rolls the log file at a user chosen frequency.
`RollingFileAppender`	This appender rolls the file to which the messages are logged when the file size reaches a certain limit. If we don't want our log files to get really huge, we can use this appender.
`ExternallyRolledFIleAppender`	This appender listens on a socket for a message to roll the current log file.

An Example Using Socket Appenders

In this section, we will write a small example to emphasise the use of socket appenders. A client will use socket appenders to write messages to a remote socket and a server will receive these messages, handle multiple client calls, and write the messages to the console.

The SocketLoggingClient Class

In this section we will have a look at the source code for the client that sends the log messages:

```
package logging;

import org.apache.log4j.Category;
import org.apache.log4j.net.SocketAppender;

public class SocketLoggingClient {

  public SocketLoggingClient() {}

  public static void main(String args[]) throws Exception {
```

Create a socket appender sending messages to a server socket running on the same server and listening on port 3000:

```
    SocketAppender appender = new SocketAppender("localhost", 3000);
```

Get the root category and set the appender for the root category as the remote socket appender:

```
    final Category cat = Category.getRoot();
    cat.addAppender(appender);
```

Send the information messages to the remote socket:

```
    for(int i = 0; i < 5; i++) {
      cat.info("Message(" + i + ") from client");
    }
```

Clean up and close the appender:

```
    appender.cleanUp();
    appender.close();
  }
}
```

The socket appender sends the messages encapsulated in the class `LoggingEvent`. This information is sent as a serialized object. The server socket can read the object stream and cast the object to a type `LoggingEvent` and call the various methods for getting the event details.

The SocketLoggingServer Class

The server will listen on a server socket and when a connection comes in from the client it passes the resultant socket to a thread. The thread reads the `LoggingEvent` object from the stream and prints the message:

```
package logging;

import java.net.Socket;
import java.net.ServerSocket;
import java.io.ObjectInputStream;
import java.io.IOException;
import org.apache.log4j.spi.LoggingEvent;
```

```
public class SocketLoggingServer {

  public SocketLoggingServer() {}

  public static void main(String[] args) throws Exception {
```

Open a new server socket on port 3000:

```
    ServerSocket srv = new ServerSocket(3000);
```

Listen on the server socket in an infinite loop:

```
    while(true) {
```

Accept the incoming socket connection in a blocking read:

```
      Socket socket = srv.accept();
```

Pass the incoming socket to an instance of the SocketHandler class that implements the Runnable interface and pass that object to a thread:

```
      Thread th = new Thread(new SocketHandler(socket));
```

Start the thread:

```
      th.start();
    }
  }
```

This static inner class implements the Runnable interface:

```
  private static class SocketHandler implements Runnable {
```

A reference to the stream used for reading the LoggingEvent objects:

```
    private ObjectInputStream stream;

    public SocketHandler(Socket socket) throws IOException {
```

Store a reference to the socket input stream wrapped in an ObjectInputStream object:

```
      stream = new ObjectInputStream(socket.getInputStream());
    }

    public void run() {
      try {
```

Read the `LoggingEvent` objects from the stream and print the message:

```
      LoggingEvent event = (LoggingEvent)stream.readObject();
      while(event != null) {
        System.out.println(event.getMessage());
        event = (LoggingEvent)stream.readObject();
      }

    } catch(EOFException eofEx) {
        System.out.println("End of stream reached");
    } catch(Exception ex) {
        ex.printStackTrace();
```

Close the resources in the `finally` block:

```
    } finally {
        try {
          stream.close();
        } catch (Exception e) {
            e.printStackTrace();
        }
    }
   }
  }
}
```

Running the Application

Make sure that `log4j.jar` is in the current directory, and compile the classes using the following command at the command prompt:

```
javac -cp .;log4j.jar logging\*.java
```

Start the server by typing the following command at the command prompt:

```
java -cp .;log4j.jar logging.SocketLoggingServer
```

Open a new window and start the client by typing the following command at the command prompt:

```
java -cp .;log4j.jar logging.SocketLoggingClient
```

You can see the following output at the console that is running the server:

```
C:\WINNT\System32\cmd.exe - java -cp .;log4j.jar logging.SocketLoggingServer

C:\ProJSPSiteDesign\Chapter07>java -cp .;log4j.jar logging.SocketLoggingServer
Message(0) from client
Message(1) from client
Message(2) from client
Message(3) from client
Message(4) from client
End of stream reached
```

Adding Appenders

A category may have multiple appenders registered with it using the addAppender() method. When a logging method is called, all the registered appenders will receive the logging event. Additionally, the appenders registered with all the ancestor categories will also receive the logging events:

```
package logging;

import org.apache.log4j.Category;
import org.apache.log4j.Priority;
import org.apache.log4j.SimpleLayout;
import org.apache.log4j.ConsoleAppender;
import org.apache.log4j.FileAppender;

public class TestAdding {

  public static void main(String args[]) {
    try {
      Category root = Category.getRoot();
      root.addAppender(new FileAppender(new SimpleLayout(), "log.txt"));

      Category child = Category.getInstance("logging.TestLogging");
      child.setPriority(Priority.WARN);
      child.addAppender(new ConsoleAppender(new SimpleLayout()));

      root.warn("Root Message");
      child.warn("Child Message");
    } catch (Exception e) {
      e.printStackTrace();
    }
  }
}
```

The first message is written only to the log file whereas the second log message is sent both to the console and to the log file. Appender additivity for categories may be controlled using the setAdditivity() method defined in the Category class.

Layout

As we have already seen, layouts are associated with appenders. The Appender interface defines a method for setting the layout. Most of the Appender implementations take the layout as an argument for their constructors. The Log4J API uses the abstract class Layout for modeling the layout used for formatting the messages. It also provides a set of concrete classes for specifying the layouts when the appenders are created:

Layout	Purpose
HTMLLayout	This is used for logging error messages as HTML tables.
PatternLayout	This layout can be configured using pattern strings. The patterns mainly consist of literal strings and pattern replacers starting with the symbol %. For example, the pattern %c%p%M%m will output the category, priority, method, and the message. Refer to the Log4J documentation for a complete listing of pattern characters.
SimpleLayout	This can be used to print the priority followed by a hyphen and the message.

Layout	Purpose
`XMLLayout`	The output of `XMLLayout` consists of a series of event elements as defined in the `log4j.dtd`. It does not output a complete well-formed XML file. The output is designed to be included as an external entity in a separate file to form a correct XML file.
`TTCCLayout`	TTCC layout format consists of time, thread, category, and nested diagnostic context information. Nested diagnostic context (NDC) is a technique used for identifying log messages from different contexts, for example multiple threads. Log4J API provides a class called `NDC` for implementing this feature. `NDC` objects can be created by HTTP handlers like JSP pages and servlets per user thread from the user information present in the request objects.

In this next example, the front controller servlet pushes the information regarding the user for the current thread into the `NDC` class. Then it calls the request delegate to process the request. The request delegate may call business objects that may in turn call data access objects. However, within the current thread all the calls to categories for logging messages will print the user information if the associated appenders use a TTCC layout:

```
public void processRequest(ServletRequest request,
                           ServletResponse response) {
  NDC.push(request.getRemoteUser());
  RequestDelegateFactory.getDelegate(request).processRequest(
                                                    request, response);
  NDC.pop();
}
```

The pushed information is popped out towards the end of the method calls. The nested diagnostic context that is pushed and popped is relative only to the current thread.

A deeply nested data access object involved in the current thread has the following code:

```
Category child = Category.getInstance("logging.TestLogging");
child.addAppender(new ConsoleAppender(new SimpleLayout());
root.warn("Root Message");
child.warn("Child Message");
```

If the principal associated with the current thread has the user name `user01`, the following message is emitted by the appender if it is configured with a TTCC layout:

```
0 [main] WARN database.TestDAO user01 - Warning Message
```

Configuration

In our previous examples we have been creating categories and setting priorities, appenders, and layouts within the code before calling the logging methods. In practical scenarios we may want to configure all the category hierarchy, priorities, appenders, and layouts in an external file and perform logging by just retrieving the named category and not bothering to set the logging preferences. This will provide use with three advantages. It will:

- Reduce the code size.
- Make logging configurable with out changing the code.
- Allow dynamic changing of the logging scheme by changing and reloading the configuration without disrupting the application. For this the application can have a dedicated thread listening for commands to reload the configuration.

The Log4J API also allows the definition of new category hierarchies, proprieties, appenders, and layouts. This is done in an external file that can be used to initialize the logging framework on application startup. The files can be written either in XML or in the Java properties file format.

Property Files

The information stored in property files can be used to initialize the Log4J setup using the class `PropertyConfigurator`. This class defines a static method `configure()` that takes the fully qualified path of the file that contains the configuration information. For example:

```
PropertyConfigurator.configure("c:/errors/myLog.properties");
```

The contents of the property file define the category hierarchies and logging preferences:

```
log4j.rootCategory=debug, stdout

log4j.appender.stdout=org.apache.log4j.ConsoleAppender
log4j.appender.stdout.layout=org.apache.log4j.TTCCLayout

log4j.category.com.db.dao=INFO, ra

log4j.appender.ra=org.apache.log4j.RollingFileAppender
log4j.appender.ra.File=myLog.txt

log4j.appender.ra.MaxFileSize=1000KB
log4j.appender.ra.MaxBackupIndex=2

log4j.appender.ea.layout=org.apache.log4j.SimpleLayout
```

In the above example:

- The root category defines the logging priority as debug level
- The root category defines an appender called `stdout` that functions as a console appender
- The layout for this appender is defined as TTCC layout

- A category called `com.db.dao` is defined and it overrides the message priority to information level
- It also uses an extra appender called `ra` that is a rolling file appender
- The name of the file is set to `myLog.txt`, the maximum size is set to `1000KB`, and the number of backup files that need to be kept is set to `2`
- This appender uses a simple layout

Once the above configuration is loaded, the classes can start logging with a single line of code as shown below:

```
package com.db.dao;

public class EmployeeDAO {

  public static Category logger =
                        Catgeroy.getInstance(EmployeeDAO.class.getName());

  public void EmployeeDAO() {
    logger.info("EployeeDAO created");
  }
}
```

Example Error Page

We have seen that in a Model 2 system with a JSP page and JavaBean acting as a front controller, all the expected checked exceptions may be passed back to the user with the error messages stored as request scope beans. We have also seen that the request delegates and business objects can throw a `SystemException` wrapping the source exception in case of unexpected checked and runtime exceptions.

The controller bean can throw this exception to the enclosing JSP page and the JSP page can use the error page attribute to handle this exception. Since we have defined priority levels for our system exception, we will use those in conjunction with the Log4J SMTP appender for sending an error message to the system administrator if a fatal error occurs. The excerpt below illustrates how it is done:

```
<%@ page isErrorPage="true" import="org.apache.log4j.*,errors" %>

<%
  if(exception instanceof SystemException) {
    SystemException ex = (SystemException)exception;
    if(ex.getPriority() == Severity.FATAL_ERROR) {
      Category error = Category.getInstance("error.fatal");
```

Create an SMTP appender. The default constructor will send an e-mail when a message of error priority is logged using a category instance to which the appender is associated:

```
      SMTPAppender appender = new SMTPAppender();
```

Set the layout:

```
        appender.setLayout(new TTCCLayout());
```

Set the to sender address, recipient address, subject, and the SMTP server used for sending the error message:

```
        appender.setFrom("admin@application.com");
        appender.setTo("admin@application.com");
        appender.setSubject("Fatal Error");
        appender.setSMTPHost("Mail Server");
```

Add the appender to the category:

```
        error.addAppender(appender);
```

Log the message:

```
        error.error(ex.getMessage(), ex);
      }
    }
  %>
```

A more elegant solution would be to use a custom tag to encapsulate all the above code, with attributes for setting the SMTP host, sender address, and recipients address:

```
  <error:sendMail host="MailServer"
                  to="admin@application.com"
                  from="admin@application.com"/>
```

The exception object can be extracted using the page context within the custom tag.

JDK 1.4 Logging API

In this section, we'll take a quick look at the logging API provided with JDK 1.4. The logging classes provided by JDK 1.4 belong to the package `java.util.logging`. The API provides facilities for delivering plain text and XML messages to memory streams, output streams, the console, files, and sockets as well as the logging facilities available in the host operating system like NT event log and the UNIX `syslog` daemon.

The JDK 1.4 logging API mainly uses three types of objects:

- **Loggers**
  These objects are similar in functionality to categories
- **Handlers**
  These objects are similar in functionality to appenders
- **Formatters**
  These objects are similar in functionality to layouts

These three entities are represented by abstract classes named `Logger`, `Handler`, and `Formatter` respectively. Priority levels are handled by a class called `Level`. This class exposes the following priority levels (in descending priority): `SEVERE`, `WARNING`, `INFO`, `CONFIG`, `FINE`, `FINER`, and `FINEST`.

Loggers

Loggers are the entities used by logging classes to log messages. They are named entities similar to Log4J categories. However, JDK 1.4 loggers also allow creation of anonymous loggers. The loggers are managed by a class called `LogManager` that can have globally registered handlers. The `Logger` class provides methods for:

- Adding and removing handlers
- Creating named and anonymous logger instances
- Logging severe, warning, info, config, fine, finer, and finest messages
- Logging, entering, and exiting information for methods

The methods provided by this class are:

Method	Purpose

`void addHandler(Handler handler)`
`Handler[] getHandlers()`
`void removeHandler(Handler handler)`
	Adds, removes, and gets a handler to the logger

`void config(String message)`	Logs a message with `config` priority
`void fine(String message)`	Logs a message with `fine` priority
`void finer(String message)`	Logs a message with `finer` priority
`void finest(String message)`	Logs a message with `finest` priority
`void info(String message)`	Logs a message with `info` priority
`void severe(String message)`	Logs a message with `severe` priority
`void warning(String message)`	Logs a message with `warning` priority
`void setLevel(Level level)` `Level getLevel()`	Gets and sets logging levels
`Logger getLogger(String name)` `Logger getAnonymousLogger()`	Gets the logger instances
`Formatter getFormatter()` `void setFormatter(Formatter formatter)`	Gets and sets the formatter

Handlers

Handlers are responsible for sending the log messages to the configured destinations. A logger can have more than one handler registered with it. Additionally, loggers are by default configured to use global handlers registered with the `LogManager` class. Logging levels can be set at both logger level and handler level. For example, a logger can enable all the messages with finest priority. However, it can selectively disable some of its handlers for the same priority. The JDK 1.4 API provides the following concrete implementations of the `Handler` interface:

- `MemoryHandler`
  This class functions in the same way as the `AsyncAppender` that comes with Log4J API
- `ConsoleHandler`
  Publishes the log messages to `System.err`
- `FileHandler`
  Publishes the messages to a file
- `SocketHandler`
  Publishes the messages to a remote socket

Formatters

Formatters are used for formatting the error messages and are associated with handlers. Formatters are represented by an abstract class and JDK 1.4 provides the following concrete implementations:

- `SimpleFormatter`
  Similar to the `SimpleLayout` class in Log4J. Prints a brief summary of the log message in a human readable format. The summary will typically be one or two lines.
- `XMLFormatter`
  Formats a log message into a standard XML format.

The LogManager Class

This class handles all the logging namespaces. This class also has a set of global handlers registered with it. The global log manager can be retrieved using the static method `getLogManager()` as shown below:

```
LogManager logManager = LogManager.getLogManager();
```

The system property `java.util.logging.manager` can be used for retrieving the default log manager. By default the log manager reads the configuration properties from the file `logging.properties` file located in the `lib\` directory of the JRE. Alternatively, the system property `java.util.logging.config.file` can be used for specifying the file.

Configuration

The default configuration shown below registers two global handlers, one for a file in the temporary directory and another for the console and logs only high priority messages:

```
# Set the logging level for the root of the namespace.
# This becomes the default logging level for all Loggers.
.level= INFO
```

```
# List of global handlers
handlers = java.util.logging.FileHandler, \
           java.util.logging.ConsoleHandler

# Properties for the FileHandler
java.util.logging.FileHandler.limit = 50000
java.util.logging.FileHandler.count = 3
java.util.logging.FileHandler.pattern = %t/java%u.%g.log

# Default level for ConsoleHandler. This can be used to
# limit the levels that are displayed on the console even
# when the global default has been set to a trace level.
java.util.logging.ConsoleHandler.level = INFO
```

However, the above properties can be overridden.

J2SE 1.4 Assertions

J2SE 1.4 introduces a new keyword called `assert` that can be used for evaluating boolean expressions. This keyword can be used in two different ways:

```
assert expr1;
assert expr1:expr2;
```

In both cases, the expression `expr1` should evaluate to a boolean value. If the runtime value of the expression is `false`, an instance of `AssertionError` is thrown. This is a subclass of `Error` and hence need not be explicitly caught in code. In the second case, the result of `expr2` is passed to the constructor of `AssertionError`.

An assertion is a statement that evaluates a boolean expression that is supposed to be true when the statement is executed. By checking that the boolean expression is true, it is guaranteed that the program is free of errors. Assertion checking may be disabled for increased performance, and is normally enabled during development but disabled during deployment. Hence, it must not be assumed that the boolean expressions contained in assertions will always be evaluated.

Assertions should not be used for checking the arguments in public methods. Argument checking is typically part of the interface exposed by the method, and invalid arguments should result in runtime exceptions like `IllegalArgumentException` being thrown.

The example below shows the how assertions are used. The private method assumes that the passed amount is guaranteed to be greater than 0:

```
private void debit(double amount) {
  assert (amount <= 0):"Invalid amount";
}
```

In the above example if a negative amount is passed, an `AssertionError` with the message "Invalid Amount" is thrown.

One typical use of assertions is in the use of switch statements where we don't expect the default to be executed, as shown below:

```
switch(dice) {
  case 1:
    ......
    break;
  case 2:
    ......
    break;
  case 3:
    ......
    break;
  case 4:
    ......
    break;
  case 5:
    ......
    break;
  case 6:
    ......
    break;
  default:
    assert false;
}
```

In the above case if a value outside the range of 1 to 6 is passed to the switch block, an `AssertError` is thrown.

By default, assertions are disabled. They can be enabled or disabled both programmatically and using command line switches, for example:

```
java -ea StartServer
```

The above snippet enables assertion for all classes, while the following explicitly enables assertion for all classes belonging to the package `com.db` and its subpackages and disables assertion for the classes belonging to `com.db.dao` and its subpackages. The assert keyword used in a class with assertion disabled is ignored by the JVM:

```
java -ea:com.db -da:com.db.dao StartServer
```

`java.lang.ClassLoader` defines the following methods for handling assertions:

- `setDefaultAssertionStatus(boolean enabled)`
  Sets the assertion status for the newly loaded classes
- `setClassAssertionStatus(String cls, boolean enabled)`
  Sets the assertion status for the named class
- `setPackageAssertionStatus(String pkg, boolean enabled)`
  Sets the assertion status for the classes belonging to the named package
- `clearAssertionStatus()`
  Restores the default assertion status

Summary

In this chapter, we have seen the fundamentals of error handling. We have also seen the different error handling patterns and techniques in J2EE web applications for handling expected and unexpected checked exceptions and runtime exceptions. We have covered the fundamentals of logging, tracing, and notification and the two popular logging APIs, Log4J from Apache Software Foundation and JDK 1.4 logging API. We have also covered the JDK 1.4 assertion features.

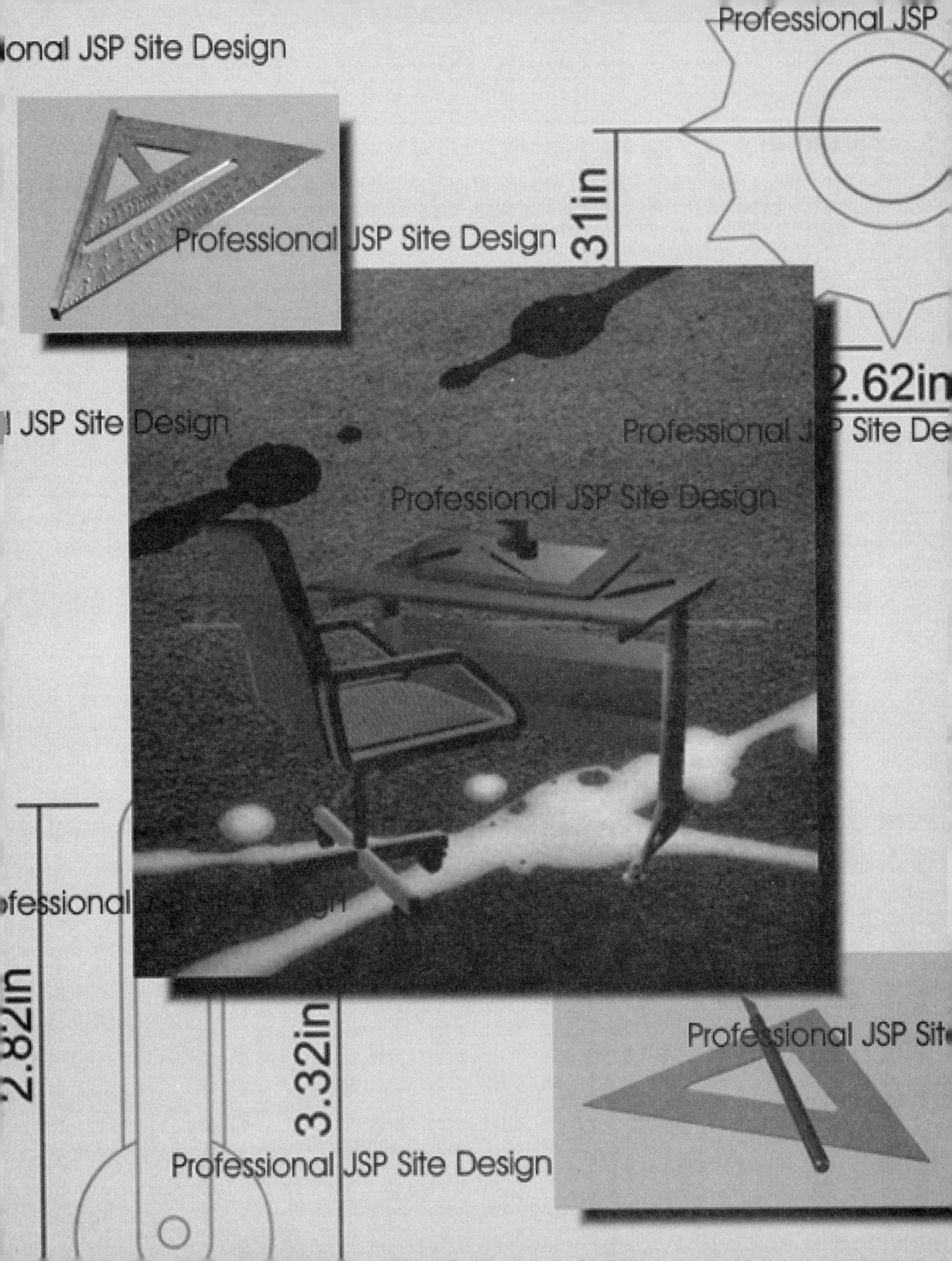
Professional JSP
Professional JSP Site Design
31in
2.62in
Professional JSP Site Design
3.32in
Professional JSP Site Design

8

Data Access Patterns

Almost all commercial enterprise applications access data stored in external resource managers; in most cases, the enterprise data is stored in a relational database management system (RDBMS). Java provides a variety of methods for accessing data stored in external RDBMSs, mainly based on JDBC and SQLJ. In this chapter we will cover a few of the more popular data access patterns used for developing web applications using Java, looking in turn at:

- Enterprise JavaBeans
- SQLJ
- Java Data Access Objects
- Reflection proxies for strongly typing abstract data structures
- A Data Access Object pattern using JDBC

Once we have covered the fundamentals of data access patterns, we will develop a data aware J2EE web application using the last of these patterns. To simplify the development of the presentation tier we will use the popular Struts Framework from the Apache Software Foundation (as described in Chapter 2).

Enterprise JavaBeans

Enterprise Java Beans are used for building component based distributed applications. The latest (recently released) specification of EJB is 2.0, which is implemented by a few of the mainstream application server vendors like Bea WebLogic Server 6.1. In the previous version (EJB 1.1) all EJB components are remote objects, where as version 2.0 brings in the concept of local EJB components. In this section we will be looking briefly at the persistent EJB components as defined by the EJB 1.1 specification. The persistence model defined for version 2.0 is significantly different from that in version 1.1.

An in-depth coverage of EJB is beyond the scope of this chapter – please refer to Professional EJB from Wrox Press (ISBN 1-861005-08-3) for an exhaustive coverage.

EJB components run in and are serviced by a managed environment. These services include transactions, life cycle management, security, and instance pooling. The EJB 1.1 specification defines two types of components:

- **Session Bean**
  Session beans function as an extension to the client applications that are using them. Multiple clients do not share session bean instances. You can have **stateful** session beans that persist the value of the instance variables across multiple method calls and **stateless** session beans that don't have that capability. However, for neither kind of session bean is the state persisted to long-term storage.

- **Entity Bean**
  Entity beans are components that model entities that are persisted to long-term storage. For example, these entities might include your enterprise's data like employee information, payroll information, account information etc that you need to store in a persistent storage for a long time. Multiple clients can share their instances, though the container serializes (synchronizes) method calls on the entity beans. Like session beans, entity beans have also two flavors. The beans for which the code to persist them are provided by the bean developer are called **BMP** (Bean Managed Persistence) entity beans and those that rely on the container to generate the persistence code are called **CMP** (Container Managed Persistence) entity beans.

EJB 2.0 supports a third type called message driven beans that are activated by asynchronous messages received by JMS destinations.

The EJB Working Model

All EJB components, regardless of whether they are of the entity type or session type, are composed of two mandatory interfaces and one mandatory class. They may also refer to additional classes like business exceptions and helper classes. Entity EJBs that represent database records with composite primary keys may also refer to classes that represent the respective primary keys.

The first interface is called the **home interface**, and should extend the `javax.ejb.EJBHome` interface, which in turn extends the `java.rmi.Remote` interface. The bean provider defines the home interface and specifies the methods within the home interface for creating a new bean instance, finding bean instances from the persistent storage in case of entity beans, and removing the enterprise beans.

The second interface is the **remote interface** and should extend `javax.ejb.EJBObject`; this in turn extends the `java.rmi.Remote` interface. The remote interface specifies the business methods for the bean.

The class is the actual **bean class** that implements the business and lifecycle methods defined in the remote and home interfaces. This implementation is entirely different from the implementation of interfaces in the Java language semantics. In fact, the lifecycle methods defined in the home interface will be prefixed with the string `ejb` when they are implemented in the bean class. The business methods should have the same name and signature in both the remote interface and the bean class.

All the session bean classes should implement the interface `javax.ejb.SessionBean` that provides methods for managing the bean instances, like activating an instance, passivating the instance temporarily, or removing the instance. Similarly, all entity bean classes should implement the interface `javax.ejb.EntityBean` and define methods for storing and loading the state of the bean to a long-term persistent storage in addition to the instance management methods.

Deployment Descriptor

One of the biggest advantages of EJB components is that their behavior can be tailored without changing their code. EJBs are servived components that rely on the EJB container within which they operate for low level services like transactions, security, resource management, persistence etc. This means you can take a compiled EJB component and make it transactional, secure, and persistent by defining these properties in an XML deployment descriptor file that is external to the beans' code. This deployment descriptor should be called `ejb-jar.xml`. For example, the deployment descriptor for an EJB component defines:

- The type of the bean (session or entity).
- Whether a session bean is stateful or stateless.
- The persistence mechanism for an entity bean – whether the persistence is bean-managed (BMP) or container-managed (CMP).
- The persistent state of an entity bean. This lets us define the instance fields within an entity bean that should be persisted to the database. With version 1.1 the persistent field should be declared public and should of either primitive type or a few classes like `java.lang.String` or `java.sql.Date`. In version 2.0, you need to specify the persistent fields of the entity EJB using abstract accessor and mutator methods.
- The security context for the methods defined in the bean. We can specify the role required for the security principal associated with the thread invoking the method. For example, in the deployment descriptor you can specify that the method for amending a salary can be called only by users with the `manager` role. The real mapping of users to roles is done in a container-specific way.
- The transactional nature of the methods defined in the bean – we can specify whether a method should execute in a transactional context. Transaction attributes for a method specify whether the container should start a new transaction, continue with the current transaction, or suspend the current transaction when the method is executed. Session beans may use either container-managed or bean-managed transactions, whereas entity beans can have only container-managed transactions. Bean-managed transactions are demarcated using the `UserTransaction` interface (part of the Java Transaction API) that should be made available though a JNDI namespace by the container provider. The transaction manager enlists the resource managers that are accessed by methods participating in the current transaction. This means that writing to a database using JDBC and sending a message using JMS can be done in a single transaction.

In addition to the deployment descriptor explained above, a deployment descriptor specific to the container might be needed to define the actual persistence mapping (in other words, mapping fields to database columns), or making the home objects available in the JNDI namespace of the application server.

Method Interposition

We have seen above that we can declare the transactional and security attributes of bean methods in a deployment descriptor. However, if we don't have the logic in the code, how does this work?

This is where method interposition comes in. We have seen that the home and remote interfaces of a bean extend the `java.rmi.Remote` interface. Hence, when a bean is deployed using container-specific tools, the tools generate classes that implement the home and the remote interfaces as well stubs and skeletons for those classes depending on the remote protocol you are using. Note that Java Remote Method Protocol (JRMP) functions differently from Internet Inter ORB (Object Request Broker) Protocol (IIOP). EJB specification supports both JRMP and IIOP. The advantage with IIOP is that it is interoperable across containers from different vendors. The client applications need to be aware only of the interface exposed by the home and the remote objects. The bean class itself is seldom exposed to the client. For example, a business method call on the remote interface is marshalled to the container. The container accepts the method call and redirects it to an instance of the actual bean class, checking and applying the security and transaction properties defined in the deployment descriptor for the bean.

The home objects are made available in the JNDI namespace of the application server during deployment. The client applications look up these objects using JNDI and use them for creating, finding, and removing remote objects. These remote objects are used for invoking the business methods on the bean.

Sample EJB Code

In this section, we will have a look at some sample EJB code for accessing a simple employee entity using container-managed persistence. The purpose of this section is only to give a feel of the EJB code and we won't be going into the details of deploying it and running it on a target application server. We will look at EJB integration patterns more closely in chapter 9.

The Remote Interface

First, we will define the remote interface for the bean. Remote methods should throw a `java.rmi.RemoteException`, together with any other business exception as declared by the method implementation within the bean class. In our remote interface we will define three methods to get the name and id of the employee, and set the employee's name:

```
import javax.ejb.EJBObject;
import java.rmi.RemoteException;

public interface Employee extends EJBObject {
  //Gets the ID
  public Integer getId() throws RemoteException;
  //Gets the name
  public String getName() throws RemoteException;
  //Sets the name
  public void setName(String name) throws RemoteException;
}
```

The Home Interface

The home interface will define the methods for creating a new employee entity, finding an employee entitity, and finding all the employee entities. The finder methods should return a remote interface for single object finders and a collection for multi object finders.

The method to create the entity should throw `javax.ejb.CreateException` and `java.rmi.RemoteException`, whereas the methods for finding entities should throw `javax.ejb.FinderException` and `java.rmi.RemoteException`. There must be a mandatory finder method called `findByPrimaryKey()` that gets the remote object representing the entity with the specified primary key:

```
import javax.ejb.EJBHome;
import javax.ejb.CreateException;
import javax.ejb.FinderException;
import java.rmi.RemoteException;
import java.util.Collection;

public interface EmployeeHome extends EJBHome {
  //Create a new employee instance
  public Employee create(Integer id, String name)
                        throws RemoteException, CreateException;

  //Find the employee with the specified ID.
  public Employee findByPrimaryKey(Integer id)
                        throws RemoteException, FinderException;

  //Finds all the employees
  public Collection findAll() throws RemoteException, FinderException;

}
```

All create methods must start with the string "`create`" and all the finder methods with "`find`", as in `findPrimaryKey()`. For bean-managed persistence, all creator and finder methods should have implementations in the bean class. But there are a few differences in the method signatures:

- The names of the methods are the names of the corresponding methods defined in the home interface prefixed with the string `ejb`.
- The `create()` method in the home interface returns the remote interface whereas the corresponding method in the bean class returns the primary key class.
- The single object finder methods in the home interface return the remote interface, whereas the corresponding method in the bean class returns the primary key class.

For container-managed persistence we don't need to define any finder methods, as they are defined in the container-generated persistence helper classes.

The Bean Class

Now that we have defined the home and remote interfaces, we will define the bean class. For container managed entity beans we need to define:

- The `ejbCreate()` methods corresponding to all the `create()` methods in the home interface
- All the business methods defined in the remote interface
- The methods defined by the interface `javax.ejb.EntityBean`

In our case there will be one `ejbCreate()` method, which takes the values passed by the client and assigns them to the instance variables that represent the bean's persistent state:

```
import javax.ejb.EntityBean;
import javax.ejb.EntityContext;
import java.rmi.RemoteException;

public class EmployeeBean implements EntityBean {
```

Instance fields that represent the persistent state:

```
public Integer id;
public String name;
```

The create method returns a `null` value for CMP beans, whereas it should return the valid primary key value for BMP beans. This is because for CMP beans primary key values are managed by the container:

```
/**
 * Create an employee instance
 */
public Integer ejbCreate(Integer id, String name) {
  this.id = id;
  this.name = name;
  return null;
}
```

`ejbPostCreate()` is a mandatory method that is called by the container after the create method:

```
public void ejbPostCreate(Integer id, String name) {}
```

Next, we must implement the business methods:

```
public Integer getId(Integer _id) {
  return id;
}

public String getName() {
  return name;
}

public void setName(String name) {
  this.name = name;
}
```

These are the methods defined by the `EntityBean` interface:

```
public void setEntityContext(EntityContext ctx) {}
public void unsetEntityContext() {}
```

These next two methods are related to pooling of bean instances and are called after and before a bean instance is activated and passivated respectively:

```
public void ejbActivate() {}
public void ejbPassivate() {}
```

The final three methods are persistence-related methods. The load method is called immediately after the instance fields are updated from the database, the store method is called immediately before the data is written back to the database, and the remove method is called immediately before the entity is removed from the database. For CMP beans these may be used for data enrichment and for BMP beans these may be used for the actual persistence code:

```
    public void ejbLoad() {}
    public void ejbStore() {}
    public void ejbRemove() {}
  }
```

The Deployment Descriptor

The example below shows the deployment descriptor for the above bean:

```
<?xml version="1.0"?>

<ejb-jar>
  <display-name>Employee</display-name>
  <enterprise-beans>
```

We start to define an entity bean:

```
    <entity>
      <description>Employee</description>
```

We need to specify, in turn, the name of the bean:

```
      <ejb-name>EmployeeBean</ejb-name>
```

The class of the home interface:

```
      <home>EmployeeHome</home>
```

The class of the remote interface:

```
      <remote>Employee</remote>
```

The class of the bean itself:

```
      <ejb-class>EmployeeBean</ejb-class>
```

The persistence type:

```
      <persistence-type>Container</persistence-type>
```

Define the class of the primary key:

```
      <prim-key-class>java.lang.Integer</prim-key-class>
```

Define whether the bean is re-entrant or not (re-entrant beans allow callbacks):

```
      <reentrant>False</reentrant>
```

Lastly in this section, we define the bean's container-managed fields:

```
      <cmp-field><field-name>id</field-name></cmp-field>
      <cmp-field><field-name>name</field-name></cmp-field>
      <primkey-field>id</primkey-field>
    </entity>
  </enterprise-beans>
```

Our final step is to define the transaction attribute as `required` for all the methods. This means that when a method is called by the container, and there is no transaction already associated with the thread, a new transaction will be started:

```
  <assembly-descriptor>
    <container-transaction>
      <method>
        <ejb-name>EmployeeBean</ejb-name>
        <method-name>*</method-name>
      </method>
      <trans-attribute>Required</trans-attribute>
    </container-transaction>
  </assembly-descriptor>

</ejb-jar>
```

The Client Code

Now let's look at a simple client that looks up the home interface and creates an employee entity. This example assumes that the bean is already deployed and that the home interface is made available in a JNDI namespace by the name `EmployeeHome`:

```
import javax.naming.InitialContext;

public class TestClass {

  public static void main(String args[]) throws Exception {
```

There are three steps we must perform; firstly, we create a JNDI initial context:

```
    InitialContext ctx = new InitialContext();
```

Next, we look up the home object in that context:

```
    EmployeeHome home = (EmployeeHome)ctx.lookup("EmployeeHome");
```

Finally, we create a new entity bean instance using the `create()` method; this creates the employee entity in the underlying persistent storage:

```
    Employee remote = home.create(1,"Meeraj");
  }
}
```

Guidelines on Using EJBs

So, when would we want to use EJBs for data access and other serviced tasks within an application? Well, some of the advantages of doing so are:

- Since the container provides services such as transaction management and security, the system can be built faster and more reliable.
- It is standards based technology and it is easier to recruit new technicians who are experienced in the EJB technology. If you use your own persistence framework, you will have to spend time in getting new developers in the team familiar with the framework.
- EJBs have evolved into a mature technology in last few years.
- It is easier to separate the web tier from the enterprise tier.

However, there are also some potential reasons for not using EJB in an application:

- The application is a simple web application that doesn't need immense enterprise capabilities,
- The application has an existing persistence layer that works fine.
- The application doesn't have a lot of transaction processing and is more of a decision support system with bulk reads and writes to the database.
- EJB has limitations restricting use of threading, native code, and static variables. The EJB specification restricts the use of certain language features and resource access within the EJB code.

SQLJ

SQLJ is a series of specifications, published by ANSI, for using SQL in the Java language; the specifications may be downloaded from http://www.sqlj.org/. SQLJ provides three main features:

- Embedded SQL statements within Java code
- Static method calls on Java classes from SQL stored procedures and functions
- Java classes as data types within SQL

It's the first of these that is of particular interest to us here.

Embedded SQL

SQLJ/OLB (Object Language Binding) is Part 0 of the SQLJ specification, and defines how SQL statements can be embedded within Java classes, for example:

```
int id = 1;
String name = "Meeraj";
#sql {INSERT INTO employee VALUES (:id,:name)};
```

This inserts a record into the `employee` table. There are a number of points of interest here:

- SQLJ statements start with `#sql`
- SQLJ statements end with semi-colon '`;`'
- SQLJ variables that are referenced within SQLJ statements should be prefixed with a colon '`:`'
- SQL text is enclosed within curly braces '`{}`'

Java classes that contain SQLJ statements need to be passed through a SQLJ translator provided by the SQLJ vendor for the database. Most of the database vendors provide proriatory SQLJ translators, such as the translator provided by Oracle Corporation. The diagram below shows the translation of a SQLJ file to a Java class. Depending on the implementation, the SQLJ translator may replace the SQLJ statements with method calls to the JDBC API:

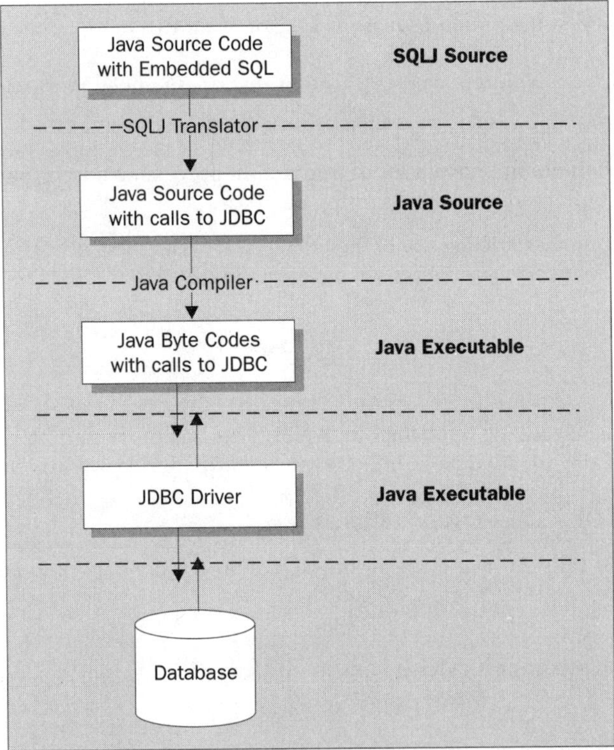

SQLJ has the following advantages over JDBC:

- SQLJ source programs are relatively smaller than JDBC programs.
- SQLJ uses database connections to check the syntax of the static SQL code during translation, whereas JDBC doesn't do this as it is a dynamic API.
- JDBC doesn't support the use of host variables within SQL statements as in SQLJ. Host variables are variables defined in the host language (Java for example) within the embedded SQL statements.

- SQLJ provides strong type checking of input and output parameters to the SQL statement at translation phase.

However, SQLJ inevitably has some disadvantages too, including:

- The need to use provider-specific tools for generating provider-specific persistence code during the translation phase
- An extra step of translation is required for generating the Java source files from the SQLJ files

Java Data Objects

Java Data Objects (JDO) is a specification for transparent persistence of Java objects into conventional data stores. Transparent persistence lets application developers make arbitrary Java objects persistent, without worrying about the intricacies of the persistence mechanism. It promotes a standard interface between Java objects that are persisted and the data store in which they are persisted (relational data stores, object data stores, or file stores). A few vendors implement the JDO specification, for example the Transparent Persistence Module available with Forte for Java, Internet Edition from Sun (http://www.sun.com/forte/ffj/).

One of the main concerns when writing object-oriented database driven applications is the intricacy associated with object to relational mapping, which is often not as seamless as desired. Application developers mostly use OR (Object Relational Mapping) tools like TopLink and CocoBase and JDBC for persisting the state of Java objects. JDO automates the mapping between persistent Java objects and the underlying data stores.

JDO circumvents the problem, associated with both JDBC and SQLJ, that application developers have to learn an extra language like SQL on top of Java. It isolates the application developer from the underlying data store and lets the JDO implementation perform the persistence of the object into a data store.

Features

The main features of JDO are:

- Application developers can write Java objects to implement the business logic without worrying about the logic for persisting the state of those objects. This frees developers from the tedious task of writing SQL statements.
- The mapping between the Java object and how it is represented in the underlying data store is determined by the JDO implementation at runtime. JDO can manage and persist a complex web of objects maintaining their interdependencies as is done in object serialization.
- The interface to the application is uniform, regardless of the type of data store used. This makes it easier to use a plug-n-play model for the underlying data stores.
- Transactional issues like data integrity, concurrency, and synchronization.
- Connection pooling based on the J2EE connector architecture.
- Scalability issues like large data sets, fine grained objects, caching, and locking.

Architecture

Writing applications using JDO involves a number of steps:

- First, we must develop application classes that perform the business logic. Object instances of some of these classes may need to be persisted to a permanent storage.
- The next stage involves the enhancement of the Java objects that need to be persisted to permanent storage, by implementing the `PersistenceCapable` interface provided by the JDO specification. Most JDO implementations achieve this by performing byte code enhancement, modifying the byte code of the compiled class so that it implements the `PersistenceCapable` interface. JDO provides an XML specification for mapping the business objects to the JDO implementation, which may be used by the class enhancers.
- The last stage uses these enhanced classes to develop the business application. If the persistence tasks are performed using the JDO interfaces, the actual mechanism of performing those tasks is transparent to the application developer.

JDO Interfaces

The JDO specification defines a number of interfaces that are implemented by JDO vendors and can be used by application developers for persisting persistence capable classes:

- `PersistenceManager`
  This interface manages transactions, reads, writes, updates, and deletes of persistence capable classes.
- `PersistenceManagerFactory`
  Instances of this interface are provided by the vendors, and can be configured and stored in external namespaces like JNDI. They act as factory objects for creating `PersistenceManager` classes.
- `Transaction`
  This interface is modeled after the OMG `UserTransaction`, and provides transaction features like atomicity, concurrency, integrity, and durability.
- `Query`
  This interface allows users to search for objects matching specified predicates, and supports ordering.
- `PersistenceCapable`
  This is the interface that must be implemented by the class whose objects are persistence capable. Developers may hand-code the classes to implement this interface. However, the preferred way of doing this is via byte code modification by external class enhancers. The interface defines methods for finding out whether the instance is transacted, new, or dirty.

JDO Sample Code

An in-depth coverage of JDO is beyond the scope of this chapter and the book; you can learn more about JDO at http://access1.sun.com/jdo/ or by reading *Professional Java Data*, Wrox Press, ISBN 1-861004-10-9. Hence, we will conclude this section with a small snippet showing how the JDO interfaces are used in application code.

We start by creating a new JNDI initial context object:

```
Context ctx = new InitialContext();
```

Our next step is to look up the persistence manager factory in the JNDI namespace:

```
PersistenceManagerFactory pmf =
        (PersistenceManagerFactory)ctx.lookup("pmfFactory");
```

We can then use the factory to obtain a persistence manager:

```
PersistenceManager pm = pmf.getPersistenceManager();
```

With the groundwork done, we can create a new employee instance. Note that the byte code of the `Employee` class needs to have been enhanced to implement the `PersistenceCapable` interface, and that the Employee class here is not the same as the EJB bean class we saw earlier:

```
Employee emp = new Employee();
emp.setId(1);
emp.setName("Meeraj");
```

Finally, we create the employee in the underlying data store:

```
pm.makePersistent(emp);
```

The activity diagram below shows the basic steps in using JDO within an application:

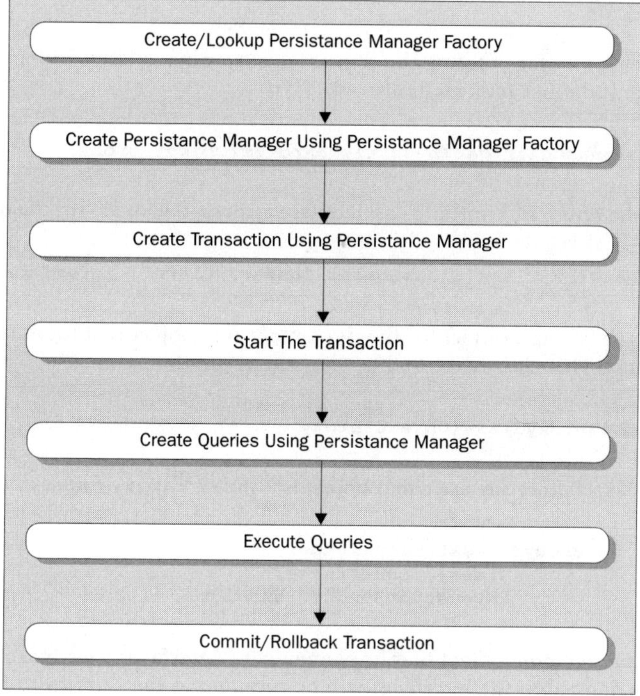

Even though quite a lot of O/R mapping and ODBMS vendors provide a JDO implementation, the JDO specification is only in the proposed final draft stage and not yet finalized. The Proposed Final Draft was published in May 2001; the Reference Implementation preliminary release was publised in June 2001; and the final Reference Implementation and Technology Compatibility Kit are expected by the end of 2001.

Dynamic Proxies

The dynamic proxy API, added to the Java Reflection API in JDK 1.3, is not directly related to data access patterns. It is, however, a quite powerful way of strongly typing abstract data structures, and in this section we will take an overview of dynamic proxies and have a look at an example of using the dynamic proxy API.

Dynamic proxies let us create objects, at runtime, that implement any interface we want. This is very useful in defining interfaces that model different entities and have varying implementation based on abstract data structures. For example, you can have an interface that represents a customer entity and uses a hashmap rather than individual instance variables to store the customer data.

At the heart of the dynamic proxy API are a class called `Proxy` and an interface called `InvocationHandler`. The `Proxy` class defines factory methods for creating dynamic objects that implement a set of interfaces, specified at run time in arrays passed as one of the method arguments. The calls on the object that implement these interfaces are rerouted to an object that implements the `InvocationHandler` interface. This object is also passed as an argument to the factory method that creates the dynamic object.

The Proxy Class

This class acts as the factory for creating the dynamic proxy objects and implementing interfaces specified at run time. It defines four methods:

```
static InvocationHandler getInvocationHandler(Object proxy)
```

This method returns the `InvocationHandler` interface associated with the specified dynamic proxy object.

```
static Class getProxyClass(ClassLoader loader, Class[] interfaces)
```

This method returns the `Class` object for the dynamic proxy object that implements all the interfaces specified as arguments. This class is created by the VM at run time.

```
static boolean isProxyClass(Object proxy)
```

This method identifies whether the specified object is a proxy object or not.

```
static Object newProxy(ClassLoader loader,
                       Class[] interfaces,
                       InvocationHandler handler)
```

This method returns a dynamic object that implements the interfaces specified in the argument list. The calls to the methods defined in the interfaces will be rerouted to the `InvocationHandler` interface specified as the argument.

The InvocationHandler Interface

This interface defines a single method that must be implemented by the classes used by the proxy class. The method calls on the proxy class are rerouted to the callback method defined by the interface, so that when a method on the dynamic proxy object is called, the invocation handler's `invoke()` method is passed the actual method, arguments and the proxy object:

```
Object invoke(Object proxy, Method method, Object[] args)
```

The first argument defines the dynamic proxy object, the second represents the method that was invoked on the interface, and the third represents the arguments passed to the method.

Using Dynamic Proxies

In this section we will develop a small application that uses dynamic proxies for strongly typing an abstract data structure. We will define an interface that represents a persistent entity stored in a data store. Then we will use the dynamic proxy API to get a proxy object that implements this interface. The state of the persistent entity is modeled using a hashmap and the invocation handler associated with the proxy will translate the data in the hashmap into the typed information specified by the interface.

The IEmployee Interface

This interface represents an employee entity that is persisted in the database. The interface defines methods for getting the employee's id, name, and salary:

```
package com.wrox.dynamicproxy;

public interface IEmployee {
  public int getId();
  public String getName();
  public double getSalary();
}
```

The GenericInvocationHandler Class

Now we will define a class that will implement the `InvocationHandler` interface and provide the logic for returning appropriate data depending on the calls made on the `IEmployee` interface. The objects of this class will store the data as a `HashMap` and, when a call that represents an accessor method comes in (we assume all the accessor methods will start with the string `get`), we strip the first three characters from the method name. The object stored in the `HashMap` against the key represented by the rest of the method name is returned. For example, when the `getId` method is called the object stored against the key `"Id"` is returned:

```
package com.wrox.dynamicproxy;

import java.lang.reflect.InvocationHandler;
import java.lang.reflect.Method;
import java.util.HashMap;

public class GenericInvocationHandler implements InvocationHandler {
```

We declare the HashMap that stores the data for the persistent entity:

```
    HashMap data;
```

The constructor initializes the data in the HashMap:

```
    public GenericInvocationHandler(HashMap data) {
      this.data = data;
    }

    public Object invoke(Object obj, Method method, Object[] obj2)
           throws Throwable {
```

First we get the name of the method that is being invoked:

```
      String methodName = method.getName();
```

Then, since all our methods are getXXX() accessor methods, we simply return the data that is stored in the HashMap with a name corresponding to the accessor method:

```
      return data.get(method.getName().substring(3));
    }
  }
```

This class can be used for any entity, as long as we enforce a naming convention for the accessor methods defined in the interfaces representing the entities and the keys under which the data is stored in the HashMap.

The EmployeeDAO Class

Now we can write a class that will provide the data access logic for the employee entity. This class can use any data access technique to populate the HashMap, and uses the Proxy class to create a dynamic object that implements the IEmployee interface.

The instance of GenericInvocationHandler is initialized by passing the HashMap that contains the data for the employee entity. In the example below, we have hard-coded the values stored in the HashMap for simplicity:

```
  package com.wrox.dynamicproxy;

  import java.util.HashMap;
  import java.lang.reflect.Proxy;
  import java.lang.reflect.InvocationHandler;

  public class EmployeeDAO {

    public EmployeeDAO() {}
```

This is a data access method for getting an employee entity by id:

```
    public IEmployee getEmployeeById(int id) {
```

Populate the HashMap:

```
    HashMap data = new HashMap();
    data.put("Id", new Integer(id));
    data.put("Name", "Meeraj");
    data.put("Salary", new Double(45000));
```

Initialize the invocation handler by passing the data:

```
    InvocationHandler handler = new GenericInvocationHandler(data);
```

Create an array of interfaces that need to be implemented:

```
    Class[] interfaces = {IEmployee.class};
```

Get the current class loader:

```
    ClassLoader loader = getClass().getClassLoader();
```

Return the dynamic proxy:

```
    return (IEmployee)Proxy.newProxyInstance(loader, interfaces, handler);
  }
}
```

The TestClient Class

Finally, we will write a small test client to use the data access object built using dynamic proxies:

```
package com.wrox.dynamicproxy;

public class TestClient {

  public static void main(String args[]) {
```

Create the data access object and get the employee entity by specifying the id:

```
    IEmployee employee = new EmployeeDAO().getEmployeeById(1);
```

Print the attributes of the employee entity:

```
    System.out.println("ID:" + employee.getId());
    System.out.println("Name:" + employee.getName());
    System.out.println("Salary:" + employee.getSalary());
  }
}
```

Compile all the classes using the following command.

```
> javac com\wrox\dynamicproxy\*.java
```

Run the test client by typing the following command:

```
> java com.wrox.dynamicproxy.TestClient
```

This will produce the following output:

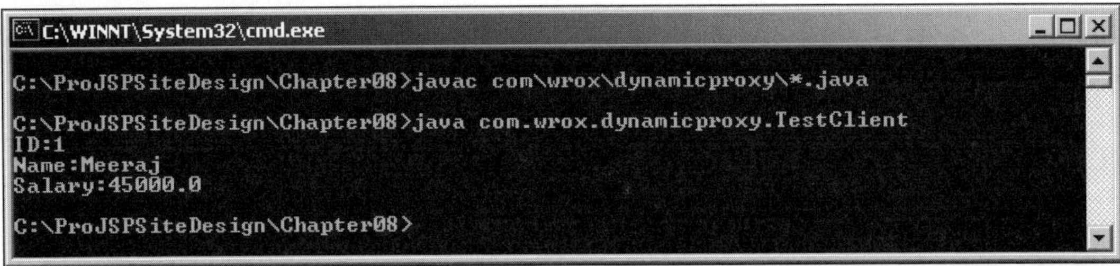

A Generic Data Access Pattern

We have looked at a number of different data access techniques so far. Even though all the patterns we have discussed have definite advantages, they have their weaknesses as well. In this section we will show a simple data access pattern for the data-driven case study we will develop in the second half of the chapter.

The data access objects that we discuss in this section are used to transform database records into entity class instances that model the real world persistent data, and vice-versa; there is a one-to-one correspondance between entity objects and database tables. The data access objects encapsulate the database calls and isolate other parts of the application from SQL statements, and so there is also a one-to-one correspondence between entity objects and data access objects. Each data access object encapsulates the database calls for:

- Creating the entity in the database
- Updating the state of the entity in the database
- Removing the entity from the database
- Finding the entity or a collection of entities from the database

This is illustrated in the diagram below; the business objects can then use the data access objects to create, find, update, and remove entity objects:

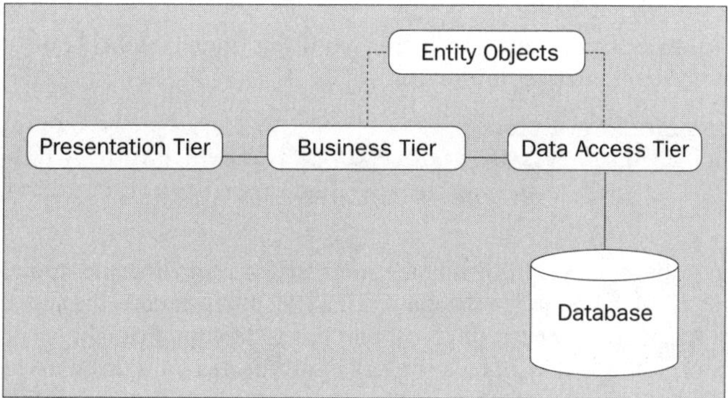

The constructors for the data access objects take instances of JDBC connections that can be used for sending SQL statements to the relational database. This is useful for demarcating transactions outside the data access objects in a business object. For example, a business object to remove a department from an employee information database may get a connection, start the transaction, pass the connection to data access objects representing employees and departments, and perform the persistence operations in a single transaction.

The methods defined by the data access object classes can be categorized as:

- A method for creating the entity in the database. This stores the persistent fields of the entity into a corresponding database table or collection of tables.
- A method for removing the entity from the database.
- A method for updating the information regarding an existing entity.
- One or more methods for finding the entities from the database for specific criteria. One mandatory method is the one to find a single entity for the specified primary key.

Exception Handling in Data Access Objects

The data access objects use a specialized set of exceptions to handle error conditions, which we'll look at first.

An instance of `CreateException` is thrown if the create method fails to create the entity in the database for some reason. The source code for the exception is shown below:

```
public class CreateException extends Exception {

  public CreateException(String message) {
    super(message);
  }
}
```

All the other exceptions follow the same pattern. They are:

- `DuplicateKeyException`
  This exception is a specialized subclass of the `CreateException` and is thrown if the create method fails to create the entity because another entity already exists in the database for the specified primary key.

- `FinderException`
  An instance of `FinderException` is thrown if the finder method fails to find the entity or collection of entities due to some reason.

- `ObjectNotFoundException`
  This is a specialized subclass of `FinderException`, which is thrown in single object finder methods, when an entity matching the specified criteria is not found in the database.

- `NoSuchEntityException`
  This unexpected exception is thrown in the methods for removing and updating entities when the specified entity is not found in the database. This exception extends the system exception `java.lang.RuntimeException`. Note that this is different from the `ObjectNotFoundException`. `NoSuchEntityException` is thrown when an entity is not found when it is expected to be found, whereas `ObjectNotFoundException` is thrown when a method is called to locate an entity in the database and without the client being certain about it will be found to exist. For example, you call an update method to update an entity that exists in the datastore, where as finder method is never certain whether the entity is going to be there in the datastore.

Create Methods

In this section, we will have a look at the methods for creating entities in the database. These methods take as arguments instances of the corresponding entities. Each data access object defines one create method, which can throw a `CreateException`. The steps involved in implementing the create method are:

- If the connection is closed, throw an `IllegalStateException`.
- Create a `PreparedStatement` from the connection, passing the insert SQL specific to the entity being created, as an argument. (Prepared statements are pre-compiled by supporting drivers to enhance performance.)
- Set the input parameters of the `PreparedStatement` from the attributes of the entity object passed to the method.
- Execute the SQL. If the update count is not equal to one, throw a `CreateException`.
- If a `SQLException` is thrown in any of the above steps, check whether an entity already exists in the relevant table for the specified primary key. If yes, throw a `DuplicateKeyException`; otherwise throw a `RuntimeException`.
- Finally, close the `PreparedStatement`. If a `SQLException` is thrown in the process, catch it and re-throw as a `RuntimeException`. (The reason for this is that under normal circumstances we don't expect a `SQLException` to be thrown at this point.)

Update Methods

Next, we will have a look at the methods for updating the entities in the database. Each data access object defines one update method, which needs to be passed an instance of the corresponding entity. The steps involved in implementing the create method are:

- If the connection is closed, throw an `IllegalStateException`.

- Create a `PreparedStatement` from the connection, passing the update SQL specific to the entity being updated, as an argument. If you intend to use database store procedures, you may want to use `CallableStatement`.
- Set the input parameters of the `PreparedStatement` from the attributes of the entity object.
- Execute the SQL. If the update count is not equal to one, throw a `NoSuchEntiyException`.
- If a `SQLException` is thrown in any of the above steps, throw a `RuntimeException`.
- Finally, close the `PreparedStatement`. If a `SQLException` is thrown in the process, catch it and re-throw it as a `RuntimeException`.

Remove Methods

The penultimate set of methods comprises those that remove entities from the database. These methods take the primary key of the corresponding entities as arguments. Each data access object defines one remove method, and the steps involved in implementing it are:

- If the connection is closed, throw an `IllegalStateException`.
- Create a `PreparedStatement` from the connection, passing the SQL command to delete the entity.
- Set the input parameters of the `PreparedStatement` from the entity object.
- Execute the SQL. If the update count is not equal to one, throw a `NoSuchEntityException`.
- If a `SQLException` is thrown in any of the above steps, throw a `RuntimeExecption`.
- Finally, close the `PreparedStatement`. If a `SQLException` is thrown in the process, catch it and re-throw it as a `RuntimeException`.

Finder Methods

The data access objects may define one or more finder methods to retrieve an entity or a collection of entities from the database. The one mandatory finder method takes as a parameter a primary key value, and returns an entity instance populated with the data corresponding to that primary key value. Additional finder methods may be added to suit your requirements. If the finder methods fail due to some unknown reason, they throw instances of `FinderException`.

Finder methods fall into two categories depending on whether they are single object or multi object finders. Single object finder methods return a single instance of the entity, and if no record is found in the table meeting the specified criteria an `ObjectNotFoundException` is thrown.

Multi object finders return a collection of zero or more entity instances; if no entities are found in the database matching the specified criteria, an empty collection is returned.

Single Object Finders

Let's look at the logic for implementing single object finders. The number and type of arguments taken by a finder method is specific to the particular `WHERE` condition in the SQL statement for querying the database; the method for finding an entity by primary key takes the corresponding primary key value as an argument. The steps involved in implementing a single object finder method are:

- If the connection is closed, throw an `IllegalStateException`.
- Create a `PreparedStatement` from the connection, passing it the select SQL specific to the entity being selected.
- Set the input parameters of the `PreparedStatement` from the input arguments passed to the method.
- Execute the SQL. If the result set is empty, throw an `ObjectNotFoundException`.
- Create an entity instance, set the attribute values from the result set columns, and return the entity instance.
- If a `SQLException` is thrown in any of the above steps, throw a `RuntimeException`.
- Finally, close the `PreparedStatement`. If a `SQLException` is thrown in the process, catch it and re-throw as a `RuntimeException`.

Multi Object Finders

Our very last category of methods are the multi object finders, which are useful for finding a collection of items matching particular criteria, such as a list of all employees in a given department. The number and type of arguments is specific to the `where` condition for the particular SQL statement used to query the database. The steps involved in implementing the multi object finder methods are:

- If the connection is closed, throw an `IllegalStateException`.
- Create a `PreparedStatement` from the connection, passing it the relevant SQL statement for the search being performed.
- Set the input parameters of the `PreparedStatement` from the input arguments passed to the method.
- Execute the SQL.
- Create an instance of `ArrayList`.
- While there are more records in the result set, create entity instances, set the attributes from the result set columns, and add to the `ArrayList`.
- Return the `ArrayList`.
- If a `SQLException` is thrown in any of the above steps, throw a `RuntimeException`.
- Finally, close the `PreparedStatement`. If a `SQLException` is thrown in the process, catch it and re-throw as a `RuntimeException`.

Case Study – An Online Auction System

Now we have seen some different data access patterns, we will develop a data-driven J2EE web application that uses the data access pattern explained in the last section. To simplify the task of developing the presentation tier of the web application, we will be using the Struts Framework (http://jakarta.apache.org/struts/) from Apache Software Foundation. In the case study we will cover:

- Proper partitioning of J2EE web applications using presentation, business, and data access tiers
- Different aspects of the Struts Framework
- Database connection pooling using the standard J2EE datasource factory

Requirements Analysis

The application will let registered users add items for auction, bid for items posted by other users, and accept the highest bid posted by other users against their items. The use cases associated with the users of the system are shown below:

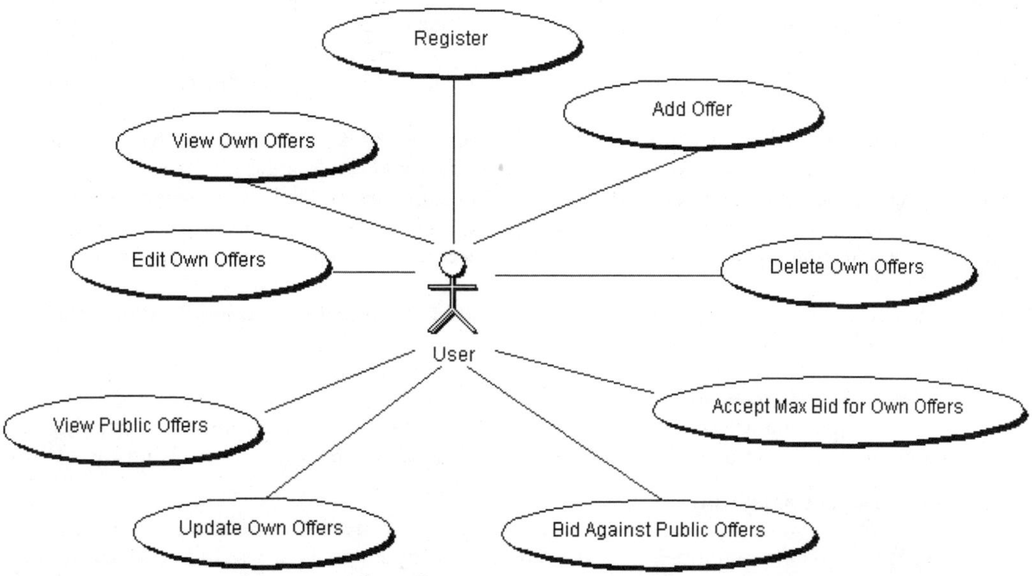

When the maximum bid of an offer is accepted by the owner of the offer, the details regarding the offer and all the bids associated with the offer are removed from the system; we could also add the ability to send confirmation e-mails to both the offering and bidding counter parties.

Choosing the Right Technology

Once we have the requirements, the next step is to choose the technology we will use for developing and implementing the system. As in previous chapters, we will use Tomcat 4.0 as the J2EE web container for deploying our web application. We will use MySQL (see http://www.mysql.com/) as the relational datastore, with the `org.gjt.mm.mysql.Driver` JDBC driver. For details of how to obtain these, see Appendix B.

Application Architecture

We next need to consider an appropriate architectural model for developing our web application. The important factors that we need to consider in formulating the architectural solution for the system include:

- Proper partitioning of the application
- Modularized design
- Separating presentation from content
- Maintainability
- Component based design
- Decoupling of application components

Keeping all the above factors in mind, we will use the MVC/Model 2 paradigm for implementing the system, using JSP pages to implement the application views. The next step is to design the controller element in the MVC paradigm. Rather that reinventing the wheel, we will use a third party off-the-shelf product for implementing our MVC framework. The Apache Struts Framework is an obvious choice because of its rich tag libraries and the variety of utilities and resources available from sites such as http://husted.com/struts/. Please refer to Chapter 2 for detailed coverage of Struts.

A task we need to accomplish if we are using Struts is to identify the different request URIs and map them to the action classes and form beans. An important thing we need to keep in mind is to partition our application properly and avoid tight coupling between the application components – loose coupling between the components help you build systems that are more flexible and extensible. The use of Struts obviously partitions the application into a set of view components, a controller element, and the application model.

The next step is to identify the components that will build the model for our applications. The model components can be broadly classified into:

- **Business logic components**
  These components are responsible for implementing the business logic for maintaining the various entities in the system like offers, users, and bids. We will call these components **Business Objects**.

- **System state components**
  These components provide the object incarnations for the system state stored in the underlying relational model. We will call these components **Entities**. In our scenario, the entities will also function as the Struts action form beans.

We can also identify a need for components that will implement the data access logic for transforming the records in the underlying relational data model to our system state components, as well as storing the state of our system state components back to the relational models. We will call these components **Data Access Objects**.

The requests coming from the browser can be broadly classified into data retrieval requests and data modification requests. These requests will be routed to the appropriate action classes by the action servlet, depending on the mapping information provided in the Struts configuration file.

These requests will be handled by the business objects, which will in turn use the data access objects for modifying the underlying relational data and extracting the data for the next view. The entities returned from the business objects will be stored in an HTTP request attribute, and the response will be forwarded to the relevant JSP page defined as a local forward for the action mapping. The JSP pages will use the appropriate Struts tags to retrieve and render the information.

The diagram below depicts the high-level view of the system we are going to develop:

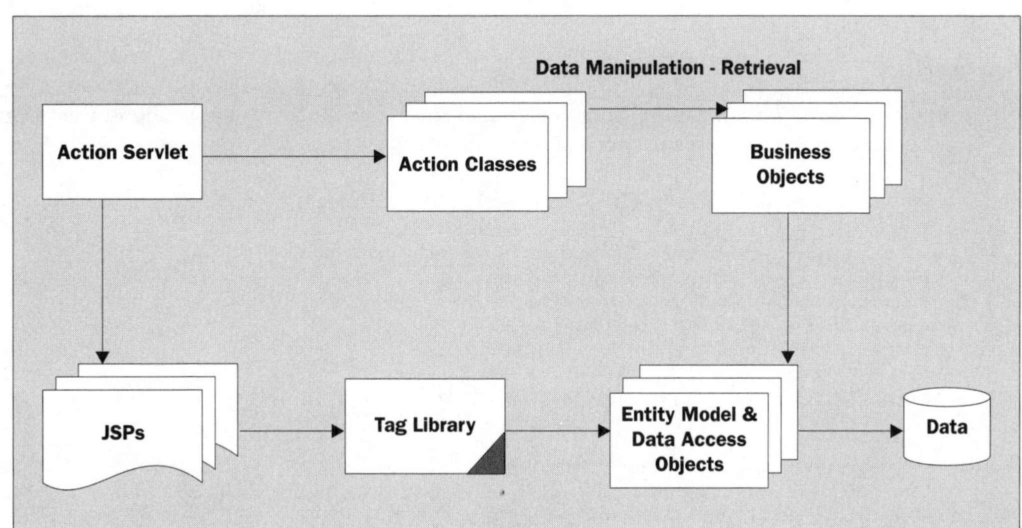

In the rest of the chapter we will:

- Plan the security system for the application
- Identify and implement our entities
- Implement the data access objects
- Implement the business objects
- Design the web tier
- Develop the Struts action class
- Implement the JSPs

Security

In this section we will describe the security settings for the application. For more detail on the methods used, see Chapter 10.

Defining the Authentication Scheme

The authentication to be used within the web application can be specified in the deployment descriptor (`web.xml`). In our web application, we will use HTTP Form Based authentication and the snippet from the web application deployment descriptor shows how the authentication scheme is specified:

```
<login-config>
  <auth-method>FORM</auth-method>
  <form-login-config>
    <form-login-page>/login.jsp</form-login-page>
    <form-error-page>/login.jsp</form-error-page>
  </form-login-config>
</login-config>
```

The snippet above specifies the authentication scheme as HTTP Form Based authentication and defines the logon page as `login.jsp` and the page to be displayed on authentication failure as `login.jsp` as well.

Authorization

J2EE promotes resource authorization using declarative roles. For J2EE web applications, the resources may be secured by defining the security constraints in the deployment descriptor, as shown below:

```
<security-constraint>
  <web-resource-collection>
    <web-resource-name>Secure resources</web-resource-name>
    <url-pattern>/editUser.do</url-pattern>
    <url-pattern>/updateUser.do</url-pattern>
    <url-pattern>/listOffer.do</url-pattern>
    <url-pattern>/editOffer.do</url-pattern>
    <url-pattern>/createOffer.do</url-pattern>
    <url-pattern>/updateOffer.do</url-pattern>
    <url-pattern>/deleteOffer.do</url-pattern>
    <url-pattern>/acceptBid.do</url-pattern>
    <url-pattern>/bid.do</url-pattern>
    <http-method>GET</http-method>
    <http-method>POST</http-method>
  </web-resource-collection>

  <auth-constraint>
    <role-name>user</role-name>
  </auth-constraint>
</security-constraint>
```

This code snippet states that the web resources accessed by the request URIs listed (`/editUser.do` and so on) can be accessed only by users having the role `user`. The mapping of these logical roles to physical users and groups on the target web container is performed by the application deployer.

In our application, all resources except the home page and page for registering new users may be accessed only by authenticated users. For this we define a logical role called `user` and define a security constraint in the deployment descriptor to restrict access to the secure resources only to those users who have the `user` role.

Security Realms

Since we are going to deploy our web application with Apache Tomcat, we need to decide how we're going to set up the security realm for the application. As users can register themselves with the system and immediately start using the system by specifying their user id and password, we need to use a dynamic realm for our application.

Luckily, Tomcat provides a JDBC realm that primarily uses two tables for performing authentication and authorization. The first table needs to store the user names and passwords, and the second table is needed to define the roles each user has been assigned.

The names of the database tables and columns holding the relevant data are defined in the `server.xml` file that can be found in the `conf\` directory under the Tomcat installation. In our case there is a one-to-one mapping between users and roles, as all the authenticated users should have the `user` role, and so we will store the user id, password, and role in the same table.

The snippet below shows the excerpt for defining the JDBC realm from the Tomcat `server.xml` file:

```
<Realm className="org.apache.catalina.realm.JDBCRealm"
       driverName="org.gjt.mm.mysql.Driver"
       connectionURL="jdbc:mysql://localhost/auction"
       userTable="user"
       userNameCol="user_id"
       userCredCol="password"
       userRoleTable="user"
       roleNameCol="role" />
```

This defines:

- The name of the class that performs the tasks for authentication and authorization; this class is provided by Tomcat.
- The name of the JDBC driver used for accessing the database.
- The JDBC URL for the database.
- The name of the table and columns that store user names and passwords. For this we will be using the table in which we store user details, so that whenever a new user is registered this table is populated with the user id and password and the realm class can use the information in the table to authenticate the users if they decide to logon to the system after registration. We will store the same table to store the role as well.

The `user` table is discussed in detail in the next section.

Identifying the Entities

The next thing we will do is to identify the entities that model the system state of the application. These entities represent the persistent data that is stored in the underlying database. The entities map to relational tables within the underlying database. From the initial requirements analysis, and the discussion on security realms, we can identify three major entities that will be used with in the system:

- `User`
  This entity represents the registered users and their details
- `Offer`
  This represents the offers added to the system by the registered users
- `Bid`
  This represents the bids raised by registered users against an available offer

Users have a one-to-many unidirectional relation with offers, and offers have the same with bids. After identifying the attributes associated with each of the entities, we arrive at the class diagram overleaf depicting the entity model for our system:

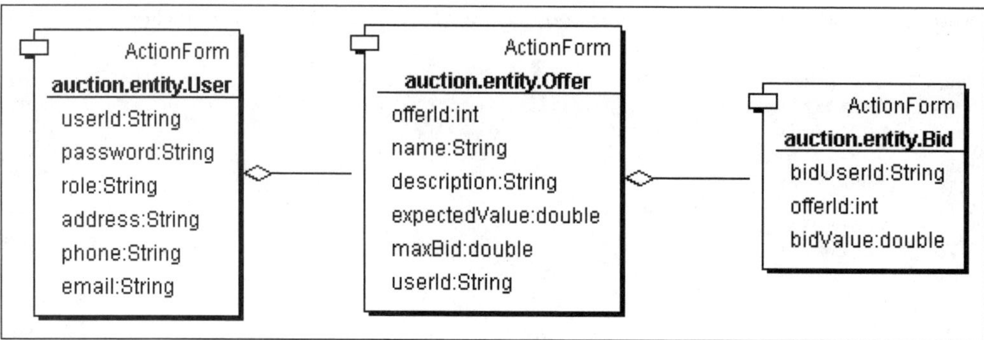

Implementing the Entities

We need to implement the entities as both database tables and Java classes.

Database Scripts

The snippet below defines the data definition script for the `user` table; the primary key identified for the table is `user_id`, and all the columns in the table are defined as not nullable:

```
CREATE TABLE user (
     user_id VARCHAR(30) NOT NULL PRIMARY KEY,
     password VARCHAR(30) NOT NULL,
     address VARCHAR(60) NOT NULL,
     phone VARCHAR(30) NOT NULL,
     email VARCHAR(30) NOT NULL,
     role VARCHAR(30) NOT NULL);
```

The primary key identified for the `offer` table is `offer_id`, which is defined to have values that are automatically incremented by the DBMS when records are inserted. All the columns in the table are defined as not nullable:

```
CREATE TABLE offer (
     offer_id INT NOT NULL PRIMARY KEY AUTO_INCREMENT,
     name VARCHAR(30) NOT NULL,
     description VARCHAR(60) NOT NULL,
     expected_value DOUBLE NOT NULL,
     max_bid DOUBLE NOT NULL,
     user_id VARCHAR(30) NOT NULL);
```

The `bid` table defines a composite primary key comprising of `bid_user_id` and `offer_id`, as a bid is uniquely identified by the combination of the item that is offered and the user who makes the bid. The snippet below defines the data definition script for the `bid` table:

```
CREATE TABLE bid (
     offer_id VARCHAR(15) NOT NULL,
     bid_user_id VARCHAR(15) NOT NULL,
     bid_value DOUBLE NOT NULL,
     PRIMARY KEY (bid_user_id,offer_id))
     TYPE=BDB
```

The database scripts defined in this section are specific to MySQL; you will need to amend the scripts if you wish to use a different target DBMS.

Java Classes

Now we will define the Java classes, in the `auction.entity` package, that will model our entities; the classes will also serve as Struts `ActionForm` beans that can be associated with the forms for entering the user, offer, and bid details. Therefore, these three classes extend `org.apache.struts.action.ActionForm`.

The User Class

The `User` class models the `user` table, and defines the attributes that represent the columns in the table. The class also defines accessors and mutators for all the attributes:

```
package auction.entity;

import org.apache.struts.action.ActionForm;

public class User extends ActionForm {

  private String userId;
  private String password;
  private String role;
  private String address;
  private String phone;
  private String email;

  // Getter and setter methods for the above attributes ...

}
```

The Offer Class

The `Offer` class models the `offer` table and defines the attributes that represent the columns in the table, together with accessors and mutators for all the attributes:

```
package auction.entity;

import org.apache.struts.action.ActionForm;

public class Offer extends ActionForm {

  private int offerId;
  private String name;
  private String description;
  private double expectedValue;
  private double maxBid;
  private String userId;

  // Getter and setter methods for the above attributes ...

}
```

The Bid Class

The `Bid` class models the `bid` table and, unsurprisingly, defines the attributes that represent the columns in the table together with accessor and mutator methods for the attributes:

```
package auction.entity;

import org.apache.struts.action.ActionForm;

public class Bid extends ActionForm {

  private String bidUserId;
  private int offerId;
  private double bidValue;

  // Getter and setter methods for the above attributes ...

}
```

Pooling Database Connections

In a properly designed enterprise application, connections to external resource managers are always pooled to improve performance and enhance efficiency, rather than opening a new connection each time the resource manager is accessed. Such resources include network sockets, connections to JMS providers, and JDBC connections.

Since we are going to use a relational datastore in our web application, we need to come up with a scheme for pooling JDBC connections, so that we maintain a "pool" of connections to the underlying resource. Client classes using the pool can request a connection from the pool, and return it back to the pool after use.

There are two ways of getting a database connection using the JDBC API:

- Using the `java.sql.DriverManager` class in the JDBC core API
- Using the `javax.sql.DataSource` interface in the JDBC extension API, which can be used as a factory for creating connections

According to the J2EE specification, all complying containers should provide an implementation of `DataSource` available for the applications running within the container. Tomcat 4.0 provides an implementation that can be configured and made available for JNDI lookup by the client application by means of an entry in the `server.xml` file:

```
<Resource name="jdbc/AuctionDB" auth="Container "
          type="javax.sql.DataSource"/>
<ResourceParams name="jdbc/AuctionDB">
  <parameter>
    <name>driverClassName</name>
    <value>org.gjt.mm.mysql.Driver</value>
  </parameter>
  <parameter>
    <name>driverName</name>
    <value>jdbc:mysql://localhost/auction</value>
  </parameter>
 </ResourceParams>
```

This snippet makes a `DataSource` implementation available for JNDI lookup by the applications, under the name `java:comp/env/jdbc/AuctionDB`. The datasource uses the MySQL JDBC driver, and the JDBC URL points to the `auction` MySQL database running locally.

The ConnectionPool Class

Instead of exposing the intricacies of JNDI lookup and getting a connection from the datasource implementation, we will provide a singleton class that will encapsulate all this functionality and act as a pool for database connections. (Singleton is a design pattern that ensures only one instance of a given class is made available per VM per classloader.) The source code is shown below:

```
package auction.db.util;

import java.sql.SQLException;
import java.sql.Connection;
import javax.sql.DataSource;

import javax.naming.Context;
import javax.naming.InitialContext;
import javax.naming.NamingException;

import java.util.Properties;

public class ConnectionPool {
```

We start by declaring the necessary variables, starting with a static variable that defines the name under which we can look up the datasource implementation instance in the JNDI namespace:

```
  private static String JNDI_NAME = "java:comp/env/jdbc/AuctionDB";
```

Our singleton instance will need to store the datasource that should be used for creating connections to the database; this instance is looked up from the JNDI namespace of the container:

```
  private DataSource ds;
```

We also need to maintain a static reference to the singleton instance itself:

```
  private static ConnectionPool mySelf;
```

The constructor is defined as private to avoid being instantiated outside the class itself; it needs to be passed the `DataSource` that it is controlling access to:

```
  private ConnectionPool(DataSource ds) {
    this.ds = ds;
  }
```

The `getInstance()` method returns the singleton instance of the `ConnectionPool` class:

```
  public static ConnectionPool getInstance() {
    try {
```

If the singleton instance is not already instantiated, we look up the DataSource in the JNDI namespace and instantiate the ConnectionPool instance. Once we are sure a ConnectionPool instance exists, we return it:

```
        if(mySelf == null) {
          Context initCtx = new InitialContext();
          DataSource ds = (DataSource)initCtx.lookup(JNDI_NAME);

          mySelf = new ConnectionPool(ds);

        }

        return mySelf;
      } catch(NamingException ex) {
          ex.printStackTrace();
          throw new RuntimeException("error.unexpected");
      }
    }
```

Lastly, the getConnection() method obtains a connection from the datasource and sets its auto commit mode:

```
    public Connection getConnection(boolean autoCommit) throws SQLException {
      Connection con = ds.getConnection();
      con.setAutoCommit(autoCommit);
      return con;
    }
  }
```

The diagram overleaf shows the sequence of events involved in obtaining the connection:

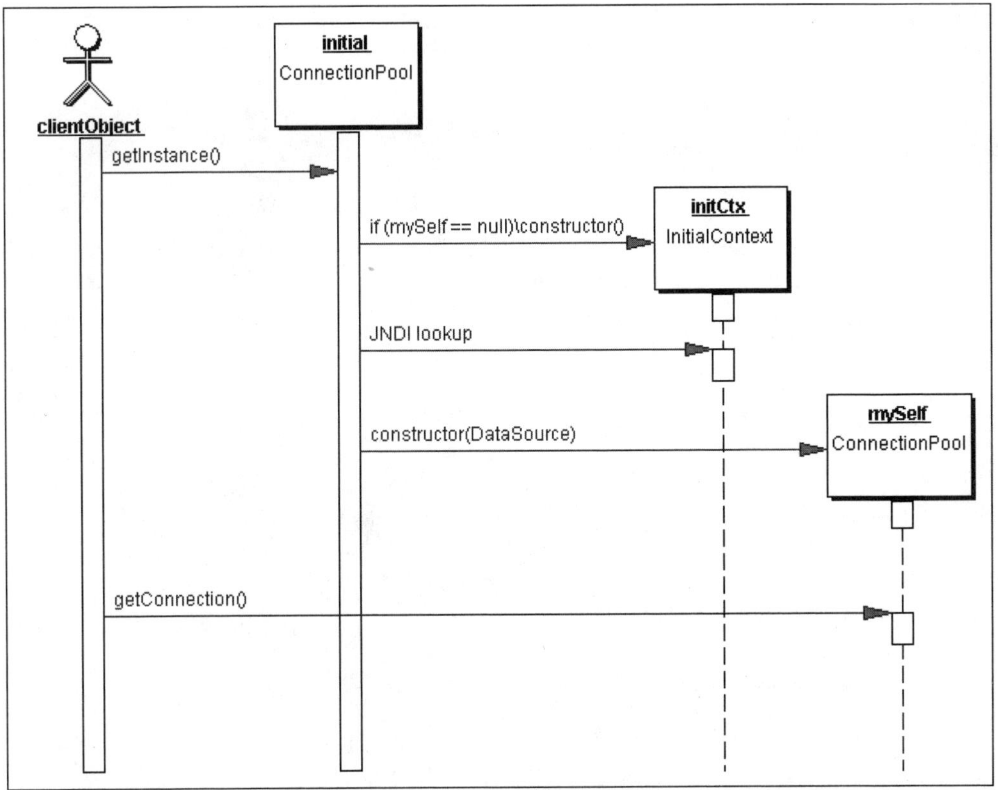

Data Access Objects

With our access to the database itself sorted out, we will now have a look at the data access objects (DAO) used for persisting user, offer, and bid entities. We will only show the error checking for the first class as it is very similar for them all, but the full source code can be downloaded from http://www.wrox.com/.

The UserDAO Class

The `UserDAO` class encapsulates the data access calls for maintaining the state of the `User` entities:

```
package auction.db;

import auction.entity.User;

import java.sql.Connection;
import java.sql.PreparedStatement;
import java.sql.ResultSet;
import java.sql.SQLException;

import java.util.Collection;
import java.util.ArrayList;

public class UserDAO {
```

In the constructor, we are passed the JDBC connection that we should use for sending SQL statements to the relation datastore; please refer back to the section on data access patterns for more details:

```
private Connection con;

public UserDAO(Connection con) {
  this.con = con;
}
```

The `create()` method takes an instance of the `User` class. A `PreparedStatement` is created that we will use for executing the `INSERT` SQL statement:

```
public void create(User user) throws CreateException {

  PreparedStatement ps = null;

  String sql = "INSERT INTO user VALUES (?,?,?,?,?,?)";

  try {
    if(con.isClosed()) {
      throw new IllegalStateException("error.unexpected");
    }

    ps = con.prepareStatement(sql);
    ps.setString(1,user.getUserId());
    ps.setString(2,user.getPassword());
    ps.setString(3,user.getAddress());
    ps.setString(4,user.getPhone());
    ps.setString(5,user.getEmail());
    ps.setString(6,user.getRole());
```

If the method fails to create the record, a `CreateException` is thrown:

```
    if(ps.executeUpdate() != 1) {
      throw new CreateException("error.create.user");
    }
```

If the failure is due to an already existing record with the same primary key (which we check by looking for an existing user with this user ID), a `DuplicateKeyException` is thrown:

```
  } catch(SQLException e) {
      try {
        findByPrimaryKey(user.getUserId());
      } catch(FinderException fe) {
         System.out.println(fe.getMessage());;
         throw new RuntimeException("error.unexpected");
      }
      throw new DuplicateKeyException("error.duplicate.user");
  } finally {
      try {
        if(ps != null) {
          ps.close();
        }
      } catch(SQLException e) {
         System.out.println(e.getMessage());;
         throw new RuntimeException("error.unexpected");
      }
  }
}
```

The `update()` method again takes an instance of the `User` class. An instance of `PreparedStatement` is created, which we use to execute the `UPDATE` SQL statement. If the specified record is not found a `NoSuchEntityException` is thrown:

```
public void update(User user) {

  PreparedStatement ps = null;

  String sql = "UPDATE user " +
               "SET password = ?," +
               "role = ?," +
               "address = ?," +
               "phone = ?," +
               "email = ? " +
               "WHERE user_id = ?";

  try {
    if(con.isClosed()) {
      throw new IllegalStateException("error.unexpected");
    }

    ps = con.prepareStatement(sql);
    ps.setString(1,user.getPassword());
    ps.setString(2,user.getRole());
    ps.setString(3,user.getAddress());
    ps.setString(4,user.getPhone());
    ps.setString(5,user.getEmail());
    ps.setString(6,user.getUserId());

    if(ps.executeUpdate() != 1) {
      throw new NoSuchEntityException("error.removed.user");
    }

  } catch(SQLException e) {
      System.out.println(e.getMessage());
      throw new RuntimeException("error.unexpected");
  } finally {
      try {
        if(ps != null) {
          ps.close();
        }
      } catch(SQLException e) {
          System.out.println(e.getMessage());;
          throw new RuntimeException("error.unexpected");
      }
  }
}
```

The `remove()` method takes the `userId` identifying the user record to be removed; it creates a `PreparedStatement` and uses it to execute the `DELETE` SQL statement. If the specified record is not found a `NoSuchEntityException` is thrown:

```
public void remove(String userId) {

  PreparedStatement ps = null;

  String sql = "DELETE FROM user WHERE user_id = ?";
```

```
    try {
      if(con.isClosed()) {
        throw new IllegalStateException("error.unexpected");
      }

      ps = con.prepareStatement(sql);
      ps.setString(1,userId);

      if(ps.executeUpdate() != 1) {
        throw new NoSuchEntityException("error.removed.user");
      }

    } catch(SQLException e) {
        System.out.println(e.getMessage());;
        throw new RuntimeException("error.unexpected");
    } finally {
        try {
          if(ps != null) {
            ps.close();
          }
        } catch(SQLException e) {
            System.out.println(e.getMessage());;
            throw new RuntimeException("error.unexpected");
        }
    }
  }
```

Finally, the `findByPrimaryKey()` method takes the `userId` for which the user record needs to be found. As you would expect, it creates a `PreparedStatement` and uses it to execute the `SELECT` SQL statement. If the record is not found an `ObjectNotFoundException` is thrown:

```
  public User findByPrimaryKey(String userId) throws FinderException {

    PreparedStatement ps = null;
    ResultSet rs = null;
    User user = null;

    String sql = "SELECT * FROM user WHERE user_id = ?";

    try {
      if(con.isClosed()) {
        throw new IllegalStateException("error.unexpected");
      }

      ps = con.prepareStatement(sql);
      ps.setString(1,userId);
      rs = ps.executeQuery();

      if(rs.next()) {
        user = new User();
        user.setUserId(rs.getString(1));
        user.setPassword(rs.getString(2));
        user.setAddress(rs.getString(3));
        user.setPhone(rs.getString(4));
        user.setEmail(rs.getString(5));
        user.setRole(rs.getString(6));

        return user;
```

```
            } else {
               throw new ObjectNotFoundException("error.removed.user");
            }

         } catch(SQLException e) {
            System.out.println(e.getMessage());;
            throw new RuntimeException("error.unexpected");
         } finally {
            try {
               if(ps != null) {
                  ps.close();
               }
               if(rs != null) {
                  rs.close();
               }
            } catch(SQLException e) {
                  System.out.println(e.getMessage());;
                  throw new RuntimeException("error.unexpected");
            }
         }

      }
   }
```

The OfferDAO Class

The `OfferDAO` class encapsulates the data access calls for maintaining the state of the `Offer` entities. We will not look at the entire source code, as it is very similar to that of `UserDAO`.

The `create()` method takes an instance of `Offer` class and executes the appropriate `INSERT` SQL statement. If the method fails to create the record, a `CreateException` is thrown. This method would never throw a `DuplicateKeyException` as the primary key for the `offer` table is automatically generated by the database:

```
   public void create(Offer offer) throws CreateException {

      PreparedStatement ps = null;

      String sql = "INSERT INTO offer " +
                   "(name,description,expected_value,max_bid,user_id) " +
                   "VALUES (?,?,?,?,?)";

      // Catch connection closed error

      ps = con.prepareStatement(sql);
      ps.setString(1,offer.getName());
      ps.setString(2,offer.getDescription());
      ps.setDouble(3,offer.getExpectedValue());
      ps.setDouble(4,0);
      ps.setString(5,offer.getUserId());

      // Error handling
   }
```

The `update()` method takes an instance of `Offer` class and executes the appropriate `UPDATE` SQL statement. If the specified record is not found a `NoSuchEntityException` is thrown:

```
public void update(Offer offer) {

  PreparedStatement ps = null;

  String sql = "UPDATE offer " +
               "SET name = ?," +
               "description = ?," +
               "expected_value = ?," +
               "max_bid = ?," +
               "user_id = ? " +
               "WHERE offer_id = ?";

  // Catch connection closed error

  ps = con.prepareStatement(sql);
  ps.setString(1,offer.getName());
  ps.setString(2,offer.getDescription());
  ps.setDouble(3,offer.getExpectedValue());
  ps.setDouble(4,offer.getMaxBid());
  ps.setString(5,offer.getUserId());
  ps.setInt(6,offer.getOfferId());

  // Error handling
}
```

The `remove()` method takes the `offerId` identifying the `offer` record to be removed and performs the relevant `DELETE` SQL statement. If the specified record is not found a `NoSuchEntityException` is thrown:

```
public void remove(int offerId) {

  PreparedStatement ps = null;

  String sql = "DELETE FROM offer WHERE offer_id = ?";

  // Catch connection closed error

  ps = con.prepareStatement(sql);
  ps.setInt(1,offerId);

  // Error handling
}
```

There are three finder methods, firstly `findByPrimaryKey()`. This takes the `offerId` for which the offer record needs to be found and executes the appropriate `SELECT` SQL statement to locate the offer. If the record is not found an `ObjectNotFoundException` is thrown:

```
public Offer findByPrimaryKey(int offerId) throws FinderException {

  PreparedStatement ps = null;
  ResultSet rs = null;
  Offer offer = null;

  String sql = "SELECT * FROM offer WHERE offer_id = ? ";
```

```
    // Catch connection closed error

    ps = con.prepareStatement(sql);
    ps.setInt(1,offerId);
    rs = ps.executeQuery();

    if(rs.next()) {
      offer = new Offer();
      offer.setOfferId(rs.getInt(1));
      offer.setName(rs.getString(2));
      offer.setDescription(rs.getString(3));
      offer.setExpectedValue(rs.getDouble(4));
      offer.setMaxBid(rs.getDouble(5));
      offer.setUserId(rs.getString(6));

      return offer;
    } else {
        throw new ObjectNotFoundException("error.removed.offer");
    }

    // Error handling
  }
```

The `findMyOffers()` method returns all the records from the `offer` table owned by the specified user and returns them as a collection of `Offer` entity instances. If an unexpected `SQLException` is thrown, it is caught and re-thrown as a `RuntimeException`:

```
  public Collection findMyOffers(String userId) {

    PreparedStatement ps = null;
    ResultSet rs = null;
    ArrayList list = new ArrayList();

    String sql = "SELECT * FROM offer WHERE user_id = ? ";

    // Catch connection closed error

    ps = con.prepareStatement(sql);
    ps.setString(1,userId);
    rs = ps.executeQuery();

    while(rs.next()) {
      Offer offer = new Offer();
      offer.setOfferId(rs.getInt(1));
      offer.setName(rs.getString(2));
      offer.setDescription(rs.getString(3));
      offer.setExpectedValue(rs.getDouble(4));
      offer.setMaxBid(rs.getDouble(5));
      offer.setUserId(rs.getString(6));

      list.add(offer);

    }

    return list;

    // Error handling
  }
```

The `findPublicOffers()` method returns all the records from the `offer` table not owned by the specified user and returns them as a collection of `Offer` entity instances. If an unexpected `SQLException` is thrown, it is caught and re-thrown as a `RuntimeException`:

```
   public Collection findPublicOffers(String userId) {

      PreparedStatement ps = null;
      ResultSet rs = null;
      ArrayList list = new ArrayList();

      String sql = "SELECT * FROM offer WHERE user_id != ? ORDER BY name";

      // Catch connection closed error

      ps = con.prepareStatement(sql);
      ps.setString(1,userId);
      rs = ps.executeQuery();
```

The following `while` block is identical to the one in `findMyOffers()`:

```
      while(rs.next()) {
         ...
      }

      // Error handling
   }
}
```

The BidDAO Class

The `BidDAO` class encapsulates the data access calls for maintaining the state of the `Bid` entities. Again, we won't look at the full listing, as `BidDAO` is very similar to the two classes above.

The `create()` method takes an instance of `Bid` class, and uses a `PreparedStatement` to perform the relevant SQL `INSERT` statement. If the method fails to create the record, a `CreateException` is thrown. This method would never throw a `DuplicateKeyException` as the primary key for the `bid` table is automatically generated by the database:

```
   public void create(Bid bid) throws CreateException {

      PreparedStatement ps = null;

      String sql = "INSERT INTO bid VALUES (?,?,?)";

      // Catch connection closed error

      ps = con.prepareStatement(sql);
      ps.setInt(1,bid.getOfferId());
      ps.setString(2,bid.getBidUserId());
      ps.setDouble(3,bid.getBidValue());

      // Error handling
   }
```

The `update()` method again takes an instance of `Bid` class and executes the appropriate `UPDATE` SQL statement. If the specified record is not found a `NoSuchEntityException` is thrown:

```
public void update(Bid bid) {

  PreparedStatement ps = null;

  String sql = "UPDATE bid SET bid_value = ? " +
               "WHERE offer_id = ? AND bid_user_id = ?";

  // Catch connection closed error

  ps = con.prepareStatement(sql);
  ps.setDouble(1,bid.getBidValue());
  ps.setInt(2,bid.getOfferId());
  ps.setString(3,bid.getBidUserId());

  // Error handling
}
```

The `remove()` method takes the `offerId` and `bidUserId` identifying the `bid` record to be removed, and executes the relevant SQL `DELETE` statement. If the specified record is not found a `NoSuchEntityException` is thrown:

```
public void remove(int offerId, String bidUserId) {

  PreparedStatement ps = null;

  String sql = "DELETE FROM bid " +
  "WHERE offer_id = ? " +
  "AND bid_user_id = ?";

  // Catch connection closed error

  ps = con.prepareStatement(sql);
  ps.setInt(1,offerId);
  ps.setString(2,bidUserId);

  // Error handling
}
```

The `findByPrimaryKey()` method takes the `offerId` and `bidUserId` for which the `bid` record needs to be found, and performs the `SELECT` SQL statement that will locate the bid. If the record is not found an `ObjectNotFoundException` is thrown:

```
public Bid findByPrimaryKey(int offerId, String bidUserId)
                            throws FinderException {

  PreparedStatement ps = null;
  ResultSet rs = null;
  Bid bid = null;

  String sql = "SELECT * from bid " +
               "WHERE offer_id = ? AND bid_user_id = ?";

  // Catch connection closed error
```

```
    ps = con.prepareStatement(sql);
    ps.setInt(1,offerId);
    ps.setString(2,bidUserId);
    rs = ps.executeQuery();

    if(rs.next()) {
      bid = new Bid();
      bid.setOfferId(rs.getInt(1));
      bid.setBidUserId(rs.getString(2));
      bid.setBidValue(rs.getDouble(3));

      return bid;
    } else {
        throw new ObjectNotFoundException("error.removed.bid");
    }

    // Error handling
  }
```

The `findByOfferId()` method returns all the records from the `bid` table and returns them as a collection of `Bid` instances for the specified `offerId`. If an unexpected `SQLException` is thrown, it is caught and re-thrown as a `RuntimeException`:

```
  public Collection findByOfferId(int offerId) {

    PreparedStatement ps = null;
    ResultSet rs = null;
    ArrayList list = new ArrayList();

    String sql = "SELECT * from bid " +
    "where offer_id = ?";

    // Catch connection closed error

    ps = con.prepareStatement(sql);
    ps.setInt(1,offerId);
    rs = ps.executeQuery();

    while(rs.next()) {
      Bid bid = new Bid();
      bid.setOfferId(rs.getInt(1));
      bid.setBidUserId(rs.getString(2));
      bid.setBidValue(rs.getDouble(3));

      list.add(bid);
    }

    return list;

    // Error handling
  }
```

The `findMaxBid()` method takes the `offerId` and returns the `bid` record with the maximum bid value. An instance of `PreparedStatement` is created that is used for executing the `SELECT` SQL statement. If there are no bids associated with the offer, a `Bid` object with the bid value as zero is returned:

```
    public Bid findMaxBid(int offerId) throws FinderException {

      PreparedStatement ps = null;
      ResultSet rs = null;
      Bid bid = null;

      String sql = "SELECT * from bid (offer_id, nod_user_id, bid_value) " +
                   "WHERE offer_id = ? ORDER BY bid_value";

      // Catch connection closed error

      ps = con.prepareStatement(sql);
      ps.setInt(1,offerId);
      rs = ps.executeQuery();

      bid = new Bid();
      bid.setOfferId(offerId);

      if(rs.next()) {
        bid.setBidUserId(rs.getString(2));
        bid.setBidValue(rs.getDouble(3));
      } else {
        bid.setBidValue(0);
      }

      return bid;

      // Error handling
    }
  }
```

Business Objects

That's our entity objects dealt with; the next step is to implement our business objects. These encapsulate the business rules associated with maintaining the entities in the system, but delegate the data access logic to the data access objects. In our application, we need to have business objects for maintaining `User`, `Offer`, and `Bid` entities.

Exception Handling

The business objects use specialized exceptions for handling error conditions. There are three such exceptions, one each for user, offer, and bid maintenance, which are in the `auction.business` package. The code for each is virtually identical to the exceptions we saw earlier when we were considering the data access tier. The exceptions are:

- `UserException`
  This exception is thrown in the methods for maintaining `User` entities
- `OfferException`
  This exception is thrown in the methods for maintaining `Offer` entities
- `BidException`
  This exception is thrown in the methods for maintaining `Bid` entities

The UserBO Class

The `UserBO` class encapsulates the business logic for maintaining the `User` entities:

```
package auction.business;

import auction.entity.User;

import auction.db.UserDAO;

import auction.db.util.ConnectionPool;

import java.sql.SQLException;
import java.sql.Connection;

import java.util.Iterator;

public class UserBO {
```

When the UserBO object is instantiated, we obtain the connection pool instance and store it as an instance variable:

```
  private ConnectionPool pool;

  public UserBO() {
    pool = ConnectionPool.getInstance();
  }
```

The class exposes three public methods for maintaining `User` entities; first up is the `getUser()` method. This performs the following tasks:

- Get a connection from the pool
- Create an instance of `UserDAO`
- Use the data access object to find the `User` entity by primary key
- If an error occurs, a `UserException` is thrown

Note that the connection is retrieved with the autcommit mode set to on:

```
  public User getUser(String userId) throws UserException {

    Connection con = null;

    try {
      con = pool.getConnection(true);
```

We then use the connection to create a new `UserDAO` object, then invoke its `findByPrimaryKey()` method to retrieve the `User` object:

```
      UserDAO userDAO = new UserDAO(con);
      return userDAO.findByPrimaryKey(userId);

    } catch(Exception e) {
```

```
            throw new UserException(e.getMessage());
        } finally {
            try {
                if(con != null) {
                    con.close();
                }
            } catch(SQLException sqle) {
                System.out.println(sqle.getMessage());;
                throw new UserException("error.unexpected");
            }
        }
    }
```

The `registerUser()` and `updateUser()` methods perform the following tasks:

- Get a connection from the pool
- Validate the user and throw an exception if the received data is invalid
- Create an instance of the user data access object
- Create or update the user entity using the data access object
- If an error occurs, the transaction is rolled back and a `UserException` is thrown

```
    public void registerUser(User user) throws UserException {

      validateUser(user);

      Connection con = null;

      try {
```

Again, we start by retrieving a connection from the pool – note, however, that this time we specify that we don't want auto-commit mode. We then pass it to the `UserDAO` constructor:

```
        con = pool.getConnection(false);

        UserDAO userDAO = new UserDAO(con);
```

With that done, we create the user, and attempt to commit the transaction:

```
        userDAO.create(user);

        con.commit();
```

If a problem arises, we then roll back the transaction and throw a `UserException`:

```
      } catch(Exception e) {
          try {
            if(con != null) {
              con.rollback();
            }
            throw new UserException(e.getMessage());
          } catch(SQLException sqle) {
```

```
                System.out.println(e.getMessage());;
                throw new UserException("error.unexpected");
            }
        } finally {
            try {
                if(con != null) {
                    con.close();
                }
            } catch(SQLException sqle) {
                System.out.println(sqle.getMessage());;
                throw new UserException("error.unexpected");
            }
        }
    }
```

updateUser() is almost identical to registerUser():

```
    public void updateUser(User user) throws UserException {

        validateUser(user);

        Connection con = null;

        try {
            con = pool.getConnection(false);

            UserDAO userDAO = new UserDAO(con);
            userDAO.update(user);

            con.commit();

        } catch(Exception e) {
            try {
                if(con != null) {
                    con.rollback();
                }
                throw new UserException(e.getMessage());
            } catch(SQLException sqle) {
                System.out.println(e.getMessage());;
                throw new UserException("error.unexpected");
            }
        } finally {
            try {
                if(con != null) {
                    con.close();
                }
            } catch(SQLException sqle) {
                System.out.println(sqle.getMessage());;
                throw new UserException("error.unexpected");
            }
        }
    }
```

Finally, the private method validateUser() checks whether all the necessary details have been entered for the user entity that is created or updated:

```
  private void validateUser(User user) throws UserException {

    if(user.getUserId().trim().equals("")) {
      throw new UserException("error.missing.userId");
    }

    if(user.getPassword().trim().equals("")) {
      throw new UserException("error.missing.password");
    }

    if(user.getAddress().trim().equals("")) {
      throw new UserException("error.missing.address");
    }
```

A possible enhancement here would be to validate the entered data for a valid phone number according to local requirements:

```
    if(user.getPhone().trim().equals("")) {
      throw new UserException("error.missing.phone");
    }

    if(user.getEmail().trim().equals("")) {
      throw new UserException("error.missing.email");
    }

  }
}
```

The OfferBO Class

The `OfferBO` class encapsulates the business logic for maintaining the `Offer` entities; it starts in the same way as `UserBO`:

```
package auction.business;

import auction.entity.Offer;
import auction.entity.User;
import auction.entity.Bid;

import auction.db.OfferDAO;
import auction.db.UserDAO;
import auction.db.BidDAO;

import auction.db.util.ConnectionPool;

import java.sql.SQLException;
import java.sql.Connection;

import java.util.Iterator;
import java.util.Collection;

public class OfferBO {

  private ConnectionPool pool;

  public OfferBO() {
    pool = ConnectionPool.getInstance();
  }
```

This class exposes three public methods for maintaining `Offer` entities: `getOffer()`, `getPublicOffers()`, and `getMyOffers()`. The `getOffer()` method performs the following tasks:

- Get a connection from the pool
- Create an instance of `OfferDAO`
- Use the data access object to find the `Offer` entity by primary key
- If an error occurs, a `OfferException` is thrown

```
public Offer getOffer(int offerId) throws OfferException {

  Connection con = null;

  try {
    con = pool.getConnection(false);

    OfferDAO offerDAO = new OfferDAO(con);
    return offerDAO.findByPrimaryKey(offerId);

  } catch(Exception e) {
      try {
        if(con != null) {
          con.rollback();
        }
        throw new OfferException(e.getMessage());
      } catch(SQLException sqle) {
          System.out.println(e.getMessage());;
          throw new OfferException("error.unexpected");
      }
  } finally {
      try {
        if(con != null) {
          con.close();
        }
      } catch(SQLException sqle) {
          System.out.println(sqle.getMessage());;
          throw new OfferException("error.unexpected");
      }
  }
}
```

The `getPublicOffers()` and `getMyOffers()` methods call the private `getOffers()` method, passing the `isPublic` indicator as `true` and `false` respectively:

```
public Collection getPublicOffers(String userId) throws OfferException {
  return getOffers(true, userId);
}

public Collection getMyOffers(String userId) throws OfferException {
  return getOffers(false, userId);
}
```

The `getOffers()` method performs the following steps:

- Get a connection from the pool
- Create an instance of the offer data access object

- If the isPublic indicator is true it calls the findPublicOffers() method on the data access object, or else it calls the findMyOffers() methods on the data access object
- If an error occurs, the transaction is rolled back and a OfferException is thrown

```
private Collection getOffers(boolean isPublic, String userId)
                                    throws OfferException {

  Connection con = null;

  try {
    con = pool.getConnection(false);

    OfferDAO offerDAO = new OfferDAO(con);
    if(isPublic) {
      return offerDAO.findPublicOffers(userId);
    } else {
        return offerDAO.findMyOffers(userId);
    }

  } catch(Exception e) {
      try {
        if(con != null) {
          con.rollback();
        }
        throw new OfferException(e.getMessage());
      } catch(SQLException sqle) {
          System.out.println(e.getMessage());;
          throw new OfferException("error.unexpected");
      }
  } finally {
      try {
        if(con != null) {
          con.close();
        }
      } catch(SQLException sqle) {
          System.out.println(sqle.getMessage());;
          throw new OfferException("error.unexpected");

  }
}
```

The addOffer() and updateOffer() methods performs the following tasks:

- Get a connection from the pool
- Validate the offer
- Create an instance of the user data access object
- Check whether the user id specified for the offer
- Create an instance of the offer data access object
- Create or update the offer entity using the data access object
- If an error occurs, the transaction is rolled back and an OfferException is thrown

```
public void addOffer(Offer offer) throws OfferException {

  validateOffer(offer);

  Connection con = null;

  try {

    con = pool.getConnection(false);

    UserDAO userDAO = new UserDAO(con);
    userDAO.findByPrimaryKey(offer.getUserId());

    OfferDAO offerDAO = new OfferDAO(con);
    offerDAO.create(offer);

    con.commit();

  } catch(Exception e) {
      try {
        if(con != null) {
          con.rollback();
        }
        throw new OfferException(e.getMessage());
      } catch(SQLException sqle) {
          System.out.println(e.getMessage());;
          throw new OfferException("error.unexpected");
      }
  } finally {
      try {
        if(con != null) {
          con.close();
        }
      } catch(SQLException sqle) {
          System.out.println(sqle.getMessage());;
          throw new OfferException("error.unexpected");
      }
  }
}

public void updateOffer(Offer offer) throws OfferException {

  validateOffer(offer);

  Connection con = null;

  try {
    con = pool.getConnection(false);

    UserDAO userDAO = new UserDAO(con);
    userDAO.findByPrimaryKey(offer.getUserId());

    OfferDAO offerDAO = new OfferDAO(con);
    offerDAO.update(offer);

    con.commit();

  } catch(Exception e) {
      try {
        if(con != null) {
```

```
                con.rollback();
            }
            throw new OfferException(e.getMessage());
        } catch(SQLException sqle) {
            System.out.println(e.getMessage());;
            throw new OfferException("error.unexpected");
        }
    } finally {
        try {
            if(con != null) {
                con.close();
            }
        } catch(SQLException sqle) {
            System.out.println(sqle.getMessage());;
            throw new OfferException("error.unexpected");
        }
    }
}
```

The `deleteOffer()` method performs the following steps:

- Get a connection from the pool
- Create an instance of the offer data access object
- Remove the offers
- Create an instance of the bid data access object
- Get all the bids associated with the offer
- Remove all the bids
- Commit the transaction. (The transaction is explicitly started with the first SQL statement that is executed with the connection, as the autocommit mode is set to `false`.)
- If an error occurs the transaction is rolled back and an `OfferException` is thrown

```
public void deleteOffer(int offerId) throws OfferException {

  Connection con = null;

  try {
    con = pool.getConnection(false);
```

First we create the offer data access object, and remove the entry for the specified offer id from the database:

```
    OfferDAO offerDAO = new OfferDAO(con);
    offerDAO.remove(offerId);
```

Then, we create the bid data access object and remove all the bid entities from the database for the specified offer id:

```
    BidDAO bidDAO = new BidDAO(con);
    Iterator it = bidDAO.findByOfferId(offerId).iterator();
```

```
        while(it.hasNext()) {
          Bid bid = (Bid)it.next();
          bidDAO.remove(bid.getOfferId(),bid.getBidUserId());
        }

        con.commit();

      } catch(Exception e) {
          try {
            if(con != null) {
              con.rollback();
            }
            throw new OfferException(e.getMessage());
          } catch(SQLException sqle) {
              System.out.println(e.getMessage());;
              throw new OfferException("error.unexpected");
          }
      } finally {
          try {
            if(con != null) {
              con.close();
            }
          } catch(SQLException sqle) {
              System.out.println(sqle.getMessage());
              throw new OfferException("error.unexpected");
          }
      }
    }
```

The `validateOffer()` method checks whether all the necessary details have been entered for the offer entity that is created or updated:

```
  private void validateOffer(Offer offer) throws OfferException {

    if(offer.getUserId().trim().equals("")) {
      throw new OfferException("error.missing.userId");
    }

    if(offer.getName().trim().equals("")) {
      throw new OfferException("error.missing.name");
    }

    if(offer.getDescription().trim().equals("")) {
      throw new OfferException("error.missing.description");
    }
  }
}
```

The BidBO Class

The `BidBO` class encapsulates the business logic for maintaining the `Bid` entities:

```
package auction.business;

import auction.entity.Offer;
import auction.entity.User;
import auction.entity.Bid;
```

```
import auction.db.OfferDAO;
import auction.db.UserDAO;
import auction.db.BidDAO;
import auction.db.DuplicateKeyException;

import auction.db.util.ConnectionPool;

import java.sql.SQLException;
import java.sql.Connection;

import java.util.Iterator;

public class BidBO {

  private ConnectionPool pool;

  public BidBO() {
    pool = ConnectionPool.getInstance();
  }
```

The `addBid()` method performs the following steps:

- Get a connection from the pool.
- If the bid value is less than or equal to zero, throw a `BidException`.
- Create an instance of the offer data access object.
- Check whether the offer specified for the bid is valid. This is to make sure that the offer for which the bid is made has not been removed by the owner of the offer.
- Create an instance of the user data access object.
- Check whether the bidding user specified is valid.
- Create an instance of the bid data access object.
- If the bid doesn't already exist it is created; otherwise, the bid value is updated.
- The highest bid value is found, and if it is greater than the current maximum bid stored for the offer, update the offer.
- Commit the transaction.
- If an error occurs, the transaction is rolled back and a `BidException` is thrown.

```
  public void addBid(Bid bid) throws BidException {

    Connection con = null;

    try {
      con = pool.getConnection(false);

      if(bid.getBidValue() <= 0) {
        throw new BidException("error.negative.bid");
      }
```

Create a user data access object and and find the `User` object for the bidding user:

```
UserDAO userDAO = new UserDAO(con);
userDAO.findByPrimaryKey(bid.getBidUserId());
```

Create an offer data access object and and find the offer entity for the bid:

```
OfferDAO offerDAO = new OfferDAO(con);
Offer offer = offerDAO.findByPrimaryKey(bid.getOfferId());
```

Try to create the bid in the database:

```
BidDAO bidDAO = new BidDAO(con);
try {
  bidDAO.create(bid);
} catch(DuplicateKeyException ex) {
```

If the bid already exists, the bid value is updated instead:

```
    bidDAO.update(bid);
}
```

We find the current highest bid and, if this bid's value is greater than the current maximum bid, we update the maximum bid value in the offer table:

```
Bid maxBid = bidDAO.findMaxBid(bid.getOfferId());

if(maxBid.getBidValue() > offer.getMaxBid()) {
  offer.setMaxBid(maxBid.getBidValue());
  offerDAO.update(offer);
}
```

Finally, we commit the transaction and do the requisite error handling:

```
    con.commit();

  } catch(Exception e) {
    try {
      if(con != null) {
        con.rollback();
      }
      throw new BidException(e.getMessage());
    } catch(SQLException sqle) {
        System.out.println(e.getMessage());;
        throw new BidException("error.unexpected");
    }
  } finally {
    try {
      if(con != null) {
        con.close();
      }
    } catch(SQLException sqle) {
        System.out.println(sqle.getMessage());;
        throw new BidException("error.unexpected");
    }
  }
}
```

The `acceptBid()` method performs the following steps:

- Get a connection from the pool
- Create an offer data access object and get the offer for the specified offer id
- Get the user id for the offer
- Create a user data access object and get the user object for the offering user
- Create a bid data access object and get the bid object corresponding to the maximum bid for the offer
- If the maximum bid value is less than or equal to zero a `BidException` is thrown
- Get the user id for the maximum bid
- Get the user object corresponding to the user with the maximum bid
- (At this point we could send e-mails to the bidding and offering users with the transaction details)
- Remove the offer, and all the bids associated with the offer
- Commit the transaction
- If an error occurs the transaction is rolled back and a `BidException` is thrown

```
public void acceptBid(int offerId) throws BidException {

  Connection con = null;

  try {
    con = pool.getConnection(false);
```

Create data access objects for offer, bid and user entities:

```
    OfferDAO offerDAO = new OfferDAO(con);
    BidDAO bidDAO = new BidDAO(con);
    UserDAO userDAO = new UserDAO(con);

    Offer offer = offerDAO.findByPrimaryKey(offerId);
```

Find the user entity that owns the offer:

```
    User offerUser = userDAO.findByPrimaryKey(offer.getUserId());
```

Find the bid entity that represents the maximum bid for the offer:

```
    Bid bid = bidDAO.findMaxBid(offerId);
```

If the maximum bid is not greater than zero, throw an exception:

```
    if(bid.getBidValue() <= 0) {
      throw new BidException("error.negative.bid");
    }
```

Find the user who owns the highest bid:

```
      User bidUser = userDAO.findByPrimaryKey(bid.getBidUserId());
```

Remove the offer:

```
      offerDAO.remove(offer.getOfferId());
```

Remove all the bids associated with the offer:

```
      Iterator it = bidDAO.findByOfferId(offerId).iterator();

      while(it.hasNext()) {
        Bid otherBid = (Bid)it.next();
        bidDAO.remove(otherBid.getOfferId(),otherBid.getBidUserId());
      }
```

Here we could add code that uses JavaMail to sending email to the offering and bidding users.

Finally, we commit the transaction and do any necessary exception handling:

```
      con.commit();

    } catch(Exception e) {
      try {
        if(con != null) {
          con.rollback();
        }
        throw new BidException(e.getMessage());
      } catch(SQLException sqle) {
          System.out.println(e.getMessage());;
          throw new BidException("error.unexpected");
      }
    } finally {
      try {
        if(con != null) {
          con.close();
        }
      } catch(SQLException sqle) {
          System.out.println(sqle.getMessage());;
          throw new BidException("error.unexpected");
      }
    }
  }
}
```

Implementing the Web Tier

In the last few sections, we have covered the design and development of the components for the application tier. It's time to discuss the web tier of our system, looking in turn at:

- Struts action forms
- Error messages and internationalization

- Using dynamic web page templates
- Implementing a role based menu
- Struts action classes
- The internal system interactions corresponding to all the use cases

Struts Actions Forms

In the section on the entity objects, we mentioned that we would be reusing our entity objects as the Struts action forms as well. We identified `User`, `Offer`, and `Bid` classes as the action form bean types associated with the forms for maintaining users, offers, and bids, and these classes accordingly extend `org.apache.struts.action.ActionForm`.

The excerpt shown below from the Struts configuration file illustrates how the action form beans are declared:

```
<form-beans>
  <form-bean name="userForm" type="auction.entity.User"/>
  <form-bean name="offerForm" type="auction.entity.Offer"/>
  <form-bean name="bidForm" type="auction.entity.Bid"/>
</form-beans>
```

This defines three action form beans by the logical names `userForm`, `offerForm`, and `bidForm`, with the types `User`, `Offer`, and `Bid` respectively. These names will be later used in the action mapping elements for associating the beans with action classes.

Error Handling and Internationalization

Proper handling of exceptions, and informing the users about expected and unexpected error conditions, is a vital element of enterprise application development. In this section, we will have a look at how we can implement an efficient error handling mechanism for our application. One important aspect of sending error messages to the end users is that they should be sent in the user's preferred language. Hence, error handling and internationalization are inter-related.

As we have seen in the section on application architecture, the HTTP requests coming in from the browser are routed to appropriate action classes. The action classes may use business objects and data access objects to fulfil the request, depending on the type of request. The method calls on these objects may throw both expected and unexpected exceptions; for example, business exceptions thrown by business objects would be expected to occur at some point, but runtime exceptions thrown from the data access layer due to unexpected SQL failure would be considered unexpected exceptions.

Method calls on instances of `UserBO`, `OfferBO`, and `BidBO` may throw instances of `UserException`, `OfferException`, or `BidException` respectively. Similarly, method calls on data object instances may throw instances of `CreateException`, `RemoveException`, or `FinderException` for expected error conditions, and instances of subclasses of `RuntimeException` for unexpected error conditions.

If we start hard-coding the error messages in the calls to the exception constructors, it will be difficult to internationalize the application. Therefore, when creating an exception object we will specify a message key instead of a descriptive error message, which can be matched up with an entry in a localized resource bundle. When an exception is thrown in a business object or a data access object it bubbles up to the action class, which will catch the exception and create an instance of the Struts `ActionError` class, passing the exception message in the constructor.

This ActionError instance is then added to an instance of the Struts ActionErrors class, which is added to the request object against the default error key using the saveErrors() method defined in the org.apache.struts.action.Action. The response is then redirected back to the input resource that caused the current action. That resource may use the Struts <html:errors> tag to query the resources file specific to the end user's preferred locale and render the error message.

The table below shows the message keys used for the data access exceptions:

Exception	**Data Access Object**	**Message Key**
CreateException	UserDAO	error.create.user
	OfferDAO	error.create.offer
	BidDAO	error.create.bid
DuplicateKeyException	UserDAO	error.duplicate.user
	OfferDAO	error.duplicate.offer
	BidDAO	error.duplicate.bid
ObjectNotFoundException	UserDAO	error.removed.user
	OfferDAO	error.removed.offer
	BidDAO	error.removed.bid
NoSuchEntityException	UserDAO	error.removed.user
	OfferDAO	error.removed.offer
	BidDAO	error.removed.bid
RuntimeException	UserDAO	error.unexpected
	OfferDAO	error.unexpected
	BidDAO	error.unexpected

The table below shows the message keys used for the business exceptions:

Exception	**Business Object**	**Message Key**
UserException	UserBO	error.missing.userId
		error.missing.password
		error.missing.address
		error.missing.phone
		error.missing.email
OfferException	OfferBO	error.missing.name
		error.missing.description
BidException	BidBO	error.negative.bid

If the business exception is caused by an exception thrown from a data access object call, the message key for the business exception will be the same as that defined for the root exception. However, if the business exception is thrown by the validation methods defined in the business object, the message key will be one of the keys defined in the above table.

The contents of the file `AuctionResources.properties`, which is the message resources file for the default locale on the server, are shown below:

```
error.removed.user=<font color="red">Selected user has been removed</font>
error.create.user=<font color="red">Unable to create the user</font>
error.duplicate.user=<font color="red">Specified user already exists</font>

error.removed.bid=<font color="red">Selected bid has been removed</font>
error.create.bid=<font color="red">Unable to create the bid</font>
error.duplicate.bid=<font color="red">Specified bid already exists</font>

error.removed.offer=<font color="red">Selected offer has been removed</font>
error.create.offer=<font color="red">Unable to create the offer</font>
error.duplicate.offer=<font color="red">Specified offer already
exists</font>

error.missing.userId=<font color="red">Please enter the user id</font>
error.missing.password=<font color="red">Please enter the password</font>
error.missing.address=<font color="red">Please enter the address</font>
error.missing.phone=<font color="red">Please enter the phone number</font>
error.missing.email=<font color="red">Please enter the email</font>

error.missing.name=<font color="red">Please enter the name</font>
error.missing.description=<font color="red">Please enter the description</font>

error.negative.bid=<font color="red">Bid should be greater than zero</font>

error.unexpected=<font color="red">Unexpected error, Please contact
webmaster</font>
```

Note that the name of the resources file without the extension needs to be passed to the action servlet as an initial parameter, using the name `application`. All of the message resources files should be available to the web application classloader, for example by storing them in the `WEB-INF\classes\` directory.

Role Based Menu

Our next task is to implement a generic menu JSP page that can be included in all our web pages. The links we need to display on the menu can be categorized as:

- The links that need to be displayed for both public and authenticated users
- The links that need to be displayed only for public users
- The links that need to be displayed only for authenticated users

A single link needs to be displayed to both public and authenticated users:

- **Home**
  This link points to welcome page of the online auction system

Only for public users should be shown these two links:

- **Logon**
  This link can be used by registered users for logging on to the system. When users click on this link, the system presents a logon form and on successful authentication, the system presents a form populated with the details for the logged on user.
- **Register**
  This link can be used for registering new users. When users click on this link, the system presents a form to enter the user details.

The links that need to be displayed only for authenticated users include:

- **Add Offer**
  Presents a form for adding new offer
- **My Offers**
  Lists all the offers owned by the current logged in user
- **Public Offers**
  Lists all the offers not owned by the current logged in user
- **Edit Details**
  Presents a form for updating the details of the current logged in user

The figures below show the menu for public and authenticated users respectively:

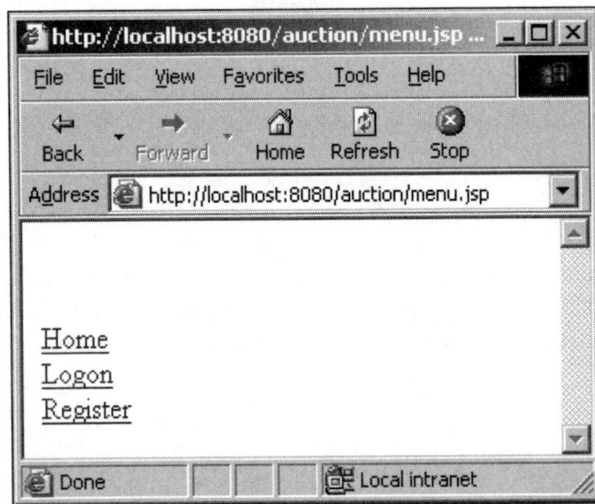

The menu JSP Page

So, how do we achieve this? Let's look at the source of `menu.jsp`:

```
<%@ taglib uri="/html" prefix="html" %>
<%@ taglib uri="/logic" prefix="logic" %>

<br/>
<br/>
```

Render the link to display the welcome page:

```
<html:link href="index.jsp">Home</html:link>
 
<br/>
```

If the user is not logged on, we display the links for logging on and registering new users. (The `<logic:notPresent role="user">` tag only renders its contents if the current user is not logged in as a `user`:

```
<logic:notPresent role="user">
   <html:link href="editUser.do?actn=edit">Logon</html:link>
    
   <br/>
   <html:link href="newUser.jsp">Register</html:link>
    
   <br/>
</logic:notPresent>
```

For authenticated users we display the links to add new offers, list public and own offers, and edit the user's details:

```
<logic:present role="user">
   <html:link href="newOffer.jsp">Add Offer</html:link>
    
   <br/>
   <html:link href="listOffer.do?actn=mine">My Offers</html:link>
    
   <br/>
   <html:link href="listOffer.do?actn=public">Public Offers</html:link>
    
   <br/>
   <html:link href="editUser.do?actn=edit">Edit Details</html:link>
    
   <br/>
</logic:present>
```

Note that the links for logging on and editing the user details both point to the *same* server-side resource for displaying the details for the currently logged on user. The only difference is that in the first case the user will first be prompted to enter their user id and password, as they are not already logged on.

Dynamic Page Template

In Chapter 5, we saw the importance of using dynamic templates for modularizing web page layouts; it would be good to come up with a dynamic template for our web pages. These will all have:

- A header section for displaying a banner
- A menu section
- A footer section for displaying the logon status
- A main section for displaying the "real" content of the page

We can implement our dynamic template using the Struts template tags; to do this we need to create a template JSP page and include it in all the other main JSP pages. We will define the template using a HTML table with the following layout:

- The first row contains a single cell for displaying the banner. Since the banner is going to be the same for all the JSP pages we can hard-code the banner in the template JSP page.
- The second row contains two cells. The first cell will contain the menu; since the logic for populating the menu is done using the Struts logic tags, and the JSP file for the menu is always the same, we can include the `menu.jsp` file using the `<jsp:include>` action. The second cell will contain the main content, which is pushed in by the JSP pages using the template. Hence, in this cell we can use the Struts `<template:get>` tag to get the content pushed in by the JSP pages using the Struts `<template:put>` tag.
- The third row will contain a single cell for displaying the information on the currently logged on user.

Here is the template in diagramatic form:

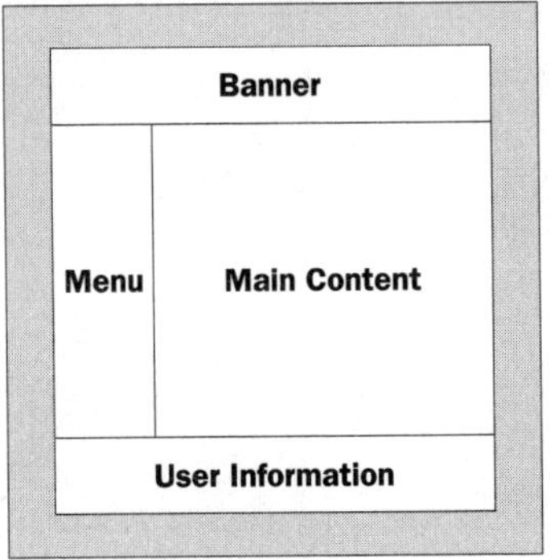

The template JSP Page

OK, let's have a look at the source code for `template.jsp`:

```
<%@ taglib uri="/template" prefix="template" %>
<%@ taglib uri="/logic" prefix="logic" %>

<html>

  <head>
    <title>
      Welcome to The Online Auction System
    </title>
  </head>

  <body>
    <center>
      <table height="100%" width="100%" cellpadding="0" cellspacing="0">
        <tr height="50" bgcolor="#CCCCCC">
```

Include the banner:

```
          <td valign="center" align="center" colspan="3">
            <h1><i>Online Auction System</i></h1>
          </td>
        </tr>
        <tr>
```

Include the menu using <jsp:include> action:

```
          <td width="15%" bgcolor="#CCCCCC" align="right" valign="top">
            <jsp:include page="menu.jsp"/>
          </td>
```

Include the main content using the Struts <template:get> tag:

```
          <td valign="top" align="center">
            <template:get name="content"/>
          </td>
          <td width="10%" bgcolor="#CCCCCC">
          </td>
        </tr>
        <tr height="10%" bgcolor="#CCCCCC">
```

We use the Struts <logic:present> with its `role` attribute tag to display the information on the currently logged on user. This information is displayed only if the currently logged on user has the `user` role:

```
          <td valign="center" align="center" colspan="3">
            <logic:present role="user">
              You are currently logged on as
              <i><%= request.getRemoteUser() %></i>
            </logic:present>
          </td>
        </tr>
      </table>
    </center>
  </body>
</html>
```

System Interactions

In this section we will cover the sequence of events within the system in response to the various actions performed by the end users. We will also identify the various Struts action mapping elements, as well as the JSP pages involved in rendering the screens.

Rather than creating Struts action classes for each end user action, we will try to categorize the end user actions and associate them with common Struts action classes. Within the action classes we will identify each request by an extra request parameter passed to the server, called `actn`. The actions are categorized as shown below:

- All user-related actions will be handled by the class `auction.action.UserAction`. This class will handle the actions for editing the user details, updating the user details, and creating new users.
- All offer-related actions will be handled by the class `auction.action.OfferAction`, which will handle the actions for adding new offers, editing offers, updating offers, deleting offers, listing own offers, and listing public offers.
- All bid-related actions will be handled by the class `auction.action.BidAction`, which will handle the actions for raising new bids and accepting the maximum bid.

The request URI for most of these actions will be mapped to the Struts action servlet, and hence to the relevant action classes, depending on the action mappings defined in the configuration file. The action classes delegate the data modification and data retrieval tasks to the business objects.

The data retrieval requests will store the data as request scope beans, so that the JSP pages that render the next view can extract them from the request attribute list. If the task is performed successfully, the action class returns the local forward corresponding to the logical name success back to the action servlet. Please refer to chapter 2 on Struts for comprehensive coverage on local and global forwards. For data retrieval requests, the JSP pages render the next view, and for data modification requests they show a simple confirmation page stating the request has been successfully processed.

Requests that don't involve either data modification or data retrieval will be mapped directly to JSP files, rather than going through Struts action classes. To map the requests that need to be handled by Struts, we will declare the Struts action servlet in the web application deployment descriptor and add a servlet mapping element to map the request URI pattern `*.do` to the action servlet, as shown below:

```
<servlet>
  <servlet-name>action</servlet-name>
  <servlet-class>org.apache.struts.action.ActionServlet</servlet-class>
  <init-param>
    <param-name>application</param-name>
    <param-value>AuctionResources</param-value>
  </init-param>
  <load-on-startup>2</load-on-startup>
</servlet>

<servlet-mapping>
  <servlet-name>action</servlet-name>
  <url-pattern>*.do</url-pattern>
</servlet-mapping>
```

Note how the servlet takes an initialization parameter defining the name of the resource files.

Home Page

The home page displays the menu for logging on and registering new users. It will also display a welcome message and a brief description of the system. The screenshot below shows the home page:

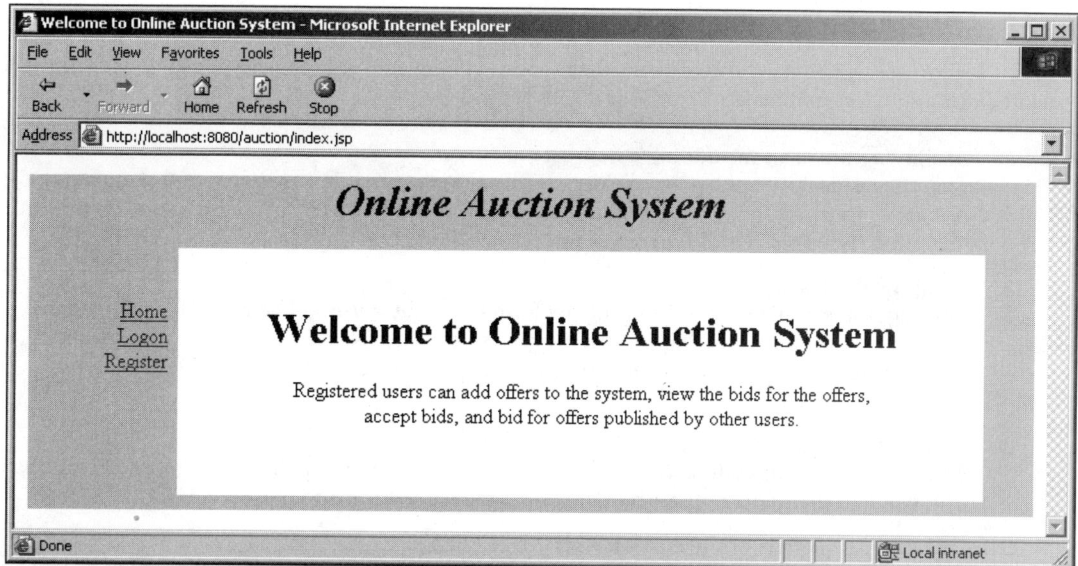

The index JSP

This JSP page, `index.jsp`, uses the Struts `<template:insert>` tag to insert the file `template.jsp`, and pushes the contents of the file `indexContent.jsp` into the template using the Struts `<template:put>` tag:

```
<%@ taglib uri="/template" prefix="template" %>

<template:insert template="template.jsp">
  <template:put name="content" content="indexContent.jsp"/>
</template:insert>
```

The indexContent JSP Page

`indexContent.jsp` just displays a brief description of the system, as in the screenshot above.

The BeanNames Interface

This interface enumerates the names which the action classes will use to store beans in request scope. Bean names are defined for user form, offer form, and list of offers:

```
package auction.action;

public interface BeanNames {
  public static final String USER_FORM = "userForm";
  public static final String OFFER_FORM = "offerForm";
  public static final String OFFER_LIST = "offerList";
}
```

User Related Actions

In this section we will cover the action class, action mappings, and JSP pages associated with the user related actions. These actions are:

- **Displaying the form for adding a new user**
  This request is initiated by the clicking on the Register link in the menu, and points to the resource `newUser.jsp`. Note that as the request is sent directly to the JSP page, there is no mapping associated with the request.

- **Creating new users**
  This request is initiated by submitting the form to add new users. The request is mapped to `registerUser.do`, which is in turn mapped to the `UserAction` class using the Struts configuration file. The value of the `actn` request parameter associated with this request is `create`.

- **Editing the details of the current user**
  The request is mapped to `editUser.do`, which is in turn mapped to the `UserAction` class. The value of the `actn` request parameter associated with this request is `edit`.

- **Updating the details of the current user**
  The request is mapped to `updateUser.do`, which is in turn mapped to the `UserAction` class. The value of the `actn` request parameter associated with this request is `update`.

The UserAction Class

OK, so let's see the code for the `auction.action.UserAction` class. The `perform()` method for this class extracts the value of the `actn` request parameter and performs the following tasks depending on the value:

- If the value is `create` it will call the `registerUser()` method on an instance of `UserBO`, passing it the action form.
- If the value is `update` it will call the `updateUser()` method on an instance of `UserBO`, again passing it the action form.
- If the value is `edit` it will call the `getUser()` method on an instance of `UserBO`, passing it the currently logged on user id. The returned `User` instance is then stored as a request scope bean.

If there is no error the class returns a local forward defined by the logical name `success'`.

```
    public ActionForward perform(ActionMapping mapping,
                                 ActionForm form,
                                 HttpServletRequest request,
                                 HttpServletResponse response)
                                 throws IOException,ServletException {
```

Get the value of the `actn` parameter:

```
        String action = request.getParameter("actn");
```

Create an instance of `UserBO` and perform the task based on the value of the `actn` parameter:

```
    UserBO userBO = new UserBO();

    if(action.equals("create")) {
      userBO.registerUser((User)form);
    } else if(action.equals("edit")) {
      User user = userBO.getUser(request.getRemoteUser());
      request.setAttribute(BeanNames.USER_FORM, user);
    } else if(action.equals("update")) {
      userBO.updateUser((User)form);
    }
```

Forward to the next view:

```
    return mapping.findForward("success");
  }
```

New User

The screenshot below displays the form for adding new users:

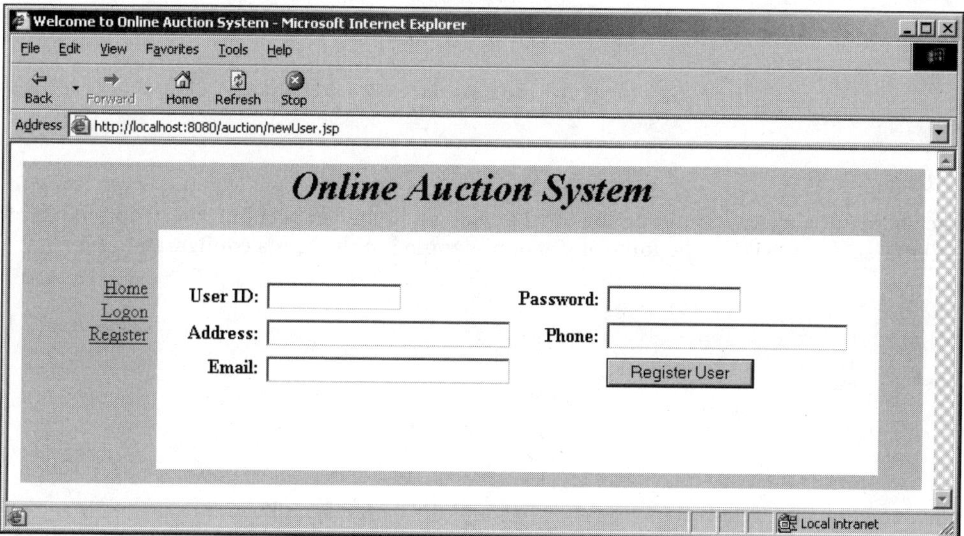

The request for displaying the form for adding new users is forwarded to the file `newUser.jsp`. This JSP page uses the Struts `<template:insert>` tag to insert the file `template.jsp` and push the contents of the file `newUserContent.jsp` into the template:

```
<%@ taglib uri="/template" prefix="template" %>

<template:insert template="template.jsp">
 <template:put name="content" content="newUserContent.jsp"/>
</template:insert>
```

The JSP `newUserContent.jsp` displays the form for entering new user details using the Struts form tags. The action for this form is to the Struts action mapping `registerUser`:

```
<%@ taglib uri="/bean" prefix="bean" %>
<%@ taglib uri="/html" prefix="html" %>
<%@ taglib uri="/logic" prefix="logic" %>
<%@ taglib uri="/template" prefix="template" %>
```

Use the Struts `<html:errors>` tag to displaying error messages if the form is sent back due to validation error:

```
  <br/>
    <html:errors/>
  <br/>

  <table cellpadding="2">
```

Render the HTML form for entering the new user details:

```
    <html:form action="/registerUser.do" focus="userId">
```

We use a hidden parameter for the role for the new user; this is hard coded to `user`:

```
      <html:hidden property="role" value="user"/>
      ...
```

Register User

This action is initiated by submitting the form explained in the last section. The action for this form is `registerUser.do` that has the following action mapping in the Struts configuration file:

```
<action path="/registerUser"
        type="auction.action.UserAction"
        input="/newUser.jsp"
        name="userForm"
        scope="request">
  <forward name="success" path="/confirm.jsp"/>
</action>
```

The mapping uses the action class `UserAction` and the action form bean `userForm`. If an error occurs the response is sent to `newUser.jsp`; otherwise it is sent to `confirm.jsp`. The `actn` request parameter associated with this request is `create`.

Edit User

The screenshot below displays the form for editing existing users:

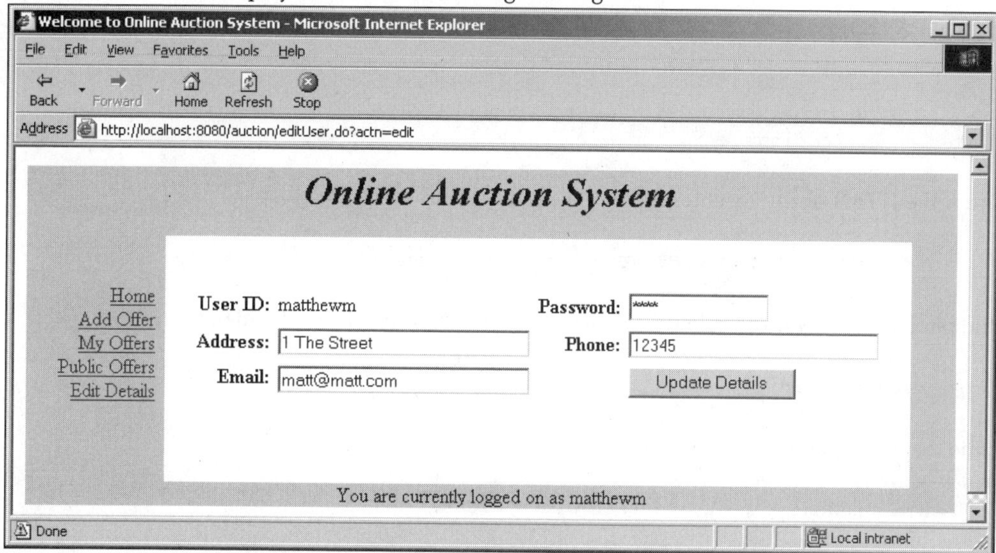

The action mapping for the above action is as follows:

```
<action path="/editUser"
        type="auction.action.UserAction">
  <forward name="success" path="/editUser.jsp"/>
</action>
```

The above action is instigated by clicking on the logon link in the unauthenticated state, and on the edit details link in the authenticated state. The `actn` request parameter associated with this request is `edit`. The action is mapped to the `UserAction` class, which will use the user business object to get the details of the currently logged on user, store the data as a request scope bean, and forward the response to `editUser.jsp`.

The request for editing existing user details is forwarded to the file `editUser.jsp`. This JSP page uses the Struts template tags to insert the file `template.jsp` and push the contents of `editUserContent.jsp` into it:

```
<%@ taglib uri="/template" prefix="template" %>

<template:insert template="template.jsp">
  <template:put name="content" content="editUserContent.jsp"/>
</template:insert>
```

The JSP page `editUserContent.jsp` displays the form for entering new user details using the Struts form tags. The action for this form is set to the Struts action mapping `updateUser`:

```
<%@ taglib uri="/bean" prefix="bean" %>
<%@ taglib uri="/html" prefix="html" %>
<%@ taglib uri="/logic" prefix="logic" %>
<%@ taglib uri="/template" prefix="template" %>
```

Use the Struts <html:errors> tag to displaying error messages if the form is sent back due to validation error:

```
<br/>
  <html:errors/>
<br/>

<table cellpadding="2">
```

Render the HTML form for entering the new user details.

```
    <html:form action="/updateUser.do" focus="userId">
```

A hidden parameter for the role for the new user; note that this is hard coded to `user`:

```
      <html:hidden property="role" value="user"/>
```

Define the `actn` parameter value as `update`:

```
    <html:hidden property="actn" value="update"/>
    ...
```

Update User

This action is initiated by submitting the form explained in the previous section. The action for this form is `updateUser.do`, which has the following action mapping in the Struts configuration file:

```
<action path="/updateUser"
        type="auction.action.UserAction"
        input="/editUser.jsp"
        name="userForm"
        scope="request">
  <forward name="success" path="/confirm.jsp"/>
</action>
```

The mapping uses the action class `UserAction` and the action form bean `userForm`. If an error occurs the response is sent to `editUser.jsp` or else it is sent to `confirm.jsp` (a simple JSP page that confirms the action). The `actn` request parameter associated with this request is `update`.

Offer Related Actions

In this section we will cover the action class, action mappings, and JSPs associated with the offer related actions. These actions are:

- **Displaying the form for adding a new offer**
  This request is initiated by clicking on the Add Offer link in the menu, and points to the resource `newOffer.jsp`.

- **Creating new offers**
  This request is initiated by submitting the form to add new offers. The request is mapped to `createOffer.do`, which is in turn mapped to the `OfferAction` class. The value of the `actn` request parameter associated with this request is `create`.

- **Editing the details of an offer**
  The request is mapped to `editOffer.do`, which is in turn mapped to the `OfferAction` class. The value of the `actn` request parameter associated with this request is `edit`.

- **Updating the details of an offer**
  The request is mapped to `updateOffer.do`, which is in turn mapped to the `OfferAction` class. The value of the `actn` request parameter associated with this request is `update`.

- **Deleting an offer**
  The request is mapped to `deleteOffer.do`, which is in turn mapped to the `OfferAction` class. The value of the `actn` request parameter associated with this request is `delete`.

- **Listing public offers**
  The request is mapped to `listOffer.do`, which is in turn mapped to the `OfferAction` class. The value of the `actn` request parameter associated with this request is `public`.

- **Listing own offers**
  The request is mapped to `listOffer.do`, which is in turn mapped to the `OfferAction` class. The value of the `actn` request parameter associated with this request is `mine`.

The OfferAction Class

In this section we will have a look at the source code for the `auction.action.OfferAction` class. The `perform()` method for this class extracts the value of the `actn` request parameter and performs the following tasks depending on the value:

- If the value is `create` it will call the `addOffer()` method on an instance of `OfferBO`, passing the action form.
- If the value is `update` it will call the `updateOffer()` method on an instance of `OfferBO`, passing the action form.
- If the value is `edit` it will call the `getOffer()` method on an instance of `OfferBO`, passing the offer id. The returned `Offer` instance is then stored as a request scope bean.
- If the value is `public` it will call the `getPublicOffers()` method on an instance of `OfferBO`, passing the user id. The returned `Collection` of `Offer` instances is then stored as a request scope bean.
- If the value is `mine` it will call the `getMyOffers()` method on an instance of `OfferBO`, passing the user id. The returned `Collection` of `Offer` instances is then stored as a request scope bean.
- If the value is `delete` it will call the `deleteOffer()` method on an instance of `OfferBO`, passing the offer id.

If there is no error, the class returns a local forward defined by the logical name `success'`.

```
public ActionForward perform(ActionMapping mapping,
                             ActionForm form,
                             HttpServletRequest request,
                             HttpServletResponse response)
                             throws IOException,ServletException {

  ActionErrors errors = new ActionErrors();
```

Get the value of the actn parameter:

```
      String action = request.getParameter("actn");
```

Create the offer business object:

```
      OfferBO offerBO = new OfferBO();
```

Get the currently logged on user:

```
      String user = request.getRemoteUser();
```

Perform the processing based on the value of the actn parameter as explained below. If the value of the actn parameter is:

- public Get all the offers posted by the other users
- mine Get all the offeres posted by the current user
- edit Get the selected offer for editing
- create Create a new offer
- update updates the selected offer
- delete Delete the selected offer

```
      if(action.equals("public")) {
        Collection col = offerBO.getPublicOffers(user);
        request.setAttribute(BeanNames.OFFER_LIST, col);
      } else if(action.equals("mine")) {
        Collection col = offerBO.getMyOffers(user);
        request.setAttribute(BeanNames.OFFER_LIST, col);
      } else if(action.equals("edit")) {
        int offerId = Integer.parseInt(request.getParameter("offerId"));
        Offer offer = offerBO.getOffer(offerId);
        request.setAttribute(BeanNames.OFFER_FORM, offer);
      } else if(action.equals("create")) {
        Offer offer = (Offer)form;
        offer.setUserId(request.getRemoteUser());
        offerBO.addOffer(offer);
      } else if(action.equals("update")) {
        Offer offer = (Offer)form;
        offer.setUserId(request.getRemoteUser());
        offerBO.updateOffer(offer);
      } else if(action.equals("delete")) {
        int offerId = Integer.parseInt(request.getParameter("offerId"));
        offerBO.deleteOffer(offerId);
      }
```

Forward to the next view:

```
      return mapping.findForward("success");
   }
```

New Offer

The screenshot below displays the form for adding new offers:

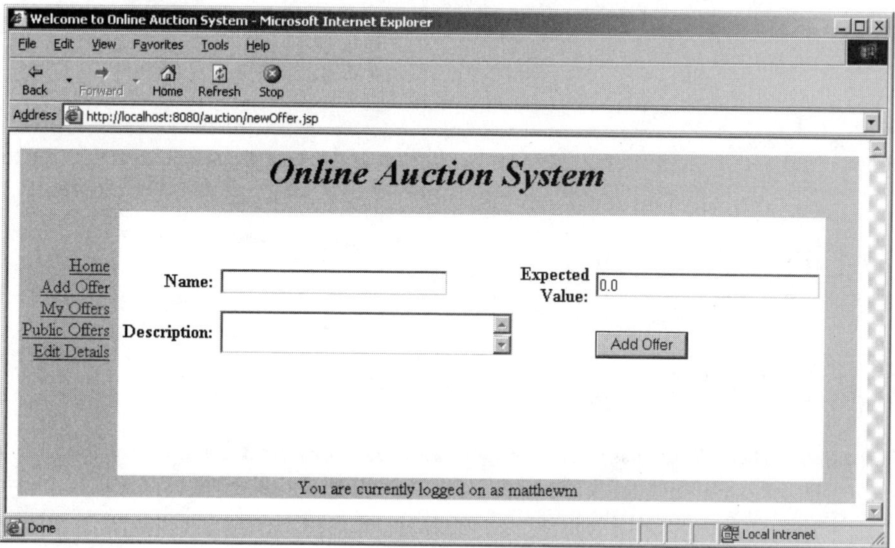

The request for displaying the form for adding new offers is forwarded to the file `newOffer.jsp`. This JSP page uses the Struts template tags to insert the file `template.jsp` and push the contents of `newOfferContent.jsp` into it:

```
<%@ taglib uri="/template" prefix="template" %>

<template:insert template="template.jsp">
  <template:put name="content" content="newOfferContent.jsp"/>
</template:insert>
```

The JSP page `newOfferContent.jsp` displays the form for entering new user details using the Struts form tags. The action for this form is set to the Struts action mapping `createOffer`:

```
<%@ taglib uri="/bean" prefix="bean" %>
<%@ taglib uri="/html" prefix="html" %>
<%@ taglib uri="/logic" prefix="logic" %>
<%@ taglib uri="/template" prefix="template" %>

<br/>
```

We use the Struts `<html:errors>` tag to display any error messages if the form is sent back due to validation error:

```
  <html:errors/>
<br/>

<table cellpadding="2">
```

Render the form for adding new offers:

```
<html:form action="/createOffer.do" focus="name">
<html:hidden property="actn" value="create"/>
<html:hidden property="maxBid" value="0"/>
...
```

Create Offer

This action is initiated by submitting the form explained in the last section. The action for this form is `createOffer.do` that has the following action mapping in the Struts configuration file:

```
<action path="/createOffer"
        type="auction.action.OfferAction"
        input="/newOffer.jsp"
        name="offerForm"
        scope="request">
  <forward name="success" path="/confirm.jsp"/>
</action>
```

The mapping uses the action class `OfferAction` and the action form bean `offerForm`. If an error occurs the response is sent to `newOffer.jsp`; otherwise it is sent to `confirm.jsp`. The `actn` request parameter associated with this request is `create`.

List Offers

The requests for listing public and own offers are mapped to the URI `listOffer.do`, and hence share the same action class `OfferAction` and the JSP page `listOffer.jsp`. The only difference is that the `actn` parameter value is `public` in the first case and `mine` in the second case. Depending on this value the action class retrieves different collections of offers and the JSP page renders different controls. The diagram below shows the list of public offers:

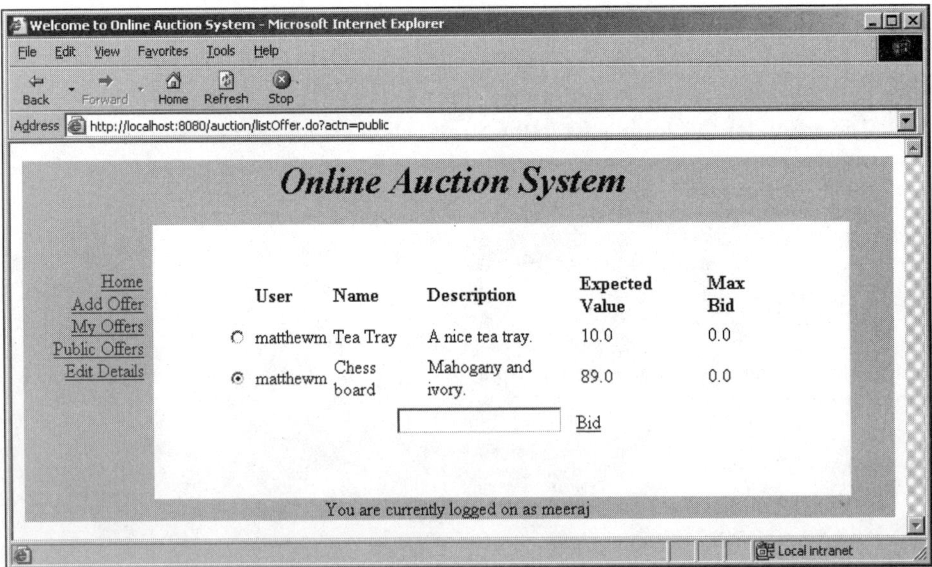

Please note that the screen displays all the offers not owned by the current user including the offer details and current maximum bid for the offer. It also has a radio button for selecting an offer. There is a field for entering a bid value for a selected offer, and a link for sending that bid.

The list of own offers displays the same information, but instead of having the controls for bidding on a selected offer, it will have controls for editing, deleting and accepting the maximum bid on a selected offer. This is depicted in the screenshot shown below:

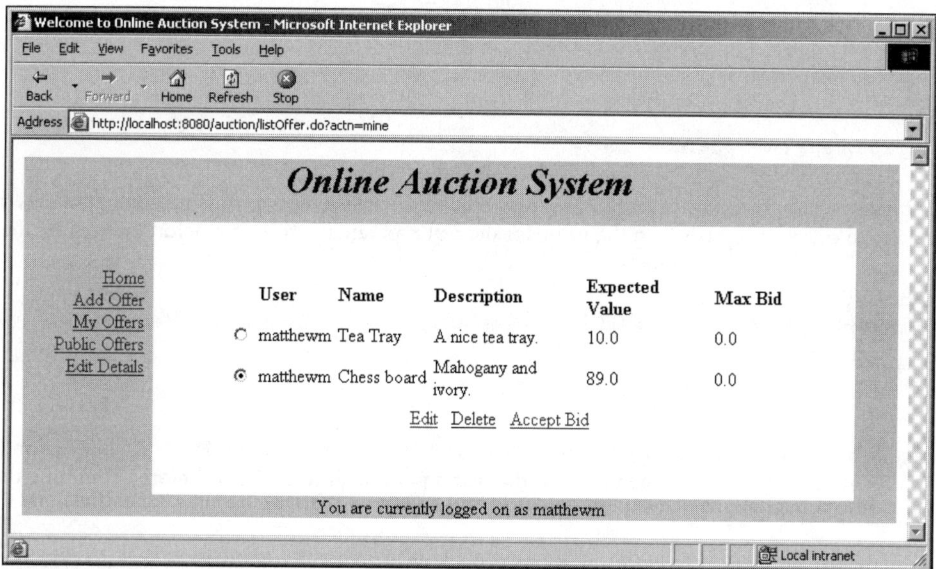

The snippet below shows the action mapping for listing the offers:

```
<action path="/listOffer"
        type="auction.action.OfferAction">
  <forward name="success" path="/listOffer.jsp"/>
</action>
```

The action class for the mapping is defined as `OfferAction`, and the JSP is `listOffer.jsp`. The request for editing existing user details is forwarded to `listOffer.jsp`, which uses the Struts template tags to insert `template.jsp` and push `listOfferContent.jsp` into it:

```
<%@ taglib uri="/template" prefix="template" %>

<template:insert template="template.jsp">
  <template:put name="content" content="listOfferContent.jsp"/>
</template:insert>
```

The JSP `listOfferContent.jsp` displays the list of public or own offers and controls for manipulating the offers:

```
<%@ taglib uri="/bean" prefix="bean" %>
<%@ taglib uri="/html" prefix="html" %>
<%@ taglib uri="/logic" prefix="logic" %>
<%@ taglib uri="/template" prefix="template" %>

<br/>
```

Use the Struts `<html:errors>` tag to displaying error messages if the form is sent back due to validation error:

```
  <html:errors/>
<br/>

<script language="Javascript">
```

The first Javascript function, `editOffer()`, is for editing the selected offer; the function below sets the action for the form to `editOffer.do` and the value for the `actn` parameter to `edit` before submitting the form:

```
function editOffer() {
  offerList.action = "editOffer.do ";
  offerList.actn.value = "edit";
  offerList.submit();
}
```

The next Javascript function, `deleteOffer()`, is for deleting the selected offer. It sets the action for the form to `deleteOffer.do` and the value for the `actn` parameter to `delete` before submitting the form:

```
function deleteOffer() {
  offerList.action = "deleteOffer.do";
  offerList.actn.value = "delete";
  offerList.submit();
}
```

The Javascript function, `acceptBid()`, is for accepting the maximum bid on the selected offer. The function sets the action for the form to `acceptBid.do` and the value for the `actn` parameter to `accept` before submitting the form:

```
function acceptBid() {
  offerList.action = "acceptBid.do";
  offerList.actn.value = "accept";
  offerList.submit();
}
```

The `bid()` function for is bidding the selected offer. The function sets the action for the form to `bid.do` and the value for the `actn` parameter to `bid` before submitting the form:

```
function bid() {
  offerList.action = "bid.do";
  offerList.actn.value = "bid";
  offerList.submit();
}
```

```
  </script>

  <form name="offerList">

    <input type="hidden" name="actn"/>
    ...
```

We then use the <logic:iterate> tag to loop though the list of offers:

```
        <logic:iterate name="offerList"
                       id="offer"
                       scope="request"
                       type="auction.entity.Offer">

          <tr>
```

Use the Struts <bean:define> tag to define the offer id as a scripting variable:

```
            <bean:define id="offerId" name="offer" property="offerId"/>
          <td>
```

Define a radio button whose value is the offer id for the current offer in the list. This value is sent back to the server when the form is submitted with the offer selected:

```
            <input type="radio" name="offerId" checked
                   value="<%= offerId %>"/>
          </td>
          <td>
```

Write the user id owning the offer:

```
            <bean:write name="offer" property="userId"/>
          </td>
          <td>
```

Write the name of the offer:

```
            <bean:write name="offer" property="name"/>
          </td>
          <td>
```

Write the offer description:

```
            <bean:write name="offer" property="description"/>
          </td>
          <td>
```

Write the offer's expected value:

```
            <bean:write name="offer" property="expectedValue"/>
          </td>
          <td>
```

Write the current maximum bid:

```
            <bean:write name="offer" property="maxBid"/>
          </td>
        </tr>

      </logic:iterate>

      <tr>
        <td colspan="6" align="center">
```

If the list of offers is not owned by the current user, render the controls for bidding against the selected offer:

```
          <logic:equal parameter="actn" value="public">
            <input type="text" name="bidValue"/>
             
            <a href="javascript:bid()">Bid</a>
          </logic:equal>
```

If the list of offers is owned by the current user, render the controls for editing, deleting and accepting the maximum for the selected offer:

```
          <logic:equal parameter="actn" value="mine">
            <a href="javascript:editOffer()">Edit</A>
             
            <a href="javascript:deleteOffer()">Delete</a>
             
            <a href="javascript:acceptBid()">Accept Bid</a>
             
          </logic:equal>

        </td>
      </tr>
    </table>

  </form>
```

Edit Offer

The form for editing an offer is displayed when the **edit offer** link is clicked with an offer selected from the list of the user's own offers. The screenshot below shows the form for editing an offer:

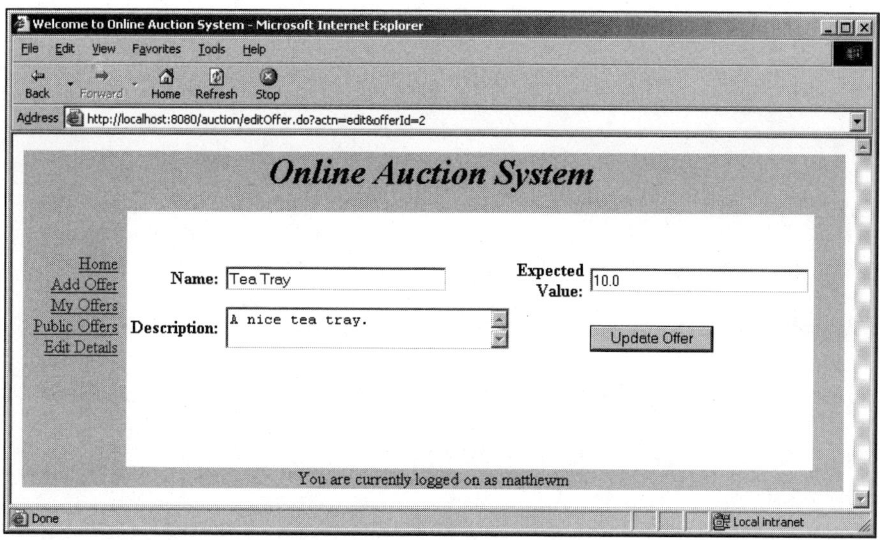

The request mapping for the action is shown below:

```
<action path="/editOffer"
        type="auction.action.OfferAction">
  <forward name="success" path="/editOffer.jsp"/>
</action>
```

The action class for the mapping is defined as `OfferAction`, and the JSP is `editOffer.jsp`. This JSP uses the Struts template tags to insert `template.jsp` and push the contents of `editOfferContent.jsp` into it:

```
<%@ taglib uri="/template" prefix="template" %>

<template:insert template="template.jsp">
  <template:put name="content" content="editOfferContent.jsp"/>
</template:insert>
```

The JSP `editOfferContent.jsp` creates the the form for editing the selected offer. The action for this form is set to the Struts action mapping `updateOffer`:

```
<%@ taglib uri="/bean" prefix="bean" %>
<%@ taglib uri="/html" prefix="html" %>
<%@ taglib uri="/logic" prefix="logic" %>
<%@ taglib uri="/template" prefix="template" %>

<br/>
```

We use the `<html:errors>` tag to display any error messages if the form is sent back due to validation error:

```
  <html:errors/>
<br/>

<table cellpadding="2">
```

Define the form for editing the selected offer:

```
<html:form action="/updateOffer.do" focus="name">
```

Render the offer id as a hidden parameter; this is used for finding the offer entity to be updated:

```
<html:hidden property="offerId"/>
```

Render the maximum bid as a hidden parameter:

```
<html:hidden property="maxBid"/>
```

Render the `actn` parameter as a hidden parameter, with the value set to `update`:

```
<html:hidden property="actn" value="update"/>
...
```

Update Offer

This action is initiated by submitting the form explained in the last section. The action for this form is `updateOffer.do`, which has the following action mapping in the Struts configuration file:

```
<action path="/updateOffer"
        type="auction.action.OfferAction"
        input="/editOffer.jsp"
        name="offerForm"
        scope="request">
  <forward name="success" path="/confirm.jsp"/>
</action>
```

The mapping uses the action class `OfferAction` and the action form bean `offerForm`. If an error occurs the response is sent to `editOffer.jsp`; otherwise it is sent to `confirm.jsp`. The `actn` request parameter associated with this request is `update`.

Delete Offer

This action is initiated by selecting an offer and clicking on the Delete link. The action for this form is `deleteOffer.do`, which has the following action mapping in the Struts configuration file:

```
<action path="/deleteOffer"
        type="auction.action.OfferAction">
  <forward name="success" path="/confirm.jsp"/>
</action>
```

The mapping uses the action class `OfferAction` and the action form bean `offerForm`. The `actn` request parameter associated with this request is `delete`.

Bid Related Actions

The final part of this section covers the action class, action mappings and JSPs associated with the bid related actions. These actions are:

- **Accepting the maximum bid for a selected offer**
  This request is initiated by clicking on the Accept Bid link in the user's own offer list and points to the resource `acceptBid.do`. The value of the `actn` request parameter associated with this request is `accept`.

- **Bidding for a selected offer**
  This request is initiated by clicking on the Bid link in the public offer list and points to the resource `bid.do`. The value of the `actn` request parameter associated with this request is `bid`.

BidAction

The `auction.action.BidAction` class implements these actions; its `perform()` method extracts the value of the `actn` request parameter and performs the following tasks depending on the value:

- If the value is `accept` it will call the `acceptBid()` method on an instance of `BidBO`, passing the action form
- If the value is `bid` it will call the `addBid()` method on an instance of `BidBO`, passing the action form

If there is no error the class returns a local forward defined by the logical name `success`. The source for the class is shown below:

```
  public ActionForward perform(ActionMapping mapping,
                               ActionForm form,
                               HttpServletRequest request,
                               HttpServletResponse response)
                               throws IOException,ServletException {

    ActionErrors errors = new ActionErrors();
```

Get the value of the `actn` parameter:

```
    String action = request.getParameter("actn");
```

Create the bid business object:

```
    BidBO bidBO = new BidBO();
```

Get the currently logged on user:

```
    String user = request.getRemoteUser();
```

Get the offer id:

```
    int offerId = Integer.parseInt(request.getParameter("offerId"));
```

Perform the appropriate task, depending on the value of the actn parameter:

```
    if(action.equals("accept")) {
      bidBO.acceptBid(offerId);
    } else if(action.equals("bid")) {
        Bid bid = (Bid)form;
        bid.setBidUserId(user);
        bidBO.addBid(bid);
    }
```

Forward to the next view:

```
    return mapping.findForward("success");
  }
```

Bid

This action is initiated by selecting an offer and clicking on the Bid link. The action for this form is bid.do, which has the following action mapping:

```
<action path="/bid"
        type="auction.action.BidAction"
        input="/listOffer.do?actn=public"
        name="bidForm"
        scope="request">
  <forward name="success" path="/confirm.jsp"/>
</action>
```

The mapping uses the action class Bid and the action form bean bidForm. The actn request parameter associated with this request is bid.

Accept Bid

This action is initiated by selecting an offer and clicking on the Accept Bid link. The action for this form is bid.do, which has the following action mapping in the Struts configuration file:

```
<action path="/acceptBid"
        type="auction.action.BidAction"
        input="/listOffer.do?actn=mine"
        name="bidForm"
        scope="request">
  <forward name="success" path="/confirm.jsp"/>
</action>
```

The mapping uses the action class Bid and the action form bean bidForm. The actn request parameter associated with this request is acceptBid.

web.xml

We ought to recap by looking at a complete listing of the deployment descriptor:

```
<?xml version="1.0" encoding="ISO-8859-1"?>
```

```
<!DOCTYPE web-app
  PUBLIC "-//Sun Microsystems, Inc.//DTD Web Application 2.3//EN"
  " http://java.sun.com/dtd/web-app_2_3.dtd ">

<web-app>
```

Declare the Struts action servlet:

```
  <!-- Standard Action Servlet Configuration (with debugging) -->
  <servlet>
    <servlet-name>action</servlet-name>
    <servlet-class>org.apache.struts.action.ActionServlet</servlet-class>
    <init-param>
      <param-name>application</param-name>
      <param-value>AuctionResources</param-value>
    </init-param>
    <load-on-startup>2</load-on-startup>
  </servlet>
```

Map all the `*.do` requests to the action servlet:

```
  <!-- Standard Action Servlet Mapping -->
  <servlet-mapping>
    <servlet-name>action</servlet-name>
    <url-pattern>*.do</url-pattern>
  </servlet-mapping>
```

Make sure our `index.jsp` is counted as a "welcome file":

```
  <welcome-file-list>
    <welcome-file>index.jsp</welcome-file>
  </welcome-file-list>
```

Define the tag library URIs:

```
  <!-- Struts Tag Library Descriptors -->
  <taglib>
    <taglib-uri>/bean</taglib-uri>
    <taglib-location>/WEB-INF/struts-bean.tld</taglib-location>
  </taglib>

  <taglib>
    <taglib-uri>/html</taglib-uri>
    <taglib-location>/WEB-INF/struts-html.tld</taglib-location>
  </taglib>

  <taglib>
    <taglib-uri>/logic</taglib-uri>
    <taglib-location>/WEB-INF/struts-logic.tld</taglib-location>
  </taglib>

  <taglib>
    <taglib-uri>/template</taglib-uri>
    <taglib-location>/WEB-INF/struts-template.tld</taglib-location>
  </taglib>
```

Define the secure resources:

```
<security-constraint>

  <web-resource-collection>
    <web-resource-name>Secure resources</web-resource-name>
    <url-pattern>/editUser.do</url-pattern>
    <url-pattern>/updateUser.do</url-pattern>
    <url-pattern>/listOffer.do</url-pattern>
    <url-pattern>/editOffer.do</url-pattern>
    <url-pattern>/createOffer.do</url-pattern>
    <url-pattern>/updateOffer.do</url-pattern>
    <url-pattern>/deleteOffer.do</url-pattern>
    <url-pattern>/acceptBid.do</url-pattern>
    <url-pattern>/bid.do</url-pattern>
    <http-method>GET</http-method>
    <http-method>POST</http-method>
  </web-resource-collection>

  <auth-constraint>
    <role-name>user</role-name>
  </auth-constraint>

</security-constraint>
```

Define login configuration as form-based login:

```
  <login-config>
    <auth-method>FORM</auth-method>
    <form-login-config>
      <form-login-page>/login.jsp</form-login-page>
      <form-error-page>/login.jsp</form-error-page>
    </form-login-config>
  </login-config>

</web-app>
```

Building the Application

Finally, let's run through how to build the application itself:

- Create a directory in the Tomcat file structure for the web application: `<TOMCAT_HOME>\webapps\auction\`.
- Create a directory called `WEB-INF\` under `auction`, and two directories called `classes\` and `lib\` under `WEB-INF\`.
- Copy the files `web.xml` and `struts-config.xml` to `WEB-INF\`.
- Copy all the JSP pages to `auction\`. Copy all the Struts tag library descriptors to `WEB-INF\`.
- Copy the file `AuctionResources.properties` to `WEB-INF\classes\`.
- Create all the database tables from the scripts provided.
- Compile all the Java classes with the `-d` option set to `auction\WEB-INF\classes\`. You should have `jdbc2_0-stdext.jar` and `struts.jar` (both from the Struts download), as well as `servlet.jar` in the compiler's classpath.

- Copy `struts.jar` file to `WEB-INF\lib` directory.
- Copy the JDBC driver JAR file (`mm-mysql.jar`) to `common\lib\` directory of Tomcat.
- Add the following entry into the Tomcat `server.xml` file:

```
<Context path="/auction" docBase="auction" debug="0" reloadable="true">

 <!-- Datasource factory for our application -->
 <Resource name="jdbc/AuctionDB" auth="Container"
          type="javax.sql.DataSource"/>
 <ResourceParams name="jdbc/AuctionDB">
   <parameter>
     <name>driverClassName</name>
     <value>org.gjt.mm.mysql.Driver</value>
  </parameter>
  <parameter>
    <name>driverName</name>
    <value>jdbc:mysql://localhost/auction</value>
  </parameter>
  </ResourceParams>

  <!-- JDBC realm for our application -->
  <Realm className="org.apache.catalina.realm.JDBCRealm"
         debug="99"
         driverName="org.gjt.mm.mysql.Driver"
         connectionURL="jdbc:mysql://localhost/auction"
         userTable="user"
         userNameCol="user_id"
         userCredCol="password"
         userRoleTable="user"
         roleNameCol="role" />

</Context>
```

To run the application, you will need to:

- Start your database server
- Start Tomcat
- Open a browser and access the URL http://localhost:8080/auction/, assuming you are running Tomcat locally on port 8080

Summary

Database access is a key element of any dynamic web application, but one that often causes difficulties with implementation. This chapter started by looking at a variety of data access patterns for web applications, looking in turn at Enterprise JavaBeans (EJB), SQLJ, Java Data Objects (JDO), and using the dynamic proxy facilities in JDK 1.3.

We then turned to examine a generic data access pattern suitable for many types of web application, based on entity objects to encapsulate the data itself, and data access objects that map the entities into relational database tables.

Lastly, we designed and implemented a real world web application using this pattern and built on Struts. In the course of so doing, we saw:

- All aspects of the analysis, design, development, and deployment phases of the project
- Security concerns like authentication, authorization, and custom security realms
- Use of Model 2 architecture for properly partitioning the web application
- Use of business objects and data access objects.
- Database connection pooling and JNDI
- Dynamic template management

Of course, you will sometimes find yourself working within a J2EE application server environment. The next chapter looks at how we can integrate access to the EJB tier into web applications.

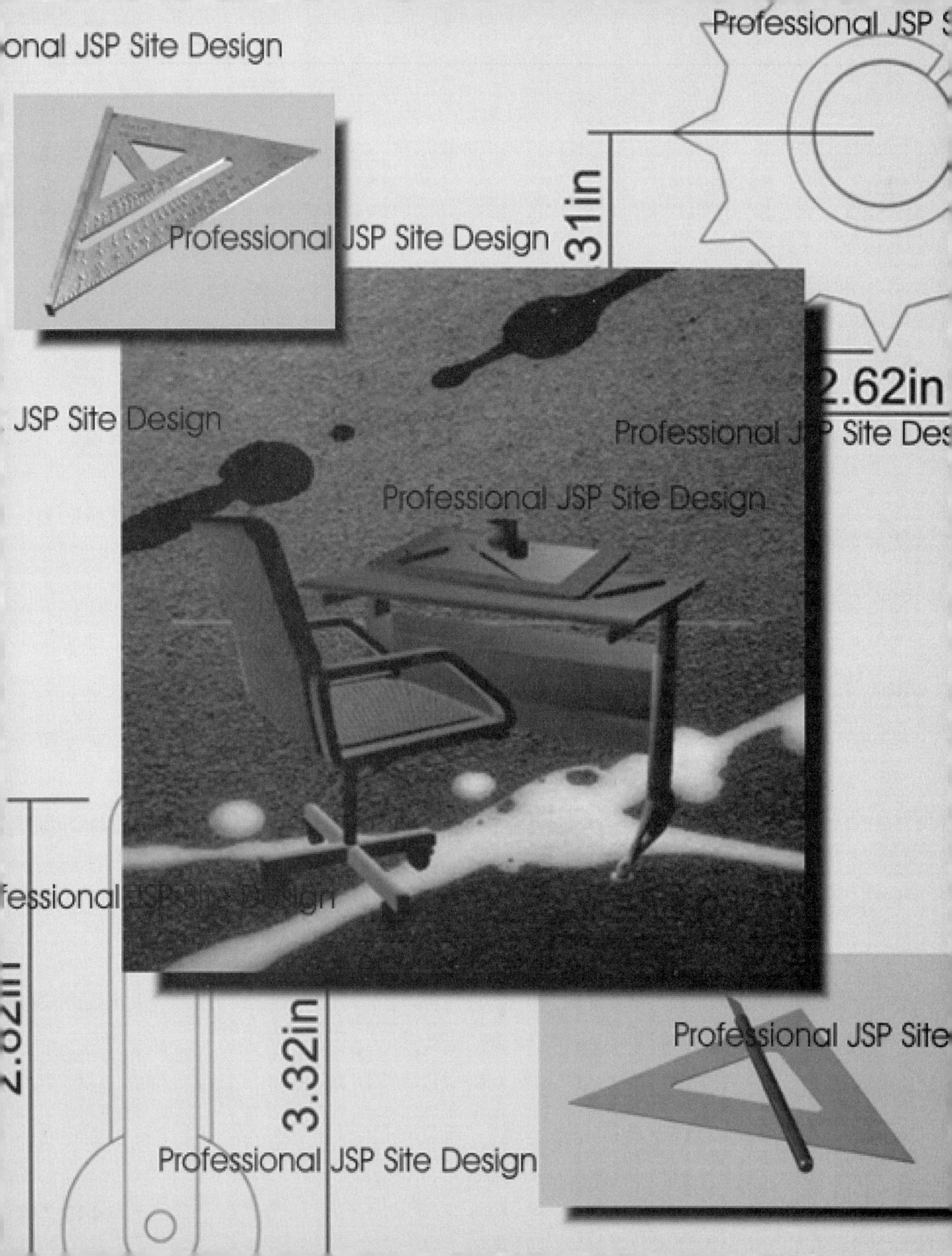
Professional JSP Site Design
31in
Professional JSP Site Design
Professional JSP Site Design
3.32in
Professional JSP Site Design

9

J2EE Integration

So far in this book we've discussed how to use the Servlet and JSP APIs to build dynamic web applications. Enterprise class web applications perform a lot more than just providing a browser-based user interface to the enterprise's data. These tasks include handling transactions, managing security, interacting with external legacy applications and relational databases, interfacing with message oriented middleware, and processing XML data.

If we were to use only the Servlet and JSP APIs for building our web applications, we would have to spend a considerable amount of time building the classes that perform the aforementioned system level services. Luckily, these APIs are only one part of Java 2 Enterprise Edition (J2EE), which provides a whole suite of APIs and technologies that can be used to build robust enterprise level applications.

In this chapter, we will provide a high level overview of some the technologies in J2EE. We'll also look at how they can be integrated with the components running in the J2EE web tier. In particular, we'll look at:

- A high level overview of J2EE architecture and the technologies that make up J2EE
- The different ways of integrating the J2EE web tier with the components built using the other J2EE technologies
- The J2EE security model
- The different issues associated with assembling and deploying J2EE applications as enterprise archive files and issues related to resolving dependencies between individual components that constitute the application
- Case studies depicting the integration of the J2EE web tier with other J2EE APIs

We don't have the space to cover these subjects in depth; we'll simply provide you with a taste of what J2EE has to offer. For more information on how to build applications that use all these J2EE technologies you should refer to *Professional Java Server Programming J2EE 1.3 Edition* from *Wrox Press (ISBN: 1-861005-37-7).*

Java 2 Enterprise Edition

J2EE provides enterprise class services that are reliable, scalable, robust, and highly available. They also integrate with existing Enterprise Information Systems (EIS). These may include the enterprise's existing data that reside in RDBMS systems, legacy applications, and Enterprise Resource Planning Systems (ERP) like SAP/R3 and PeopleSoft.

J2EE is a multi-tiered architecture that enables functionality to be implemented in the most appropriate location. In a typical scenario, a middle tier implements the services that interact with the existing EISs. The middle tier separates the client tier (which provides the user interface to the system) from the intricacies of the EIS tier.

The many different J2EE technologies are defined in a set of specifications (http://java.sun.com/j2ee/download.html#platformspec). A vendor will provide implementations for those interfaces and classes detailed in the specification.

The specification only states what the methods, fields, and properties of a class or interface must be – it is up to the vendor to actually implement the functionality. For example, the `javax.servlet.ServletRequest` interface defined in the Servlet specification models an incoming request. However, different vendors who provide J2EE web containers provide different implementations for this interface. This is true for most of the J2EE technologies. Some of these interfaces are implemented by the platform vendors whereas the rest are implemented by application developers.

Sun provide a reference implementation of the J2EE specifications (http://java.sun.com/j2ee/sdk_1.3/). In J2EE terminology, a piece of software that implements the J2EE technologies is called a J2EE server. J2EE servers provide an environment for the different J2EE components to operate, and may contain two important entities called web containers and EJB (Enterprise JavaBean) containers.

Web containers provide the operating environment for web components like JSP pages and servlets. EJB containers host EJB components. Sun provides a compatibility test suite that can be used by the container vendors to test whether their products comply with the J2EE specification. Tomcat is the reference web container implementation. Reputed J2EE server vendors include BEA Systems, IBM, Oracle Corporation, and Sybase Inc. Jboss (http://www.jboss.org/) is a very popular EJB container from the open source freeware community.

The main elements of the J2EE architecture that enables scalable enterprise application development are:

- A standard application model for developing n-tier applications
- A standard platform for hosting these applications
- A compatibility test suite to verify whether the platform conforms to the specification
- A reference implementation that provides a platform that supports the different technologies specified in the J2EE specification

The elements that constitute J2EE-based systems may be broadly classified into four areas:

- **Application components**
  Application components are applications written in the Java programming language that runs on the user's desktop. These components are typically GUI applications.

- **Applet components**
  Applets are GUI components that execute within the sandbox of the users' web browsers.

- **Web components**
  Web components are servlets, JSP pages, filters, and event listeners that run within J2EE web containers. These components may be used to generate contents of various formats like HTML or XML in response to HTTP requests.

- **EJB components**
  EJB components typically contain the business and data access logic and they run within the EJB containers.

J2EE Technologies

The J2EE specification defines various technologies used for building enterprise class applications. Some of these technologies are implemented by application developers for building the J2EE components, whilst the rest are implemented by container vendors that provide the different enterprise services to these components and include:

- **Enterprise Java Beans (EJB)**
  A technology for building transaction aware, distributed components. EJBs are one of the most popular of the J2EE technologies. EJB components can rely on the container in which they run for system level services like transaction management, persistence, security, and resource pooling. This helps application developers concentrate more on building the application logic rather than worrying about the system level services.

- **Servlets and JavaServer Pages**
  A technology for building web components. Servlets and JSP pages comprise the most popular component based architecture for generating dynamic content for different client devices ranging from palm-held devices to UNIX workstations.

- **Java Transaction API/Java Transaction Service**
  JTA and JTS provide the services for handling transactions. In most cases, application developers will deal with the high-level JTA for handling transactions programmatically and will seldom use the low-level JTS API. However, if you use EJBs and rely on the container for transaction handling, you won't need JTA either. If you don't use EJBs, you can use JTA to handle transactions programmatically within your web components.

- **JDBC extensions**
  Optional extensions to the JDBC core API. The JDBC optional package provides useful facilities like database connection pooling and XA compliant distributed transaction resources.

- **Java Authentication and Authorization Service**
  API for security management. JAAS provides a pluggable model for authentication and authorization services.

- **Java Messaging Service**
  API for enabling enterprise messaging. JMS is a very effective technology for implementing systems architected using message-oriented middleware (MOM). MOM based systems are very useful in implementing a loosely coupled and disconnected architecture.

- **JavaMail**
  API for implementing e-mail functionality.

- **Java API for XML Processing (JAXP)**
  A parser independent API for parsing and transforming XML data.

- **Java Connector Architecture (JCA)**
  API for accessing legacy systems and ERPs (Enterprise Resource Planning) like SAP/R3, Peoplesoft etc.

The diagram below shows what a typical J2EE application would look like:

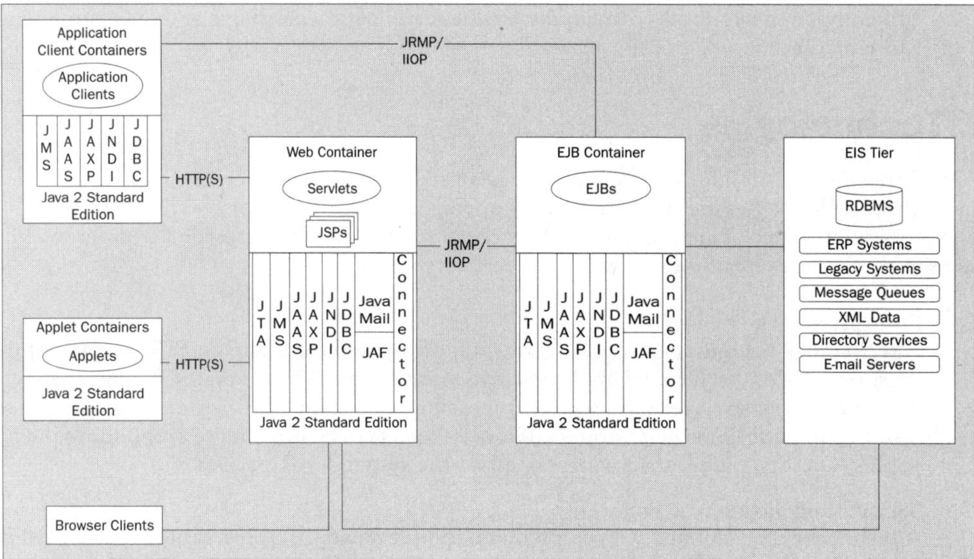

Managing Transactions

Transactions are essential elements of enterprise class web applications. Assume you are building an online banking system. If your system fails at the credit stage of a transfer of funds, the system may be in an inconsistent state if it is non-transactional. This means that someone will end up losing money. However, in transactional systems, you can perform the above in a single transaction. This guarantees that if the credit action fails, the debit is rolled back.

The key features of transactional systems are atomicity, consistency, isolation, and durability, known as ACID properties:

- **Atomicity**
  Ensures that all operations that constitute a transaction are considered as a single atomic operation

- **Consistency**
  Ensures that the state of the system is left in a consistent state after and before the transaction

- **Isolation**
  Ensures that multiple transactions can occur in a system in isolation from each other

- **Durability**
  Ensures that system state is persisted after a transaction is committed

J2EE supports application programming for distributed transaction management through the Java Transaction API (JTA) and Java Transaction Service (JTS). Developers can define the transactional properties of EJB components during design or deployment using declarative statements in the deployment descriptor.

J2EE compliant product vendors should support transactions that span across multiple components accessing XA compliant resources like JDBC connections and JMS sessions. J2EE supports both declarative and programmatic transactions. Declarative transactions are managed by the container and are relevant only to EJBs. The transaction attributes for the bean methods are defined in the deployment descriptor and the container is required to demarcate the transactions accordingly before the respective methods are called.

Programmatic transaction demarcation is achieved using the `javax.transaction.UserTransaction` interface defined by JTA. This interface defines methods for starting, committing, and rolling back transactions. This is the preferred method of demarcating transactions in servlets and JSP pages. The J2EE specification states that filters and lifecycle event listeners should not be using this interface for demarcating transactions.

UserTransaction within Web Components

The following points are pertinent when using JTA from J2EE web components:

- The J2EE platform should provide an object whose class implements the `UserTransaction` interface to all the web components. This object should be available for lookup using the standard JNDI API by the name `java:comp/env/UserTransaction`. The JNDI API is explained in detail in a later section.
- If a web component invokes a method on an EJB within a transaction, the container should propagate the transaction context to the EJB. For example, if the web component explicitly starts a transaction and the method that is invoked on the EJB has the transaction attribute set to `required`, the container doesn't need to start a new transaction.
- The transaction context needs to be propagated to the EJB only if both the web and EJB component run within the same J2EE server instance.
- Threads that are newly spawned from web components participating in transactions won't be propagated with the current transaction context.
- The transaction manager doesn't need to propagate transactions from a client component to a web component.
- Transactions shouldn't span across multiple life cycle methods of a web component. For example, a transaction started in the `doGet()` method of a Servlet should be committed or rolled back before the thread returns from that method.
- It is recommended not to store transactional resources like JDBC connections and JMS sessions in static and instance fields as it increases the risk of them being accessed from multiple threads. This is because in a multithreaded servlet, the servlet instance can be accessed by multiple threads and the instance and static variables will be exposed to all the threads accessing the servlet instance.
- Web components that provide serialized access by implementing the `SingleThreadModel` interface may store such resources in instance fields.

Working examples of using user transactions within J2EE web components are explained in the *Web Tier Integration* section.

JDBC Optional Extension

If your web applications access databases, you may want to pool your database connections. One solution is to write your own pool based on a popular resource pooling algorithm (see Chapter 12 for an example of this). However, the JDBC optional extensions provide the functionality for implementing JDBC connection factories. It also provides classes and interfaces that provide XA compliant distributed transactional facilities.

The JDBC optional extension defines interfaces for row sets, distributed transactions, connection pooling, and connection naming through JNDI. These interfaces are defined in the `javax.sql` package and are available with J2EE 1.3 version. However, JDBC 3.0 merges both the core API and optional extension and is available with J2SE 1.4.

The most commonly used interface from the optional extension is `DataSource`, which functions as a factory for creating connections. Instances of this class may be configured and made available for lookup using the standard JNDI API. This interface sits on top of the JDBC driver provided by the database vendor for creating connections to the resource manager. Even though the J2EE vendors are recommended to implement this functionality, it is not mandated by the specification. However, most of the leading J2EE server vendors provide a `DataSource` implementation with their products.

Other important interfaces from the JDBC optional extensions include:

- `PooledConnection`
  Provides facility for connection pooling.
- `XAConnection`
  Provides facility for distributed transactions.
- `XADataSource`
  Defines factory methods for creating `XAConnection` objects.
- `RowSet`
  Extends the standard JDBC `ResultSet` interface and supports the JavaBean design pattern. Notable implementations for this interface are `CachedRowSet`, `JDBCRowSet`, and `WebRowSet` available from the Sun Java website.

Messaging

Message-oriented middleware (MOM) is an integral element of enterprise application development. It lets applications integrate in a loosely coupled and disconnected manner, enabling them to send messages to each other with out worrying about whether the application to which messages are sent is up and running.

J2EE defines the Java Messaging Service (JMS) API for enabling Java applications to exchange enterprise messages. The interfaces belonging to the JMS specification are defined in the `javax.jms` package. JMS is a mandatory feature for J2EE 1.3 and supports both publish-subscribe and point-to-point messaging. Point-to-point messaging is based on message queues and publish-subscribe messaging is based on topic hierarchies.

In point-to-point messaging, messages sent to a queue are intended for a single recipient. Once a recipient reads the message, the message is removed from the queue. Whereas, in publish-subscribe messaging, messages sent to a topic may be shared between multiple recipients that have subscribed to the topic.

Software vendors that support JMS are required to implement the interfaces defined by the JMS specification. These vendors are called JMS providers in the JMS terminology. The Java applications that connect to the JMS providers for exchanging enterprise messages are called JMS clients. All the JMS clients connect to a centralized hub that is the JMS provider for sending and receiving messages rather than connecting to each other. This is illustrated in the diagram shown below:

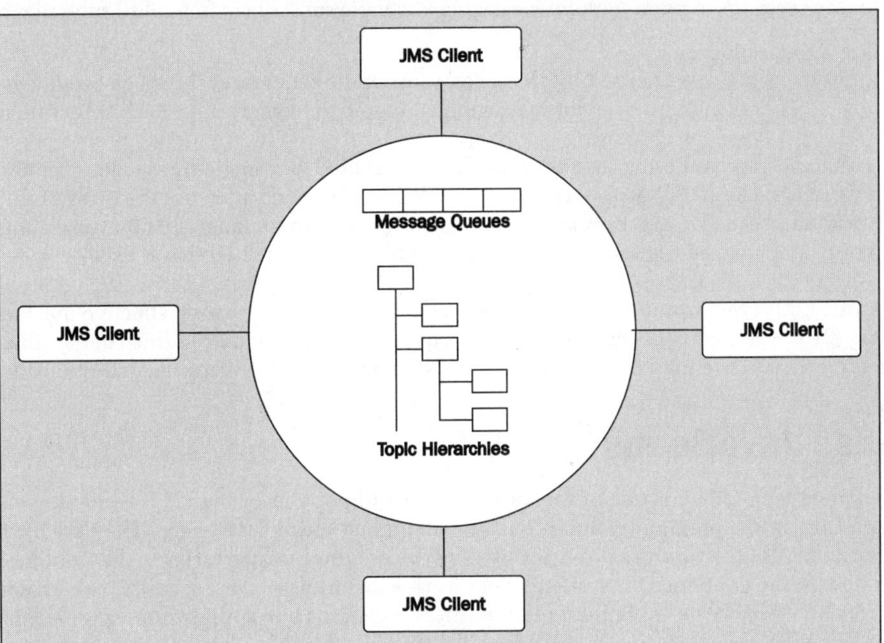

JMS clients that rely only on the interfaces defined by the JMS specification and don't use provider specific implementation classes are portable across multiple JMS providers. The interfaces defined in the JMS specification may be categorized as follows.

- **Connection factories**
  JMS defines queue and topic connection factories for creating queue and topic connections specific to point-to-point and publish-subscribe messaging respectively. Connection factories are normally configured and stored in JNDI using provider specific tools and are later looked up by JMS clients.

- **Connections**
  Connections are used for creating sessions between clients and providers. JMS defines both topic and queue connections.

- **Destinations**
  Destinations are used to model queues and topics to and from which messages are sent and received. Destinations are normally configured and stored in JNDI using provider specific tools and later looked up by JMS clients.

- **Sessions**
  Queue sessions and topic sessions are used for creating message consumers and producers as well as the messages that are exchanged.

- **Messages**
  Messages are used to exchange information between JMS clients. JMS supports messages that can carry text data, byte stream, and serialized Java objects.
- **Message consumers**
  Message consumers are used by JMS clients for receiving messages. Message consumers are called queue receivers in point-to-point messaging and topic subscribers in publish-subscribe messaging.
- **Message producers**
  Message producers are used by JMS clients for sending messages. Message producers are called queue senders in point-to-point messaging and topic publishers in publish-subscribe messaging.

Messages sent and received using JMS sessions can be included in a single transaction that accesses other resource managers, like JDBC datasources, as well. Web components may use the `UserTransaction` interface defined in the JTA specification for demarcating the transactions. EJBs may use either container managed or bean managed transactions depending on the type of the EJB that is used.

JMS supports both synchronous and asynchronous messaging and is a very effective mechanism for integrating J2EE web and EJB tiers. We will see a detailed example later in this chapter that illustrates message driven EJBs as a means of integrating the web and EJB tiers using asynchronous messaging.

Enterprise JavaBeans

EJB component technology is one of the most elegant and popular of the J2EE technologies. We briefly mentioned EJBs in the previous chapter, but we will go into more detail here. They are distributed components that use the services provided by an EJB container for performing different low-level tasks. You can rely on the container for system level services like transactions, security, resource pooling, and persistence and concentrate on building the business logic for your application.

EJB components exhibit the following characteristics:

- They may contain the business logic that operates on the enterprise data
- The state of the components expressed through their instance variables are managed by the container
- The behavior of a component may be amended during deployment by editing the deployment descriptor
- The bean components may rely on the container for services like lifecycle management, transactions, relations, and security
- Client calls to the bean components are always intercepted by the container
- Bean components that comply with the EJB specification are deployable across containers from different vendors

The different types of distributed components specified by the EJB 2.0 specification are:

- **Session Beans**
  - Components that can provide stateless services to clients
  - Components that can provide stateful services
- **Message Driven Beans**
  - A component whose service can be called by an asynchronous JMS message
- **Entity Beans**
  - Entity component that manage their states
  - Entity components whose states are managed by the container

Client View

Session and entity beans are accessed by the clients via their client views. Message driven beans don't have a client view as they are invoked by the container on reception of a JMS message. EJB clients may be other EJBs, web components, Java application, or CORBA components. The EJB 2.0 specification supports both local and remote components. Local components are accessible by clients that run in the same JVM as the components, whereas remote components are location transparent.

The client view is comprised of the following elements, regardless of whether the EJB is local or remote:

- Home interface
- Component interface
- Object identity

The home interface defines the lifecycle methods for the bean component. These methods are used for creating, finding, and removing bean instances. This remote interface is provided by the bean developer, and is implemented by the container when the bean is deployed. Home interfaces are generally made available by the container in a naming and directory service and later looked up by the clients using standard JNDI calls. Local home interfaces should extend the interface `EJBLocalHome` and remote home interfaces should extend `EJBHome` belonging to the `javax.ejb` package.

The component interface defines the business methods for the EJB. This is also a remote interface provided by the bean developer and implemented by the container provider during deployment. Instances of remote interfaces are created or found using the lifecycle methods defined in the home interface. Method calls on the remote interface are intercepted by the container before it is routed to the actual method implementation in the bean class. Local component interfaces should extend the interface `EJBLocalObject` and remote component interfaces should extend `EJBObject` belonging to the `javax.ejb` package.

Object identities of session beans are generated by the container and are not exposed to the clients whereas those of entity beans are defined by the bean provider by specifying the primary class of the component.

The following diagram depicts the client view of an EJB:

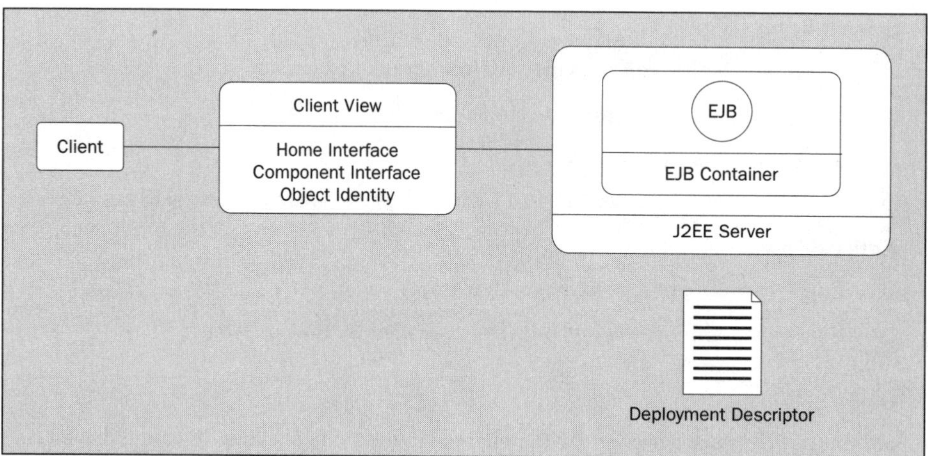

Component Contract

Component contract defines the methods that need to be implemented by the EJB class itself. Instances of EJB classes run within the managed environments of the containers and are never exposed to the clients. Clients always invoke methods against the home and remote objects and these methods are intercepted by the container before being routed to the EJB component. The component contracts for session, entity, and message driven entity beans are explained below:

- The bean provider should implement all the business methods defined in the bean's component interface in the bean class.
- Message driven beans should be provided with an `onMessage()` method.
- The bean developer should implement the `ejbCreate()`, `ejbPostCreate()`, and `ejbRemove()` methods for session and entity beans. They should also provide the `ejbFind()` methods for bean managed persistence entity beans.
- The `ejbCreate()` and `ejbFind()` methods should correspond to the `create()` and `find()` methods defined in the home interface.
- Entity beans, session beans, and message driven beans should implement the `EntityBean`, `SessionBean`, and `MessageDrivenBean` interfaces respectively.
- Entity beans with bean managed persistence should provide abstract accessor methods to the fields that are managed by the container.

The Deployment Descriptor

EJBs are normally deployed in an EJB container as a JAR file that contains the home interface, component interface, bean class, any other dependent classes, and an XML file that contains declarative information about the bean. This file is a the **deployment descriptor** and is called `ejb-jar.xml`. This file contains information about the bean such as transactional nature, security, persistence, home interface, component interface, bean class, primary key class, bean type, and so on. For example:

```
META-INF/
        ejb-jar.xml
com/example/
           ExmployeeHome.class
           Employee.class
           EmployeeEHB.class
           EmployeeKey.class
```

The above JAR file contains the following files:

- Deployment descriptor
- Home interface: `com.example.EmployeeHome`
- Component interface: `com.example.Employee`
- EJB class: `com.example.EmployeeEJB`
- Primary key class: `com.example.EmployeeKey` (primary key classes are only applicable for entity beans)

This has been a fairly quick review of EJBs, but *Professional EJB* from *Wrox Press (ISBN 1-861005-08-3)* gives more in-depth coverage.

E-Mailing

E-mailing is one of the integral elements of modern enterprise applications. There are a multitude of internet web sites that provide e-mail functionality for subscribed users. The JavaMail technology lets Java programs interface with e-mail servers to send and receive messages independent of the e-mail protocols like SMTP and POP3.

The JavaMail specification adds an e-mail framework to the J2EE suite of technologies and provides the following functionality:

- Creating mail messages with headers that can handle different mime types
- Opening sessions with mail servers to authenticate users and control access to the message stores
- Sending and receiving messages

The actual access to the different message sources is implemented by the specific protocol providers. JavaMail is normally configured by passing a `Properties` object to the `Session` object provided by the API. This object can be used for connecting to the service provider, sending and receiving messages, and so on.

Web containers may make `Session` objects pre-configured and available in a naming and directory service that can be looked up using standard JNDI calls. Web components can refer to the JNDI names using the `resource-ref` element in the deployment descriptor.

XML Parsing

XML is arguably the most exciting and powerful technology in modern day enterprise application development. It will be difficult to find a modern enterprise application that doesn't use XML in some form or an other.

XML is a very powerful model for storing structured configuration information. There are many different vendors who provide XML parsers, like the Apache Foundation, Oracle, and Sun. However, if you start using vendor specific classes in your applications, it will be difficult for you to switch vendors. JAXP provides a uniform interface to both DOM and SAX based XML parsing in a vendor independent manner.

The J2EE API defines a factory based approach for both SAX and DOM based XML parsing that is independent of the specific parser that is used. The classes defined in the Java API for XML Parsing (JAXP) belong to the package `javax.xml.parsers` package. The classes that belong to this package are:

- `DocumentBuilder`
  This class can be used for DOM based parsing as well as building DOM structures
- `DocumentBuilderFactory`
  This is a factory class used for creating DOM based parsers
- `SAXParser`
  This class can be used for SAX based parsing
- `SAXParserFactory`
  This is a factory class used for creating SAX based parsers

JAXP also supports pluggable XSLT transformation engines. All J2EE platforms are required to support at least one SAX parser, one DOM parser, and one transformation engine. The parsers are required to support various validation modes as well as namespaces.

Other J2EE APIs

The other APIs defined by the J2EE specification include:

- **Java Connector Architecture (JAC)**
  Provides a standard architecture for back-end applications such as Enterprise Resource Planning (ERP) and Customer Resource Management (CRM) systems to "plug-and-play" with any J2EE 1.3 compatible application server
- **Java Authentication and Authorization Service (JAAS)**
  Extends the Java security architecture with additional support to authenticate and enforce access controls upon users
- **Java Bean Activation Framework (JAF)**
  Determines the type of an arbitrary piece of data, encapsulates access to it, discovers the operations available on it, and instantiates the appropriate bean to perform the operations

Web Tier Integration

In this section we will have a look at the concepts behind integrating the J2EE web tier with other J2EE technology APIs including EJB, JMS, JavaMail, JDBCX, and JTA. The corner stone for integrating the web tier with the other J2EE technology APIs is naming and lookup. Common lookups are:

- EJB home objects
- JDBC datasource objects
- Mail sessions

- User transactions
- JMS connection factories
- JMS destinations

Both Java standard and enterprise editions provide a very powerful API for performing naming and directory operations. This API is called Java Naming and Directory Interface (JNDI). Before we delve into the intricacies of web tier integration, we will have a quick overview of JNDI.

Java Naming and Directory Interface

Directory services are widely used in enterprise systems for storing information about users, applications, and devices. They also provide naming facilities for identifying entities whose information has been stored. Examples of directory services are LDAP, NDS, NIS, and Microsoft Active Directory. JNDI provides a uniform API for Java applications to perform naming and directory operations independent of the directory service that is accessed. JNDI uses different SPIs (Service Provider Interface) for accessing specific directory services. This is illustrated in the diagram shown below:

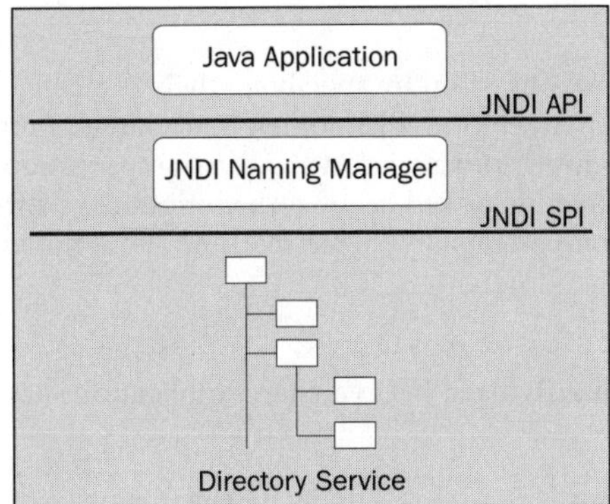

Directory services use a naming system for storing information about different resources. Client applications can later use this naming information to access the objects stored in directory services. Every object stored in a naming service is bound to a name. Multiple name-object bindings are stored in a common entity called context that is again identified by a name. For example, a context by the name `java:comp/env/jdbc` may contain two datasource objects bound to the names `EmployeeDS` and `CustomerDS`.

Contexts can be compared to nodes in a tree structure. A node may contain multiple name-object bindings. Accordingly contexts can either be root contexts or sub contexts. This is illustrated in the diagram shown below:

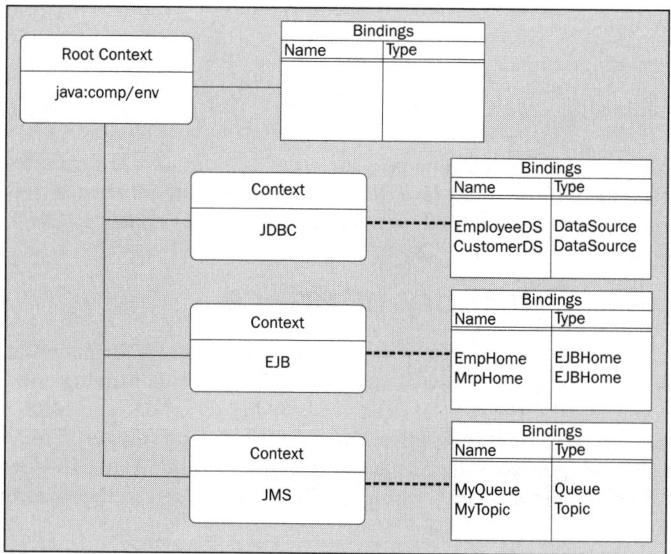

Both contexts and objects can be looked up by specifying their respective names. For example, objects that implement the different J2EE interfaces like EJB homes, datasources, destinations, and connection factories may be created, configured, and stored in JNDI namespaces supplied by the J2EE EJB and web containers. These objects can then be looked up by web components, EJB components, and client applications. Vendor neutral components only need to know about the interfaces exposed by these objects.

Contexts

The JNDI entities that are primarily used in Java client applications are:

- `Context`
  This is the most important interface defined in JNDI. It is used for creating name-object bindings, listing the name-object bindings, and looking up objects by name. The following table lists some of the important methods provided by this interface:

Method	**Description**
`Object lookup(String name)`	Looks up an object by name
`void bind(String name, Object obj)`	Binds the object to the name
`NamingEnumeration list(String name)`	Lists all the bindings

- `InitialContext`
  Initial contexts represent initial bootstrap contexts. When initial contexts are created you can specify the provider URL where the directory service is running and an initial context factory to be used by the JNDI naming manager. If this is not specified, the default values for your component's environment are used. A general practice is not to specify the provider URL and initial context factory if the namespace provider is running within the same environment as the one in which your web or EJB component is running. However, you may need to specify them if you are connecting to an external naming provider.

The example below shows how initial contexts are used:

```
InitialContext iCtx = new InitialContext();
Context ctx = (Context)iCtx.lookup("java:comp/env");
Queue myQueue = (Queue)ctx.lookup("jms/MyQueue");
```

The example below shows connecting to an external naming provider. For example, connecting from a web component running within Tomcat to a naming provider running within BEA WebLogic server:

```
Properties prop = new Properties();
prop.put(Context.INITIAL_CONTEXT_FACTORY,
             "weblogic.jndi.WLInitialContextFactory");
prop.put(Context.PROVIDER_URL, "t3:\\localhost:7001");
InitialContext iCtx = new InitialContext(prop);
Context ctx = (Context)iCtx.lookup("java:comp/env");
Queue myQueue = (Queue)ctx.lookup("jms/MyQueue");
```

In the above example the initial context factory and the provider URL is specified when the initial context is constructed.

J2EE Server Requirements

The naming requirements defined by the J2EE specification for J2EE servers allow J2EE application assemblers and deployers to customize the business logic of the components without amending the component code. It also enables component providers to access objects stored in JNDI namespaces without being aware of the real name of the objects.

Web containers are required to provide the naming environment that can be accessed using JNDI. The naming environment for a component should have the initial context bound to the name `java:comp/env`. All the references are resolved relative to this name.

Accessing EJBs from Web Components

EJB home references are declared in the web deployment descriptor using the `<ejb-ref>` element. This reference is linked to the real name of the EJB as defined in the EJB deployment descriptor. The excerpt from the web deployment descriptor before the amendment is shown below:

```
<ejb-ref>
  <description>This is an EJB reference</description>
  <ejb-ref-name>ejb/emp</ejb-ref-name>
  <ejb-ref-type>Entity</ejb-ref-type>
  <home>com.EmployeeHome</home>
  <remote>com.Employee</remote>
</ejb-ref>
```

The above reference enables the web component to look up the EJB using JNDI by specifying the name `java:comp/env/ejb/emp`. The above excerpt defines the type of the EJB, home interface class, and remote interface class. Here the web component provider doesn't need to worry about the real name of the EJB at all. It's recommended to bind all the EJBs within the `ejb/` context under the initial context. The deployer will amend the descriptor to link the above reference to a real EJB as shown below:

```
<ejb-ref>
  <description>This is an EJB reference</description>
  <ejb-ref-name>ejb/emp</ejb-ref-name>
  <ejb-ref-type>Entity</ejb-ref-type>
  <home>com.EmployeeHome</home>
  <remote>com.Employee</remote>
  <ejb-link>../EmployeeBean.jar#EmployeeBean</ejb-link>
</ejb-ref>
```

The above excerpt links the bean to the EJB by the name `EmployeeBean` in the `EmployeeBean.jar` file in the J2EE application as the web component.

Accessing Connection Factory References

Web application deployment descriptors also let you define symbolic links to resource manager factories like datasources and JMS connection factories. This lets web components refer to resource manager connection factories by logical name without worrying about the real name to which they are bound in the naming provider. The component provider may declare the resource factories in the deployment descriptor using the `<resource-ref element>`. The J2EE specification recommends the following initial contexts for the different J2EE resource factories:

- `java:comp/env/jdbc` for datasources
- `java:comp/env/jms` for JMS connection factories
- `java:comp/env/url` for URL connection factories
- `java:comp/env/mail` for mail sessions

The excerpt below shows a resource factory reference before the deployment descriptor is amended by the deployer:

```
<resource-ref>
  <description>Connections for employee DB</description>
  <res-ref-name>jdbc/empDS</res-ref-name>
  <res-type>javax.sql.DataSource</res-type>
  <res-auth>Container</res-auth>
  <res-sharing-scope>Shareable</res-sharing-scope>
</resource-ref>
```

The above example defines a datasource accessed by the name java:comp/env/jdbc/empDS. The <res-auth> element defines whether the component needs to specify the security credentials programmatically or whether the container can use the principal associated with the thread. The allowed values are Application and Container. The <res-sharing-scope> element defines whether the connections obtained are shareable or not. The deployer may use JNDI link references to map these logical names to real names to which the objects are bound.

The example below shows how a JMS connection factory is defined in the web deployment descriptor:

```
<resource-ref>
  <description>Connections for employee DB</description>
  <res-ref-name>jms/myTCF</res-ref-name>
  <res-type>javax.jms.TopicConnectionFactory</res-type>
  <res-auth>Application</res-auth>
  <res-sharing-scope>Unshareable</res-sharing-scope>
</resource-ref>
```

Accessing Resource Environment References

Resource environment references enable web components to access administered objects like JMS destinations using logical names. The example below shows how a JMS queue is defined in the web deployment descriptor:

```
<resource-env-ref>
  <description>Booking queue</description>
  <res-env-ref-name>jms/bookingQueue</res-env-ref-name>
  <res-env-type>javax.jms.Queue</res-env-type>
</resource-env-ref>
```

The above queue may be looked up by the name java:comp/env/jms/bookingQueue. You don't need to specify any authentication information for resource environment references.

Accessing UserTransactions

Containers are required to provide a UserTransaction implementation available to the components by the name java:comp/UserTransaction. The snippet below shows how a user transaction can be used within the web component:

```
InitialContext context = new InitialContext();
UserTransaction trans = (UserTransaction)ctx.lookup("java:comp/UserTransaction");
trans.start();
...
trans.commit();
```

Deployment and Assembly

In this section, we will cover how J2EE web application components (WAR) and EJB components (JAR) can be assembled into a J2EE enterprise (EAR) application.

Web Component Format

J2EE web components are normally packaged into a JAR file with the extension `.war`. As these should be familiar to you as a web programmer, we will not cover them here.

EJB Component Format

J2EE EJB components are normally packaged into a JAR file. The section below shows the contents of a typical JAR file:

```
/META-INF/
          Manifest.mf
          ejb-jar.xml
/EmployeeHome.class
/Employee.class
/EmployeeBean.class
/EmployeeKey.class
/EmployeeException.class
```

The `META-INF\` directory contains the standard EJB deployment descriptor as well as an optional manifest file. This may also contain container specific descriptors, especially for CMP entity beans. You normally store the home interface, remote interface, bean class and other dependent classes like primary key class and custom exceptions in the root directory of the JAR file.

J2EE Applications

J2EE applications are composed of web components, EJB components, application components, and an application specific deployment descriptor called `application.xml`. These files are packaged into a JAR file with the extension `.ear` (Enterprise ARchive). The diagram below depicts the structure of an EAR file:

```
/META-INF/
          Manifest.mf
          application.xml
/employee.war
/employeeBean.jar
```

The `META-INF\` directory contains the standard J2EE application deployment descriptor as well as an optional manifest file. All the J2EE components that comprise the application are stored outside this directory.

Resolving Dependencies

When you package multiple J2EE components into a single J2EE application, you may have to resolve dependencies within the components. For example, a servlet in a web component may want to access an EJB in the EJB component. For this the client view of the EJB should be exposed to the servlet. In this section, we will discover how these dependencies are resolved.

The J2EE extension mechanism architecture lets classes from one JAR file in a J2EE application refer to classes in a different JAR file in the same application. This means that a servlet in a web component can refer to an EJB in the same application without having the client view in the `WEB-INF\classes\` or `WEB-INF\lib\` directories of the web component. This is achieved by adding a `class-path` header in the manifest file of the web component. The space separated list of referenced jar file URIs relative to the parent J2EE application are defined against this header.

Consider a WAR component named `employee.war` and an EJB component called `employeeBean.jar` stored in the root directory of the J2EE application. If you have the following entry in the `/META-INF/Manifest.mf` file of the WAR component, you can access the EJB home and remote interfaces without storing the EJB client view in the classpath of the WAR component:

```
class-path: employeeBean.jar
```

Application Deployment Descriptor

The J2EE application deployment descriptor lets us define the components that make up the application as well as security roles for the application. The components that can be included in a J2EE application are:

- Web components
- EJB components
- Application components
- Resource adapter connectors

The diagram below depicts the hierarchical structure of the deployment descriptor:

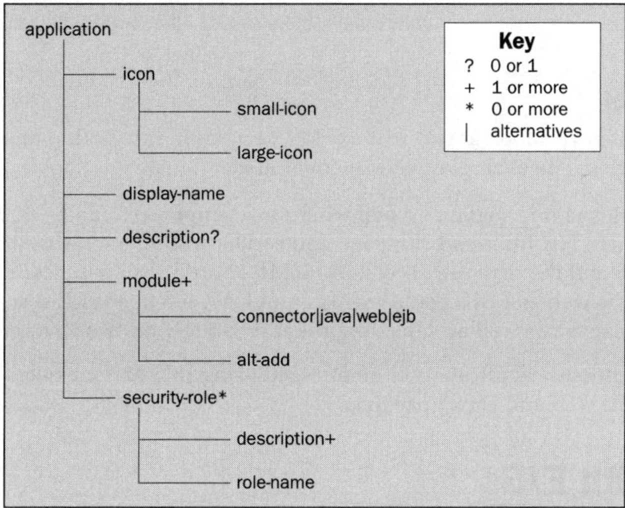

The various components that comprise the application are encapsulated in the `<module>` elements. The components we are more interested in are EJB and web components. The excerpt below shows an example web component declaration in a J2EE application deployment descriptor:

```
<module>
  <web>
    <web-uri>employee.war</web-uri>
    <context-root>/employee</context-root>
  </web>
</module>
```

The web component defines the relative URI of the WAR file in the EAR file and the context path for the web application. The excerpt below shows an EJB component definition:

```
<module>
  <ejb>employeeBean.jar</ejb>
</module>
```

The EJB component defines the relative URI of the JAR file in the EAR file. The deployment descriptor should be called `application.xml` and should be stored in the `META-INF\` directory of the EAR file. The listing below shows a complete deployment descriptor:

```
<?xml version="1.0" encoding="ISO-8859-1" ?>
<application>
  <display-name>Employee App</display-name>
  <module>
    <web>
      <web-uri>employee.war</web-uri>
      <context-root>/employee</context-root>
    </web>
  </module>
  <module>
    <ejb>employeeBean.jar</ejb>
  </module>
</application>
```

Case Studies

In this section we will have a look at two real world examples in integrating the J2EE web tier with the other J2EE technologies. The examples we will cover are:

- A small employee information system where new employees can be added through a browser based interface. The front-end JSP page and servlet will interact with the enterprise tier using a session EJB and the session EJB will use CMP entity EJBs for accessing the database. We will deploy the web and EJB components as an EAR file in a J2EE server having both web and EJB containers as well as deploying them separately on two different containers.
- The aforementioned application re-engineered using JMS and message driven beans for integrating the web and enterprise tiers.

Integrating with EJBs

In this section, we will develop an example to illustrate the integration of J2EE web and EJB tiers.

Application Architecture

The application provides a simple browser based interface for entering new employees by providing the employee id, employee name, and department id. When the form is submitted the application performs the following tasks:

- Checks whether the employee id entered is not an empty string
- Checks whether the entered employee id doesn't already exist in the employee table
- Checks whether the employee name entered is not an empty string

- Checks whether the department id entered is not an empty string
- Checks whether the department id exists in the department table
- Creates a record in the employee table

We have built similar applications in this book that accept data from the browser and manipulate database tables. However, in those examples we were writing our own data access code using JDBC and managing transactions programmatically using the connection objects. In this example we will use EJB components to delegate these tasks to the EJB container.

We will use the popular **Session Façade pattern** for implementing the EJB solution. This pattern provides a simple interface to a group of related interfaces that may be invoked individually. In our case, we will use a stateless session bean method to start a transaction. This method will use different entity bean instances for accessing the database.

The method calls on the entity beans are enlisted in the transaction stated by the container when the method on the session bean is invoked. Here we don't write any logic for transaction and persistence management and use EJB components for relying on the container for all these services.

To partition the application properly into web, business, and database tiers, we will use a servlet for request processing, a session bean for performing the business rules, and entity beans for data access. This is illustrated in the following diagram:

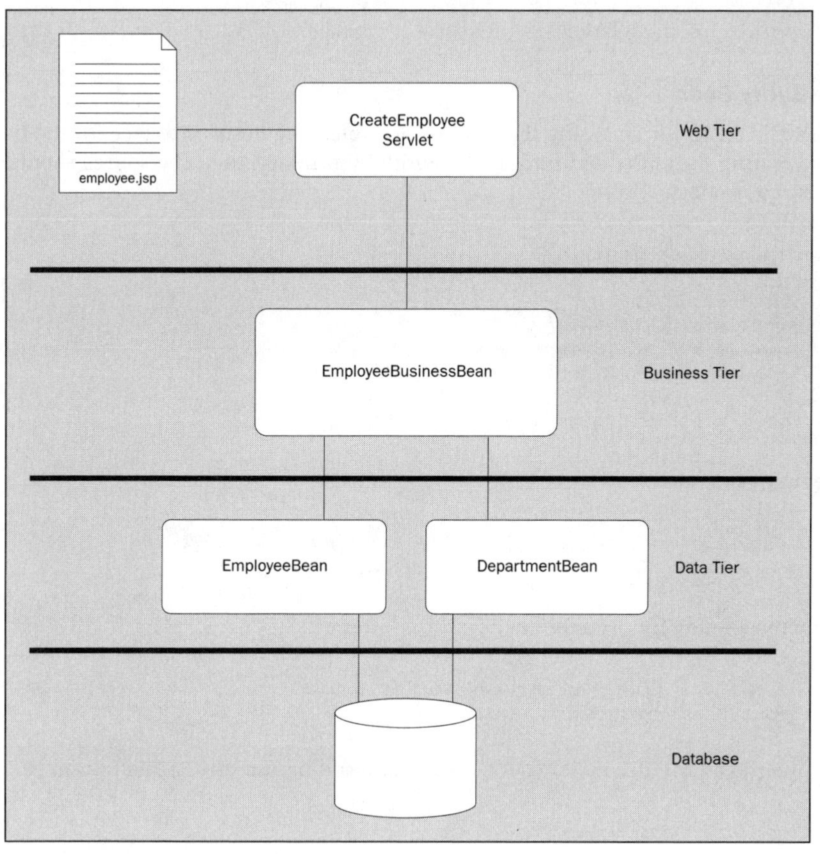

We will develop the application and first deploy it as an EAR file in a J2EE server that provides both the web and EJB containers. For this we will use the JBoss application server.

Database

As with the rest of the book we will use MySQL for storing the relational data. We will create a database called `employees` and two tables in the database called `employee` and `department`. The create script for the `employee` table is shown below. We will also create some reference data into the `department` table:

```
CREATE DATABASE employees;

USE employees;

CREATE TABLE employee (
    emp_id VARCHAR(30) PRIMARY KEY,
    emp_name VARCHAR(30) NOT NULL,
    dep_id VARCHAR(30)
);

CREATE TABLE department (
    dep_id VARCHAR(30) PRIMARY KEY,
    dep_name VARCHAR(30) NOT NULL
);

INSERT INTO department VALUES ("DEP001", "Production");
INSERT INTO department VALUES ("DEP002", "Sales");
```

The Employee Entity Bean

We will use a CMP EJB for accessing the `employee` table. The home interface for the bean provides methods for creating the entity and finding the entity by primary key. The source should be stored in a file called `EmployeeHome.java`:

```
package com.wrox.employee.ejb;

import javax.ejb.EJBHome;
import javax.ejb.CreateException;
import javax.ejb.FinderException;
import java.rmi.RemoteException;

public interface EmployeeHome extends EJBHome {
```

Create an employee entity:

```
  public Employee create(String empId, String empName, String depId)
      throws CreateException, RemoteException;
```

Find the employee entity by primary key:

```
  public Employee findByPrimaryKey(String empId)
      throws FinderException, RemoteException;
}
```

The remote interface provides methods for getting and setting the `employee` attributes:

```
package com.wrox.employee.ejb;
```

```
import javax.ejb.EJBObject;
import java.rmi.RemoteException;

public interface Employee extends EJBObject {
```

Get and set the employee id:

```
  public String getEmpId() throws RemoteException;
  public void setEmpId(String empId) throws RemoteException;
```

Get and set the employee name:

```
  public String getEmpName() throws RemoteException;
  public void setEmpName(String empName) throws RemoteException;
```

Get and set the department id:

```
  public String getDepId() throws RemoteException;
  public void setDepId(String depId) throws RemoteException;
}
```

The EJB class implements the business methods and the entity bean callback methods:

```
package com.wrox.employee.ejb;

import javax.ejb.EntityBean;
import javax.ejb.EntityContext;
import java.rmi.RemoteException;

public class EmployeeBean implements EntityBean {

  private EntityContext ctx;
```

Define the container managed fields:

```
  public String empId;
  public String empName;
  public String depId;
```

This method is called by the container just before the bean is created:

```
  public String ejbCreate(String empId, String empName, String depId) {
    this.empId = empId;
    this.empName = empName;
    this.depId = depId;

    return null;
  }

  public void ejbPostCreate(String empId, String empName, String depId) {}
```

Implement the business methods:

```
    public String getEmpId() {
      return empId;
    }

    public void setEmpId(String empId) {
      this.empId = empId;
    }

    public String getEmpName() {
      return empName;
    }

    public void setEmpName(String empName) {
      this.empName = empName;
    }

    public String getDepId() {
      return depId;
    }

    public void setDepId(String depId) {
      this.depId = depId;
    }
```

Implement the entity bean callback methods:

```
    public void setEntityContext(EntityContext ctx) {
      this.ctx = ctx;
    }

    public void unsetEntityContext() {
      this.ctx = null;
    }

    public void ejbActivate() {}
    public void ejbPassivate() {}
    public void ejbLoad() {}
    public void ejbStore() {}
    public void ejbRemove() {}
  }
```

Department Entity Bean

We will use a CMP EJB for accessing the `department` table. The home interface for the bean provides methods for creating the entity and finding the entity by primary key. The source should be stored in a file called `DepartmentHome.java`.

```
package com.wrox.employee.ejb;

import javax.ejb.EJBHome;
import javax.ejb.CreateException;
import javax.ejb.FinderException;
import java.rmi.RemoteException;

public interface DepartmentHome extends EJBHome {
```

Create a department entity:

```
    public Department create(String depId, String depName)
        throws CreateException, RemoteException;
```

Find the department entity by primary key:

```
    public Department findByPrimaryKey(String depId)
        throws FinderException, RemoteException;
}
```

The remote interface provides methods for getting and setting the `department` attributes. The source should be stored in a file called `Department.java`:

```
package com.wrox.employee.ejb;

import javax.ejb.EJBObject;
import java.rmi.RemoteException;

public interface Department extends EJBObject {
```

Get and set the department id:

```
    public String getDepId() throws RemoteException;
    public void setDepId(String depId) throws RemoteException;
```

Get and set the department name:

```
    public String getDepName() throws RemoteException;
    public void setDepName(String depName) throws RemoteException;
}
```

The EJB class implements the business methods and the entity bean callback methods. The source should be stored in a file called `DepartmentBean.java`.

```
package com.wrox.employee.ejb;

import javax.ejb.EntityBean;
import javax.ejb.EntityContext;
import java.rmi.RemoteException;

public class DepartmentBean implements EntityBean {

    private EntityContext ctx;
```

Define the container managed fields:

```
    public String depId;
    public String depName;
```

This method is called by the container just before the bean is created:

```
public String ejbCreate(String depId, String depName) {
  this. depId = depId;
  this. depName = depName;

  return null;
}

public void ejbPostCreate(String depId, String depName) {}
```

Implement the business methods:

```
public String getDepId() {
  return depId;
}

public void setDepId(String depId) {
  this.depId = depId;
}

public String getDepName() {
  return depName;
}

public void setDepName(String depName) {
  this.depName = depName;
}
```

Implement the entity bean callback methods:

```
  public void setEntityContext(EntityContext ctx) {
    this.ctx = ctx;
  }

  public void unsetEntityContext() {
    this.ctx = null;
  }

  public void ejbActivate() { }
  public void ejbPassivate() { }
  public void ejbLoad() { }
  public void ejbStore() { }
  public void ejbRemove() { }
}
```

Employee Business Bean

We will use a stateless session bean to implement the business logic for creating the employee record. This bean will provide a method for creating the employee. This bean will use the entity beans explained in the last section for validating and creating the entities. The home interface provides the method to create the remote object:

```
package com.wrox.employee.ejb;

import javax.ejb.EJBHome;
import javax.ejb.CreateException;
import javax.ejb.FinderException;
import java.rmi.RemoteException;

public interface EmployeeBusinessHome extends EJBHome {

  public EmployeeBusiness create() throws CreateException, RemoteException;

}
```

The remote interface defines a business method:

```
package com.wrox.employee.ejb;

import javax.ejb.EJBObject;
import java.rmi.RemoteException;

public interface EmployeeBusiness extends EJBObject {

  public void createEmployee(String empId, String empName, String depId)
      throws RemoteException, EmployeeException;

}
```

The bean class implements the business method and session callback methods:

```
package com.wrox.employee.ejb;

import javax.ejb.SessionBean;
import javax.ejb.SessionContext;
import javax.ejb.DuplicateKeyException;
import javax.ejb.ObjectNotFoundException;
import javax.ejb.EJBException;

import javax.naming.InitialContext;
import javax.rmi.PortableRemoteObject;
import java.rmi.RemoteException;

public class EmployeeBusinessBean implements SessionBean {

  private SessionContext ctx;

  public void ejbCreate() {}

  public void ejbPostCreate() {}
```

Implement the business method:

```
  public void createEmployee(String empId, String empName, String depId)
      throws EmployeeException {

    try {
```

Throw an exception if the entered employee id is not valid:

```
        if(empId == null || empId.equals("")) {
          throw new EmployeeException("Employee id can't be null");
        }
```

Throw an exception if the entered employee name is not valid:

```
        if(empName == null || empName.equals("")) {
          throw new EmployeeException("Employee name can't be null");
        }
```

Throw an exception if the entered department id is not valid:

```
        if(depId == null || depId.equals("")) {
          throw new EmployeeException("Department id can't be null");
        }
```

Create a JNDI initial context:

```
        InitialContext jndiContext = new InitialContext();
```

Look up the employee entity bean:

```
        Object empRef  = jndiContext.lookup("EmployeeBean");
        EmployeeHome empHome =
                    (EmployeeHome)PortableRemoteObject.narrow(empRef,
                                                    EmployeeHome.class);
```

Look up the department entity bean:

```
        Object depRef  = jndiContext.lookup("DepartmentBean");
        DepartmentHome depHome =
          (DepartmentHome)PortableRemoteObject.narrow(depRef,
                                                 DepartmentHome.class);
```

Check whether the specified department id is available in the database:

```
        depHome.findByPrimaryKey(depId);
```

Create the employee entity:

```
        empHome.create(empId, empName, depId);
      } catch(Exception ex) {
```

If an exception is thrown roll back the transaction:

```
          ctx.setRollbackOnly();
```

Throw back business exceptions as instances of EmployeeException:

```
        if(ex instanceof DuplicateKeyException) {
          throw new EmployeeException("Employee id already exists.");
        }
        if(ex instanceof ObjectNotFoundException) {
          throw new EmployeeException("Department id not found.");
        }
        if(ex instanceof EmployeeException) {
          throw (EmployeeException)ex;
        }
```

Throw unexpected exceptions as runtime exception:

```
        throw new EJBException(ex.getMessage());
      }
    }
```

Implement the session call back methods:

```
    public void setSessionContext(SessionContext ctx) {
      this.ctx = ctx;
    }

    public void unsetSessionContext() {
      ctx = null;
    }

    public void ejbActivate() {}
    public void ejbPassivate() {}
    public void ejbRemove() {}
  }
```

The business bean throws an EmployeeException when a business rule is violated. This exception is a part of the session beans client view:

```
  package com.wrox.employee.ejb;

  public class EmployeeException extends Exception {

    public EmployeeException(String msg) {
      super(msg);
    }
  }
```

Deployment Descriptors

The EJBs need to have the standard deployment descriptor. Additionally, we need to have a server specific deployment descriptor for container managed persistence. This is for mapping the entity bean instance fields to the database table columns. The standard deployment descriptor should be called ejb-jar.xml:

```
  <?xml version="1.0"?>

  <ejb-jar>
    <display-name>Employee Info System</display-name>
    <enterprise-beans>
```

Define the container managed fields, primary key field, primary key class, home interface, remote interface and bean class for the employee entity bean:

```
<entity>
  <description>Employee entity</description>
  <ejb-name>EmployeeBean</ejb-name>
  <home>com.wrox.employee.ejb.EmployeeHome</home>
  <remote>com.wrox.employee.ejb.Employee</remote>
  <ejb-class>com.wrox.employee.ejb.EmployeeBean</ejb-class>
  <persistence-type>Container</persistence-type>
  <prim-key-class>java.lang.String</prim-key-class>
  <reentrant>False</reentrant>
  <cmp-field><field-name>empId</field-name></cmp-field>
  <cmp-field><field-name>empName</field-name></cmp-field>
  <cmp-field><field-name>depId</field-name></cmp-field>
  <primkey-field>empId</primkey-field>
</entity>
```

Define the container managed fields, primary key field, primary key class, home interface, remote interface, and bean class for the department entity bean:

```
<entity>
  <description>Department entity</description>
  <ejb-name>DepartmentBean</ejb-name>
  <home>com.wrox.employee.ejb.DepartmentHome</home>
  <remote>com.wrox.employee.ejb.Department</remote>
  <ejb-class>com.wrox.employee.ejb.DepartmentBean</ejb-class>
  <persistence-type>Container</persistence-type>
  <prim-key-class>java.lang.String</prim-key-class>
  <reentrant>False</reentrant>
  <cmp-field><field-name>depId</field-name></cmp-field>
  <cmp-field><field-name>depName</field-name></cmp-field>
  <primkey-field>depId</primkey-field>
</entity>
```

Define the home interface, remote interface and bean class for the employee session bean:

```
  <session>
    <description>Employee Business</description>
    <ejb-name>EmployeeBusinessBean</ejb-name>
    <home>com.wrox.employee.ejb.EmployeeBusinessHome</home>
    <remote>com.wrox.employee.ejb.EmployeeBusiness</remote>
    <ejb-class>com.wrox.employee.ejb.EmployeeBusinessBean</ejb-class>
    <session-type>Stateless</session-type>
    <transaction-type>Container</transaction-type>
  </session>
</enterprise-beans>
```

Define the transaction demarcation attributes for the bean methods:

```
<assembly-descriptor>
  <container-transaction>
    <method>
      <ejb-name>EmployeeBean</ejb-name>
      <method-name>*</method-name>
    </method>
```

```
      <method>
        <ejb-name>DepartmentBean</ejb-name>
        <method-name>*</method-name>
      </method>
      <method>
        <ejb-name>EmployeeBusinessBean</ejb-name>
        <method-name>*</method-name>
      </method>
      <trans-attribute>Required</trans-attribute>
    </container-transaction>
  </assembly-descriptor>
</ejb-jar>
```

The JBoss specific deployment descriptor maps the bean instance variables to the database columns. This file should be called `jaws.xml`:

```
<jaws>
```

Define the data source to use. This datasource should be defined in the JBoss configuration file `jboss.jcml` (see below for the entry):

```
  <datasource>EmployeeDS</datasource>
  <type-mapping>mySQL</type-mapping>

  <enterprise-beans>
```

Define the column mappings for the employee entity:

```
    <entity>
      <ejb-name>EmployeeBean</ejb-name>
      <table-name>employee</table-name>
      <cmp-field>
        <field-name>empId</field-name>
        <column-name>emp_id</column-name>
      </cmp-field>
      <cmp-field>
        <field-name>empName</field-name>
        <column-name>emp_name</column-name>
      </cmp-field>
      <cmp-field>
        <field-name>depId</field-name>
        <column-name>dep_id</column-name>
      </cmp-field>
    </entity>
```

Define the column mappings for the department entity:

```
    <entity>
      <ejb-name>DepartmentBean</ejb-name>
      <table-name>department</table-name>
      <cmp-field>
        <field-name>depId</field-name>
        <column-name>dep_id</column-name>
      </cmp-field>
      <cmp-field>
```

```
            <field-name>depName</field-name>
            <column-name>dep_name</column-name>
          </cmp-field>
        </entity>
      </enterprise-beans>
    </jaws>
```

The excerpt below is from the JBoss configuration file for defining the datasource:

```
      <mbean code="org.jboss.jdbc.XADataSourceLoader"
        name="DefaultDomain:service=XADataSource,name=EmployeeDS">
        <attribute name="PoolName">EmployeeDS</attribute>
        <attribute name="DataSourceClass">
          org.jboss.pool.jdbc.xa.wrapper.XADataSourceImpl</attribute>
        <attribute name="Properties"></attribute>
        <attribute name="URL">jdbc:mysql://localhost/employees</attribute>
      </mbean>
```

The Employee JSP Page

This JSP defines the form for entering the employee details:

```
    <%@page contentType="text/html"%>
    <html>
      <head><title>JSP Page</title></head>
      <body>
```

Define a bean to display the error message if any. Error messages are stored as request scope beans by the request processing servlet:

```
        <jsp:useBean id="error" class="java.lang.String" scope="request"/>
        <%= error %>
```

Define the form to enter the employee details:

```
        <form action="CreateEmployee" method="post">
          <b>ID:</b><input type="text" name="empId" size="30"/>
          <br/>
          <b>Name:</b><input type="text" name="empName" size="30"/>
          <br/>
          <b>Department:</b><input type="text" name="depId" size="30"/>
          <br/>
          <input type="submit" value="Create Employee" size="30"/>
          <br/>
        </form>
      </body>
    </html>
```

The CreateEmployee Servlet

When the form defined in `employee.jsp` is submitted, the request is sent to a servlet that looks up the employee business bean and delegates the task of validating and creating the employee entity. The source for the servlet should be stored in a file called `CreateEmployee.java`:

```
package com.wrox.employee.web;

import javax.servlet.RequestDispatcher;
import javax.servlet.ServletConfig;
import javax.servlet.ServletException;

import javax.servlet.http.HttpServlet;
import javax.servlet.http.HttpServletRequest;
import javax.servlet.http.HttpServletResponse;

import java.io.IOException;
import java.io.PrintWriter;

import com.wrox.employee.ejb.EmployeeBusinessHome;
import com.wrox.employee.ejb.EmployeeBusiness;
import com.wrox.employee.ejb.EmployeeException;

import javax.rmi.PortableRemoteObject;
import javax.naming.InitialContext;
import java.util.Properties;

public class CreateEmployee extends HttpServlet {

  public void init(ServletConfig config) throws ServletException {
    super.init(config);
  }

  public void doPost(HttpServletRequest request,
                     HttpServletResponse response)
                     throws ServletException, IOException {

    try {
```

Gather the request parameters:

```
      String empId = request.getParameter("empId");
      String empName = request.getParameter("empName");
      String depId = request.getParameter("depId");
```

Create the initial context:

```
      InitialContext jndiContext = new InitialContext();
```

Look up the employee business home objects:

```
      Object empRef  = jndiContext.lookup("java:comp/env/employee");
      EmployeeBusinessHome empHome =
               (EmployeeBusinessHome)PortableRemoteObject.narrow(empRef,
                                                    EmployeeBusinessHome.class);
```

Create the remote object:

```
      EmployeeBusiness emp = empHome.create();
```

Create the employee:

```
        emp.createEmployee(empId, empName, depId);
```

Print a message if the employee is created successfully:

```
        PrintWriter writer = response.getWriter();
        writer.println("Employee successfully created.");

      } catch(Exception ex) {
```

If a business exception is thrown, store the error message as a request scope bean and forward the response back to the JSP page:

```
          if(ex instanceof EmployeeException) {
            request.setAttribute("error", ex.getMessage());
            RequestDispatcher rd =
                  getServletContext().getRequestDispatcher("/employee.jsp");
            rd.forward(request, response);
          }
          throw new ServletException(ex);
      }
    }
  }
```

Web Deployment Descriptor

The listing below shows the deployment descriptor for the web component:

```
<?xml version="1.0" encoding="ISO-8859-1"?>

<!DOCTYPE web-app
    PUBLIC "-//Sun Microsystems, Inc.//DTD Web Application 2.2//EN"
    "http://java.sun.com/dtd/web-app_2_2.dtd">

<web-app>
```

Declare the servlet for creating the employees:

```
  <servlet>
    <servlet-name>
      CreateEmployee
    </servlet-name>
    <servlet-class>
      com.wrox.employee.web.CreateEmployee
    </servlet-class>
  </servlet>
```

Define the servlet mapping for the above servlet:

```
  <servlet-mapping>
    <servlet-name>
      CreateEmployee
    </servlet-name>
```

```
    <url-pattern>
      /CreateEmployee
    </url-pattern>
  </servlet-mapping>
```

Define the EJB reference to the employee business bean:

```
  <ejb-ref>
    <ejb-ref-name>employee</ejb-ref-name>
    <ejb-ref-type>session</ejb-ref-type>
    <home>com.wrox.employee.ejb.EmployeeBusinessHome</home>
    <remote>com.wrox.employee.ejb.EmployeeBusiness</remote>
    <ejb-link>EmployeeBusinessBean</ejb-link>
  </ejb-ref>
</web-app>
```

Deploying as a J2EE EAR File

The steps involved in creating the EAR component are as follows:

- Create the EJB JAR component
- Create the web WAR component
- Resolve dependencies
- Create the EAR file

EJB component

We need will to package all the three EJBs into a single JAR file. You'll need to compile the classes we wrote earlier. To compile these classes you'll need to include the `j2ee.jar` archive that ships with the J2EE SDK. Then, create a JAR named `employeeBean.jar` that contains the following directories and files:

```
/com/wrox/employee/ejb/
                       EmployeeHome.class
                       Employee.class
                       EmployeeBean.class
                       DepartmentHome.class
                       Department.class
                       DepartmentBean.class
                       EmployeeBusinessHome.class
                       EmployeeBusiness.class
                       EmployeeBusinessBean.class
                       EmployeeException.class
/META-INF/
          ejb-jar.xml
          jaws.xml
```

Web Component

To avoid having the client view of the employee business bean, we will use the `Class-path` header in the manifest file of the WAR component. The manifest file should be called `Manifest.mf` and the content of this file is shown below:

```
Class-path: employeeBean.jar
```

The contents of the WAR file `employee.war` are:

```
/employee.jsp
/WEB-INF/
         web.xml
         classes/com/wrox/employee/web/
                                       CreateEmployee.class
/META-INF/
          Manifest.mf
```

You can use the following command to force the JAR utility not to create a new manifest file:

```
jar -cfM employee.war *
```

Creating the EAR File

The EAR file should contain the WAR and JAR components as well as the application deployment descriptor `application.xml` that is shown below:

```
<?xml version="1.0" encoding="ISO-8859-1" ?>
<application>
  <display-name>Employee App</display-name>
```

Define the web component and its context path:

```
  <module>
    <web>
      <web-uri>employee.war</web-uri>
      <context-root>/employee</context-root>
    </web>
  </module>
```

Define the EJB component:

```
  <module>
    <ejb>employeeBean.jar</ejb>
  </module>
</application>
```

The contents of the `employeeApp.ear` file are:

```
/employee.war
/employeeBean.jar
/META-INF/
          application.xml
```

Deploying the Application

First we will deploy the application in a J2EE server that provides both the web and EJB containers. For this we will use JBoss with embedded Tomcat service. This can be downloaded from http://www.jboss.org/. Perform the following steps for installing JBoss and enabling the Tomcat embedded service:

- Explode the downloaded archive to a local directory (we will call it `JBOSS_HOME`).
- This directory will contain two directories called `jboss\` and `tomcat\`, containing the files required for JBoss and Tomcat respectively.
- Add the following entry to the `<JBOSS_HOME>\jboss\conf\default\jboss.conf` file to add the Tomcat classes to the classpath:

```
<MLET CODE = "org.jboss.util.ClassPathExtension" ARCHIVE="jboss.jar"
        CODEBASE="../../lib/ext/">
    <ARG TYPE="java.lang.String" VALUE="../../../tomcat/lib/">
    <ARG TYPE="java.lang.String" VALUE="Tomcat">
</MLET>
```

- Add the following entry to the `<JBOSS_HOME>\JBoss\conf\default\jboss.jcml` file to include the Tomcat embedded service:

```
<mbean code="org.jboss.tomcat.EmbeddedTomcatServiceSX"
    name="DefaultDomain:service=EmbeddedTomcat" />
```

- Add the following J2EE deployer setting to the same file:

```
<mbean code="org.jboss.deployment.J2eeDeployer"
    name="J2EE:service=J2eeDeployer">
    <attribute name="DeployerName">Default</attribute>
    <attribute
        name="JarDeployerName">:service=ContainerFactory</attribute>
    <attribute name="WarDeployerName">:service=EmbeddedTomcat</attribute>
<mbean>
```

- Make the following changes to `<JBOSS_HOME>\tomcat\conf\server.xml` file.

  Set up the class loader hierarchy to enable VM call optimization.
  Add after the `org.apache.tomcat.context.WorkDirInterceptor` `ContextInterceptor`:

```
<ContextInterceptor
    className="org.jboss.tomcat.ContextClassLoaderInterceptor" />
```

  Add the `jboss-web.xml` parser after the `org.jboss.tomcat.ContextClassLoaderInterceptor` `ContextInterceptor`:

```
<ContextInterceptor
    className="org.jboss.tomcat.naming.JbossWebXmlReader" />
```

  Set the request thread classloader. Add before the `org.apache.tomcat.request.SessionInterceptor` `RequestInterceptor`:

```
<RequestInterceptor
    className="org.apache.tomcat.request.Jdk12Interceptor" />
```

  Map the current web user to the `SecurityAssociation` principal. Add after the `org.apache.tomcat.request.SimpleRealm` `RequestInterceptor`:

```
<RequestInterceptor className="org.jboss.tomcat.security.JbossRealm" />
```

- Make sure that JBoss has access to `tools.jar` (place it in `<JBOSS_HOME>\jboss\lib\ext\` if it doesn't). Start the MySQL database engine.
- Copy the EAR file to `<JBOSS_HOME>\jboss\deploy\` directory.
- Start JBoss by running `<JBOSS_HOME>\jboss\bin\run.bat` file.

Running the Application

Navigate to http://localhost:8080/employee/employee.jsp:

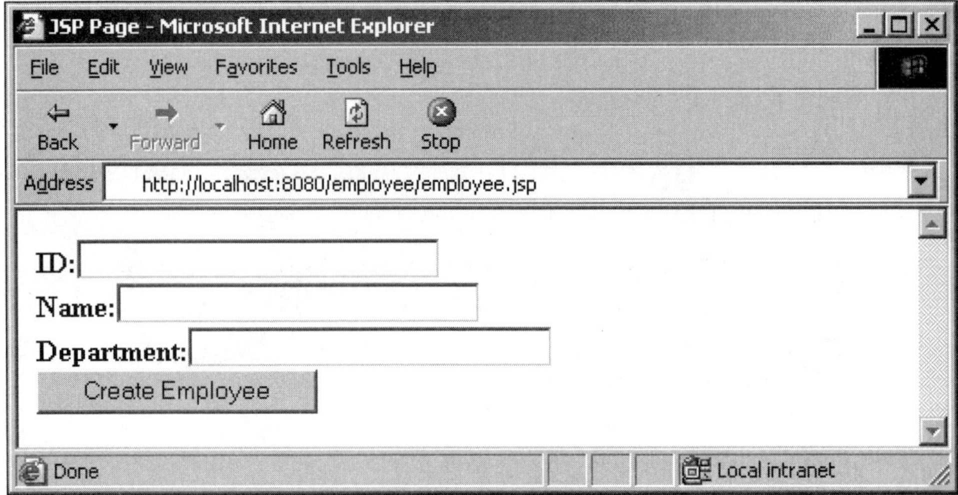

If you enter an invalid department id (DEP008 for example) and submit the form, you will be informed of the error and be presented with the form again.

Enter valid information and submit the form:

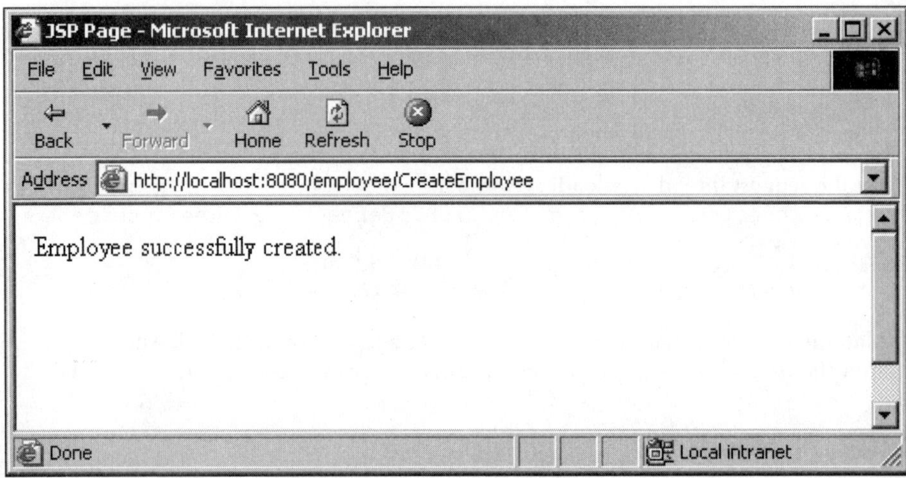

Deploying in Separate Containers

In some scenarios you may want to deploy your web and EJB components in containers running in different VMs, particularly when your EJB container is running on a different machine than the web container for performance and load balancing related issues. In such scenarios, you may need to make slight changes during deployment as explained in this section.

Now we will deploy the EJBs in a JBoss instance and the web component in an instance of Tomcat running in a different process space. The changes we need to make are listed below:

- The web component now should have the client view of the employee session bean available in the classpath. This includes `EmployeeBusinessHome`, `EmployeeBusiness`, and `EmployeeException`.
- The servlet now needs to specify the initial context factory and provider URL when the JNDI initial context.
- The JBoss specific JNDI provider classes now should be available in the classpath for the web component.
- The classes and interfaces from the `javax.ejb` package should now be available in the classpath for the web component.
- The servlet now should refer to the EJB home by the real JNDI name under which it is stored.

The excerpt below shows the amended `doPost()` method of the servlet reflecting the required changes:

```
String empId = request.getParameter("empId");
String empName = request.getParameter("empName");
String depId = request.getParameter("depId");
```

Specify the initial context factory and provider URL:

```
Properties prop = new Properties();
prop.put("java.naming.factory.initial",
                                "org.jnp.interfaces.NamingContextFactory");
prop.put("java.naming.provider.url", "localhost");

InitialContext jndiContext = new InitialContext(prop);
```

Look up the bean by the real JNDI name:

```
Object empRef  = jndiContext.lookup("EmployeeBusinessBean");
EmployeeBusinessHome empHome =
                   (EmployeeBusinessHome)PortableRemoteObject.narrow(
                                     empRef, EmployeeBusinessHome.class);
EmployeeBusiness emp = empHome.create();

emp.createEmployee(empId, empName, depId);

PrintWriter writer = response.getWriter();
writer.println("Employee successfully created.");
```

The diagram below shows the contents of the new web component file:

```
/employee.jsp
/WEB-INF/
        web.xml
        /classes/
                CreateEmployee
                EmployeeBusinessHome
                EmployeeBusiness
                EmployeeException
        /lib/
            ejb.jar
            jboss.jar
            jnpserver.jar
```

Note the following changes:

- The manifest header is no longer required
- The client view of the session bean is available in the classes directory
- EJB classes are made available in the lib directory
- The JBoss specific JNDI classes are made available in the lib directory

Web Tier Integration using JMS

With the advent of message driven beans in the EJB 2.0 specification, we have a more elegant way of integrating the web and enterprise tiers in a loosely coupled way. Message driven beans are components that are triggered by messages sent to JMS destinations. JMS can operate in both asynchronous and request-response modes.

Web components can gather the data entered by end users, create JMS messages, and send them to JMS destinations. Message driven beans listening on these destinations can accept these messages and perform further processing. This is very important for processing requests that take a long time to complete. In such cases the web components can send the message and the thread can return providing an information message to the user. The message driven bean accepts the information and performs the processing.

In our example, the servlet can gather the employee information and create a JMS message that contains this information. This message can be sent to a JMS destination that is monitored by a message driven bean. The message driven bean can extract the employee information from the incoming JMS message and call the required business method on the employee session bean. This is illustrated in the diagram shown below:

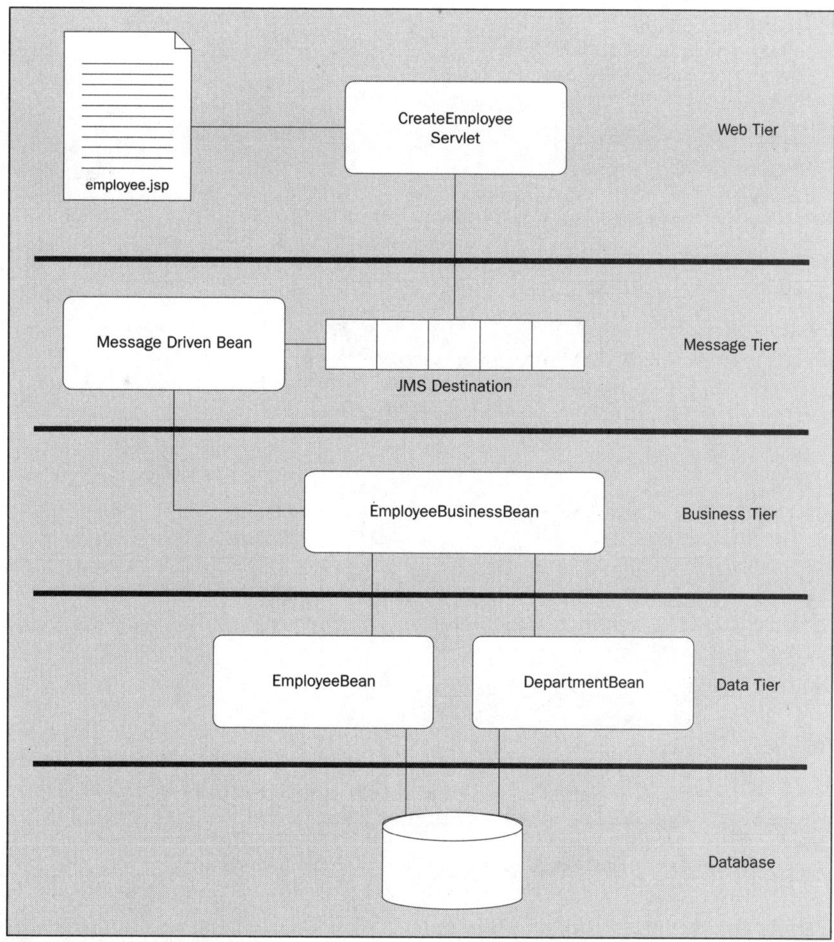

The CreateEmployee Class

Now we will modify our servlet for creating employees to send a JMS message to a destination instead of directly accessing the employee session bean:

```
package com.wrox.employee.web;

import javax.servlet.ServletConfig;
import javax.servlet.ServletException;

import javax.servlet.http.HttpServlet;
import javax.servlet.http.HttpServletRequest;
import javax.servlet.http.HttpServletResponse;

import java.io.IOException;
import java.io.PrintWriter;

import javax.jms.MapMessage;
import javax.jms.QueueConnectionFactory;
```

```
import javax.jms.Queue;
import javax.jms.QueueConnection;
import javax.jms.QueueSession;
import javax.jms.QueueSender;

import javax.naming.InitialContext;
import java.util.Properties;

  public class CreateEmployeeJMS extends HttpServlet {

    public void init(ServletConfig config) throws ServletException {
        super.init(config);
    }

    public void doPost(HttpServletRequest request,
                       HttpServletResponse response)
                       throws ServletException, IOException {

      try {
```

Get the employee details:

```
      String empId = request.getParameter("empId");
      String empName = request.getParameter("empName");
      String depId = request.getParameter("depId");
```

Create the initial context:

```
      Properties prop = new Properties();
      prop.put("java.naming.factory.initial",
               "org.jnp.interfaces.NamingContextFactory");
      prop.put("java.naming.provider.url", "localhost");

      InitialContext jndiContext = new InitialContext(prop);
```

Look up the topic connection factory and the topic:

```
      Queue queue  = (Queue)jndiContext.lookup("queue/empQueue");
      QueueConnectionFactory qcf =
                          (QueueConnectionFactory)jndiContext.lookup(
                                       "QueueConnectionFactory");
```

Create the topic connection, session and publisher:

```
      QueueConnection con = qcf.createQueueConnection();
      QueueSession sess =
               con.createQueueSession(true, QueueSession.AUTO_ACKNOWLEDGE);
      QueueSender sender = sess.createSender(queue);
```

Create a map message and store the employee details:

```
      MapMessage msg = sess.createMapMessage();
      msg.setString("empId", empId);
      msg.setString("empName", empName);
      msg.setString("depId", depId);
```

Start the connection, send the message and close the connection:

```
        con.start();
        pub.publish(msg);
        con.close();

        PrintWriter writer = response.getWriter();
        writer.println("Your request is being processed.");

      } catch(Exception ex) {
          throw new ServletException(ex);
      }
    }
  }
```

The EmployeeMDB Class

This message-driven bean monitors the `EmpTopic` JMS topic. When a message arrives, the employee details are extracted and the business method on the employee business bean is called. Message driven beans don't have a client view and hence don't have any home or remote interfaces. MDBs are required to implement the JMS interface `MessageListener` and the `MessageDrivenBean` interface:

```
package com.wrox.employee.mdb;

import javax.ejb.MessageDrivenBean;
import javax.ejb.MessageDrivenContext;
import javax.ejb.EJBException;

import javax.jms.MessageListener;
import javax.jms.Message;
import javax.jms.MapMessage;

import javax.naming.InitialContext;
import javax.rmi.PortableRemoteObject;

import ejb.EmployeeBusinessHome;
import ejb.EmployeeBusiness;

public class EmployeeMDB implements MessageDrivenBean, MessageListener {

  public void setMessageDrivenContext(MessageDrivenContext ctx) {}
  public void ejbCreate() {}
  public void ejbRemove() {}

  public void onMessage(Message message) {
    try {
      MapMessage msg = (MapMessage)message;
```

Get the employee information from the incoming message:

```
      String empId = msg.getString("empId");
      String empName = msg.getString("empName");
      String depId = msg.getString("depId");

      InitialContext jndiContext = new InitialContext();
```

Lookup the employee session home:

```
        Object empRef  = jndiContext.lookup("EmployeeBusinessBean");
        EmployeeBusinessHome empHome =
                    (EmployeeBusinessHome)PortableRemoteObject.narrow(
                                         empRef, EmployeeBusinessHome.class);
```

Create the employee session remote object:

```
        EmployeeBusiness emp = empHome.create();
```

Create the employee:

```
        emp.createEmployee(empId, empName, depId);
      } catch(Exception ex) {
        throw new EJBException(ex.getMessage());
      }
    }
  }
```

Deployment Descriptor

The deployment descriptor for the MDB is shown below. The descriptor defines the bean name, bean class, and the transaction demarcation attributes:

```
<?xml version="1.0"?>
<!DOCTYPE ejb-jar>
<ejb-jar>
  <enterprise-beans>
    <message-driven>
      <ejb-name>EmployeeMDB</ejb-name>
      <ejb-class>com.wrox.employee.mdb.EmployeeMDB</ejb-class>
      <message-selector></message-selector>
      <transaction-type>Container</transaction-type>
      <message-driven-destination>
        <destination-type>javax.jms.Queue</destination-type>
        <subscription-durability>Durable</subscription-durability>
      </message-driven-destination>
    </message-driven>
  </enterprise-beans>
  <assembly-descriptor>
    <container-transaction>
      <method>
        <ejb-name>EmployeeMDB</ejb-name>
        <method-name>*</method-name>
      </method>
      <trans-attribute>Required</trans-attribute>
    </container-transaction>
  </assembly-descriptor>
</ejb-jar>
```

Tying a message driven bean to the JNDI name of a JMS destination is performed in a container specific manner. In JBoss, this can be performed using the `jaws.xml` file as shown below:

```
<?xml version="1.0" encoding="Cp1252"?>
<jboss>
  <enterprise-beans>
    <message-driven>
```

This should refer to the EJB name specified in the standard deployment descriptor:

```
      <ejb-name>EmployeeMDB</ejb-name>
      <configuration-name>Standard Message Driven Bean</configuration-name>
```

JNDI name of the destination:

```
      <destination-jndi-name>queue/empQueue</destination-jndi-name>
    </message-driven>
  </enterprise-beans>
</jboss>
```

Deploying the Application

For deploying the application we can reuse most of the components in the last example. The MDB can go into the same EJB JAR component as the session and entity beans. You need to modify the ejb-jar.xml file to include the deployment description for the MDB explained in the last section. You should also modify the jaws.xml file to include the JMS destination specific entries for the MDB as explained in the last section.

The contents of the EJB JAR will now look as follows.

```
/ejb/
     EmployeeHome.class
     Employee.class
     EmployeeBean.class
     DepartmentHome.class
     Department.class
     DepartmentBean.class
     EmployeeBusinessHome.class
     EmployeeBusiness.class
     EmployeeBusinessBean.class
     EmployeeException.class
     EmployeeMDB.class
/META-INF/
          ejb-jar.xml
          jaws.xml
```

The contents of the WAR and EAR files remain the same. However, to include the modified version of the servlet that sends the JMS messages, add the following to `jboss.jcml`:

```
  <mbean code="org.jboss.mq.server.QueueManager"
         name="JBossMQ:service=Queue,name=empQueue"/>
```

Copy the EAR file to the deploy directory of JBoss. Start MySQL and then JBoss.

Running the Application

Navigate to http://localhost:8000/employee/employee.jsp:

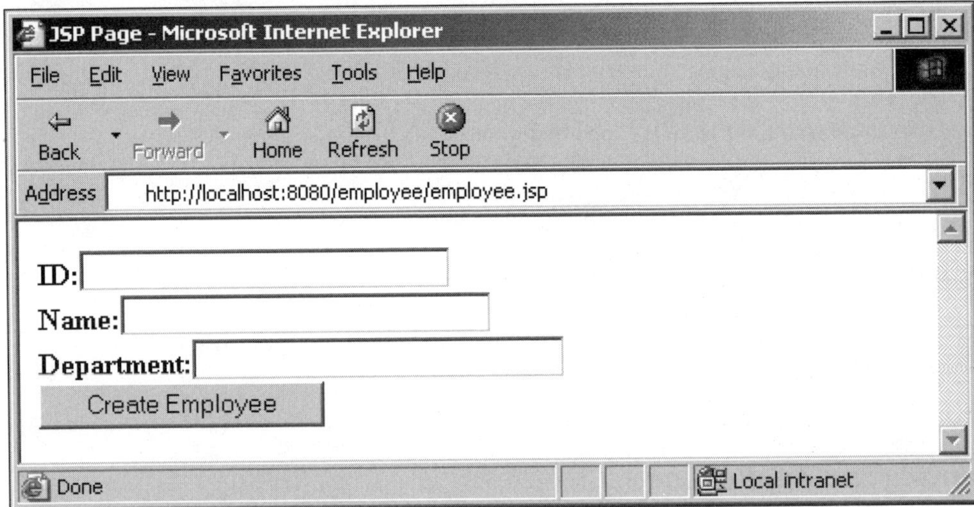

Enter valid information and submit the form:

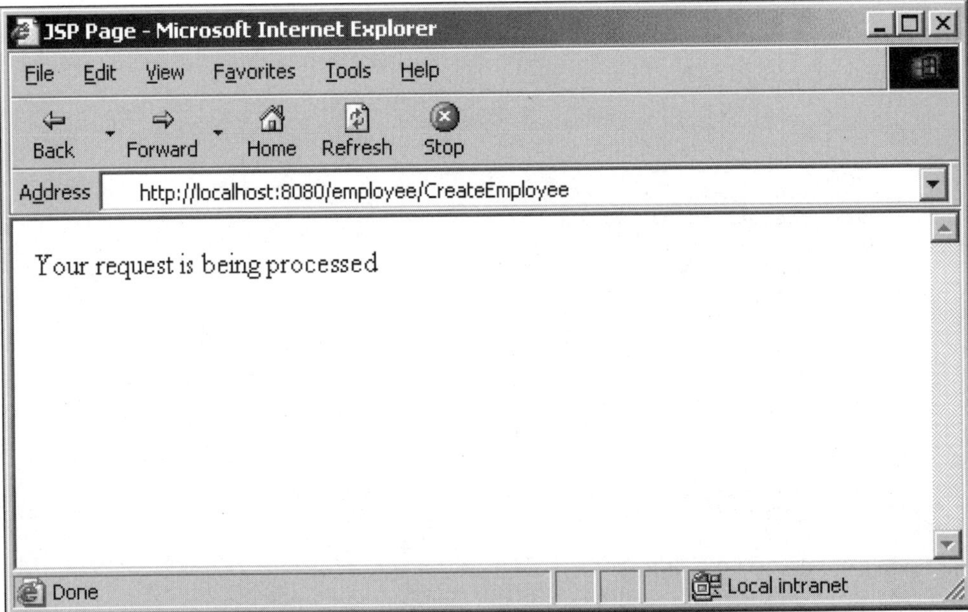

Summary

In this chapter we have covered:

- J2EE architecture
- An overview of various J2EE APIs
- An overview of the JNDI API
- Various techniques of integrating J2EE web tier with other J2EE technologies
- Deployment and assembly issues
- A real world application depicting integration, deployment, and assembly issues

The next chapter returns us to consideration of the user interface of our application, looking at security and user management in web applications.

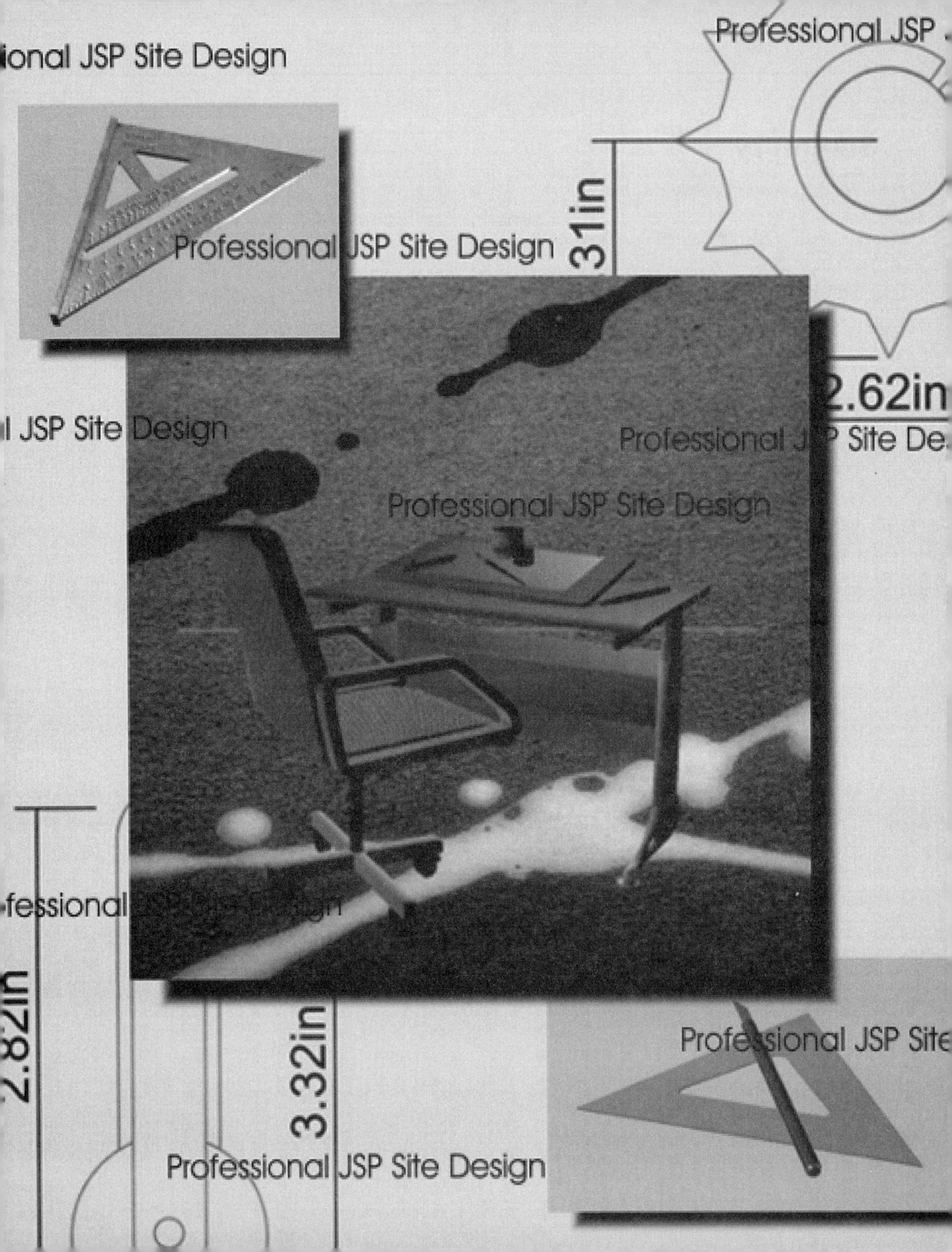
Professional JSP Site Design
31in
Professional JSP Site Design
Professional JSP Site Design
3.32in
Professional JSP Site Design

10

Security and User Management

No matter how innovative a web application is, or how wonderful the services are that it provides, if it's not secure all your good work can be undone. A web application can be left unsecured in many different ways; each will lead to a loss of user confidence in the service. After all, an unsecured e-commerce web application that leaves customers credit details or other personal information freely available is unlikely to win the confidence of its users.

There are two aspects of security to keep in mind when designing a web application:

- The security of the code we implement ourselves
- The security of the server the application will run on

The Servlet specification provides us with a range of tools to manage application and server security. However, the specification does not cover everything, and the areas that are left unsecured must be managed by the server that actually implements the specification.

In this chapter, we will examine what the Servlet specification has to say about security, and how it is implemented in Apache Tomcat 4.0. We'll look at the areas in which the level of security may be lacking, and what steps we should take to ensure that our server is secure. Then, we'll go on to look at the type of security we might have to implement for our web applications.

In particular, we will look at:

- The authentication support provided by the HTTP protocol
- The security provided by the web server
- How to implement the Secure Socket Layer and how to use Digital Certificates
- How to provide the necessary authentication using JAAS

Then, we will create our own login management system. Once a user has been identified in such a system, we might want to manage that user's interaction with the application over a time – without the user having to continually perform re-identification. We will look at how we can implement this functionality using a persistent login with our login management system. To begin with, we'll understand how we can use the security provided for in the Servlet specification.

Authentication Mechanisms

The first step in effectively securing an application against unauthorized use is to identify the user. Once this is done, we can programmatically decide what he can do or even tailor the content accordingly.

Authentication means establishing that a user is who he claims to be.

The most common approach is to ask the user for a password (although other options like certificate and biometrics are becoming increasingly common). However the user is authenticated the principle remains the same: the server asks the client for some data (which must be transmitted securely) that can be used to uniquely identify the client.

HTTP Authentication

The HTTP protocol provides some built-in authentication support. If a client attempts to access some restricted content, the following occurs:

- The client attempts to access one of the restricted pages
- The HTTP server replies that it needs special user authentication
- The client asks the user for a username and password (this information can often be saved for future use)
- The client attempts to access the page again, this time using the supplied username and password
- The client is allowed access to the page if the server accepts the name and password

If the resource that is restricted by the server is a servlet, then the server can retrieve the name of the user and the type of authorization from the servlet's `HttpServletRequest` object, using the following methods:

```
public String getRemoteuser()
public String getAuthType()
```

The server will determine whether the user is authorized to invoke the servlet, independent of the servlet calling the `getRemoteUser()` method. Still, knowing the name can come in handy for secondary authorization, session tracking, and personalization.

The Java Servlet Specification includes the following authentication mechanisms for web containers:

- HTTP basic authentication
- HTTP digest authentication
- HTTP client authentication
- Form based authentication

Basic Authentication

Basic authentication is a challenge/response security model.

> **The challenge/response security model is one in which the user is challenged by the server for identification for each protected resource it wants to access; the user then responds with appropriate identification.**

A protected resource can be, among other things, a directory, a servlet, or a JSP page. The web server maintains a database of usernames and passwords. The authentication process consists of the client sending a request and the server responding with a request of its own for a user name and password. The client subsequently requests access again, this time with a username and password. The server handles the actual validation of the username and password.

Basic authentication is a very weak form of authentication because the username and password are not encrypted but are only thinly disguised using Base64 encoding, which can easily be reversed.

Base64 encoding is defined in RFC 1521, more information about it can be found at http://www.rfc-editor.org/.

Anyone who intercepts the usernames and passwords on route from the client to the server has access to this sensitive information. This problem can be overcome by using an encrypted connection between the client and server, such as the **Secure Socket Layer (SSL)** protocol.

Digest Authentication

Like basic authentication, digest authentication is based on the challenge/response model. This was created because of basic authentication's shortcomings. The main difference is that, instead of transmitting a password over the network, a **digest** of the password is sent.

The digest is produced by taking a hash of the user name and password using the very secure MD5 encryption algorithm. Then, a data string called nonce (that is server specific) is uniquely generated each time a protected resource is requested.

The MD5 is a message digest algorithm as defined in RFC 1321.

The output of this algorithm is a 128-bit (16 byte) digest. The transactions are more secure because digests are valid for only a single URI request and nonce value. The problem is that digest authentication is not broadly supported in today's web clients and servers.

Custom Authentication

A servlet can be implemented to enforce any security policy that is not directly supported in the Servlet API. A servlet uses status codes and HTTP headers to manage its own security policy. If the user is not authorized to access a page, the server can deny access by sending SC_UNAUTHORIZED (HTTP status code 401) indicating that the request requires HTTP authentication, and a WWW-Authenticate header to tell the client about the authorization scheme and the authentication realm. The Authorization header contains the username and password encoded in Base64.

The following servlet demonstrates how custom authentication can be implemented:

```
package security;

import javax.servlet.*;
import javax.servlet.http.*;

public class CustomLogin extends HttpServlet {
  static final String USER_KEY = "CustomLogin.user";

  public void doGet(HttpServletRequest req, HttpServletResponse resp)
            throws ServletException, java.io.IOException {
    resp.setContentType("text/html");
    java.io.PrintWriter out = resp.getWriter();
    HttpSession session = req.getSession(true);

    String sessionUser = null;
    if (session != null) {
      sessionUser = (String) session.getAttribute (USER_KEY);
    }

    String user = null;
    if (sessionUser == null) {
      user = validUser(req);
    }

    if ((sessionUser == null) && (user == null)) {
      resp.setStatus(HttpServletResponse.SC_UNAUTHORIZED);
```

Set the authentication realm:

```
      resp.setHeader("WWW-Authenticate", "BASIC realm=\"users\"");

      out.println("<html>");
      out.println("<head>");
      out.println("<title>Invalid User</title>");
      out.println("</head>");
      out.println("<body>");
      out.println("Invalid User");
    } else {
      if ((sessionUser == null) && (session != null)) {
        session.setAttribute (USER_KEY, user);
        sessionUser = user;
      }
      out.println("<html>");
      out.println("<head>");
      out.println("<title>Welcome</title>");
      out.println("</head>");
      out.println("<body style=\"text-align:center\">");
      out.println("<center><h2>Welcome " + sessionUser +
                  "!</h2></center>");
    }
    out.println("</body>");
    out.println("</html>");
    out.flush();
  }

  protected String validUser(HttpServletRequest req) {
```

Get the authorization header:

```
    String encodedAuth = req.getHeader("Authorization");

    if (encodedAuth == null) {
      return null;
    }
    if (!encodedAuth.toUpperCase().startsWith("BASIC")) {
      return null;
    }
    String decoded = Decoder.base64(encodedAuth.substring(6));
    int idx = decoded.indexOf(":");
    if (idx < 0) {
      return null;
    }
    String user = decoded.substring(0, idx);
    String password = decoded.substring(idx + 1);
    if (!validateUser(user, password)) {
      user = null;
    }
    return user;
  }

  protected boolean validateUser(String user, String password) {
    boolean valid = false;
    if ((user != null) && (password != null)) {
```

A real-time check would likely use a database or LDAP server at this stage:

```
        if (user.equals("adarsh")) {
          valid = true;
        }
      }
      return valid;
    }

    public void init(ServletConfig cfg) throws ServletException {
      super.init(cfg);
    }

    public void destroy() {
      super.destroy();
    }
  }
```

Next, we create the class that decodes the encoded content:

```
package security;

public class Decoder {
  static final char[] b2c = {
    'A','B','C','D','E','F','G','H','I','J','K','L','M','N','O','P',
    'Q','R','S','T','U','V','W','X','Y','Z','a','b','c','d','e','f',
    'g','h','i','j','k','l','m','n','o','p','q','r','s','t','u','v',
    'w','x','y','z','0','1','2','3','4','5','6','7','8','9','+','/' };

  static final char pad = '=';
  static byte[] c2b = null;

  public static String base64(String s) {
    if (c2b==null) {
      c2b = new byte[256];
      for (byte b=0; b<64; b++) {
        c2b[(byte)b2c[b]]=b;
      }
    }

    byte[] nibble = new byte[4];
    char[] decode = new char[s.length()];
    int d=0;
    int n=0;
    byte b;

    for (int i=0; i<s.length(); i++) {
      char c = s.charAt(i);
      nibble[n] = c2b[(int)c];

      if (c==pad) {
        break;
      }
```

```
        switch(n) {
          case 0:
            n++;
            break;
          case 1:
            b=(byte)(nibble[0]*4 + nibble[1]/16);
            decode[d++]=(char)b;
            n++;
            break;
          case 2:
            b=(byte)((nibble[1]&0xf)*16 + nibble[2]/4);
            decode[d++]=(char)b;
            n++;
            break;
          default:
            b=(byte)((nibble[2]&0x3)*64 + nibble[3]);
            decode[d++]=(char)b;
            n=0;
            break;
        }
      }

      String decoded = new String(decode,0,d);
      return decoded;
    }
  }
```

When we navigate to http://localhost:8080/Security/Servlet/security.CustomLogin with Internet Explorer, we see this request for a username and password:

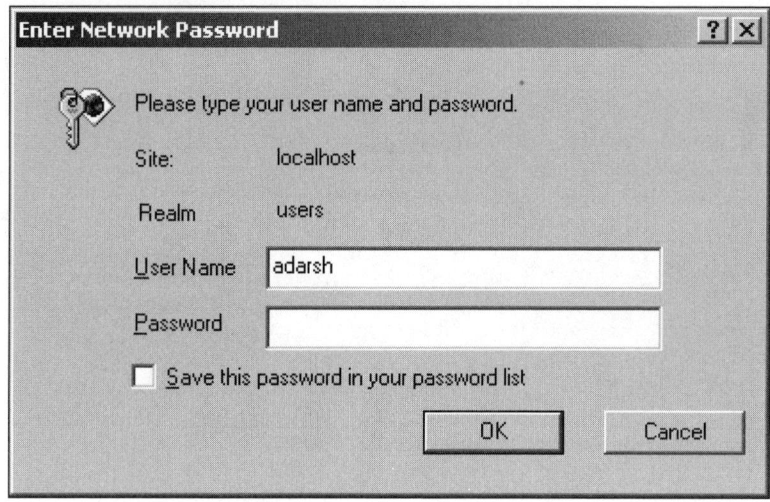

No password is required but if we enter adarsh for the username, we see the following welcome message:

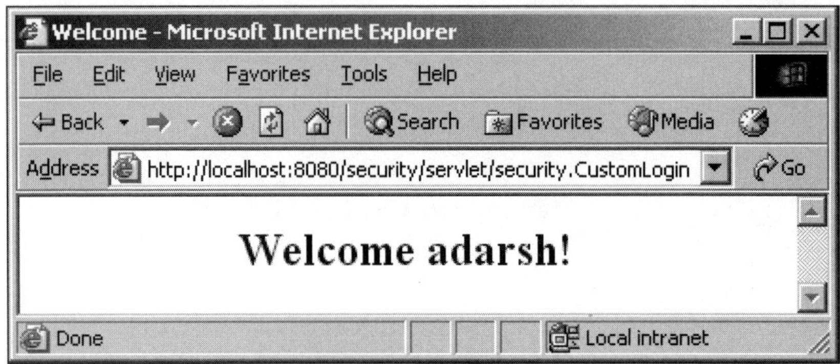

If we enter an incorrect username (in this case anything other than adarsh), we are presented with a further request for a username and password.

Form-based Authentication

Form-based authentication works just like basic and digest authentication, except that it lets you control the appearance of the login screen, which allows you to create more aesthetically pleasing login forms.

Implementing form-based authentication is relatively straightforward. First, a login page is generated like any other HTML form. The form accepts the user's name and password and submits the information to a servlet to validate the login:

```
package.login;

import javax.servlet.*;
import javax.servlet.http.*;

public class ServletLogin extends HttpServlet {
  public static String USER_KEY = "ServletLogin.user";
  public static String FIELD_USER = "username";
  public static String FIELD_PASSWORD = "password";

  public void doGet(HttpServletRequest req, HttpServletResponse resp)
              throws ServletException, java.io.IOException {
      resp.setContentType("text/html");
      java.io.PrintWriter out = resp.getWriter();
      String uri = req.getRequestURI();
```

We create a form to accept the user and password:

```
      HttpSession session = req.getSession(true);
      String user = (String) session.getValue (USER_KEY);

      if (user == null) {
        login(out, uri);
```

```
        return;
      }

      out.println("<html>");
      out.println("<head>");
      out.println("<title>Welcome</title>");
      out.println("</head>");
      out.println("<body>");
      out.println("<center><h2>Welcome!</h2>");
      out.println("</center>");
      out.println("</body>");
      out.println("</html>");
      out.flush();
    }

  public void doPost(HttpServletRequest req,
                     HttpServletResponse resp)
    throws ServletException, java.io.IOException
    {
      resp.setContentType("text/html");
      java.io.PrintWriter out = resp.getWriter();

      HttpSession session = req.getSession(true);
      String user = (String) session.getValue (USER_KEY);

      if (user == null) {
        String username = req.getParameter(FIELD_USER);
        String password = req.getParameter(FIELD_PASSWORD);

        if (!validUser(username, password)) {
          out.println("<html>");
          out.println("<title>Invalid User</title>");
          out.println("<body><center><h2>Invalid User!</h2>");
          out.flush();
          return;
        }
```

Store the username in the session:

```
        session.putValue (USER_KEY, username);
      }
```

The current user has been validated so redirect to our main site:

```
      resp.sendRedirect("http://" + req.getRequestURI());
    }

  protected void login(java.io.PrintWriter out, String uri)
                   throws java.io.IOException {
    out.println("<html>");
    out.println("<head>");
    out.println("<title>Login</title>");
```

```
    out.println("<center><h2>Welcome! Please login</h2>");
    out.println("<br><form method=POST action=\"" +
                uri + "\">");
    out.println("<table>");
    out.println("<tr><td>User ID:</td>");
    out.println("<td><input type=text name=" +
                FIELD_USER + " size=30></td></tr>");
    out.println("<tr><td>Password:</td>");
    out.println("<td><input type=password name=" +
                FIELD_PASSWORD + " size=10></td></tr>");
    out.println("</table><br>");
    out.println("<input type=submit value=\"Login\">");
    out.println("</form></center></body></html>");
  }

  protected boolean validUser(String username, String password) {
    boolean valid = false;
```

Perform a simple check to validate:

```
    if ((username != null) && (username.length() > 0)) {
      valid = username.equals(password);
    }
      return valid;
  }

  public void init(ServletConfig cfg) throws ServletException {
    super.init(cfg);
  }

  public void destroy() {
    super.destroy();
  }
}
```

If we enter identical values for User ID and Password, we see a welcome page:

If we enter incorrect values for User ID and Password, we see an error page:

Digital Certificates

Digital certificates provide integrity and better security than basic and digest authentication. This also solves the problem of confidentiality, because the communication is now encrypted. The key concept is public key cryptography in which each participant has two keys, public and private, for encrypting and decrypting information. Digital signatures help us to confirm and identify the sender.

Digital Signatures are gaining acceptance as many nations are passing laws that give them equal legal standing with hand written signatures.

Secure web transactions are already dependent on digital signatures. The digital certificate binds a public key with an identity and enables a receiver to verify the sender's digital signature. Therefore, when a secure connection is set up with a web server, a client can encrypt information that only the identified server can decrypt.

The RSA public-key crypto system and digital signature scheme are widely deployed today. The idea is that someone could form a digital signature using public key cryptography that anyone else could verify but which no one else can generate. Whitfield Diffie and Martin Hellman conceived the general idea, but the method was further developed by Rivest, Shamir, and Adleman (hence the name RSA) in 1977 and it has become a popular and proven technology.

The RSA digital signatures scheme applies the sender's private key to a message to generate a signature. The signature can then be verified by applying the corresponding public key to the message and the signature using the verification process, providing either a valid or an invalid result. These two operations of signing and verifying comprise the RSA Digital Signatures scheme. Any signature generated by the first operation will always verify correctly with the second operation if the corresponding public key is used.

To establish that the public key given by a person is in fact a real one, a third-party should vouch for the person's identity. An established certificate authority such as VeriSign Corporation usually handles this. VeriSign offers a numbers of classes of digital IDs depending on the level of trust, and individually verifies IDs with high trust rating.

Secure Socket Layer

If you design your web site for commerce and it collects credit card information or provides other confidential information, then your customers need protection. Usually, that means some form of encryption.

When users access your web site, the information they send is not encrypted by default. Someone may intercept and decipher the data sent from the user's browser to your web site. To prevent data theft you can apply a special encryption mechanism to your web site. This method employs Secured Socket Layer (SSL) technology. Accessing web sites using SSL appears different from regular sites. A normal web site might be: http://www.wrox.com/. If a web site is using SSL, then the 'http' protocol token becomes 'https' as in: https://www.wrox.com/.

Keys

To use SSL you must first create keys. Keys are the special encryption encoding that is applied to the data. Both the web site and user browser must have keys to open and read the transmitted data. Two types of keys are used, the public key and the private key. The owner of the keys holds the private key. The public key is available to anyone that wishes to exchange data. The keys are used to package data into digital envelopes that have digital signatures.

Digital Envelopes

When sending data, the sender uses the recipient's public key to encrypt the information into a digital envelope. The sender transmits the digital envelope to the recipient. Since only the recipient's private key decodes the digital envelope no one who steals the packet of data will be able to read the information. Only the intended recipient has the private key.

Digital Signatures

The sender will also add a digital signature as proof of the sender's credentials. The sender uses his private key to sign the digital envelope. The recipient uses the sender's public key to verify the digital signature. Only the sender's public key will verify the signature, ensuring that the digital envelope came from the official sender.

Certificates

The problem with just creating public/private keys and implementing SSL is that they can lull users into a false sense of security. Users think because a web site is secured, it must be a legitimate site. A rogue Web site could create keys, establish an SSL web site, and collect credit card numbers for a bogus product. To resolve this problem, before you can install any encryption keys on your web site, a Certificate Authority (CA) must certify them.

A CA ensures that your web site is a legitimate place of business. A quick search of the Internet will list hundreds of certificate authorities that can certify your keys. You must have a CA certify and assign your site a certificate before you can use SSL. Certificates remain valid until they expire or the CA revokes them. The CA maintains a list of invalid certificates in a special list called the certificate revocation list (CRL).

You can find details on SSL, encryption, cryptography, and public/private keys at http://www.rsa.com/.

Why Not Use SSL for Everything?

If securing data is as easy using SSL, why don't we use it to for all our web sites? The answer to this question is simple: performance. Using SSL dramatically affects the speed at which users can access information. Because the system must encrypt and decrypt all data, a large amount of extra processing occurs. This slows both the user and the web site. The best time to use SSL is when sending confidential data over the Internet. Whether your web site or the user sends it, confidential information should be protected.

Controlling Access to Web Resources

The Servlet API adds support for an optional mechanism to specify access control constraints for a web application. For our example, we consider Tomcat, which like any servlet container, is meant to run behind a web server, though it can run standalone also. The web server takes care of receiving HTTP requests from client browsers and the servlet container takes care of serving Servlets and JSP pages for those URLs that request them.

Tomcat's configuration is based on two files:

- `server.xml` – Tomcat's global configuration file
- `web.xml` – The default deployment descriptor

`server.xml` is Tomcat's main configuration file. Tomcat lets the user define default `web.xml` values for all contexts by putting a default `web.xml` file in the `conf` subdirectory of `%CATALINA_HOME%`. When constructing a new context, Tomcat uses the default `web.xml` file as the base configuration, and then applies the application specific `web.xml` (the application's `WEB-INF\web.xml` file) settings.

Access is granted to a **role** instead of directly to a user or group.

> **A role is an abstract grouping of users that needs to be mapped to real users and group names.**

Tomcat uses the `tomcat-users.xml` file, which is located in the `conf` directory to define users and assign them roles:

```
<tomcat-users>
  <user name="adarsh" password="pword1" roles="admin"/>
  <user name="girish" password="pword2" roles="user"/>
</tomcat-users>
```

The type of access control that should be assigned for a web application resource is defined in the `web.xml` file, located in the `WEB-INF` directory of an application.

```
<security-constraint>
  <web-resource-collection>
    <web-resource-name>admin</web-resource-name>
    <url-pattern>/data/*</url-pattern>
  </web-resource-collection>
  <auth-constraint>
    <role-name>admin</role-name>
  </auth-constraint>
</security-constraint>
<login-config>
    <auth-method>BASIC</auth-method>
    <realm-name>users</realm-name>
</login-config>
```

The `<web-resource-collection>` element defines the resources to be protected. The `<auth-constraint>` element defines the users who have access to the protected resources. The URL pattern for the protected resources is specified in the `<url-pattern>` element. The type of authentication and the name associated with the protected parts of the application (known as the realm) is defined in the `<login-config>` element. These requirements, when declared in the `web.xml` file, allow the servlet container to take care of all authentication and access control.

Using SecurityManager in Tomcat

The correct use of a SecurityManager while running Tomcat can protect your server from Trojan servlets, JSP pages, beans, and tag libraries, and even inadvertent mistakes. Using the Java SecurityManager is just one more line of defense a system administrator can use to keep the server secure and reliable. However, implementation of a SecurityManager in Tomcat has not been fully tested to ensure the security of Tomcat. No special permissions have been created to prevent access to internal Tomcat classes by JSP pages, web applications, servlets, beans, or tag libraries. Still, running with a SecurityManager is definitely better than running without one.

Permission classes are used to define what permissions a class loaded by Tomcat will have. There are a number of permission classes as part of the JDK and you can even create your own permission class for use in your own web applications. The following is the summary of the System SecurityManager permission classes applicable to Tomcat:

Class	Description
`java.util.PropertyPermission`	Controls read/write access to JVM properties such as `java.home`
`java.lang.RuntimePermission`	Controls use of some system/runtime functions like `exit()` and `exec()`.
`java.io.FilePermission`	Controls read/write/execute access to files and directories.
`java.net.SocketPermission`	Controls use of network sockets.
`java.net.NetPermission`	Controls use of multicast network connections.
`java.lang.reflect.ReflectPermission`	Controls use of reflection to do class introspection.
`java.security.SecurityPermission`	Controls access to security methods.
`java.security.AllPermission`	Allows access to all permissions, just as if you were running Tomcat without a SecurityManager.

Tomcat 4.0 provides a custom permission class called `org.apache.naming.JndiPermission`. This permission controls read access to JNDI named file based resources. The permission name is the JNDI name and there are no actions. A trailing '*' can be used to perform wild card pattern matching for a JNDI named file resource when granting permission, for example:

```
permission org.apache.naming.JndiPermission "jndi://localhost/examples/*";
```

Configuring Tomcat for Use with a SecurityManager

For Tomcat 4.0 the security policies implemented by the Java SecurityManager are configured in the `catalina.policy` file located in the `%CATALINA_HOME%/conf/` directory. The `catalina.policy` file replaces any system `java.policy` file, and can be edited by hand or by using the `policytool` application that comes with the JDK. Entries in the `catalina.policy` file use the standard `java.policy` file format.

Tomcat can be started with the SecurityManager in place by using the `-security` option. Entries in the `catalina.policy` file use the standard `java.policy` file format.

```
grant [signedBy <signer> [,codeBase <code source>] {
    permission <class> [<name> [, <action list>]];
};
```

The `signedBy` and `codeBase` entries are optional when granting permissions.

This file contains a default set of security policies to be enforced when it is executed with the `-security` option. These permissions apply to javac; shared system extensions; server startup code; servlet API classes, and to the container's core code, plus any additional libraries installed in the "server" directory. These permissions are granted by default to all web applications. In addition, a web application will be given a read FilePermission and `JndiPermission` for all files and directories in its document root. You can assign additional permissions to particular web applications by adding additional "grant" entries here. Different permissions can be granted to JSP pages, classes loaded from the `/WEB-INF/classes/` directory, all jar files in the `/WEB-INF/lib/` directory, or can even be granted to individual JAR files in the `/WEB-INF/lib/` directory.

Here is an example where, in addition to the default entries; we want to grant the example web application the ability to connect to the `localhost` SMTP port so that it can send mail:

```
grant codeBase "file:${catalina.home}/webapps/examples" {
  permission java.net.SocketPermission "localhost:25","connect";
  permission java.net.SocketPermission "localhost:1024","listen";
  permission java.util.PropertyPermission "*","read";
};
```

Working with JDBCRealm

A **Realm** component represents a mechanism by which a "database" of usernames, passwords, and their associated security roles can be linked for the purpose of authenticating users and validating security constraints. The **JDBC Realm** connects to a relational database, accessed through an appropriate JDBC driver, in order to perform lookups of usernames, passwords, and their associated roles. Because the lookup is done each time it is required, changes to the database will be immediately reflected in the information used to authenticate new logins.

In order to be used by the JDBC Realm, it must be possible to establish a JDBC connection to the database. The database must contain a table containing information about users, which must conform to the following rules:

- There must be exactly one row for each user
- There must be a column (identified by the `userNameCol` attribute) that contains the username of the user represented by this row
- There must be a column (identified by the `userCredCol` attribute) that contains the password of the user represented by this row
- The MessageDigest algorithm configured by the digest attribute must encode the password
- Usernames must be unique

The database must contain a table containing information about the roles for users, which must conform to the following rules:

- A role and user combination must be unique
- A user can appear in more than one row
- A user may have zero rows in this table, if that user is not assigned to any roles

- There must be a column (identified by the `userNameCol` attribute) that contains the username of the user whose role assignment is represented by this row
- There must be a column, (identified by the `userRoleCol` attribute) that contains the role name assigned to this user

The following set of configuration attributes let you customize the database:

Attribute	**Meaning**
`driverName`	The name of the driver needed to connect to the database
`connectionURL`	The URL used to connect to the database
`userTable`	The users table
`userNameCol`	The column in the users table that contains the name
`userCredCol`	The column in the users table that contains the password
`userRoleTable`	The users-roles table
`roleNameCol`	The column in the users table that contains a role given to a user
`connectionName`	The name to use when connecting to the database (optional)
`connectionPassword`	The password to use when connecting to the database (optional)
`digest`	The algorithm used for digest passwords, such as "MD5", "MD2", "SHA", or "No" for plain passwords

This is an example of how to set up a JDBC Realm. For this example, we use the MySQL JDBC driver:

- The `user` table – Contains the user's name and a password field
- The `role` table – Contains a single field that has the role's name
- The `user_roles` table – This table joins a set of roles to a single user and has the `user_name` and the `role_name` as its fields

```
CREATE TABLE users (
  user_name VARCHAR(15) PRIMARY KEY,
  user_pass VARCHAR(15) NOT NULL
);

CREATE TABLE roles (
  role_name VARCHAR(15) PRIMARY KEY
);

CREATE TABLE user_roles (
  user_name VARCHAR(15) NOT NULL,
  role_name VARCHAR(15) NOT NULL,
  PRIMARY KEY( user_name, role_name )
);
```

This information must be added to the `server.xml` file, for example:

```
<JDBCRealm
  debug="99"
  driverName="org.gjt.mm.mysql.Driver"
  connectionURL="jdbc:mysql://localhost/authority?user=test;password=test"
  userTable="users"
  userNameCol="user_name"
  userCredCol="user_pass"
  userRoleTable="user_roles"
  roleNameCol="role_name" />
```

To use digested passwords you need to store them in a digested form. To achieve this, you will need to use the same digest strategies that JDBCRealm uses to store the passwords. Inside JDBCRealm there is a static method:

```
final public static String digest(String password,String algorithm)
```

JDBCRealm provides this method as a tool to be used outside JDBCRealm by an application that wants to generate digested passwords to be readable. The class JDBCRealm contains a `main()` method, so it can be used as an application to generate digests and print them to `stdout`:

```
java org.apache.tomcat.modules.aaa.JDBCRealm
     -a <algorithm> <password> [<password> ...]
```

Where `<algorithm>` is a supported message digest algorithm, for example MD5, and `<password>` is a plain text password to be digested.

Single Sign-On Support

Single sign-on support makes it possible for an authenticated user scanned the first time, and then recognized across other web applications in the same environment without requiring the user to log in again. Tomcat supports that capability if it is configured as follows:

- All clients must provide support for cookies.
- As implemented in Tomcat, the scope of "single sign-on" support is the entire set of web applications registered with a single virtual host.
- The system administrator must configure the `%CATALINA_HOME%/conf/server.xml` file at the `<Engine>` or `<Host>` level, configure a `<Realm>` element that defines the database of valid users and their corresponding roles. In the default configuration shipped with Tomcat, this is done at the Engine level.

```
<Engine name="Standalone" defaultHost="localhost" debug="0">
  <Realm
    className="org.apache.catalina.realm.JDBCRealm" debug="99"
    driverName="org.gjt.mm.mysql.Driver"
    connectionURL="jdbc:mysql://localhost/authority?user=test;password=test"
    userTable="users" userNameCol="user_name" userCredCol="user_pass"
    userRoleTable="user_roles" roleNameCol="role_name" />
```

Define the default virtual host:

```
<Host name="localhost" debug="0" appBase="webapps" unpackWARs="true">
```

Nested inside the <Host> element, you must include the following element:

```
<Valve className="org.apache.catalina.authenticator.SingleSignOn"
       debug="0"/>
```

This support utilizes cookies to maintain user identity across applications, the vulnerability of information exposure apply here as when cookies are used to maintain session identity within a single web application. To overcome this limitation you can run across a secure network connection.

For more information about how to configure security with Tomcat, you should refer to the online documentation.

Authentication using JAAS

The **Java Authentication and Authorization Service (JAAS)** 1.0 is a set of Java packages that allows services to authenticate users and enforce access controls on them. JAAS extends the access control architecture of the Java 2 Platform and implements the **Pluggable Authentication Module (PAM)** framework, which allows applications to remain independent from the underlying authentication technology. This means that new authentication technologies can be plugged under an application without the application having to be modified.

J2SE 1.3 provides developers with a way to enforce access controls based on where code came from and who signed it. However, it lacks the ability to enforce similar access controls based on who *runs* the code – JAAS provides us with such support.

JAAS extends the Java security model so that it can perform checks based on the identity of the caller. It can be used to determine who is currently executing Java code and to ensure they have the necessary permissions.

Applications start the authentication process by instantiating a `LoginContext` object, which in turn references a configuration to determine the authentication technology, or `LoginModule`, to be used to perform the authentication. Typical `LoginModules` will prompt for, and verify, a username and password.

Before we can use JAAS effectively, we need to understand some concepts associated with the technology.

Subject

A subject, represented by the `javax.security.auth.Subject` class, is an identity in a system that is authenticated and assigned permissions, and could be a human user, a machine, or even another process. A subject is associated with other identities called **principals**. This association is what distinguishes a subject from other subjects. A subject has other attributes called **credentials**, which are stored in a **set**:

- Those that need to be shared are stored in a public credential set
- Those that need to be protected are stored in a private credential set

Principal

Principals implement the `java.security.Principal` interface and represents subject identities. A principal represents a subject's interactions with an authority. The following code shows how a principal can be defined:

```
import java.security.Principal;

public final class SimplePrincipal implements Principal {
  private final String name;

  public SimplePrincipal(String name) {
    if (name == null) {
      throw new IllegalArgumentException("Name cannot be null");
    }
    this.name = name;
  }

  public int hashCode() {
    return name.hashCode();
  }

  public java.lang.String getName() {
    return name;
  }

  public java.lang.String toString() {
    return "SimplePrincipal: " + name;
  }

  public boolean equals(java.lang.Object obj) {
    if (obj == null) return false;
    if (!(obj instanceof SimplePrincipal)) return false;
    SimplePrincipal other = (SimplePrincipal) obj;
    return name.equals(other.getName());
  }
}
```

Credentials

Credentials are not part of the core JAAS class library – any Java class can represent a credential. There are two interfaces related to credentials: `Refreshable` and `Destroyable`. The `Refreshable` interface provides the capability for a credential to refresh itself and has two abstract methods. The first determines if the credential is valid:

```
boolean isCurrent()
```

And the second updates or extends that validity of the credential:

```
void refresh() throws RefreshFailedException
```

Implementations of this method should perform an `AuthPermission("refreshCredential")` security check to ensure the caller has permission to refresh the credential.

The `Destroyable` interface provides the capability of destroying the contents within a credential and has two abstract methods. The first determines if the credential has been destroyed:

```
boolean isDestroyed()
```

And the second destroys and clears the information associated with this credential:

```
void destroy() throws DestroyFailedException
```

Subsequent calls to certain methods on this credential will result in an `IllegalStateException` being thrown. Implementations of this method should perform an `AuthPermission("destroyCredential")` security check to ensure the caller has permission to destroy the credential.

Client and LoginContext

In order to associate a principal with a subject, clients must log in. JAAS provides a concrete class, `LoginContext`, which acts as a session with a group of one or more authentication providers. This allows the development of applications independent of the underlying authentication technology.

The `LoginContext` consults a configuration to determine the authentication services, or `LoginModules`, configured for a particular application. This means that different `LoginModules` can be plugged in under an application without requiring any modifications to the application itself. The following code demonstrates how to use a `LoginContext`:

```
import java.util.Iterator;
import java.security.PrivilegedAction;
import javax.security.auth.Subject;
import javax.security.auth.login.LoginContext;

public class JAASClient {

  public static void main(String [] args) {
```

```
        try {
          loginAndDoSomething();
        } catch (Exception e) {
          e.printStackTrace();
        }
      }

      public static void loginAndDoSomething() throws Exception {
```

The `LoginContext` constructor prepares to authenticate based on a named configuration. In this case, the configuration is named `SimpleLogin` (more on this in a moment):

```
        LoginContext ctx = new LoginContext("SimpleLogin");
```

The call to `login()` then causes the `LoginContext` to call one or more authentication providers:

```
        ctx.login();
```

The call to `getSubject()` returns a `Subject` that contains any `Principals` that the authenticators chose to assign:

```
        Subject subj = ctx.getSubject();
        System.out.println("Login assigned these principals: ");
```

The call to `getPrincipals()` lists the principals that the login assigned to the `Subject`:

```
        Iterator it = subj.getPrincipals().iterator();
        while (it.hasNext()) {
          System.out.println("\t" + it.next());
        }

        Subject.doAs(subj,
                     new PrivilegedAction() {
                       public Object run() {
                         System.out.println("You live at "
                         + System.getProperty("user.home"));
                         return null;
                       }
                     });
        ctx.logout();
      }
    }
```

Configuration File

The `LoginContext` finds the named configuration from a configuration file that looks something like this:

```
SimpleLogin {
  SimpleLoginModule required;
};
```

This tells the `LoginContext` to load a class named `SimpleLoginModule`, which is a service provider for some authentication strategy. The `required` attribute means that this class's approval is required for the login to succeed. The `LoginContext` allows multiple authentication providers, so additional entries could appear inside the `SimpleLogin` block.

In order to authenticate a user, we need a `javax.security.auth.login.LoginContext`:

```
LoginContext lc = new LoginContext("simple.conf",
                                   new TextCallbackHandler());
```

The constructor takes two arguments:

- The name of an entry in the JAAS login configuration file
- A `CallbackHandler` object

The first argument is the name used to look up an entry for this application in the JAAS login configuration file. It specifies the classes that implement the underlying authentication technology. The classes must implement the `javax.security.auth.spi.LoginModule` interface.

In our example code, we used the `SimpleLoginModule` to perform authentication. The entry in the login configuration file we use is the name `"simple.conf"`, so that is the name we specify as the first argument to the `LoginContext` constructor:

```
LoginContext lc = new LoginContext("simple.conf",
                                   new TextCallbackHandler());
```

When a `LoginModule` needs to communicate with the user, for example to ask for a user name and password, it does not do so directly. That is because there are various ways of communicating with a user, and it is desirable for `LoginModules` to remain independent of the different types of user interaction. Rather, the `LoginModule` invokes a `javax.security.auth.callback.CallbackHandler` to perform the user interaction and set appropriate results, such as the user name and password.

An instance of the particular `CallbackHandler` to be used is specified as the second argument to the `LoginContext` constructor. The `LoginContext` forwards that instance to the underlying `LoginModule` (in our case `SimpleLoginModule`). An application either could write its own `CallbackHandler` or, more commonly, could simply specify an existing one. It is common to use `com.sun.security.auth.callback.TextCallbackHandler`, which prompts for, and reads, the username and password.

Provider

A JAAS authentication provider provides the authentication strategy, which is implemented through the `LoginModule` interface. The `LoginModule` interface gives us the ability to implement different kinds of authentication technologies that can be plugged to an application. Accordingly, our `SimpleLoginModule` must implement the `LoginModule` interface.

The `LoginContext` will call these methods in the following sequence:

1. `initialize()`
   This method instantiates a `LoginModule` with a `subject`, to which it can later attach principals to if the login succeeds, and a `CallbackHandler`. It is used to communicate with users for authentication information. The `Callback` handler decouples the service provider from the particular input devices. The shared map contains general configuration information, and the options map contains a provider-pecific configuration.

2. `login()`
   This method tells the provider to authenticate the subject. Principals are not assigned at this time.

3. `commit()`
   This method completes and finalizes the authentication process. If the authentication process was successful, then this method continues to associate relevant principals, public credentials, or private credentials with the subject. If the authentication process failed, then this method removes any previously stored authentication state, such as usernames or passwords.

4. `abort()`
   This method aborts the authentication process. The provider does not assign principals to the subject.

5. `logout()`
   This method cancels the assignment of principals to the subject.

Our `SimpleLoginModule` class is indeed very simple. It recognizes only one principal and one authentication string, both of which are hard-coded into the class.

```
import java.io.*;
import java.util.*;
import java.security.Principal;
import javax.security.auth.Subject;
import javax.security.auth.callback.CallbackHandler;
import javax.security.auth.spi.LoginModule;

public class SimpleLoginModule implements LoginModule {

  private static final int NOT_AUTHENTICATED = 0;
  private static final int AUTHENTICATED = 1;
  private static final int AUTHENTICATE_COMMITTED = 2;

private int state;
  private SimplePrincipal sp;
```

```
  private Subject sub;

  public boolean abort() {
    if ((sub != null) && (sp != null)) {
      Set prins = sub.getPrincipals();
      if (prins.contains(sp)) {
        prins.remove(sp);
      }
    }
    sub = null;
    sp = null;
    state = NOT_AUTHENTICATED;
    return true;
  }

  public boolean commit() {
    if (state < AUTHENTICATED) {
      return false;
    }
    if (sub == null) {
      return false;
    }
    Set prins = sub.getPrincipals();
    if (!prins.contains(sp)) {
      prins.add(sp);
    }
    state = AUTHENTICATE_COMMITTED;
    return true;
  }

  public void initialize(Subject s, CallbackHandler ch,
                         Map shared, Map options) {
    state = NOT_AUTHENTICATED;
    sp = null;
    sub = s;
  }

  public boolean login() {
    BufferedReader br =
               new BufferedReader(new InputStreamReader(System.in));
    System.err.println("Which publisher shares with you the knowledge "
                     + of experienced programmers? ");
    try {
      String resp = br.readLine();
      if (!resp.equalsIgnoreCase("Wrox")) {
        return false;
      }
    } catch (IOException ioe) {
      return false;
    }
    sp = new SimplePrincipal("Adarsh");
    state = AUTHENTICATED;
    return true;
  }

  public boolean logout() {
    state = NOT_AUTHENTICATED;
    sp = null;
    sub = null;
    return true;
  }
}
```

Java Policy File

A JAAS authentication provider is a highly trusted part of the system, and needs special permissions. To grant these permissions, we need to specify a Java 2 policy file in which we grant trust in the provider. In the following policy file the provider files and the JAAS API files are completely trusted:

```
grant codeBase "file:./provider/" {
  permission java.security.AllPermission;
};
```

You will need to edit the `jaas.jar codeBase` entry to point to the location of `jaas.jar` on your local system (the other URLs are relative and do not need to be edited):

```
grant codeBase "file:./client/jaas.jar" {
  permission java.security.AllPermission;
};
```

The client code is given the permissions it needs to bootstrap a `LoginContext` and to perform an authentication check:

```
grant codeBase "file:./client/" {
  permission javax.security.auth.AuthPermission "createLoginContext";
  permission javax.security.auth.AuthPermission "doAs";
```

The client is also given permission to read the `"user.home"` property, which is the 'sensitive operation' being demonstrated in our example:

```
  permission java.util.PropertyPermission "user.home", "read";
};
```

JAAS Policy File

JAAS defines a policy file format for assigning permissions to authenticated clients. The format looks very similar to the normal Java 2 policy file.

> **In J2SE 1.4, a separate JAAS policy file will not be necessary. All settings will be controlled by the standard policy.**

For JAAS 1.0, the JAAS-specific sections are in a separate file that looks like this:

```
grant Principal SimplePrincipal "Adarsh" {
  permission java.util.PropertyPermission "user.home", "read";
};
```

The permission settings look exactly like Java 2 security permission settings. The only difference is in the grant declaration, which can list a principal instead of, or in addition to, the normal `codeBase` and `signedBy` settings. This simple example gives `testUser` permission to read the `user.home` property.

Running the JAAS Application

Let's build and run the JAAS application we have discussed. You should have the following files and directories:

```
client/
       JAASClient.java
       jaas.jar
provider/
         SimpleLoginModule.java
         SimplePrincipal.java
conf/
     simple.conf
     JAASProvider.policy
     SimpleJAAS.policy
```

Then compile the Java classes (you will need to include `jaas.jar` in your classpath). With the classes compiled and the policy files in place, we can issue the following command (you will need to edit the command to specify the correct location of `jaas.jar`):

```
java -cp .;client/jaas.jar;client;provider
     -Djava.security.manager
     -Djava.security.policy=conf/JAASProvider.policy
     -Djava.security.auth.policy=conf/SimpleJAAS.policy
     -Djava.security.auth.login.config=conf/simple.conf
     JAASClient
```

If we examine the command, we see that it first turns on Java 2 security:

```
-Djava.security.manager
```

Then gives the provider the Java 2 permissions it needs:

```
-Djava.security.policy=JAASProvider.policy
```

Then gives the client the JAAS permissions it needs:

```
-Djava.security.auth.policy=SimpleJAAS.policy
```

And finally tells the `LoginContext` where to find the configuration file:

```
-Djava.security.auth.login.config=simple.conf
```

When we run the command we see something like:

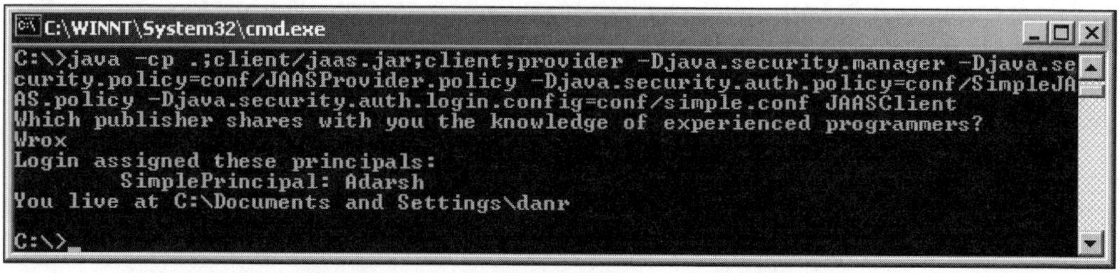

```
C:\>java -cp .;client/jaas.jar;client;provider -Djava.security.manager -Djava.se
curity.policy=conf/JAASProvider.policy -Djava.security.auth.policy=conf/SimpleJA
AS.policy -Djava.security.auth.login.config=conf/simple.conf JAASClient
Which publisher shares with you the knowledge of experienced programmers?
Wrox
Login assigned these principals:
        SimplePrincipal: Adarsh
You live at C:\Documents and Settings\danr

C:\>_
```

Although this example was quite simple, it demonstrates basics of using JAAS. However, if you develop production implementation, you should bear the following points in mind:

- You should not use `System.in` and `System.err`. The `CallbackHandler` interface is provided for this purpose. Rewrite the `SimpleLoginModule` to use a `CallbackHandler` provided by the client.
- Providers do not actually need `AllPermission`.
- In general, you do not need to write your own providers or principals. Instead, you can use a standard provider and principals that integrate with your OS login, smart card, or some other authentication provider.

That completes our overview of security on the server. Next, we'll go onto look at how we can manage users that access our web applications.

Login Management System

A login procedure becomes necessary in situations where access to sensitive data is to be given to selective users, and login would help in a business scenario, where it would help in many ways if we knew who is visiting our site. However, in many cases it will be overkill if logins are enforced – they might simply deter visitors.

In this example, we will explore ways in which JavaServer Pages can be used to implement a login management. A note of caution is that, although a portion of code could certainly be used in an actual system, it should not be treated as commercial grade. As is always the case with sample code, you are encouraged to make changes and improvements. This example can be considered as a skeleton system over which the techniques that have been discussed in the previous sections can be implemented.

The main page in this application is divided into two frames. The left frame contains the menu and the right frame is the display area. The `index.html` contains the code for this screen:

```
<html>
  <head>
    <title>Login Management</title>
    <link rel="stylesheet" type="text/css" href="style.css" />
  </head>
  <frameset cols="130,*">
```

```
    <frame src="menu.html" frameborder="0" noresize="noresize" name="menuframe">
    <frame src="welcome.html" frameborder="0" name="rightframe">
  </frameset>
</html>
```

The left frame houses the `menu.html`:

```
<html>
  <head>
    <link rel="stylesheet" type="text/css" href="style_menu.css" />
  </head>
  <body>
    <h3>
      Options
    </h3>
    <table>
      <tr>
        <td>
          <a href="Login.jsp" target="rightframe">Login</a>
        </td>
      </tr>
      <tr>
        <td>
          <a href="Page1.jsp" target="rightframe">Page 1</a>
        </td>
      </tr>
      <tr>
        <td>
          <a href="Page2.jsp" target="rightframe">Page 2</a>
        </td>
      </tr>
      <tr>
        <td>
          <a href="Logout.jsp" target="rightframe">Logout</a>
        </td>
      </tr>
    </table>
  </body>
</html>
```

The right frame initially houses `welcome.html` and will change depending on the menu item selected:

```
<html>
  <head>
     <link rel="stylesheet" type="text/css" href="style.css" />
  </head>
  <body>
    <h2>Welcome!</h2>
    <p>Please login before viewing other pages.</p>
  </body>
</html>
```

We also have a couple of stylesheets, `style_menu.css` for `menu.html`, and `style.css` for all our other pages. This is what we will see when the application starts up:

Now let's try to login, and enter the User ID and password. Clicking on the Login option in the menu will point to `Login.jsp`. This uses the `LoginProcessor` bean to check whether the user has already logged in, and if not a form is generated to accept the ID and password for logging in.

```
<jsp:useBean id="loginprocessor"
             class="login.LoginProcessor"
             scope="application" />
<jsp:useBean id="userinfo"
             class="login.UserInfo"
             scope="session" />
<%
  if (loginprocessor.alreadyLoggedIn(userinfo)) {
%>
    <jsp:forward page="AlreadyLogged.html" />
<%
  }
%>

<html>
  <head>
    <link rel="stylesheet" type="text/css" href="style.css" />
    <title>Login</title>
  </head>

  <body>
    <h2>Login</h2>
    <form name="login" method="POST"
          action="Validate.jsp" class="loginForm">
      <table>
        <tr>
          <td class="loginMenu">User ID </td>
```

```
          <td>
            <input name="user" type="text" length="9" maxlength="9" />
          </td>
        </tr>
        <tr>
          <td class="loginMenu">Password </td>
          <td>
            <input name="password" type="password"
                   length="8" maxlength="8" />
            </font>
          </td>
        </tr>
      </table>
      <p>
        <input type="submit" value="Login" class="btn" />
        <input type="reset" value="Reset" class="btn" />
      </p>
    </form>
  </body>
</html>
```

The output of the login screen looks like this:

`Validate.jsp` validates the User ID and the Password and if we have entered them correctly we will see the following page:

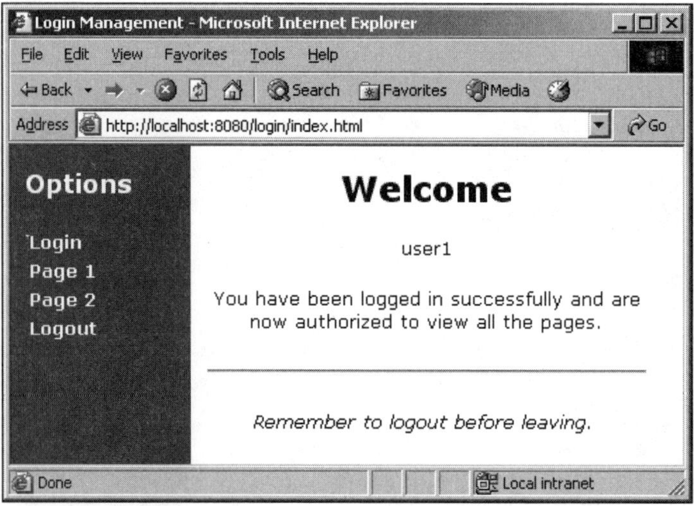

The code for `Validate.jsp` is:

```
<%@ page errorPage="Error.jsp" %>
<jsp:useBean id="loginprocessor"
             class="login.LoginProcessor"
             scope="application" />
<jsp:useBean id="userinfo"
             class="login.UserInfo"
             scope="session" />
<jsp:setProperty name="userinfo" property="*"/>
<%! String nextPage; %>
<%
  if (loginprocessor.alreadyLoggedIn(userinfo)) {
      nextPage = "AlreadyLogged.html";
  }
  else {
    if (loginprocessor.login(userinfo)) {
      userinfo.setSessionId(session.getId());
      nextPage = "Welcome.jsp";
    }
    else {
      nextPage = "LoginFailure.html";
    }
  }
%>
<jsp:forward page="<%= nextPage %>" />
```

`Welcome.jsp` generates the welcome screen:

```
<jsp:useBean id="userinfo" class="login.UserInfo"
  scope="session" />
<html>
  <head>
    <link rel="stylesheet" type="text/css" href="style.css" />
  </head>
  <body>
    <h2>Welcome</h2>
    <%= userinfo.getUser() %>
    <p>You have been logged in successfully and are now
       authorized to view all the pages.</p>
    <hr />
    <p><i>Remember to logout before leaving.</i></p>
  </body>
</html>
```

In case if either the user or password is incorrect, the `LoginFailure.html` handles this page:

```
<html>
  <head>
    <link rel="stylesheet" type="text/css" href="style.css" />
  </head>
  <body>
    <h2>Login Failed</h2>
    <p><a href="Login.jsp">Retry</a></p>
  </body>
</html>
```

`Error.jsp` handles any errors:

```
<%@ page isErrorPage="true" %>
<html>
  <head>
    <link rel="stylesheet" type="text/css" href="style.css" />
  </head>
  <body>
    <h2>An Error Occurred</h2>
    <p><%= exception.getMessage() %></p>
  </body>
</html>
```

After the user has been authenticated, they can access the other pages. The code to generate this page is in `Page1.jsp` and `Page2.jsp`, which are almost the same:

```
<%@ page errorPage="Error.jsp" %>
<jsp:useBean id="loginprocessor"
class="login.LoginProcessor"
  scope="application" />
<jsp:useBean id="userinfo" class="login.UserInfo"
  scope="session" />
<%
  if (!loginprocessor.keepAlive(userinfo,getServletInfo())) {
%>
     <jsp:forward page="NotLoggedIn.html" />
<%
  }
%>
<html>
  <head>
    <link rel="stylesheet" type="text/css" href="style.css" />
  </head>
  <body>
```

We print either Page 1 or Page 2:

```
    <h2>Page 1</h2>
  </body>
</html>
```

`AlreadyLogged.html` handles the situation when the users attempt multiple logons:

```
<html>
  <head>
    <link rel="stylesheet" type="text/css" href="style.css" />
  </head>
  <body>
    <h2>You Are Already Logged In</h2>
    <p>You can continue to view other pages.</p>
  </body>
</html>
```

`AlreadyLogged.jsp` generates the following screen:

Let's see how we can prevent unauthorized users from bypassing the login and directly accessing the other pages on the site. We need a mechanism that will permit each JSP page to determine for itself whether the user has been authenticated as part of the active session. If a user tries to access the pages for which they have not been authenticated, they are redirected to `NotLoggedIn.jsp`:

```
<html>
  <head>
   <link rel="stylesheet" type="text/css" href="style.css" />
  </head>
  <body>
    <h2>You Are Not Logged In</h2>
    <p>Please <a href="Login.jsp">Login</a> to gain access
       to other pages.</p>
  </body>
</html>
```

`NotLoggedIn.jsp` generates the following screen:

The final activity performed by the user at the end of a session is that of logging out. We have provided a **Logout** option in our menu; when selected it points to `Logout.jsp`:

```
<%@ page errorPage="Error.jsp" %>
<jsp:useBean id="loginprocessor"
class="login.LoginProcessor"
  scope="application" />
<jsp:useBean id="userinfo" class="login.UserInfo"
  scope="session" />
<%
  if (loginprocessor.alreadyLoggedIn(userinfo)) {
%>
<%
  loginprocessor.logout(userinfo);
  session.invalidate();
%>
<%
  }
%>
<%@ include file="welcome.html" %>
```

We have referenced two `useBean` actions, `UserInfo` and `LoginProcessor` in our other JSP files. The `UserInfo` bean contains the information on the users:

```
package login;

public class UserInfo {
  private String  user;
  private String  password;
  private String sessionId;
  private boolean loggedIn;
```

Then we define the usual getter and setter methods for the `user`, `password`, `sessionId`, and `loggedIn` properties before defining a constructor that sets some default values:

```
  public UserInfo( ) {
    user = "";
    password = "";
    sessionId = "";
    loggedIn = false;
  }
}
```

The `LoginProcessor` bean contains the methods that are needed for validation, and other chores in our application:

```
package login;

import java.util.*;

public class LoginProcessor {

  private Hashtable userTable;
  private Hashtable currentLogins;

  public LoginProcessor() {
```

A database connection for the user table can be initialized but to keep our example focused a hashtable is used instead:

```
    userTable = new Hashtable();
    userTable.put("user1", "pass1");
    userTable.put("user2", "pass2");
    userTable.put("user3", "pass3");

    currentLogins = new Hashtable();
  }

  public boolean alreadyLoggedIn(UserInfo userinfo) {
    boolean loggedIn = userinfo.getLoggedIn();
    return loggedIn;
  }

  public boolean keepAlive(UserInfo userinfo,
      String pageInfo) {
    if (!alreadyLoggedIn(userinfo)) {
      return false;
    }
    String user = userinfo.getUser();
    String sessionId = userinfo.getSessionId();
    synchronized (currentLogins) {
      if (currentLogins.containsKey(user)) {
          currentLogins.put(user, userinfo.getSessionId());
        }
      }
    return true;
  }

  public boolean login(UserInfo userinfo) {
    if (alreadyLoggedIn(userinfo)) {
      return false;
    }
    String user = userinfo.getUser();
    if ((userTable.get(user)).equals(userinfo.getPassword())) {
      userinfo.setLoggedIn(true);
```

A database could be used here to query for user info:

```
      currentLogins.put(user, userinfo.getSessionId());
    }
    return userinfo.getLoggedIn();
  }

  public void logout(UserInfo userinfo) {
    currentLogins.remove(userinfo.getUser());
    userinfo.setLoggedIn(false);
  }
}
```

This was a simple example of how users could be recognized and managed. Next, we'll use what we've learnt to create a more interesting application – the ubiquitous shopping cart.

Session Management

HTTP is a stateless protocol so special measures must be taken to allow a server to identify and remember a particular user during a series of transactions. The idea of maintaining state between requests to a web application is known as session tracking.

A session can be defined as a series of related interactions between a single client and the web server, which takes place over a certain period.

For example: you are shopping on-line and you add an item to your cart. When you move to the page that accepts your payment, the server needs to keep track of your orders. How does the server know what is already in your cart? Since HTTP is a stateless protocol, the web server does not automatically know which session the given request belongs to. There are two approaches to get around this problem:

- We can get the client to identify itself each time it makes a request and then store and retrieve data relating to the client
- We can send the data to the client and make the client send it back alongside each request it makes

We need to know how we are going to share this data between the different requests that the user makes. Traditionally, this is done either by URL rewriting, hidden form fields, or by using cookies. However, when developing servlets we have another option of using methods provided by Servlet API. These methods use URL rewriting and cookies under the covers and can store data about them in session objects. This can be used by any servlets during the session.

Before we start to look at how we can use the methods the Servlet API provides, it's helpful to understand how the techniques that the servlet container uses under the hood work.

Hidden Form Fields

Using hidden form fields is one of the simplest session-tracking techniques. Hidden form fields are HTML input types that are not displayed when read by a browser. We include hidden form fields with HTML elements like this:

```
<input type="hidden" name="book" value="Java" />
```

When you open this HTML document, the input types marked as hidden will not be visible. They will, however, be transmitted in the request. In a way, hidden form fields act as constant variables for a form.

As far as a servlet receiving a submitted form is concerned, there is no difference between a hidden field and a visible one. The following example shows how to use form fields in this way. For our example, we will build a form, which contains hidden fields that contain items in the shopping cart in the GET method. The servlet will then display the current items to the users:

```
import javax.servlet.*;
import javax.servlet.http.*;
```

```
import java.io.*;
import java.util.*;

public class HiddenFieldExample extends HttpServlet {

  public void init(ServletConfig config)
      throws ServletException {
    super.init(config);
  }

  public void writeHead(PrintWriter out) {
    out.println("<html>");
    out.println("<head><title>Hidden Field Example</title></head>");
    out.println("<body style=\"font-family:verdana;font-size:10pt;\">");
  }

  public void writeFoot(PrintWriter out) {
    out.println("</body></html>");
  }

  public void doGet(HttpServletRequest request,
                    HttpServletResponse response)
              throws ServletException, IOException {
    response.setContentType("text/html");
    PrintWriter out = response.getWriter();
    writeHead(out);
    out.println("<form action=\"HiddenFieldExample\" method=\"POST\">");
    out.println("<input type=\"hidden\" name=\"book\" value=" +
                "\"Beginning JSP Web Development\" />");
    out.println("<input type=\"hidden\" name=\"book\" value=" +
                "\"Professional JSP Site Design\" />");
    out.println("<input type=\"submit\" value=\"Check Out\" />");
    writeFoot(out);
    out.close();
  }

  public void doPost(HttpServletRequest request,
                     HttpServletResponse response)
              throws ServletException, IOException {
    response.setContentType("text/html");
    PrintWriter out = response.getWriter();
    writeHead(out);
    out.println("<h3> Your Shopping Basket contains </h3>");
    String[] books = request.getParameterValues("book");
    out.println("<ul>");
    for (int i=0; i<books.length; i++) {
      out.println("<li>" + books[i] + "</li>");
    }
    out.println("</ul>");
    writeFoot(out);
    out.close();
  }
}
```

The servlet we created can service both POST and GET methods. The form that contains hidden fields and an action that points to the servlet's `doPost()` method is provided in the `doGet()` method. The `doPost()` method will then parse the hidden values sent in the request and echo them back to the client:

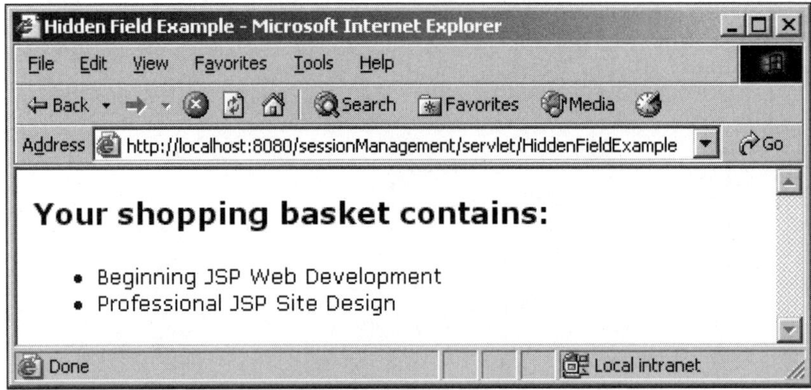

You see that hidden form fields are easy to implement, and are supported in all popular browsers. The major disadvantage with this technique is that it works only for a sequence of dynamically generated forms, which means that you will not be able to use the Back button on your browser without losing the additional fields added to the current page, and also the client can see them by viewing the source HTML sent to the client.

URL Rewriting

Simply appending some extra data at the end of each URL that identifies the session does the job, and the server can associate the session identifier with data it has stored about that session. This is a good solution and works even with browsers that do not support cookies, or where the user has disabled cookies. URL rewriting is a method in which the requested URL is modified to include a session ID.

There are several ways to perform URL rewriting. For example, the following URL is rewritten to pass a session ID of '`abc`':

```
http://server:port/servlet/rewrite (original )
http://server:port/servlet/rewrite/abc (extra path information )
http://server:port/servlet/rewrite?sessionid=abc (added parameter )
http://server:port/servlet/rewrite;$sessionid$abc (custom change )
```

A very simple example can include the user ID as a part of a URL reference by an HTML hyper-link:

```
<a href="http://localhost:8080/sessionManagement/servlet/AddItem?uid=ada">
  Add Items
</a>
```

Now when this item is clicked, the user id is passed along with the request. The `AddItem` servlet simply has to get the value of the `uid` parameter from the `HttpServletRequest` object, then refer to a database or a file on the server to produce the relevant information.

There are several disadvantages to URL rewriting:

- It poses a problem and may run into some environment limitations, such as how long the size of the URL can be.
- It is exposed to anyone who would want to intercept the request or view it in the browser's history window.
- Finally, performing a URL rewriting can be very tedious.

Cookies and Session Management

A cookie is a small piece of information that the web server sends to the browser. The browser then saves the cookie to a file. The browser sends the cookie back to the same server in every request that it makes. Cookies are often used to keep track of sessions.

A cookie contains a small amount of structured data (less than 4Kb), which gives the server information about the user's identification, preference, or past behavior. Servlets use the information in a cookie as a:

- Low-security user sign-on
- Repository of user preferences
- Means of maintaining state from one HTML page to the next

> **It's important to remember that there is no guarantee that a browser will accept a cookie you try to set, so it's important that your application can cope with this eventuality.**

Using Cookies

Servlets send cookies to clients by adding fields to HTTP response headers, and clients automatically return cookies by adding fields to HTTP request headers. The cookies have the following properties:

Property	Description
Name	Name of the cookie
Domain	Domain name of the server that created and sent the cookie
Path	Information about the path of the web page a user was in, when the cookie was sent
Expiration	It can be set to expire and is denoted in the format date–month–time
Secure	If set, the information is encrypted during transmission
Value	Specific data to be stored

Cookies are named and have a single value. They may have optional attributes, including a comment, path, and domain qualifiers, a maximum age and a version. A server can provide one or more cookies to a client, and a browser is expected to support twenty cookies per host, three hundred per user, and limit each cookie's size to 4096 bytes. The servlet should create a cookie with an initial name and value. The name of the cookie must be an HTTP/1.1 token as defined by RFC 2109, and the value can be any string.

Null values are not guaranteed to work the same way on all browsers. Also, if your servlet returns a response to the user with a writer, create the cookie before accessing the writer, because cookies are sent to the client as a header, and headers must be written before accessing the writers.

A servlet can create cookies like this:

```
Cookie cookie = new Cookie("ID", "69");
```

Then send a cookie to the client using the `addCookie()` method of `HttpServletResponse`:

```
res.addCookie(cookie);
```

A servlet can retrieve a cookie by calling the `getCookies()` method of `HttpServletRequest`:

```
Cookie[] cookies = req.getCookies();
if (cookies != null) {
  for (int i = 0; i < cookies.length; i++) {
    String name = cookies[i].getName();
    String value = cookies[i].getValue();
  }
}
```

You can set a number of attributes like version, domain restriction pattern, maximum age, path, comment etc., for a cookie in addition to its name and value. The following example shows how cookies can be used for session handling:

```
import javax.servlet.*;
import javax.servlet.http.*;
import java.io.*;
import java.util.*;

public class CookieExample extends HttpServlet {

  public void init(ServletConfig config)
       throws ServletException {
    super.init(config);
  }

  private String getUser(String value) {
    String userName = null;
```

We would select the username from a database in a real application:

```
    if (value.equals("666")) {
      userName = "Adarsh";
    }
    return userName;
  }

  public void doGet(HttpServletRequest request,
                    HttpServletResponse response)
              throws ServletException, IOException {

    Cookie[] cookieList = request.getCookies();
    String user = null;
    String responseMessage = null;
    if (cookieList != null ) {

    for (int x = 0; x < cookieList.length; x++) {
        String name = cookieList[x].getName();
        if (name.equals("sid")) {
          user = getUser(cookieList[x].getValue());
          break;
        }
      }
    }

    if (user == null) {
      response.addCookie(new Cookie("sid", "666"));
      responseMessage = "Welcome! This is a new session";
    }
    else {
      responseMessage = "Hello " + user;
    }

    response.setContentType("text/html");
    PrintWriter out = response.getWriter();
    out.println("<html>");
    out.println("<head><title>Cookie Example</title></head>");
    out.println("<body style=\"font-family:verdana;font-size:10pt\">");
    out.println(responseMessage);
    out.println("</body></html>");
    out.close();
  }
}
```

Every time a request is serviced by the `CookieExample` servlet, it checks for cookies in the `HttpServletRequest`. If the request contains cookies, the servlet iterates over the list of cookies to look for a cookie with the name `sid`. In case cookies are not found and the list does not contain a cookie with a name `sid`, you create a cookie and add it to the response. When you test this servlet, you will see:

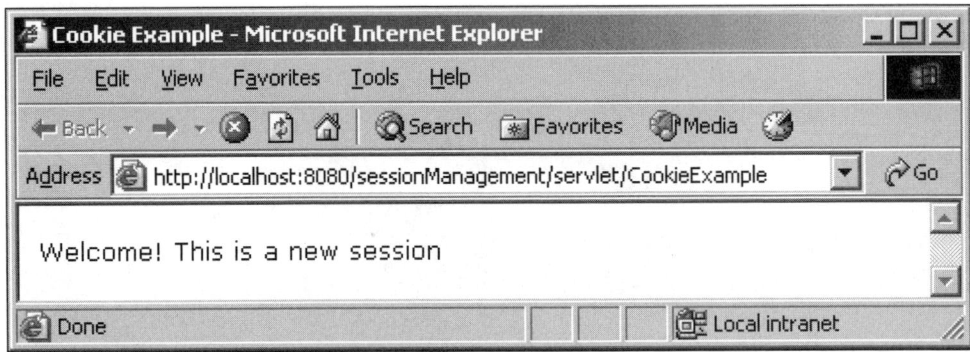

After this, press the Refresh button on your browser, and you will receive:

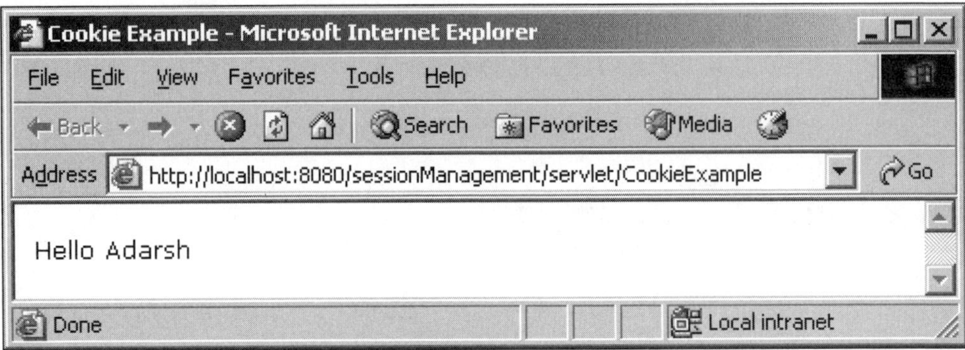

Session Tracking with Servlet API

The Servlet API provides several methods and classes to handle session tracking. However, the extent of support varies depending on the server. For example, a server could have the ability to revert to using URL rewriting when cookies fail, but Tomcat does not support this. The `HttpSession` object provides this functionality. The `HttpSession` object is defined by the `HttpSession` interface and is obtained using the `getSession()` method of the `HttpServletRequest` object. You can store any serializable Java objects in a session object. In our example, it is used to store the items of your shopping cart:

```
HttpSession session = request.getSession(true);
```

The parameter is a Boolean and has values:

- `true` to create a new session for this request if necessary
- `false` to return `null` if there's no current session

When tracking sessions in your servlets, the first thing you have to do is obtain the session object, and once this is done, you can read from or write to it. When you are finished, you can invalidate the session using the `invalidate()` method or let it expire on its own. The `setMaxInactiveInterval()` method lets you set the maximum time interval, in seconds, that the servlet container will keep this session open between client accesses. After this interval, the servlet container will invalidate the session. A negative time indicates the session should never timeout. You may want to invalidate the session if it is defined by a particular transaction that has been completed. However, if the session is simply used to track a user's action or to store their preferences, then you will probably want to leave it to expire on its own.

```
public void setAttribute(String name, Object value)
public void removeAttribute(String name)
public Object getAttribute(String name)
public Enumeration getAttributeNames()
```

To specify information, you use the `setAttribute()` method, supplying a key and a value. The `removeAttribute()` method removes the object bound to the specified name or does nothing if there is no binding. These methods can throw an `IllegalStateException` if the session being accessed is invalid.

These session objects have built in data structure that let you store any number of keys and associated values. You use `getAttribute()` method to look up a previously stored value. The return type is `Object`, so you have to cast it to a more specific type of data. The return value is null if there is no such attribute.

You can also find all the attribute names in a given session using the `getAttributeNames()` method, which returns an `Enumeration` object:

```
public String getId()
public boolean isNew()
public void invalidate()
public long getCreationTime()
public long getLastAccesedTime()
```

A user is assigned a new `HttpSession` object and a unique session ID when they first access the site. Behind the scenes, the session ID is usually saved on the client in a cookie or sent as part of a rewritten URL. A servlet can discover a session's ID with the `getId()` method.

A session either expires automatically after a set time of inactivity or when it is explicitly invalidated by a servlet. Several methods help in managing the session life cycle:

- The `isNew()` method returns `true` if the session was just created rather than being referenced by an incoming client request
- The `invalidate()` method causes the session to be invalidated, and all objects stored in the session are unbound
- The `getCreationTime()` method returns the time in milliseconds since January 1, 1970 at which the session was made
- The `getLastAccessedTime()` method returns the time at which the client last sent a request associated with this session since the January 1, 1970

The following code shows how we can use this information:

```
import javax.servlet.*;
import javax.servlet.http.*;
import java.util.*;
import java.io.*;

public class DigSessionInfo extends HttpServlet {
  public void doGet(HttpServletRequest request, HttpServletResponse response)
                  throws ServletException, IOException {
    HttpSession session = request.getSession(true);
    response.setContentType("text/html");
    PrintWriter out = response.getWriter();
    String title;
    Integer visitCount = new Integer(0);
    if (session.isNew()) {
      title = "Welcome";
    }
    else {
      title = "Welcome Again";
      Integer prevCount = (Integer)session.getAttribute("visitCount");
      if (prevCount != null) {
        visitCount = new Integer(prevCount.intValue() + 1);
      }
    }
    session.setAttribute("visitCount",visitCount);
    out.println(
      "<html>" +
      "<head><title>Session Example</title></head>" +
      "<body style=\"font-family:verdana;font-size:10pt\">" +
      "<h1>" + title + "</h1>" +
      "<h2>Information on Your Session </h2>" +
      "<table border=\"1\" style=\"font-size:10pt;\">" +
      "<tr>" +
      "<th>Info Type</th><th>Value</th>" +
      "</tr><tr>" +
      "<td>Session ID</td>" +
      "<td>" + session.getId() + "</td>" +
      "<tr>" +
      "<td>Created on</td>" +
      "<td>" + new Date(session.getCreationTime()) + "</td>" +
      "<tr>" +
      "<td>Last Accessed on</td>" +
      "<td>" + new Date(session.getLastAccessedTime()) + "</td>" +
      "<tr>" +
      "<td>Number of Visits</td>" +
      "<td>" + visitCount + "</td>" +
      "</tr>" +
      "</table>" +
      "</body></html>");
  }
  public void doPost(HttpServletRequest request, HttpServletResponse response)
```

```
                          throws ServletException, IOException {
      doGet(request, response);
   }
}
```

When you click on your browser's **Refresh** button you can see the heading change from "Welcome" to "Welcome Again" and the count of previous access incrementing:

Using the Session JSP Tag Library

The session JSP tag library (http://jakarta.apache.org/taglibs/doc/session-doc/intro.html) provides tags for reading or modifying client `HttpSession` information. To make use of this tag library the web application should be configured as follows (all these files can be downloaded from http://jakarta.apache.org/builds/jakarta-taglibs/releases/session/):

- Copy the tag library descriptor file (`session.tld`) to the `/WEB-INF` subdirectory of your web application
- Copy the tag library JAR file (`session.jar`) to the `/WEB-INF/lib` subdirectory of your web application.
- Add a `<taglib>` element to your web application deployment descriptor in `/WEB-INF/web.xml` like this:

```
<taglib>
  <taglib-uri>http://jakarta.apache.org/taglibs/session-1.0</taglib-uri>
  <taglib-location>/WEB-INF/session.tld</taglib-location>
</taglib>
```

To use the tags from this library in your JSP pages, add the following directive at the top of each page:

```
<%@ taglib uri="http://jakarta.apache.org/taglibs/session-1.0"
           prefix="sess" %>
```

sess is the tag name prefix. You can change this value to any prefix you like.

The following tags are present in this tag library:

The session Tag

This tag is used to access general information about the session:

- creationTime
  Returns the time in milliseconds since midnight January 1, 1970 GMT
- sessionId
  Returns the unique id of this session
- lastAccessedTime
  Returns the last time the client sent a request as number of milliseconds since midnight January 1, 1970 GMT
- maxInactiveInterval
  Returns the maximum time interval, in seconds, that the servlet container will keep this session open between client accesses

Here is an example of the session tag in action:

```
<sess:session id="ss" />
  The creation time in milliseconds since midnight January 1, 1970 GMT is:
<jsp:getProperty name="ss" property="creationTime" />
```

The isnew Tag

This tag is used to determine if a session is new. If value is set to false if session is not new. It also contains the body of the tag if it is new.

```
<sess:isnew>
  This session is new.
</sess:isnew>
<sess:isnew value="false">
  This session is not new.
</sess:isnew>
```

The invalidate Tag

This tag is used to invalidate a session.

```
<sess:invalidate/>
```

The maxinactiveinterval Tag

This tag is used to set the maximum inactive interval before a session times out, causing it to be removed:

```
<sess:maxinactiveinterval>900</sess:maxinactiveinterval>
```

The attribute Tag

This tag returns a single attribute value:

```
<sess:attribute name="test1"/>
```

The attributes Tag

This tag loops through all the session attribute name-value pairs:

```
<sess:attributes id="loop">
  Name: <jsp:getProperty name="loop" property="name" />
  Value: <jsp:getProperty name="loop" property="value" />
</sess:attributes>
```

The existsattribute Tag

This tag checks if an attribute exists. If `value` is set to `false` the session attribute does not exist:

```
<sess:existsattribute name="test1">
  The session attribute with name test1 exists.
</sess:existsattribute>
<sess:existsattribute name="test1" value="false">
  The session attribute with name test1 does not exist.
</sess:existsattribute>
```

The removeattribute Tag

This tag removes an attribute:

```
<sess:removeattribute name="test1"/>
```

The setattribute Tag

This tag sets an attribute:

```
<sess:setattribute name="test1">Test Value</sess:setattribute>
```

Online Store

Cyber shopping is a booming business. The following example shows you the skeletal implementation of an on-line bookstore. We will try to implement a few of the concepts we have discussed so far in this example.

Creating a Database

We will start by defining the database tables that holds information about the books we intend to sell and about our customers. We will use MySQL for this purpose (see Appendix B for details of installing MySQL). This example needs three tables, the `category` table that stores the description of the various categories under which we segregate the books, the `products` table contains the details about the books, and the `customer` table contains the details about our customers. We also include some sample data:

```
CREATE DATABASE shopping;

USE shopping;

CREATE TABLE category (
    cid INTEGER PRIMARY KEY AUTO_INCREMENT,
    cdesc VARCHAR(30)
);

CREATE TABLE products (
    pid INTEGER PRIMARY KEY AUTO_INCREMENT,
    cat INTEGER,
    pdesc VARCHAR(50),
    price FLOAT
);

CREATE TABLE IF NOT EXISTS customer (
    custno INTEGER PRIMARY KEY AUTO_INCREMENT,
    n_last VARCHAR(35),
    n_first VARCHAR(20),
    n_mi CHAR,
    a_number VARCHAR(10),
    a_street VARCHAR(25),
    a_apt VARCHAR(8),
    a_city VARCHAR(25),
    a_state CHAR(2),
    a_zip CHAR(5),
    a_zip_plus4  CHAR(4),
    a_telno CHAR(10),
    a_tel_ext CHAR(4));

GRANT ALL PRIVILEGES
    ON shopping.*
    TO adarsh@localhost IDENTIFIED BY 'hsrada';

INSERT INTO category VALUES (1,'Java');
INSERT INTO category VALUES (2, '.NET');
INSERT INTO category VALUES (3, 'Linux');
INSERT INTO category VALUES (4, 'SQL');
INSERT INTO category VALUES (5, 'XML');

INSERT INTO products VALUES
    (1861004958, 1, 'Professional JSP 2nd Edition', 59.99);
INSERT INTO products VALUES
    (1861002092, 1, 'Beginning JSP Web Development', 39.99);
INSERT INTO products VALUES #
    (1861004974, 2, 'Professional VB.NET', 59.99);
INSERT INTO products VALUES
    (1861003013, 3, 'Professional Linux Programming', 59.99);
INSERT INTO products VALUES
    (1861005474, 5, 'Professional XML Schemas', 59.99);
```

The `customer` table contains a unique id for each customer, along with name and address details. Each product belongs to a category.

Now that we have created the database, the next step is to provide it with the web interface that the visitors can use to access the bookstore. We will divide the page into two frames. The left frame persists throughout and will contain the navigational menu, and the right frame is used as the primary display area. The HTML code for `index.html`:

```
<html>
  <head>
    <title>Wrox Press</title>
  </head>
  <frameset cols="150,*">
    <frame src="Menu.html"
      frameborder="0" noresize="noresize" name="MAINMENUFRAME">
    <frame src="Welcome.jsp"
      frameborder="0" name="RIGHTFRAME">
  </frameset>
</html>
```

The code for the menu frame is in `Menu.html`:

```
<html>
  <head>
    <link rel="stylesheet" type="text/css" href="style/menu.css" />
  </head>
  <body>
    <table>
      <tr>
        <td>
          <a href="CustomerApplication.html"
             target="RIGHTFRAME">Registration</a>
        </td>
      </tr>
      <tr>
        <td>
          <a href="ProductCategories.jsp"
             target="RIGHTFRAME">Catalog</a>
        </td>
      </tr>
      <tr>
        <td>
          <a href="ShoppingCart.jsp"
             target="RIGHTFRAME">Shopping Cart</a>
        </td>
      </tr>
    </table>
    <hr />
  </body>
</html>
```

The main display area will display the contents as generated by `Welcome.jsp`. This also makes the customer bean available for use. The customer ID is set using the `<setProperty>` tag. Using the customer bean, a personalized welcome message is displayed.

```
<%@ page import="javax.servlet.http.Cookie" %>
<%@include file="CustId.jsp" %>
<jsp:useBean id="custBean" class="shopping.Customer"
  scope="session">
  <jsp:setProperty name="custBean" property="customerInfo"
    value="<%= getCustID(request) %>" />
</jsp:useBean>

<html>
  <head>
    <link rel="stylesheet" type="text/css" href="style/global.css" />
  </head>
  <body>
    <%
      String val = getCustID(request);
      if (val != null) {
    %>
    <h2>Welcome,
    <jsp:getProperty name="custBean" property="firstName" /></h2>
    <%
      }
      else {
    %>
    <h2>Welcome!</h2>
    <p>
    You have not registered before, please do so by clicking on
    <i><b>Registration</b></i> in the menu.</p>
    <%
      }
    %>
    <p>
    Welcome to Wrox Press. You can use the menu on the left to navigate.
    </p>
  </body>
</html>
```

The `Welcome.jsp`– includes the `CustId.jsp`:

```
<%! public String getCustID(HttpServletRequest request) {
    String custID = null;
    Cookie[] cookies = request.getCookies();
    if (cookies != null) {
      for (int i = 0; i < cookies.length; ++i) {
        if (cookies[i].getName().equals("customerid")) {
          custID = cookies[i].getValue();
          break;
        }
      }
    }
    return custID;
  }
%>
```

This file contains a function for checking for a cookie name `customerid` in the request and returns the cookie value, which is the unique ID of the customer. The customer bean to retrieve the customer information from the database uses this.

If the user is visiting for the first time the `Welcome.jsp` prompts the user to register by clicking on the **Registration** link on the menu frame, else the visitor is greeted with his name. The `Customer` bean contains methods to retrieve (`getCustomerInfo()` method) and store (`recordCustomer()` method) information about the customer. The code for the customer bean looks like this:

```
package shopping;

import java.sql.*;
import java.sql.Connection;
import java.sql.ResultSet;
import java.sql.SQLException;
import java.sql.Statement;
import java.text.SimpleDateFormat;
import java.util.Date;
import javax.servlet.http.Cookie;
import javax.servlet.http.HttpServletRequest;

public class Customer {

  Connection con = null;
private String customerID = "";
  private String firstName = "";
  private String lastName = "";
  private String middleInitial = "";
  private String streetNumber = "";
  private String street = "";
  private String apt = "";
  private String city = "";
  private String state = "";
  private String zip = "";
  private String zipPlusFour = "";
  private String telephoneNumber = "";
  private String telephoneExtension = "";
```

Then we define the standard getter and setter methods for these properties, we won't show them here.

```
  private static final String GET_CUSTOMER_INFO =
    "SELECT * FROM customer";

  private static final String CUSTNO_QUALIFIER =
    " WHERE custno=";

  private static final String INSERT_CUST =
    "INSERT INTO customer VALUES";

  private static final String AND = " and ";
  private static final String LPAREN = "(";
  private static final String RPAREN = ")";
  private static final String COMMA = ",";
  private static final String PERCENT = "%";
  private static final String QUOTE = "'";
```

```
private static final String NULL = "null";

public Customer() {
  Class.forName("org.gjt.mm.mysql.Driver").newInstance();
}

public void setCustomerInfo(String custno) throws Exception {
  if (custno != null) {
    customerID = custno;
    getCustomerInfo(custno);
  }
}

private String getCustomerIDno() throws SQLException {
  String cno;
  con = DriverManager.getConnection(
     "jdbc:mysql://localhost/shopping?user=adarsh&password=hsrada");
  Statement qs = con.createStatement();
  ResultSet rs = qs.executeQuery("Select * from customer");
  rs.last();
  cno = Integer.toString(rs.getInt(1));
  con.close();
  customerID = cno;
  return cno;
}

private void getCustomerInfo(String custno)  throws SQLException {
  con = DriverManager.getConnection(
     "jdbc:mysql://localhost/shopping?user=adarsh&password=hsrada");

  Statement qs = con.createStatement();
  ResultSet rs = qs.executeQuery(GET_CUSTOMER_INFO +
                                 CUSTNO_QUALIFIER +
                                 QUOTE + custno + QUOTE);
  rs.next();
  customerID = Integer.toString(rs.getInt(1));
  lastName = rs.getString(2);
  firstName = rs.getString(3);
  middleInitial = rs.getString(4);
  streetNumber = rs.getString(5);
  street = rs.getString(6);
  apt = rs.getString(7);
  city = rs.getString(8);
  state = rs.getString(9);
  zip = rs.getString(10);
  zipPlusFour = rs.getString(11);
  telephoneNumber = rs.getString(12);
  telephoneExtension = rs.getString(13);
  con.close();
}

public String recordCustomer() throws SQLException {
  con = DriverManager.getConnection(
    "jdbc:mysql://localhost/shopping?user=adarsh&password=hsrada");
```

```
    Statement st = con.createStatement();
    st.executeUpdate("INSERT INTO customer " +
                     LPAREN + "n_last" + COMMA + "n_first" +
                     COMMA + "n_mi" + COMMA + "a_number" + COMMA +
                     "a_street" + COMMA + "a_apt" + COMMA + "a_city" +
                     COMMA + "a_state" + COMMA + "a_zip" + COMMA +
                     "a_zip_plus4" + COMMA + "a_telno" + COMMA +
                     "a_tel_ext" + RPAREN + " VALUES " + LPAREN +
                     QUOTE + lastName + QUOTE + COMMA +
                     QUOTE + firstName + QUOTE + COMMA +
                     QUOTE + middleInitial + QUOTE + COMMA +
                     QUOTE + streetNumber + QUOTE + COMMA +
                     QUOTE + street + QUOTE + COMMA +
                     QUOTE + apt + QUOTE + COMMA +
                     QUOTE + city + QUOTE + COMMA +
                     QUOTE + state + QUOTE + COMMA +
                     QUOTE + zip + QUOTE + COMMA +
                     QUOTE + zipPlusFour + QUOTE + COMMA +
                     QUOTE + telephoneNumber + QUOTE + COMMA +
                     QUOTE + telephoneExtension + QUOTE + RPAREN);
    con.close();
    return getCustomerIDno();
  }
}
```

If you open the application for the first time, the initial screen would look like this:

RegisterCustomer.jsp

On clicking the Registration option, the CustomerApplication.html is displayed (see the code download for details of this HTML page):

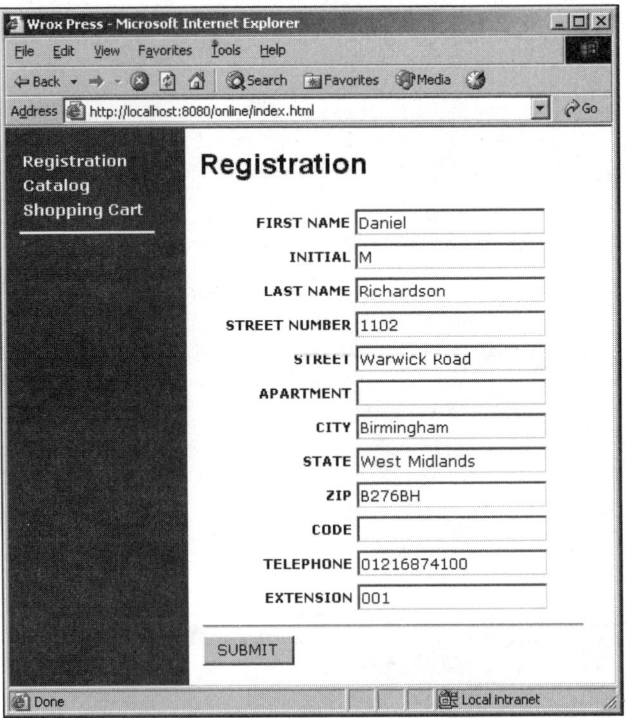

On submitting this form, `RegisterCustomer.jsp` action is executed:

```
<%@ page errorPage="Error.jsp" %>
<%@ page import="javax.servlet.http.Cookie" %>
<%@include file="CustId.jsp" %>
<jsp:useBean id="custBean" class="shopping.Customer"
  scope="session" >
</jsp:useBean>
<jsp:setProperty name="custBean" property="*" />
<html>
  <head>
    <link rel="stylesheet" type="text/css" href="style/global.css" />
  </head>
  <body>

  <%
    String ln = custBean.recordCustomer();
  %>
  <%
    String custno = custBean.getCustomerID();
  %>
```

```
<%
  Cookie c = new Cookie("customerid",custno);
  c.setVersion(1);
  c.setPath("/");
  c.setMaxAge(365 * 24 * 60 * 60);
  response.addCookie(c);
%>


  <h2>Welcome,
  <jsp:getProperty name="custBean" property="firstName" />
  </h2>
  <p>We have recorded the following data in your profile:</p>
  <table>
    <tr>
      <td class="registerTD">First Name</td>
      <td><jsp:getProperty name="custBean" property="firstName" /></td>
    </tr>
    <tr>
      <td class="registerTD">Middle Initial</td>
      <td>
        <jsp:getProperty name="custBean" property="middleInitial" />
      </td>
    <tr>
      <td class="registerTD">Last Name</td>
      <td><jsp:getProperty name="custBean" property="lastName" /></td>
    <tr>
      <td class="registerTD">Street Number</td>
      <td><jsp:getProperty name="custBean" property="streetNumber" /></td>
    </tr>
    <tr>
      <td class="registerTD">Street</td>
      <td><jsp:getProperty name="custBean" property="street" /></td>
    </tr>
    <tr>
      <td class="registerTD">Apartment</td>
      <td><jsp:getProperty name="custBean" property="apt" /></td>
    </tr>
    <tr>
      <td class="registerTD">City</td>
      <td><jsp:getProperty name="custBean" property="city" /></td>
    </tr>
    <tr>
      <td class="registerTD">State</td>
      <td><jsp:getProperty name="custBean" property="state" /></td>
    </tr>
    <tr>
      <td class="registerTD">Zip</td>
      <td><jsp:getProperty name="custBean" property="zip" /></td>
    </tr>
    <tr>
      <td class="registerTD">Code</td>
      <td><jsp:getProperty name="custBean" property="zipPlusFour" /></td>
    </tr>
```

```
        <tr>
          <td class="registerTD">Telephone</td>
          <td>
            <jsp:getProperty name="custBean" property="telephoneNumber" />
          </td>
        </tr>
        <tr>
          <td class="registerTD">Extension</td>
          <td>
            <jsp:getProperty name="custBean" property="telephoneExtension" />
          </td>
        </tr>
      </table>
    </body>
  </html>
```

This also uses the `recordCustomer()` method of the customer bean to store the customer's details in the customer table, and sends a cookie to the browser. The summary of the entry made is also displayed:

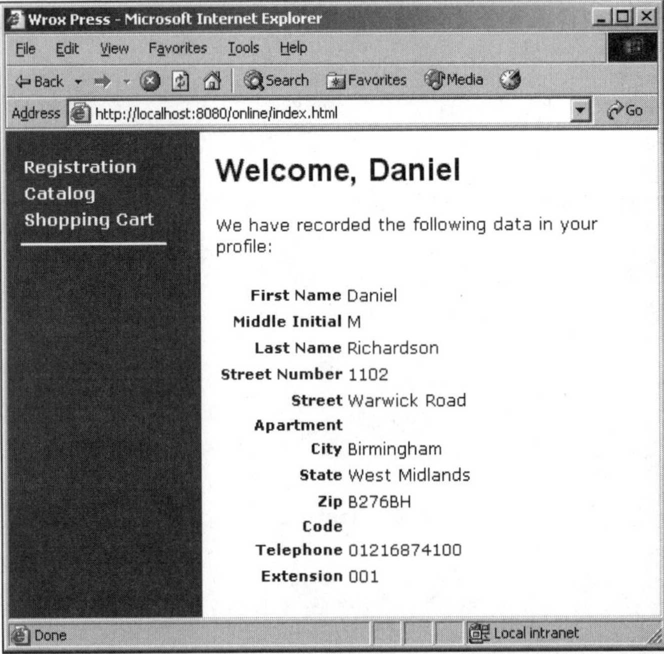

On clicking the Catalog on the menu, the `ProductCategories.jsp` is executed, which uses the `ProductBean` to iterate and display the list of categories.

```
  <jsp:useBean id="pb" class="shopping.ProductBean"
    scope="request" />
  <%
    String[] categories = pb.getCategories();
```

```
%>
<html>
  <head>
    <link rel="stylesheet" type="text/css" href="style/global.css" />
  </head>
  <body>
    <h2>Catalog</h2>
    <table>
      <%
        for (int i=0; i<categories.length; ++i) {
      %>
          <tr>
            <td>
      <%
            String anchor = "<a href=\"GetProducts.jsp?" +
                            "cat=" + categories[i]+"\">";
      %>

            <%= anchor %>
            <%=pb.getCategoryName(categories[i]) %></a>
            </td>
          </tr>
      <%
        }
      %>
    </table>
  </body>
</html>
```

The `getCategories()` action of the `ProductBean` is executed, and the categories are listed:

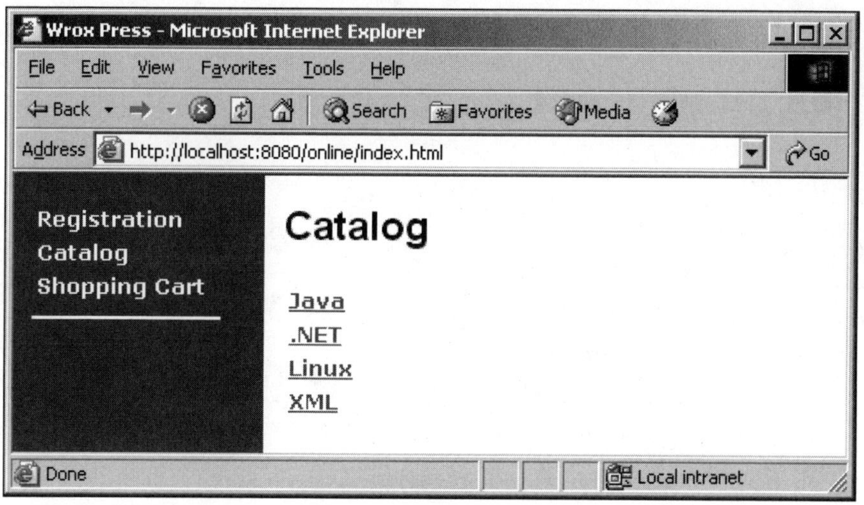

The ProductBean contains methods to retrieve the product and category names. The code for the ProductBean.java looks like this:

```
import java.util.*;

public class ProductBean {

  Connection con = null;
  private static final String AND = " AND ";
  private static final String QUOTE = "'";
  private static final String RBRAC = ")";
  private static final String COMMA = ",";

  public ProductBean() throws Exception {
    Class.forName("org.gjt.mm.mysql.Driver").newInstance();
  }

  public ProductList[] getProductEntries() throws SQLException {
    con = DriverManager.getConnection(
       "jdbc:mysql://localhost/shopping?user=adarsh&password=hsrada");

    Statement us = con.createStatement();
    ResultSet rs = us.executeQuery("SELECT * FROM products");
    Vector v = new Vector();
    while (rs.next()) {
      ProductList pl = new ProductList();
      pl.setId(rs.getInt(1));
      pl.setProduct(rs.getInt(2));
      pl.setDescription(rs.getString(3));
      pl.setPrice(rs.getFloat(4));
      v.add(pl);
    }
    con.close();
    ProductList[] plv = new ProductList[v.size()];
    for (int i = 0; i < v.size(); ++i) {
      plv[i] = (ProductList)v.elementAt(i);
    }
    return plv;
  }

  public ProductList[] getProductEntries(String cat) throws SQLException {
    con = DriverManager.getConnection(
       "jdbc:mysql://localhost/shopping?user=adarsh&password=hsrada");

    Statement us = con.createStatement();
    ResultSet rs = us.executeQuery("SELECT * FROM products WHERE " +
                                   " cat = " + cat);
    Vector v = new Vector();
    while (rs.next()) {
      ProductList pl = new ProductList();
      pl.setId(rs.getInt(1));
      pl.setProduct(rs.getInt(2));
      pl.setDescription(rs.getString(3));
      pl.setPrice(rs.getFloat(4));
```

```
      v.add(pl);
    }
    con.close();
    ProductList[] plv = new ProductList[v.size()];
    for (int i = 0; i < v.size(); ++i) {
      plv[i] = (ProductList)v.elementAt(i);
    }
    return plv;
  }

  public ProductList getProductEntry(int id) throws SQLException {
    con = DriverManager.getConnection(
       "jdbc:mysql://localhost/shopping?user=adarsh&password=hsrada");

    Statement us = con.createStatement();
    ResultSet rs = us.executeQuery("SELECT * FROM products WHERE pid = " +
                                   Integer.toString(id));
    rs.next();
    ProductList pl = new ProductList();
    pl.setId(rs.getInt(1));
    pl.setProduct(rs.getInt(2));
    pl.setDescription(rs.getString(3));
    pl.setPrice(rs.getFloat(4));
    con.close();
    return pl;
  }

  public String[] getCategories() throws SQLException {
    con = DriverManager.getConnection(
       "jdbc:mysql://localhost/shopping?user=adarsh&password=hsrada");

    Statement us = con.createStatement();
    ResultSet rs = us.executeQuery("SELECT DISTINCT cat FROM products");
    Vector v = new Vector();
    while (rs.next()) {
      String s = rs.getString(1);
      v.add(s);
    }
    con.close();
    String[] sa = new String[v.size()];
    for (int i = 0; i < v.size(); ++i) {
      sa[i] = (String)v.elementAt(i);
    }
    return sa;
  }

  public String getCategoryName(String cat) throws SQLException {
    con = DriverManager.getConnection(
       "jdbc:mysql://localhost/shopping?user=adarsh&password=hsrada");

    Statement us = con.createStatement();
    ResultSet rs = us.executeQuery("SELECT cdesc FROM category WHERE " +
                                   " cid = " + cat);
    rs.next();
```

```
        String catname = rs.getString(1);
        con.close();
        return catname;
    }
}
```

On selecting a particular product category, the `GetProducts.jsp` executes to list the products under that category:

```
<%@ page import="java.util.Hashtable" %>

<jsp:useBean id="pb" class="shopping.ProductBean"
  scope="session" />
<%
  String query = request.getQueryString();
  Hashtable qt = HttpUtils.parseQueryString(query);
  String cat = ((String[])qt.get("cat"))[0];
  shopping.ProductList[] pl = pb.getProductEntries(cat);
%>
<html>
  <head>
    <link rel="stylesheet" type="text/css" href="style/global.css" />
  </head>
  <body>
    <h2>Product List</h2>
    <table>
      <%
        for (int i = 0; i < pl.length; ++i) {
        String href = "<a href=\"SelectItem.jsp?" +
                      "pid=" + pl[i].getId() + "\">";
      %>
      <tr>
        <td>
          <%= href %>
          <%= pl[i].getId() %>
        </td>
        <td>
          <%= pl[i].getDescription() %>
        </td>
      </tr>
    <%
      }
    %>
  </body>
</html>
```

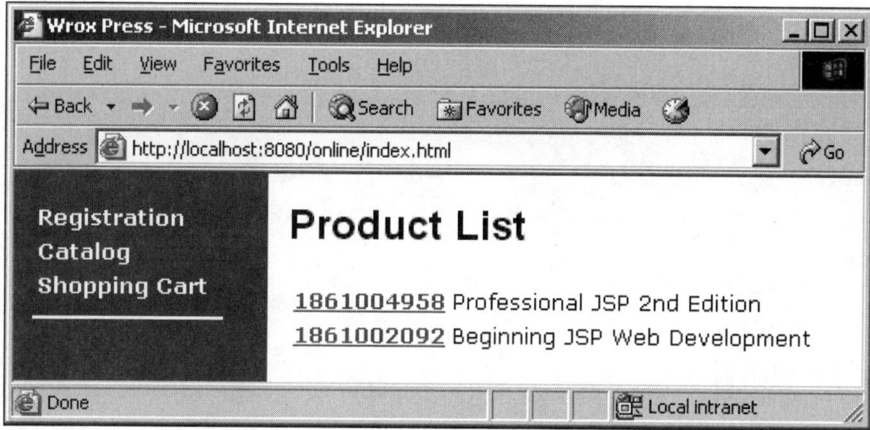

The product ID is a link to the `SelectItem.jsp`. This uses the `ProductBean` to list the products in the shopping cart as a table. It generates a form to accept the quantity details for each product.

```
<%@ page import="java.util.Hashtable" %>
<jsp:useBean id="pb" class="shopping.ProductBean"
  scope="session" />
<%
  String query = request.getQueryString();
  Hashtable qt = HttpUtils.parseQueryString(query);
  String idString = ((String[])qt.get("pid"))[0];
  int id = Integer.parseInt(idString);
  shopping.ProductList pl = pb.getProductEntry(id);
  String action = "AddItem.jsp?" +
    "pid=" + idString + "\"";
%>
<html>
  <head>
    <link rel="stylesheet" type="text/css" href="style/global.css" />
  </head>
  <body>
    <h2>Add Item to Shopping Cart</h2>
    <form method="POST" action="<%= action %>">
      <table class="registerTable">
        <tr>
          <td class="registertd">
            ID
          </td>
          <td>
            <%= pl.getId() %>
          </td>
        </tr>
        <tr>
          <td class="registertd">
            Description
          </td>
          <td>
            <%= pl.getDescription() %>
```

```
          </td>
        </tr>
        <tr>
          <td class="registertd">
            Price
          </td>
          <td>
            <%= pl.getPrice() %>
          </td>
        </tr>
      </table>
      <p>Enter how many of the above items you would like to order.</p>
      <p>Then click on "ADD TO SHOPPING CART".</p>
      Quantity:
      <input type="text" name="quantity" size="5" />
      <input type="submit" name="submit" value="ADD TO SHOPPING CART">
    </form>
  </body>
</html>
```

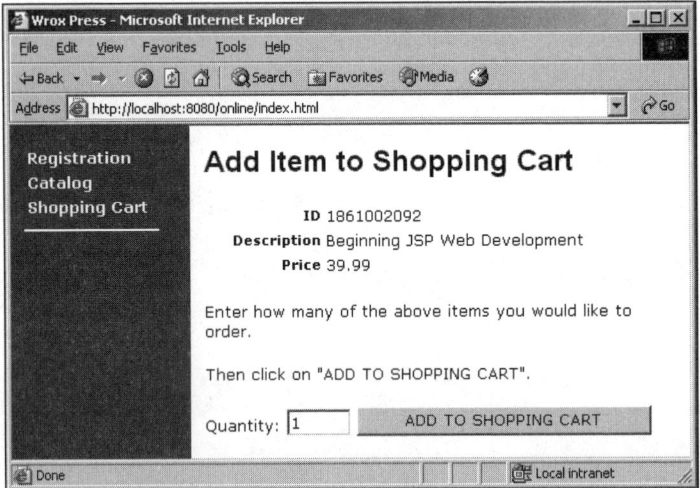

On specifying the quantity, and submitting the form, the `AddItem.jsp` action is executed, which calls the `addItem()` method of the `ShoppingCart` bean.

```
<%@ page import="java.util.Hashtable" %>

<jsp:useBean id="pb" class="shopping.ProductBean"
             scope="session" />
<jsp:useBean id="cart" class="shopping.ShoppingCart"
             scope="session" />
<%
  String query = request.getQueryString();
  Hashtable qt = HttpUtils.parseQueryString(query);
  int id = Integer.parseInt(((String[])qt.get("pid"))[0]);
  shopping.ProductList pl = pb.getProductEntry(id);
```

```
    int qty = Integer.parseInt(request.getParameter("quantity"));
    cart.addItem(new shopping.OrderItem(pl,qty));
    shopping.OrderItem[] contents = cart.getContents();
%>
<jsp:forward page="ShoppingCart.jsp" />
```

The `ProductList` class identifies the book order:

```
import java.util.Hashtable;
import java.util.StringTokenizer;

public class ProductList {
```

All these properties have the appropriate getter and setter methods:

```
  public int product;
  public int id;
  public String description;
  public float price;

  public ProductList() {}

  public boolean matchesDesc(String keywords,boolean all) {
    String dl = description.toLowerCase();
    StringTokenizer kst = new StringTokenizer(keywords);
    String[] keys = new String[kst.countTokens()];
    while (kst.hasMoreTokens()) {
      String tok = kst.nextToken();
      int ix = dl.indexOf(tok.toLowerCase());
      if (ix >= 0) {
        if (!all) {
return true;
        }
      }
      else {
        if (all) {
          return false;
        }
      }
    }
    return (all) ? true: false;
  }
}
```

The `OrderItem` class extends `ProductList`. This identifies the book along with the quantity ordered:

```
public class OrderItem extends ProductList {
  int quantity;

  public OrderItem(ProductList pl, int quantity) {
    setProduct(pl.getProduct());
    setId(pl.getId());
    setDescription(pl.getDescription());
```

```
    setPrice(pl.getPrice());
    this.quantity = quantity;
  }

  public int getQuantity() {
    return quantity;
  }

  public void setQuantity(int quantity) {
    this.quantity = quantity;
  }
}
```

The ordered item is added to the shopping cart, through a `<jsp:forward>` action to the `ShoppingCart.jsp`. This generates a page containing the list of items currently ordered. The same action is executed on clicking the Shopping Cart on the menu frame:

```
<jsp:useBean id="cart" class="shopping.ShoppingCart"
  scope="session" />
<%
  shopping.OrderItem[] contents = cart.getContents();
  if (contents.length == 0) {
%>
    <jsp:forward page="NoItems.html" />
<%
  }
%>
<html>
  <head>
    <link rel="stylesheet" type="text/css" href="style/global.css" />
  </head>
  <body>
    <h2>Shopping Cart</h2>
    <form method="POST" action="CheckOut.html">
      <table class="registerTable">
<%
        for (int i=0; i<contents.length; ++i) {
      %>
          <tr>
            <td class="center">
              <%= contents[i].getId() %>
            </td>
            <td class="right">
              <%= contents[i].getDescription() %>
            </td>
            <td class="right">
              <input type="input" size="3"
                name="<%= contents[i].getId() %>"
                value="<%= contents[i].getQuantity() %>">
            </td>
            <td class="right">
              <%= contents[i].getPrice() %>
            </td>
```

```
          <td class="right">
            <%= cart.totalAsString(contents[i].getId()) %>
          </td>
        </tr>
    <%
      }
    %>
      <tr>
        <td></td>
        <td></td>
        <td></td>
        <td></td>
        <td class="right">
          <%= cart.totalAsString() %>
        </td>
      </tr>
    </table>
    <hr />
    <table>
      <tr>
        <td>
          <input type="submit" name="checkout" value="CHECK OUT">
        </td>
      </tr>
    </table>
  </form>
 </body>
</html>
```

The `ShoppingCart` bean provides methods to:

- Empty the cart
- Check whether the cart is empty
- Retrieve the contents of the cart
- Set the quantity to an existing item
- Add items to the cart

```
package shopping;

import java.text.NumberFormat;
import java.util.Enumeration;
import java.util.Hashtable;

public class ShoppingCart {

  Hashtable contents;

  public ShoppingCart() {
    contents = new Hashtable();
  }
```

```
  public void empty() {
    contents.clear();
  }

  public boolean isEmpty() {
    return (contents.size() > 0);
  }

  public OrderItem[] getContents() {
    OrderItem[] sca = new OrderItem[contents.size()];
    int i = 0;
    for (Enumeration e = contents.elements(); e.hasMoreElements();) {
      sca[i++] = (OrderItem)e.nextElement();
    }
    return sca;
  }

  public void setQuantity(String id, int quantity) {
    if (!contents.containsKey(id)) {
      return;
    }
    if (quantity == 0) {
      contents.remove(id);
      return;
    }
    OrderItem item = (OrderItem)contents.get(id);
    item.setQuantity(quantity);
    contents.put(id,item);
  }

  public void addItem(OrderItem item) {
    String id = Integer.toString(item.getId());
    if (contents.containsKey(id)) {
      OrderItem itemInCart =
        (OrderItem)contents.get(id);
item.setQuantity(item.getQuantity() +
        itemInCart.getQuantity());
    }
    contents.put(id,item);
  }

  public String totalAsString(int id) {
    OrderItem item =
      (OrderItem)contents.get(Integer.toString(id));
    NumberFormat nf = NumberFormat.getCurrencyInstance();
    return nf.format((double)item.getQuantity() *
      (double)item.getPrice());
  }

  public String totalAsString() {
    double total = 0;
    for (Enumeration e = contents.elements(); e.hasMoreElements();) {
      OrderItem item = (OrderItem)e.nextElement();
        total = total + (double)item.getQuantity() *
```

```
            (double)item.getPrice();
        }
        NumberFormat nf = NumberFormat.getCurrencyInstance();
        return nf.format(total);
    }
}
```

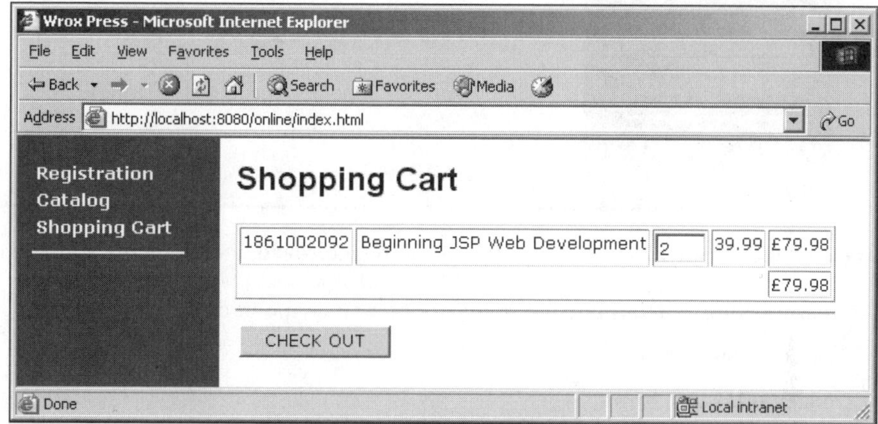

When no items are selected to the shopping cart the `NoItems.html` page is displayed:

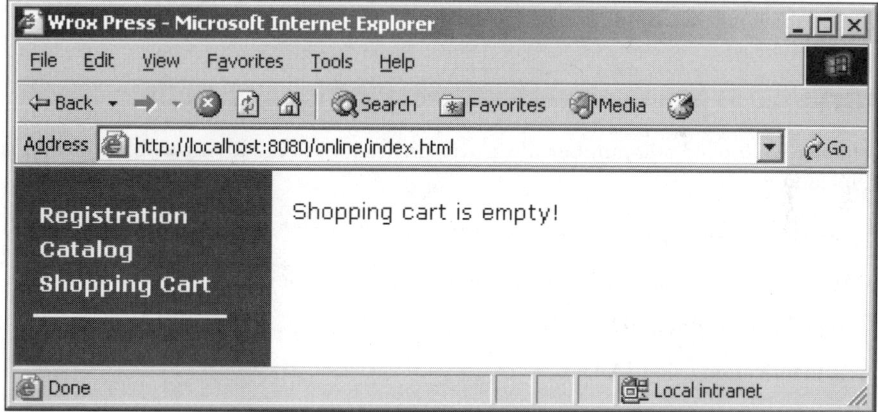

When the form in the `ShoppingCart.jsp` is submitted by clicking on the Check Out button, the `CheckOut.html` page is displayed:

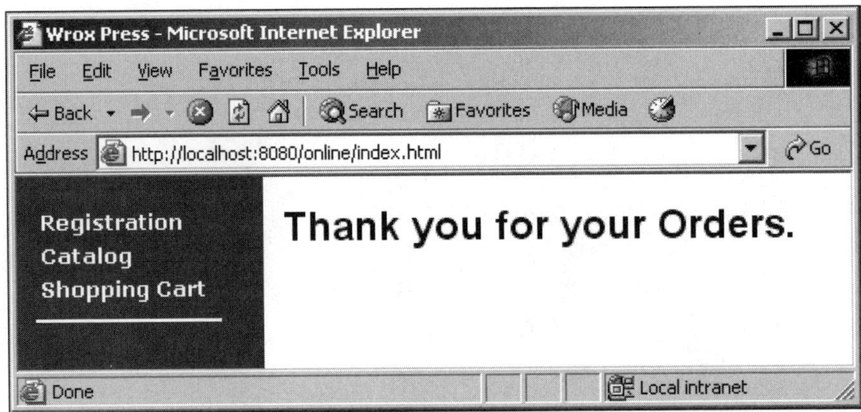

There are a number of ways that this application can be improved, including the addition of:

- Order tracking to determine the status of order at any point of time
- Customer feed back form
- Product evaluation forms
- Special schemes for regular shoppers

I would encourage you to use this application, and the techniques we've covered in this chapter, as a starting point for your own applications.

Summary

In this chapter we looked at a number of security issues that relate to our web applications and servers, including:

- The authentication mechanisms of HTTP protocol
- Methods we can use to implement custom authentication
- Digital certificates and Secure Sockets Layer (SSL)
- Authentication using JAAS

Then we went on to look at how we can manage users that access our site. We saw a number of simple examples that demonstrated various user management techniques, including an implementation of a simple login management system and a shopping cart.

In the next chapter, we will continue to learn how to manage users. We will see how we can track users as they navigate our site, and use the information we gather about users to tailor the content and style of our site appropriately.

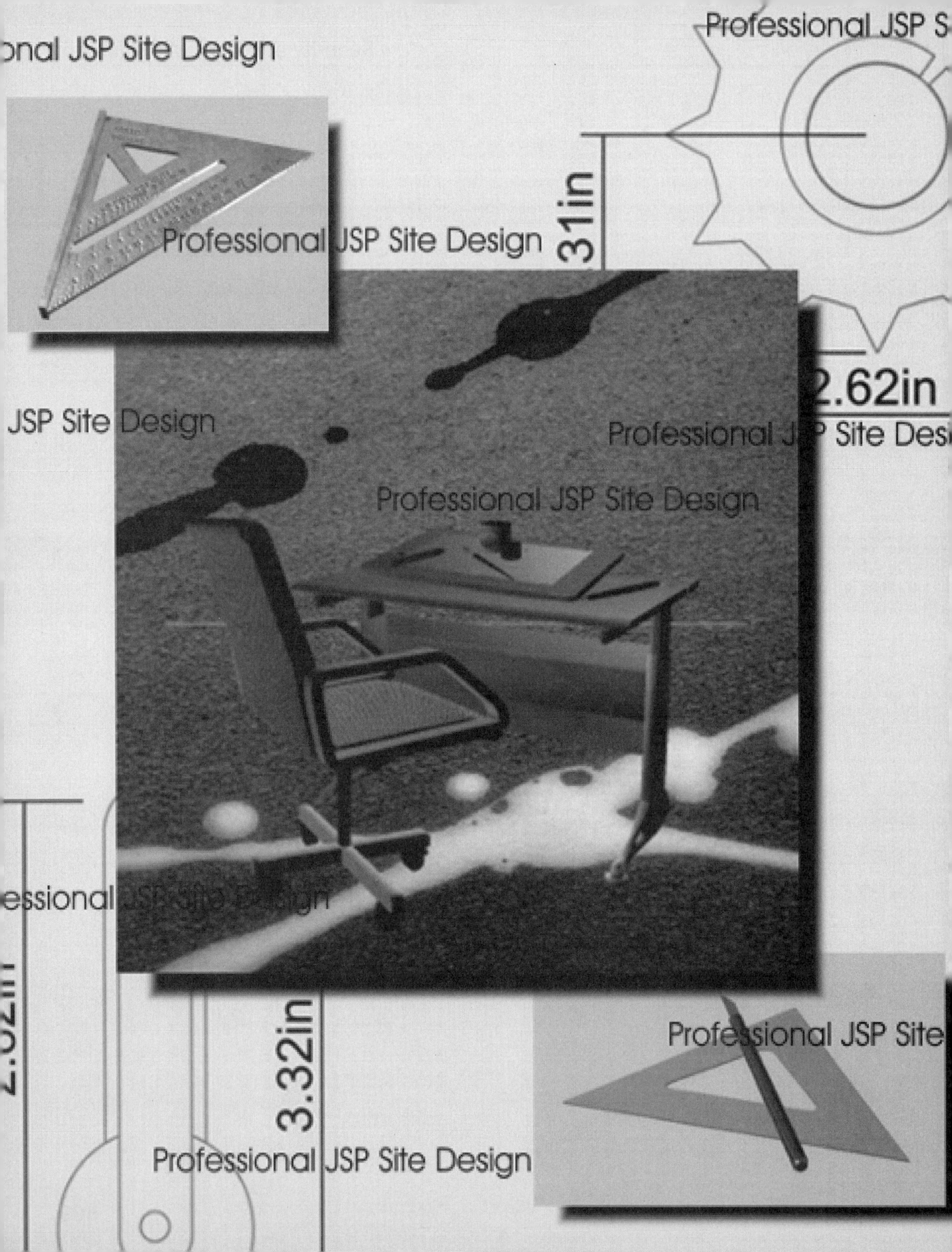
Professional JSP Site Design
31in
2.62in
Professional JSP Site Design
3.32in
Professional JSP Site Design

11

Visitor Tracking and Personalization

Not all visitors to your site are the same. They won't all want to see the same content, and they'll all have different ideas about the importance of the content they do see. Visitors might even enjoy your site more if the layout was slightly different, or a different color scheme was used.

In this chapter, we'll look at how we can tailor content for a particular user. Of course, in order to tailor the content for a user we need to be able to identify the user. In Chapter 10, we saw how we can keep track of users across sessions, and in this chapter, we will put those techniques to practical use.

It's also very useful to get an idea of how visitors use your site. What pages do they visit? In what order do they visit them? We can learn a great deal about a client by examining the request parameters and HTTP headers that they send when they access a site. We can then use this information to build a better picture of our users, and tailor the content of the site accordingly. However, we don't want to have to create the code to keep track of our users ourselves. It would be much better to use a pre-existing application to do this tedious job for us, so we'll look at some software that performs this role.

Specifically, we'll look at:

- How we can gather information from a request by a client, and what sort of information is available
- How we can use visitor-tracking software to keep track of the pages that are accessed on our site

Then, we'll go onto to build an example web application that provides personalized content to users. It will allow users to register and logon with the system, and then specify the layout, content, and colors used on the site. This application will make use of the techniques that we learnt in Chapter 10, as well as demonstrating the practicalities of personalization.

First, we'll look at what we can learn about visitors to our site.

Snooping on Request

It's often useful to know details about clients, and information about the requests that a web application is handling. Servlets have a number of methods available to gain access to this information. This information can then be used for security purposes and for identifying the client. It is retrieved from the `ServletRequest` object using this method:

```
public String getRemoteUser()
```

This method returns the name of the user making the request. This information can be used for authorization purposes, as well as give information about each client, which can be used over time to save an individual's preferences. It returns a null if the client has not been authenticated.

For the servlet to find out what the client has requested, it accesses request parameters associated with the request. Every request a servlet receives can have any number of request parameters. These parameters are always name-value pairs. The servlet gets its request parameters as a part of the query string for GET requests, or as encoded data for POST requests. However, they *retrieve* their parameters in the same way, by using these methods from `ServletRequest`:

```
public String getParameter(String name)
public String[] getParameterValues(String name)
```

In addition, a servlet can access parameter names using the following method of `ServletRequest`, which returns all the parameter names as an enumeration of `String` objects:

```
public Enumeration getParameterNames()
```

An HTTP request includes extra file information to indicate a file on the server. Servlets don't need this support, but a CGI program cannot interact with its server and so cannot receive the path parameter. To overcome this deficiency, there is a need to support extra path information, which is encoded in the URL. A servlet can access this information and can translate it into the real path using these methods of `ServletRequest`:

```
public String getPathInfo()
public String getPathTranslated()
```

The path information is only useful for a servlet if it knows the actual location of the file. For example the path `/index.html` isn't very useful until we need to translate it to the actual file system location of the file in the path information, for example: `/tomcat/webapps/test/index.html`.

The servlet can use several methods to find out exactly what file or servlet the client requested. We can use the `getRequestURL()` method of `HttpUtils`:

```
public static StringBuffer getRequestURL(HttpServletRequest request)
```

And the `getRequestURI()` and `getServletPath()` methods of `HttpServletRequest`:

```
public String getRequestURI()
public String getServletPath()
```

A servlet mostly needs only the request URI (which can be thought of as a URL without scheme, host, port, and query string for a normal servlet). For servlets in a chain, the request URI is always that of the first servlet in the chain. The `getServletPath()` method is used when it is enough to know the servlet name under which it was invoked.

The details about the manner in which the request was made can also be made available by using the `getScheme()` and `getProtocol()` methods of `ServletRequest`:

```
public String getScheme()
public String getProtocol()
```

With the help of the `getScheme()` method the servlet can find out whether the request was made over a secure connection (as indicated by the scheme "https") or it is an insecure request (as indicated by the scheme "http"). The other schemes may include "ftp", "jdbc", or "rmi". The servlet uses the `getProtocol()` to get the protocol and version number. The protocol and version number are separated by a slash, for example "vHTTP/1.0v" or "vHTTP/1.1".

The HTTP headers also provide some additional information about the request. The server deals directly with most of the details of the headers. For example, when a server receives a request for a restricted page, it checks that the request includes an appropriate Authorization header. However, servlets may want to read a few headers on occasion. A header value can be retrieved as a `String`, a `long`, or an `int` using these methods of `HttpServletRequest`:

```
public String getHeader(String name)
public long getDateHeader(String name)
public int getIntHeader(String name)
```

Some of the headers that a servlet may want to read are:

- `Accept`
  Specifies the media (MIME) type the client prefers to accept. A servlet can use this header to determine the type of content to return. For example, `Accept: text/*`
- `User-Agent`
  Gives information about the browser name and version that can be used to customize its response
- `Authorization`
  This includes the username and password (the client's authorization to access the resource), which can be used for custom authorization

Other headers are used by the servlets, but only indirectly. Let's put together an example that uses the methods discussed above:

```
import javax.servlet.*;
import javax.servlet.http.*;
import java.io.*;
import java.util.*;

public class RequestSnoop extends HttpServlet {

  public void doGet(HttpServletRequest request,
                    HttpServletResponse response)
                    throws ServletException, IOException {

    response.setContentType("text/html");
    PrintWriter out = response.getWriter();
    out.println("<html>\n" +
    "<head><title>Request Snoop</title></head>\n" +
    "<body style=\"font-family:verdana;font-size:8pt\">\n" +
    "<h3>Request information:</h3>\n" +
    "Request method : " + request.getMethod() + "<br>" +
    "Request URI : " + request.getRequestURI() + "<br>" +
    "Request scheme: " + request.getScheme() + "<br>" +
    "Request protocol : " + request.getProtocol() + "<BR>" +
    "Servlet path : " + request.getServletPath() + "<br>" +
    "Path info : " + request.getPathInfo() + "<br>" +
    "Path translated : " + request.getPathTranslated() + "<br>"+
    "Server name : " + request.getServerName() + "<br>" +
    "Server port : " + request.getServerPort() + "<br>" +
    "Remote user : " + request.getRemoteUser() + "<br>" +
    "Remote address : " + request.getRemoteAddr() + "<br>" +
    "Remote host : " + request.getRemoteHost() + "<br>"+
    "Authorization : " + request.getAuthType() + "<br>");

    Enumeration enum = request.getHeaderNames();

    if (enum.hasMoreElements()) {
      out.println("<h3>Request headers:</h3>");
      while (enum.hasMoreElements()) {
        String name = (String)enum.nextElement();
        out.println(" " + name + " : " + request.getHeader(name) + "<BR>");
      }
    }
    out.println("</body></html>");
  }
}
```

If we navigate to this servlet, we get something like the following response:

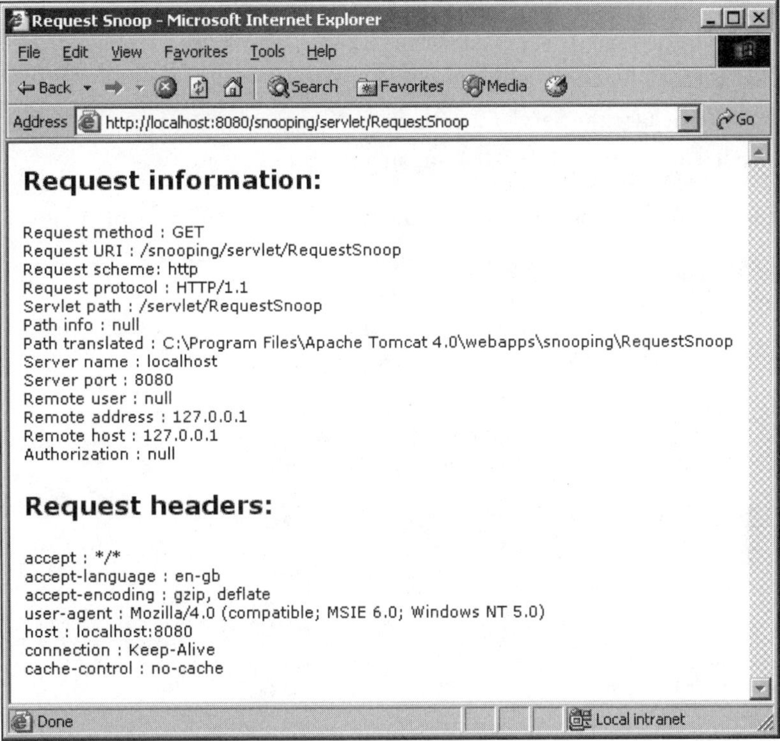

Visitor Tracking Using Clickstream

One of the components of OpenSymphony is **Clickstream**. It is a small utility to show the current users on your site, and where they've been, in detail.

> *An online demo and download is available at* http://www.opensymphony.com/clickstream/, *which displays the list of visitors currently on the site, and provides details about the visitor.*

Clickstream allows you to track the 'traffic paths' across your site. It starts tracking when users sessions begin, and track information with each click the user makes. It is designed to log the complete click stream to a file or `PrintStream` when the users' session ends. It also tries to discover whether the user is a bot, and filters accordingly – currently over 250 bots are detected.

> *A bot is a piece of software used to dig through data. They are commonly employed by search engines to compile their databases of sites on the Web.*

Clickstream is still quite basic – for example, click streams are not yet logged to a file. The code itself is very simple and contains:

- A filter to track requests – `ClickstreamFilter`
- A class to check for bots – `BotChecker`
- A class to listen for the Servlet 2.3 events – `ClickstreamLogger`
- A bean to store details of the click stream – `Clickstream`

These class files should be copied into the `\WEB-INF\classes` directory of your web application:

```
\WEB-INF\classes\
                 Clickstream.class
                 ClickstreamFilter.class
                 ClickstreamLogger.class
                 BotChecker.class
```

We also need to place two JSP files in the application directory, `clickstreams.jsp` and `viewstream.jsp`. Finally, add the following to your `web.xml` file:

```
<filter>
  <filter-name>Clickstream Filter</filter-name>
  <filter-class>ClickstreamFilter</filter-class>
</filter>

<filter-mapping>
  <filter-name>Clickstream Filter</filter-name>
  <url-pattern>/*.jsp</url-pattern>
</filter-mapping>

<filter-mapping>
  <filter-name>Clickstream Filter</filter-name>
  <url-pattern>/*.html</url-pattern>
</filter-mapping>

<listener>
  <listener-class>ClickstreamLogger</listener-class>
</listener>
```

This currently tracks any click on a JSP or HTML file. If you want to track other clicks (for example, TXT or PDF files), just add more filter mappings.

Let's add ClickStream to the shopping cart web application we created in Chapter 10. For the filter to work on Tomcat 4.0, we need to make some modifications to the downloaded files. Essentially, we need to make the software compatible with the Servlet 2.3 specification.

We need to update the `ClickstreamFilter` class to the latest API by renaming the `setFilterConfig()` method to `init()` and adding an empty `destroy()` method:

```
public void init(FilterConfig filterConfig) {
         this.filterConfig = filterConfig;
}

public void destroy() {}
```

As Tomcat 4.0 doesn't automatically place compiled JSP pages in the default package we need to put our Clickstream classes in a package of their own, and then import this package into each JSP page. Add the following line to each Clickstream class:

```
package clickstream;
```

Then put the source files into a `clickstream` directory, before recompiling them. Then add the following line to both JSP pages:

```
<%@ page import="clickstream.*" %>
```

We also need to make some changes to `web.xml`:

- Move the `<listener>` element to after the `<filter>` and `<filter-mapping>` elements, so that they match the order required by the deployment descriptor DTD.
- Change the mapping from `/*.html` and `/*.jsp` to `*.html` and `*.jsp`, as Tomcat enforces the rule that prohibits using a slash.
- Update the value of the `<filter-class>` element to `clickstream.ClickstreamFilter`, to reflect the changes we made earlier to the packaging.
- Update the value of the `<listener-class>` element to `clickstream.ClickstreamLogger`, to reflect the changes we made earlier to the packaging.

If you don't want to make these changes, you can find the updated files at http://www.wrox.com/.

Re-deploy the shopping cart web application. Then to see who is currently on your site, simply navigate to clickstreams.jsp:

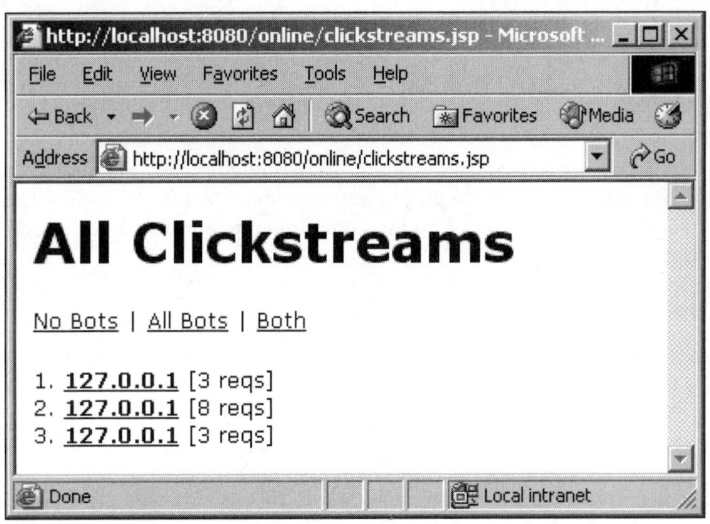

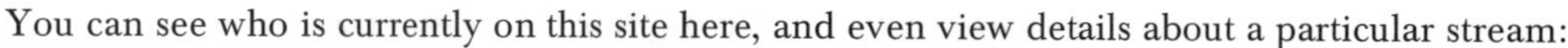

You can see who is currently on this site here, and even view details about a particular stream:

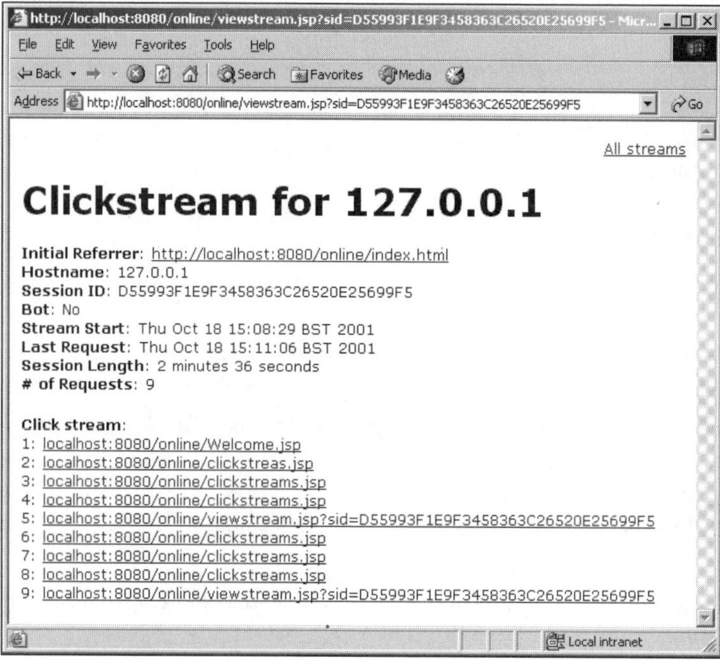

As you can see, Clickstream can provide you with potentially very useful information about visitors to your site that would otherwise be tedious to collect.

Clickstream is a work in progress, so you should refer to the online documentation for the latest information, as well as details of future releases.

Personalization

The key to personalization is in the use of databases, which allow users to store their preferences and tailor the site to their taste. We'll create an example application that will allow the user to customize some of the visual elements of the site, like the color scheme, and the layout of the screen. The specific areas of customization are:

- Allow the navigation to be laid out on the right, or on the left
- Select a color scheme independent of the layout
- Show sections that are of interest to the user

This application will be quite limited in functionality; our aim here is to demonstrate the essentials of personalization. Accordingly, the different sections of the site will not actually be created – they will simply be represented by disabled links within the navigation menu.

All these options have to be explicitly selected by the user, which are stored in a database. These attributes are then later referred to in order to present the layout when the user visits the site again.

Our next task is to create a database to store the information that enables personalization of the site. The following listing shows the SQL commands that create these tables. Each table has an ID field that uniquely identifies each element in the table. Use the following script to create the database, the tables, and some sample data:

```
CREATE DATABASE personalization;

USE personalization;

CREATE TABLE users (
    userid INTEGER AUTO_INCREMENT PRIMARY KEY,
    name CHAR(30),
    password CHAR (30),
    style CHAR(10),
    color CHAR(10)
);

CREATE TABLE usersections (
    sectionid INTEGER AUTO_INCREMENT PRIMARY KEY,
    name TEXT
);

CREATE TABLE sections (
    sectionid INTEGER PRIMARY KEY,
    name TEXT
);

GRANT ALL PRIVILEGES
    ON personalization.*
    TO wrox@localhost IDENTIFIED BY 'adarsh';

INSERT INTO sections VALUES (1, "News");
INSERT INTO sections VALUES (2, "New Releases");
INSERT INTO sections VALUES (3, "Future Titles");
INSERT INTO sections VALUES (4, "Resources");
INSERT INTO sections VALUES (5, "Book Reviews");
INSERT INTO sections VALUES (6, "Support");
INSERT INTO sections VALUES (7, "Features");
```

The user table assigns each user a unique ID and stores the name and password. In addition, it also stores the selected layout style and the color schema. The sections table contains the description of the various sections of the site. The `usersections` table contains the selection of interested sections of a particular user. The user's selection of sections contains multiple values and so the values are stored in a separate table named `usersections`, which is joined to the user table through the `userid` field. The `usersection` table contains entries of sections that the user wants to view.

Once the table has been designed, it is possible to consider what pages will be needed, which in turn points to the beans that need to be written.

> *We won't show the complete source code for this chapter, as we want to concentrate on what's important. Items such as CSS stylesheets have been left out completely, but as usual, the complete source code is available for download from* http://www.wrox.com/.

The `UserInfoBean` drives the entire personalization of the site:

```
package personalization;

import javax.servlet.*;
import javax.servlet.http.*;
import java.util.*;
import java.sql.*;

public class UserInfoBean implements java.io.Serializable {
```

The constructor populates our bean with some default values:

```
  public UserInfoBean() {
    loggedIn = false;
    style = "navleft";
    color = "blue";
  }
```

We have some constants that make working with our database easier:

```
  private static String DATABASE_URL =
         "jdbc:mysql://localhost/personalization?user=wrox&password=adarsh";
  private static String DRIVER = "org.gjt.mm.mysql.Driver";
```

We also create a helper method, which returns a connection to our database:

```
  private Connection getConnection() {
    Connection con = null;
    try {
      Class.forName(DRIVER).newInstance();
      con = DriverManager.getConnection(DATABASE_URL);
    } catch (Exception e) {
      e.printStackTrace(System.err);
    }
    return con;
  }
```

We create the following properties for our bean: `name`, `password`, `request`, `userid`, `loggedin`, `style`, and `color`. The only non-standard method associated with these properties is the setter method for `request`:

```
  public void setRequest(Object request) {
    this.request = (HttpServletRequest) request;
    setName(this.request.getParameter("name"));
  }
```

We have an array to keep track of the sections:

```
  private int sections[];
```

Next we have methods that allow us to retrieve and set information about the user from the database. The `select()` method:

```
  public void select() {
    StringBuffer sbQuery = new StringBuffer("SELECT * FROM users");
    StringBuffer sbWhereClause = new StringBuffer("");
    boolean hasWhere = false;
    Vector vec = new Vector();
```

Construct the WHERE clause of the SQL statement:

```
    if (name != null && password != null) {
      hasWhere = true;
      sbWhereClause.append("name = '" + getName() + "'" +
                           " AND password = '" + getPassword() + "'");
    }

    if(hasWhere) {
      sbQuery.append(" WHERE " + sbWhereClause.toString());
    }

    String query = sbQuery.toString();

    try {
      Connection con = getConnection();
      Statement st   = con.createStatement();
      ResultSet r  = st.executeQuery(query);

      if(r.next()) {
        loggedIn = true;
        userid = r.getInt("userid");
        color = r.getString("color").trim();
        style = r.getString("style").trim();
        r.close();

        r = st.executeQuery("SELECT sectionid from usersections " +
                            "WHERE userid = " + userid);
        while(r.next()) {
          vec.addElement(new Integer(r.getInt("sectionid")));
        }
        sections = new int[vec.size()];
        for(int i=0;i<vec.size();i++) {
          sections[i] = ((Integer) vec.elementAt(i)).intValue();
        }

        vec.removeAllElements();
        r.close();
        st.close();
        setColor(color);
        setStyle(style);
      }
    } catch (Exception e) {
      System.err.println(query);
      e.printStackTrace(System.err);
    }
  }
```

The nameInUse() method checks if the name a user has chosen is unique:

```
public boolean nameInUse() {
  boolean res = true;
  try {
    Connection con = getConnection();
    Statement st   = con.createStatement();
    ResultSet r  = st.executeQuery("SELECT * from users where name = '" +
                                   name + "';");
    res = r.next();
    r.close();
    st.close();
  } catch (Exception e) {
    System.err.println("Unable to get user info");
    e.printStackTrace(System.err);
  }
  return res;
}
```

The wantsSection() method checks if a user wants to see a particular section displayed:

```
public boolean wantsSection(int section) {
  if (sections == null) {
    return false;
  }
  for(int i=0;i<sections.length;i++) {
    if(sections[i] == section) {
      return true;
    }
  }
  return false;
}
```

The insert() method inserts new user data into the database:

```
public void insert() {
  try {
    Connection con = getConnection();
    Statement st   = con.createStatement();
    st.executeUpdate("INSERT INTO Users(name,password,style,color) " +
                     "VALUES('" + name + "','" + password +
                     "','navleft','blue')");
    ResultSet r  = st.executeQuery("SELECT userid FROM users WHERE " +
                                   "name = '" + name + "'");
    if (r.next()) {
         userid = r.getInt("userid");
    }
    loggedIn = true;
    r.close();
    st.close();
  } catch (Exception e) {
    System.out.println("Unable to insert");
    e.printStackTrace();
  }
}
```

The `setSections()` method gets all the sections, and then removes any unwanted ones:

```
public void setSections(String sectionsS[]) {
  int s[] = new int[sectionsS.length];
  Vector v = new Vector();
  int sectIds[] = SectionHolder.getIds();

  for (int i=0;i<sectionsS.length;i++) {
    try {
        s[i] = Integer.parseInt(sectionsS[i].trim());
    } catch (NumberFormatException e) {
        s[i] = -1;
    }
  }

  for(int i=0;i<sectIds.length;i++) {
    boolean listed = false;
    for(int j=0;j<s.length && !listed;j++) {
        listed = (sectIds[i] == s[j]);
    }
    if(listed) {
      v.addElement(new Integer(sectIds[i]));
    }
  }

  sections = new int[v.size()];
  for(int i=0;i<sections.length;i++) {
    sections[i] = ((Integer) v.elementAt(i)).intValue();
  }
}
```

Finally, the `update()` method updates the user's preferences:

```
  public void update() {
    try {
      Connection con = getConnection();
      Statement st   = con.createStatement();
      st.executeUpdate("UPDATE users SET style = '" + style +
                       "', color = '" + color + "' WHERE name = '" +
                       name + "'");
      ResultSet r  = st.executeQuery("SELECT userid FROM users WHERE " +
                                     "name = '" + name + "'");
      if (r.next()) {
        userid = r.getInt("userid");
      }
      st.executeUpdate("DELETE from usersections WHERE userid = " + userid);
      for (int i=0;i<sections.length;i++) {
          st.executeUpdate("INSERT INTO usersections VALUES(" +
                           sections[i] + "," + userid + ")");
      }
      st.close();
    } catch (Exception e) {
      System.err.println("Unable to update");
      e.printStackTrace();
    }
    select();
  }
}
```

The `SectionHolder` is a simple class that handles the storing and retrieval of sections:

```
package personalization;

import java.sql.*;
import java.util.*;

public class SectionHolder {
  private static String names[];
  private static int ids[];

  static String tst;

  public static String[] getNames() {
    return names;
  }

  public static int[] getIds() {
    return ids;
  }

  public static String getName(int id) {
    for(int i=0;i<ids.length;i++) {
      if(ids[i] == id) {
        return names[i];
      }
    }
    return null;
  }

  public SectionHolder() {
    try {
      Class.forName("org.gjt.mm.mysql.Driver").newInstance();
      Connection con = DriverManager.getConnection(
        "jdbc:mysql://localhost/personalization?user=wrox&password=adarsh");
      Statement st   = con.createStatement();
      ResultSet rs   = st.executeQuery("SELECT * FROM Sections");

      Vector namesV = new Vector();
      Vector idsV   = new Vector();

      while(rs.next()) {
        namesV.addElement(rs.getString(2));
        idsV.addElement(new Integer(rs.getInt(1)));
      }
      tst = (String) namesV.lastElement();

      rs.close();
      st.close();

      names = new String[namesV.size()];
      ids   = new int[namesV.size()];

      for(int i=0;i<namesV.size();i++) {
        names[i]  = (String) namesV.elementAt(i);
        ids[i] = ((Integer) idsV.elementAt(i)).intValue();
      }
    } catch (Exception e) {
      e.printStackTrace(System.err);
    }
  }
}
```

At the top of each page, we include `setup.jsp`:

```
<jsp:useBean id="user"
             class="personalization.UserInfoBean"
             scope="session">
  <jsp:setProperty name="user" property="*"/>
</jsp:useBean>

<jsp:useBean id="sections"
     class="personalization.SectionHolder"
     scope="application"/>
```

The JSP starts by accessing a `UserInfoBean`, which it uses to present the section name and a customized greeting to the user. Then we have the header, which also appears on each page:

```
<html>
  <head>
    <title>
      Wrox Press
    </title>
    <link rel="stylesheet" type="text/css" href="style/global.css" />
    <link rel="stylesheet" type="text/css"
```

Based on the information stored in the `UserInfoBean` we include a stylesheet that includes the styles for the appropriate color scheme:

```
          href="style/<jsp:getProperty name="user"
                                       property="color" />.css" />
  </head>
```

And a welcome message that is inserted into every page:

```
<h2>Welcome To Wrox Press</h2>
<hr />
```

For the purpose of this example, the content of the site is left blank. The default page for the web application is `index.jsp`:

```
<%@include file="setup.jsp" %>

<%
  if(user.getStyle().equals("navright")) {
%>
    <jsp:forward page="index_right.jsp"/>
<%
  } else {
%>
      <jsp:forward page="index_left.jsp"/>
<% } %>
```

Based on the required layout, index.jsp forwards the request to one of:

- index_right.jsp
- index_left.jsp

The code for all these pages is identical, except the code to display the navigation is placed in different locations based on the user's choice. The UserInfoBean and SectionHolder beans are made available. The JSP page generates the HTML code based on these properties.

The JSP page checks whether the user is logged in and the preferences are set accordingly. If the user is logged in the content section contains a link to set preferences or create a new account. The navigation section gets the list of sections names from SectionHolder and iterates through all sections, displaying each. It also contains a form to log in a user and a link to create a new account.

index_left.jsp places the navigation to the left:

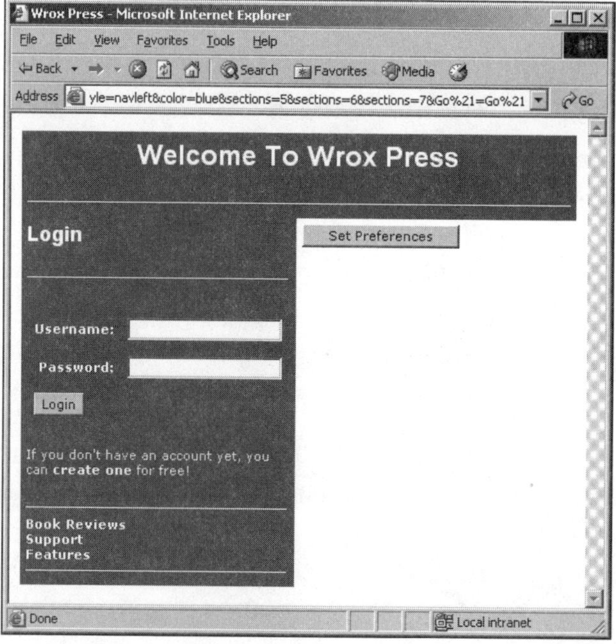


```
<%@include file="setup.jsp" %>
<%@include file="header.html" %>

  <body>
    <table class="bodyTable">
      <tr>
        <td class="header" colspan="2">
          <%@include file="welcome.html" %>
        </td>
      </tr>
```

```
        <tr>
          <td class="navBar">
            <%@include file="navBar.jsp" %>
          </td>
          <td>
            <%@include file="content.jsp" %>
          </td>
        </tr>
      </table>
    </body>
  </html>
```

And index_right.jsp places the navigation to the right:

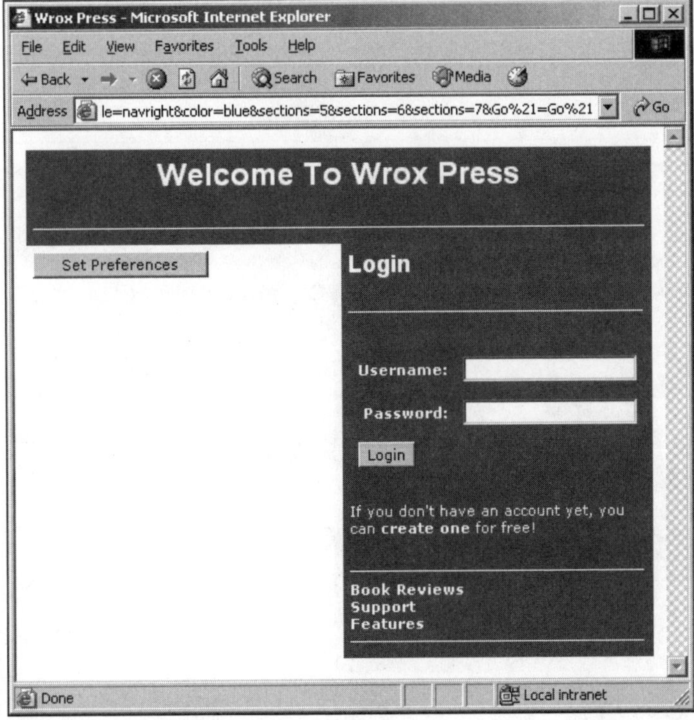


```
  <%@ include file="setup.jsp" %>
  <%@include file="header.html" %>

    <body>
      <table class="bodyTable">
        <tr>
          <td class="header" colspan="2">
            <%@include file="welcome.html" %>
          </td>
        </tr>
```

```
        <tr>
          <td>
            <%@include file="content.jsp" %>
          </td>
          <td class="navBar">
            <%@include file="navBar.jsp" %>
          </td>
        </tr>
      </table>
    </body>
  </html>
```

Our example allows users to create their own account on the site. The account creation page is shown below:

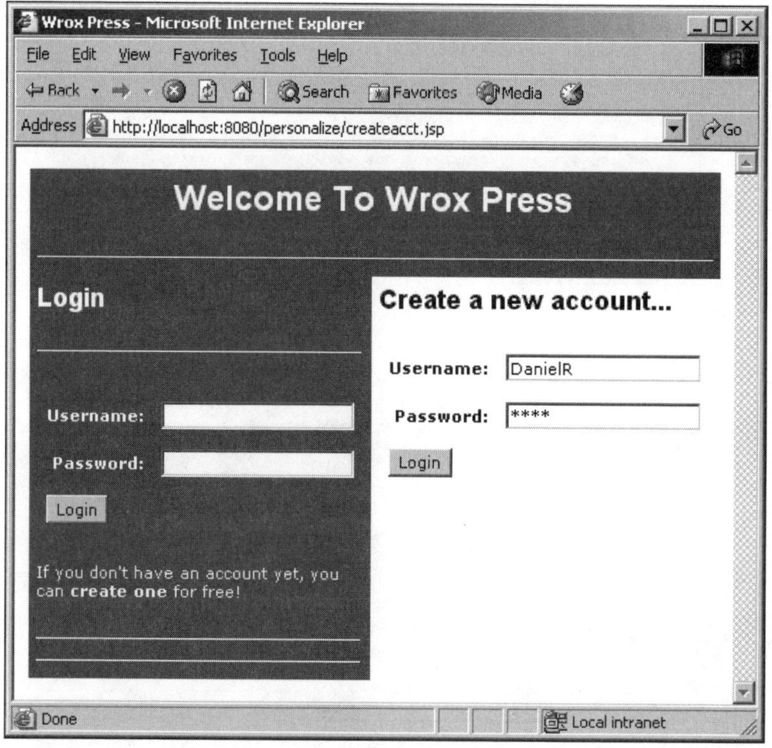


```
<%@include file="setup.jsp" %>
<%@include file="header.html" %>

  <body>
    <table class="bodyTable">
      <tr>
        <td class="header" colspan="2">
          <%@include file="welcome.html" %>
        </td>
      </tr>
```

```
      <tr>
        <td class="navBar">
          <%@include file="navBar.jsp" %>
        </td>

       <td>
       <% if(request.getParameter("name") != null) { %>

           <jsp:setProperty name="user" property="*"/>

           <% if(user.nameInUse()) { %>
             <h3>Sorry, that name is already in use.  Please choose
                 another.</h3>
             <jsp:include page="accountForm.jsp" flush="true"/>
             <% } else { %>
                  <% user.insert(); %>
                  <p>
                    Account created for
                    <jsp:getProperty name="user" property="name" />
                  </p>
                  <p>Return to the Wrox Press
                    <a
                    href="index.jsp?name=<%=request.getParameter("name")%>">
                      Home Page
                    </a>
                    or set your
                    <a
               href="userprefs.jsp?name=<%=request.getParameter("name")%>">
                      Preferences
                    </a>
                  </p>
                 <% } %>
            <% } else { %>
              <h3>Create a new account...</h3>
              <jsp:include page="accountForm.jsp" flush="true"/>
            <% } %>
            </td>
          </tr>
        </table>
      </body>
    </html>
```

When this JSP page is invoked with the name and a password, it will check the database to see if the name is in use via the `UserInfoBean`'s `nameInUse()` method. If the name is not yet in use, the new account will be created; otherwise, the user will be notified that the name is not available. If the JSP page is called without a name and password, the form will be presented again.

This page can be improved so that the user is prompted to enter the password twice to verify it. Alternatively, many sites also allow the user to specify a challenge consisting of a question and the correct response. If the user forgets his password, the site can issue the challenge, and if the user responds properly, the password is revealed.

When an account is first created, the user is automatically logged in. On subsequent visits, the user will have to log in from the navigation section. The login form is submitted to `index_select.jsp`:

```
<%@include file="setup.jsp" %>

<% user.select(); %>

<%
  if(user.getStyle().equals("navright")) {
%>
    <jsp:forward page="index_right.jsp"/>
<%
  } else {
%>
      <jsp:forward page="index_left.jsp"/>
<% } %>
```

If a username and password has been provided, the bean will check whether that combination exists in the database. If so, the bean will set the user's `loggedIn` flag and retrieve all the user's preferences. If not, the user will be asked to log in again.

Once a user has logged in, they can customize the site. The page and the code are shown next:

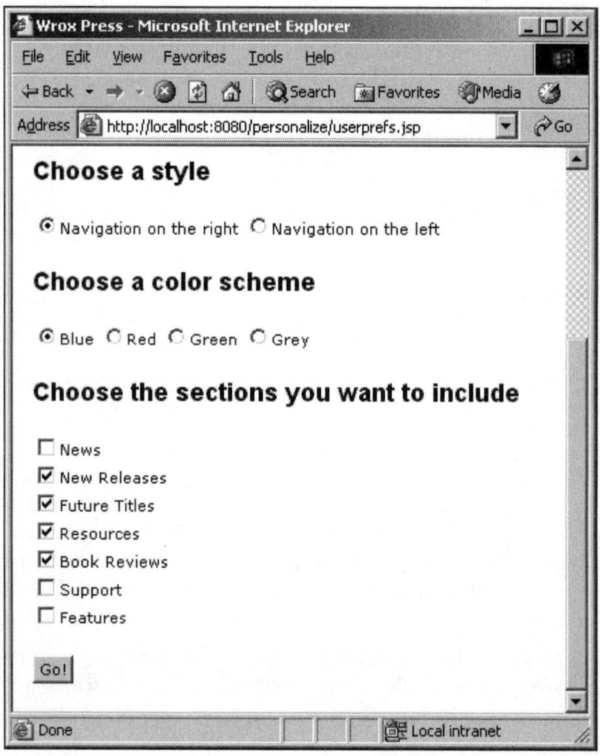

```
<%@ include file="setup.jsp" %>
<%@include file="header.html" %>

<table class="bodyTable">

  <tr>
    <td class="header">
      <%@ include file="welcome.html" %>
    </td>
  </tr>

  <tr>
    <td>
      <h2>User Preferences</h2>
      <p>Welcome <%= user.getName() %>.
      Use this page to configure Wrox site to your choice.
      You can select a style for pages, a color scheme,
      and add or remove sections from your personal edition.</p>

      <form action="setprefs.jsp" method="GET">

        <h3>Choose a style</h3>
        <p>
            <% String na = request.getParameter("name"); %>
            <% String nl = "<input type=\"hidden\" name=\"name\"
                                    value=\""+na+"\"></P>"; %>
            <%= nl %>

            <input type="radio" name="style" value="navright"
            <% if(user.getStyle().equals("navright")) { %>
             checked
            <% } %>>Navigation on the right
            <input type="radio" name="style" value="navleft"
            <% if(user.getStyle().equals("navleft")) { %>
             checked
            <% } %>>Navigation on the left
        </p>

        <h3>Choose a color scheme</h3>
        <p>
            <input type="radio" name="color" value="blue"
            <% if(user.getColor().equals("blue")) { %>
             checked
            <% } %>>Blue
            <input type="radio" name="color" value="red"
            <% if(user.getColor().equals("red")) { %>
             checked
            <% } %>>Red
            <input type="radio" name="color" value="green"
            <% if(user.getColor().equals("green")) { %>
             checked
            <% } %>>Green
            <input type="radio" name="color" value="grey"
            <% if(user.getColor().equals("grey")) { %>
             checked
            <% } %>>Grey
         </p>
```

```
        <h3>Choose the sections you want to include</h3>

        <p>
          <% String sectionNames[] = sections.getNames(); %>
          <% int sectionIds[] = sections.getIds(); %>

            <% for (int i=0;i<sectionIds.length;i++) { %>
              <input type="checkbox" name="sections"
               value="<%= sectionIds[i] %>"
               <% if(user.wantsSection(sectionIds[i])) { %>
               checked
               <% } %>><%= sectionNames[i] %><br />
            <% } %>
        <p>

        <p><input type="submit" name="Go!" value="Go!"></p>
      </td>
      </tr>
    </table>
  </body>
</html>
```

The form generated by this JSP page is in turn submitted to `setprefs.jsp` which is similar to `index.jsp`, the only interesting portion being the lines in which the values are changed in the bean and the database is updated:

```
<jsp:setProperty name="user" property="*"/>
<% user.update(); %>
```

This completes our analysis of this example web application. Although it is simple and has plenty of room for improvement, it demonstrates how we can personalize sites for individual users. It should have given you plenty of ideas for how you can add personalization to your site.

Summary

In this chapter, we continued our coverage of keeping track of users. We began by looking at the type of information that a client makes available during a request, and how we can access this information. Then, we looked at how we can use software such as Clickstream to keep track of users as they access our site. This information, if properly analyzed, can help us to better design our site to fulfill the needs of our visitors.

We went on to create an example web application that provides personalized content to users, including the page layout, content, and color scheme. This application demonstrated many of the techniques we learnt in this chapter and Chapter 10, including:

- Managing the logon of users
- Keeping track of a particular user across a session using hidden form fields and URL rewriting

In the next chapter, we're going to continue to look at how we can manage the content that is presented on our site. To do this we'll develop a news management application that will allow us to post new content to our site, as well as manage existing content.

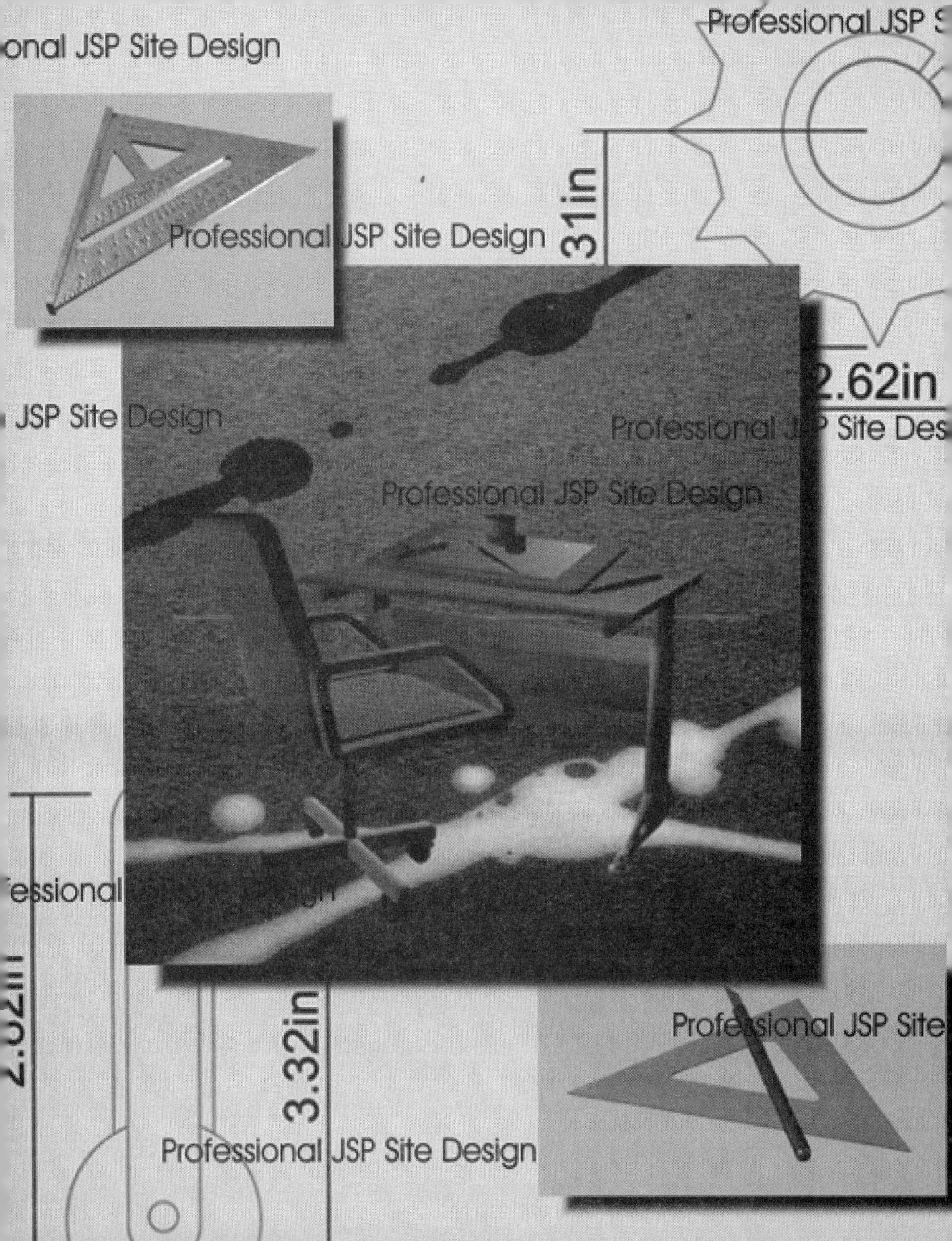
Professional JSP Site Design
Professional JSP Site Design
Professional JSP Site Design
3.32in
Professional JSP Site Design

12

Content Management

Eye candy brings them in, but content brings them back, especially if that content is kept up-to-date and topical. Armed with a good tool, we can convert the effort needed to keep a site current from an everyday struggle into a daily pleasure. This chapter steps through a case study that develops an article management system for a news site, or any site that posts articles on a regular basis.

We'll build on this example throughout this chapter and the next two. In this chapter, the application is a simple news posting utility. Then we will use it to provide the articles as subscription content to other sites. Finally, we will enhance the search capabilities to make the articles easier to find.

We will be building the application using the Struts Framework, introduced in Chapter 2. If your own applications are built with Struts, our news poster could be plugged in as a JAR library, and the control-flow mappings copied into your own Struts configuration file. The articles case study is a simple database application that demonstrates best practices you can use in other Struts projects.

Before we get started, let's discuss why a news poster is a good choice for a content management case study.

Managing Timely Content

Most of the work in content management today revolves around:

- Separating content from the presentation layer
- Making updated content available wherever it is needed
- Organizing and searching content

The conventional approach for separating content from presentation is to use XML to store the content, which is then formatted at run time using a stylesheet. See Chapter 12 of *Professional JSP 2nd Edition* from *Wrox Press (ISBN 1-861004-95-8)* for more about using XML with JSP pages.

However, using XML and stylesheets this way is still a developing technology. Initiatives like **Apache Cocoon** (http://xml.apache.org/cocoon/) and **Apache Slide** (http://jakarta.apache.org/slide/) are going to have a lot to offer us in the near future, but are not quite ready for everyday use in a production site. For most working web sites, the last two points, keeping content update fresh and making it easy to find, are the issues that need to be addressed today.

HTML is a capable format for creating static pages, and with JSP, dynamic pages can be created without much effort. However, a problem many web sites still have is that continually adding new content to the site requires knowledgeable personnel who can be trusted to add a new page without disrupting the others. Adding a new page often means updating another index page so that the visitors can find it. So, the person adding the page has to know how to do that too, and be trusted to do it correctly.

Where this tends to happen most often is with articles that are posted to a site on a regular basis. These may be news articles, a column, or just "what's new" snippets. Generally, the latest posting replaces the previous posting, which is relegated to an archive.

A way to streamline posting material like this is to use a news posting utility. This is the most common approach to content management today. News posters are running many popular sites, like SlashDot (http://slashdot.org/) and NewsForge (http://www.newsforge.com/). See Chapter 14 for more about these sites, where we cover another popular approach to content management – portals. While there is no shortage of news posting applications for other platforms like PHP, there is very little available for Java web applications. So, let's fill that gap with a news posting application of our own.

Articles

First, to give us a place to start, let's set out a simple workflow for our base application, and highlight some technical requirements the application must meet.

Workflow

A **workflow** is the flow or progress of work done by a company, industry, department, or person. Sometimes an entire workflow can be represented within an application. More often, an application represents only part of a greater workflow. A point-of-sale application may record the sale and order inventory, but it doesn't put the merchandise into the bag and hand it to the customer.

Our news poster is part of a greater workflow that would include identifying articles to write, writing the articles, and perhaps approving them for publication. For now, let's look at that portion of the overall workflow that must be handled by our example application for it to be useful:

- Contributors log in to the application
- Contributors complete a web form with the article's title, author, and content as a text paragraph or HTML
- Contributors may edit or delete their own articles, and the articles of other contributors
- Visitors may list current articles by date entered, or search for specific articles by title, author, or content

Requirements

In the workflow, we talked about how things happened in context – what needs to be done when. In contrast, the requirements itemize which features we will need to complete the workflow, without specifying in what sequence they might be used. To borrow a concept from database development, the requirements are a "normalized" version of the workflow.

From our simple workflow, we can determine our application's minimum requirements:

- Store the title, author, and content of an article
- List articles by descending entry order (newest to oldest)
- Filter and list articles by title, author, or content
- Authenticate contributors (via some form of login)
- Be adaptable to any web layout
- Be extensible to meet future requirements
- Be easily plugged into other applications and environments
- Run within a JSP 1.1 and Servlet 2.2 environment

Further Enhancements

In Chapter 13, we will add a full text search of author, title, keywords, and other fields, using the Lucene search engine. In Chapter 14, we will add syndication of content (using RDF Site Summary (RSS)) to the application.

Based on our discussion of content management, other functionality that could be useful to add to the application would be:

- Storing additional attributes, including topic, short description, keywords, and status code
- Including images with an article
- Allowing editorial approval before public release
- Entry of articles to be displayed at a later data
- Automatic expiration of articles
- Including content from an uploaded HTML file
- Integrated search of articles and other web pages
- Support for HTTP PUT and WebDAV file transfers
- Support a hierarchical subject structure (for example, Jakarta Slide)

While most of these features would be useful, they are not required for our initial workflow. Our goal should then be to create an extensible, component-driven application that we can use today and enhance tomorrow.

Design Complications

Even the simplest application comes with complications. Let's try to anticipate the design complications, tier by tier:

- **Client Tier**
  Since it caters to public news sites, and cannot control how a browser is configured, our application should not rely on JavaScript. If JavaScript is used, it should simply enhance the user experience, and be simple enough to work with any browser.

- **Presentation Tier**
  The design of a web site often changes, so it's important that our presentation be easy to integrate into any layout. Since custom tags look and feel like HTML, they can be easily moved around a layout by web page authors. Our presentation should rely on custom tags, rather than scriptlets, to display the articles.

- **Business Tier**
  A major feature is being able to select an assortment of articles using various criteria. It should be easy to implement new search methods into the application.

- **Integration Tier**
  The current application is being designed for a Java 2 Standard Edition web server. However, data access and helper objects (or components) should be used so that it could hook up with a Java 2 Enterprise Edition application server instead. For more about J2EE integration, see Chapter 9. Likewise, the SQL commands should be isolated so that they could be optimized for a particular DBMS platform, or migrated to J2EE, if desired.

Custom Components

The toolset provided by the Struts Framework will provide most of what we will need for the client and presentation tiers, but we will need some additional components in the business and integration tiers, namely:

- A database schema designed to store our information
- SQL commands to manage our information
- Data access and helper objects to fetch information from persistent storage (for example, DBMS)

We will cover each of these components in detail over the remainder of the chapter.

First Steps

Since the application is based on the Struts Framework, we will focus on what we have to add to an application based on the Struts "blank application" template. We will not be reviewing the standard Struts classes, configuration files, or tag extensions in detail, or how other prerequisites, like the JDBC classes, work. This material is better covered elsewhere. For more about Struts, see Chapter 2. The example application will also use a component-based design. See Chapter 1 for more about designing applications with components.

It's usually helpful to start an application with **storyboard** pages. A storyboard depicts the application as a series of static pages – a "non-working" demo:

- A storyboard gives us an idea of how the application will look to the user, how they will interact with the data, and how navigation will flow from page to page
- A storyboard does not tell us exactly what components we will need on the backend, but it does tell us a lot about what the components will have to do
- A storyboard does not help us define the underlying workflow, but it does demonstrate how we might represent a workflow as a web application

Let's take a look at how we expect our pages to work when we are finished. We will keep the layout very simple, so the code can be adapted for use in other web pages.

Storyboard

To realize our initial workflow, it looks like we will need four pages:

- **The Menu Page**
  To select operations and enter search phrases
- **The Entry Page**
  To enter new articles
- **The Article Page**
  To display articles in full
- **The List Page**
  To display a found set of articles

> **At the storyboard stage we are not interested in how these pages will be implemented. We don't need to worry about the business logic of the application yet; rather we are considering how the content is presented to the user.**

The Menu Page

This is a simple menu that we can use to test the application. We can easily select a list of current articles, posted in the last day, week, or month. The LATEST NEWS button displays the last ten articles posted. If a user is looking for something specific, they can also search by title, author, or the article content:

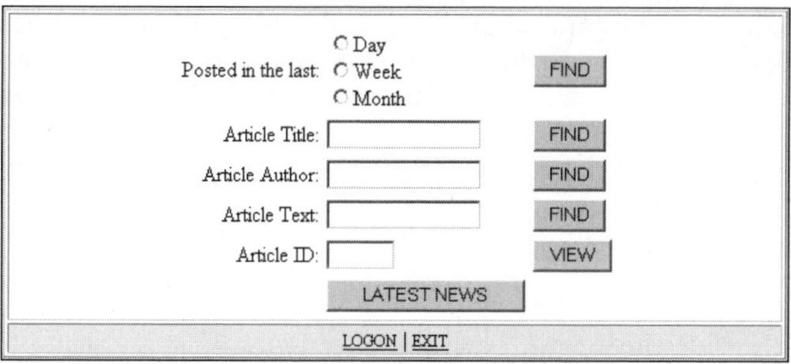

All of these forms, buttons, or links will be implemented with custom tags, and so can be easily integrated with your own application's look and feel.

The Entry Page

This page is the data entry form for our contributors to use:

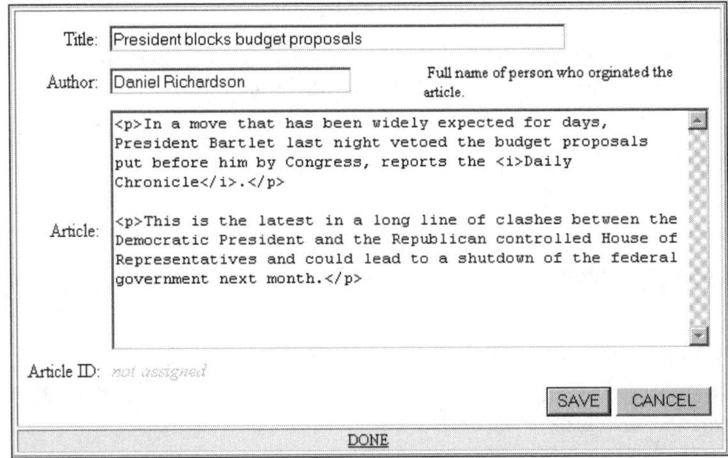

If a contributor is not logged in the user is challenged for identification, and must provide a valid username and password.

The List Page

This page lists our articles. The same page should be used for all types of searches, making the addition of new selections easy:

The Article Page

`article.jsp`, the heart of the application, displays the full text of the article, along with the title and author. The editing controls at the bottom will only display for authorized users. We do not have to create two versions of the page – the page intelligently renders the correct page for the user:

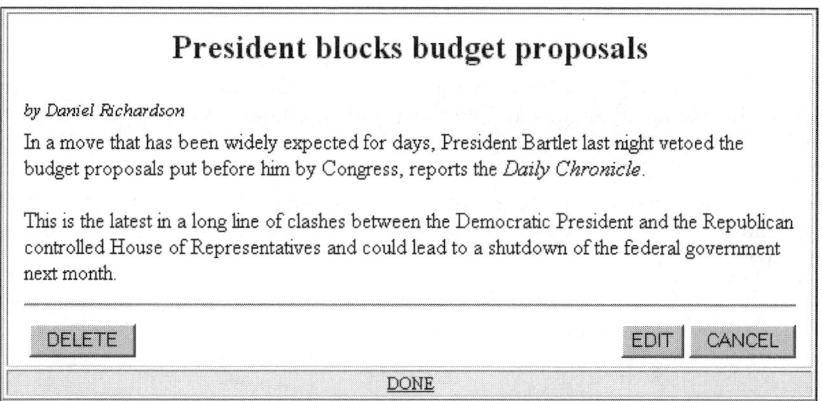

The EDIT button will display the entry page, so that the article can be revised and re-submitted. The DELETE button marks the article so that it will not display on searches, and can be permanently removed at a later date. These buttons only display to contributors, and will not be available to anonymous visitors to the site.

Now that we understand what we expect our application do be able to do, it's time to start thinking about how to implement this functionality – beginning with how the content itself is to be stored.

Database Schema

Based on our requirements and storyboards, we can design our first database schema. Our database will have two tables: `primary_keys` and `article`.

The primary_keys Table

The de facto standard for database management is a relational database accessed via SQL. Relational database designs generally rely on a primary key for a table. The best primary keys tend to be simple, arbitrary numbers that are not exposed to the users and not subject to change (such as a serial number). Some database implementations offer a auto-increment function which can create primary keys in serial form, but it is not a standard SQL feature.

To provide our own auto-increment feature, we can use a table to store the table name and a counter. A SQL query can then retrieve the next key for a table, increment it, and update the table for the next record. Here's our auto-increment, or `primary_keys`, table:

Label	Remarks	Name	Type	Index
`Next Key`	Use and increment	`next`	`INTEGER`	
`Table Name`	Table name	`name`	`VARCHAR(31)`	PRIMARY KEY

The article Table

In addition to the primary key and what is needed to fulfill our storyboard pages, we will add some tracking fields to the `article` table. These are included to provide a brief audit trail in case there is a question about the history of an article. The `user` and `host` fields are provided as part of the HTTP request.

Rather than instantly delete an article, we've provided a field so that it can be marked for deletion instead. Our standard SQL queries will exclude any article that is "marked". This gives us a chance to undelete the article later:

Label	Remarks	Name	Type	Index
`Article ID`	From keys table	`article`	`INTEGER`	PRIMARY KEY
`Article Text`	Memo field for story, if not uploaded	`content`	`TEXT`	
`Author Name`	Author's full name	`creator`	`VARCHAR(79)`	
`Contributed`	Date first contributed	`contributed`	`TIMESTAMP`	
`Contributed By`	Original contributor (principal)	`contributor`	`CHAR(15)`	
`Marked`	Marked as deleted?	`marked`	`BIT`	NON-UNIQUE
`Modified By`	Last principal to update	`user`	`CHAR(15)`	
`Modified From`	IP of last principal to update	`host`	`CHAR(15)`	
`Modified On`	Date last updated	`modified`	`TIMESTAMP`	
`Title`	Top level title for article	`title`	`VARCHAR(255)`	

Quick Start

If you want the full source for reference as we walk through the application, the WAR with complete source is available from http://www.wrox.com/. Here are the quick start installation notes for Tomcat 4.0:

- Update `<TOMCAT_HOME>\conf\tomcat-users.xml` to include:

```
<user name="articles" password="articles" roles="manager,contributor" />
```

- Place the `articles.war` in the `webapps\` folder and let it deploy

The connection pool (discussed later in *The Connection Pool* section) requires three standard JARs to be available: `jdbc2_0-std-ext.jar`, `jta.jar`, and `xerces.jar`. Make sure that these are in the `<TOMCAT_HOME>\common\lib\` folder:

- Remove `jaxp.jar` from the `<TOMCAT_HOME>\lib\` directory (so Tomcat uses Xerces instead)
- Review `WEB-INF\classes\poolman.xml` for any changes needed for setup, like your JDBC driver
- Create a folder `\var\lucene\articles\` for use in Chapter 13
- Optionally, create a folder `\var\applogs\` for the connection pool log
- Restart Tomcat so the changes take affect

Lock It Up

We'll be using **role-based security** with our application so that only authorized users will be able to submit and edit articles. Certain resources will only be made available to users who are logged in and have been assigned the correct role. A user can be given more than one role. User roles are like the user groups used by most operating systems, including Unix and NT.

> *For information about configuring the security of your web applications, see Chapter 10.*

First let's secure the appropriate resources by adding security constraints to `web.xml`. This way we can identify which roles can access a resource by its URI.

In developing our application, we will be routing all the control through Struts `ActionMappings`, and not linking directly to any JSP pages. This will let us put the sensitive pages under an `/admin/` mapping. We can then use that pattern to add declarative security to our web application. For browser compatibility, we will use BASIC/EBasic authentication. See Chapter 10 for more about web application security and the consequences of these choices:

```
<security-constraint>
  <web-resource-collection>
    <web-resource-name>Administrative</web-resource-name>
    <!-- Define the context-relative URL(s) to be protected -->
    <url-pattern>/admin/*</url-pattern>
  </web-resource-collection>
  <auth-constraint>
    <!-- Anyone with one of the listed roles may access this area -->
    <role-name>manager</role-name>
    <role-name>contributor</role-name>
  </auth-constraint>
</security-constraint>
<login-config>
  <auth-method>BASIC</auth-method>
  <realm-name>EBasic Authentication Area</realm-name>
</login-config>
```

With this in place, if you try to access http://localhost:8080/articles/do/admin/edit the container will display a login dialog and demand your credentials. For example, using Internet Explorer we see:

But Don't Throw Away the Key

While the Servlet specification defines how to configure security constraints, it does not define how to provide logins to the container.

Many containers, including Tomcat and Resin, offer **JDBCRealm** authentication. This allows us to define a JDBC database in `web.xml`, which the container will use to lookup a user's credentials. In a production site, this is an excellent feature, since we can manage our users and roles from within the web application itself. There is an example of JDBC authentication in Chapter 8.

Tomcat also offers a simpler option: we can add users to an XML configuration file in the Tomcat `conf\` directory. Here's the `tomcat-users.xml` with our default `articles` user and roles added:

```
<tomcat-users>
  <user name="tomcat" password="tomcat" roles="tomcat" />
  <user name="role1"  password="tomcat" roles="role1"  />
  <user name="both"   password="tomcat" roles="tomcat,role1" />

  <user name="articles" password="aticles" roles="manager,contributor" />

</tomcat-users>
```

If you add this line to your `<TOMCAT_HOME>\conf\tomcat-users.xml`, and restart Tomcat, you'll be able to answer the challenge, and access the URIs located under `admin`.

Real Code

In the "real code" phase, we will:

- Create the database tables
- Create the data access utilities
- Create the JSP Pages

Creating the Database Tables

Rather than provide a generic SQL script we can feed to our DBMS from the command line, let's use a Struts administrative `Action` to create the database for us.

So what do we need to bootstrap a database for our application? Our design caveats mentioned keeping the SQL statements distinct from the Data Access Objects (DAO), so they could be optimized for a different DBMS or migrated to J2EE. In practice, I find it handy to have both a low-level and high-level Data Access Object. That makes for three main classes:

- `Commands`
  The SQL commands as static strings
- `Data`
  The high-level DAO exposed to the application
- `Statements`
  The low-level DAO that accesses the resource tier (DBMS)

Since this is a database-driven application, we'll be using a number of SQL related classes.

The Commands Class

We'll create a SQL package under `articles`, and a `Commands` class to store these and other SQL commands for searching and updating articles (see the code download for a full listing):

```
package com.wrox.articles.sql;

public final class Commands {
```

First, let's define some static variables to store the names of our tables:

```
    public static final String KEYS_TABLE = "primary_keys";
    public static final String ARTICLE_TABLE = "article";
```

Referring to our database schema, we can define the strings that would create our tables, using the SQL Database Description Language (DDL). These are actually DDL fragments that we can use with the table names (above) to generate a complete statement:

```
    public static final String KEYS_CREATE =
        "(name CHAR(15) NOT NULL PRIMARY KEY," +
        "marked BIT NOT NULL DEFAULT 0," +
        "next INTEGER NOT NULL DEFAULT 0" + ");";

    public static final String ARTICLE_CREATE =
        "(article     INTEGER NOT NULL PRIMARY KEY,"+
        "marked       BIT NOT NULL," +
        "modified     TIMESTAMP," +
        "user         CHARACTER(15)," +
        "host         CHARACTER(15)," +
        "contributed TIMESTAMP," +
        "contributor CHARACTER(15)," +
```

```
        "creator      VARCHAR(79) NOT NULL," +
        "title        VARCHAR(255) NOT NULL," +
        "content      TEXT," +
        "INDEX marked_index (marked)," +
        "INDEX title_index (title,creator)" + ");";
```

The two following strings are used to insert a starter primary key for the `article` table:

```
    public static final String PRIMARY_KEY_INIT = "101";

    public static final String ARTICLE_KEY_INIT =
        "INSERT INTO primary_keys " +
        "(name,next) VALUES ('article'," + PRIMARY_KEY_INIT + ");";
}
```

The Data Class

Conventional design patterns encourage the use of Data Access Objects to connect to a database, or other persistent store, and hide the implementation from the rest of the application. That's the strategy we will use here. Our main DAO is a class named `Data` with all static methods. The methods here will be specific to our application, and make calls to more generic methods in `Statements`, another class of static methods. Not all the methods are shown but they all follow the same pattern.

> **The `Data` class retrieves the appropriate SQL statement from the `Commands` class, and passes it to a library method in `Statements` to execute. Our application is only exposed to the methods in the `Data` class, and has no idea where the data actually comes from, or what commands are used to fetch it. In practice, this makes `Data` the de facto interface for the application's business tier.**

Our first two methods in `Data` are `keysCreateTable()` and `articleCreateTable()`. These are called by the `CreateTables` Struts `Action` as "black boxes". All `CreateTables` knows is that they might throw a `SQLException`. The rest of the implementation is hidden:

```
package com.wrox.articles.sql;

import java.sql.Connection;
import java.sql.SQLException;
import java.sql.PreparedStatement;
import java.sql.ResultSet;
import java.sql.Timestamp;
import java.util.Collection;
import java.util.Date;

public final class Data {
```

`keysCreateTable()` creates the `primary_keys` table. It's a wrapper to pass `KEYS_TABLE` and `KEYS_CREATE` to `Statements.createTable()` (we'll cover the `Statements` class next), and encapsulate the implementation. If the create succeeds, we insert starter primary keys for the `article` table with a call to `Statements.executeUpdate()`:

```
    public static final void keysCreateTable() throws SQLException {
      int result = Statements.createTable(Commands.KEYS_TABLE,
                                          Commands.KEYS_CREATE);
      result = Statements.executeUpdate(Commands.ARTICLE_KEY_INIT);
    }
```

`articleCreateTable()` creates the `article` table. Again, this is a wrapper to pass `ARTICLE_TABLE` and `ARTICLE_CREATE` to `createTable()`, thereby encapsulating the implementation:

```
    public static final void articleCreateTable() throws SQLException {
      Statements.createTable(Commands.ARTICLE_TABLE,
                             Commands.ARTICLE_CREATE);
    }
  }
```

The Statements Class

As mentioned, both the `keysCreateTable()` and the `articleCreateTable()` methods reuse code the old-fashioned way by calling library methods in `Statements`. Let's take a look:

```
package com.wrox.articles.sql;

import java.sql.Connection;
import java.sql.SQLException;
import java.sql.PreparedStatement;
import java.sql.Statement;
import java.sql.ResultSet;

public final class Statements {
```

`executeUpdate()` prepares a command using SQL statements and executes it with the DBMS configured with the connection pool (we'll cover that next). The command may be an `INSERT`, `UPDATE`, or `DELETE`:

```
    public static final int executeUpdate(String command)
      throws SQLException {

      Connection connection = null;
      Statement statement = null;
      int result = 0;
      try {
        connection = ConnectionPool.getConnection();
        statement = connection.createStatement();
        result = statement.executeUpdate(command);
      }

      finally {
        try {
          if (statement != null) {
            statement.close();
          }
```

```
        if (connection!= null) {
          connection.close();
        }
      } catch (SQLException sqle) {
          // non-fatal; only closing if pooled
          // don't overthrow original exception
      }
    }
    return result;
  }
```

The other library method we'll need from `Data` is `createTable()`. This creates a new database table in an existing database by passing `CREATE TABLE` and the DDL fragments we defined in `Data` as parameters. The existing database is the one configured with the connection pool. For safety, this method does not drop the tables first. To recreate tables, we must first drop them ourselves from the DBMS command line or a management utility. The method returns the result of `executeUpdate()`:

```
  public static final int createTable(String tableName, String tableCreate)
    throws SQLException {
    return executeUpdate("CREATE TABLE " + tableName + " " + tableCreate);
  }
}
```

You need to create the database yourself. The method for creating a database varies among vendors, so consult your DBMS documentation. This method will also not replace an existing table, so you would need to drop that yourself if you want it recreated. However, it's still much easier than piping a SQL script from the command line.

The ConnectionPool Class

While Struts provides a simple connection pool, named `GenericDataSource`, it is difficult to use this class in a layered application. Why? Struts exposes the datasource through the `ServletContext`, and our Data Access Objects do not have direct access to that layer. However, since the Struts `GenericDataSource` is an optional package, it is just as easy to use something else (and in a production environment, I would recommend that you do, since this Struts package is really not designed for intensive use).

As an alternative, we will use the very capable PoolMan package, which can be downloaded from http://www.codestudio.com/.

PoolMan is a popular open source package available under the GNU Lesser General Public License and permits unrestricted commercial use of the unmodified `poolman.jar`. See the `LICENSE` file in the PoolMan download for details. Our layered approach makes it easy for us to swap in another connection pool (so long as it is not bound to the `ServletContext`).

Our data access routines all request a connection from the `ConnectionPool` class. They don't actually know or care that we are using a pool – they just ask for a connection, and are given one – with the proviso that they close it as soon as they are through with it. Closing a connection is especially important with a pool, since it frees the connection for use by someone else.

Here is the ConnectionPool class that, working with PoolMan, returns the connections:

```
package com.wrox.articles.sql;

import java.sql.Connection;
import java.sql.SQLException;
import javax.sql.DataSource;
import com.codestudio.sql.PoolMan;

public final class ConnectionPool {
```

First, let's define the static we need to access the database through PoolMan. This must match the same token used in \WEB-INF\classes\poolman.xml (described next):

```
  public static final String DATASOURCE_KEY = "articles";
```

In case something goes awry, let's provide an exception message to throw if findDataSource() returns null:

```
  public static final String DATASOURCE_ERROR =
        "Connection pool not available. " +
        "Is poolman.jar and poolman.xml on the CLASSPATH? " +
        "Is the database service running?";
```

The getConnection() method returns a JDBC connection from the connection pool:

```
  public static final Connection getConnection() throws SQLException {
    DataSource ds = PoolMan.findDataSource(DATASOURCE_KEY);
    if (ds==null) {
      throw new SQLException(DATASOURCE_ERROR);
    }
    return(ds.getConnection());
  }
}
```

Since this is a pooled connection, it must be used and closed promptly. The method is also written so that it will not return null (an exception is thrown instead). This saves extra tests later.

The PoolMan Configuration File – poolman.xml

On the installation side, you may also need to add the database driver for your DBMS to the Tomcat lib\ folder (if you have not done so already for another example in the book), or adjust the settings in the WEB-INF\classes\poolman.xml file to match your own setup. Here's the one to use with a standard installation of MySQL:

```
<?xml version="1.0" encoding="UTF-8"?>

<poolman>
  <management-mode>local</management-mode>
  <datasource>
```

```
    <dbname>articles</dbname>
    <jndiName>jdbc/articles</jndiName>
    <driver>org.gjt.mm.mysql.Driver</driver>
    <url>jdbc:mysql://localhost/articles</url>
    <username>root</username>
    <password></password>
    <minimumSize>0</minimumSize>
    <maximumSize>10</maximumSize>
    <connectionTimeout>600</connectionTimeout>
    <userTimeout>12</userTimeout>
    <shrinkBy>10</shrinkBy>
    <logFile>/var/applogs/poolman.log</logFile>
    <debugging>false</debugging>
    <cacheEnabled>true</cacheEnabled>
    <cacheSize>20</cacheSize>
    <cacheRefreshInterval>120</cacheRefreshInterval>
  </datasource>
</poolman>
```

If you would like to use another connection pool instead, you only need to amend the `ConnectionPool` class and rebuild it with the appropriate values set for your connection pool. No other changes to the application would be required.

The CreateTables Action

All this leaves the `CreateTables` action very little to do. We just need to subclass the standard Struts action, and provide a few calls to our helper classes:

```
package com.wrox.articles.http;

import java.io.IOException;
import java.io.PrintWriter;
import java.sql.SQLException;
import javax.servlet.ServletException;
import javax.servlet.http.HttpServletRequest;
import javax.servlet.http.HttpServletResponse;
import org.apache.struts.action.Action;
import org.apache.struts.action.ActionForm;
import org.apache.struts.action.ActionForward;
import org.apache.struts.action.ActionMapping;
import org.apache.struts.action.ActionServlet;
import com.wrox.articles.sql.Data;

public final class CreateTables extends Action {

  public ActionForward perform(ActionMapping mapping,
                               ActionForm form,
                               HttpServletRequest request,
                               HttpServletResponse response)
    throws IOException, ServletException {
```

Since this is an "internal-use" `Action`, like the Struts administrative `Actions`, we just return plain text to the client, rather than bother with a JSP page. To prepare for this, we setup a standard `PrintWriter`, as we would with any generic HTTP servlet:

```
response.setContentType("text/plain");
PrintWriter writer = response.getWriter();
try {
```

First, we tell the client that we are working on the `primary_keys` table, and call the `Data.createTable()` method. If an exception is returned, we interpose the word "NOT" to signal the error. The actual exception is logged, so we can study it later. If all goes well, the screen will read: KEYS TABLE CREATED.

If it does not go well, it would read: KEYS TABLE NOT CREATED:

```
  writer.print("KEYS TABLE ");
  Data.keysCreateTable();
} catch (SQLException sqle) {
    servlet.log("SQL Exception: " + sqle);
    writer.print("NOT ");
}
writer.println("CREATED.");
```

We repeat the process with the `article` table. Since the exception was caught and logged, this will proceed even if there is an error with creating the `primary_keys` table:

```
try {
  writer.print("ARTICLE TABLE ");
  Data.articleCreateTable();
} catch (SQLException sqle) {
    servlet.log("SQL Exception: " + sqle);
    writer.print("NOT ");
}
writer.println("CREATED.");
```

If more tables are needed in a future version, we can continue the process for each table here. When all tables are complete, we indicate that to the client, and return null to the Struts controller. This tells the controller that we handed the response ourselves, and there is nothing else for it to do:

```
      writer.println("DONE");
      return(null);
   }
}
```

We'll be using this same data access strategy throughout the application:

- The SQL statements and low-level data access code are each kept in their own classes
- The high-level `Data` class puts the two together, and presents a high-level interface to the application
- The application only has to call the `Data` class methods, handle any exceptions, and make any flow control decisions

The CreateTables Mapping

Of course, a Struts Action is no good without an ActionMapping. Here's the struts-config.xml mapping for our CreateTables Action:

```
<action-mappings>

  <action path="do/admin/CreateTables"
          type="com.wrox.articles.http.CreateTables"/>

</action-mappings>
```

To create a database using MySQL, run mysql from the command line, and enter:

```
CREATE DATABASE articles;
```

In a production environment, we would also create a special user for the application, and restrict access to the database. See your product's documentation for details.

With a database on board, we can run CreateTables for the first time. After starting the container, we can run CreateTables like the standard Struts administrative Actions by navigating to http://localhost:8080/articles/admin/CreateTables. You will see this security screen:

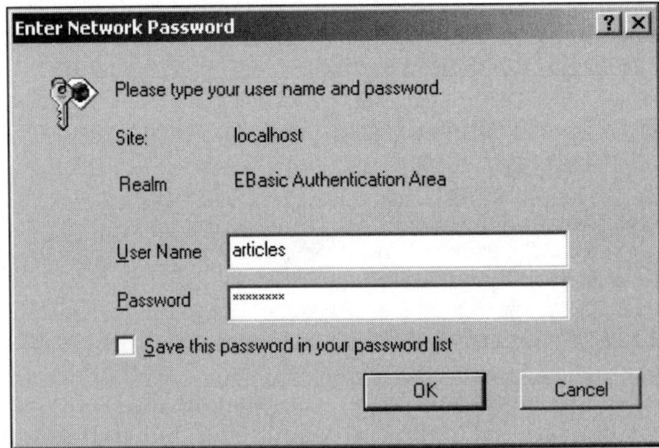

Enter articles and articles as the username and password after which your screen will look something like this:

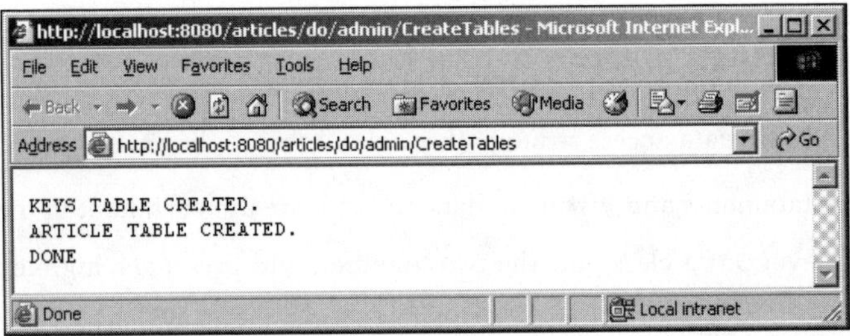

The Data Access Operations

A core requirement of the application is to store and select data from a persistent store. Since this is a common requirement for web applications, it's handy to have a reusable set of objects to perform the basic operations: create, retrieve, update, and delete (CRUD).

Struts is a BYOM framework (Bring Your Own Model) in that it doesn't provide any basic classes or interfaces for data access. This is helpful for developers porting a project to Struts, but not so helpful when we are trying to build a web database application from scratch.

> *Of course, few developers ever build any application completely from scratch. There are usually classes from one application that we can adapt for another. In the Articles application, we've isolated the resuable components into a separate packaged, named `ext`. The key classes for our CRUD operations will be subclassed from the `ext` package. In this chapter, we will discuss how the `ext` classes are used in the Articles application, but leave the implementation as a black box. The source code for the `ext` package is provided in the WAR, and copiously documented if you are interested in how it works.*

Extending ext

To put the `ext` package to work, we need to implement three classes, an `AccessBean` helper, an `AccessForm`, and an `Access Action` to handle the client requests. We'll discuss each in turn, but here's an overview:

- `AccessForm` is a subclass of `ActionForm` that implements utility methods expected by the `Access Action`.
- `AccessBean` provides helper properties for creating multi-row lists in a view, as in a hit list from a search. We will use it to implement the specific data access code for our tables, and let the `Access Action` handle the Struts `ActionErrors` and `ActionForwards`.
- `Access` is a "framework" `Action` that can be used to manage CRUD operations for any table in any Struts application. Once we define our `AccessBean` helper and the `ActionForm` for our application, we can pass them to a utility method in `Access`. The `Access` class then copes with the Struts error handling and forwards.

The ArticleForm Class

Our first `ActionForm` is `ArticleForm`. This represents the data-entry screen for a new article, as shown on our storyboards. The properties here will be retained by the database, and so also represent fields from our database schema:

```
package com.wrox.articles.http;

import java.io.IOException;
import java.util.Map;
import javax.servlet.http.HttpServletRequest;
import org.apache.struts.action.Action;
import org.apache.struts.action.ActionError;
import org.apache.struts.action.ActionErrors;
import org.apache.struts.action.ActionForm;
import org.apache.struts.action.ActionMapping;
import org.apache.struts.util.BeanUtils;
import ext.http.AccessForm;
```

`ArticleForm` extends `AccessForm` from the `ext` package. `AccessForm` is a base class that provides default functionality for transferring the properties of a bean via a `Map`. These methods use reflection, and so do not have to be overridden. However, we do have to provide the usual accessors and mutators for our bean's properties:

```
public class ArticleForm extends AccessForm {

   protected String article = null;

   public String getArticle() {
     return (this.article);
   }

   public void setArticle(String article) {
     this.article = article;
   }

   protected String contributor = null;

   public String getContributor() {
     return (this.contributor);
   }

   public void setContributor(String contributor) {
     this.contributor = contributor;
   }

   protected String creator = null;

   public String getCreator() {
     return (this.creator);
   }

   public void setCreator(String creator) {
     this.creator = creator;
   }

   protected String title = null;

   public String getTitle() {
     return (this.title);
   }

   public void setTitle(String title) {
     this.title = title;
   }

   protected String content = null;

   public String getContent() {
     return (this.content);
   }

   public void setContent(String content) {
     this.content = content;
   }
```

Aside from the "map" methods, the `DataBean` interface has a second set of methods, designed to help with data access between layers and beans. In practice, many JavaBeans represent a set of fields that has a unique identifier. In a database application, like ours, this is usually the primary key for the table. We'll override the default "key" methods to use our article property, which stores the primary key:

```
    public String getKey() {
      return getArticle();
    }

    public void setKey(String article) {
      setArticle(article);
    }
```

Our `validate()` method checks that required properties are not null and not blank:

```
    public ActionErrors validate(ActionMapping mapping,
                                 HttpServletRequest request) {

      ActionErrors errors = new ActionErrors();
      if ((creator == null) || ("".equals(creator))) {
        errors.add(ActionErrors.GLOBAL_ERROR,
                   new ActionError("errors.required","Author"));
      }
      if ((title == null) || ("".equals(title))) {
        errors.add(ActionErrors.GLOBAL_ERROR,
                   new ActionError("errors.required","Title"));
      }
      if ((content == null) || ("".equals(content))) {
        errors.add(ActionErrors.GLOBAL_ERROR,
                   new ActionError("errors.required","Article text"));
      }
        return (errors);
    }
```

Our `reset()` method sets the bean properties to null:

```
    public void reset(ActionMapping mapping, HttpServletRequest request) {
      this.article = null;
      this.contributor = null;
      this.creator = null;
      this.title = null;
      this.content = null;
    }
  }
```

The ArticleHelper Class

`AccessBean` is an abstract class, but the `ext` package offers a concrete subclass, `AccessBeanList`. We will use this as the basis for our own helper class, `ArticleHelper`.

Following the same model we used in `CreateTables`, `ArticleHelper` calls `Data` to handle the actual access. `Data` in turn combines the SQL commands with SQL prepared statements, and returns the result as a `List`. The `ArticleHelper` stores the list, and is also the object returned to the presentation layer:

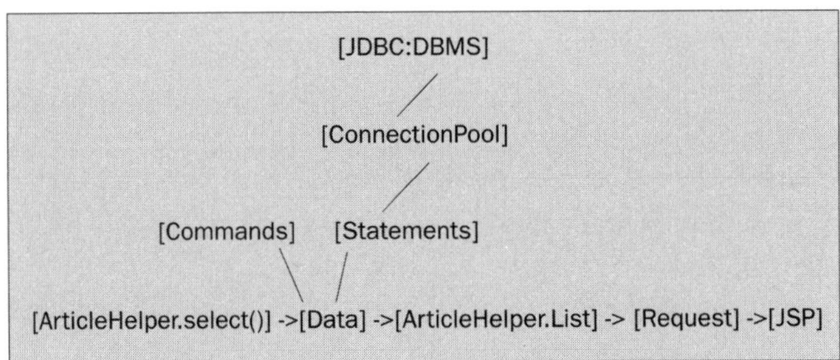


```
package com.wrox.articles;

import java.sql.SQLException;
import java.util.Map;
import java.util.Iterator;
import java.util.List;
import java.util.ArrayList;
import ext.sql.DataAccess;
import ext.sql.AccessBeanList;
import ext.util.DataBean;
import com.wrox.articles.http.ArticleForm;
import com.wrox.articles.sql.Data;
import com.wrox.articles.search.Engine;

public final class ArticleHelper extends AccessBeanList {
```

In our `Client` class (discussed next), we will pass our `ActionForm` to the `ArticleHelper` when it is instantiated using this convenience constructor. It creates a single-element list for the `ActionForm`. A default constructor is also provided, per the JavaBean conventions:

```
  public ArticleHelper(Object object) {
    super();
    ArrayList list = new ArrayList(1);
    list.add(object);
    setRows(list);
  }

  public ArticleHelper() {
    super();
  }
```

The first methods in `ArticleHelper` are required by the `ext.DataAccess` interface implemented by our ancestor class. These must be overridden to provide functionality. (The default methods do nothing.)

The `allocateKey()` method simply calls a corresponding method in the `Data` class. This will reserve and return the next available key for the article table:

```
  public int allocateKey() throws SQLException {
    return Data.articleAllocateKey();
  }
```

The ancestor `AccessBean` class provides a list of beans to use in an operation. The `insert()` method retrieves beans from that list, and calls a method in `Data` to insert a new article. Since our `ArticleForm` implements the `ext.DataBean` interface, we can use a standard `Map` to transfer the data:

```
public int insert() throws SQLException {
  int count = 0;
  while (rows.hasNext()) {
    DataBean thisForm = (DataBean) rows.next();
    // Set primary key for next insert
    thisForm.setKeyInt(allocateKey());
    Map thisMap = thisForm.toMap();
    Data.articleInsert(
      (String) thisMap.get("article"),
      (String) thisMap.get("contributor"),
      (String) thisMap.get("creator"),
      (String) thisMap.get("title"),
      (String) thisMap.get("content")
    );
    count++;
  }
  return count;
}
```

Like the `insert()` method, `update()` extracts the data for the updated article, and passes it to a static method in the `Data` class:

```
public int update() throws SQLException {
  int count = 0;
  while (rows.hasNext()) {
    DataBean thisForm = (DataBean) rows.next();
    Map thisMap  = thisForm.toMap();
    Data.articleUpdate(
      (String) thisMap.get("article"),
      (String) thisMap.get("contributor"),
      (String) thisMap.get("creator"),
      (String) thisMap.get("title"),
      (String) thisMap.get("content")
    );
    count++;
  }
  return count;
}
```

The `select()` method handles the various searches the application performs. By providing custom search routines designed for content management, this is the method that distinguishes Articles from other database applications. Without this component, the application is just a shoebox of articles.

First, we get the column property from our helper as a local string, and set the helper's list to null. The following routines will then try to populate the list with a set of matching articles:

```
public int select() throws SQLException {
  String column = getColumn();
  setRows(null);
  TASK: {
```

This block will select all of the articles if the helper is passed an empty key.

The `Data.articleSearchCurrent()` method returns a collection of beans, using the `ArticleForm` bean as a template. All of the following blocks use the same technique. `Data` is called to return a collection of beans, and the result is set as the `ArrayList` provided by our helper:

```
if (("".equals(key))) {
  setRows( Data.articleSearchCurrent(new ArticleForm()) );
  break TASK;
}
```

This block will select a specific article by ID, if a key is given but the column is blank:

```
if (("".equals(column)) ||
    (DataAccess.KEY.equals(column)) ||
    ("article".equals(column))) {
  setRows(Data.articleSelect(getKeyInt(), new ArticleForm()));
  break TASK;
}
```

This block selects the last *n* articles:

```
if (("last".equals(column))) {
  setRows( Data.articleSearchLast(getKeyInt(), new ArticleForm()) );
  break TASK;
}
```

This block selects an article by how long ago it was created in hours:

```
if ("hours".equals(column)) {
  setRows(Data.articleSearchHours(getKeyInt(), new ArticleForm()));
  break TASK;
}
```

This block selects an article by finding a string in its title:

```
if ("title".equals(column)) {
  setRows(Data.articleSearchTitle(getKey(), new ArticleForm()));
  break TASK;
}
```

This block selects an article by finding a string in its author property:

```
if ("author".equals(column)) {
  setRows(Data.articleSearchCreator(getKey(), new ArticleForm()));
  break TASK;
}
```

This block selects an article by finding a string in its content:

```
        if ("content".equals(column)) {
          setRows(Data.articleSearchContent(getKey(), new ArticleForm()));
          break TASK;
        }
      }
```

Once these tests have been applied, the number of matches on our helper list is returned. If nothing matched, and the list is still null, then zero would be returned:

```
      return getRowCount();
    }
```

The `delete()` method is another wrapper around a static `Data` method:

```
    public int delete() throws SQLException {
      int count = 0;
      while (rows.hasNext()) {
        DataBean thisForm = (DataBean) rows.next();
        Data.articleDelete(thisForm.getKeyInt());
        count++;
      }
      return count;
    }
  }
```

The Client Class

On the back end, all that's left to implement is our subclass of `ext.Access`. As with `CreateTables`, at this point, there's not much left to do, just support code for control-flow and error-handling:

```
package com.wrox.articles.http;

import java.io.IOException;
import java.sql.SQLException;
import java.util.Map;
import javax.servlet.ServletException;
import javax.servlet.http.HttpServletRequest;
import javax.servlet.http.HttpServletResponse;
import org.apache.struts.action.ActionError;
import org.apache.struts.action.ActionErrors;
import org.apache.struts.action.ActionForm;
import org.apache.struts.action.ActionForward;
import org.apache.struts.action.ActionMapping;
import org.apache.struts.action.ActionServlet;
import ext.http.Access;
import ext.sql.DataAccess;
import com.wrox.articles.ArticleHelper;
import com.wrox.articles.sql.Data;

import com.wrox.articles.sql.ConnectionPool;
```

```
public final class Client extends Access {

  public ActionForward perform(ActionMapping mapping,
                               ActionForm form,
                               HttpServletRequest request,
                               HttpServletResponse response)
    throws IOException, ServletException {
```

First we check to see if the request was cancelled, rather than submitted. This is a standard Struts `Action` tied to the `<html:cancel>` tag. If the request was cancelled, we return our "cancel" forwarding, and exit:

```
    if (isCancelled(request)) {
      return (mapping.findForward("cancel"));
    }
```

A prime purpose of a Struts `Action` is error handling, so we need to instantiate an `ActionErrors` collection for this request. We also instantiate an array of strings to collect confirmation messages and their replaceable parameters:

```
    ActionErrors errors = new ActionErrors();
    ArticleForm thisForm = (ArticleForm) form;
    String[] confirm = new String[Access.CONFIRM_MAX];
```

Now we create our `ArticleHelper` object that has been specialised to handle our tables.

```
    ArticleHelper thisHelper = new ArticleHelper(form);
```

To do the real work of this `Action`, we pass our helper objects to a utility method of the `ext.Access` class. The source is available in the application WAR if you are interested. Basically, it calls the appropriate method of our `ArticleHelper` object and returns the result:

```
    int result = crud(mapping,thisForm,request,errors,confirm,thisHelper);
```

When the `crud()` method returns, we check our error handler for any messages. If there were errors, we forward to our input page, if there is one:

```
    if (!errors.empty()) {
      saveErrors(request, errors);
      if (mapping.getInput()!=null) {
        return (new ActionForward(mapping.getInput()));
      }
```

Or, look for an "error" forwarding if our input property is null:

```
      return (mapping.findForward("error"));
    }
```

If there were no errors, we call a utility method in our ancestor class to transfer any confirmation message from the `Confirm` array to the errors collection. Our JSP page can then display them using the same tags as errors, but they will be read by the user as confirmation messages instead:

```
    saveConfirm(errors,confirm);
    if (!errors.empty()) {
      saveErrors(request, errors);
    }
```

And, if we make it here, all is well, and we can return a standard "continue" to the controller.

```
    return (mapping.findForward("continue"));
  }
}
```

The First Shall Be Last

With this infrastructure in place, we draft our JSP pages and complete the application.

The menu JSP Page

The menu page is the default starting point for the example application. In practice, this page might be integrated into a larger layout, or provided in separate sections. Since the layout is based on custom tags, it can fit easily into any layout.

The different forms on this page use the `key` and `col` parameters from `AccessBean` to identify different search patterns. The `col` determines which property of field to search, and the `key` what to look for. The internal methods know whether or not `key` is a primary key field, and so use exact or fuzzy "like" searches as appropriate. Note how the forms and their parameters correlate to the methods in `ArticleHelper`:

```
<%@ page language="java" %>
<%@ taglib uri="/tags/struts-html" prefix="html" %>
<%@ taglib uri="/tags/struts-bean" prefix="bean" %>
<%@ taglib uri="/tags/struts-logic" prefix="logic" %>
<%@ taglib uri="/tags/request" prefix="req" %>

<html:html/>
  <head>
    <html:base/>
```

All of the pages refer to a stylesheet, to simplify presentation changes and to keep extra markup out of the JSP page:

```
    <link rel="stylesheet" type="text/css" href="../styles/global.css" />
    <title>Admin - Menu</title>
  </head>
  <body>
    <table class="parent">
      <tr>
        <td align="center">
          <table class="child">
            <tr>
```

Each page also has a section to display error messages. Confirmation messages, like "1 record added", will also display here. If there are no confirmations or errors, the cell is empty:

```
        <td colspan="3">
          <html:errors/>
        </td>
      </tr>
```

This is the search form at the top of the page. It offers radio buttons to select articles by their age. The actual selection is in hours, but the equivalent calendar period is shown to the user (day, week, month):

```
      <html:form action="/Search">
        <input type="hidden" name="col" value="hours">
        <tr>
          <td align="right">Posted in the last:</td>
          <td align="left">
            <input type="radio" name="key" value="24">Day<br>
            <input type="radio" name="key" value="168">Week<br>
            <input type="radio" name="key" value="720">Month
          </td>
          <td align="left">
            <html:submit property="submit" value=" FIND "/>
          </td>
        </tr>
      </html:form>
```

This is the search by title form. Notice that it submits to the same Struts `ActionMapping`, but uses a different value for `col`. The first form used `hours`, this form uses `titles`. Of course, this is a hidden field, and not displayed on the page:

```
      <html:form action="/Search">
        <input type="hidden" name="col" value="title">
        <tr>
          <td align="right">Article Title:</td>
          <td align="left">
            <input type="text" name="key" size="16"
           maxlength="45">
          </td>
          <td align="left">
            <html:submit property="submit" value=" FIND "/>
          </td>
        </tr>
      </html:form>
```

The search by author form:

```
      <html:form action="/Search">
        <input type="hidden" name="col" value="author">
        <tr>
          <td align="right">Article Author:</td>
          <td align="left">
            <input type="text" name="key" size="16"
           maxlength="45">
          </td>
          <td align="left">
            <html:submit property="submit" value=" FIND "/>
          </td>
        </tr>
      </html:form>
```

The search by content form:

```
<html:form action="/Search">
  <input type="hidden" name="col" value="content">
  <tr>
    <td align="right">Article Text:</td>
    <td align="left">
      <input type="content" name="key" size="16"
      maxlength="45">
    </td>
    <td align="left">
      <html:submit property="submit" value=" FIND "/>
    </td>
  </tr>
</html:form>
```

The article ID form submits to `/View` rather than `/Search`. As the ID is unique, we can bypass searching and go directly to the article:

```
<html:form action="/View">
  <input type="hidden" name="col" value="article">
  <tr>
    <td align="right">Article ID:</td>
    <td align="left">
      <input type="text" name="key" size="5" maxlength="10">
    </td>
    <td align="left">
      <html:submit property="submit" value=" VIEW "/>
    </td>
  </tr>
</html:form>
```

The final form on this page is a button that fires a search for the "last" articles. The setting of the `key` value tells the `Action` to return the last 10 articles added to the database:

```
<html:form action="/Search">
  <input type="hidden" name="col" value="last">
  <tr>
    <td align="right"> </td>
    <td align="left">
      <input type="hidden" name="key" value="10">
       <html:submit property="submit" value=" LATEST NEWS "/>
    </td>
    <td align="left"></td>
  </tr>
</html:form>
```

With role-based security active, the `<req>` tag will only provide this form to users in the contributor role, so only contributors will have the ADD ARTICLE button.

> *The `<req>` tag is from the Jakarta Taglibs Request Library (http://jakarta.apache.org/taglibs/). The JAR is provided with the Articles WAR.*

```
<req:isUserInRole role="contributor">
  <tr>
    <td colspan="3">
      <hr>
    </td>
   </tr>
   <tr>
     <td> </td>
     <td>
       <html:form action="/admin/Input">
         <html:submit>ADD ARTICLE</html:submit>
       </html:form>
     </td>
     <td> </td>
   </tr>
 </req:isUserInRole>
```

Likewise, role-based security will only display this form to users in the manager role, so only managers will be shown the administrative menu:

```
<req:isUserInRole role="manager">
  <tr>
    <td> </td>
    <td>
      <table border="1" cellpadding="8" width="100%">
        <tr>
          <td>
             
            <html:link forward="createTables">
              CREATE TABLES
            </html:link></br>
             
            <html:link forward="reload">
              RELOAD CONFIG
            </html:link>
          </td>
        </tr>
      </table>
    </td>
    <td> </td>
  </tr>
</req:isUserInRole>
```

This table prints at the bottom of the page, as a footer. The LOGON link goes through a second mapping to this page, /do/admin/Menu. Since this URI is "under" admin, the container will prompt for a login before allowing access. If the login is successful, the same JSP page will be displayed, but additional controls will appear according to the user's role:

```
          </table>
        </td>
        </tr>
        <tr>
          <td class="options">
            <html:link forward="logon">LOGON</html:link> |
            <html:link forward="exit">EXIT</html:link>
          </td>
        </tr>
      </table>
    </table>
  </body>
</html>
```

The entry JSP page

This page displays the data-entry form for adding or editing articles:

```
<%@ page language="java" %>
<%@ taglib uri="/tags/struts-html" prefix="html" %>
<%@ taglib uri="/tags/struts-bean" prefix="bean" %>
<%@ taglib uri="/tags/struts-logic" prefix="logic" %>

<html:html/>
  <head>
   <html:base/>
   <link rel="stylesheet" type="text/css" href="../styles/global.css" />
   <title>Articles - Article Entry Form</title>
  </head>
  <body>
    <table class="parent">
      <tr>
        <td>
          <table class="child">
            <tr>
              <td colspan="3">
                <html:errors/>
              </td>
            </tr>
```

Note that this form submits to the `Store Action`. This is where the `SMART_STORE` parameter from our `ArticleHelper` class comes in. When `SMART_STORE` is true, the `Action` will check the form's key to see if it is null. If so, it changes the operation to `INSERT`. If the key is not null, it changes it to `UPDATE`. This lets us use one form for both operations.

Since `Store` is "under" admin, unauthorised users cannot submit a request to this resource:

```
            <html:form action="/admin/Store">
              <tr>
                <td align="right" nowrap>Title:</td>
                <td align="left" colspan="2">
                  <html:text property="title" size="50"
                             maxlength="255" accesskey="T"/>
                </td>
              </tr>
              <tr>
                <td align="right" nowrap>Author:</td>
                <td align="left">
                  <html:text property="creator" size="30"
                             maxlength="75" accesskey="A"/>
                </td>
                <td align="left">
                  Full name of person who orginated the article.
                </td>
              </tr>
              <tr>
```

Struts does provide a tag for displaying text areas, but it does not support the "wrap" property, which is not part of the formal standard. However, since the property is supported by the popular browsers, and users expect it, we use a trick to write the content inside a regular `textarea` tag:

```
          <td align="right" nowrap>Article:</td>
          <td align="left" colspan="2">
            <textarea name="content" rows="12" cols="50"
                      accesskey="a" tabindex="2" wrap="soft">
              <bean:write name="articleForm" property="content"/>
            </textarea>
          </td>
        </tr>
        <tr>
```

Note the treatment of the article ID on this page. To provide a consistent presentation, the article ID is included for both an insert and an update. When the article ID is not present (or "null"), the form says "Not Assigned" in dim text. When the article ID is present, it prints the ID as text, rather than in a field. (Primary keys should not be edited by users.) This is the same technique used to decide whether to add or update an article on the server side:

```
          <td align="right" nowrap>Article ID:</td>
          <logic:notPresent name="articleForm" property="key">
            <td align="left"><i>
              <html:hidden property="key"/>
              not assigned
            </i></td>
          </logic:notPresent>
          <logic:present name="articleForm" property="key">
            <td align="left">
              <html:hidden property="key"/>
              <bean:write name="articleForm" property="key"/>
            </td>
          </logic:present>
          <td> </td>
        </tr>
```

Our buttons:

```
        <tr>
          <td colspan="3" align="right">
            <html:submit accesskey="S">
              SAVE
            </html:submit>
            <html:cancel  accesskey="C">
              CANCEL
            </html:cancel>
          </td>
        </tr>
        <html:hidden property="key"/>
      </html:form>
    </table>
  </td>
</tr>
<tr>
  <td class="options">
    <html:link forward="done" accesskey="D">
      DONE
    </html:link>
  </td>
</tr>
</table>
```

The article JSP Page

The article page crops up often in our workflow. It is displayed as a confirmation page after an insert or update. It is also displayed as the "detail" for a link on the `list.jsp` (covered next). This is probably the simplest page, since it just displays a single record using `<bean:write>`:

```
<%@ page language="java" %>
<%@ taglib uri="/tags/struts-html" prefix="html" %>
<%@ taglib uri="/tags/struts-bean" prefix="bean" %>
<%@ taglib uri="/tags/struts-logic" prefix="logic" %>
<%@ taglib uri="/tags/request" prefix="req" %>

<html:html/>
  <head>
    <html:base/>
    <link rel="stylesheet" type="text/css" href="../styles/global.css" />
    <title>Articles - Article</title>
  </head>
  <body>
    <table class="parent">
      <tr>
        <td>
          <table class="child">
            <tr>
              <td colspan="3">
                <html:errors/>
              </td>
            </tr>
            <tr>
              <td colspan="3" align="center">
                <h2>
                  <bean:write name="articleForm" property="title"/>
                </h2>
              </td>
            </tr>
            <tr>
              <td colspan="3" class="author">
                by <bean:write name="articleForm" property="creator"/>
              </td>
            </tr>
            <tr>
```

By setting `filter=false`, Struts will not escape HTML so that any markup entered into the content field will be rendered:

```
              <td colspan="3">
                <bean:write name="articleForm" property="content"
                 filter="false"/>
              </td>
            </tr>
```

When role-based security is active, the following set of buttons will only be displayed to users in the contributor role:

```
              <req:isUserInRole role="contributor">
                <tr>
                  <td colspan="3">
                    <hr />
                  </td>
                </tr>
                <tr>
                  <html:form action="/admin/Delete">
                    <td align="left">
                      <html:submit>DELETE</html:submit>
                    </td>
                    <html:hidden property="key"/>
                  </html:form>
                  <html:form action="/admin/Edit">
                    <td colspan="2" align="right">
                      <html:submit>EDIT</html:submit>
                      <html:cancel>CANCEL</html:cancel>
                    </td>
                    <html:hidden property="key"/>
                  </html:form>
                </tr>
              </req:isUserInRole>
            </table>
          </td>
        </tr>
        <tr>
          <td class="options">
            <html:link forward="done">DONE</html:link>
          </td>
        </tr>
      </table>
    </body>
  </html>
```

The list JSP Page

This page displays a simple list of articles meeting a search request. The list is carried by the `ArticleHelper` object, which was subclassed from `ext.AccessBeanList`. The heart of the page is inside the Struts `iterate` tag, which loops through the list passed in the request:

```
<%@ page language="java" %>
<%@ taglib uri="/tags/struts-bean" prefix="bean" %>
<%@ taglib uri="/tags/struts-html" prefix="html" %>
<%@ taglib uri="/tags/struts-logic" prefix="logic" %>

<html:html/>
  <head>
    <html:base/>
    <link rel="stylesheet" type="text/css" href="../styles/global.css" />
    <title>Articles - Article List</title>
  </head>
  <body>
   <table class="parent">
     <tr>
       <td align="center">
```

This is the page heading for our match set. The `rowCount` and `parameter` properties are provided by the `ArticleHelper` class through its ancestor class, `ext.AccessBeanBase`. The name of the attribute, `"RESULT"`, is documented in the source as `ext.DataAccess.HELPER_KEY`:

```
          <table class="child">
            <tr>
              <td align="center" colspan="3">
                <bean:write name="RESULT" property="rowCount"/>
                matches for
                <bean:write name="RESULT" property="parameter"/>
              </td>
            </tr>
```

The `logic` tag will only print the column headers and list items if the row count is not zero:

```
            <logic:notEqual name="RESULT" property="rowCount" value="0">
              <tr bgcolor="#FFFFEE">
                <th>
                  <span style="text-transform: uppercase">id</span>
                </th>
                <th>
                  <span style="text-transform: uppercase">article</span>
                </th>
              </tr>
              <tr>
```

The scriptlets here alternate the background colours on the rows, making the list easier to read:

```
                <% int i = 0; %>
                <logic:iterate name="RESULT" property="rows" id="row">
                  <% i++;
                     if ( i % 2 == 0) { %>
                  <tr bgcolor="#EEEEEE">
                  <% } else { %>
                  <tr bgcolor="#FFFFFF">
                  <% } %>
                    <td align="left">
                      <bean:write name="row" property="article"/>
                    </td>
                    <td align="left" width="100%">
```

The `<html:link>` tag hyperlinks the list items to the detail for the article:

```
                      <html:link forward="article" paramName="row"
                        paramProperty="key" paramId="key">
                        <bean:write name="row" property="title"/>
                      </html:link>
                    </td>
                  </tr>
                </logic:iterate>
              </tr>
            </logic:notEqual>
          </table>
        </td>
      </tr>
      <tr>
        <td class="options">
          <html:link forward="done">DONE</html:link>
        </td>
      </tr>
    </table>
  </body>
</html>
```

The Action Mappings

Finally, here are the Action mappings for this application:

```
<action-mappings>

  <!-- Article Menu (guests) -->
  <action
    path="/Menu"
    forward="/pages/menu.jsp">
  </action>

  <!-- Article Menu (admin) -->
  <action
    path="/admin/Menu"
    forward="/pages/menu.jsp">
  </action>

  <!-- Input Article (admin) -->
  <action
    path="/admin/Input"
    type="com.wrox.articles.http.Client"
    name="articleForm"
    scope="request"
    validate="false"
    parameter="input">
     <forward
       name="continue"
       path="/pages/entry.jsp"/>
  </action>

  <!-- List action mapping -->
  <action
    path="/List"
    type="com.wrox.articles.http.Client"
    name="articleForm"
    scope="request"
    validate="false"
    parameter="select">
     <forward
            name="continue"
            path="/pages/list.jsp"/>
  </action>

  <!-- View Article action mapping -->
  <action
    path="/View"
    type="com.wrox.articles.http.Client"
    name="articleForm"
    scope="request"
    validate="false"
    parameter="select">
     <forward
       name="continue"
```

```
        path="/pages/article.jsp"/>
    </action>

    <!-- Article Edit action mapping (admin) -->
    <action
      path="/admin/Edit"
      type="com.wrox.articles.http.Client"
      name="articleForm"
      scope="request"
      validate="false"
      parameter="select">
        <forward
          name="continue"
          path="/pages/entry.jsp"/>
    </action>

    <!-- Article Store action mapping (admin) -->
    <action
      path="/admin/Store"
      type="com.wrox.articles.http.Client"
      name="articleForm"
      scope="request"
      validate="true"
      input="/pages/entry.jsp"
      parameter="store">
        <forward
          name="continue"
          path="/pages/article.jsp"/>
    </action>

    <!-- Article Search action mapping -->
    <action
      path="/Search"
      type="com.wrox.articles.http.Client"
      name="articleForm"
      scope="request"
      validate="false"
      parameter="select">
        <forward
          name="continue"
          path="/pages/list.jsp"/>
    </action>

    <!-- Article Edit action mapping (admin) -->
    <action
      path="/admin/Delete"
      type="com.wrox.articles.http.Client"
      name="articleForm"
      scope="request"
      validate="false"
      parameter="delete">
        <forward
          name="continue"
          path="/pages/menu.jsp"/>
```

```
    </action>

    <!-- Create Tables action mapping (admin) -->
    <action
      path="/admin/CreateTables"
      type="com.wrox.articles.http.CreateTables"/>

    <!-- The standard administrative actions available with Struts -->
    <!-- These are protected by security -->
    ...

  </action-mappings>
```

Summary

In this chapter we built a simple news posting application that you can adopt, adapt, and extend for use on your own web site.

In building the Articles application, we:

- Developed a workflow and requirements to help plan our application
- Anticipated complications and customizations early in the design
- Used a storyboard to plan the application's flow and demonstrate the feature set
- Developed a database schema to fulfill our workflow, requirements, and storyboard
- Implemented security at the outset as part of the application's design
- Created the database tables using a Struts `Action` class
- Installed our connection pool as a "pluggable" component
- Deployed our database operations using a standard class that can be reused in other applications
- Customized which controls appear on our Java ServerPages according to the user's security role

In the next chapter, we will continue to develop our Articles application. In doing so we will explore the power and benefits that effective searching can bring to a site.

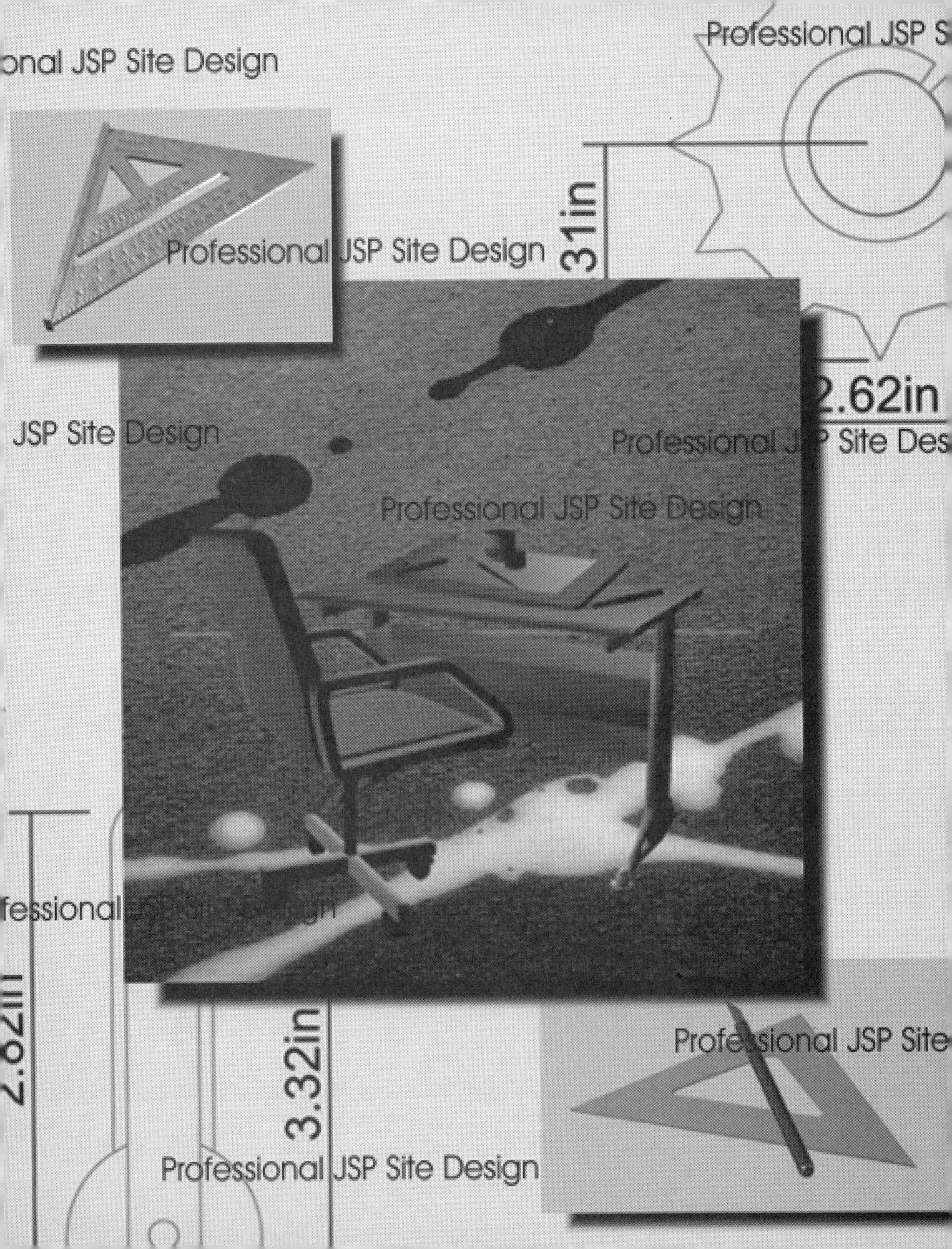

Professional JSP S
onal JSP Site Design
31in
Professional JSP Site Design
2.62in
JSP Site Design
Professional JSP Site Des
Professional JSP Site Design
3.32in
Professional JSP Site
Professional JSP Site Design

13

Searching

So much content, so little time... A good search tool is an essential part of any professional web site. If users can spend less time finding content, they can spend more time enjoying it.

Search What?

Most applications can benefit from a good search utility, and web applications are no exception. Bulletin boards need to search messages, help desks need to search incident reports, portals need to search channels, and general content sites need to search all the pages in their web. Some of these materials are found on disk files, and others are found in structured documents and databases. A good web search tool should be able to find information in any or all of these sources, and whisk users straight to the source.

Search How?

While a brute-force approach may work well on the desktop, a multi-user application really needs to pre-index content for better performance. Getting `grep` to crawl our web site isn't going to cut it on a production site. Enter the search engines.

Most search engines implement some type of keyword search on an **inverted index**. The index is basically a list of words with a link to where the word can be found. Often the index is maintained as a **balanced binary tree**, and usually updated all at once as a batch process.

For some applications, batch updates can be problematic, if they are dealing with live feeds or documents that change continually. So the best search engine packages also provide for incremental index updates.

Of course, not every word needs to be indexed. Common background words, like "the" and "and" can bloat an index and contribute nothing to a search. Most engines let us provide a list of **stop words** to omit from the index, or may just ignore short words altogether. Others generate stop words statistically, or use a combination of these strategies.

To be helpful, some search utilities come ready to look for pages to index. Of course, this doesn't help much if our information is trapped in a database or other structured file. Likewise, it's important that a search engine can read the file formats our site uses. Many engines can read only HTML documents, and ignore other formats, like text files, Java ServerPages, and PDFs.

More advanced techniques used by search engines include:

- **Content Tagging**
  Many web pages include meta tags, with names like `AUTHOR` and `DESCRIPTION`. One use of content tagging would be to search for a name just within a page's `AUTHOR` tag. If the name appeared in the body of the page, it would be ignored. Content tagging can be very useful in searching databases, where we might want to "tag" each field for independent searches.

- **Stemming**
  Words often take more than one form. A stemming feature also looks for the plural (or singular) form of a word, or for the word as a gerund. So "colors" would also match "color", and "run" would also match "running". Stemming is language-specific, so an algorithm for stemming an English document may produce unlikely results if used against a Spanish document instead.

- **Internationalization**
  Many search engines presume that the underlying language is English. This can cause problems when searching non-English documents.

- **Concurrency**
  Most web sites are expected to run 24x7. An advanced search engine can (concurrently) update its index while people are conducting searches.

The gateway to an engine's features, simple or advanced, is usually a search query. Today's tools support a variety of query types:

- **Simple Keyword**
  Here the content is scanned for the occurrence of a single word or sequence of characters.

- **Boolean**
  A complex keyword search that lets the user search for the presence of two or more keywords. A full boolean search also lets us look for one keyword, but omit another. For example, a mineralogist might search for documents that contain "rock" but do not contain "roll".

- **Soundex**
  Similar to stemming, a soundex search finds words that sound alike. This can be very helpful when searching things like family names, so that "Smith" will also match "Smythe". (This is why soundex was first invented – to help government agencies index names.)

- **Proximity**
  Something like a boolean search, a proximity search looks for words that appear together. In a regular boolean search, the words can appear anywhere in the search document. In a proximity search, they are required to appear within so many words of each other.

- **Relevance**
  Simple search engines return hits in the order they are found. More advanced engines will rank documents so that those which appear more relevant are listed first.

It's a rare engine that supports everything; many simply look for a keyword or two.

Many applications simply rely on using database queries for their searching. While easy to implement, this approach has its drawbacks when compared to a true search engine:

- By ANSI default, SQL text searches are case-sensitive, so a search for "explorer" would miss "Explorer".
- A SQL wildcard search sees the text as a string, rather than as a collection of words (or **tokens**). So a search for "explorers" would miss "explorer".
- Standard SQL queries don't support essential searching features like relevance. This means hits are returned in an arbitrary order.
- Complex boolean queries, with multiple AND and OR statements, can be a performance bottleneck for a SQL DBMS.

Of course, some DBMS implementations do provide some very handy search options. MySQL (which is used extensively throughout this book) is a good example. MySQL supports case-insensitive searching and full text indices that index words and return results ordered by relevance. However, the full text searches do not use stemming, or give the developer any control over stop words.

MySQL also supports searching with queries that use regular expressions. This can give the clever developer a way to perform some types of boolean searches, and even look for words rather than strings. However, regular expressions do not support relevance, so the search results come back in an arbitrary order.

Other vendors may offer similar extensions, but relying on any of these lock us into a vendor's implementation and features may fall short of what true search engines offer.

Search Who?

Let's look at adding a true full text search to Articles, the news poster we introduced in Chapter 12. Keeping some other requirements in mind, like the portals we will discuss in Chapter 14, we would also like a package that:

- Can search database records, text documents, web pages, and JSP pages
- Provides word-based full-text searches
- Can provide full boolean searches, that can include one term but exclude another
- Can search within a date range
- Will list matches by relevance

- Can be updated incrementally or by using a batch job
- Can be internationalized

There are several products available that we might use in our application, Swish-E (http://sunsite.berkeley.edu/SWISH-E/), Glimpse (http://webglimpse.org/), libibex (available as part of the GNOME Evolution project http://developer.gnome.org/tools/cvs.html), freeWAIS (http://ls6-www.informatik.uni-dortmund.de/ir/projects/freeWAIS-sf/), iSearch (http://www.etymon.com/Isearch/), to name a few, but the one that caught our eye is **Lucene**.

Lucene

Lucene is a leading choice for high-performance Java web applications, and is very easy to use. Applications already using Lucene include:

- Websearch (http://www.i2a.com/websearch/)
- Jive Forums (http://www.jivesoftware.com/)
- Eyebrowse (http://eyebrowse.tigris.org/)
- The FAQs and forum searches at jGuru (http://www.jguru.com/)

Lucene, an open source package, was originally hosted at SourceForge, but has recently joined the Apache Jakarta project (http://jakarta.apache.org/lucene/).

Lucene was originally created by Doug Cutting, based on over a decade of experience with information retrieval projects for luminaries like Xerox's Palo Alto Research Center, Apple's Advanced Technology Group, Excite, and Grand Central. Lucene was released as open source in 2000, and donated to the Apache Software Foundation in August 2001. As an ASF project, the development of Lucene is managed by a team of volunteer developers, to help ensure that work on the codebase continues.

Under the Apache Software License (http://www.apache.org/LICENSE/), we can modify and/or redistribute the Lucene source, so long as the original copyright is acknowledged and appropriate credit given.

Lucene's Main Features

Scalable, high-performance indexing:

- Over 200Mb/hour on Pentium II/266
- Incremental indexing as fast as batch indexing
- Small RAM requirements (only 1MB heap)
- Index size roughly 30% of the size of text indexed

Powerful, accurate, and efficient search algorithms:

- Ranked searching – best results returned first
- Boolean and phrase queries
- Fielded searching (for example, title, author, contents)

- Date-range searching

Simple APIs allow developers to:

- Incorporate new document types
- Localize for language
- Develop new user interfaces

Cross-platform solution:

- 100%-pure Java (not yet certified)

Common applications of Lucene:

- **Searchable e-mail**
  Search large e-mail archives instantly; update index as new messages arrive
- **CD-ROM-based online documentation search**
  Search large publications quickly with platform-independent system
- **Search previously-visited web pages**
  Re-locate a page seen weeks or months ago
- **Web site searching**
  Let users search all the pages on a website
- **Document servers and content management systems**
  Search any collection of documents

Getting to know Lucene

The foundation of Lucene's searching and indexing is an object called `Document`. A `Document` is a logical construct, the source of which may be a web page, a PDF, or a database record. It's all the same to Lucene. We can even mix all of these different data sources into the same index.

To Lucene, a document is simply a set of fields. A `Field` is another Lucene object.

Each `Field` has a name and a text value. It also has boolean properties for `isStored` and `isIndexed`.

- A `Field` that is **stored** is returned when the search hits on the `Document`, either for display or for reference
- A Field that is **indexed** can be part of a search query

To access the source of the `Document`, one of the stored `Fields` must uniquely identify it for retrieval, by a URI or primary key, for example.

In sum, `Document` objects are a collection of `Field` objects and constitute the unit of indexing and searching.

First Steps

Getting up and running with Lucene is simply a matter of reading in our data source, and then adding it, `Field` by `Field`, to a `Document` object. In some cases, there may just be two `Field` objects, the content of the datasource and a second `Field` to identify it again later. The `Document` objects are then turned over to a Lucene `Index` object for processing. Later, a `Query` object from the Lucene `search` package is used to examine one or more `Index` objects, and return a list of matching `Documents` – the hits.

Here is the Lucene workflow, from datasource to `Index` and back to hits:

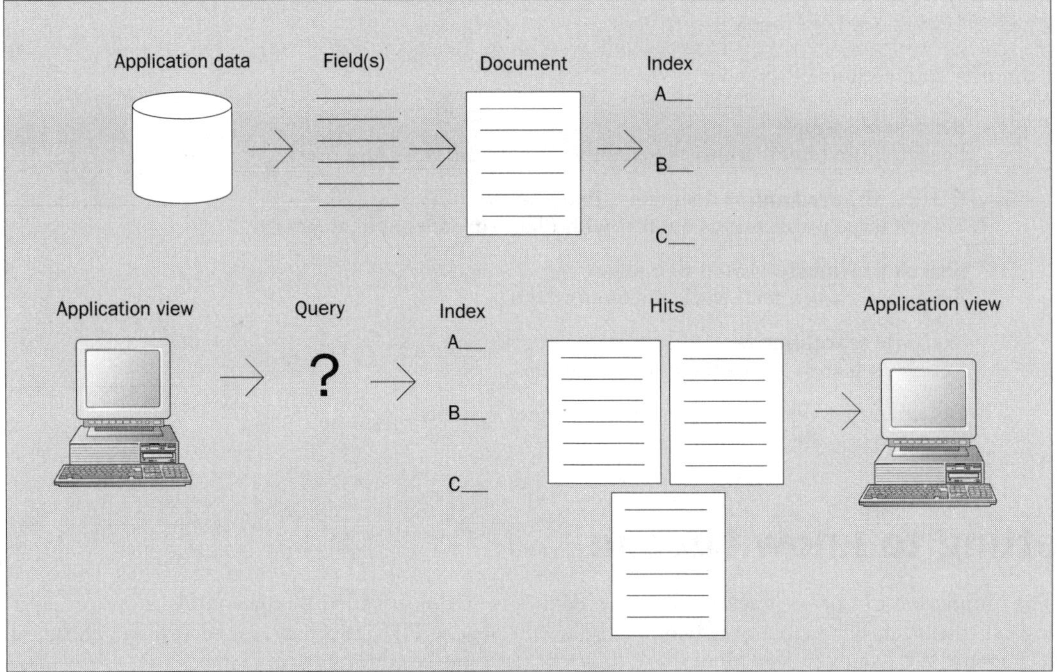

The foundation classes for all of these objects are abstract, so we can roll our own, but Lucene comes complete with useful concrete implementations of each key class, so we can use it out of the box. This makes Lucene both an extensible framework *and* a ready-to-use toolkit.

Let's run through a quick example of indexing a file using the concrete implementations that ship with Lucene. This example is straight from the Lucene package (`demo.IndexFiles` and `demo.FileDocument`). The demo is designed to index a single document, or an entire folder.

Let's present the full source first, and then review the key points.

The IndexFiles Class

```
package demo;

import com.lucene.analysis.StopAnalyzer;
import com.lucene.index.IndexWriter;
```

```
import java.io.File;
import java.util.Date;

class IndexFiles {
```

The `main()` method creates a new set of index segments in a folder named `index`:

```
public static void main(String[] args) {
    try {
      IndexWriter writer = new IndexWriter("index",
        new StopAnalyzer(), true);
```

The `indexDocs()` method is called to add a single document or entire directory to the index:

```
      // call method below
      indexDocs(writer, new File(args[0]));

      writer.optimize();
      writer.close();

    } catch (Exception e) {
      System.out.println(" caught a " + e.getClass() +
             "\n with message: " + e.getMessage());
    }
  }
```

The `indexDocs()` method checks to see if the parameter is a file or a directory. If it is a directory, it recurses through it adding each file to the `IndexWriter`. If it is a file, it adds the document to the `IndexWriter`:

```
public static void indexDocs(IndexWriter writer, File file)
       throws Exception {

    if (file.isDirectory()) {
      String[] files = file.list();
      for (int i = 0; i < files.length; i++)
    indexDocs(writer, new File(file, files[i])); // recursive
    } else {
      System.out.println("adding " + file);
      // Call static method from utility class in package (below)
      writer.addDocument(FileDocument.Document(file));

    }
  }
}
```

The FileDocument Class

```
package demo;

import java.io.File;
import java.io.Reader;
```

```
import java.io.FileInputStream;
import java.io.BufferedReader;
import java.io.InputStreamReader;
import com.lucene.document.Document;
import com.lucene.document.Field;
import com.lucene.document.DateField;

public class FileDocument {
```

Within the `IndexWriter.addDocument()` call, the file is converted to a document using the static method `Document()`. This method does most of the actual work:

```
  public static Document Document(File f)
       throws java.io.FileNotFoundException {
```

First, it creates a new document object, and adds the file path:

```
    Document doc = new Document();
    doc.add(Field.Text("path", f.getPath()));
```

Then it also adds a `modified` property, so that the date the file was modified can be indexed and used in a search:

```
    doc.add(Field.Keyword("modified",
              DateField.timeToString(f.lastModified())));
```

Finally, it reads in the file, and adds the contents as a text field:

```
    FileInputStream is = new FileInputStream(f);
    Reader reader = new BufferedReader(new InputStreamReader(is));
    doc.add(Field.Text("contents", reader));

    return doc;
  }

  private FileDocument() {}
}
```

Control returns to the `IndexWriter`, and the writer is closed, committing the index segments to disk.

Searching the Index

Later, the index can be searched using code like this:

```
  Searcher searcher = new IndexSearcher("index");
  Analyzer analyzer = new StopAnalyzer();

  Query query = QueryParser.parse(queryString, "contents", analyzer);

  Hits hits = searcher.search(query);
```

`Hits` is a collection of JavaBeans that represents the documents being searched. We'll present more code like this later, when we add a full text search to the Articles case study from Chapter 12.

Keeping it Fresh

Of course, once we create an index, it's important to keep it updated. Lucene supports both incremental and batch indexing. Stop words are handled by a nifty analyzer mechanism, which also handles the tokenizing process. A filtering mechanism is supported so virtually any file format can be indexed.

Lucene can accept data from any `java.io.InputStream` or `String` a developer can deliver. Lucene's field objects can be used for content tagging. Almost all popular query features are supported, with the exception of a soundex search.

One of Lucene's real innovations is its approach to indexing. Rather than maintain a single monolithic index, Lucene maintains several **index segments**. When a new document needs to be indexed, Lucene creates a new index segment, and conducts searches by scanning each segment.

Lucene maintains a balance between the number of segments and the number of entries in each segment. If a segment is not fully populated, Lucene may want to add new entries to it. When segments need to be combined, Lucene does not modify the segments in place, but merges them into a new segment, and then deletes the old ones. This avoids having to lock segments during updates:

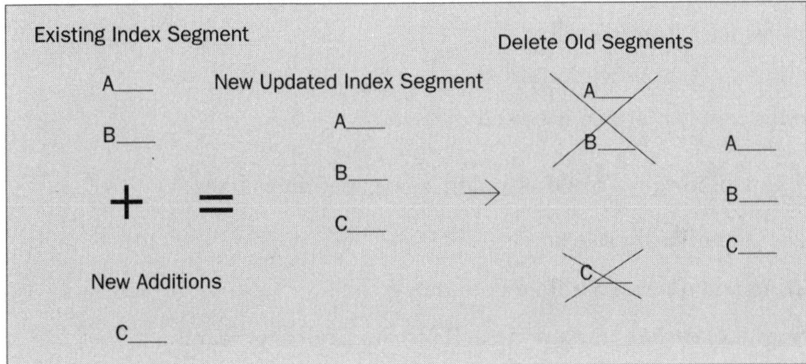

Integrating Lucene

Adding a full-text searching package like Lucene to our application might seem like quite a chore at first, but in practice it can be very simple. Let's integrate Lucene with the Articles application introduced in Chapter 12.

> **If you are following along, be sure to install the Articles WAR for Chapter 13 from the Wrox website (http://www.wrox.com/). To use Lucene in your own web applications, simply place a copy of the `lucene.jar` in your `WEB-INF\lib\` folder. This is available with the download of Articles, or from the Lucene website (http://jakarta.apache.org/lucene/). Of course, there is additional documentation for Lucene in the distribution, so be sure to look at that, too.**

Our Articles Trip-Ticket

To review, Articles is an application for posting, editing, and displaying articles. When we left Articles, it offered searching by recent date, title, author, text, and article ID:

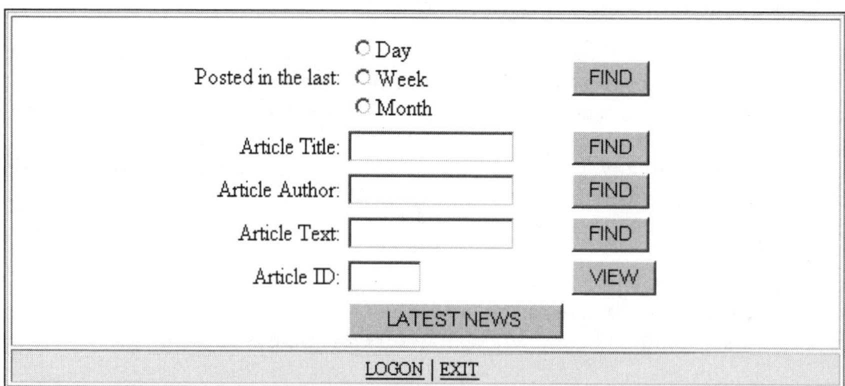

Working from the existing feature set, the requirements for our Lucene integration would be to:

- Query articles by field, including title, author, and text
- Create document objects from the database records for each article
- Index all articles from scratch
- Update index when article is added
- Update index when article is edited or deleted

Given Lucene's capabilities, we could also add new capabilities like:

- Listing text queries by relevance
- Restricting text queries within a date range
- Querying title, author, and article at once for a full-text search
- Giving the title in a full-text search greater weight than other text
- Parsing HTML from articles so only real content is indexed

However, implementing these capabilities would require additional changes to the Articles application. Here we will just focus on integrating Lucene with the existing feature set, and implement the first set of requirements.

Since Articles already presents an administrative menu to authorized users, we should plan on adding our batch update command there. Once created, we can have Lucene update the indexes as articles are added or changed.

Getting Under the Hood

So how does Articles insert and update records? How about searching? Where will we add the Lucene integration?

Articles accesses the database through its `ArticleHelper` class. Following a tiered design `ArticleHelper` is called by the `Client Action`, and then calls a data access object, which talks to the database. To integrate Lucene with Articles, all of our work will happen in `ArticleHelper`. Here we can redirect the calls for selecting articles to Lucene, and piggy-back updating Lucene for inserts, updates, and deletes. Happily, the use of a helper object will make integrating Lucene into Articles a clean and simple operation.

To perform its own searches, Articles uses a simple "field=keyword" design. It collects a column and key property, where the column is the property to be searched, and the key is the value to search with. For a primary key column, the match will be exact. For other types of columns, it may not. To retrieve an article by its primary key, we could use a URI like: http://localhost/articles/do/View?key=14.

Jumpstart

So to get there from here, let's start with a simple utility to create the Lucene index and seed it with any articles that may have already been added to Articles. Articles uses an `Action` called `CreateTables` to initialized the database tables, so let's do the same for Lucene, and setup a `CreateIndex Action`.

For `CreateIndex`, we will need to:

- Create a Lucene `Index` object
- Retrieve each article from the database
- Create a `Document` object
- Add each field from the article to the Lucene `Document` object
- Write the `Document` to the `Index`
- Close the `Index` when we are done

Adding the fields to the documents is a key design decision when integrating Lucene with an application. For each field, we can set three properties: `store`, `index`, and `tokenize`. If we **store** a field, Lucene will keep a copy of the string in the index. Then we can retrieve the field from the index, rather than going back to the datasource. If we **index** a field, then it can be used in a search query. If we **tokenize** a field, Lucene will break it down into one or more terms.

By setting these boolean properties in different combinations, we can build an efficient index that meets the exact needs of our application. For example, we will need to store a page name or primary key with each document so we can retrieve it later. However, we would not want to tokenize that, since it is a single term. We also might not need to index it, since this field might not be exposed to the user.

Setting Field Properties

Lucene provides several static methods with descriptive names to help us easily set the field properties. This makes it very easy to create the field we need without staring at an anonymous array of boolean values. Each is just called with the field name and value. Here's a rundown of the static methods provided by the `Field` class:

- **Keyword**
  Constructs a String-valued `Field` that is not tokenized, but is indexed and stored. Useful for non-text fields, e.g. "date" or "url".
- **Text**
  Constructs a String-valued `Field` that is tokenized and indexed, and is stored in the index, for return with hits. Useful for short text fields, like "title" or "subject".
- **UnIndexed**
  Constructs a String-valued `Field` that is not tokenized or indexed, but is stored in the index, for return with hits. Useful for storing key fields or URLs to locate the document later.
- **UnStored**
  Constructs a String-valued `Field` that is tokenized and indexed, but that is not stored in the index. Useful for fields that are not displayed as part of a hit list, like large text fields.

The `Text()` method is also overloaded to take a `java.io.Reader`:

- **Text**
  Constructs a Reader-valued `Field` that is tokenized and indexed, but is not stored in the index verbatim. Useful for longer text fields, like "body".

For our index, we can use the `Keyword()` method to add the primary key, `Text()` for the title, and `UnStored()` for the rest, since we might want to search on them, but they don't show up on the search list.

Additions to Data

For completeness, we will need to add a new data access method to Articles – one that retrieves a block of records in first-in, first-out order. Lucene assigns a sequential ID to the documents as they are indexed, and this will let us keep the original order intact, in case we need to use it later. Happily, there is already an underlying query and resource access method that we can use, so we only need to add one very simple method, `articleSelect()`, to `Data`:

```
public static final Collection articleSelect(Object target)
        throws SQLException {
  return Statements.getCollection(Commands.ARTICLE_SELECT,target);
}
```

The CreateIndex Class

To generate the index, we will need to add a new class, `CreateIndex`:

```
package com.wrox.articles.http;

import java.io.IOException;
import java.io.PrintWriter;
import java.sql.SQLException;
import java.util.ArrayList;
import javax.servlet.ServletException;
import javax.servlet.http.HttpServletRequest;
import javax.servlet.http.HttpServletResponse;
import org.apache.struts.action.Action;
import org.apache.struts.action.ActionForm;
```

```
import org.apache.struts.action.ActionForward;
import org.apache.struts.action.ActionMapping;
import org.apache.struts.action.ActionServlet;

import com.lucene.analysis.StopAnalyzer;
import com.lucene.document.Document;
import com.lucene.document.Field;
import com.lucene.index.IndexWriter;

import com.wrox.articles.http.ArticleForm;
import com.wrox.articles.search.Engine;
import com.wrox.articles.sql.Data;

public final class CreateIndex extends Action {

  public ActionForward perform(ActionMapping mapping,
                               ActionForm form,
                               HttpServletRequest request,
                               HttpServletResponse response)
      throws IOException, ServletException {
```

Since this is an "internal-use" `Action`, like the Struts administrative `Actions`, it just returns plain text to the client, rather than bother with a JSP page. To prepare for this, we set up a standard `PrintWriter`, as we would with any generic HTTP servlet:

```
    response.setContentType("text/plain");
    PrintWriter printWriter = response.getWriter();
    ArrayList list = null;
    ArticleForm article = null;
```

First, we create a new index writer and start a new index:

```
    try {
      IndexWriter index = new IndexWriter(
        INDEX_PATH,
        new StopAnalyzer(),
        true);
```

Using our new `Data` method, we retrieve all the existing articles in the order they were first created:

```
      list = (ArrayList)
      Data.articleSelect(new ArticleForm());
```

Now we loop through the list of articles:

```
      for (int i=0; i<list.size(); i++) {
        article = (ArticleForm) list.get(i);
```

For each article, we create a new document object and add the record properties as document fields. The `blankNull()` utility method exchanges an empty string for any nulls, since can't index a null:

```
        Document document = new Document();
        document.add(Field.Keyword("article",
        blankNull(article.getArticle())));
        document.add(Field.Text("title",
        blankNull(article.getTitle())));
        document.add(Field.UnStored("contributor",
        blankNull(article.getContributor())));
        document.add(Field.UnStored("creator",
        blankNull(article.getCreator())));
        document.add(Field.UnStored("content",
        blankNull(article.getContent())));
```

We then add the populated document object to the index for analysis, and report our progress:

```
        index.addDocument(document);
        printWriter.print(i); printWriter.print(':');
        printWriter.println(article.getTitle());
      }
```

When the loop completes, we print the document count, and then optimize and close the index. For best performance, always optimize an index after adding a new group of documents:

```
      printWriter.print(index.docCount());
      printWriter.println(" articles indexed.");
      index.optimize();
      index.close();
```

Since this class is designed to index all the documents at once, we exit the process on any exception:

```
    } catch (Exception e) {
        e.printStackTrace();
        StringBuffer sb = new StringBuffer("Exception: " + e);
        printWriter.println(sb.toString());
    }
    printWriter.println("DONE");
    return(null);
  }
```

Here we document the system path to use for the index. Later in the chapter, we will change this into a public method for better flexibility:

```
  public static String INDEX_PATH = "/var/lucene/articles";
```

The `blankNull()` utility method exchanges a blank string for any null properties, since Lucene can't index nulls:

```
  private static String BLANK_STRING = "";

  public static final String blankNull(String string) {
    if (string==null) {
```

```
        return BLANK_STRING;
      } else {
        return string;
      }
    }
  }
```

If the database contained a large number of articles to index, we would need to amend this code to process the records in blocks. However, we just did the entire database at once, with the assumption it holds fewer than a hundred articles. Once the initial index is in place, Lucene can maintain it incrementally. To index a greater number of database records, we would make additional calls to the database and simply add each block to the index.

To expose our new command to the framework, we need to add an `ActionMapping` to the Struts configuration file (`struts-config.xml`):

```
<!-- Create Index action mapping (admin) -->
    <action
        path="/admin/CreateIndex"
        type="org.apache.struts.articles.http.CreateIndex"/>
```

Finally, we add a command to the default menu page (menu.jsp), putting it inside the admin block with the others:

```
<req:isUserInRole role="manager">
  <tr>
    <td> </td>
    <td><table border="1" cellpadding="8" width="100%"><tr><td>
       <html:link forward="createTables">CREATE TABLES</html:link></br>
       <html:link forward="createIndex">CREATE INDEX</html:link></br>
       <html:link forward="reload">RELOAD CONFIG</html:link>
    </td></tr></table>
    </td>
    <td> </td>
  </tr>
</req:isUserInRole>
```

The First Mile

Then, if we login (username "articles", password "articles") we'll get a plain, but helpful display, looking something like this:

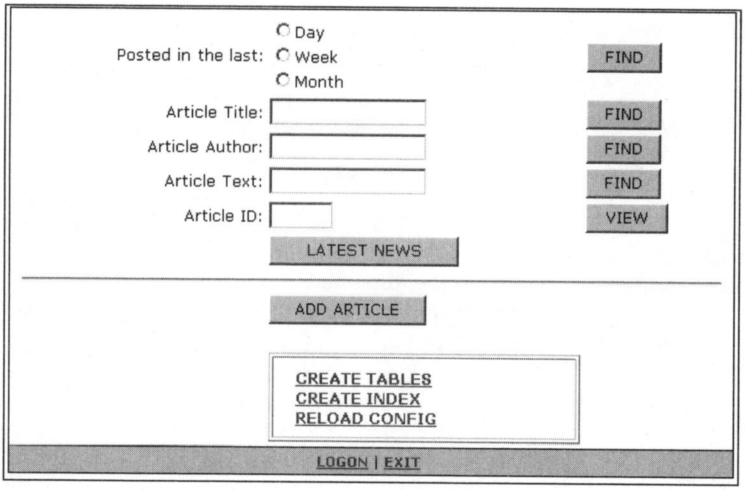

Day
Posted in the last: Week
Month
FIND
Article Title: FIND
Article Author: FIND
Article Text: FIND
Article ID: VIEW
LATEST NEWS
ADD ARTICLE
CREATE TABLES
CREATE INDEX
RELOAD CONFIG
LOGON | EXIT

Are We There Yet?

Now that we have an index, we can start the switch from using SQL queries for searching to using Lucene queries instead. As promised, this all happens within the `ArticleHelper` class. This class is called by the Struts `Action`, and in turns calls the resource layer helpers to retrieve the data. This very useful design now lets us call the Lucene resource layer instead of the DBMS resource layer, without the rest of the application knowing the difference.

For a search, the `ArticleHelper` class had been doing things like:

```
// --  --
if ("title".equals(column)) {
  setRows((List) Data.articleSearchTitle(getKey(),new ArticleForm()));
  break TASK;
}
```

This did a SQL "like" search on the title field, using a key string provided by the user.

From Lucene's perspective, this would be a **TermQuery** against the title field. This will not yield the same result as a "like" search using SQL, but with stemming, it should return an equivalent result. The "like" search returns a match if the key string appears anywhere within the field. For example, "tim" would match "time". This will not happen with Lucene, since it tokenizes the field, and knows about words. With stemming, Lucene will match "searching" for "search", since the stemmer knows to drop the "ing" (at least in English).

The SQL version of search title goes like this:

- Call data access method with key string and target object
- Call resource access method with SQL query, key string, and target object
- Setup and execute the SQL query, and return a collection of the target object

The Lucene version of search title starts out like this:

- Call `QueryParser` with key string to setup query object
- Call `IndexSearcher` with the index and query object
- Setup and execute the `IndexSearch`, and return a collection of `Document` objects (`Hits`).
- Process the hits to return a collection of the target object

Let's redraft the search title block to use Lucene as outlined:

```
// --  --
if ("title".equals(column)) {
  try {
    Searcher searcher = new IndexSearcher(getIndexPath());
    Query query = QueryParser.parse(key,column,new StopAnalyzer());
    Hits hits = searcher.search(query);
    ArrayList list = new ArrayList();
    for (int i=0; i<hits.length(); ++i) {
      ArticleForm form = new ArticleForm();
      Document doc = hits.doc(i);
      form.setArticle(doc.get("article"));
      form.setTitle(doc.get("title"));
      list.add(form);
    }
    setRows(list);
  } catch (Exception e) {
      throw (new SQLException(e.toString()));
  }
  break TASK;
}
```

This code plugs right into Articles, and returns a result list from the index rather than a SQL query. It then uses a SQL query to retrieve the rest of the article. So, technically, we have arrived, and to complete the integration, we could just repeat this pattern for the author and text methods.

Did Someone Say Pattern?

When you think about it, the types of access methods we need for a search engine are very similar to those we need for data access. So, why not follow the same design pattern? Let's put together a suite of access methods for searching, just like the ones we already use for SQL.

> **So where we had a `Data` access class for SQL, let's have an `Engine` access class for our searching. And where we populated a collection of beans from a `ResultSet`, let's populate a collection of beans from the `Hits`.**

Since Lucene allows for the `Searcher` and `Analyzer` objects to be subclassed, we can also provide convenience methods to return the default choices for Articles. If we change our mind later, we can make the change in one place, and return a different subclass for either of these key objects.

The Engine Class

Corresponding to the `Data` class in the Articles application, we'll add a `search.Engine` class for our search engine:

```
package com.wrox.articles.search;

import java.io.IOException;
import java.util.Collection;

import com.lucene.analysis.Analyzer;
import com.lucene.analysis.StopAnalyzer;

import com.lucene.document.Document;
import com.lucene.document.Field;

import com.lucene.index.IndexReader;
import com.lucene.index.IndexWriter;
import com.lucene.index.Term;

import com.lucene.queryParser.QueryParser;
import com.lucene.queryParser.ParseException;

import com.lucene.search.Hits;
import com.lucene.search.IndexSearcher;
import com.lucene.search.Query;
import com.lucene.search.Searcher;

import ext.search.LuceneUtils;

public final class Engine {
```

The `getAnalyzer()` method returns the `StopAnalzyer` as a default. An ancestor class could override this to provide a different analyzer with new capabilities:

```
  public static final Analyzer getAnalyzer() {
    return new StopAnalyzer();
  }
```

The `getIndexPath()` method returns the default path for our index segments. This path must exist on the host system. You could also replace the hard-coded path here with a routine that read the path from a configuration file. Each Lucene index needs its own directory (since the index is managed in multiple segments):

```
  public static final String getIndexPath() {
    return "/var/lucene/articles";
  }
```

The `getSearcher()` method returns a default `Searcher` object for the application. Here we return a standard `IndexSearcher`:

```
  public static final Searcher getSearcher() throws IOException {
    return new IndexSearcher(getIndexPath());
  }
```

The `getIndexWriter()` method returns a default `IndexWriter`. We just return the default `IndexWriter` that uses the file system to store the index. The index could also be stored in some other location, like a database, by providing our own `IndexWriter` object:

```
public static final IndexWriter getIndexWriter(Boolean create)
        throws IOException {
  return new IndexWriter(
    getIndexPath(),
    getAnalyzer(),
    create);
}
```

The `getHits()` method returns a `Hits` object, using, default searcher:

```
public static final Hits getHits(Query query) throws IOException  {
  return getSearcher().search(query);
}
```

The `getQuery()` method takes the `key` and `column` properties used by Articles, and passes them to a standard Lucene query parser, along with our `Analyzer`, and then returns a Lucene `Query` object:

```
public static final Query getQuery(String key, String column)
        throws ParseException {
  return QueryParser.parse(key,column, getAnalyzer());
}
```

The `articleSearchTitle()` method calls on other library methods to perform a search on our Lucene index for documents matching a given title. Using a method from our `LuceneUtils` class (covered next), it creates a collection of JavaBeans from the Lucene `Hits` list. Any JavaBean with public setters that match public getters on the Lucene `Hits` object can be used as the target class:

```
  public static final Collection articleSearchTitle(String key,
                                                    Object target)
          throws Exception {
    return LuceneUtils.getCollection(target,
    getHits(getQuery(key,"title")));
  }
}
```

The LuceneUtils Class

We also add an `ext.search.LuceneUtils` class corresponding to the `ResultSetUtils` in the Articles application. The methods here help us populate an arbitrary JavaBean from the Lucene `Hits` object. The `ResultSetUtils` class in Articles does the same thing, only with `ResultSets`:

```
package ext.search;

import java.lang.reflect.InvocationTargetException;

import java.util.ArrayList;
import java.util.Collection;
import java.util.Enumeration;
```

```
import java.util.HashMap;
import java.util.Map;

import com.lucene.document.Document;
import com.lucene.document.Field;
import com.lucene.search.Hits;

import org.apache.struts.util.BeanUtils;

public class LuceneUtils {
```

The `populate()` method makes efficient use of reflection to transfer data from a Lucene document to some other JavaBean. When a setter on the target bean matches a field name in the Lucene document, the JavaBean property is set with the contents of the field.

The underlying utility class, `BeanUtil.populate()`, is also used by Struts to populate `ActionForms` from HTTP requests and by Articles to populate arbitrary JavaBeans from `ResultSets`:

```
public static void populate(Object bean, Document document)
        throws Exception {

    // Build a list of relevant fields and values
    HashMap properties = new HashMap();

    // Iterator of field names
    Enumeration fields = document.fields();

    while (fields.hasMoreElements()) {
      Field field = (Field) fields.nextElement();
      properties.put(field.name(),field.stringValue());
    }

    // Set the corresponding properties of our bean
    try {
      BeanUtils.populate(bean, properties);
    } catch (Exception e) {
        throw new Exception("BeanUtils.populate: " + e.toString());
    }
}
```

The `getCollection()` method builds on `populate()` to return a collection of the target JavaBeans from a Lucene `Hits` object:

```
public static Collection getCollection(Object target, Hits hits)
        throws Exception {

    // Use ArrayList to maintain sequence
    ArrayList list = new ArrayList();

    // Acquire target class
    Class factory = target.getClass();
```

```
      try {
        // Scroll to each document; populate bean, and add to list
        for (int i=0; i<hits.length(); ++i) {
          Object bean = factory.newInstance();
          Document doc = hits.doc(i);
          populate(bean,doc);
          list.add(bean);
        }
      } catch (Throwable t) {
          throw new Exception("LuceneUtils.getCollection: " + t.toString());
      }
      return ((Collection) list);
    }
  }
```

The Last Mile

We now have what we need to search the Articles database using Lucene queries in place of SQL queries. Of course, an indexed search is only as good as the index it searches: we will need to keep it updated as articles are added, updated, and even deleted.

Indexing one article is the same as indexing them all, so we will be able to take the code we need from `CreateIndex` and turn it into a helper. Then whenever a record is inserted, we can call a companion helper to have the search engine add it to the index (likewise for a delete). For an update, we do both, first delete the article from the index, and then add it back again.

Here is the rest of the `Engine` class, and the complete `ArticleHelper` class after all the additions. The changes we made for Lucene are highlighted.

The Engine Class Continued

Like `articleSearchTitle()`, `articleSearchCreator()` and `articleSearchContent()`, are high-level methods to return a hit list matching a given creator or content. These are partial searches, so any word will match:

```
    public static final Collection articleSearchCreator(String key,
                                         Object target) throws Exception {

      return LuceneUtils.getCollection(target,
                                    getHits(getQuery(key,"creator")));
    }

    public static final Collection articleSearchContent(String key,
                                         Object target) throws Exception {

      return LuceneUtils.getCollection(target,
                                    getHits(getQuery(key,"content")));
    }
```

The `articleIndex()` method adds an article record (from the database) to the index. The first property, `article`, is the primary key, so that the article can be easily retrieved from the database later. The utility method, `blankNull()`, ensures that an empty string is used instead of a null, since Lucene chokes on nulls:

```
public static final void articleIndex (String article,
                                       String contributor,
                                       String creator,
                                       String title,
                                       String content,
                                       IndexWriter index
                                       ) throws Exception {

  Document document = new Document();
  document.add(Field.Keyword("article", Engine.blankNull(article)));
  document.add(Field.Text("title", Engine.blankNull(title)));
  document.add(Field.UnStored("contributor",
                              Engine.blankNull(contributor)));
  document.add(Field.UnStored("creator", Engine.blankNull(creator)));
  document.add(Field.UnStored("content", Engine.blankNull(content)));
  index.addDocument(document);
}
```

The `articleInsert()` method simply calls `articleIndex()`. This allows `articleIndex()` also to be used by `articleUpdate()`:

```
public static final void articleInsert(String article,
                                       String contributor,
                                       String creator,
                                       String title,
                                       String content
                                       ) throws Exception {

  articleIndex(article, contributor, creator,
               title, content, getIndexWriter(false));
}
```

The `articleDelete()` method removes the article from the index. It does not change how the article is stored in the database. Later, this will be called by a helper method that will also call `Data.articleDelete()` to update the database. It is also called by `Engine.articleUpdate()`:

```
public static final void articleDelete(String article) throws Exception {

  IndexReader reader = getIndexReader().delete(new term("article",
                                                        article));
}
```

The `articleUpdate()` method first deletes the existing index entry, and then adds the new one. Both steps are through calls to other methods in the class:

```
public static final void articleUpdate(String article,
                                       String contributor,
                                       String creator,
                                       String title,
                                       String content
                                       ) throws Exception {

  articleDelete(article);
```

```
    articleInsert(article, contributor, creator, title, content);
  }
```

The ArticleHelper Class

Here's the `ArticleHelper` class, updated to use our new Lucene methods. The changes are minor. For a full treatment of `ArticleHelper`, see Chapter 12:

```
...

  public synchronized int insert() throws SQLException {
    int count = 0;
    while (rows.hasNext()) {
      DataBean thisForm = (DataBean) rows.next();
      thisForm.setKeyInt(allocateKey());
      Map thisMap = thisForm.toMap();
      try {
        Engine.articleInsert((String) thisMap.get("article"),
                             (String) thisMap.get("contributor"),
                             (String) thisMap.get("creator"),
                             (String) thisMap.get("title"),
                             (String) thisMap.get("content"));
      } catch (Exception e) {
          throw (new SQLException(e.toString()));
      }

      Data.articleInsert((String) thisMap.get("article"),
                         (String) thisMap.get("contributor"),
                         (String) thisMap.get("creator"),
                         (String) thisMap.get("title"),
                         (String) thisMap.get("content"));
      count++;
    }
    return count;
  }

  public int update() throws SQLException {
    int count = 0;
    while (rows.hasNext()) {
      DataBean thisForm = (DataBean) rows.next();
      Map thisMap  = thisForm.toMap();
      try {
        Engine.articleUpdate((String) thisMap.get("article"),
                             (String) thisMap.get("contributor"),
                             (String) thisMap.get("creator"),
                             (String) thisMap.get("title"),
                             (String) thisMap.get("content"));
      } catch (Exception e) {
          throw (new SQLException(e.toString()));
      }
      Data.articleUpdate((String) thisMap.get("article"),
                         (String) thisMap.get("contributor"),
                         (String) thisMap.get("creator"),
                         (String) thisMap.get("title"),
```

```
                         (String) thisMap.get("content"));
      count++;

      return count;
  }

  public int select() throws SQLException {
    ...

      // -- --
      if ("title".equals(column)) {
        try {
          setRows((List) Engine.articleSearchTitle(getKey(),
          new ArticleForm()));
        } catch (Exception e) {
            throw (new SQLException(e.toString()));
        }
        break TASK;
      }
      // -- --
      if ("author".equals(column)) {
        try {
          setRows((List) Engine.articleSearchCreator(getKey(),
          new ArticleForm()));
        } catch (Exception e) {
            throw (new SQLException(e.toString()));
        }
        break TASK;
      }
      // -- --
      if ("content".equals(column)) {
        try {
          setRows((List) Engine.articleSearchContent(getKey(),
          new ArticleForm()));
        } catch (Exception e) {
            throw (new SQLException(e.toString()));
        }
        break TASK;
      }
    }
    return getRowCount();
  }

  public int delete() throws SQLException {
    int count = 0;
    while (rows.hasNext()) {
      DataBean thisForm = (DataBean) rows.next();
      try {
        Engine.articleDelete(thisForm.getKey());
      } catch (Exception e) {
          throw (new SQLException(e.toString()));
      }
      Data.articleDelete(thisForm.getKeyInt());
      count++;
```

```
        }
        return count;
    }
}
```

Home Again

It's interesting to note that in all of this, we have made no changes to the Struts Action, and added but one menu item to a JavaServer Page. Since Articles uses a layered design, we were able to switch from searching with SQL queries to Lucene indexed search just by changing the backend packages.

Crawling Files

The Lucene distribution has several examples for indexing files. The basic process is to read the file in as a stream, and then to add it to the document where we added properties from the database records. We could even add them to the same index, and provide a combined database\web page searching application.

A good source for more about crawling files is **WebSearch**, a project started by Donald Duddleston. This is a ready-to-run web application that we can integrate with our site. Look for more about WebSearch on the Lucene site or at the developer's site (http://www.i2a.com/websearch/).

Summary

Searching is a vital feature for any application, especially a web application. We covered the basic features and concepts used by search engines generally, and then focused on a particular package, Lucene.

If your own application is well designed, adding a search engine like Lucene can be surprisingly simple. Lucene uses a clean, object-orientated design that many toolkits and applications would do well to emulate.

The Lucene tookit features five key objects: `Document`, `Field`, `Analyzer`, `Index`, and `Query`. Each of these objects is based on interfaces and abstract implementations, so you can create your own, but Lucene also provides useful concrete implementations so you can use it out of the box.

A Lucene `Document` is comprised of one or more fields. The `Document` is a logical construct, and can represent any type of data source: HTML page, database record, or whatever else you might use. Each field can be stored, indexed, or tokenized in any combination. As a developer, you create the `Document` objects, and add fields to it from the datasource. You also create or open the `Index`, which can be stored as a file.

As you add each document to an `Index`, it is streamed through an `Analyzer`. The `Analyzer` tokenizes the stream, skips over stop words, and may provide other special functions, like stemming. Later, you can create a `Query` object to search the `Index` for a set of documents. There are `Query` objects for various types of searches, like term, phrase, or boolean, and a general purpose query object that parses a command line. The `Query` returns a collection of documents in a `Hits` object.

You can use the `Hits` object to display the matches. One of the fields in your document should uniquely identify it so you can retrieve the data source if the document.

Lucene's toolkit approach makes it easy to integrate into your existing application. You can also use Lucene as part of a standalone application to crawl your site and search through its files. WebSearch is one such application that you could start using on your web site today.

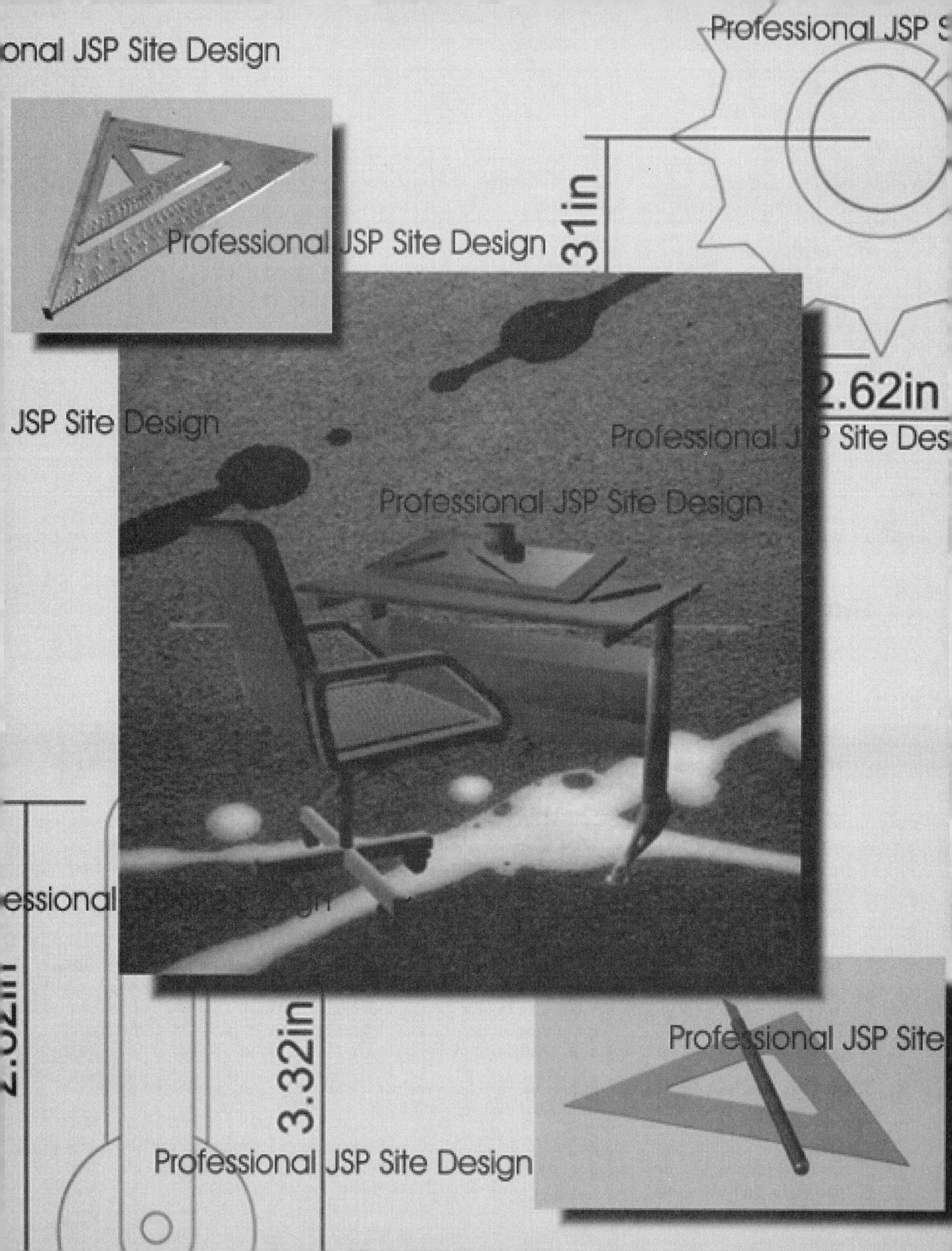

Professional JSP Site Design
31in
2.62in
Professional JSP Site Design
3.32in
Professional JSP Site Design

14

Portals

Portals are the darlings of the Internet and of intranets worldwide. The promise of a portal is to give every visitor instant access to whatever content they desire. Whether you have a new product, press release, job opening, or a link to information, it can be put on a portal and made available for all.

A portal is a web page designed as an entry point to information and services for a target audience. Portals for a general audience might offer a collection of information on your local weather, TV listings, news, sports, horoscope, or stock portfolio. On the services side, there are calendars, e-mail, bill payment, message boards, and even diet tracking. These smaller pieces of information are called **portlets**. There are also many specialized portals too, which cater to a huge range of interests.

Of course, the corporate world has not overlooked the utility of portals. **Enterprise Information Portals (EIPs)** are designed for use over a corporate intranet or some other secure network. An EIP provides information and services specific to a given enterprise, which may include its employees, partners, suppliers, and customers. EIPs may offer data warehousing tools and sale automation, group and project schedulers, personnel directories, and other business-to-business portlets.

A key feature of today's portals is personalization. In addition to content, some portals also let you choose your own theme or "skin". Users can customize the fonts, colors, and layout of your portal to suit their own tastes. Not all portal pages are private affairs; they might offer individual **weblogs** – personal web sites that can be shared with other users, sites, or even portals.

Portals often provide access to various "channels" of content. Channels may be provided by large news sites or by weblog, or by any kind of site in between. This is known as **syndication**.

In this chapter, we'll:

- Look at how and where portals originated.
- Learn about the technology that developed alongside portals.
- See how we can implement a portal on our own site. There are several products available for Perl and PHP, but the **Jetspeed** Portal Server from the Apache Jakarta project can be used to provide portals on a Java based site. We can use Jetspeed along with the new Portlet API.
- Develop our own starter portal using Struts and hook it up to the Articles news poster we developed in Chapter 12.

The Origin of Portals

When the web was young, it was common to find a list on every homepage with links to the owner's favorite sites. Over time some of these lists grew and became sites of their own. One such site, run by a couple of graduate students, began asking guests to suggest new links for the page. Soon, this directory was so large and so popular that it had to be moved from the college campus where it began and became the world-famous Yahoo!.

People came to recognize sites like Yahoo! as a portal to the Internet. Many browsers that were once greeted by http://home.netscape.com turned elsewhere in search of new content. Netscape needed a way to bring them back and so in 1999, My Netscape Network (MNN) was born. In an effort to find a way to add more content to its portal, MNN introduced a file format dubbed **RDF Site Summary (RSS)** as a combination **channel-description-framework** and **content-gathering mechanism**.

Combining these two ideas together was an exciting concept, since it enabled people to both describe and distribute content at the same time in a single file. RSS was initially released as version 0.9, in a public beta-test of the nascent format.

> ***Resource Description Framework*** *(RDF) is a W3C specification (http://www.w3.org/TR/REC-rdf-syntax/) designed to catalog metadata.*

RDF Site Summary

Although simple, RSS is an effective means to describe and syndicate content. To syndicate content, all someone needs to do is post a text file on a site in a plain format that anyone could code by hand. Here is an annotated example of a RSS .09 document:

```
<?xml version="1.0"?>
  <rdf:RDF xmlns:rdf="http://www.w3.org/1999/02/22-rdf-syntax-ns#"
          xmlns="http://my.netscape.com/rdf/simple/0.9/">
```

<channel> is the top-level element for the file. Everything else in the file is part of the channel. The channel can have a descriptive title, and a link to the channel's entry or "welcome" page:

```
<channel>
  <title>wrox.com</title>
  <link>http://www.wrox.com</link>
  <description>Wrox: Programmer to Programmer</description>
</channel>
```

The original RSS format provided for a single image, or icon, that could be displayed along with the channel:

```
<image>
  <title>wrox.com</title>
  <url>http://www.wrox.com/Includes/images/channel.gif</url>
  <link>http://www.wrox.com </link>
</image>
```

Each channel can include one or more items. The items in turn have their own title and a brief description of the content. A hyperlink is also provided, so the reader can access the actual content:

```
<item>
  <title>JSP Standard Tag Library Early Access</title>
  <description>
    Quietly, almost surreptitiously, a (very early) early
    access release of the long-awaited JSP Standard Tag Library (JSPTL)
    is upon us as promised at JavaOne this year. So, what's in it and
    what does it tell us about the future of JSP?
  </description>
  <link>
    http://www.wrox.com/News/viewReview.asp?art_type=new&amp;id=583
  </link>
</item>
<item>
  <title>The Many Faces of Wrox</title>
  <description>
    At Wrox Press we are well-known for our policy of putting
    pictures of our authors on the covers of our books. But how did this
    come about and what's the reasoning behind it? In-house author Chris
    Ullman explains.
  </description>
  <link>
    http://www.wrox.com/Features/viewReview.asp?section=
                                              3&art_type=fea&id=590
  </link>
</item>
```

An interesting feature of the RSS format is the `<textinput>` element. Each channel is entitled to one of these (like the image). The `<textinput>` element can be used to create a simple one-line HTML form, usually to launch a search:

```
<textinput>
  <title>Search</title>
  <description>Search the Wrox database</description>
  <name>textfield</name>
  <link>http://www.wrox.com/Search/Search.asp</link>
```

```
    </textinput>
</rdf:RDF>
```

A portal engine could then perform a GET operation on the file via HTTP, transform it to XML, and then render it alongside other channels. People clicking on our item's link are whisked to our site for the rest of the story – but they came to the portal first. The portal as well as our site see an increase in traffic.

The portal specializes on exposing content, but leaves others to develop it.

Although Netscape discontinued its RSS initiative, the format has continued to grow in popularity. Shortly after Netscape introduced RSS, David Winer of UserLand released another version, 0.91, and recast the acronym RSS as **Rich Site Summary**.

This new version added several elements from the UserLand **ScriptingNews** format (http://my.userland.com/stories/storyReader$11/), and strayed from the format's RDF roots. In December 2000, the **RSS-DEV Working Group** released RDF Site Summary 1.0. (http://groups.yahoo.com/group/rss-dev/files/specification.html). This format builds on the original 0.9 specification and provides for extensibility via XML namespace modules. The format is backward compatible with 0.9 and is on its way to becoming the syndication standard.

Syndicated Content

Many sites immediately saw the value of syndicated content. At the popular **SlashDot** (http://www.slashdot.org/) authors can post stories that, once approved by an editor, automatically become part of the SlashDot home page. These new additions are also made available via SlashDot's RSS channel. This lets other sites merge headlines from SlashDot into their own home page. This information is contained in a document at http://www.slashdot.com/slashdot.xml. A recent example looked like this:

```
<?xml version="1.0" ?>
<backslash xmlns:backslash="http://slashdot.org/backslash.dtd">
  <story>
    <title>XFree86 Drivers For Solaris</title>
    <url>http://slashdot.org/article.pl?sid=01/08/29/133225</url>
    <time>2001-08-29 13:36:38</time>
    <author>timothy</author>
    <department>sincere-flattery</department>
    <topic>102</topic>
    <comments>26</comments>
    <section>articles</section>
    <image>topicsun.gif</image>
  </story>
```

And so on with other stories:

```
  <story>
    <title>File System Round-Up Interview</title>
    <url>http://slashdot.org/article.pl?sid=01/08/29/1241237</url>
    <time>2001-08-29 13:01:24</time>
```

```
    <author>Hemos</author>
    <department>fsck-in-record-time</department>
    <topic>164</topic>
    <comments>39</comments>
    <section>developers</section>
    <image>topicupgrades.gif</image>
  </story>
</backslash>
```

Note that SlashDot uses its own DTD. Another version of the same channel, using the latest version of RSS, is available at http://www.slashdot.com/slashdot.rss. *For compatibility, many sites often offer multiple versions of the same channel.*

Sites like SlashDot and **NewsForge** (http://newsforge.com/) are now nothing but channel. The site is structured around their syndicated channels, and the home pages are a listing of the latest summaries.

Aggregators

RSS has quickly become the standard for free content syndication on the Internet. There are now so many channels and portals, it's very difficult to keep track of them all. Enter the **aggregators**, such as UserLand (http://www.userland.com/) and XmlTree (http://www.xmltree.com/). These sites act as a registry for syndicates; they are a place where portals can find new channels to offer.

UserLand also offers a site (http://my.userland.com/) where we can register and customize our own channel feeds, thereby creating a portal.

Weblogs

Of course, this being the Internet, pretty soon everyone wants to host their own channel. A popular way to do this is via a **weblog**, which is the Internet version of public access TV. A weblog is a personal web site that is hosted within a larger site, and is usually maintained with automated tools. A weblog will typically let us publish written essays, annotated links, documents, graphics, and multimedia. These are often syndicated using portals and act like personal webzines or electronic op-ed columns.

When using Windows or MacIntosh, a neat way to keep a weblog updated is to use **UserLand Radio**. We can "upstream" our weblog to a host site, and also subscribe to RSS channels. So, like a HAM radio, we can use it to both send and receive (publish and subscribe).

Developers can also extend UserLand Radio, and it's not hard to imagine a corporate Intranet using weblogs and UserLand Radio as a publishing medium. Here's a quote from David Winer:

For example, if you're the information maven in your organization, you could produce an HTML page for everyone in your organization to read, or e-mail it to them at 8am, and at the same time publish it in RSS so other radio users can benefit from your research and the way you put the news together.

Investigating that more closely is not within the scope of this chapter. For more about UserLand radio, visit their web site at http://radio.userland.com/.

Newswires

As the syndication food chain grew, a slot opened up for yet another player – the **newswire**. A newswire is basically a channel of channels. The newswire host uses aggregators to acquire new channels, often in a specialized area. These channels are then offered through an API to other sites. A newswire may also offer a search facility, to that people can build their own custom portal on the fly.

An excellent example of an open API newswire is O'Reilly's **Meerkat** (http://www.oreillynet.com/meerkat/), which encourages people to include its aggregated content into their own sites. Meerkat offers a well-documented API that can be used to return a selection of stories, and return them in various formats. One flavor is JavaScript, which makes it very easy to include a Meerkat query into any web site.

Plug and Play Portals

There are several prewritten portal solutions for Perl and PHP. We will quickly overview these for background, and then move on to the plug and play offerings that run on Java.

As the portal concept exploded, prewritten applications quickly appeared. A popular choice for PHP is **PHP-Nuke** (http://phpnuke.org/), which, like many portal packages, adds features like reader comments and surveys to the basic newsfeed. The software used to run SlashDot is also available as open source, and has its own web site, **SlashCode** (http://slashcode.com/). It is not particularly portable, as it expects to be run on an Apache web server with `mod_perl` and MySQL.

For those looking for something on another platform, the SlashCode site keeps a short list of "Slash-Alikes" (http://slashcode.com/slashalikes.shtml). There are currently several packages for PHP and even one for ASP, but nothing for JSP or Java.

In the closed source arena, a popular offering is UserLand's **Manilla**. This very interesting product is part of the Frontier package, which combines content management, discussion groups, mailing lists, and portals into a complete web site solution.

Frontier is available for Windows and MacIntosh, and is sold on a subscription basis. For a moderate fee, you are entitled to use Frontier and obtain all updates and fixes made available during that time. After the subscription lapses, you can continue to use Frontier as-is. It's rather like a magazine subscription. When it runs out, you don't receive any more issues, but can continue to use what you have already received. If you're lucky, you might be able to try Manilla online for free at ManillaSites (http://www.manilasites.com/). However, only so many free sites are available, and the "no vacancy" sign may be hung out when you try.

The last free version of Frontier is also still available for download at (http://www.scripting.com/frontier5/downloads/). This version is only available as-is. For new features and fixes, you would need to subscribe to the current version.

Java Based Portals

On the Java side, the Jakarta **Jetspeed** project (http://jakarta.apache.org/jetspeed/) is working hard to bring a plug-and-play portal to our Java web site. We'll spend some more time with Jetspeed later, but for now, note that it is a standalone web application that we can install and then administer with a GUI. It's designed so that any webmaster can maintain the portal without being a Java engineer. And, being an Apache project, it is also open source and free.

The WebSphere Portal Server (http://www-4.ibm.com/software/webservers/portal/) builds on the Jetspeed API to provide an extensible portal framework. Like Jetspeed, the WebSphere product comes with several ready-to-run portlets, and encourages developers to add their own. WebSphere also bundles their Personalization Server, which cooperates with other IBM products. We'll spend more time with the joint WebSphere/Jetspeed Portlet API later this in this chapter.

Other Portals

Along with WebSphere, many vendors now offer Java portal frameworks with their applications servers. iPlanet, Oracle, and Silverstream all offer products designed to help administrators and developers create portals within and between their web applications. Feature-by-feature reviews of these products are outside the scope of this chapter, but we can spare a quick tour:

- **iPlanet Portal Server** (http://www.iplanet.com/)
  Emphasizes key features like membership management, personalization, aggregation, security, integration services, and search services. At this writing, the original product was being repackaged into Standard and Enterprise versions, designed to serve different segments of the marketplace.

- **Oracle9iAS Portal** (http://otn.oracle.com/)
  Designed to integrate "web-based resources such as web pages, applications, business intelligence reports, and syndicated content feeds, within standardized, reusable information components called portlets". Like Jetspeed and WebSphere, Oracle is taking a framework approach that can allow third parties to develop portlets that plug-in and are ready-to-use.

- **SilverStream ePortal** (http://www.silverstream.com/)
  Also based on a framework that provides core features including personalization, content management, a component framework, and a library of components. Business users create personalization rules, workflows, and content with intuitive tools while developers write ePortal components, conditions, and actions for the rules engine.

- **JCorporate** (http://www.jcorporate.com/)
  A new portal solution that will be a "value-added" integration of Apache Jetspeed and their own Expresso framework. JCorporate's offering will give subscribers the use of Jetspeed within a scalable J2EE environment, along with JCorporate's premium support package.

Edge Side Includes

Another up-and-coming player on the portal landscape is **Edge Side Includes** (http://www.edge-delivery.org/). This is a specification for an open API that is garnering a lot of industry support. While ESI is being written so that it can be used on any platform, it also includes a specification for a JSP tag library, JESI. Unfortunately, there is no implementation available at this time, but we can overview the proposed specification.

The ESI open standard specification is being co-authored by Akamai, ATG, BEA Systems, Circadence, Digital Island, IBM, Interwoven, Oracle, and Vignette.

> **Edge Side Includes accelerates dynamic web-based applications by defining a simple markup language to describe cacheable and non-cacheable web page components that can be aggregated, assembled, and delivered at the network edge.**

ESI builds on the idea of dynamic includes offered by the Apache SSI module and JavaServer Pages. The underlying model is that we should provide web pages as individual fragments, which can each be cached at different points of the delivery system and for different lengths of time (or not at all).

Each fragment has its own cache and access profile. These are set in HTTP headers or configuration files. We might want to cache the template for several days, but only cache a particular fragment, say an advertisement or stock quote, for a few seconds or minutes. Other fragments, such as an account total, may be declared entirely non-cacheable.

There is only a small set of JESI tags on the drawing board, which should be relatively easy to integrate into existing JSP solutions:

Tag	Description
`<jesi:include>`	Used in a template page to indicate to the ESI processor how the fragments are to be assembled
`<jesi:control>`	Assign an attribute (e.g. expiration) to templates and fragments
`<jesi:template>`	Used to contain the entire content of a JSP container page within its body
`<jesi:fragment>`	Encapsulate individual content fragments within a JSP page
`<jesi:codeblock>`	Specify that a particular piece of code needs to be executed before any other fragment is executed (a database connection established or user id computed)
`<jesi:invalidate>`	Explicitly remove and/or expire selected objects cached in an selected objects cached in an ESI processor
`<jesi:personalize >`	Insert personalized content into a page where the content is placed in cookies and inserted into the page by the ESI processor

Jetspeed

Apache Jetspeed began as a groupware portal to keep people on the road in touch with home base and evolved into a platform for building Enterprise Information Portals with XML. Along the way it blossomed into a framework supporting several source formats and display engines, and has even become the host of an open API.

> *Note that Jetspeed is still under active development. At this writing, a production release was not available. However, development releases are being used on both public sites and for intranet portals. If you are interested in acquiring a portal, or writing your own, Jetspeed is definitely worth a look.*

Jetspeed's Features

Standards-based:

- Fully portable across all platforms that support Java 1.2 and the Servlet 2.2 specification
- Supports the open Portlet API specification (planned for version 1.3)

Allows easy configuration and integration through:

- XML-based configuration registry of portlets
- Integration with popular packages like Cocoon, WebMacro, and Velocity

Allows the syndication of content through:

- Rich Site Summary
- Open Content Syndication (another emerging standard)
- Synchronization with external services, like AvantGo

The content can be sent quickly to the user through the use of:

- Local buffering of remote content including XML and remote images
- In-memory cache for quick page rendering

Content can be customized for individual users using:

- Database user authentication
- Profiler Service to access pages based on user, access rights, media types, and language
- Persistence service available to all portlets to easily store state per user per page
- Custom default home page configuration

It is easy to create content for a variety of devices, and to deploy that content:

- Template-based layouts including JSP and ECS
- Wireless Markup Language (WML) support
- Web application development infrastructure
- Full Web Application Archive (WAR) support

Installing Jetspeed

Jetspeed is distributed as a web application, which makes it easy to take for a test drive. Jetspeed should work with any Servlet 2.2 and Java 2 container, but I would recommend starting with Tomcat 4 first. Following my own advice, Jetspeed 1.3a2 was up and running out of the box with Tomcat 4.0 in just a few minutes.

> **Be sure to get version a2 or later, since several defaults have changed from a1. At this writing a2 was only available from the CVS repository on the Jetspeed web site. You may also download the `jetspeed-1a2.war` from the Wrox web site (http://www.wrox.com/).**

Quick Start

To get started using Jetspeed with Tomcat 4 you should:

- Download the Jetspeed binary as detailed above and extract `jetspeed.war` from the archive. Place the WAR in `<TOMCAT_HOME>\webapps\`.
- Start the container and then navigate to http://localhost:8080/jetspeed/. If everything was set up correctly you will see the Jetspeed homepage.

Out of the box, Jetspeed comes with two predefined users, `admin` and `turbine`. Both are documented on the initial, getting-started homepage. Each of these users has different profiles designed to demonstrate the flexibility of Jetspeed:

- The `admin` user has access to a control panel that displays runtime information about Jetspeed. The administrator can also start and stop Jetspeed services, set access permissions for users, create new security roles, and post stories to the Jetspeed content channels.
- The `turbine` user shows how a regular user, with an interest in Turbine (a web application framework), might set up a portal page. The configuration for the turbine user includes live RSS feeds that will change day to day (or even hour to hour).

Turbine and Hypersonic

Turbine is an open source web application framework that spun off from Jetspeed. Turbine provides user authentication, page layout, scheduling, and other services to Jetspeed. Turbine is an active open source project in its own right (available at http://jarkarta.apache.org/turbine/) and is used with many other web applications.

The user information is stored in a standard JDBC database. The database uses the Turbine security model, which allows us to set up both roles and groups to help manage user access rights. Out of the box, Jetspeed uses the all-Java Hypersonic DBMS. Jetspeed should work with any JDBC SQL database, but I would recommend using it with Hypersonic for a while before trying something else.

Internally, Jetspeed is dependent on several other open source projects including Castor, Cocoon, Element Construction Kit, Velocity, Xerces, and Xalan, but everything we need to get started is in the Jetspeed WAR.

Using Jetspeed

We are going to get started with Jetspeed by:

- Creating a user
- Customizing the user's color scheme and home page
- Adding a channel to Jetspeed to which users can subscribe
- Changing the Jetspeed logo

Creating a User

To create a new user, start by going to the login screen, and then selecting Create new user. After we enter the user's details, Jetspeed will create a new account.

Once a user is logged in, they can customize their home page display to use any of the portlets available to Jetspeed – each box, or pane, on the home page is a separate portlet. To help us get started, Jetspeed comes with over a dozen ready-to-use portlets, many available for both HTML and WAP.

Customizing an Account

Jetspeed gives the user a good deal of control over the layout of their portal page. Users can also select their own color scheme. After creating an account, a Customize link appears on the home page. By following this link, users can select a color scheme from a drop down box.

Each user has a default home portlet that is configured by the portal administrator. Each user can choose what other portlets should appear on their page, and whether to display them in different panes. The panes act like sub-pages, and can be displayed as tabs or in a menu. The user can also determine in what order the portlets or panes display. Each portlet has its own title bar, which includes icons for editing, exiting, maximizing, and minimizing the portlet. These work like any GUI control, we just point-and-click.

Next we will see how to configure Jetspeed to use additional portlets. Once this is done users will be able to add new portlets to their home page, just as they do for those that ship with Jetspeed.

Adding a Portlet for a RSS Channel

Of course, to get the most use out of Jetspeed, we will want to add new portlets to our Jetspeed configuration, or remove any which don't apply. One of the easiest portlets to configure is another RSS channel. Let's walk through this process to get a feel of how Jetspeed is configured.

Jetspeed stores the user customizations, and other configuration settings, using **Portlet Structure Markup Language** (an XML application). One of the configuration files is the **portlet registry**, which contains information about all portlets registered in the system. To configure new content channels for our Jetspeed installation, we can add them to the portlet registry file in the Jetspeed web application (`WEB-INF\conf\portlets.xreg`). Let's add a NewsForge channel to our configuration.

In Jetspeed, everything is a portlet, including a RSS channel. Our channel can use the Jetspeed `RSSPortlet`, which renders RDF Site Summary format and presents it to the user as HTML. Jetspeed allows us to reuse portlets, so that we do not have to actually load a separate object for every portlet. Since several other channels are based on the `RSSPortlet`, we can add our feed just by adding another reference to the `RSSPortlet`. Here's how to register a new channel for NewsForge:

```
<portlet-entry name="Newsforge" hidden="false" type="ref"
               parent="RSS" application="false">
  <meta-info>
    <title>NewsForge</title>
    <description></description>
  </meta-info>
  <url>http://www.newsforge.com/newsforge.rdf</url>
</portlet-entry>
```

First, stop the container, then add this element into the portlet registry file, after the other `<portlet-entry>` element, and restart the container. When we reopen Jetspeed, the new channel will be listed alongside the others on the Customize screen.

Of course, it's also important to be able to reverse the process and remove a portlet from the portlet registry file. To prevent new subscriptions, stop the container, clip the element from the portlet registry file, and restart.

However, if a portlet for a RSS channel has already been installed on a user's page, it will continue to function even after we remove it, so we will need to be careful about which channels we provide to begin with. Also, be sure that the portlet is not on the default page for anonymous users or the default page for new users, or they will still have access to that RSS channel.

One portlet that we might want to keep on board is **Jetspeed Content**, as this comes with several predefined channels that we can use to syndicate our own stories. To add new content, login as `admin` and look for the `JetspeedContent` portlet. Fill out the dialog, and our story is in syndication.

> **If you want your stories to be syndicated to other sites, your Jetspeed content syndication file must be found at http://{yourSite}/{yourJetspeedApp}/rss/jetspeed.rss.**

Adding a Logo

Once we've begun customizing the channels, we might want to really make the Jetspeed installation our own by changing the default layout. For a quick and easy customization, we can swap in a copy of your logo for the default. It's stored at `<JETSPEED>\images\jetspeed-logo.gif`.

Jetspeed: The Next Generation

Jetspeed's original API was rooted in the Turbine web application framework, and exposed many elements of Turbine through its interfaces. In cooperation with IBM, Jetspeed has developed a generic version of the Portlet API that can be implemented in many different frameworks and environments.

The **WebSphere Portlet Server** (http://www-4.ibm.com/software/webservers/portal/) is based on the joint **Apache Portlet API 2**.

> *At this writing, the new API had not yet been implemented in Jetspeed. Like any new API, some details may be subject to change as Jetspeed, and possibly other products, put theory into practice. Drafts of the WebSphere and new Jetspeed APIs are available on the Wrox web site (http://www.wrox.com/). At some point, the APIs are planned to merge.*

Since future versions of Jetspeed will be based on the new API, it warrants a closer look.

The Apache Portlet API

The high-level concept behind the API is that portlets are in fact web applications, simply running within another web application. Accordingly, the Portlet API follows the specification for web applications, right down to using PAR files to deploy portlets (rather than WAR files). This makes the API intuitive to anyone already developing Java web applications.

Another key aspect of the Portlet API is that it is designed to be platform-neutral. Its supporters would like to see it adopted in many environments, leading to a standard mechanism for the deployment of portlets.

These two principles, **portlets-as-applications** and **framework-neutrality**, play very well together in practice. Within the API, portlet classes and interfaces are defined using variations on the corresponding servlet class names. For example, a servlet receives a `ServletRequest` and a portlet receives a `PortletRequest`, and uses it in the same way. This pattern is strictly followed throughout the API. This makes learning the API easy for any Java web developer, and relatively easy to incorporate in another framework.

> **The goal of the Portlet API is to allow the creation of customizable, multi-device portal components (portlets) that can be aggregated on a single page, as part of a larger application.**

Requirements

The API has several formal requirements, which can be helpful in understanding the design. The Portlet API should be:

- **Self-Contained**
  It must not expose any intrinsic properties of the underlying platform (for example, Jetspeed, WebSphere Portal Server) so that it can be implemented on different code bases by different vendors, and position itself as a standard.

- **Encapsulated**
  It should clearly separate data that exists per portal, per user, per portlet, per user/per portlet, per session, or per request. This is to permit scalable and thread-safe implementations.

- **Similar**
  It should be similar to the Servlet API since it needs to do many of the same things for the same reasons.
- **Pluggable**
  It should allow for definition of service interfaces and for registration of services that implement the interfaces. For example:
  - **User info**
    For getting user info such as name, address, and age
  - **Persistence**
    For storing per-user, per-portlet settings
  - **Location**
    For obtaining the user's location
  - **Personalization**
    For storing/getting personalization info
  - **Data**
    For access to databases, schema-to-object mappings
  - **Content**
    For access to syndicated content
  - **Cache**
    For access to URLs via caches
- **Flexible**
  It should allow rendering using various technologies (JSP, XSLT/XSL) and markup languages (XML, WML, XHTML, HTML, VoiceXML). This permits portal implementations for different output devices.
- **Abstract**
  It should provide abstract base classes for common portlet types, based on a generic interface. This balances quick implementation of portlets with the development of new portlet types.
- **XML output**
  It should provide only well-formed XML output. This guarantees that the portal can always post-process the portlet output if needed.

Elements

A portal application consists of portlets and other standard web application elements as defined by the Java Servlet specification 2.2. A portlet application exists as a structured hierarchy of directories contained within a web application. The structures defined by the API can exist in an open file system, an archive file, or some other form for deployment purposes. It is recommended, but not required, that portlet containers support this structure as a runtime representation.

Corresponding to the `WEB-INF\` folder, the API defines a `PORTLET-INF\` folder for all things related to the portlet that aren't in the root of the hierarchy. The structure of `PORTLET-INF\` follows `WEB-INF\`, and includes a deployment descriptor named `portlet.xml`. The API also provides for a PAR file, in standard JAR format, to automatically deploy the portlet within a web application.

Here's an example deployment descriptor for a portlet application from the API proposal. The idea is that it is to be very similar to the deployment descriptor for a web application. Details may change when the API is finalized, and implemented in Jetspeed 1.3:

```
<!DOCTYPE portlet-app PUBLIC "-//Apache//DTD Portlet Application
     x.x//EN" "http://<whatever>.dtd">

<portlet-app>
  <portlet-app-name>A PIM Application</portlet-app-name>
  <context-param>
    <param-name>Webmaster</param-name>
    <param-value>webmaster@yourco.com</param-value>
  </context-param>
  <portlet>
    <portlet-name>YourCo. Mail</portlet-name>
    <portlet-class>com.yourco.portlets.MailPortlet</portlet-class>
    <allows>
      <minimize/>
      <maximize/>
      <close/>
    </allows>
    <supports>
      <default document='yes'/>
      <personalize fragment='yes'/>
    </supports>
    <config-param>
      <param-name>default_max_items</param-name>
      <param-value>5</param-value>
      <param-name>default_sort</param-name>
      <param-value>date, desc</param-value>
    </config-param>
  </portlet>
  <portlet>
    <portlet-name>YourCo. Calendar</portlet-name>
    <portlet-class>com.yourco.portlets.CalendarPortlet</portlet-class>
    <title>Your Personal Calendar</title>
    <title mime-type='application/vnd.wap.wml'>Calendar</title>
    <keywords>calendar,date,appointment</keywords>
    <language locale='de'>
      <title>Ihr Persönlicher Kalender</title>
      <title mime-type='application/vnd.wap.wml'>Kalender</title>
      <keywords>Kalendar,Datum,Verabredung,Termin</keywords>
    </language>
    <supports>
      <default fragment='yes'/>
      <personalize fragment='yes' mime-type='text/html'/>
      <help fragment='yes'/>
    </supports>
    <config-param>
      <param-name>default_view</param-name>
      <param-value>month</param-value>
    </config-param>
  </portlet>
</portlet-app>
```

Advanced Features

A fully functional portlet server provides several features in addition to those provided by a standard web container, including:

- A protected `PORTLET-INF\` folder
- A portlet deployment descriptor that is observed by the container and its class loader
- Individual classes and lib folders that are observed by the container's class loader
- Deployments using a PAR file, with robust runtime updates

The rationale behind these features is to give portlet applications the same facilities as web applications, so that we can easily plug a portlet into our application without conflicts. The portlet server prevents conflicts between portlets in the same way that a web container prevents conflicts between web applications.

The Portlet API also provides many useful features that can be instantiated in a standard web container. Without a portlet server, portlet applications would have to be installed by hand and more carefully integrated into the larger web application.

The Apache Portlet API

As mentioned, the Portlet API is deliberately modeled on the Servlet API. The `Portlet` class has a `service()` method which like that of the servlet method takes a request and a response. The portlet version takes a `PortletResponse` and `PortletRequest`, which in turn have familiar methods like `getParameter()`, as well as some unfamiliar methods, like `getDynamicData()`.

Let's focus on the unfamiliar methods in order to get a feel for what the Portlet API does that is different from servlets.

The proposed API is available in the Jetspeed development CVS. For your convenience, a copy of the proposal is also available on the book site (http://www.wrox.com/).

The Portlet Container

At the top of the Portlet API food chain is a **portlet container** or **portlet server**. The container is responsible for handling the plug-and-play aspects for portlets, much the same way a web container handles the plugging in of servlets.

In practice, the portlet container may simply be a servlet – for example Jetspeed is built over a single Turbine servlet.

Normally the portlet container will receive the requests for all portlets in the application, and select which one should process a given request. The container is then responsible for initializing a portlet and then passing it requests, just as a web container is responsible for initializing a servlet and then passing it requests.

Like a servlet, a portlet can be instantiated and have its `init()` method called on startup or sometime afterward (but always before the first request for the portlet is handled). When the container instantiates the portlet using `init()`, it passes a `PortletConfig` object.

The PortletConfig Object

The `PortletConfig` object is larger than its servlet counterpart and includes properties to describe how the portlet can be used within the portal, including whether the portlet can be moved, resized, closed, minimized, or maximized.

Portlets are meant to be available on multiple devices and so `PortletConfig` has a method to see if a given **client** (device) supports a given **capability**:

```
supports(Portlet.Mode mode, Client client)
```

The portlet `Client` object has no servlet counterpart; it returns various strings to indicate, among other things, its manufacturer, mime types, and user agent. It can also return another portlet specific object – `Capability`. The Portlet API predefines capabilities as static instances that hold a Boolean value indicating if the capability is supported by the device. Capabilities include things like `HTML_JAVASCRIPT`, `HTML_CSS`, and `WML_TABLE`.

The `PortletRequest` object (covered later) provides a `getClient()` method. So, to determine if the calling device supports frames, we can call:

```
portletRequest.getClient().isCapableOf(Capability.HTML_FRAME);
```

The `PortletConfig` also provides a method to check whether a portlet supports a given locale:

```
if (portletConfig.supports(myLocale)) { …
```

The Portlet API defines several modes a portlet may assume:

- **Configure**
  Allows the portlet to bring its own configuration screen if required. This would be used by an administrator to set global defaults for a portlet that would apply to all users. The configuration screen would usually be an HTML form representing the portlet's configuration file, but the API does not specifically define this.

- **Personalize**
  Allows the portlet to capture user-specific parameterization, which leads to a personalized view of the portlet. This is the mode that would be used to capture the user's city setting for a weather portlet, or their star sign for an astrology portlet. Like the configure mode, this would usually be an HTML form representing a configuration file. The API does not define the location and format of the configuration file.

- **Help**
  A portlet should provide useful online help in this mode. Usually this would be a description of the portlet's content or controls.

- **Default**
  The standard "one-of many" portlet view on a page.

The PortletContext Object

The PortletConfig also provides access to the PortletContext. Like the ServletContext, this interface defines a set of methods that a portlet uses to communicate with its portlet container. Via the PortletContext, a portlet can write a log file and access external resources, as well as send messages to other portlets, retrieve localized text, and manage listeners.

> **The Portlet interface does not provide for retaining a link to the PortletContext, or the properties it exposes. This is left to the abstract and concrete portlet classes, as it is for servlets.**

Here are some of the PortletContext methods that are used most often:

Method	Description
`String getText( String bundle, String key, Locale locale)`	The Portlet API provides several additional methods for localizing applications. This method returns a localized String based on a key for a given Locale. This could form the basis of an entire localization sub-system, as is found in the Struts Framework.
`void send( String portletName, PortletMessage message, PortletRequest request)`	A PortletMessage can be used for inter-portlet communications. This method sends the specified message to all portlets on the same page that have the specified name. The PortletMessage interface is empty, leaving all functionality to the developer.
`PortletLog getLog()`	Returns the portlet log which allows the portlet to write informational, warning, or error messages to a log. The PortletLog interface defines several useful methods, including error(String aText), error(String aText, Throwable aCause), info(String aText), isEnabled(), and warn(String aText). The type and location of the log is a matter of implementation.
`void include( String path, PortletRequest request, PortletResponse response)`	Allows the portlet to delegate the rendering to another resource as specified by the given path.

The DynamicData Object

An important extension made in the Portlet API is the DynamicData object. DynamicData is a collection of attributes (name-value pairs) that the portlet can use to store information (both temporarily and persistently). We could also think of it as a private context that a portlet can use as an alternative to the request context or session context. Each of the Configuration, Request, Session, and User objects provides two accessors that return a DynamicData object:

```
DynamicData getData()
```

This method returns the default `DynamicData` object for this portlet – conceptually equivalent to `HttpServletRequest.getSession()`:

```
DynamicData getData(String name)
```

This method returns the dynamic data as it is held by the configuration in the shared section with the given name. A shared section in the configuration allows state to be shared among portlets, even if they are of different type. A portlet needs to know the name of a section to gain access. In addition, advanced implementations can restrict access to portlets that have been previously authorized to access a certain shared section.

While the request and the session already have attribute manipulation, the dynamic data object was created to introduce named sections of attributes for configuration and personalized data. It adds a uniform interface to attribute manipulation, plus it provides functionality for multi-value attributes and en-bloc copying.

Accordingly, the `DynamicData` class provides several useful and familiar methods:

Method	Description
`void addAllFrom(DynamicData aData)`	Adds all attributes from the given data to this data.
`Object getAttribute(String name)`	Returns the value of the attribute with the given name, or null if no such attribute exists.
`Enumeration getAttributeNames()`	Returns an enumeration of all available attributes names.
`void removeAll()`	Removes all attributes.
`void removeAttribute(String name)`	Removes the attribute with the given name.
`void setAttribute(String name, Object value)`	Sets the attribute with the given name and value.
`service(PortletRequest request, PortletResponse response)`	Once a portlet is instantiated, it can begin to service requests and provide the appropriate responses. `PortletRequest` and `PortletResponse` are covered in the following sections.

The PortletRequest and PortletSession Objects

Like its servlet counterpart, the `PortletRequest` plays a key role, and provides several important methods. These include familiar methods like `getAttribute()`, `getAttributeNames()`, `getLocale()`, `getMethod()`, `getParameter()`, `getParameterMap()`, `isSecure()`, and `setAttribute()`. Others, like `getClient()` and `getMode()`, are not found in `ServletRequest`, but their meaning should be clear.

A few others are specific to portlets, or have special features, such as the `getSession()`, `getUser()`, and `getWindows()` methods of `PortletSession`:

```
PortletSession getSession(boolean create)
```

This method returns the current session or, if there is no current session and the given flag is true, it creates one and returns it.

Within an application, there is only one object instance of each portlet class, yet each user has a personalized view of that portlet instance. The portlet session carries vital information for the portlet to create a personalized user experience. Portlet instance plus session creates a virtual instance of the portlet.

This is similar to the way a servlet relates to its servlet container. In a typical web application, individual information for a user may be carried in the request or session context. In a portlet application, the same type of information can be carried in the `PortletSession`. This way individual portlets do not have to share namespaces with other portlets and worry about naming conflicts – each gets its own session object.

As a consequence, the portlet should not attempt to store the portlet session or any other user-related information as instance or class variables. In fact, instance variables of a portlet can be considered to have similar behavior as class variables, because there is ever only one instance, which is shared by multiple threads. Therefore, any instance information has to be either read-only (as is the case for the portlet configuration), or, if it must be read-write, then carefully protected by the `synchronized` keyword.

Of course, since the portlet is multithreaded with all requests for the portlet, it is also important that the code runs as quickly as possible. This means that the use of `synchronized` should be minimized, and sharing access to instance information should be avoided.

The `PortletSession` provides a place where a portlet can share personal data, but there still may be circumstances where access to instance information, or other data objects, must be shared. If this is the case then we have to use synchronization so that only one thread accesses the shared data at once. Otherwise, we may create a race condition, and users may end up with a mixture of each other's data. Synchronization degrades performance in any web application, and can be a serious bottleneck when a good number of our current users may be sharing access to the same portlet object.

The User Object

The Servlet API includes an `HttpServletRequest.getUserPrincipal()` method that returns a `java.security.Principal` object containing the name of the current authenticated user. The `PortletSession` exposes a standard `User` object that defines a fixed set of attributes along with access to a `DynamicData` object as well. It's possible that the pre-defined attributes will be re-visited in a future version of the API. Here are some methods provided by the `User` object:

Method	Return Value
`DynamicData getData()`	Returns the dynamic data of this user profile
`String getFamilyName()`	Returns the family name of the user
`String getGivenName()`	Returns the given name of the user
`String getID()`	Returns the user id

Method	Return Value
`long getLastLoginTime()`	Returns the point of time that this was last logged in, or null if this information is not available
`String getMiddleNames()`	Returns the middle names of the user
`String getNickName()`	Returns the nickname of the user

The PortletPage Object

Another portlet-specific object provided in the `PortletRequest` is `PortletPage`. This object contains information about the currently visible page. Although this is a simple object, with only `getName()` and `getData()` methods, it represents one of the more complex parts of an application, that of writing the view. If the portlet is run in help or configure mode, the dynamic data is not accessible and the `getData()` methods will return null:

The PortletWindow Object

As the `PortletPage` represents the current page displayed in a portlet, the `PortletWindow` object represents the window that encloses a portlet. The portlet window can send events on manipulation of its various window controls, like the minimize or close buttons. However, a portlet can also interrogate the portlet window about its current visibility state. For example, a portlet may render its content differently depending on whether its window is maximized or not:

Method	Description
`void addWindowListener( WindowListener listener)`	Adds the given listener to receive window events from this portlet window
`boolean isClosed()`	Returns whether this portlet window is currently closed
`boolean isDetached()`	Returns whether this portlet window is currently detached
`boolean isMaximized()`	Returns whether this portlet window is currently maximized
`boolean isMinimized()`	Returns whether this portlet window is currently minimized
`void removeWindowListener( WindowListener listener)`	Removes the given listener from receiving window events from this portlet window
`void setClosed(boolean aFlag)`	Sets this window to be closed
`void setDetached(boolean aFlag)`	Sets this window to be detached

Table continued on following page

Method	Description
`void setMaximized(boolean aFlag)`	Sets this window to be maximized
`void setMinimized(boolean aFlag)`	Sets this window to be minimized
`void setTitle(PortletTitle title)`	Sets the given title to be the title of this window

The closed, detached, maximized, and minimized properties are events that are passed to any `WindowListener`.

The PortletResponse Object

The `Portlet` is also passed a `PortletResponse` object that represents the response sent to the client device. It is up to the portlet container to enhance, extend, or modify the response as required before it is actually sent to the client device:

Method	Description
`void addActionListener( ActionListener listener)`	Adds the given listener to receive action events when one of the portlet URIs is called that will be part of this response.
`PortletURI createURI ( Portlet.Mode mode)`	Create a portlet URI for the given portlet mode. The returned URI can be further extended by adding portlet-specific parameters and by attaching actions.
`String encodeURI(String path)`	Returns the encoded URI of the resource at the given path. Encoding may include things like prefixing or conversion to an absolute URL.
`PrintWriter getWriter()`	Returns the writer object that can be used to contribute markup to the portlet response. It is important to note that the markup generated by the portlet is either a full document or just a fragment of the markup. A corresponding setting in the deployment descriptor has to be made.

Portlet Events

The Portlet API provides a simple event notification system that developers will find easy to extend. There are three event classes, which all implement the base `Event` interface:

- `ActionEvent`
  Sent by the portlet container when an HTTP request is received that is associated with one or more actions

- `MessageEvent`
  Sent by the portlet container if one portlet sends a message to another
- `WindowEvent`
  Sent by a portlet window whenever the user or the portal interacts with its controls

The `ActionEvent` and `MessageEvent` interfaces specify a `getAction()` and `getMessage()` method respectively. The `WindowEvent` class defines several constants for windowing events, like closing, maximizing, minimizing, moving, resizing, and restoring.

Each has a `Listener` interface (`ActionListener`, `MessageListener`, `WindowListener`), and an abstract "adapter" class, which is recommended as the basis for our own implementations.

The base `Event` interface defines two key methods:

Method	Description
`PortletRequest getRequest()`	Returns the portlet request that has caused this event
`PortletSession getSession()`	Returns the portlet session of the virtual instance that receives this event

The portlet container delivers all events to the respective event listeners (and thereby the portlets) before the content generation is started. Should a listener, while processing the event, find that another event needs to be generated, that event will be queued by the portlet container and delivered at a point in time that is at the discretion of the portlet container. It is only guaranteed that it will be delivered and that it will happen before the content generation phase.

This also means that no further events will be delivered once the content generation phase has started. For example, messages cannot be sent from within the `service()` methods. The resulting message event will not be delivered and essentially discarded.

The API recommends that intelligent portlet containers provide a cyclic event detection mechanism, so that if two or more portlets happen to send each other events that are triggered by each other, the portlet container does not come to a halt.

The Portlet API certainly has its place, but let's look at some simpler alternatives that we can start using in our own applications right away.

My Website Portal

Many observers feel that the difference between a true portal and an ordinary web site is personalization. If we can login and make the page our own, it's a portal. If not, it's just another web site. Of course, this means managing a profile for each of our users.

One way to manage the storage of profiles is to create a file or folder for each user, based on their login. Another approach is to store the profile in a database. In either case, the usual approach is to create a bean representing the profile in a user session when they log in, and then refer to that bean throughout the application. Anonymous visitors are given a default bean to use until they login.

The simplest way to manage the user configurations can be to define one or more beans, and then save these as XML documents. There are several utilities that can help with this, including Castor's XML Mapper, available from http://www.castor.org/xml-mapping.html.

A lesser known, but extremely useful, package is Sixbs, an open source package by Tagtraum Industries, available from http://www.tagtraum.com/sixbs.html. This library is capable of writing and reading beans to and from XML using their public properties, and does it quite well. Here's a very simple example of how to "round-trip" a bean with Sixbs:

```
MyBean b1 = new MyBean();
SIXBSWriter out = new SIXBSWriter(new FileWriter("myBean.xml"));
```

Serialize b1:

```
out.write(b1);
out.close();
SIXBSReader in = new SIXBSReader(new FileReader("myBean.xml"));
```

De-serialize b2:

```
MyBean b2 = (MyBean)in.readObject();
```

Complete personalization should also include letting the user select themes or skins. These can simply be Cascading Style Sheets (CSS). The CSS file to use can be passed in the request or session context, or be part of some user profile bean our application already uses. Here's a simple example, using the Struts bean tag, which expects a dynamic path to a CSS file to be stored under styleSheetName:

```
<link rel="stylesheet"
      href="<bean:write name="styleBean" property="styleSheetName">"
      type="text/css" />
```

Content Management

Most news portals are based on the use of syndicated content. The RSS 0.91 format is especially designed for distributing news channels this way, and provides several enhancements over the original RSS 0.9. It also provides for a text entry field, which makes for a nice gateway into another application.

For example, the "My Netscape Weather" portlet starts out by displaying the weather for several large cities. If you press edit, you're given the chance to specify the cities. If you click the name of any city, or enter a name in the text box, you get a full page rundown of that city's weather. All this functionality could be provided using a dynamic RSS channel.

Many syndicated channels are provided as static XML files that are periodically refreshed with the latest additions, and are returned via a simple HTTP GET request. **Dynamic channels** create the XML on the fly, according to specified parameter, and return the XML in response. Meerkat is a good example of a portal using dynamic channels. Of course, the query can also be delivered via other delivery mechanisms such as POST or XML-RPC to achieve the same result: a custom channel file in response to the given query.

Let's put together a starter portal that can display several channels at once. This code could be used as the basis for a complete portal application using syndicated content.

Channel Beans

Today, most professional web applications are designed using Model 2 or Model-View-Controller (MVC) design patterns, and portals should be no exception. We should be sure to stick to Model 2 patterns from the ground up, remembering that:

- The content for a portlet should be placed into a JavaBean
- The JavaBean should be passed to the portlet view for display

The underlying format of RSS 0.91 is XML. Since direct display or transformation of XML is still beyond most web browsers these days, we need to transform the XML into HTML. One approach to this is to use XSL, or a similar technology, to transform the XML to HTML inside a JSP page. However, since we would like to use a Model 2 design, we really should transform the XML into a JavaBean and then pass that object to the portlet. Then the JSP page can simply accesses the bean's properties and render the HTML, as it would any other brand of dynamic content. We could also pass the JavaBean to a WAP portlet and have it render markup for a WAP device.

Chomping Channels

One good tool for transforming XML to Java objects is the **Jakarta-Commons Digester**, which is used by the Struts Framework to parse its configuration file. The digester is now available as a general development tool, and includes a package for parsing RSS files. The package includes a handy `Channel` JavaBean to represent the content of a RSS 0.91 file. We can pass this bean to our portlets, and let them use it to render the channel.

Getting the Digester

The digester is available through the Jakarta web site (http://jakarta.apache.org/commons/). You can also download the version used here from the Wrox web site (http://www.wrox.com/). The digester package is well documented, and you might find it useful in your other projects. For our news portal, using it is just plug and play.

> *The digester uses `jaxp.jar` and `crimson.jar` (versions 1.1). These need to be exposed to our web application, usually by including them in the `lib\` folder. In the case of Tomcat, it is important to use the Tomcat version of `crimson.jar` to avoid sealing violations.*

To get a feel of how easy the RSS digester is to use, here's a test `Action` for Struts that reads a given RSS file, parses the file into a `Channel` object, and then uses the object to render the file back as XML again. On the screen, this has the appearance of simply piping the XML to the screen, but it's actually "round-tripping" the file.

Here's the `Render Action` for Struts:

```
package com.wrox.portal.http;

import java.io.IOException;
import java.io.PrintWriter;

import java.sql.SQLException;
```

```
import java.util.Iterator;

import javax.servlet.ServletException;
import javax.servlet.http.HttpServletRequest;
import javax.servlet.http.HttpServletResponse;

import org.apache.commons.digester.rss.Channel;
import org.apache.commons.digester.rss.Item;

import ext.sql.AccessBean;
import com.wrox.articles.ArticleHelper;
import com.wrox.articles.http.ArticleForm;

import org.apache.struts.action.Action;
import org.apache.struts.action.ActionError;
import org.apache.struts.action.ActionErrors;
import org.apache.struts.action.ActionForm;
import org.apache.struts.action.ActionForward;
import org.apache.struts.action.ActionMapping;
import org.apache.struts.action.ActionServlet;
```

The `Render` class takes a path, reads in a RSS document, and parses the RSS document into a `Channel` JavaBean. The `Channel` bean makes the content of the RSS document available through standard accessors:

```
public final class Render extends Action {

  public ActionForward perform(ActionMapping mapping,
                               ActionForm form,
                               HttpServletRequest request,
                               HttpServletResponse response)
                       throws IOException, ServletException {
```

We are just going to write the XML as the response. We set the content type as text so the browser won't try to render it as HTML:

```
    response.setContentType("text/plain");
    PrintWriter writer = response.getWriter()
```

Here, we add some flexibility to the class by obtaining the path as part of the URL, or from the Struts action mapping:

```
    String path = request.getParameter("path");
    if (path==null) {
      path = mapping.getParameter();
    }
```

We now instantiate the `RSSDigester` object and create a `Channel` object. The digester's `parse()` method reads in the XML document and returns a `Channel` JavaBean. If the `Channel` comes back null for any reason, we report the errors as "No Data". This usually means the path is missing or invalid:

```
        try {
          RSSDigester digester = new RSSDigester();
          Channel channel = (Channel) digester.parse(path);
          if (channel!=null) {
            channel.render(writer);
          } else {
            writer.print("No data!");
          }
        } catch (Throwable t) {
          writer.print(t.toString());
        }
        return(null);
    }
}
```

To put the `Action` to work, we also need to add the following to the Struts configuration file. Note that we are providing an URL to a known RSS document, so that `Render` has a default to use when a path is not given in the URL:

```
<action
     path="/Render"
     type="org.apache.struts.portal.http.Render"
     parameter= "http://www.apacheweek.com/issues/apacheweek-headlines.xml"
/>
```

If you want to try this, either by rolling your own or by downloading the news portal WAR, here are some channels you can fetch:

- **ApacheWeek** – http://www.apacheweek.com/issues/apacheweek-headlines.xml
- **Jetspeed** – http://jakarta.apache.org/jetspeed/channels/jetspeed.rss
- **Struts** – http://jakarta.apache.org/jetspeed/channels/struts.rss
- **Turbine** – http://jakarta.apache.org/jetspeed/channels/turbine.rss

To check these out, you would open:
http://localhost:8080/articles/do/render?path=http://www.apacheweek.com/issues/apacheweek-headlines.xml

and so forth.

If you have Jetspeed installed, you can also fetch your internal Jetspeed channel at:
http://{yourhost}/jetspeed/rss/jetspeed.rss

Fetch, Struts, Fetch

Let's expand on the `Render Action` to provide one we can use in production. What's needed is an `Action` that will fetch any given RSS file, digest it, save the JavaBean, and continue. The continue step might then display the channel as a HTML file. However, the Action doesn't need to know that.

Here's a new `Action`, `Fetch`, that is based on the `Render Action`. We'll highlight the changes between the two:

```
package com.wrox.portal.http;

import java.io.IOException;
import java.io.PrintWriter;

import java.sql.SQLException;

import java.util.Iterator;

import javax.servlet.ServletException;
import javax.servlet.http.HttpServletRequest;
import javax.servlet.http.HttpServletResponse;

import org.apache.commons.digester.rss.Channel;
import org.apache.commons.digester.rss.Item;

import ext.sql.AccessBean;
import com.wrox.articles.ArticleHelper;
import com.wrox.articles.http.ArticleForm;

import org.apache.struts.action.Action;
import org.apache.struts.action.ActionError;
import org.apache.struts.action.ActionErrors;
import org.apache.struts.action.ActionForm;
import org.apache.struts.action.ActionForward;
import org.apache.struts.action.ActionMapping;
import org.apache.struts.action.ActionServlet;

final class Fetch extends Action {

  public ActionForward perform(ActionMapping mapping,
                               ActionForm form,
                               HttpServletRequest request,
                               HttpServletResponse response)
                       throws IOException, ServletException {
```

Since we'll be passing this through the request, we need to give the bean a name. We'll just use CHANNEL as a name:

```
  public static final String CHANNEL_KEY = "CHANNEL";

  public ActionForward perform(ActionMapping mapping,
                               ActionForm form,
                               HttpServletRequest request,
                               HttpServletResponse response)
                       throws IOException, ServletException {
```

Since we won't be writing directly to output, we'll need a Struts ActionErrors collection to store the errors for handling elsewhere:

```
    ActionErrors errors = new ActionErrors();
    Channel channel = null;
    String path = request.getParameter("path");
```

```
      if (path==null) {
        path = mapping.getParameter();
      }
      try {
        RSSDigester digester = new RSSDigester();
        channel = (Channel) digester.parse(path);
      } catch (Throwable t) {
```

In Render, we just wrote the error out in the response. Here, we add it to the errors collection instead (if it occurs). We then look for an input page to handle the error:

```
        errors.add(ActionErrors.GLOBAL_ERROR,
                   new ActionError("rss.access.error"));
                   servlet.log(t.toString());
      }
      if (!errors.empty()) {
        saveErrors(request, errors);
        if (mapping.getInput()!=null) {
          return (new ActionForward(mapping.getInput()));
        }
```

If there is no input page, look for an "error" forwarding instead:

```
        return (mapping.findForward("error"));
      }
```

If we reach this point, there was no error, so we can save the bean, and continue:

```
      request.setAttribute(CHANNEL_KEY,channel);
      return (mapping.findForward("continue"));
    }
  }
```

Here's a quick test page to see if our "round tripping" is still working:

```
<%@ page import="org.apache.commons.digester.rss.Channel"%>
<%@ page import="java.io.Writer"%>
<jsp:useBean id="CHANNEL" scope="request"
             type="org.apache.commons.digester.rss.Channel"/>
<% response.setContentType("text/plain"); %>
<% Writer writer = (Writer) out; %>
<% CHANNEL.render(writer); %>
```

And the Struts configuration entry to pull it all together:

```
<action
  path="/Fetch"
  type="org.apache.struts.portal.http.Fetch"
  parameter="http://www.apacheweek.com/issues/apacheweek-headlines.xml">
     <forward name="continue" path="/WEB-INF/pages/render.jsp" />
</action>
```

All Aboard – renderHtml.jsp

The round-trips are fun, but our destination is HTML. Now that we know everything is working smoothly, let's write a JSP page to output the `Channel` bean as HTML. The Struts Framework provides a handy `write` tag in its `bean` tag library. Here's how we can render the `Channel` bean in HTML using the Struts `<bean:write>` tag:

```
<%@ page language="java" %>
<%@ taglib uri="/tags/struts-bean" prefix="bean" %>
<%@ taglib uri="/tags/struts-logic" prefix="logic" %>
<html:html/>
  <head>
```

Here's the title from the channel bean:

```
    <title><bean:write name="CHANNEL" property="title"/></TITLE>
    <meta http-equiv="Content-Type" content="text/html;
          charset=iso-8859-1">
    <html:base/>
  </head>
  <body>
    <table cellspacing="2" cellpadding="4" width="90%" align="center">
      <tr>
```

Here we render the image from the channel bean, the title again, this time with a hyperlink to the channel's home page, followed by the description for the channel itself:

```
        <td>
          <img src="<bean:write name="CHANNEL" property="image.URL"/>">
        </td>
        <td width="100%">
          <a href="<bean:write name="CHANNEL" property="link"/>">
            <bean:write name="CHANNEL" property="title"/>
          </a>
        </td>
      </tr>
      <tr>
        <td colspan="2">
          <bean:write name="CHANNEL" property="description"/>
        </td>
      </tr>
    </table>
```

We now write each item in the channel in turn, showing the title and description for each. Following the description is a "... more" hyperlink to the "rest of the story":

```
    <logic:iterate name="CHANNEL" property="items" id="ITEM">
      <hr width="90%">
      <table cellspacing="2" cellpadding="4" width="90%" align="center">
        <tr>
          <td><h4><bean:write name="ITEM" property="title"/></h4></td>
        </tr>
        <tr>
```

```
        <td><bean:write name="ITEM" property="description"/></TD>
      </tr>
      <tr>
        <td align="right">
          ...
          <a href="<bean:write name="ITEM" property="link"/>">more</a>
        </td>
      </tr>
    </table>
  </logic:iterate>
  <hr width="90%">
 </body>
</html>
```

To move from our roundtrip `Fetch` to the HTML version, we need only change the Struts configuration file, and have it "continue" to the HTML page instead. The `Action` remains the same:

```
<action
  path="/Fetch"
  type="org.apache.struts.portal.http.Fetch"
  parameter="http://jakarta.apache.org/jetspeed/channels/struts.rss">
    <forward name="continue" path="/WEB-INF/pages/renderHtml.jsp" />
</action>
```

In fact, we don't even need to stop the server, update the config file and navigate to http://{yourhost}/portal/do/admin/Reload. This will put the new configuration into effect. Navigate to http://{yourhost}/portal/do/Fetch and view the `Channel` as HTML.

If we wanted specific actions for specific channels, we could just add them to the config file like this:

```
<action
  path="/fetch/Struts"
  type="org.apache.struts.portal.http.Fetch"
  parameter="http://jakarta.apache.org/jetspeed/channels/struts.rss">
    <forward name="continue" path="/WEB-INF/pages/render.jsp" />
</action>
```

Well, this is a great for a single channel, but what about a portal layout, where we need to display several channels? No problem. Since all our channels can be represented as URIs, we simply need an action that can take several URIs and create a corresponding bean for each. Our JSP page can then iterate over the beans, and display each channel in turn.

Following the previous examples let's set this up so a default can be passed as an `ActionMapping` parameter, and be overridden by a setting passed in the session or request context, or on the query line:

```
public final class Channels extends Action {

  public static final String CHANNELS_KEY = "CHANNELS";

  public ActionForward perform(ActionMapping mapping,
                               ActionForm form,
                               HttpServletRequest request,
                               HttpServletResponse response)
```

```
                        throws IOException, ServletException {

    ActionErrors errors = new ActionErrors();
    org.apache.commons.digester.rss.Channel channel = null;
```

Manufacture a list of channels for demonstration purposes:

```
    ArrayList channels = new ArrayList();
    channels.add("http://www.newsforge.com/newsforge.rss");
    channels.add("http://xmlhack.com/rss.php");
    channels.add("http://lwn.net/headlines/rss");
```

Loop through the channels:

```
    ArrayList channelBeans = new ArrayList(channels.size());
    try {
      for (int i=0; i<channels.size(); i++) {
        RSSDigester digester = new RSSDigester();
        channelBeans.add(digester.parse((String)channels.get(i)));
      }
    } catch (Throwable t) {
     errors.add(ActionErrors.GLOBAL_ERROR,
                  new ActionError("rss.access.error"));
      servlet.log(t.toString());
    }
```

As before, we will handle any errors, and then save the bean and continue if all is well:

```
    if (!errors.empty()) {
      saveErrors(request, errors);
      if (mapping.getInput()!=null) {
        return (new ActionForward(mapping.getInput()));
      }       return (mapping.findForward("error"));
    }    request.setAttribute(CHANNELS_KEY,channelBeans);
    return (mapping.findForward("continue"));
  }
}
```

Creating a JSP page to display the channels can be as easy as using an `Iterator` and creating a simple page called `channels.jsp`:

```
<body>
  <logic:iterate name="CHANNELS" id="CHANNEL">
    <table cellspacing="2" cellpadding="4" width="90%" align="center">
      <tr>
        <td>
          <img src="<bean:write name="CHANNEL" property="image.URL"/>">
        </td>
        <td width="100%">
          <a href="<bean:write name="CHANNEL" property="link"/>">
            <bean:write name="CHANNEL" property="title"/>
```

```
            </a>
          </td>
        </tr>
        <tr>
          <td colspan="2">
            <bean:write name="CHANNEL" property="description"/>
          </td>
        </tr>
      </table>
      <logic:iterate name="CHANNEL" property="items" id="ITEM">
        <hr width="90%">
        <table cellspacing="2" cellpadding="4" width="90%" align="center">
          <tr>
            <td><h4><bean:write name="ITEM" property="title"/></h4></td>
          </tr>
          <tr>
            <td><bean:write name="ITEM" property="description"/></td>
          </tr>
          <tr>
            <td align="right">
              ...
              <a href="<bean:write name="ITEM" property="link"/>">
                more
              </a>
            </td>
          </tr>
        </table>
      </logic:iterate>
      <hr width="90%">
  </logic:iterate>
  </body>
```

Add a node to the Struts configuration file, and we're riding the wave:

```
<action
  path="/Channels"
  type="com.wrox.portal.http.Channels">
    <forward name="continue" path="/WEB-INF/pages/channels.jsp" />
</action>
```

For a multi-column layout, a list for each column can be passed.

Too Much of a Good Thing

While syndicated channel files are dynamic, they are not *that* dynamic. Ideally, a portal application should buffer all the RSS files it reads so that they are not read more than once an hour or so. Whether or not this is strictly necessary depends on how many people are using our portal.

Jetspeed includes the **DiskBuffer** package (`org.apache.jetspeed.cache.disk`) that does just that. To integrate with an application like this, we would check the buffer before calling the digester. When checked, the cache will retrieve or refresh the document, or decide to use a cached version. The buffer can return an input stream to the file in its cache, which we can pass to the digester. Integrating a package like DiskBuffer into our application can be quite a bit of work, so we should be sure it is needed before we put in the effort.

Another approach might be to buffer the `Channel` objects themselves. This would use more RAM, compared to using space on disk, but it would eliminate the need to read the channel from a file and render the XML to a bean each time it is used. To avoid threading issues during channel updates, this type of implementation would need to pass copies of the `Channel` bean to the request rather than a reference to the original, or provide some other mechanism to keep the `Channel` object from being refreshed while it was being rendered as HTML. Again, implementing this would be non-trivial, so be sure it is needed first.

Returning the Favor

The `Channel` bean from the RSS digester package can also be used to create an RSS channel file. Here's an action for the Articles application from Chapter 12 that returns a query as a dynamic RSS file.

This can be called with a URI like http://localhost:8080/articles/do/rss/Search?col=last to return the last ten articles posted. Other queries can be formed using `col={field}&key={text}` where `{field}` is `author` or `title` and `{text}` is a string to match.

The Articles application was not written to support RSS channels from the ground up. However, it does use a similar approach. The search returns a list with an element for each of the articles found. This is the same basic idea of a channel containing `Item` objects. Rather than write a new search routine, we will just take the `ArticleList` and convert it to a `Channel`.

Here's our `Render Action` for the Articles application:

```
package com.wrox.articles.http;

import java.io.IOException;
import java.io.PrintWriter;

import java.sql.SQLException;

import java.util.Iterator;

import javax.servlet.ServletException;
import javax.servlet.http.HttpServletRequest;
import javax.servlet.http.HttpServletResponse;

import org.apache.commons.digester.rss.Channel;
import org.apache.commons.digester.rss.Item;

import ext.sql.AccessBean;
import com.wrox.articles.ArticleHelper;
import com.wrox.articles.http.ArticleForm;

import org.apache.struts.action.Action;
```

```
import org.apache.struts.action.ActionError;
import org.apache.struts.action.ActionErrors;
import org.apache.struts.action.ActionForm;
import org.apache.struts.action.ActionForward;
import org.apache.struts.action.ActionMapping;
import org.apache.struts.action.ActionServlet;
```

The Articles Render Action transforms the list of found articles from its own ArticleList bean, containing a collection of ArticleForm objects, into a Channel bean containing a collection of Item objects:

```
public final class Render extends Action {

  public ActionForward perform(ActionMapping mapping,
                               ActionForm form,
                               HttpServletRequest request,
                               HttpServletResponse response)
                   throws IOException, ServletException {
```

First we set up the ActionErrors object, in case we need it, and the channel object, just as we did for the Portal Render Action:

```
    ActionErrors errors = new ActionErrors();
    Channel channel = new Channel();
```

The ArticleHelper handles the data access for the Articles application. This Action expects the ArticleHelper to already exist in the request. We will set this up so a regular Search Action is run first to create the ArticleHelper, so that we can then use it here. The helper is required, so we generate an error if it is missing:

```
    ArticleHelper helper = (ArticleHelper)
    request.getAttribute(AccessBean.HELPER_KEY);
    if (helper==null) {
      errors.add(ActionErrors.GLOBAL_ERROR,
      new ActionError("access.missing.parameter"));
    }
```

We now know the helper exists and can get busy with the rest of our Action. First, we set some defaults:

```
    if (errors.empty()) {
      try {
         channel.setTitle("Articles");
         channel.setDescription(
                "The Articles application is your passport to currency.");
```

This links back to the Articles application at our web site:

```
         channel.setLink("http://localhost:8080/articles/");
```

We now loop through the ArticleForm beans and convert them to Item beans:

```
        Iterator rows = helper.getRows();
        while (rows.hasNext()) {
          ArticleForm article = (ArticleForm) rows.next();
          Item item = new Item();
          item.setTitle(article.getTitle());
```

This links the item back to the article in our application.

```
          item.setLink(
                   "http://localhost:8080/articles/do/articler/View?key=" +
                   article.getArticle());
          channel.addItem(item);
        }
```

If any errors occur, we handle them in the usual Struts fashion. This is the "top" of the application, so we should catch all exceptions here. There's no one else above us:

```
      } catch (Exception e) {
        errors.add(ActionErrors.GLOBAL_ERROR,
                   new ActionError("rss.access.error"));
        servlet.log(e.toString());
      }
    }
    if (!errors.empty()) {
      saveErrors(request, errors);
      if (mapping.getInput()!=null) {
        return (new ActionForward(mapping.getInput()));
      }

return (mapping.findForward("error"));
    }
```

Here, we return the XML back as the response. Ironically, our portal application will read this back in to create a new `Channel` bean, but we don't know that. Any application that supports RSS could request our syndicated content this way. This realises the high purpose of XML – to transfer data between applications:

```
    response.setContentType("text/plain");
    channel.render(response.getWriter());
    return(null);
  }
}
```

Here are the entries for the Struts configuration file in the Articles application:

```
<action
  path="/rss/Search"
  type="com.wrox.articles.http.Client"
  name="articleForm"
  scope="request"
  validate="false"
```

```
    parameter="select">
    <forward name="continue" path="/do/rss/Render"/>
  </action>

  <action
    path="/rss/Render"
    type="com.wrox.articles.http.Render"
    scope="request"
    validate="false">
  </action>
```

Notice that we start out by using the existing search action to put a result bean in the request, but then forward it to the `Render Action`. Here we take the result bean and use it create the channel bean, which is rendered as the response. So now we can call our own Articles application from our own Portal application and return the articles as a RSS channel, along with the others.

Summary

The backbone of today's portals is still syndicated content. We reviewed the origins of portals, and the development of syndication formats, such as RDF Site Summary. There are several portal-in-a-box packages available for various platforms, though the pickings for Java are still slim. We outlined some of the high-end portal servers available today, and walked through an initial installation of Apache Jetspeed.

An up-and-coming force in Java portal development is the Apache Portal API. This open standard is being shared by WebSphere Portal Server and Apache Jetspeed, and holds much promise for the future. We took a close look at the API's architecture so you know what's coming.

To close the chapter, we examined some simple ways to build portals into your own applications, including code for creating JavaBeans from Rich Site Summary channels and using them to write JavaServer Pages. Finally, we demonstrated creating your own RSS file using the same JavaBean.

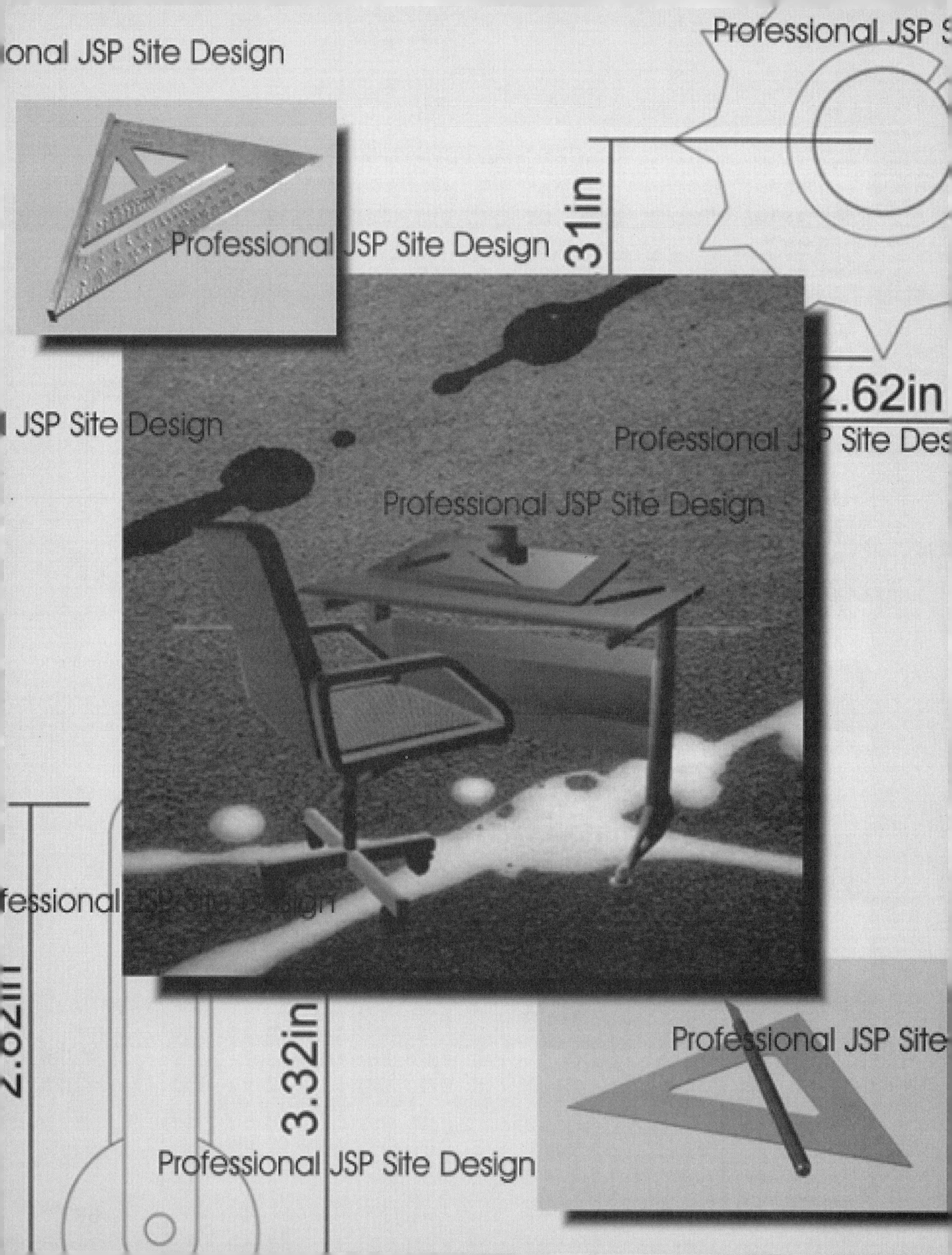
Professional JSP Site Design
31in
Professional JSP Site Design
3.32in
Professional JSP Site Design

15

An XML-JSP Framework–1

There are many web application frameworks based on the Model 2 architecture that can be used to build JSP web applications, and they all share certain characteristics. Any such framework needs to be able to store data and pass it from one part of the framework to another; this data is known as the **model data**. Most frameworks use JavaBeans to store this model data, which often leads to a large number of bean classes that correspond to the different views in the system.

XML is increasingly used as the 'glue' between the tiers in an application. The data that a web application relies on is often available as XML, so if a web application is to be able to present that data to clients in a straightforward way it is important that it can easily accept, generate, and render XML.

There are many JSP custom tag libraries that can render XML for web pages, but most of them rely on XSLT transformations of a well-formed Document Object Model (DOM). We saw in Chapter 2 how Struts provides a request-processing and data-rendering framework together with a host of custom tag libraries that provide useful features. These features included linking JavaBean instances with HTML forms and form elements. What we lack is a web application framework that seamlessly integrates the presentation tier with the underlying XML model in the same way.

A framework that uses XML to store the model data will provide three benefits not available to frameworks that use JavaBeans:

- Regardless of the variety or complexity of the view, the data can be easily abstracted as XML nodes
- We can use XML schemas to create a generic validation engine, which can be used to validate the data sent by a client
- We can use XSL transformations to easily render content to a variety of devices

Such a framework could be used to develop the presentation tier of an enterprise application that produces and consumes XML data. For example, it could be used to develop a web front to a set of web services that provide access to the enterprise data.

In this, and the following two chapters, we will develop a JSP web application framework that uses XML to represent the model data. Our framework will be able to generate, validate, accept, and render XML. This XML could be a well-formed DOM, an XML node, or a document fragment. The framework will also provide custom tag libraries that will be able to:

- Link HTML forms and form elements with the underlying XML data
- Extract data from XML nodes
- Iterate over a list of nodes
- Render HTML forms and populate the form elements with data extracted from XML nodes

The main framework code and the tag libraries will be detailed in Chapter 16, and in Chapter 17 we will develop a sample application using our framework. This application will have two distinct layers: the web tier that will be built on our framework and the web services tier built using Simple Object Access Protocol (SOAP), which will provide the business services to the web tier.

As usual, the code for both the framework and the example application is available for download at http://www.wrox.com/.

The design and development of our JSP-XML framework will be broken down into several distinct steps:

- We will analyze what the framework is required to do, which will involve a detailed discussion of the framework's functionality
- Most of our custom tags and XML parsing classes will make use of **XPath** expressions so we will look at the XPath specification and understand how XPath expressions provide us with an easy way to access information from XML nodes
- We will look at how we can use XML schemas to implement a generic validation engine
- We will look at how our framework will generate XML documents

Once this is done we can design and implement a push MVC web framework that can produce, consume, render, and validate XML.

Analyzing the Requirements

Before we can do anything else, we need to analyze, in detail, the functional requirements of our web application framework.

> **Our aim is to create an application framework that can be used to build web applications that can function as a front end for enterprise systems that generate and consume XML.**

The framework must perform six functions. It must be able to:

- **Generate XML**
  The framework should provide the users with functionality for generating XML nodes from the incoming request data
- **Validate XML**
  The framework should provide application developers with a generic validation engine, which can be used to validate the data sent by clients
- **Handle errors and render XML**
  If data validation errors occur the framework should present the original HTML form back to the user complete with all the data previously entered
- **Delegate requests**
  The framework should provide the functionality to delegate request URIs to classes that are capable of processing the requests
- **Manage views**
  Users of the framework should be able to declaratively map logical names to physical resources for rendering the next view and link these names to specific request URIs

Let's look in detail at each of these, and discuss what implications they hold for the design of the framework.

XML Generation

Users should be able to generate XML nodes from a request. As the generated XML may need to be passed to external applications users must have complete control over the structure of the generated XML. This can be achieved if the framework exposes a common interface for which users write their own implementations.

This technique of exposing an interface for which the user implements a class that contains the required functionality is common to many applications. We will encounter it a number of times in the design of our framework.

Application developers should be able to declaratively link their XML generation implementation classes to specific request URIs. This is similar to the way we can map request URIs to particular servlets in a standard web application deployment descriptor. A user may even want to switch off XML generation for selected request URIs. For example, if a request doesn't have any request parameters, there may be no point in generating any XML.

XML Validation

The framework should provide a generic validation engine that developers can use to validate data entered by a client.

We are not validating XML sent by the client itself – rather we are validating the XML that is generated from the request URI sent by the client.

We should be able to define our own XML schemas and, just as we did for XML generation, declaratively link them to specific request URIs. As with XML generation, we should be able to switch off validation completely for selected request URIs.

Error Handling

If an error occurs when validating the data submitted from an HTML form the framework should return the original HTML form to the client. The form should be returned complete with the data that was originally entered. In order to do this the framework will need to link HTML forms with the XML nodes that are generated on submission of the form. The framework will also need to be able to render the form.

XML Rendering

The framework must be able to return the original HTML form back to the user retaining all the data previously entered. This should include both read-only and editable data. To do this, the framework will require custom tags that can render HTML forms and form elements.

The form rendering tag must be able to link the rendered HTML form to the XML node that was generated on submission of the form. The framework should also provide additional custom tags that allow the iteration over a list of XML nodes, or the discovery of the value of a given node. These tags will be used for the rendering of a list of XML nodes as a read-only list. Such a tag would be used to populate the options list of an HTML `SELECT` control.

Declarative Request Delegation

Developers must be able to delegate request URIs to classes that are capable of processing the requests. As with XML generation the framework will provide an interface and the developer will provide classes that perform the actual processing. These classes will be declared in a configuration file and will be mapped to the URI of the request they are designed to process. Then, when a request is received, the framework can load the class that will handle the request and delegate the processing of the request to it. The framework itself only needs to know about the interface, and the type of the class to delegate the processing to. The framework knows nothing about the actual implementation of the class.

The interface the framework exposes should provide developers with the request and response associated with the URI as well as any XML generated for the URI. The interface should also provide users with the information required to select the next view.

Declarative View Management

We should be able to declare mappings of logical names to the physical resources responsible for rendering the next view. We should also be able to link these logical names to specific request URIs.

The framework must pass this information to the request delegate classes, which can then choose the next view based on the outcome of processing the request. For every view mapping we must be able to define whether the view is redirected to the client, or whether it is forwarded using the request dispatcher interface. If the view is redirected the servlet container will send the response to the client and, by using the appropriate request headers, tell the client to access the new view. However, the forwarding of views is done at the server, without a trip to the client.

High Level Architecture

We are clear about the functionality our framework must provide, and we have discussed how some parts of the framework will interact (both with clients and other parts of the framework). Now we are ready to set out in more detail how the framework is to be implemented, including design issues that are not directly related to the functionality of the framework. Our main design goals at this stage are that the framework should:

- Manage resources efficiently
- Handle errors robustly
- Have a interface based design
- Reuse components
- Be both extensible and flexible
- Be easy to configure

The following activity diagram depicts the high level architecture of our framework:

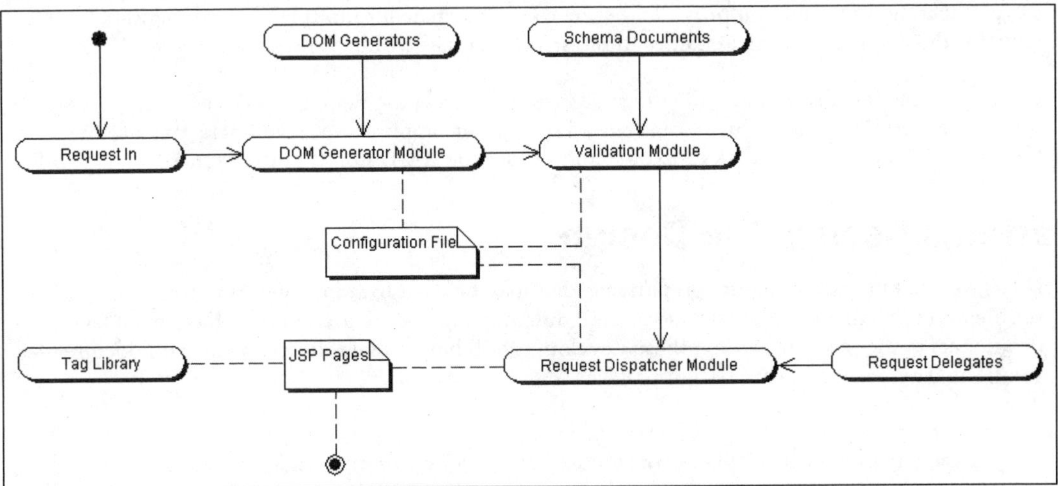

The architecture is based on a push MVC paradigm. Incoming HTTP requests are routed to objects that handle the requests using a **command pattern**.

> *The Command pattern allows a request to be passed to a specific object. The choice of object depends on some parameterized information. A command pattern provides a common interface for all the objects that are capable of processing the request. However, the client class only needs to know about the interface.*

These objects will access and process the request data. They will also push the data required for the next view into JavaBeans that have request scope. The JSP pages responsible for rendering the views will then use custom tags (provided by the framework) to extract and render the data.

The incoming requests will pass first through the **DOM Generator Module**. This module will check the configuration file to find the **DOM Generator** class to be used to generate the XML for the particular request URI. The generator module will then accept the generated XML node and store it in a JavaBean that has request scope. The name of the request attribute under which the XML node is stored can be defined in the configuration file.

At this stage the generated XML can be validated against an XML schema. If the XML generated for a request URI is to be validated, an entry must be made in the configuration file that maps a request URI to the location of the relevant schema. The **Validation Module** will then validate the generated XML against this schema.

If the validation fails, the framework will return control back to the page that instigated the current request. This page should then render the original data provided by the client. This is done using custom tags that extract the data from the XML node that was stored as a request attribute by the generator module. If the validation was successful, control will be forwarded to the **Request Dispatcher Module**.

The request dispatcher module will pass the validated XML node, the request and response objects, and any configuration information to the **Request Delegates**. The request delegates process the request and store the information required for rendering the next view as XML nodes in the request attribute list. They also select the resource that is responsible for rendering the next view. This selection is made from the configuration information provided by the request dispatcher module. The configuration file contains the mapping of logical names to physical resources within the web application.

Finally, the request dispatcher will either forward or redirect the response to a resource selected by the specific request delegate. If this resource is a JSP page the application developers may use the custom tags provided by the framework to extract and render the XML stored in the request scope JavaBeans.

Patterns Used in the Design

Next, we need to discuss the **design patterns** that may be used to implement this architecture. The problems and challenges that we face in designing our framework are likely to have been faced by many developers in the past. Hopefully, these developers will have solved the problems and documented the solutions. These solutions are design patterns.

> **Design patterns are "well known solutions for well known problems".**

Erich Gamma, Richard Helm, Ralph Johnson, and John Vlissides – the gang of four (GoF) – documented twenty-three patterns in *Design Patterns: Elements of Reusable Object-Oriented Software* from *Addison-Wesley (ISBN 0-201-63361-2)*, which document solutions for common design problems encountered in object-orientated programming Most modern patterns are based on one of these twenty-three.

Also worth mentioning are the J2EE patterns documented by Sun at http://java.sun.com/j2ee/blueprints/design_patterns/. These patterns address design problems associated with enterprise application development. In fact, most of these patterns have their roots in the GoF patterns.

Our aim is to identify which patterns are used within our framework. Once we have identified which patterns are used we can apply one or more of the "well known solutions".

Decorating Filter Pattern

The DOM generator and validation modules perform pre-processing on the request object. Filter modules accept the request and then generate and validate XML nodes from the request parameters before storing them as request attributes. This addition of information is known as **decorating** the requests.

> **The Decorator pattern, as defined by the GoF, is one in which additional responsibilities are dynamically attached to an object.**

An example of a Decorator pattern in action is the stream readers and writers in the Java IO package that convert byte streams to Unicode streams. In our framework we need to pass request objects through decorators so that their contents can be dynamically modified.

The decorator pattern is refined in the J2EE patterns to become the **Decorating Filter pattern**. The purpose of decorating filters is to provide pre- and post-processing for the requests and responses. This pattern may be used to perform tasks common to a group of requests such as authentication, logging, and data transformation.

The Decorating Filter pattern is illustrated in the following sequence diagram:

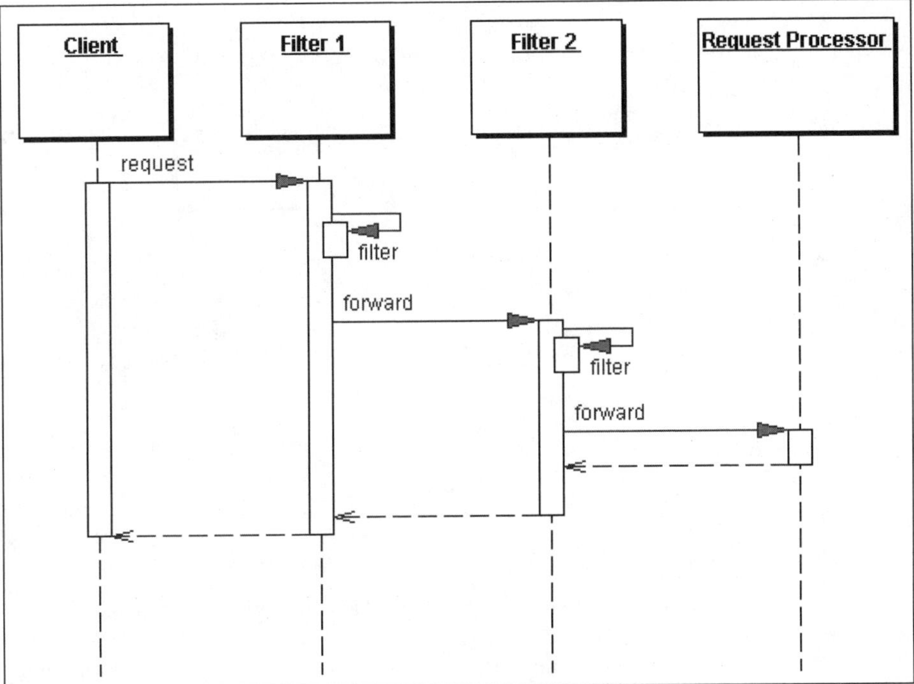

The request from the client will go to the first filter, which performs the filter logic before forwarding the request and response to the second filter. In our framework the first filter will be the generator module that creates an XML node from the request data and stores it as a request attribute. The XML generation will actually be delegated to classes provided by the application developers that implement the XML generation interface.

The second filter also performs filtering logic before forwarding the request and response to the ultimate destination of the request, where it is processed. In our framework, the second filter will be the validation module, which will validate the XML node generated by the generator module.

Once the request is processed, control is passed back to the client by tracing the filter path in reverse order.

Front Controller Pattern

The **Front Controller pattern** (as defined in the J2EE pattern catalogue) provides a centralized controller that processes requests. This allows us to ensure that all the requests routed to the controller pass through a common set of filters that perform logging or authentication. The controller can also make decisions on how a request is processed and what resource should render the next view.

Usually the controller will delegate the request processing and view dispatching tasks to helper classes, in which cast the controller will implement the classic **Mediator pattern** (from the GoF) to orchestrate the various tasks performed by these helper classes. The mediator pattern is defined as a behavioral pattern used to define an object that encapsulates how a set of objects should interact. This pattern promotes loose coupling between objects by preventing them from making explicit references to one another.

The controller may be implemented as a servlet or a JSP page. However, servlets are considered the standard method of implementing a controller element. The request URIs that should be routed to the controller can be defined in the deployment descriptor using the `servlet-mapping` element.

The following sequence diagram depicts a typical implementation of the Front Controller pattern:

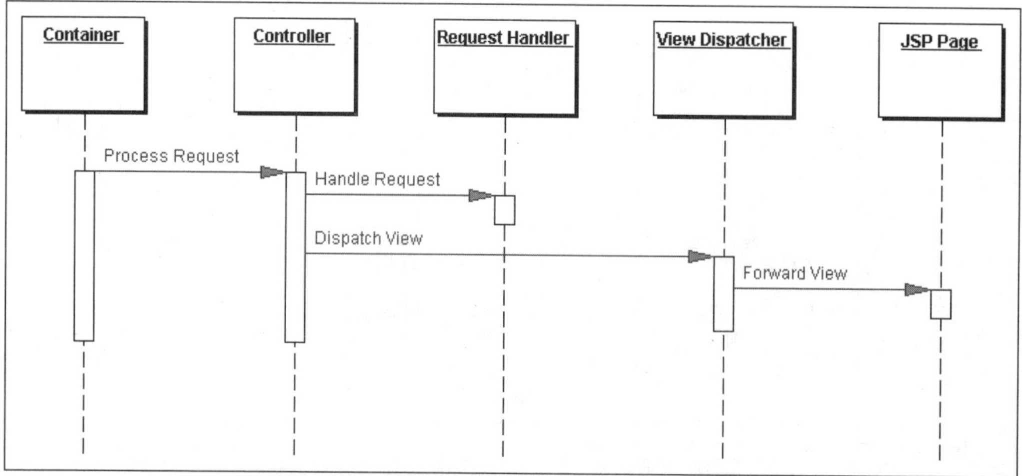

The container passes the request to the controller servlet. The controller servlet will then identify an appropriate request handling helper class to handle the request. Once a helper class is found the controller will delegate the request-handling task to it. Finally, the controller delegates the task of selecting the next view to a view dispatcher helper class.

In our framework the controller will be implemented as a servlet and application developers will be provided with a common set of interfaces for classes that handle requests. Application developers will need to write implementations of these interfaces and register them in the configuration file against required request URIs.

When our framework's controller servlet receives a request, the following will happen:

- The controller will retrieve an object from a pool of request handlers (identified from the configuration information)
- The controller will use the GoF **command pattern** to delegate the request-handling task to the selected request handler, passing it the request and response objects, any XML node generated for the current request, and any configuration information required by the request delegate to select the next view
- The request delegate will return the information required to render the next view back to the controller
- The controller will then use the servlet `RequestDispatcher` interface to dispatch the next view

Command Pattern

Command pattern is a GoF behavioral pattern used to define an abstraction of performing a command. The main entities that participate in the pattern are the invoker object, the abstract command, and the concrete command implementations. The pattern may optionally configure the concrete implementations with receivers that can receive the result of executing the command.

> **The Command pattern is a very powerful pattern to use when writing frameworks in which the core of the framework deals with a set of abstractions to which the systems that use the framework provide implementations.**

The following class diagram depicts the implementation of a command pattern:

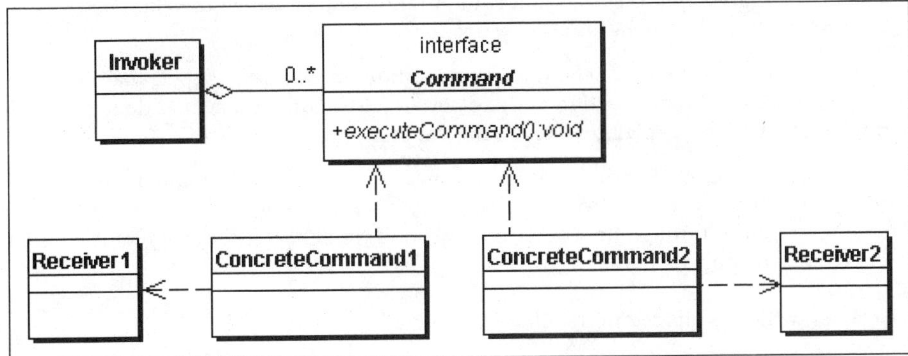

Concrete implementations are provided for the `Command` interface. An `Invoker` object may be configured with multiple implementations. On receiving an event, the `Invoker` may choose a specific implementation depending on the event and delegate the task of executing the command. The `Invoker` doesn't need to anything about the concrete implementations.

In our framework the Command pattern is used to implement the DOM generation module and the request dispatcher module.

Implementing the DOM Generation Module

In this module, the framework exposes an interface, `framework.xml.DOMGenerator`, to which application developers write implementations. Developers then link these implementations to request URIs in the configuration file.

The DOM generation filter will call the specific implementation upon receiving a request with the relevant information. The DOM generator will create the XML node and store it as a request attribute using the name specified in the configuration file. In our framework, the DOM generating filter is the invoker, the DOM generator abstraction is the abstract command, the concrete implementation is the concrete command, and the request object is the receiver. This is further illustrated in the following class diagram:

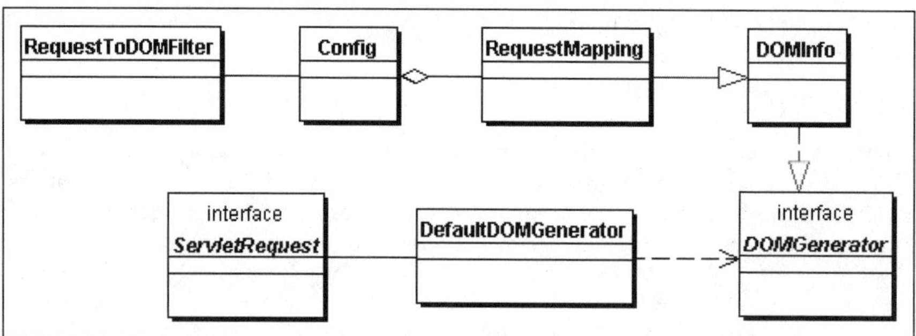

There are some interesting points to note here:

- The aggregation shown between `RequestToDOMFilter` and `DOMGenerator` will be implemented through a configuration object.
- The actual aggregation is stored in a configuration object, which the class `RequestToDOMFilter` holds a reference to.
- The framework provides a default implementation for `DOMGenerator` that iterates through the request parameter collection and creates an XML node (the actual details of the implementation are explained later in the chapter).
- The `RequestToDOMFilter` holds an instance of `Config` object that contains a hash map of request URIs and concrete `RequestMapping` instances. The `RequestMapping` instances hold a reference (through the `DOMInfo` object) to the `DOMGenerator` that is configured for the request mapping.

All these classes will be explained in detail later in the chapter.

Implementing the Request Dispatcher Module

In this module, the framework exposes an interface, `framework.controller.RequestHandler`, to which application developers write implementations. Developers then link the request handlers to request URIs in the configuration file.

The dispatcher servlet calls a specific implementation upon receiving a request that passes the relevant information. The request generators may interact with the relevant business proxy to perform the business task. The handlers will pass information (which depends on the outcome of the business task) back to the dispatcher servlet so that the next view can be chosen.

In our framework the dispatcher servlet is the invoker, the request handler abstraction is the abstract command, and the concrete handler implementations are the concrete commands (in this case we don't have a receiver object). All this is further illustrated in the following class diagram:

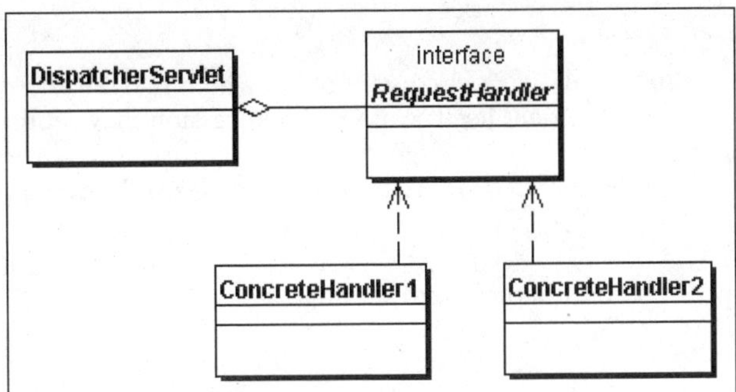

It is important to note that:

- The aggregation shown between `DispatcherServlet` and `RequestHandler` is implemented through a configuration object
- The actual aggregation is stored in a configuration object, which the class `DispatcherServlet` holds a reference to

The details of the implementation are explained later in the chapter.

Configuring the Framework

The framework should be extensible and configurable, and should allow developers to declaratively link request URIs to XML DOM generators, schema documents, and request handlers. In this section we will design and implement the configuration module, which consists of a configuration XML file and a set of configuration classes.

> *We can't store this configuration information in* `web.xml` *because the configuration information you can store in the deployment descriptor is restricted by the deployment descriptor DTD. The only customized information you can include is servlet, filter and context init parameters. For extra flexibility an external configuration file is always necessary.*

Before we delve into the design intricacies of the configuration module, we need to take a brief look at XPath expressions, as we will be using them quite extensively to read our configuration data and in the design of our tag libraries.

An Overview of XPath

XPath is a set of expressions, formulated by the W3C (http://www.w3c.org/), and used to access parts of XML documents relative to a given node. XPath expressions allow us to access nodes or lists of nodes that are descendants, siblings and ancestors. XPath expressions also allow us to filter the node lists by specifying conditions that must be met. XPath also provides expressions for manipulating strings, numbers, and booleans.

> **We only have space here to take a whirlwind tour of XPath. For more information you should refer to *Professional Java XML* from *Wrox Press* (*ISBN 1-861004-01-X*) or *Java XML Programmer's Reference* from *Wrox Press* (*ISBN 1-861005-20-2*).**

XPath expressions are evaluated relative to a context node, which may be an arbitrary node within the document or the document root element itself. An XPath expression may return one of the following:

- A set of nodes that contain zero or more unordered nodes without duplicates
- A Boolean
- An IEEE compliant 64-bit floating point number
- A string

Location Paths

The most commonly used XPath expression is a **location path**. This selects a set of nodes relative to the context node. Location paths may be expressed as absolute paths starting from the document root or relative to the context node. If it is expressed as an absolute path it starts with the character '`/`'. Location paths allow both expanded and abbreviated syntaxes and we will cover both.

Location paths are composed of one or more **location steps**, separated by the character '`/`'. An absolute location path always starts with the '`/`' character and is relative to the document root, whereas a relative location path is always relative to the context node.

Location Steps

Location steps are the building blocks for location paths. A location step mainly consists of three parts:

- **An axis**
  This specifies the relationship that the node we want to select has with the context node. For example, the `child` axis specifies that the selected nodes should be the children of the context node.
- **A node test**
  This tests the name of the node from the node list selected by the axis
- **Zero or more predicates**
  These may be used to further filter down the nodes from the node list

Location steps are expressed as the axis and the node test separated by a double colon followed by the predicates in square braces. An example for a location step is:

```
child::skill[position() = 1]
```

This selects the first child node with the name `skills` of the context node. If it was used with the following XML, with `<skills>` as the context node:

```
<skills>
  <skill id="1"><skill-name>Java</skill-name></skill>
  <skill id="2"><skill-name>C++</skill-name></skill>
```

```
    <skill id="3"><skill-name>Cobol</skill-name></skill>
  </skills>
```

it would select the `<skill id="1"><skill-name>Java</skill-name></skill>` node.

Location paths may also be composed of multiple location steps. For example:

```
child::skill[position() = 1]/child::skill-name
```

This selects all the `skill-name` children of the first `skill` child of the context node. The expression shown above will select the `skill-name` element with the content as `Java` when evaluated using the `skills` element as the context node.

Axes

The axes available in XPath are:

Axis	Description
`child`	The immediate children of the context node
`descendant`	All descendants of the context node
`parent`	The immediate parent of the context node
`ancestor`	All ancestors of the context node
`following-sibling`	All the next siblings of the context node
`preceding-sibling`	All the preceding siblings of the context nodes
`following`	All the nodes following the context node in the document excluding descendants, namespaces and attributes
`preceding`	All the nodes preceding the context node in the document excluding descendants, namespaces, and attributes
`attribute`	All the attributes of the context node
`namespace`	All the namespace declarations within the context node
`self`	The context node itself
`descendant-or-self`	All the descendants of the context node and the context node itself
`ancestor-or-self`	All the ancestors of the context node and the context node itself

Node Tests

Every axis in XPath has an associated principal node type decided by the type of the axis:

- An attribute axis has the node type "attribute"
- A namespace axis has the node type "namespace"
- All other axes have the type "element"

A node test only returns those nodes if both of the following conditions are met:

- The node type matches the principal node type of the associated axis
- The expanded name exactly matches the defined node test

The principal node types include elements, text content, comments and processing instructions. For example in the following location path:

```
child::fName
```

Only the child elements of the context node with the name `fName` are selected when evaluated against the element `name` in this XML fragment:

```
<name fName="This is an attribute">
  <fName>This is element content</fName>
</name>
```

Even if the context node has an attribute by the name `fName`, it is not selected.

The character '*' can be used for all the nodes with types matching the principal node type of the axis. For example, in the location path shown below, all the child elements of the context node are selected:

```
child::*
```

The above expression will select both child elements `fName` and `lName` when evaluated against the element `name` in the XML fragment below:

```
<name
  <fName>Luca</fName>
  <lName>Vialli</lName>
</name>
```

In addition the XPath specification defines the following predefined node tests:

Test	Description
`text()`	Selects all the text node children of the context node
`comment()`	Selects all the comment node children of the context node
`processing-instruction()`	Selects the processing instructions children of the context node

Abbreviated Syntax

If we want to select all the `first-name` attributes of the `name` child of the first `employee` child of the context node, we can write this:

```
child::employee[postion() = 1]/child::name/attribute::first-name
```

However, this syntax is cumbersome and tedious to write – this is where abbreviated syntax steps in. Abbreviated syntax lets us use an abbreviated notation for axes. In this particular example abbreviated syntax means that the child axis becomes the default axis and the attribute axis is shortened to the character '@'. This means that the above location path can also be written as:

```
employee[position() = 1]/name/@first-name
```

Some of the other commonly used abbreviations are:

- The expression "." represents the self axis
- The expression ".." represents the parent axis
- The expression ".//" represents the descendants axis
- The predicate `[position() = 1]` may be abbreviated to `[1]`

Xalan and XPathAPI

The XPath specification only defines the syntax for the location paths and other details. To use XPath expressions you need to use software that implements the specification and provides an API for executing XPath expressions. The core framework code explained in this chapter uses Xalan 2 from the Apache Software Foundation, which can be downloaded from http://xml.apache.org/.

The Xalan API provides a class called `org.apache.xpath.XPathAPI` that provides a set of static methods that are used to execute XPath expressions relative to a context node. These methods return either a single node or a list of nodes. There are two methods that are used quite extensively in our framework:

```
public static NodeList selectNodeList(Node contextNode, String expr)
                       throws TransformerException
```

This method selects a list of nodes defined by the expression relative to the specified context node. If there are no nodes available for the specified arguments, an empty node list is returned.

```
public static NodeList selectSingleNode(Node contextNode, String expr)
                       throws TransformerException
```

This method selects a single node defined by the expression relative to the specified context node. If there is no node available for the specified arguments, `null` is returned. If there is more than one node, the first node is returned.

Designing the Configuration System

We are now ready to design the configuration system, including:

- The XML data model used for the configuration file
- The classes that compose the configuration module
- The Servlet 2.3 application event listeners used to initialize the configuration objects

Designing the XML Data Model

In this section we will identify the elements and attributes we need to define in our configuration file the requirements we extracted from our analysis earlier in the chapter. The result of this will be a DTD that can be used to validate an XML configuration file.

Document Element

We will call the document element `config`:

```
<!ELEMENT config (...)>
```

The next task is to define the content model for our document element.

DOM Generators

In the requirements analysis section we mentioned that we should define a pool of DOM generators that could be used by multiple request URIs. To implement this we need to uniquely identify all the DOM generators used within the system in the configuration file so that the configuration system can read and initialize instances of those classes. Accordingly, the first element in the content model for the document element is an element that encapsulates all the DOM generators. We will call this element `dom-generators`:

```
<!ELEMENT config(dom-generators,...)>
<!ELEMENT dom-generators(...)>
```

Next we need to identify the content model for the element `dom-generators`. This element will include zero or more elements that uniquely identify the DOM generators used within the system. These elements should have unique identifiers so that they can be linked to the request URIs. We will also need to define the fully qualified class names for these implementations. We will call this element `dom-generator` and define two attributes named `id` and `class`:

```
<!ELEMENT dom-generators(dom-generator*)>
<!ELEMENT dom-generator EMPTY>
<!ATTLIST dom-generator id ID #REQUIRED
                        class CDATA #REQUIRED>
```

Request Handlers

In the requirements analysis section we mentioned that we should define a pool of request handlers that could be reused by multiple request URIs. To do this we need to uniquely identify all the request handlers used within the system in the configuration file, so that the system can read and initialize instances of these classes. Accordingly, the next element in the content model of the document element is an element that encapsulates all the request handlers. We will call this element `request-handlers`:

```
<!ELEMENT config(dom-generators,request-handlers,...)>
<!ELEMENT request-handlers(...)>
```

The next step is to identify the content model for the element `request-handlers`. This element will contain zero or more elements that uniquely identify the request handlers used within the system. These elements should have unique identifiers so that they can be linked to the request URIs. We will also need to define the fully qualified class names for these implementations. We will call the element `request-handler` and define two attributes named `id` and `class`:

```
<!ELEMENT request-handlers(request-handler*)>
<!ELEMENT request-handler EMPTY>
<!ATTLIST request-handler id ID #REQUIRED
                          class CDATA #REQUIRED>
```

Request Mapping

Next we need to map the request URIs to request handlers, DOM generators, and schema documents. We will also define a mapping for each request URI that maps logical names to resources within the web application responsible for rendering the next view for the URI. The object modeling the request mapping information will be passed to the request handler implementation so that it can select a resource for rendering the next view by specifying a logical name, depending on the outcome of processing the request. We will also have to define a special kind of resource that can be used by the handlers for forwarding the page that issued the current request if any validation errors occur.

We will call the outermost element `request-mapping`. A request mapping is uniquely identified by a URI so we will define an attribute called URI for this element. The document element may contain zero or more request mapping elements. Hence the content model for the document element will be:

```
<!ELEMENT config(dom-generators, request-handlers, request-mapping*)>
<!ELEMENT request-mapping(...)>
<!ATTLIST request-mapping URI CDATA #required>
```

We need to define the content model for the `request-mapping` element. It should have a link to the `request-handler` element declared earlier in the `request-handlers` element so we will define an element called `handler` that has an attribute `ref` of type `IDREF` that links to the `id` attribute of the relevant `request-handler` element:

```
<!ELEMENT request-mapping(handler,...)>
<!ELEMENT handler EMPTY>
<!ATTLIST handler ref IDREF #required>
```

We need to define a link to the `dom-generator` element declared earlier. We will define an element called `dom` that has an attribute `ref` of type `IDREF` that links to the `id` attribute of the relevant `dom-generator` element. This element should also define the name and scope under which the generated XML node is stored (the only scopes allowed are request and session). Hence we will define two more attributes called `dom-name` and `dom-scope` of type `CDATA`. This element is optional, which allows users to selectively choose URIs for which XML nodes are not generated:

```
<!ELEMENT request-mapping(handler,generator?,...)>
<!ELEMENT dom EMPTY>
<!ATTLIST dom ref IDREF #required
          dom-name CDATA #required
          dom-scope CDATA #required>
```

We need to define an optional schema that is associated with the request, which can be used by the validating module to validate the data entered by the users. We will define an element called `schema` with three attributes named `location`, `namespace-aware` and `target-namespace`. The first one is a mandatory attribute of type `CDATA` that identifies the physical location of the schema document. The second one is an enumerated attribute called with a list of values as `yes` and `no` (with the default value as `no`). The third attribute defines the target namespace if the schema is namespace aware:

```
<!ELEMENT request-mapping(handler,generator?,schema?,...)>
<!ELEMENT schema EMPTY>
<!ATTLIST schema location CDATA #required
              namespace-aware (yes|no) "no"
              target-namespace CDATA #implied>
```

We define a collection of resources as a map of logical names to physical resources. We will also define whether a resource should be redirected or forwarded to the browser (with the default as forwarded). Here we will define a container element called `forwards` that contains zero or more `forward` elements. Each `forward` element will have two mandatory attributes of type `CDATA` named `name` and `resource`. An enumerated attribute called `redirect` with a list of values as `true` and `false` is also defined (with the default value as `false`):

```
<!ELEMENT request-mapping(handler,generator?,schema?,forwards,...)
<!ELEMENT forwards(forward*)>
<!ELEMENT forward EMPTY>
<!ATTLIST forward name CDATA #required
               resource CDATA #required
               redirect (true|false) "false">
```

Lastly, we will define an element named `input` that will contain the information regarding the resource that rendered the page that triggered the current request. This element will have a single mandatory attribute named `resource` of type `CDATA`:

```
<!ELEMENT request-mapping(handler,generator?,schema?,forwards,input?)
<!ELEMENT input EMPTY>
<!ATTLIST input resource CDATA #required>
```

Putting it all Together

Let's take a look at the completed DTD for the configuration file:

```
<!ELEMENT config(dom-generators, request-handlers, request-mapping*)>
<!ELEMENT dom-generators(dom-generator*)>
<!ELEMENT dom-generator EMPTY>
<!ELEMENT request-handlers(request-handler*)>
<!ELEMENT request-handler EMPTY>
<!ELEMENT request-mapping(handler,generator?,schema?,forwards,input?)>
<!ELEMENT handler EMPTY>
<!ELEMENT dom EMPTY>
<!ELEMENT schema EMPTY>
<!ELEMENT forwards(forward*)>
<!ELEMENT forward EMPTY>
<!ELEMENT input EMPTY>
<!ATTLIST dom-generator id ID #REQUIRED
          class CDATA #REQUIRED>
<!ATTLIST request-handler id ID #REQUIRED
          class CDATA #REQUIRED>
<!ATTLIST handler ref IDREF #required>
<!ATTLIST dom ref IDREF #required
          dom-name CDATA #required
          dom-scope CDATA #required>
<!ATTLIST schema location CDATA #required
          namespace-aware (yes|no) "no"
          target-namespave CDATA #IMPLIED>
```

```
<!ATTLIST forward name CDATA #required
          resource CDATA #required
          redirect (true|false) "false">
<!ATTLIST input resource CDATA #required>
```

Sample Configuration File

An example of the configuration file for our framework is shown here:

```
<config>
  <request-handlers>
    <request-handler id="create-handler"
                     class="application.handlers.EmployeeCreateHandler"/>
  </request-handlers>

  <dom-generators>
    <dom-generator id="create-generator"
                   class="application.xml.EmployeeDOMGenerator"/>
  </dom-generators>
```

This is the request mapping for the URI `EmployeeList.do`. The request URI we use should be mapped to the controller servlet used within the framework. In this example, all the request URIs that match `*.do` are mapped to the controller servlet in the web application deployment descriptor.

```
  <request uri="EmployeeCreate.do">
```

We need a reference to the declared request handler responsible for handling the request. Of course, a request handler can be shared by more than one mapping:

```
    <handler ref="create-handler"/>
```

Now we have a reference to the declared DOM generator that is responsible for generating the XML node for the request. Like a request handler, a DOM generator may be shared by more than one mapping. The name and scope under which the generated XML node is stored are also defined:

```
    <generator ref="create-generator"
               dom-name="employee"
               dom-scope="request"/>
```

Here we declare the schema validation details:

```
    <schema namespace-aware="false"
            location="http://localhost:8080/employee/schema/employee.xsd"/>
```

Now we define the forward list:

```
    <forwards>
      <forward name="SUCCESS" resource="EmployeeList.jsp" redirect="false"/>
    </forwards>
```

Finally, we define the resource to which the request should be forwarded if a validation error occurs:

```
    <input resource="/EmployeeNew.do"/>
  </request>
</config>
```

Mapping Configuration XML to Java Classes

In this section we will map our XML data model to a set of Java classes. The advantage of modeling the configuration data as XML is that we can cache the configuration information in memory using a bean with application scope so that our filters and servlets can easily access it. We will have classes that encapsulate:

- The configuration file
- DOM generator mappings
- Request handler mappings
- Request mapping information
- Schema information
- Forwards
- DOM generation information

The following is the class diagram for the configuration module:

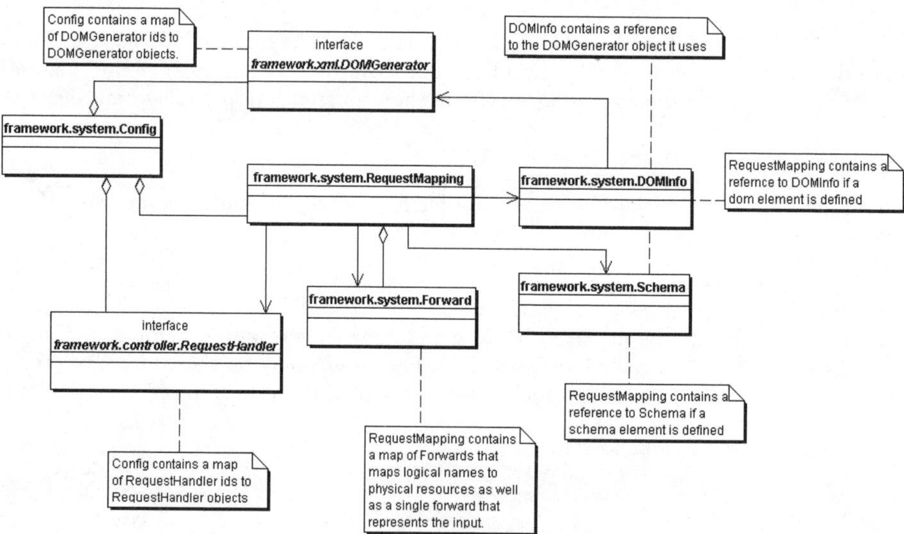

Before we delve into the details of the classes shown above we need to cover three other classes used to define constants and handling exceptions.

The AttributeNames Interface

The `AttributeNames` interface defines:

- The name by which the configuration object is stored as a servlet context attribute
- The name by which error messages are stored as request attributes by the validation engine

Let's take a look at the code for this interface:

```
package framework.system;

public interface AttributeNames {
```

Define the name under which the configuration object is stored as a servlet context attribute:

```
   public static final String CONFIG = "CONFIG";
```

Define the name under which error messages are stored within the request scope on validation and business rules violation errors:

```
    public static final String ERROR_MESSAGE = "ERROR_MESSAGE";
}
```

Error Handling

The framework provides an exception class and an interface that can be used for severity based exception handling. You should refer to Chapter 7 for coverage of severity based error handling. The exception class provides exception nesting and provides a host of overloaded constructors for passing messages, severity levels, and root exceptions. The methods to print the stack trace are overloaded so as to print the stack trace of the parent exception as well.

The Severity Interface

```
package framework.system;

public interface Severity {
```

Create static fields to indicate expected and unexpected errors:

```
  public static final int EXPECTED = 0;
  public static final int UNEXPECTED = 1;
}
```

The FrameworkException Class

```
package framework.system;

import java.io.PrintStream;
import java.io.PrintWriter;

public class FrameworkException extends Exception {
```

Define fields to hold the severity of the exception and the parent exception:

```
  private int severity;
  private Throwable parent;
```

This constructor can be used to create an exception instance by specifying the message, root exception and the severity level:

```
  public FrameworkException(String message,
                            Throwable parent,
                            int severity) {
    super(message);
    this.parent = parent;
    this.severity = severity;
  }
```

This constructor can be used to create an exception instance by specifying the message and the root exception. The severity level defaults to expected exception:

```
public FrameworkException(String message, Throwable parent) {
  this(message, parent, Severity.EXPECTED);
}
```

This constructor can be used to create an exception instance by specifying the message and the severity level. The root exception is a null reference in this case:

```
public FrameworkException(String message, int severity) {
  this(message, null, severity);
}
```

This constructor can be used to create an exception instance by specifying the severity and the root exception. The message defaults to that of the root exception:

```
public FrameworkException(Throwable parent, int severity) {
  this(parent.getMessage(), parent, severity);
}
```

This constructor can be used to create an exception instance by specifying the message. The severity level defaults to expected exception and the root exception is a null reference:

```
public FrameworkException(String message) {
  this(message, null, Severity.EXPECTED);
}
```

This constructor can be used to create an exception instance by specifying the root exception. The message defaults to that of the root exception and the severity defaults to expected level:

```
public FrameworkException(Throwable parent) {
  this(parent.getMessage(), parent, Severity.EXPECTED);
}
```

Define a method to return the severity level:

```
public int getSeverity() {
  return severity;
}
```

Finally, the `printStackTrace()` methods are overridden to print the stack trace of the root exception (if available) before printing that of the current exception:

```
public void printStackTrace() {
  if(parent != null) {
    parent.printStackTrace();
  }
  super.printStackTrace();
}

public void printStackTrace(PrintStream ps) {
  if(parent != null) {
    parent.printStackTrace(ps);
  }
  super.printStackTrace(ps);
}
```

```
    public void printStackTrace(PrintWriter pw) {
      if(parent != null) {
        parent.printStackTrace(pw);
      }
      super.printStackTrace(pw);
    }
  }
```

The Forward Class

The `Forward` class encapsulates information about the resource to be used to render the next view. This class is also used to create objects that store information about the input page that should be sent back to the client if validation errors occur for specific URIs.

The class declares two attributes that correspond to the `resource` and `redirect` attributes defined in the `action` element of the configuration DTD. The first attribute is a string that identifies the resource path and the second one is a Boolean that states whether or not the response should be redirected back to the client.

For the objects modeling the `input` element of the configuration DTD, the value of the redirect attribute is always false. The class defines getter methods for the attributes and the initial values of the attributes are set in the constructor:

```
  package framework.system;

  public class Forward {

    protected String resource;
    protected boolean redirect;

    public String getResource() {
      return resource;
    }

    public boolean isRedirect() {
      return redirect;
    }

    public Forward(String resource, boolean redirect) {
      this.resource = resource;
      this.redirect = redirect;
    }
```

We also have an overloaded constructor that allows us to set the initial value of the `redirect` attribute to `false`:

```
    public Forward(String resource) {
      this(resource, false);
    }
  }
```

The Schema Class

The `Schema` class models the `schema` element defined in the configuration DTD. It defines three attributes corresponding to the attributes defined for the element in the DTD as well as standard getter and setter methods for these attributes:

```
package framework.system;

public class Schema {
```

We define the attributes to store information on the schema associated with a given request URI. The first attribute defines whether the schema is namespace aware. This attribute defines whether the XML documents generated by the DOM generator module are namespace aware. The DOM generator module uses the value of this attribute to decide whether to add additional information in the generated XML node that can be used by the schema processor (the namespace awareness of XML documents validated using schemas are explained in the section on XML schemas):

```
  private boolean namespaceAware;

  public boolean isNamespaceAware() {
    return namespaceAware;
  }

  public void setNamespaceAware(boolean namespaceAware) {
    this.namespaceAware = namespaceAware;
  }
```

The second attribute defines the physical location of the schema that can be used to validate the generated DOM:

```
  private String location;

  public String getLocation() {
    return location;
  }

  public void setLocation(String location) {
    this.location = location;
  }
```

The third attribute defines the target namespace:

```
  private String targetNamespace;

  public String getTargetNamespace() {
    return targetNamespace;
  }

  public void setTargetNamespace(String targetNamespace) {
    this.targetNamespace = targetNamespace;
  }
}
```

The DOMInfo Class

The `DOMInfo` class encapsulates information about the details of DOM generation for a given URI. An instance of this class stores a reference to the object that implements the `DOMGenerator` interface for the relevant request URI. (The `DOMGenerator` interface is discussed in detail later in this chapter.)

Instances of `DOMInfo` only store a *reference* to the `DOMGenerator` implementation stored in a pool of `DOMGenerator` implementations – they do not store their own copy.

DOMInfo also has attributes that identify the name and scope under which the generated XML node is stored:

```
package framework.system;

import framework.xml.DOMGenerator;

public class DOMInfo {

  private String domName;
  private String scope;
  private DOMGenerator domGenerator;

  public String getDOMName() {
    return domName;
  }

  public void setDOMName(String domName) {
    this.domName = domName;
  }

  public String getScope() {
    return scope;
  }

  public void setScope(String scope) {
    this.scope = scope;
  }

  public DOMGenerator getDOMGenerator() {
    return domGenerator;
  }

  public void setDOMGenerator(DOMGenerator domGenerator) {
    this.domGenerator = domGenerator;
  }

  public DOMInfo() {
  }
}
```

The RequestMapping Class

The RequestMapping class encapsulates the information about a request URI mapping, including:

- A reference to the DOMInfo associated with the request (if a dom element is defined for the request mapping in the configuration file).
- A reference to the Schema associated with the request (if a schema element is defined for the request mapping in the configuration file).
- A reference to a Forward object that represents the resource that will be used to render the page when the request is sent back to the client if validation errors occur.
- A map of names to Forward objects, which maps the logical name of the forwards defined in the configuration file to actual instances of Forward. The scope of the logical names is a given request URI mapping.

- A reference to the RequestHandler object that is responsible for handling the requests with the request URI matching the URI attribute defined for the request-mapping element. Objects of this class only store a reference to the RequestHandler implementation stored in a pool of RequestHandler implementations rather than storing their own copy.

```
package framework.system;

import framework.xml.DOMGenerator;
import framework.controller.RequestHandler;

import java.util.HashMap;

public class RequestMapping {

  private DOMInfo domInfo;
  private HashMap forwardMap;
  private Forward input;
  private RequestHandler requestHandler;
  private Schema schema;
```

Define the standard getter and setter methods for the domInfo, input, requestHandler, and schema attributes:

```
  public DOMInfo getDOMInfo() {
    return domInfo;
  }

  public void setDOMInfo(DOMInfo domInfo) {
    this.domInfo = domInfo;
  }

  public Forward getInput() {
    return input;
  }

  public void setInput(Forward input) {
    this.input = input;
  }

  public RequestHandler getRequestHandler() {
    return requestHandler;
  }

  public void setRequestHandler(RequestHandler requestHandler) {
    this.requestHandler = requestHandler;
  }

  public Schema getSchema() {
    return schema;
  }

  public void setSchema(Schema schema) {
    this.schema = schema;
  }
```

The getter and setter methods for forwardMap are somewhat different from the standard forms. We declare a method to get a Forward object by specifying the name defined in the configuration file:

```
  public Forward getForward(String name) {
    return (Forward)forwardMap.get(name);
  }
```

Finally, we declare a method to set the map of `Forward` objects for a given request URI mapping:

```
  public void setForwardMap(HashMap forwardMap) {
    this.forwardMap = forwardMap;
  }
}
```

The Config Class

The `Config` class is designed to be a wrapper for all the configuration information it stores:

- A map of `RequestHandler` ids to `RequestHandler` objects, which is initialized from the `request-handlers` element in the configuration file.
- A map of `DOMGenerator` ids to `DOMGenerator` objects, which is initialized from the `dom-generators` element in the configuration file.
- A map of request URIs to `RequestMapping` objects, which is populated from the various `request-mapping` elements defined in the configuration file. The `RequestMapping` objects store references to `RequestHandler` objects stored in the `RequestHandler` map. They also store references to `DOMGenerator` objects stored in the `DOMGenerator` map through the `DOMInfo` object.

This class defines only one public method, which returns a `RequestMapping` object for a given request URI. Once we have a reference to the `RequestMapping` object we access all the information we need, such as the `DOMGenerator`, or `RequestHandler`, that is associated with the request. Accordingly, `Config` will be used in our filters and dispatcher servlet to pass information on the request mapping to the associated request handlers and DOM generators.

The constructor for this class takes the location of the configuration file and parses the XML in it. XPath expressions are then used to navigate the DOM, allowing us to extract the information required to create the relevant objects.

The events that occur are shown in the following activity diagram:

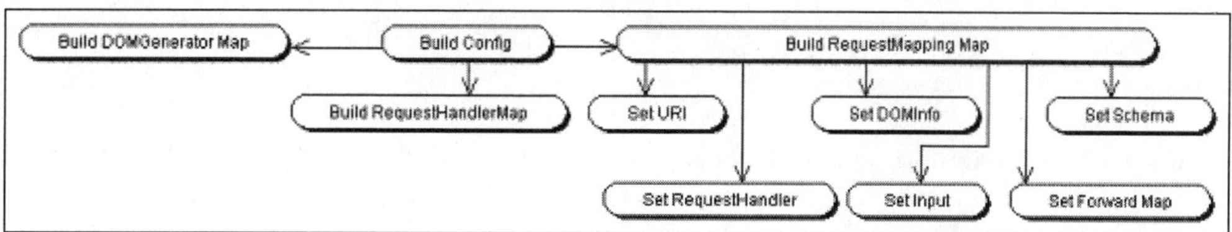

The configuration file is read and parsed into an XML DOM. Next, all the child elements of the `request-handlers` element are read, and a map is created of the request handler ids and the associated request handler objects. The request handler objects are instantiated by dynamically loading the `class` attribute value defined for the `request-handler` elements.

Similarly, all the child elements of the dom-generators element are read and a map is created of the DOM generator ids to the DOM generator objects. The DOM generator objects are instantiated by dynamically loading the class attribute value defined for the dom-generator elements.

The request-mapping elements are read one at a time and a map of the request URI defined for by the URI attribute of the elements to RequestMapping objects is created. When creating the RequestMapping object the following sequence of events occurs:

- The request handler reference is retrieved from the request handler map and stored as an instance variable. We mentioned earlier that the id attribute of request-handler elements defined within the request-handlers element is of type ID and the ref attribute of the handler element defined within the request-mapping elements is of type IDREF. These two attributes are linked to each other.
- If a dom child element is specified for the request-mapping element, a DOMInfo object is created and stored in the RequestMapping object. This object stores a reference to the relevant DOMGenerator class from the DOM generator map. We mentioned that the id attribute of dom-generator elements defined within the dom-generators element is of type ID and the ref attribute of the generator element defined within the request-mapping elements is of type IDREF. These two attributes are linked to each other. The DOMInfo object also stores the name and scope under which the generated XML node is stored.
- If a schema child element is specified for the request-mapping element, a Schema object is created and stored in the RequestMapping object. The Schema object stores the location and target namespace of the schema as well as whether or not the schema is namespace aware.
- A map of logical forward names to the Forward objects are created from the forwards element of the request-mapping element, and stored in the RequestMapping object. The forward names are extracted from the name attribute of the forward elements defined within the forwards element. The Forward objects store information on the path to the resource and whether the resource should be redirected or forwarded.
- If an input child element is specified for the request-mapping element, a Forward object is created and stored in the RequestMapping object. The Forward object stores information on the path to the input resource and the redirect attribute is always false.

Let's take a look at the source code for the Config class:

```
package framework.system;

import java.util.HashMap;
import java.io.InputStream;
import java.io.IOException;
```

This time we need to import the interfaces specified by the W3C that model the various XML entities:

```
import org.w3c.dom.Node;
import org.w3c.dom.NodeList;
import org.w3c.dom.NamedNodeMap;
import org.w3c.dom.Document;

import org.xml.sax.SAXException;
import javax.xml.transform.TransformerException;
```

```
import javax.xml.parsers.DocumentBuilderFactory;
import javax.xml.parsers.DocumentBuilder;
import javax.xml.parsers.ParserConfigurationException;

import framework.controller.RequestHandler;

import framework.xml.DOMGenerator;

import org.apache.xpath.XPathAPI;
import java.util.Collection;

public class Config {
```

We declare the attributes to store the map of DOM generators, request handlers, and request mappings:

```
  protected HashMap domGeneratorMap = new HashMap();
  protected HashMap requestHandlerMap = new HashMap();
  protected HashMap requestMappingMap = new HashMap();
```

The constructor takes an input stream to the configuration file, parses it into an XML document, and calls the private methods to create the configuration objects.

```
  public Config(InputStream stream) throws FrameworkException {
    try {
      DocumentBuilderFactory builderFactory =
                               DocumentBuilderFactory.newInstance();
      DocumentBuilder builder = builderFactory.newDocumentBuilder();
      Document document = builder.parse(stream);
      Node root = document.getDocumentElement();
      buildConfig(root);
```

If the parser classes are available in the classpath and the configuration XML is well formed and valid no exceptions will be thrown, which is why the exceptions are marked as unexpected when they are re-thrown in the `catch` clause:

```
    } catch(ParserConfigurationException e) {
        throw new FrameworkException(e, Severity.UNEXPECTED);
    } catch(SAXException e) {
        throw new FrameworkException(e, Severity.UNEXPECTED);
    } catch(IOException e) {
        throw new FrameworkException(e, Severity.UNEXPECTED);
    }
  }
```

There is only one public method, which returns a reference to a `RequestMapping` object for a given URI:

```
  public RequestMapping getRequestMapping(String uri) {
    return (RequestMapping)requestMappingMap.get(uri);
  }
```

We declare a private method that populates the three maps:

```
  private void buildConfig(Node root) throws FrameworkException {
    buildDOMGeneratorMap(root);
    buildRequestHandlerMap(root);
    buildRequestMappingMap(root);
  }
```

We declare a method that builds the DOM generator map. This calls another utility method, `buildClassMap()`, by passing the XPath expression to the `dom-generator` elements, the context node as the document element, and a reference to the map in which the information should be stored:

```
private void buildDOMGeneratorMap(Node root) throws FrameworkException {
  String expr = "dom-generators/dom-generator";
  buildClassMap(root, expr, domGeneratorMap);
}
```

We declare a method that builds the request handler map. Again, this calls `buildClassMap()`, by passing the XPath expression to the `request-handler` elements, the context node as the document element, and a reference to the map in which the information should be stored:

```
private void buildRequestHandlerMap(Node root) throws FrameworkException {
  String expr = "request-handlers/request-handler";
  buildClassMap(root, expr, requestHandlerMap);
}
```

We declare a utility method used to populating the DOM generator and request handler maps. This method takes as arguments the context node, the required XPath expression, and the map to which the information should be stored. The `id` and `class` attributes of individual elements are read using XPath. The objects are dynamically instantiated from the `class` attribute value and stored in the map against the `id` attribute value:

```
private void buildClassMap(Node node, String expr, HashMap map)
            throws FrameworkException {
  try {
    NodeList nodes = XPathAPI.selectNodeList(node, expr);
    for(int i = 0;i < nodes.getLength();i++) {
      Node childNode = nodes.item(i);
      NamedNodeMap attributeMap =
      childNode.getAttributes();
      String name = attributeMap.getNamedItem("id").getNodeValue();
      String cls = attributeMap.getNamedItem("class").getNodeValue();
      map.put(name, Class.forName(cls).newInstance());
    }
  } catch(TransformerException e) {
      throw new FrameworkException(e, Severity.UNEXPECTED);
  } catch(ClassNotFoundException e) {
      throw new FrameworkException(e, Severity.UNEXPECTED);
  } catch(InstantiationException e) {
      throw new FrameworkException(e, Severity.UNEXPECTED);
  } catch(IllegalAccessException e) {
      throw new FrameworkException(e, Severity.UNEXPECTED);
  }
}
```

We declare a method that builds the map of request URIs to `RequestMapping` objects:

```
private void buildRequestMappingMap(Node root) throws FrameworkException {
  try {
```

We read all the `request-mapping` elements and iterate through the list one at a time:

```
    String expr = "request";
    NodeList requestList = XPathAPI.selectNodeList(root, expr);
    for(int i = 0;i < requestList.getLength();i++) {
      RequestMapping requestMapping = new RequestMapping();
```

Then read the next node in the list:

```
Node requestNode = requestList.item(i);
```

Then read the value of the uri attribute:

```
expr = "@uri";
Node uriNode = XPathAPI.selectSingleNode(requestNode, expr);
String uri = uriNode.getNodeValue();
```

We read the value of the ref attribute, which can be used to extract a RequestHandler object from the request handler map and store this reference in the RequestMapping object:

```
expr = "handler/@ref";
Node requestHandlerNode = XPathAPI.selectSingleNode(
                                                    requestNode, expr);
RequestHandler requestHandler = null;
if(requestHandlerNode != null) {
  requestHandler = (RequestHandler)requestHandlerMap.get(
                                  requestHandlerNode.getNodeValue());
}
requestMapping.setRequestHandler(requestHandler);
```

Next we call the method that returns the DOMInfo object associated with the request mapping and store it in the RequestMapping object. The request mapping object holds a reference to the DOMInfo object that in turn holds a reference to the concrete DOMGenerator instance. The RequestToDOMFilter will use this information for delegating the DOM generation task to the concrete DOMGenerator class associated with the current request:

```
requestMapping.setDOMInfo(getDOMInfo(requestNode));
```

Then we call the method that returns the Schema object associated with the request mapping and store it in the RequestMapping object. The RequestMapping object holds a reference to the Schema object that in turn holds a reference to the location of the schema file that will be used to validate the DOM generated by the RequestoDOMFilter. The DOMGenerator instances will use this information for adding extra information into the generated DOM that will be used by the schema processor:

```
requestMapping.setSchema(getSchema(requestNode));
```

We call the method that returns the Forward map object associated with the request mapping and store it in the RequestMapping object:

```
requestMapping.setForwardMap(getForwardMap(requestNode));
```

We then read the value of resource attribute of the input element (if it is defined) and create a Forward object setting the redirect attribute as false. We store this reference in the RequestMapping object:

```
expr = "input/@resource";
Node inputNode = XPathAPI.selectSingleNode(requestNode, expr);
Forward input = null;
if(inputNode != null) {
  input = new Forward(inputNode.getNodeValue(), false);
}
requestMapping.setInput(input);
```

Finally, we add the `RequestMapping` object to the request-mapping map against the URI:

```
        requestMappingMap.put(uri, requestMapping);
      }
    } catch(TransformerException e) {
      throw new FrameworkException(e, Severity.UNEXPECTED);
    }
  }
```

Now we declare a method that constructs a map of `Forward` objects associated with the request mapping:

```
  private HashMap getForwardMap(Node requestNode)
                  throws FrameworkException {
    try {
      String expr = "forwards/forward";
      NodeList forwardList = XPathAPI.selectNodeList(requestNode, expr);
      HashMap forwardMap = new HashMap();

      for(int i = 0;i < forwardList.getLength();i++) {
        Node forwardNode = forwardList.item(i);
        expr = "@name";
        Node nameNode = XPathAPI.selectSingleNode(forwardNode, expr);
        String name = nameNode.getNodeValue();
        expr = "@resource";
        Node resourceNode = XPathAPI.selectSingleNode(forwardNode, expr);
        String resource = resourceNode.getNodeValue();

        expr = "@redirect";
        Node redirectNode = XPathAPI.selectSingleNode(forwardNode, expr);
        boolean redirect = false;
        if(redirectNode != null) {
          redirect = Boolean.TRUE.equals(redirectNode.getNodeValue());
        }

        Forward forward = new Forward(resource, redirect);
        forwardMap.put(name, forward);
      }

      return forwardMap;

    } catch(TransformerException e) {
          throw new FrameworkException(e, Severity.UNEXPECTED);
    }
  }
```

We declare a method that returns the `DOMInfo` object associated with the request mapping if the `dom` element is specified:

```
  private DOMInfo getDOMInfo(Node requestNode) throws FrameworkException {
    try {
      String expr = "generator";
      Node domInfoNode = XPathAPI.selectSingleNode(requestNode, expr);
        if(domInfoNode == null) {
          return null;
        }

      DOMInfo domInfo = new DOMInfo();

      expr = "@dom-name";
      Node domNameNode = XPathAPI.selectSingleNode(domInfoNode, expr);
```

```
      String domName = domNameNode.getNodeValue();
      domInfo.setDOMName(domName);

      expr = "@scope";
      Node scopeNode = XPathAPI.selectSingleNode(requestNode, expr);
      String scope = "request";
      if(scopeNode != null) {
        scope = scopeNode.getNodeValue().toLowerCase();
      }
      if(!scope.equals("request") && !scope.equals("session")) {
        throw new FrameworkException("Invalid scope: " + scope,
                                               Severity.UNEXPECTED);
      }
      domInfo.setScope(scope);

      expr = "@ref";
      Node domGeneratorNode = XPathAPI.selectSingleNode(domInfoNode, expr);
      DOMGenerator domGenerator = null;
      domGenerator = (DOMGenerator)domGeneratorMap.get(
                                   domGeneratorNode.getNodeValue());
      domInfo.setDOMGenerator(domGenerator);

      return domInfo;
    } catch(TransformerException e) {
        throw new FrameworkException(e, Severity.UNEXPECTED);
    }
  }
```

We declare the method that constructs the Schema object associated with the request mapping (if the schema element is defined):

```
  private Schema getSchema(Node requestNode) throws FrameworkException {
    try {
      String expr = "schema";
      NodeList schemaList = XPathAPI.selectNodeList(requestNode, expr);

      if(schemaList.getLength() <= 0) {
        return null;
      }

      Schema schema = new Schema();

      expr = "schema/@namespace-aware";
      Node namespaceAwareNode = XPathAPI.selectSingleNode(
                                              requestNode, expr);
      schema.setNamespaceAware("YES".equalsIgnoreCase(
                             namespaceAwareNode.getNodeValue()));

      expr = "schema/@location";
      Node locationNode = XPathAPI.selectSingleNode(requestNode, expr);
      schema.setLocation(locationNode.getNodeValue());

      if(schema.isNamespaceAware()) {
        expr = "schema/@target-namespace";
        Node targetNamespaceNode = XPathAPI.selectSingleNode(
                                             requestNode, expr);
        schema.setTargetNamespace(targetNamespaceNode.getNodeValue());
      }

      return schema;
```

```
        } catch(TransformerException e) {
            throw new FrameworkException(e, Severity.UNEXPECTED);
        }
    }
}
```

Initializing and Storing the Configuration Object

Next we will have a look at where and how we will initialize the configuration object and where it will be stored. One obvious choice is to use a load-on-startup servlet but the Servlet 2.3 API provides an even more elegant mechanism for performing tasks on application initialization and destruction, as well as on session establishment and invalidation. For these purposes the Servlet 2.3 API provides four interfaces:

- `javax.servlet.ServletContextListener`
  This interface defines call back methods related to application startup and shutdown. The J2EE web container calls these methods when the web application is loaded and destroyed.
- `javax.servlet.ServletContextAttributesListener`
  This interface defines call back methods related to adding and removing attributes to the servlet context. The J2EE web container calls these methods when attributes are added to and removed from the servlet context.
- `javax.servlet.HttpSessionListener`
  This interface defines call back methods related to establishment and invalidation of sessions. The J2EE web container calls these methods when sessions are established, invalidated, or expired.
- `javax.servlet.HttpSessionAttributesListener`
  This interface defines call back methods for adding and removing attributes to the session. The J2EE web container calls these methods when attributes are added to and removed from the sessions.

We will use the `ServletContextListener` interface to initialize the configuration object and store it as a servlet context attribute. For this we need to write a class that implements this interface and provides the logic in the call back method that is invoked on application startup that:

- Reads the configuration file
- Creates the configuration object
- Stores the configuration object as a servlet context attribute.

We will also have to declare this class as a listener in the web application deployment descriptor and define the location of the configuration file as a context initialization parameter.

Let's take a look at the source code for `ServletContextListener`:

```
package framework.system;

import javax.servlet.ServletContextListener;
import javax.servlet.ServletContextEvent;
import javax.servlet.ServletContext;

public class Initializer implements ServletContextListener {
```

```
    public void contextInitialized(ServletContextEvent event) {
      try {
        System.out.println("Application starting.");
```

Get the servlet context from the servlet context event:

```
        ServletContext ctx = event.getServletContext();
```

Read the location of the configuration file as a context init parameter:

```
        String configFile = ctx.getInitParameter("config");
```

Create the configuration object and store it as a servlet context attribute:

```
        Config config = new Config(ctx.getResourceAsStream(configFile));
        ctx.setAttribute(AttributeNames.CONFIG, config);

        System.out.println("Application initialized.");
      } catch(FrameworkException e) {
          e.printStackTrace();
          throw new RuntimeException(e.getMessage());
      }
    }

    public void contextDestroyed(ServletContextEvent event) {}
  }
```

The following is an excerpt from the web application deployment descriptor that shows how the context init parameter and the context listener are registered:

```
    <context-param>
      <param-name>config</param-name>
      <param-value>/config/config.xml</param-value>
    </context-param>

    <listener>
      <listener-class>framework.system.Initializer</listener-class>
    </listener>
```

Summary

This chapter was the first of three that deal with a web application framework that allows J2EE web applications to easily handle XML.

We discussed why it would be useful for a web application to be built using a framework that allowed the seamless integration of the presentation tier with the underlying XML data model – just as Struts ties instances of JavaBeans to HTML forms and form elements.

Our aim was to create a framework that would allow data to be:

- Easily abstracted as XML nodes
- Validated by a generic validation engine using user supplied XML schemas
- Easily rendered to a variety of devices

In this chapter we explored the requirements of the framework in general and decided on an MVC based architecture. We then went on to design and build some of the interfaces and classes required for the framework. In doing this it was necessary for us to briefly introduce XPath, as well as some of the latest additions to the Servlet 2.3 API. Finally, we designed a flexible system for configuring applications that are built using the framework.

In the next chapter we will continue to build our framework. The next step is to implement the filters that will allow DOM generation and validation. We will also design and implement a custom tag library that can render the data stored in an XML DOM.

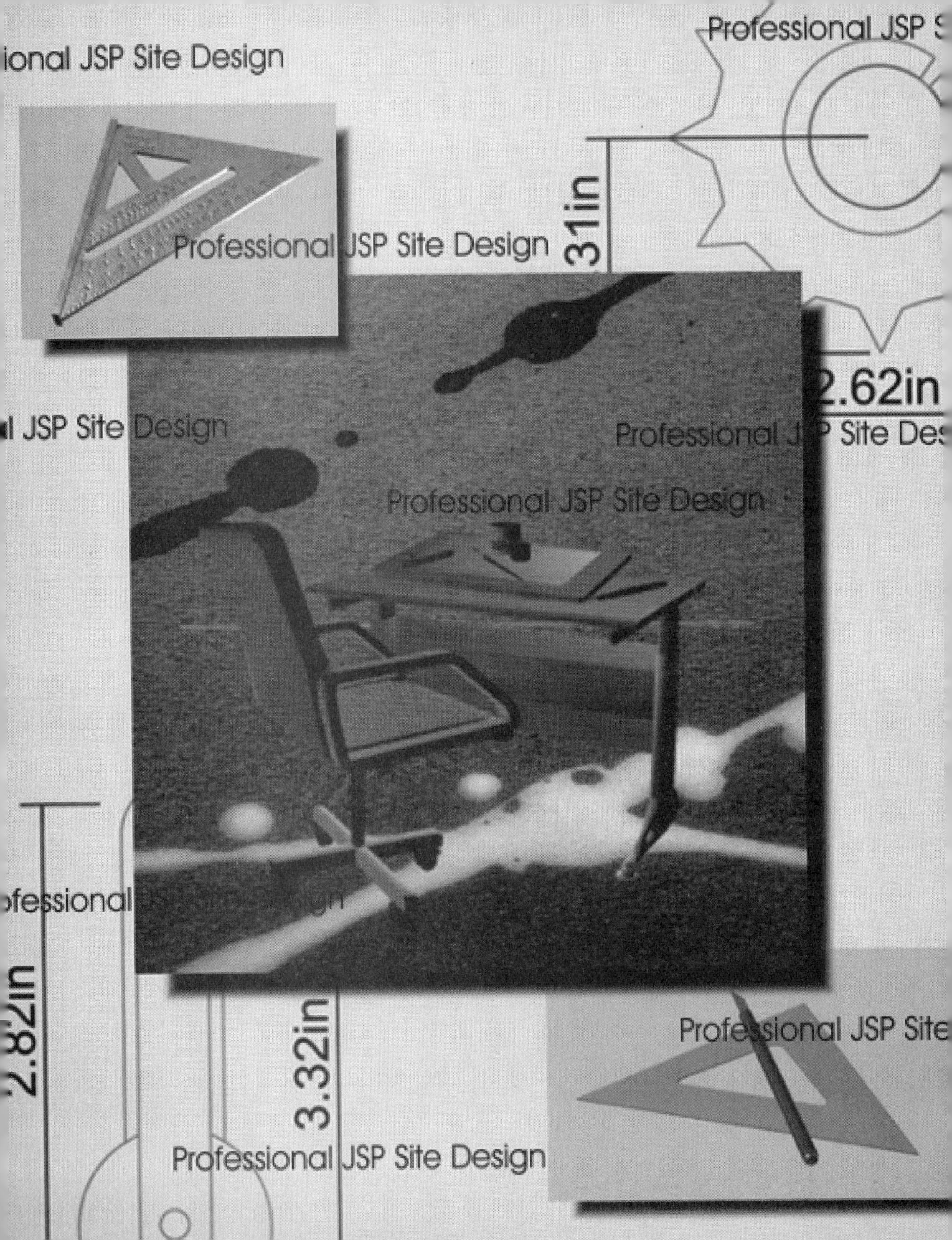
Professional JSP Site Design
31in
Professional JSP Site Design
2.62in
Professional JSP Site Design
3.32in
Professional JSP Site Design

16

An XML-JSP Framework – 2

In the last chapter we began the construction of an XML-JSP framework that can be used to build web applications that could function as a front end for enterprise systems generating and consuming XML. We looked in detail at the design of our framework, and identified patterns in the design that pointed us towards possible implementation solutions.

In this chapter we will complete our implementation of the framework. There are two parts of the framework still to be created:

- The filters that will generate and validate XML
- Two custom tag libraries: one to render HTML forms and the other to perform various actions on XML nodes

Implementing the Filters

We mentioned in Chapter 15 that we will use filters to generate XML nodes and to validate the data sent by clients, although we didn't go into any detail about how they would be implemented. The validation of the data is dependant on XML schemas that the application developer will link to specific collections of request URIs. For example, we could configure our application to use one schema to validate request URIs that match `input/*` and to use another schema to validate request URIs that match `display/*`.

We will begin by looking at how we can use a filter to generate XML nodes.

Abstract HTTP Filter

The filter API makes use of interfaces found in the `javax.servlet` package – in particular `ServletRequest` and `ServletResponse`. Our framework will use HTTP requests only, so we will need to write an implementation of the `Filter` interface that filters HTTP requests specifically. We will call this implementation `AbstractHttpFilter`. We will then extend `AbstractHttpFilter` in order to create filters that actually contain the required functionality.

These filters will need to have access to the configuration information (stored in the configuration file we designed in Chapter 15). As every filter will need access to this information, the required functionality should be implemented in `AbstractHttpFilter`. Then every class that extends `AbstractHttpFilter` will automatically have access to the configuration information. Recall that an object containing the configuration information is stored in the servlet context. `AbstractHttpFilter` can extract this object in its `init()` method and store it as a protected instance variable – thus allowing all the filters that extend `AbstractHttpFilter` access to it.

The following class diagram shows how our abstract HTTP filter, and the concrete sub-classes we need to create, are related:

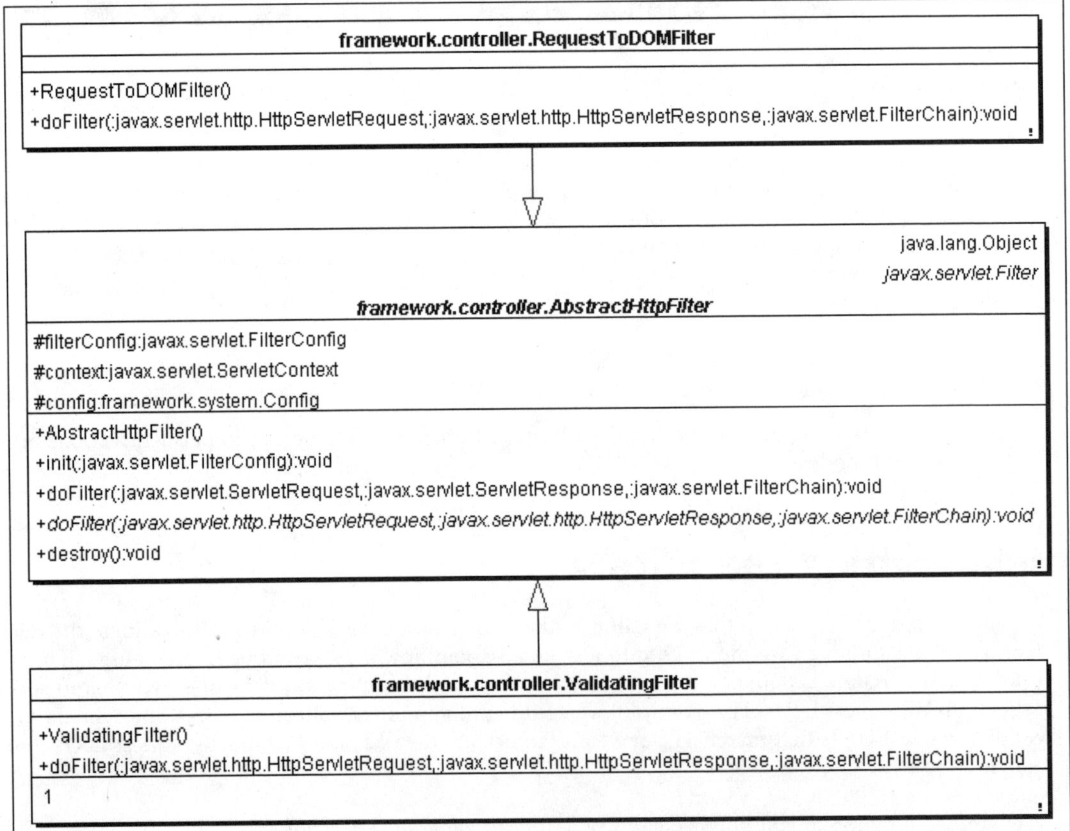

`AbstractHttpFilter` provides an implementation of all the methods defined in the `Filter` interface.

> *For more information on the methods that a filter must implement, and on filters in general, you should refer to Chapter 3.*

`AbstractHttpFilter` also declares an abstract overload of the `doFilter()` method defined in the `Filter` interface. However, instead of taking arguments of type `ServletRequest` and `ServletResponse`, our abstract method takes arguments of type `HttpServletRequest` and `HttpServletResponse`.

We still have to implement the original `doFilter()` method, as this is the method that the container will call. Therefore, in our implementation we cast the request and response to their HTTP equivalents and then pass them to the abstract `doFilter()` method. When we create concrete subclasses of `AbstractHttpFilter` we will need to provide an implementation of the abstract `doFilter()` method. Let's look at the complete source code for `AbstractHttpFilter`:

```
package framework.controller;

import javax.servlet.Filter;
import javax.servlet.FilterConfig;
import javax.servlet.ServletRequest;
import javax.servlet.ServletResponse;
import javax.servlet.FilterChain;
import javax.servlet.ServletException;
import javax.servlet.ServletContext;

import javax.servlet.http.HttpServletRequest;
import javax.servlet.http.HttpServletResponse;

import java.io.IOException;

import framework.system.Config;
import framework.system.AttributeNames;

public abstract class AbstractHttpFilter implements Filter {

  protected FilterConfig filterConfig;
  protected ServletContext context;
```

We declare an instance of the `Config` object, which can be used by the subclasses to access the configuration information. Then, in the `init()` method we can retrieve the `Config` object from the servlet context:

```
  protected Config config;

  public void init(FilterConfig filterConfig) {
    this.filterConfig = filterConfig;
    context = filterConfig.getServletContext();
    config = (Config)context.getAttribute(AttributeNames.CONFIG);
  }
```

In our required implementation of `doFilter()` we cast the request and response to their HTTP equivalents and call an abstract version of the `doFilter()` method:

```
  public void doFilter(ServletRequest request,
                       ServletResponse response,
                       FilterChain chain)
              throws IOException, ServletException {
    if(request instanceof HttpServletRequest) {
      doFilter((HttpServletRequest)request,
               (HttpServletResponse)response,
               chain);
    }
  }
```

We declare the abstract method that will be implemented by subclasses of `AbstractHttpFilter`:

```
  public abstract void doFilter(HttpServletRequest request,
                                HttpServletResponse response,
                                FilterChain chain)
                       throws IOException, ServletException;
```

Finally, we can perform any necessary cleanup of resources in the `destroy()` method:

```
  public void destroy() {
    filterConfig = null;
  }
}
```

DOM Generator Module

The next stage is to create the DOM generator module. Recall from Chapter 15 that the DOM generator module is responsible for converting the incoming request data to a DOM. To perform this conversion the module makes use of an interface named `DOMGenerator`, and two classes named `RequestToDOMFilter` and `DefaultDOMGenerator`:

- `DOMGenerator`
  This interface provides a method that is implemented in XML node generators created by the application developer. Specific implementations of this interface are tied to specific collections of request URIs. This is done in the configuration file.

- `RequestToDOMFilter`
  This class extends `AbstractHTTPFilter`. It is responsible for delegating the generation of a DOM to an implementation of `DOMGenerator`. It performs this delegation based on the information stored in the `DOMInfo` object (which in turn was populated from the information stored in the configuration file).

- `DefaultDOMGenerator`
  This class is a default implementation of `DOMGenerator` provided by the framework.

Next, we'll look in detail at the implementation of these interfaces and classes.

The DOMGenerator Interface

This interface defines a single method that takes the current request and request mapping and returns an XML node. We pass the mapping object so that the implementations of this interface can use it to retrieve the schema associated with the XML node:

```
package framework.xml;

import javax.servlet.ServletRequest;
import javax.servlet.http.HttpServletRequest;
import org.w3c.dom.Node;
import framework.system.*;

public interface DOMGenerator {

  public Node generateDOM(HttpServletRequest request,
                          RequestMapping mapping)
          throws FrameworkException;
}
```

The RequestToDOMFilter Class

The `RequestToDOMFilter` class is at the heart of the DOM generator module. It is implemented as a servlet filter as specified in the Servlet 2.3 specification. `RequestToDOMFilter` retrieves a request mapping object that corresponds to the request URI from the configuration object. It then uses the information in the request mapping object to first delegate the generation of the DOM and then validate the generated XML:

```
package framework.controller;

import javax.servlet.*;
import javax.servlet.http.*;
import framework.system.*;
import framework.xml.DOMGenerator;
import java.io.IOException;
import org.w3c.dom.Node;

public class RequestToDOMFilter extends AbstractHttpFilter {

  public void doFilter(HttpServletRequest request,
                       HttpServletResponse response,
                       FilterChain chain)
          throws IOException, ServletException {
    try {
```

We use the `getServletPath()` method of `request` to return the request URI (but we exclude the host address, port number, context path, and query string):

```
      String uri = request.getServletPath().substring(1);
```

Now we can get the `RequestMapping` that corresponds to the request URI. Recall that we created a protected variable, `config`, in the super class `AbstractHttpFilter` that stores a reference to the `Config` object:

```
    RequestMapping mapping = config.getRequestMapping(uri);
```

Now we have the request mapping we can retrieve the `DOMInfo` object:

```
    DOMInfo domInfo = mapping.getDOMInfo();
```

If the value of `DOMInfo` object is null, we simply send the request to the next filter in the chain and return:

```
    if(domInfo == null) {
      chain.doFilter(request,response);
      return;
    }
```

If the value of `DOMInfo` isn't null we get the `DOMGenerator` implementation instance for the request URI and delegate the task of XML node generation to it:

```
    DOMGenerator domGen = domInfo.getDOMGenerator();
    Node inputDOM = domGen.generateDOM(request, mapping);
```

We need to get the scope and name of the attribute in which the generated XML node is to be stored:

```
    String scope = domInfo.getScope();
    String domName = domInfo.getDOMName();
```

Now we can store the generated XML node as an attribute with the correct scope:

```
    if("request".equals(scope)) {
      request.setAttribute(domName, inputDOM);
    } else {
        request.getSession().setAttribute(domName, inputDOM);
    }
```

Finally, we send the request to the next filter in the chain:

```
    chain.doFilter(request,response);

  } catch(FrameworkException e) {
     throw new ServletException(e);
  }
 }
}
```

The DefaultDOMGenerator Class

DefaultDOMGenerator provides a default implementation for the DOMGenerator interface. This class iterates through the request parameter names and creates an XML node with the following properties:

- The node name is retrieved from the DOMInfo object
- Child elements are created with names set from the names of the request parameters
- The content of each child element is set from the value of the request parameters

If there is a Schema object associated with the RequestMapping object then DefaultDOMGenerator sets the schema attributes to the root node of the generated DOM. Let's look at the implementation in detail:

```
package framework.xml;

import java.util.Enumeration;
import javax.xml.parsers.*;
import org.w3c.dom.*;
import framework.system.*;
import javax.servlet.ServletRequest;
import javax.servlet.http.HttpServletRequest;

public class DefaultDOMGenerator implements DOMGenerator {

  public Node generateDOM(HttpServletRequest request,
                          RequestMapping mapping)
             throws FrameworkException {
    try {
```

We get the Schema associated with RequestMapping:

```
      Schema schema = mapping.getSchema();
```

Then we get an enumeration of the request parameters, before starting to build our DOM:

```
      Enumeration enum = request.getParameterNames();
      DocumentBuilderFactory factory = DocumentBuilderFactory.newInstance();
      factory.setNamespaceAware(true);
      DocumentBuilder builder =  factory.newDocumentBuilder();
      Document document = builder.newDocument();
```

We retrieve the DOMInfo from the RequestMapping and create a element with a name set to the value set in the DOMInfo object (this name was originally defined in the configuration file):

```
      DOMInfo domInfo = mapping.getDOMInfo();
      Element root = document.createElement(domInfo.getDOMName());
```

If the Schema object is not null, we set the schema attributes:

```
    if(schema != null) {
      Attr schemaNS = document.createAttribute("xmlns:xsi");
      schemaNS.setValue("http://www.w3.org/2001/XMLSchema-instance");
      root.setAttributeNode(schemaNS);
```

If the schema is namespace aware, we set the target namespace as well as the schemaLocation. For the schemas with target namespace, the schemaLocation attribute in the instance document is a pair of values with the first one in the pair indicating the schema location and the second one indicating the target namespace:

```
      if(schema.isNamespaceAware()) {
        Attr targetNamespace = document.createAttribute("xmlns");
        targetNamespace.setValue(schema.getTargetNamespace());
        root.setAttributeNode(targetNamespace);
        Attr schemaLoc = document.createAttribute("xsi:schemaLocation");
        schemaLoc.setValue(schema.getLocation() + " " +
                           schema.getTargetNamespace());
        root.setAttributeNode(schemaLoc);
      } else {
```

If the schema doesn't have a target namespace, we set the value for the attribute to noNamespaceSchemaLocation:

```
        Attr schemaLoc =
              document.createAttribute("xsi:noNamespaceSchemaLocation");
        schemaLoc.setValue(schema.getLocation());
        root.setAttributeNode(schemaLoc);
      }
    }
```

We iterate through the request parameters and append child elements to the document element. The names and element contents determined by the names and values of the request parameters:

```
    String param= null;
    String values[] = null;

    while(enum.hasMoreElements()) {
      param = (String)enum.nextElement();
      values[] = request.getParameterValues(param);

      for(int i = 0;i < values.length;i++) {
        if(values[i] != null && !"".equals(values[i].trim())) {
          Element child = document.createElement(param);
          root.appendChild(child);

          String value = values[i];
          Text text = document.createTextNode(values[i]);
          child.appendChild(text);
        }
      }
    }
```

Finally, we return the document element:

```
            return root;
        } catch(ParserConfigurationException e) {
            throw new FrameworkException(e, Severity.UNEXPECTED);
        }
    }
}
```

Validation Module

The validation module provides two public classes and an anonymous inner class:

- `ValidatingFilter` – extends `AbstractHTTPFilter` and provides the core validation code.
- `Serializer` – a utility class that is used to serialize an XML node to an input stream.
- The anonymous inner class functions as the error handler for the XML parser. All the call back methods simply re-throw the `SAXParseException` passed in as the argument.

`ValidatingFilter` receives from the `Config` object the `RequestMapping` object for the current request. The `DOMInfo` and `Schema` objects can then be retrieved from the `RequestMapping` object. If these objects are not null the name and scope used to store the XML node can be retrieved from the `DOMInfo` object. These can then be used to retrieve the actual XML node from the `DOMInfo` object.

Once the validation module has the XML node it can go about validating it. First, a parser object is created using the standard JAXP API, which can be used to parse the XML node. If the parse process throws a `SAXParseException`, the input `Forward` object is retrieved from the `DOMInfo` object, the error message is stored as a request attribute, and the request is sent back to the resource indicated by the input `Forward` object. If no error occurs, the parsing is successfully completed and the request is forwarded to the next filter in the chain.

With this overview of the validation process in mind, let's look in detail at the implementation of the classes in this module.

The Serializer Class

The `Serializer` class uses the `XMLSerializer` class that is provided with Xerces. This class is used to transform an XML node into an input stream. We need to make this transformation because none of the overloaded `parse()` methods defined in JAXP take an XML node as an argument.

We implement `Serializer` as a **Singleton**. A Singleton pattern ensures that there is only ever one instance of a particular class within the virtual machine, which allows us to provide a single point of access to it.

```
package framework.xml;

import org.w3c.dom.*;
import java.io.*;
import org.apache.xml.serialize.XMLSerializer;

public class Serializer {
```

Declare the singleton instance:

```
private static Serializer instance;
```

We provide a private constructor to avoid the class being initialized from outside the class:

```
private Serializer() {}
```

Now we define the singleton access method:

```
public static Serializer getInstance() {
  synchronized {
     if(instance == null) {
        instance = new Serializer();
     }
  }
  return instance;
}
```

In the `serialize()` method we use the Xerces `XMLSerializer` class to write the contents of a node to a byte array, which we then return:

```
  public InputStream serialize(Node node) throws IOException {
    XMLSerializer serializer = new XMLSerializer();
    ByteArrayOutputStream output = new ByteArrayOutputStream();
    serializer.setOutputByteStream(output);
    serializer.serialize((Element)node);
    byte[] byteArray = output.toByteArray();
    output.close();

    return new ByteArrayInputStream(byteArray);;
  }
}
```

The ValidatingFilter Class

Next, we'll look at the source code for the validating filter:

```
package framework.xml;

import org.w3c.dom.*;
import javax.servlet.*;
import javax.servlet.http.*;
import java.io.IOException;
import framework.system.*;
import framework.xml.Serializer;
import javax.xml.parsers.*;
import org.xml.sax.*;

public class ValidatingFilter extends AbstractHttpFilter {

  public void doFilter(HttpServletRequest request,
                       HttpServletResponse response,
                       FilterChain chain)
           throws IOException, ServletException {
```

The first thing to do is to get the current request URI. Once we have that we can extract the `RequestMapping` object from the `Config` object, which we can then use to get the `DOMInfo` object:

```
String uri = request.getServletPath().substring(1);
RequestMapping mapping = config.getRequestMapping(uri);
DOMInfo domInfo = mapping.getDOMInfo();
```

If `domInfo` is null we should just forward the request to the next resource in the chain and return:

```
if(domInfo == null) {
  chain.doFilter(request,response);
  return;
}
```

If the `Schema` object associated with the `RequestMapping` object is null we should forward the request to the next resource in the chain and return:

```
if(mapping.getSchema() == null) {
  chain.doFilter(request, response);
  return;
}
```

Next, we get the name and scope of the attribute used by `RequestToDOMFilter` to store the generated XML node:

```
String scope = domInfo.getScope();
String domName = domInfo.getDOMName();
```

Using these, we can extract the XML node:

```
Node inputDOM;
if("request".equals(scope)) {
  inputDOM = (Node)request.getAttribute(domName);
} else {
   inputDOM = (Node)request.getSession().getAttribute(domName);
}

try {
```

We need to create a namespace-aware validating parser using the standard JAXP API:

```
DocumentBuilderFactory factory = DocumentBuilderFactory.newInstance();
factory.setValidating(true);
factory.setNamespaceAware(true);
DocumentBuilder parser = factory.newDocumentBuilder();
DocumentBuilderFactory factory = DocumentBuilderFactory.newInstance();
factory.setValidating(true);
factory.setNamespaceAware(true);
DocumentBuilder parser = factory.newDocumentBuilder();
```

We set the error handler as an anonymous inner class so that all the call back methods simply re-throw the exception passed to them:

```
      parser.setErrorHandler(new ErrorHandler() {

        public void error(SAXParseException ex) throws SAXException {
          throw ex;
        }

        public void fatalError(SAXParseException ex) throws SAXException {
          throw ex;
        }

        public void warning(SAXParseException ex) throws SAXException {
          throw ex;
        }
      });
```

The next step is to serialize the XML node, parse it, and then send the request to the next resource in the chain:

```
      Serializer serializer = Serializer.getInstance();

      parser.parse(
            new InputSource(Serializer.getInstance().serialize(inputDOM)));
      chain.doFilter(request, response);

    } catch(ParserConfigurationException e) {
      throw new ServletException(e);
```

If a `SAXException` is thrown, the exception message is stored as a request attribute specified by `AttributeNames.ERROR_MESSAGE`. Then we forward the request to the resource specified by the `RequestMapping` object's `input` attribute. The error message key can then be used by display pages to extract and display the error message:

```
    } catch(SAXParseException e) {
      request.setAttribute(AttributeNames.ERROR_MESSAGE, e.getMessage());
      Forward input = mapping.getInput();
      RequestDispatcher rd =
                        request.getRequestDispatcher(input.getResource());
      rd.forward(request, response);

    } catch(SAXException e) {
      e.printStackTrace();
      throw new ServletException(e);
    }
  }
}
```

Request Dispatcher Module

In this section we'll have a look at the request dispatcher module, which provides an interface and a class:

- `RequestHandler`
  This interface provides a method to be implemented by request handlers created by application developers. Specific implementations of this interface are tied to request URIs in the configuration file. In the Chapter 15 we saw how the request mapping elements in the configuration file refer to a request handler element that defines the concrete implementation of the interface that handles the request. The dispatcher module can then load an instance of the request handler class corresponding to the current request and delegate the request handling task to it.
- `DispatcherServlet`
  This class extends `HttpServlet`. It retrieves the `RequestMapping` object corresponding to the current request and then extracts the instance of the `RequestHandler` implementation instance. Then it can delegate the request-handling task by passing the request, response, generated XML node, and request mapping to the handler. The `Forward` object returned by the handler is then used to forward or redirect the resource used for rendering the next view. The request that needs to be handled by the framework should be mapped to this servlet in the deployment descriptor. If we wanted to incorporate the XML generation and validation, we would need to map the filters to all the requests handled by the `DispatcherServlet`.

The details of how this is done are explained when we describe the deployment descriptors.

The RequestHandler Interface

```
package framework.controller;

import javax.servlet.http.*;
import org.w3c.dom.Node;
import framework.system.*;

public interface RequestHandler {

  public Forward processRequest(HttpServletRequest request,
       HttpServletResponse response, RequestMapping mapping, Node inputDOM)
                                              throws FrameworkException;
}
```

The DispatcherServlet Class

Much of the code for `DispatcherServlet` is familiar:

```
package framework.controller;

import org.w3c.dom.*;
import javax.servlet.*;
import javax.servlet.http.*;
```

```
import java.io.*;
import framework.system.*;

public class DispatcherServlet extends HttpServlet {

  private Config config;

  public void init(ServletConfig config) throws ServletException {
    super.init(config);
    this.config =
          (Config)getServletContext().getAttribute(AttributeNames.CONFIG);
  }

  public void doPost(HttpServletRequest request,
                     HttpServletResponse response)
                       throws IOException, ServletException {
    doGet(request, response);
  }

  public void doGet(HttpServletRequest request,
                    HttpServletResponse response)
                      throws IOException, ServletException {

    try {
      String uri = request.getServletPath().substring(1);
      RequestMapping mapping = config.getRequestMapping(uri);
      RequestHandler handler = mapping.getRequestHandler();
      DOMInfo domInfo = mapping.getDOMInfo();
      Node inputDOM = null;

      if(domInfo != null) {
        inputDOM = (Node)request.getAttribute(domInfo.getDOMName());
      }
```

We delegate the request-handling task to the `RequestHandler` implementation and receive the `Forward` object in return. The `RequestMapping` object is passed to the `RequestHandler` so that the implementing classes can use it to find a `Forward` object by specifying a logical name:

```
      Forward forward = handler.processRequest(request, response,
                                               mapping, inputDOM);
```

Then we forward to the resource that is responsible for rendering the next view (specified by the `Forward` object):

```
      if(forward.isRedirect()) {
        response.sendRedirect(forward.getResource());
      } else {
          RequestDispatcher rd =
                  request.getRequestDispatcher(forward.getResource());
          rd.forward(request, response);
      }
    } catch(FrameworkException e) {
      throw new ServletException(e);
    }
  }

  public void destroy() {}
}
```

Deployment Descriptor

We need to perform four tasks in the deployment descriptor. We need to:

- Map all the requests that should be handled by the framework to the dispatcher servlet
- Of these requests, map those that need XML node generation to the `RequestToDOMFilter`
- Of these requests, map those that need validation to `ValidatingFilter`
- Declare the context listener to initialize the configuration object

We can take a common approach to:

- Mapping a URI pattern to the dispatcher servlet
- Mapping the dispatcher servlet to both the generating and validating filters

XML node generation and validation can be switched off selectively for request URIs by not defining `dom` and `schema` elements within the request mapping elements for those URIs. This is particularly useful for those requests that don't have any parameters associated with them.

An example deployment descriptor is shown below:

```
<?xml version="1.0" encoding="ISO-8859-1"?>

<!DOCTYPE web-app
    PUBLIC "-//Sun Microsystems, Inc.//DTD Web Application 2.3//EN"
    "http://java.sun.com/j2ee/dtds/web-app_2_3.dtd">

<web-app>
```

Define a context parameter that points to the location of the configuration file:

```
  <context-param>
    <param-name>config</param-name>
    <param-value>/config/config.xml</param-value>
  </context-param>
```

Declare the `RequestToDOMFilter`:

```
  <filter>
    <filter-name>RequestToDOM</filter-name>
    <filter-class>framework.controller.RequestToDOMFilter</filter-class>
  </filter>
```

Declare the `ValidatorFilter`:

```
  <filter>
    <filter-name>Validator</filter-name>
    <filter-class>framework.controller.ValidatingFilter</filter-class>
  </filter>
```

Map `RequestToDOMFilter` to the dispatcher servlet:

```
<filter-mapping>
  <filter-name>RequestToDOM</filter-name>
  <servlet-name>Dispatcher</servlet-name>
</filter-mapping>
```

Map `ValidatorFilter` to the dispatcher servlet:

```
<filter-mapping>
  <filter-name>Validator</filter-name>
  <servlet-name>Dispatcher</servlet-name>
</filter-mapping>
```

Declare the application context listener:

```
<listener>
  <listener-class>framework.system.Initializer</listener-class>
</listener>
```

Declare the dispatcher servlet:

```
<servlet>
  <servlet-name>Dispatcher</servlet-name>
  <servlet-class>framework.controller.DispatcherServlet</servlet-class>
</servlet>
```

Finally, we map all the requests ending with `.do` to the dispatcher servlet:

```
  <servlet-mapping>
    <servlet-name>Dispatcher</servlet-name>
    <url-pattern>*.do</url-pattern>
  </servlet-mapping>

</web-app>
```

That completes our implementation of the filters required by our framework. Our next task is to create the custom tag libraries.

Custom Tag Libraries

Our next task is to design and develop two custom tag libraries to be used in conjunction with our XML-JSP framework. They are:

- An HTML Tag Library that will contain custom tags that renders HTML forms and form controls. The tags in this library will associate forms with request mapping elements in the configuration file. This will allow us link an XML DOM validation schema to an HTML form through the configuration element.
- An XML Tag Library that will contain custom tags to perform various actions on XML nodes. These actions include iterating over a list of nodes, selecting a list of nodes, extracting the value of a node, and comparing the values of nodes.

Both tag libraries will make extensive use of XPath expressions. However, before we get into the specifics of the implementation we should take a look at the functional requirements of the tag libraries, beginning with the HTML Tag Library.

HTML Tag Library – Functional Requirements

The HTML Tag Library is designed to be able to render HTML forms. To do this it must be able to render textboxes, radio buttons, checkboxes, dropdown select lists (and the options within them), and buttons, so it will need to be able to render the following HTML controls: `form`, `input`, `textarea`, `select`, and `option`.

When a client submits a form the request will first go through the DOM generation module. A DOM will be generated and will be stored as a request or session attribute (the name and scope of this attribute is defined in the configuration file). If validation of the data fails, the page will be sent back to the client. At this stage the HTML tag library must be able to extract from the attribute the information originally sent by the client and repopulate the form controls accordingly.

In order to perform this repopulation the tags in the HTML tag library will need to have a `path` attribute defining an XPath expression that points to the XML node containing the appropriate value. The XPath expression will be evaluated relative to the XML node extracted by the enclosing form tag and can return either a single node or a node list.

Those tags within the library that render controls like a select list box, or a group of associated radio buttons will need to be able to extract multiple data values for the same name. Our custom XML tag library will provide this functionality.

XML Tag Library – Functional Requirements

The XML Tag Library contains tags that can:

- Iterate over a node list
- Extract the value of a node

In both these cases we need to be able to specify either the node list to be iterated over, or the node whose value should be extracted. We will select a node list to be iterated over by using an XPath expression to identify the node list from a specified context node. We will need to specify attributes in the tag that identify the context node and the XPath expression. The tag should also be used to expose the current item in the node list to the enclosing JSP page. We will identify a node whose value should be extracted by specifying the XPath expression to the node in the tag.

Implementing the HTML Tag Library

With the functional requirements of our tag libraries specified, we can begin to think about exactly how we will implement that functionality, beginning with the form tag in the HTML tag library:

- The form tag should be implemented as a normal tag that extends `TagSupport`. We don't need a body tag, as we will never want to suppress the body content of the tag.
- The form tag should extract the bean that is used to store the generated XML node and expose is so that any nested tags can access it.

- Of course, the form tag will only contain a valid XML node when the form is to be sent back to the client because of an error during validation.
- The form tag will also expose attributes that correspond to those of a standard HTML form, for example, `method` and `action`.

Next, we consider the implementation of those tags used to render form controls. All the form control tags will have a common ancestor that will define attributes common to all. These attributes include the name and value of the tag, as well as the XPath expression pointing to the node that holds the value to be used to populate the control. We will name this ancestor tag `BaseTag`, and it will define protected methods that provide subclasses access to the first value in the list, or the entire list of values produced by evaluating the XPath expression. The XPath expression is always used to extract a single value or a list of values from the XML node stored by the enclosing form tag, and is defined using the `path` attribute defined in the `BaseTag`.

Of course, the value attribute will need to be interpreted differently for different form controls:

- For the `select` tag the value attribute is irrelevant.
- For the `textarea`, `text`, and `password` tags, the value attribute is used to render the text that is displayed within the control. If this attribute is omitted the tag will need to try to retrieve the value from the XML node defined in the parent form (using the specified XPath expression).
- For the hidden and submit tags the value attribute is used to define the request parameter value that is sent back to the server when the form is submitted. If this attribute is not specified the tag will try to extract the value from the XML node stored in the parent form tag.
- For the radio and checkbox tags the value attribute is used to define the request parameter value sent back to the server when the form is submitted with a particular radio button or checkbox selected. For radio and checkbox tags this attribute must be mandatory because its value will be compared to the list of values retrieved from the XML node stored by the form tag (using the defined XPath expression). This comparison allows us to decide whether the control should be rendered as checked.

The `select` and `textarea` tags will directly subclass `BaseTag`, and will incorporate their own logic to render their respective controls.

All the tags used to render HTML input elements will have a base class, `InputTag`, which will also subclass `BaseTag`. `InputTag` will encapsulate the logic to render the controls. In addition, the `checkbox`, `radio`, `submit`, and `hidden` tags will subclass `InputTag`.

The `text` and `password` tags will extend a class, `EditableInputTag`, which will have attributes that define the maximum length and size for the controls. `EditableInputTag` will itself extend `InputTag`.

The tag that renders the `option` element will need to have an attribute to define the name of the bean used to store the XML node that contains the data for the element. It will also require two additional attributes containing the XPath expressions that point to the value and the label for the control. The `option` tag will need to collaborate with the enclosing `select` tag to decide whether the option element should be rendered as selected.

The class diagram that follows shows all the classes, and the relationships between them, in the HTML Tag Library:

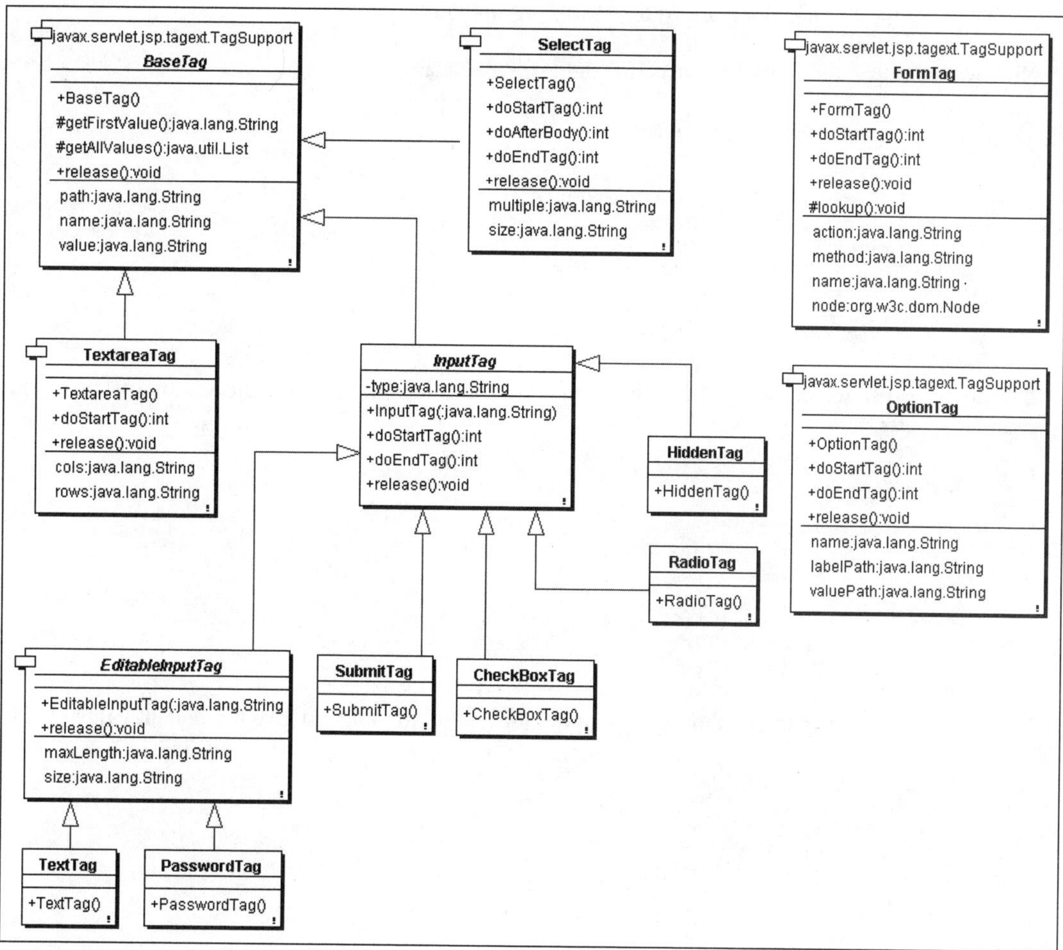

The next stage is to implement the classes required for our tag library.

The FormTag Class

This class is used as the handler for implementing the tag used to render HTML form elements. The class will execute the following sequence of events when the `doStartTag()` method is executed:

- It will use the value specified for the `action` attribute to extract the `RequestMapping` object from the `Config` object
- It will then use the `DOMInfo` object stored in the `RequestMapping` object to extract the name and scope by which the generated XML node is stored
- Then it will try to extract the XML node and stores it as an instance variable

- If it can't find the node it won't throw an error because the generated XML node will be present only when the form is sent back due to validation errors
- Finally, it writes the markup for rendering the HTML form

Now we will have a look at the source for the `FormTag` class:

```
package framework.taglib.html;

import java.io.IOException;
import javax.servlet.ServletContext;
import javax.servlet.http.*;
import javax.servlet.jsp.*;
import org.w3c.dom.Node;
import framework.system.*;

public class FormTag extends TagSupport {
```

Define the attribute, along with the standard getter and setter methods for the action attribute. This is a mandatory attribute:

```
  protected String action = null;

  public String getAction() {
    return action;
  }

  public void setAction(String action) {
    this.action = action;
  }
```

Define the attribute for the method by which the form is submitted, and give it a default value of "POST":

```
  protected String method = "POST";

  public String getMethod() {
    return method;
  }

  public void setMethod(String method) {
    this.method = method;
  }
```

Define the attribute for the name of the form:

```
  protected String name = null;

   public String getName() {
     return name;
  }

  public void setName(String name) {
    this.name = name;
  }
```

This variable is used to store the generated XML node that is associated with this form:

```
  protected Node node;
```

The tags that render the form controls to access the XML data behind the form may use this method:

```
public Node getNode() {
  return node;
}
```

Look up the XML node that is associated with this form:

```
public int doStartTag() throws JspException {
  lookup();
```

Then write the HTML markup for the start tag:

```
    HttpServletResponse response =
                        (HttpServletResponse) pageContext.getResponse();
    StringBuffer results = new StringBuffer("<form");
    results.append(" name=\"");
    results.append(name);
    results.append("\"");
    results.append(" method=\"");
    results.append(method);
    results.append("\" action=\"");
    results.append(action);
    results.append("\"");
    results.append(">");

    JspWriter writer = pageContext.getOut();
    try {
      writer.print(results.toString());
    } catch (IOException e) {
        throw new JspException(e.getMessage());
    }

    return (EVAL_BODY_INCLUDE);
  }

  public int doEndTag() throws JspException {
```

Write the HTML markup to render the form's end tag:

```
    StringBuffer results = new StringBuffer("</form>");
    JspWriter writer = pageContext.getOut();
    try {
      writer.print(results.toString());
    } catch (IOException e) {
        throw new JspException(e.getMessage());
    }

    return (EVAL_PAGE);
  }
```

We set all the instance variables to default values. We need to do this because the J2EE web container may be reusing tag instances from an instance pool (this is a standard pattern used in designing custom tags to ensure that the tag handler classes have proper default values when the container reuses them):

```
    public void release() {
      super.release();
      action = null;
      method = "POST";
      name = null;
    }
```

This method looks up the generated XML node (if present) that is associated with this form:

```
    private void lookup() throws JspException {
```

Retrieve the instance of the `Config` object stored in the application context:

```
      ServletContext context = pageContext.getServletContext();
      Config config = (Config)context.getAttribute(AttributeNames.CONFIG);
```

Extract the `RequestMapping` object with the URI attributing same way as the action attribute defined for the form:

```
      RequestMapping mapping = config.getRequestMapping(action);
```

Retrieve the `DOMInfo` object. If there is no `DOMInfo` object present, return silently, as XML node generation for request URIs can be switched off selectively:

```
      DOMInfo domInfo = mapping.getDOMInfo();
      if(domInfo == null) {
        return;
      }
```

Find the name under which the XML node is stored and try to retrieve it. If the node is not found, return silently. This is because the node will be present only when the form is sent back to the end user because of validation errors:

```
      String domName = domInfo.getDOMName();

      Object obj = pageContext.findAttribute(domName);
      if(obj != null && obj instanceof Node) {
        node = (Node)obj;
      }
    }
  }
```

The following table shows the attributes defined for this tag:

Name	Required	Runtime Expression	Comment
`action`	Yes	`True`	The form's action. This may be used find the `RequestMapping` object associated with the form.
`method`	No	`True`	The method by which the form is submitted.
`name`	No	`True`	The name of the form that may be used in client side scripts.

This is the start of the HTML tag library descriptor (`html.tld`):

```
<?xml version="1.0" encoding="UTF-8"?>
<!DOCTYPE taglib
          PUBLIC "-//Sun Microsystems, Inc.//DTD JSP Tag Library 1.1//EN"
          "http://java.sun.com/j2ee/dtds/web-jsptaglibrary_1_1.dtd">

<taglib>
  <tlibversion>1.0</tlibversion>
  <jspversion>1.1</jspversion>
  <shortname>SKLN Form Tags</shortname>

  <tag>
    <name>form</name>
    <tagclass>framework.taglib.html.FormTag</tagclass>
    <bodycontent>JSP</bodycontent>
    <attribute>
      <name>action</name>
      <required>true</required>
      <rtexprvalue>true</rtexprvalue>
    </attribute>
    <attribute>
      <name>method</name>
      <required>false</required>
      <rtexprvalue>true</rtexprvalue>
    </attribute>
    <attribute>
      <name>name</name>
      <required>false</required>
      <rtexprvalue>true</rtexprvalue>
     </attribute>
  </tag>
```

Using the Form Tag

Let's look at a simple example of using the `form` tag. First we would define a request mapping element in the configuration file:

```
<request uri="EmployeeCreate.do">
    <schema namespace-aware="false" location="employee.xsd"/>
    <handler ref="create-handler"/>
    <generator ref="create-generator" dom-name="employee"
               dom-scope="request"/>
    <forwards>
        <forward name="SUCCESS" resource="EmployeeList.jsp" />
    </forwards>
    <input resource="/EmployeeNew.jsp"/>
</request>
```

The following snippet of code would then render our form – of course, we're not yet in a position to add form controls:

```
<html:form action="EmployeeCreate.do"/>
      <!-- Add form controls -->
</html:form>
```

The following sequence of events happen when the form is submitted:

- The DOM generator module will create an XML node from the request data and store it with the name `employee` in the request scope.
- The validation module validates the DOM using the schema file, `employee.xsd`. If the validation is successful, the request is forwarded to the request dispatcher module.
- If the validation fails, the request is sent back to the resource defined by the `input` element, in this case `EmployeeNew.jsp`, which contains the form tag.
- The tag handler class will find the name and scope of the attribute under the generated XML DOM is stored, in this case `employee` and request scope, from the configuration object. This XML node is exposed using a public method by the tag handler class.
- The child tags that are responsible for rendering the various HTML controls can access the XML node to get the data previously entered by the end user and render the controls pre-populated.

The BaseTag Class

This class defines the common attributes used by all the other tags to render form controls like text boxes and radio buttons. The attributes defined in this class are explained below:

Attribute	Description
`name`	The name of the form control.
`value`	The value attribute for the form control.
`path`	The XPath expression that is used to find the value or list of values that may be used to render the form control. The expression is evaluated against the generated XML node stored in the enclosing form class object.

This class also has methods used to get a single value and a list of values from the XML node stored in the form tag class:

```
package framework.taglib.html;

import javax.servlet.jsp.tagext.TagSupport;
import javax.servlet.jsp.JspException;
import java.util.*;
import org.w3c.dom.*;
import org.apache.xpath.XPathAPI;
import javax.xml.transform.TransformerException;

public abstract class BaseTag extends TagSupport {
```

Define the `path`, `name`, and `value` attributes:

```
private String path;

public String getPath() {
  return path;
}

public void setPath(String path) {
  this.path = path;
}

protected String name = null;

public String getName() {
  return name;
}

public void setName(String name) {
  this.name = name;
}

protected String value = null;

public String getValue() {
  return value;
}

public void setValue(String value) {
  this.value = value;
}
```

This method returns a single value by evaluating the XPath expression against the XML node stored by the parent form tag:

```
protected String getFirstValue() throws JspException {
  try {
```

Now get the parent form tag by class. The `findAncestorWithClass()` method is used to get the form tag handler class within which the element is embedded.

```
    FormTag parentForm = (FormTag)findAncestorWithClass (this,
          FormTag.class);

    if(parentForm == null) {
      return null;
    }
```

Extract the XML node from the parent form tag. If the node is null, return silently. This is because the request mapping corresponding to this form may have XML node generation switched off or the form could be being rendered for the first time, in either case there won't be generated XML node available:

```
      Node node = parentForm.getNode();
      if(node == null) {
        return null;
      }
```

Select a single node and return the node value using the Xalan XPathAPI class:

```
      Node searchNode = XPathAPI.selectSingleNode(node, path);

      if(searchNode != null) {
        return searchNode.getNodeValue();
      } else {
          return "";
      }

      } catch(TransformerException e) {
          throw new JspException(e.getMessage());
      }
    }
```

This method returns a list of values by evaluating the XPath expression against the XML node stored by the parent form tag:

```
  protected List getAllValues() throws JspException {
    try {
      List list = new ArrayList();
```

Get the parent tag by this tag's class:

```
      FormTag parentForm =
      (FormTag)findAncestorWithClass(this, FormTag.class);
      if(parentForm == null) {
        throw new JspException("Parent form not found.");
      }
```

Again, extract the XML node from the parent form tag and if the node is null, return an empty list:

```
      Node node = parentForm.getNode();
      if(node == null) {
        return list;
      }
```

Select a list of single nodes and return the node values as a list using the Xalan XPathAPI class:

```
      NodeList valueList = XPathAPI.selectNodeList(node, path);
        for(int i = 0;i < valueList.getLength();i++) {
          list.add(valueList.item(i).getNodeValue());
        }
        return list;
```

```
    } catch(TransformerException e) {
      throw new JspException(e.getMessage());
    }
  }

  public void release() {
    path = null;
    name = null;
    value = null;
  }
}
```

The InputTag Class

This class acts as the base class for all the tag handler classes used to render form controls of HTML `input` type and extends `BaseTag`. The class defines a single attribute called `type` to identify the type of the input element. This attribute is not a tag attribute and is populated in the constructor. This is an abstract class and the specific subclasses invoke the super class constructor by passing appropriate values for the type attribute when they are created. This class also defines the logic for rendering the input element:

```
package framework.taglib.html;

import java.io.IOException;
import javax.servlet.jsp.*;

public abstract class InputTag extends BaseTag {
```

This attribute defines the type of input element that is rendered:

```
  private String type;

  public InputTag(String type) {
    this.type = type;
  }

  public int doStartTag() throws JspException {
    StringBuffer results = new StringBuffer("<input type=\"");
```

Define the type of the input element:

```
    results.append(type);
    results.append("\" name=\"");
    results.append(name);
    results.append("\"");
```

If the type is text or password, set the `maxLength` and `size` attribute by type casting the tag instance to the relevant subclass:

```
    if (type.equalsIgnoreCase("text") ||
        type.equalsIgnoreCase("password")) {
      results.append(" maxlength=\"");
```

The handler classes for text and password elements share the common ancestor class `EditableInputTag`:

```
    String maxLength = ((EditableInputTag)this).getMaxLength();
    results.append(((EditableInputTag)this));
    results.append("\"");

    results.append(" size=\"");
    String size = ((EditableInputTag)this).getSize();
    results.append(((EditableInputTag)this));
    results.append("\"");
  }

  results.append(" value=\"");
```

If the value attribute is not null, set the value attribute of the input element to that specified by the `value` attribute of the input tag. Please note that this attribute is mandatory for radio and checkbox tags:

```
  if (value != null) {
    results.append(value);
```

If the value attribute is not specified and the tag is not checkbox or radio tag, set the value attribute of the input element by extracting it from the XML node stored in the parent form tag. This is because the value attribute is treated differently for radio buttons and check boxes, as it defines the value that is sent back when the form is submitted with the control checked.

```
  } else if(!type.equalsIgnoreCase("radio") &&
            !type.equalsIgnoreCase("checkbox")) {
          String value = getFirstValue();
          if (value == null) {
            value = "";
          }
          results.append(value);
  }
  results.append("\"");
```

If the tag is checkbox or radio, get the list of values defined by the XPath expression from the XML node stored in the parent form tag. If the value attribute specified for the tag is present in the returned list, select the control as selected:

```
  if(type.equalsIgnoreCase("radio") ||
     type.equalsIgnoreCase("checkbox")) {

      if(getAllValues().contains(value)) {
        results.append(" checked ");
      }
  }
  results.append(">");
```

Write the markup to the enclosing JSP writer:

```
String maxLength = ((EditableInputTag)this).getMaxLength();
        results.append(maxLength);
        results.append("\"");

        results.append(" size=\"");
        String size = ((EditableInputTag)this).getSize();
        results.append(size);
        results.append("\"");
      }

      results.append(" value=\"");
```

Reset the instance variables:

```
    public void release() {
      super.release();
      type = null;
    }
  }
```

The RadioTag Class

This tag is used to render HTML radio input elements and directly subclasses `InputTag`. The only thing this class does is call the super class constructor by passing the type as `radio`:

```
package framework.taglib.html;

public class RadioTag extends InputTag {

  public RadioTag() {
    super("radio");
  }
}
```

Tag Attributes

The table below shows the attributes defined for this tag:

Name	Required	Runtime Expression	Comment
`name`	Yes	`true`	The request parameter name that is sent back to the server for this control
`path`	No	`true`	The XPath expression that points to the node that contains the data for this control
`value`	Yes	`true`	The value that is sent back to the server when the form is submitted with the control as selected

We add the following to the HTML tag library descriptor:

```
<tag>
  <name>radio</name>
  <tagclass>framework.taglib.html.RadioTag</tagclass>
  <attribute>
    <name>name</name>
    <required>true</required>
    <rtexprvalue>true</rtexprvalue>
  </attribute>
  <attribute>
    <name>path</name>
    <required>true</required>
    <rtexprvalue>true</rtexprvalue>
  </attribute>
  <attribute>
    <name>value</name>
    <required>true</required>
    <rtexprvalue>true</rtexprvalue>
  </attribute>
</tag>
```

The CheckBoxTag Class

This tag is used to render HTML checkbox input element and directly subclasses `InputTag`. The only thing this class does is call the super class constructor by passing the type as `checkbox`:

```
package framework.taglib.html;

public class CheckBoxTag extends InputTag {

  public CheckBoxTag() {
    super("checkbox");
  }
}
```

Tag Attributes

The table below shows the attributes defined for this tag:

Name	Required	Runtime Expression	Comment
`name`	Yes	`true`	The request parameter name that is sent back to the server for this control
`path`	No	`true`	The XPath expression that points to the node that contains the data for this control
`value`	Yes	`true`	The value that is sent back to the server when the form is submitted with the control as selected

We add the following to the HTML tag library descriptor:

```
<tag>
  <name>checkbox</name>
  <tagclass>framework.taglib.html.CheckBoxTag</tagclass>
  <attribute>
    <name>name</name>
    <required>true</required>
    <rtexprvalue>true</rtexprvalue>
  </attribute>
  <attribute>
    <name>path</name>
    <required>true</required>
    <rtexprvalue>true</rtexprvalue>
  </attribute>
  <attribute>
    <name>value</name>
    <required>true</required>
    <rtexprvalue>true</rtexprvalue>
  </attribute>
</tag>
```

The SubmitTag Class

This tag is used to render a HTML submit input element and directly subclasses `InputTag`. The only thing this class does is call the super class constructor by passing the type as `submit`:

```
package framework.taglib.html;

public class SubmitTag extends InputTag {

  public SubmitTag () {
    super("submit");
  }
}
```

Tag Attributes

The table below shows the attributes defined for this tag:

Name	Required	Runtime Expression	Comment
`name`	No	`true`	The request parameter name that is sent back to the server for this control
`value`	No	`true`	The value that is sent back to the server when the form is submitted with the control as selected

We add the following to the HTML tag library descriptor:

```
<tag>
  <name>submit</name>
  <tagclass>framework.taglib.html.SubmitTag</tagclass>
  <attribute>
    <name>name</name>
    <required>true</required>
    <rtexprvalue>true</rtexprvalue>
  </attribute>
  <attribute>
    <name>value</name>
    <required>true</required>
    <rtexprvalue>true</rtexprvalue>
  </attribute>
</tag>
```

The HiddenTag Class

This tag is used to render the HTML hidden input element and directly subclasses `InputTag`. The only thing this class does is call the super class constructor by passing the type as `hidden`:

```
package framework.taglib.html;

public class HiddenTag extends InputTag {

  public HiddenTag() {
    super("hidden");
  }
}
```

Tag Attributes

The table below shows the attributes defined for this tag:

Name	Required	Runtime Expression	Comment
`name`	Yes	`true`	The request parameter name that is sent back to the server for this control
`path`	No	`true`	The XPath expression that points to the node that contains the data for this control
`value`	No	`true`	The value that is sent back to the server when the form is submitted

We add the following to the HTML tag library descriptor:

```
<tag>
  <name>hidden</name>
  <tagclass>framework.taglib.html.HiddenTag</tagclass>
  <attribute>
    <name>name</name>
    <required>true</required>
    <rtexprvalue>true</rtexprvalue>
  </attribute>
  <attribute>
    <name>path</name>
    <required>true</required>
    <rtexprvalue>true</rtexprvalue>
  </attribute>
  <attribute>
    <name>value</name>
    <required>true</required>
    <rtexprvalue>false</rtexprvalue>
  </attribute>
</tag>
```

The EditableInputTag Class

This class defines two extra attributes for specifying the size and the maximum length of the controls. It is an abstract class that extends `InputTag` and serves as the super class for the tags used to render HTML text and password input elements:

```
package framework.taglib.html;

public abstract class EditableInputTag extends InputTag {

  public EditableInputTag(String type) {
    super(type);
  }

  private String maxLength;

  public String getMaxLength() {
    return maxLength;
  }

  public void setMaxLength(String maxLength) {
    this.maxLength = maxLength;
  }

  private String size;

  public String getSize() {
    return size;
  }

  public void setSize(String size) {
    this.size = size;
  }

  public void release() {
    super.release();
    maxLength = null;
    size = null;
  }
}
```

The TextTag Class

This tag is used to render HTML text input element and directly subclasses `EditableInputTag`. The only thing this class does is call the super class constructor by passing the type as `text`:

```
package framework.taglib.html;

public class TextTag extends EditableInputTag {

  public TextTag() {
    super("text");
  }
}
```

Tag Attributes

The table below shows the attributes defined for this tag:

Name	Required	Runtime Expression	Comment
`name`	Yes	`true`	The request parameter name that is sent back to the server for this control
`path`	No	`true`	The XPath expression that points to the node that contains the data for this control
`value`	No	`true`	The text that may be pre-populated in the control
`maxLength`	No	`true`	The maximum number of characters that may be entered into the control
`size`	No	`true`	The number of character that are visible simultaneously in the control

We add the following to the HTML tag library descriptor:

```
  <tag>
    <name>text</name>
    <tagclass>framework.taglib.html.TextTag</tagclass>
    <attribute>
      <name>maxlength</name>
      <required>false</required>
      <rtexprvalue>true</rtexprvalue>
    </attribute>
    <attribute>
      <name>name</name>
      <required>true</required>
      <rtexprvalue>true</rtexprvalue>
    </attribute>
    <attribute>
      <name>path</name>
```

```
      <required>true</required>
      <rtexprvalue>true</rtexprvalue>
    </attribute>
    <attribute>
      <name>size</name>
      <required>false</required>
      <rtexprvalue>true</rtexprvalue>
    </attribute>
    <attribute>
      <name>value</name>
      <required>false</required>
      <rtexprvalue>true</rtexprvalue>
    </attribute>
  </tag>
```

The PasswordTag Class

This tag is used to render a HTML password input element and directly subclasses `EditableInputTag`. The only thing this class does is call the super class constructor by passing the type as `password`:

```
package framework.taglib.html;

public class PasswordTag extends EditableInputTag {

  public PasswordTag () {
    super("password");
  }
}
```

Tag Attributes

The table below shows the attributes defined for this tag:

Name	Required	Runtime Expression	Comment
`name`	Yes	`true`	The request parameter name that is sent back to the server for this control
`path`	No	`true`	The XPath expression that points to the node that contains the data for this control
`value`	No	`true`	The text that may be pre-populated in the control
`maxLength`	No	`true`	The maximum number of characters that may be entered into the control
`size`	No	`true`	The number of character that are visible simultaneously in the control

We add the following to the HTML tag library descriptor:

```
<tag>
  <name>password</name>
  <tagclass>framework.taglib.html.PasswordTag</tagclass>
  <attribute>
    <name>maxlength</name>
    <required>false</required>
    <rtexprvalue>true</rtexprvalue>
  </attribute>
  <attribute>
    <name>name</name>
    <required>true</required>
    <rtexprvalue>true</rtexprvalue>
  </attribute>
  <attribute>
    <name>path</name>
    <required>true</required>
    <rtexprvalue>true</rtexprvalue>
  </attribute>
  <attribute>
    <name>size</name>
    <required>false</required>
    <rtexprvalue>true</rtexprvalue>
  </attribute>
  <attribute>
    <name>value</name>
    <required>false</required>
    <rtexprvalue>true</rtexprvalue>
  </attribute>
</tag>
```

The TextareaTag Class

This class extends `BaseTag` and is used to render HTML textarea elements:

```
package framework.taglib.html;

import java.io.IOException;

import javax.servlet.jsp.JspException;
import javax.servlet.jsp.JspWriter;

public class TextareaTag extends BaseTag {

  protected String cols = null;

  public String getCols() {
    return cols;
  }

  public void setCols(String cols) {
    this.cols = cols;
```

```
  }

  protected String rows = null;

  public String getRows() {
    return rows;
  }

  public void setRows(String rows) {
    this.rows = rows;
  }

  public int doStartTag() throws JspException {
```

Start creating the markup for the textarea element:

```
    StringBuffer results = new StringBuffer("<textarea");
    results.append(" name=\"");
    results.append(name);
    results.append("\"");
```

Define the number of columns in the textarea:

```
    if (cols != null) {
      results.append(" cols=\"");
      results.append(cols);
      results.append("\"");
    }
```

Define the number of rows in the textarea:

```
    if (rows != null) {
      results.append(" rows=\"");
      results.append(rows);
      results.append("\"");
    }

    results.append(">");
```

Define the textarea content:

```
    if (value != null) {
      results.append(value);
    } else {
        String value = getFirstValue();
        if (value == null) {
          value = "";
        }
        results.append(value);
    }

    results.append("</textarea>");
```

Write the markup to the enclosing JSP writer:

```
      JspWriter writer = pageContext.getOut();
      try {
        writer.print(results.toString());
      } catch (IOException e) {
          throw new JspException(e.getMessage());
      }

      return (EVAL_BODY_INCLUDE);

    }

    public void release() {
      super.release();
      cols = null;
      rows = null;
    }
  }
```

Tag Attributes

The table below shows the attributes defined for this tag:

Name	Required	Runtime Expression	Comment
`name`	Yes	`true`	The request parameter name that is sent back to the server for this control
`path`	No	`true`	The XPath expression that points to the node that contains the data for this control
`value`	No	`true`	The text that may be pre-populated in the control
`cols`	No	`true`	The number of columns in the textarea
`rows`	No	`true`	The number of rows in the textarea

We add the following to the HTML tag library descriptor:

```
    <tag>
      <name>textarea</name>
      <tagclass>framework.taglib.html.TextareaTag</tagclass>
      <attribute>
        <name>cols</name>
        <required>false</required>
        <rtexprvalue>true</rtexprvalue>
      </attribute>
      <attribute>
        <name>name</name>
        <required>true</required>
        <rtexprvalue>true</rtexprvalue>
```

```
    </attribute>
    <attribute>
      <name>path</name>
      <required>true</required>
      <rtexprvalue>true</rtexprvalue>
    </attribute>
    <attribute>
      <name>rows</name>
      <required>false</required>
      <rtexprvalue>true</rtexprvalue>
    </attribute>
    <attribute>
      <name>value</name>
      <required>false</required>
      <rtexprvalue>true</rtexprvalue>
    </attribute>
  </tag>
```

The SelectTag Class

This class directly extends `BaseTag` and is used to render HTML select elements. The select tag may contain nested option tags within them that are used to render the individual elements in the select list:

```
package framework.taglib.html;

import java.io.IOException;

import javax.servlet.jsp.JspException;
import javax.servlet.jsp.JspWriter;

public class SelectTag extends BaseTag {
```

Define the attribute for the `multiple` property. This property defines whether the control is rendered as a dropdown list box or a multi-select list box:

```
  protected String multiple = null;

  public String getMultiple() {
    return multiple;
  }

  public void setMultiple(String multiple) {
    this.multiple = multiple;
  }
```

Define the attribute for the size property. This property defines the number of displayable items in the list:

```
  protected String size = null;

  public String getSize() {
    return (this.size);
```

```
  }

  public void setSize(String size) {
    this.size = size;
  }

  public int doStartTag() throws JspException {
    StringBuffer results = new StringBuffer("<select");
    results.append(" name=\"");
    results.append(name);
    results.append("\"");
```

Write the `multiple` and `size` properties:

```
    if (multiple != null) {
      results.append(" multiple");
    }

    if (size != null) {
      results.append(" size=\"");
      results.append(size);
      results.append("\"");
    }

    results.append(">");
```

Write the `select` element start tag to the enclosing container:

```
    JspWriter writer = pageContext.getOut();
    try {
      writer.print(results.toString());
    } catch (IOException e) {
        throw new JspException(e.getMessage());
    }

    return (EVAL_BODY_INCLUDE);
  }

  public int doAfterBody() throws JspException {
    return SKIP_BODY;
  }

  public int doEndTag() throws JspException {
```

Write the `select` element end tag to the enclosing writer:

```
    JspWriter writer = pageContext.getOut();
    try {
      writer.print("</select>");
    } catch (IOException e) {
        throw new JspException(e.getMessage());
```

```
      }

      return (EVAL_PAGE);

    }

    public void release() {
      super.release();
      multiple = null;
      size = null;
    }
  }
```

Tag Attributes

The table below shows the attributes defined for this tag.

Name	Required	Runtime Expression	Comment
`name`	Yes	`true`	The request parameter name that is sent back to the server for this control
`path`	No	`true`	The XPath expression that points to the node that contains the data for this control
`multiple`	No	`true`	Whether the control allows multi-select
`size`	No	`true`	The number of items displayed simultaneously

We add the following to the HTML tag library descriptor:

```
<tag>
  <name>select</name>
  <tagclass>framework.taglib.html.SelectTag</tagclass>
  <bodycontent>JSP</bodycontent>
  <attribute>
    <name>multiple</name>
    <required>false</required>
    <rtexprvalue>true</rtexprvalue>
  </attribute>
  <attribute>
    <name>name</name>
    <required>true</required>
    <rtexprvalue>true</rtexprvalue>
  </attribute>
  <attribute>
    <name>path</name>
    <required>true</required>
    <rtexprvalue>true</rtexprvalue>
  </attribute>
  <attribute>
    <name>size</name>
    <required>false</required>
    <rtexprvalue>true</rtexprvalue>
  </attribute>
</tag>
```

The OptionTag Class

This class acts as the tag handler class for the tag used to render HTML `option` elements. The value and the label for the `option` element rendered will come from an XML node stored as a bean. The tag specifies attributes to define the name of the attribute under which the XML node is stored, and XPath expressions to the nodes relative to the context node that contain the data for rendering the option value and label. This tag also interacts with the parent select tag to decide whether the item should be rendered as selected:

```
package framework.taglib.html;

import java.io.IOException;
import javax.servlet.jsp.*;
import javax.servlet.jsp.tagext.*;
import javax.xml.transform.TransformerException;
import org.w3c.dom.*;
import org.apache.xpath.XPathAPI;

public class OptionTag extends TagSupport {
```

Define properties for the name under which the XML node that contains the data for the option element is stored; the XPath expression to contain the data for the option label relative to the XML node specified by the name attribute; and the XPath expression to contain the data for the option value relative to the XML node specified by the name attribute:

```
  protected String name = null;

  public String getName() {
    return name;
  }

  public void setName(String name) {
    this.name = name;
  }

  protected String labelPath = null;

  public String getLabelPath() {
    return labelPath;
  }

  public void setLabelPath(String labelPath) {
    this.labelPath = labelPath;
  }

  protected String valuePath = null;

  public String getValuePath() {
    return valuePath;
  }

  public void setValuePath(String valuePath) {
```

```
    this.valuePath = valuePath;
  }

  public int doStartTag() throws JspException {
    return SKIP_BODY;
  }

  public int doEndTag() throws JspException {
    try {
```

Get the XML node that contains the data for the option element:

```
      Object obj = pageContext.findAttribute(name);
      if(obj == null || !(obj instanceof Node)) {
        System.out.println(name + " is null");
        return EVAL_PAGE;
      }
      Node node = (Node)obj;

      String value = null;
```

Get the label data using the XPath expression defined by `labelPath`:

```
      if(valuePath != null) {
        Node valueNode;
        valueNode = XPathAPI.selectSingleNode(node, valuePath);
        if(valueNode != null) {
          value = valueNode.getNodeValue();
        }
      }
```

Get the value data using the XPath expression defined by `valuePath`:

```
      String label = null;
      if(labelPath != null) {
        Node labelNode;
        labelNode = XPathAPI.selectSingleNode(node, labelPath);
        if(labelNode != null) {
          label = labelNode.getNodeValue();
        }
      }

      if(value == null) {
        value = label;
      }
```

Get the parent select tag:

```
      SelectTag parentTag = (SelectTag)findAncestorWithClass(
                                                    this, SelectTag.class);

      if(parentTag == null) {
        return EVAL_PAGE;
      }

      StringBuffer results = new StringBuffer();
```

Start producing the HTML markup required to render the option element:

```
      results.append("<option value=\"");
      results.append(value);
      results.append("\" ");
```

If the list of values for the parent select tag contains the value for the option element, render it as selected:

```
      if(parentTag.getAllValues().contains((value))) {
        results.append(" selected ");
      }

      results.append(">");
      results.append(label);
      results.append("</option>\r\n");
```

Write the markup to the enclosing JSP writer:

```
      JspWriter writer = pageContext.getOut();
      writer.print(results.toString());

    } catch (IOException e) {
        throw new JspException(e.getMessage());
    } catch (TransformerException e) {
        throw new JspException(e.getMessage());
    }
    return EVAL_PAGE;
  }

  public void release() {
    super.release();
    labelPath = null;
    valuePath = null;
  }
}
```

Tag Attributes

The table below shows the attributes defined for this tag:

Name	Required	Runtime Expression	Comment
`name`	Yes	`true`	The name under which the XML node that contains the data is stored
`labelPath`	No	`true`	The XPath expression that points to the node that contains the data for the option label
`valuePath`	No	`true`	The XPath expression that points to the node that contains the data for the option value

We add the following to the HTML tag library descriptor:

```
    <tag>
      <name>option</name>
      <tagclass>framework.taglib.html.OptionTag</tagclass>
      <bodycontent>empty</bodycontent>
      <attribute>
        <name>name</name>
        <required>true</required>
        <rtexprvalue>true</rtexprvalue>
      </attribute>
      <attribute>
        <name>labelPath</name>
        <required>true</required>
        <rtexprvalue>true</rtexprvalue>
      </attribute>
      <attribute>
        <name>valuePath</name>
        <required>false</required>
        <rtexprvalue>true</rtexprvalue>
      </attribute>
    </tag>

  </taglib>
```

XML Tag Library

Our XML tag library contains two tags:

- A tag to extract the value of a node selected using a specified XPath expression relative to a specified context node
- A tag to iterate over a list of nodes (selected relative to a specified context node) using a specified XPath expression that exposes each node in the list as a page scope bean by the specified name

The ValueOfTag Class

This tag takes two attributes:

- The first attribute specifies the name of the attribute under which the context node is stored. The tag handler will try to find an attribute by the specified name of type `org.w3c.xml.Node` in page, request, session and application scope using the `findAttribute()` method on the `pageContext` object.
- The second attribute specifies the XPath expression that is used to select the node whose value is to be extracted. The tag handler will evaluate the XPath expression defined by this attribute against the context node defined by the last attribute to extract the value that is to be rendered.

```
package framework.taglib.xml;

import javax.servlet.jsp.tagext.TagSupport;
import javax.servlet.jsp.JspException;
import org.w3c.dom.*;
import javax.xml.transform.TransformerException;
import java.io.IOException;
import org.apache.xpath.XPathAPI;

public class ValueOfTag extends TagSupport {
```

Define attributes for the name of the attribute under which the XML node is stored and the XPath expressions that are used for selecting the node whose value is to be extracted:

```
  private String node;

  public String getNode() {
    return node;
  }

  public void setNode(String node) {
    this.node = node;
  }

  private String path;

  public String getPath() {
    return path;
  }

  public void setPath(String path) {
    this.path = path;
  }

  public int doStartTag() throws JspException {
    try {
```

Extract the specified context node:

```
        Object obj = pageContext.findAttribute(node);
        if(obj == null) {
          throw new JspException("Specified node not found.");
        } else if(obj == null) {
            return EVAL_BODY_INCLUDE;
        }

        Node xmlNode = null;
        if(obj instanceof Node) {
          xmlNode = (Node)obj;
        } else {
            throw new JspException("Specified node not found.");
        }
```

Select the node relative to the context node using the specified XPath expression and write the value of the node to the enclosing JSP writer:

```
        Node searchNode = XPathAPI.selectSingleNode(xmlNode, path);
        if(searchNode != null) {
          pageContext.getOut().println(searchNode.getNodeValue());
        }

        return EVAL_BODY_INCLUDE;

      } catch(TransformerException e) {
          throw new JspException(e.getMessage());
      } catch(IOException e) {
          throw new JspException(e.getMessage());
      }
    }
  }
```

Tag Attributes

The table below shows the attributes defined for this tag.

Name	Required	Runtime Expression	Comment
`node`	Yes	`true`	The name under which the context node is stored
`path`	Yes	`true`	The XPath expression that points to the node whose values is to be extracted

We add the following to the XML tag library descriptor (`xml.tld`):

```
<tag>
  <name>valueOf</name>
  <tagclass>framework.taglib.xml.ValueOfTag</tagclass>
  <info> Displays info from a XML node </info>
  <attribute>
    <name>path</name>
    <required>true</required>
    <rtexprvalue>true</rtexprvalue>
  </attribute>
  <attribute>
    <name>node</name>
    <required>true</required>
    <rtexprvalue>true</rtexprvalue>
  </attribute>
</tag>
```

The ForEachTag Class

This tag will iterate over a list of nodes selected from a context node using an XPath expression and expose each item in the list as a page scope bean.

This tag uses the `IteratorTag` feature introduced in JSP 1.2, which is similar to both body tags (in that its body can be evaluated more than once) and simple tags (in that their body content doesn't need to be written explicitly):

```
package framework.taglib.xml;

import javax.servlet.jsp.tagext.TagSupport;
import javax.servlet.jsp.JspException;

import org.w3c.dom.Node;
import org.w3c.dom.NodeList;
import org.w3c.dom.Document;

import javax.xml.transform.TransformerException;

import org.apache.xpath.XPathAPI;

public class ForEachTag extends TagSupport {
```

Define attributes for the name under which the context node is stored and the XPath expression that is used to select the list of nodes:

```
  private String name;

  public String getName() {
    return name;
  }

  public void setName(String name) {
    this.name = name;
  }

  private String path;

  public String getPath() {
    return path;
  }

  public void setPath(String path) {
    this.path = path;
  }
```

This is an instance variable used to track the index of the current item in the list:

```
  private int count = 0;
```

This is the attribute that stores the selected lists of nodes:

```
    private NodeList nodeList;

    public int doStartTag() throws JspException {
      try {
        count = 0;
        nodeList = null;
```

Retrieve the context node:

```
        Object obj = pageContext.findAttribute(name);
        if(obj == null) {
          throw new JspException("Specified node not found.");
        }

        Node xmlNode = null;
        if(obj instanceof Node) {
          xmlNode = (Node)obj;
        }
```

Select the list of nodes specified by the XPath expression:

```
        nodeList = XPathAPI.selectNodeList(xmlNode, path);
```

If the selected list contains one or more nodes, make the first node in the list available as a page scope bean by the name specified by the id attribute:

```
        if(nodeList.getLength() > 0) {
          pageContext.setAttribute(id, nodeList.item(count++));
          return EVAL_BODY_INCLUDE;
        }

        return SKIP_BODY;

      } catch(TransformerException e) {
          throw new JspException(e.getMessage());
      }
    }

    public int doAfterBody() {
```

While there are more nodes in the list, make the next node in the list available as a page scope bean by the name specified by the attribute:

```
      if(count >= nodeList.getLength()) {
        return SKIP_BODY;
      }

      pageContext.setAttribute(id, nodeList.item(count++));
      return EVAL_BODY_AGAIN;

    }
  }
```

Tag Attributes

The table below shows the attributes defined for this tag:

Name	Required	Runtime Expression	Comment
name	Yes	true	The name under which the context node is stored
path	Yes	true	The XPath expression that is used to select the list of nodes
id	Yes	true	The name of the page scope bean that contains the current node in the list

We add the following to the XML tag library descriptor:

```
<tag>
  <name>forEach</name>
  <tagclass>framework.taglib.xml.ForEachTag</tagclass>
  <info> Iterates over a list of XML nodes </info>
  <attribute>
    <name>path</name>
    <required>true</required>
    <rtexprvalue>true</rtexprvalue>
  </attribute>
  <attribute>
    <name>id</name>
    <required>true</required>
    <rtexprvalue>true</rtexprvalue>
  </attribute>
  <attribute>
    <name>name</name>
    <required>true</required>
    <rtexprvalue>true</rtexprvalue>
  </attribute>
</tag>
```

Summary

We spent this chapter completing our implementation of the XML-JSP framework. We had already implemented the configuration of the framework in Chapter 15, and so our task in this chapter was to develop the classes that are at the heart of our framework, including:

- The filters that generate and validate XML
- A custom tag library to generate HTML form and form controls
- A custom tag library to perform actions on XML nodes

These filters and tag libraries provide the functionality we require of our framework. Used with the configuration classes we created in Chapter 15, we now have the ability to create web applications that can easily generate and validate XML.

In the next chapter we will design and build a web application that communicate with web services, which is exactly what our framework was designed to implement easily. The application will allow us to demonstrate the ease of use and power of the framework we have created.

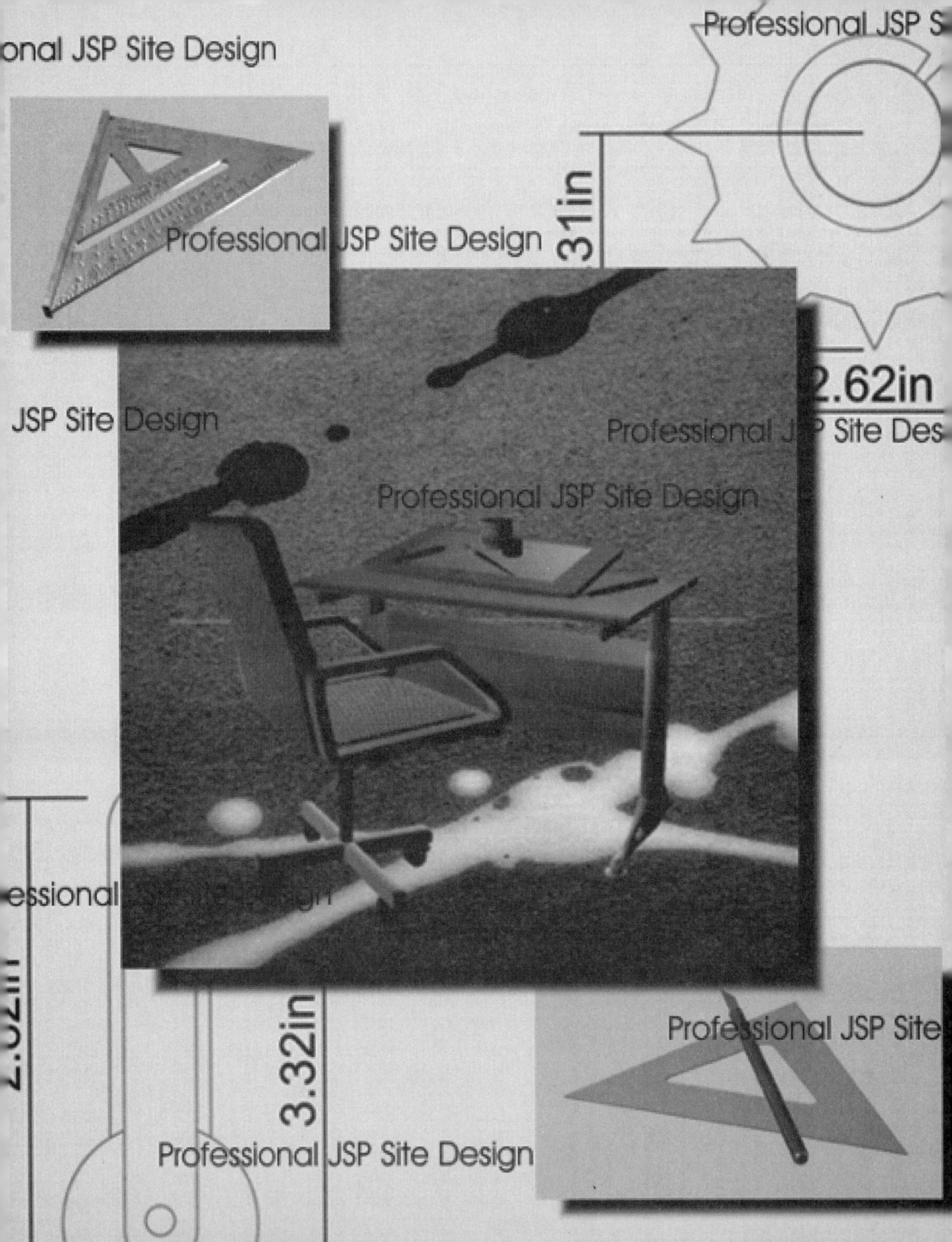
Professional JSP Site Design
31in
2.62in
Professional JSP Site Design
3.32in
Professional JSP Site Design

17

An XML-JSP Framework – 3

We've spent the last two chapters developing an XML-JSP Framework that we can use to develop web applications that can generate, consume, and render XML. In this chapter, we will use this framework to develop just such an application, which will act as a web tier that maintains data stored using XML. This application will make use of many of the features provided by the framework including XML generation, schema validation, error handling, request delegation, and custom tag libraries.

The application will interact with a set of **Simple Object Access Protocol (SOAP)** based web services. These web services will perform the actual manipulation of the underlying data. Our web application will use XML to communicate with the web services, which will be easy to program because the application will be built with our XML-JSP Framework. The web application will use the framework to generate XML from client input; send the request as SOAP envelopes to the web services; receive the response from the web services as SOAP envelopes; and finally render the XML embedded in the SOAP envelope to the client.

The design and creation of our sample application will follow these steps:

- We will take a high-level look at the architecture of the application
- Our application will make extensive use of SOAP, so, we will spend some time understanding the basic concepts of SOAP
- We will analyze how our application will be used and use this information to design its configuration
- We will need to create the web services that perform the manipulation of the underlying data
- We will create and deploy the classes required by the framework, including the request handlers and JSP pages
- Finally, we will deploy and test our application

Application Architecture

Our application will function as a simple web-based employee information system. It will provide users will screens that can be used to:

- List current employees
- Add new employees

To make the application more interesting, and to better demonstrate the power of the XML-JSP framework, we will isolate the web and business tiers of the applications by making use of SOAP based web services:

- The business tier will be implemented as a set of web services that will access and modify the underlying data
- The presentation tier will provide a user interface to the XML that is retrieved from the web services, and will provide users with the ability to amend the data

We will need to create web services that can:

- Retrieve a list of current employees and departments
- Add new employees

The request handlers within the web tier can then pass SOAP requests to these web services. The web services will gather the information in the SOAP envelope, perform the required processing, and return the response as a SOAP envelope. The request handlers will receive the envelope, extract the data stored in the envelope as XML nodes, and store these nodes as beans with either request or session scope. The JSP pages responsible for rendering the next view can then use the appropriate custom tags to retrieve and display the data from the stored XML nodes.

However, before we can delve into the details of the design and implementation of our sample application, we need to have an understanding of the SOAP specification, and the Apache SOAP implementation that we will make use of.

Simple Object Access Protocol

> **Simple Object Access Protocol (SOAP) is a lightweight protocol based on XML, which is used for the exchange of typed information in a decentralized and distributed environment.**

SOAP consists of four parts:

- An envelope that describes a framework to define what a document is and how to process it
- A set of encoding rules for representing application specific data types in XML vocabulary
- A convention for representing remote procedure calls and responses in XML
- A binding convention for exchanging messages using an underlying data transport protocol

The most common use of SOAP is to represent the remote procedure calls and responses involved in web services, and the **Web Services Description Language (WSDL)** specification defines a SOAP binding that representing the remote procedure calls, parameters, and responses using SOAP.

Contrary to popular belief SOAP doesn't specify anything about the physical routing of messages. Applications such as BizTalk that are built on top of SOAP provide routing information by defining custom SOAP headers.

This is an example of a simple SOAP message:

```
<env:Envelope xmlns:env="http://www.w3.org/2001/06/soap-envelope">
  <env:Header>
    <auth:authentication xmlns:auth="http://mutant.com/cdrs/authentication">
      <auth:userId>ranieri</auth:userId>
      <auth:password>chelseaFC</auth:password>
    </auth:authentication>
  </env:Header>
  <env:Body>
    <app:getCustomer xmlns:app="http://mutant.com/cdrs/application">
      <app:custId>122</app:custId>
    </app:getCustomer>
  </env:Body>
</env:Envelope>
```

If you have a look at the above example, you can see that it contains vocabularies from three namespaces:

- `http://www.w3.org/2001/06/soap-envelope`
- `http://mutant.com/cdrs/authentication`
- `http://mutant.com/cdrs/application`

The first of these, which appears in the first line, contains the SOAP envelope vocabulary such as `Envelope`, `Header`, and `Body`. This namespace is specific to SOAP version 1.2. The second and third namespaces contain the vocabulary that is specific to our application. We define a namespace to the authentication header, and another for the remote procedure call to get the details of a customer.

Fundamentals of SOAP

All SOAP messages are XML documents that contain vocabularies belonging to the SOAP namespace as well as custom application namespaces. The SOAP specification defines the following terms to identify the different entities involved in SOAP based message interchange:

Term	Description
SOAP Message	A SOAP message is a basic unit of communication in a message interchange.
SOAP Binding	SOAP binding is the formal set of rules for carrying SOAP messages on top of an underlying data transport protocol.

Table continued on following page

Term	Description
SOAP Node	A SOAP node is the entity that processes a SOAP message according to the conventions defined by the SOAP specification. Zero or more SOAP nodes may process a SOAP message before it reaches the ultimate recipient from the message originator.
SOAP Envelope	A SOAP envelope is the outermost syntactic construct of a SOAP message. This is represented by the document element `Envelope`, which belongs to the SOAP namespace.
SOAP Block	A SOAP block is an atomic unit of information that may be deciphered by a SOAP node processing the node. In our example, the `authentication` and `getCustomer` elements are SOAP blocks.
SOAP Header	A SOAP envelope may contain an optional child represented by the element `Header`, which may contain zero or more SOAP blocks. The SOAP header is used to add arbitrary information to the SOAP message in a decentralized way.
SOAP Body	A SOAP envelope should contain a child represented by the element `Body`, which may contain zero or more SOAP blocks. The SOAP Body elements are primarily used for storing the payload of the data interchange. The contents of the body are always intended for the ultimate recipient of the message.
SOAP Fault	This is a special SOAP block contained in the SOAP body and contains the error information generated by a SOAP node.
SOAP Sender	A SOAP sender is the SOAP node that transmits a SOAP message.
SOAP Receiver	A SOAP receiver is the SOAP node that receives a SOAP message.
Initial SOAP Sender	An initial SOAP sender is a SOAP node that originates a message.
Ultimate SOAP Receiver	An ultimate SOAP receiver is the SOAP node that is the ultimate destination of the SOAP message.
SOAP Intermediary	SOAP intermediaries are SOAP nodes that process the message before it reaches the ultimate SOAP receiver.
Message Path	A message path consists of an initial sender, an ultimate receiver, and zero or more intermediaries.

Message Processing and SOAP Headers

SOAP provides a flexible mechanism for extending a SOAP message in a decentralized and modular way, without there being prior knowledge between the communicating parties. Typical examples of extensions that can be implemented as SOAP header blocks are authentication, transaction management, and payment.

All immediate children of SOAP Header elements are called header blocks, which must all be namespace qualified. The header blocks may use the `actor` and `mustUnderstand` attributes that belong to the SOAP namespace to identify the SOAP node that will process the header block.

The actor Attribute

A SOAP message travels from an initial SOAP sender to an ultimate SOAP receiver along a SOAP message path. Along the way, it can pass through a set of SOAP intermediaries. The intermediaries and the ultimate SOAP receiver are identified by a URI specified using the `actor` attribute. A SOAP intermediary to which a header block is addressed should process the block and remove it before the message is propagated further in the message path. The intermediary should not modify the SOAP body information.

If the `actor` attribute is not specified, the header block is addressed to the ultimate recipient. The SOAP intermediaries interrogate the `actor` attribute associated with all the header blocks and identify the header blocks addressed to them.

The mustUnderstand Attribute

The `mustUnderstand` attribute identifies whether a SOAP node can ignore a header block that is addressed to it. If the `mustUnderstand` attribute is set to a value of `1`, the SOAP node is mandated to process the message; if it can't process the message it should raise a SOAP fault and abort the propagation of the message further down the message path.

The default value of this attribute is `0`. Our example contains an optional header block called `authentication`, addressed to the ultimate receiver:

```
<auth:authentication xmlns:auth="http://mutant.com/cdrs/authentication">
  <auth:userId>ranieri</auth:userId>
  <auth:password>chelseaFC</auth:password>
</auth:authentication>
```

Header blocks are good candidates for sending authentication information. In our application, most of the messages won't have SOAP intermediaries, so the header blocks will be mandatory ones addressed to the ultimate receivers.

SOAP Fault

SOAP fault is a special body block added by a SOAP node that indicates a fault in processing the message. For example:

```
<env:Body>
  <env:Fault>
    <faultcode>MustUnderstand</faultcode>
    <faultstring>One or more mandatory headers not understood</faultstring>
  </env:Fault>
</env:Body>
```

The `Fault` element may also contain optional child elements named `faultActor` that identify the SOAP node that caused the fault. The `Fault` element can also contain a `detail` element that contains details of the fault that occurred. When an exception is thrown during processing of the message, some Java implementations use the `detail` element to pass the stack trace back to the sender.

The SOAP specification defines the following fault codes:

Fault Code	**Cause**
`VersionMismatch`	Faults caused by namespace mismatches
`MustUnderstand`	Faults caused when a SOAP node can't process a mandatory header block
`Client`	Faults caused by incorrect information in the message sent by the client
`Server`	Faults caused during message processing at the server

SOAP Encoding

SOAP encoding specifies how application specific data types are represented within the SOAP message. The specification for SOAP encoding is closely related to the XML schema specification.

The namespace URI http://www.w3.org/2001/06/soap-encoding defines the set of default SOAP encoding rules. The encoding rule used by any element in SOAP blocks may use the `encodingStyle` attribute to specify the encoding used within that element. This attribute belongs to the SOAP namespace. The SOAP encoding rule supports simple types, compound types, and arrays. All simple values are represented as element content and the types of the values should be specified using one of the following:

- The `xsi:type` attribute in the containing element
- The containing element instance is itself contained within an element containing an `enc:arrayType` attribute (this is applicable for arrays)
- The name of the element bears a definite relation to the type, that type can then be determined from a schema

Simple types are always represented as character data and the enclosing element will specify the type using the `xsi:type` attribute. A compound value is encoded as a sequence of elements, each accessor represented by an embedded element whose name corresponds to the name of the accessor. A multi-reference simple or compound value is encoded as an independent element containing a local, unqualified attribute named `id` and of type `ID`. Each accessor to this value is an empty element having a local, unqualified attribute named `href` and have type `uri-reference`. Arrays are compound values defined as having a type of `enc:Array`.

You should refer to the SOAP specification for an exhaustive coverage of SOAP encoding rules. However, most off-the-shelf SOAP implementations have the object serialization and the framework will handle encoding rules transparently.

SOAP RPC

In this section, we will have a look at the scheme for representing a remote procedure call (RPC) and the responses using SOAP. If SOAP RPC is used on top of HTTP, the SOAP RPC represents the HTTP request and the HTTP response maps to the RPC result. To invoke an RPC using SOAP the following information is required:

- The URI of the target SOAP node
- A method name and an optional method signature
- The parameters to the method
- Optional header data

Both RPC invocation and responses are stored as body content. An RPC invocation is modeled as a complex type with accessors representing each parameter. The name of the compound type should map to the method name. Each parameter is viewed as an accessor, with a name corresponding to the name of the parameter and type corresponding to the type of the parameter. These appear in the same order as in the procedure or method signature. The response is viewed as a compound type containing an accessor for the return. The name of the return value element and the body block is not relevant. SOAP also supports OUT and IN/OUT parameters. For RPC responses the OUT and IN/OUT parameter elements follow the return value element. An invocation fault is encoded as a SOAP fault.

The example below shows a typical RPC encoded using SOAP:

```
<env:Envelopexmlns:env="http://www.w3c.org/2001/06/soap-envelope"
  xmlns:xsi="http://www.w3.org/2001/XMLSchema-instance"
  xmlns:xsd="http://www.w3.org/2001/XMLSchema" >
  <env:Body>
    <app:getClosingValue
      xmlns:app="mutant.com"
      env:encodingStyle="http://www.w3.org/2001/06/soap-encoding" >
      <app:sedol xsi:type="xsd:string">00098765</app:sedol>
    </app:getClosingValue>
  </env:Body>
</env:Envelope>
```

Most SOAP implementations provide a simple API for invoking the RPC and handle most of the tedious tasks like generating the SOAP envelope that represent the RPC, and serializing the parameters. Some of them also let you do SOAP based messaging where you need to create the SOAP envelopes that represent the RPC – even though this sounds a bit complicated, it allows you to have finer control over the information you interchange.

SOAP Features

In summary, the main features of SOAP are:

- It supports HTTP tunneling as a transport binding
- It supports RPC handling as a service

- It can support disconnected operations if the transport supports disconnected operations, including SMTP, and MOM
- The encoding rules are quite complicated and closely related to XML Schema specification
- Even though simple SOAP envelopes are decipherable by human readers, relatively complicated ones may need machine assistance
- General protocol efficiency was not a design goal and consequently SOAP doesn't support multiplexing channels
- Even though `actor` and `mustUnderstand` attributes promote decentralized processing of messages, no implementation details have bennspecified.
- Security and authentication are not directly specified. However, most of the implementations provide added security features

Apache SOAP Implementation

We've covered the part of the SOAP specification, but to write SOAP aware web services and clients we need to have software that *implements* the SOAP specification. For our sample application we will use the SOAP implementation from the Apache Software Foundation, which provides a framework for writing SOAP RPC as well as messaging services and clients.

The SOAP RPC implementation provides a sophisticated way of passing parameters and getting results using remote procedure calls. Behind the scenes, the framework will take care of SOAP translation, encoding, transport, and routing.

SOAP messaging is a bit more complicated. We need to create the SOAP envelopes and the framework will perform transport and message routing. However, SOAP messaging gives us finer grained control than SOAP RPC. In our sample application we will be implementing our web services as SOAP messaging services and writing SOAP clients that will exchange SOAP envelopes with the web services.

We won't be covering the Apache SOAP implementation exhaustively in this section. Instead, we will be covering only those concepts, classes, and methods that will enable us to write simple SOAP messaging services and clients required for our particular application.

Installing Apache SOAP

The binary distribution for Apache SOAP may be downloaded from http://xml.apache.org/dist/soap/version-2.2/. To actually make use of Apache SOAP, you will also need the following:

- A JAXP compliant, namespace aware, XML parser. Xerces was used to build the sample application and is available from http://xml.apache.org/xerces2-j/.
- The JavaMail API, which is available from http://java.sun.com/products/javamail/.
- The JavaBeans Activation Framework, which is available from http://java.sun.com/products/javabeans/glasgow/jaf.html.

The SOAP implementation from Apache is a J2EE web application that can be run in any J2EE web container. The unpacked SOAP distribution has a directory called `webapps` under the root SOAP directory. This directory contains the WAR file for the web application, which you should expand and copy to the `webapps` directory of Tomcat.

You may need to add more classes to your SOAP web application when you write services. To ensure that the necessary classes are available you should add the following files to the `WEB-INF\lib` directory of the expanded SOAP web application:

- `xerces.jar`
- `mail.jar`
- `activation.jar`

We also need these JAR files to write SOAP clients as well as for compiling our web services and client classes.

To test the SOAP installation you should start Tomcat and navigate to http://localhost:8080/soap/servlet/messagerouter/. If you get the following screen, your SOAP installation has been successful:

Writing SOAP Messaging Services

Let's look at how to develop and deploy a SOAP message service with our installation of Apache SOAP. Message services are responsible for the message content from the SOAP envelope passed on to them by the message router.

The Apache SOAP API provides the infrastructure classes to create a SOAP envelope, to add content to it, to send it to a message router, and to read the contents of the envelope. SOAP message services may participate in a request-response paradigm with the SOAP client. SOAP message services give us more control over the data that is interchanged between the web service clients and the web services, such that it allows any XML node to be passed as a SOAP body block.

SOAP message services are defined as methods against a class. These methods are required to conform to the signature shown below:

```
public void nameOfService (SOAPEnvelope requestEnvelope,
                           SOAPContext requestContext,
                           SOAPContext responseContext)
```

Where `nameOfService` is the name of the service. The class `SOAPEnvelope` models a SOAP envelope with methods for adding and extracting header and body entries. The reference `requestEnvelope` contains the incoming message and the references `requestContext` and `responseContext` point to the `SOAPContext` associated with the request and response respectively.

The services may use `responseContext` to send messages back to clients. A typical sequence of events involved in writing a SOAP message service participating in a request-response paradigm is:

- Receive the incoming message using the registered service
- Read the body of the request envelope and then read the body blocks from the body
- Perform processing and then create a new envelope to send back to the client
- Create a new body and add body blocks
- Add the body to the response envelope
- Marshall the envelope and send it back to the client using the response context

> *We will have a look at some example web services written using SOAP message service when we start writing our sample application.*

The following code snippet illustrates how this sequence of events is implemented:

```
public void msg(SOAPEnvelope reqEnvelope,
                SOAPContext reqContext,
                SOAPContext resContext) {

  Body reqBody = reqEnvelope.getBody();
  Vector reqBodyEntries = reqBody.getBodyEntries();
  Node bodyNode = (Node)reqBodyEntries.elementAt(0);
```

Perform processing:

```
  Envelope resEnvelope = new Envelope();
  Vector resBodyEntries = new Vector();
  Body resBody = new Body();
```

Add body blocks to the body:

```
  resBody.setBodyEntries(resBodyEntries);
  resEnvelope.setBody(resBody);

  StringWriter sw = new StringWriter();
  XMLJavaMappingRegistry reg = new XMLJavaMappingRegistry();
  resEnvelope.marshall(sw, reg, resContext);
  resContext.setRootPart(sw.toString(), "text/xml");
  System.out.println("getEmployeeList: End");
}
```

Deploying a Message Service

Once we have written a service, we need to deploy it on the server so that the clients can access it. The Apache SOAP web application that we installed earlier on Tomcat can be used to deploy services. We will see how to use this web-based administration when we come to deploy the web services we create for use with our sample application.

Writing SOAP Message Clients

SOAP message clients access the SOAP message services and send SOAP envelopes. If they work within a request-response paradigm, they will also receive the response envelopes sent back by the services. A typical sequence of events in writing a SOAP message client working in a request-response paradigm is:

- Create a new request envelope.
- Create a new body.
- Create a new body block. The body block is an XML node, the name of the root element of this node should match the name of the targeted method, and the name space URI should match the id of the targeted object.
- Add the body block to the body and the body to the envelope.
- Create a new `Message` object. Use the `send()` method on the `Message` object to send the envelope by specifying the URL of the Apache SOAP message router servlet.
- Receive the response envelope using the `Message` object. Extract the body, and body blocks, and perform the processing.

The code that follows illustrates how this sequence of events is implemented:

```
Envelope reqEnv = new Envelope();
Body body = new Body();
Vector bodyEntries = new Vector();
bodyEntries.addElement(soapRequestNode);
body.setBodyEntries(bodyEntries);
reqEnv.setBody(body);

Message msg = new Message();
msg.send(new URL(ROUTER), "urn", reqEnv);

Envelope resEnvelope = msg.receiveEnvelope();
Vector resBodyEntries = resEnvelope.getBody().getBodyEntries();
Node resNode = (Node)resBodyEntries.elementAt(0);
```

Now that we have the XML-JSP framework ready and have enough information to write SOAP aware web services and clients, we can start to implement our sample employee information system.

Sample Application Use Cases

When the users access the system, the web tier will display a list of employees. For this the web tier will access the web service that provides the list of employees. The web service reads this information from an XML file held locally.

When the users click on the link to add a new employee, the web tier will present a form for entering the employee information. The form will let the users choose a department from a list of departments. For this the web tier will access the web service that provides the list of departments.

When the user submits the form, the web tier will first validate the user input and then call the web service to create the new employee. The web service will add the new employee to the XML file and call the service to get the new list of employees. This service will return the new list of employees to the web tier, and the web tier can then display this list.

Application Configuration

From our analysis of how the application will be used, it is evident that there will be three types of requests going from the client browser to the framework:

- Requests for the list of employees
- Requests for a new form for entering employee details
- Requests for creating a new employee

Our task is to come up with a matrix that maps request URIs to handlers, generators, schema documents, and JSP pages, and use this to come up with the configuration file for the application.

The matrix below maps request URIs to DOM generators, schema documents, and request handlers:

URI	DOM Generator	Schema	Handler
`EmployeeList.do`	None	None	`EmployeeList Handler`
`EmployeeNew.do`	None	None	`EmployeeNew Handler`
`EmployeeCreate.do`	`EmployeeDOMGenerator`	`employee.xsd`	`EmployeeCreate Handler`

The `EmployeeList.do` requests will have DOM generation and schema validation switched off and the `EmployeeListHandler` class will handle the requests. This class will:

- Access the relevant web service to get the list of employees
- Store the list as a request scope bean in the form of an XML node
- Forward it to the appropriate JSP page responsible for rendering the information

The `EmployeeNew.do` requests will have DOM generation and schema validation switched off and the `EmployeeNewHandler` class will handle the requests. This class will:

- Access the relevant web service to get the list of departments
- Store the list as a request scope bean in the form of an XML node
- Forward it to the appropriate JSP page responsible for rendering the information

The `EmployeeCreate.do` requests will use the class `EmployeeDOMGenerator` for generating the XML node and validate it using the XML document called `employee.xsd` and the request will be handled by the class `EmployeeCreateHandler`. This class will:

- Access the relevant web service to create the employee
- Receive the new list of employees
- Store the list as a request scope bean in the form of an XML node
- Forward it to the appropriate JSP page responsible for rendering the information

The matrix below shows the mapping between request URIs to the resources that render the response on successfully processing the request as well as failing to process the request:

URI	Resource on Success	Resource on Failure
`EmployeeList.do`	`EmployeeList.jsp`	None
`EmployeeNew.do`	`EmployeeNew.jsp`	None
`EmployeeCreate.do`	`EmployeeList.jsp`	`EmployeeNew.do`

The request handler for `EmployeeList.do` requests will forward the response to the `EmployeeList.jsp` on successfully processing the request. This JSP page will use the custom tags from the XML tag library to iterate over the list of employees stored as an XML node and render the information. If the processing is not successful due to some unknown exception, the response is sent to the servlet container's error page.

The request handler for `EmployeeNew.do` requests will forward the response to the `EmployeeNew.jsp` on successfully processing the request. This JSP page will use the custom tags from the XML and HTML tag libraries to render the form for entering the employee information. If the form is sent back to the users because of validation errors the custom tags will retain the original data entered by the users by extracting them from the XML node generated when the form was submitted last time. If the processing is not successful due to some unknown exception, the response is sent to the servlet container's error page.

The request handler for `EmployeeCreate.do` requests will forward the response to the `EmployeeList.jsp` on successfully processing the request. This JSP will use the custom tags from the XML tag library to iterate over the list of employees stored as an XML node and render the information. If the processing is not successful due to validation errors, the response is sent to the resource `EmployeeNew.do`. It is sent to `EmployeeNew.do` instead of `EmployeeNew.jsp` because the request going to `EmployeeNew.do` will access the request handler `EmployeeNewHandler` and the handler will populate the list of departments.

The full listing of the configuration file is shown below:

```
<config>
```

Declare the request handlers:

```
  <request-handlers>
    <request-handler id="list-handler"
                     class="application.handlers.EmployeeListHandler"/>
    <request-handler id="new-handler"
                     class="application.handlers.EmployeeNewHandler"/>
    <request-handler id="create-handler"
                     class="application.handlers.EmployeeCreateHandler"/>
  </request-handlers>
```

Declare the DOM generators:

```
  <dom-generators>
    <dom-generator id="create-generator"
                   class="application.xml.EmployeeDOMGenerator"/>
  </dom-generators>
```

Declare the mapping for `EmployeeList.do` requests:

```
  <request uri="EmployeeList.do">
    <handler ref="list-handler"/>
    <forwards>
      <forward name="SUCCESS" resource="EmployeeList.jsp"
               redirect="false"/>
    </forwards>
  </request>
```

Declare the mapping for `EmployeeNew.do` requests:

```
  <request uri="EmployeeNew.do">
    <handler ref="new-handler"/>
    <forwards>
      <forward name="SUCCESS" resource="EmployeeNew.jsp"
               redirect="false"/>
    </forwards>
  </request>
```

Mapping for `EmployeeCreate.do` requests:

```
  <request uri="EmployeeCreate.do">
```

Define the schema information:

```
      <schema namespace-aware="false"
              location="http://localhost:8080/employee/schema/employee.xsd"/>
      <handler ref="create-handler"/>
```

Define the DOM generator information:

```
      <generator ref="create-generator" dom-name="employee"
                 dom-scope="request"/>
      <forwards>
        <forward name="SUCCESS" resource="EmployeeList.jsp"
                 redirect="false"/>
      </forwards>
```

Finally, define the resource used to send the response back on validation errors:

```
      <input resource="/EmployeeNew.do"/>
    </request>
  </config>
```

The Web Services

Now we will have a look at the web services used in the system. From our earlier analysis, it is evident that we need three services to:

- Get the list of employees
- Get the list of departments
- Create new employees

We will define the services related to employees in one class and the department service in another.

The EmployeeService Class

The `EmployeeService` class will define the methods for the services to get the current list of employees and create a new employee. The instance of this class is defined (in the deployment descriptor) to live for the entire lifecycle of the application. Hence, when the instance is constructed, the class reads an XML file that contains the employee data, parses it to an XML DOM, and stores it in an instance variable.

When a request comes for the current list of employees, the class returns the document element of the employee DOM wrapped in a SOAP envelope. When a request comes in to add a new employee, the class extracts the employee information stored as an XML node from the request envelope and adds it to the employee DOM. It will also serialize the employee DOM and write it to the persistent backup:

```
package services;

import java.io.*;
```

```
import java.util.Vector;
import javax.xml.parsers.DocumentBuilder;
import org.apache.soap.*;
import org.apache.soap.util.xml.*;
import org.w3c.dom.*;
import org.xml.sax.InputSource;

public class EmployeeService {
```

We define the location of the employee XML file (you will need to change this to reflect the set up on your system):

```
  private static final String DATA_LOCATION =
          "c:/employee.xml";
```

This is the in-memory copy of the employee DOM:

```
  private Document employeeDOM;
```

The employee XML is read, parsed and stored as an in-memory DOM in the constructor:

```
  public EmployeeService() throws Exception {
    try {
      FileReader fr = new FileReader(DATA_LOCATION);
      DocumentBuilder xdb = XMLParserUtils.getXMLDocBuilder();
      employeeDOM = xdb.parse(new InputSource(fr));
      fr.close();

    } catch(Exception e) {
        e.printStackTrace();
        throw e;
    }
  }
```

Next, we declare a method that gets a list of employees:

```
  public void getEmployeeList(Envelope reqEnvelope, SOAPContext reqContext,
                              SOAPContext resContext) throws Exception {
    try {
```

Create a new SOAP envelope:

```
      Envelope resEnvelope = new Envelope();
```

Create a vector to hold the body blocks:

```
      Vector resBodyEntries = new Vector();
```

Create a new body:

```
      Body resBody = new Body();
      synchronized(this) {
```

Add the document element of the employee DOM as a body block:

```
        resBodyEntries.addElement(employeeDOM.getDocumentElement());
      }
```

Set the body entries:

```
        resBody.setBodyEntries(resBodyEntries);
```

Set the body:

```
      resEnvelope.setBody(resBody);
```

Marshal the envelope and send it back to the client.

```
      StringWriter sw = new StringWriter();
      XMLJavaMappingRegistry reg = new XMLJavaMappingRegistry();
      resEnvelope.marshall(sw, reg, resContext);
      resContext.setRootPart(sw.toString(), "text/xml");
      System.out.println("getEmployeeList: End");

    } catch(Exception e) {
      e.printStackTrace();
      throw e;
    }
  }
```

We also need a method to add an employee:

```
  public void addEmployee(Envelope reqEnvelope, SOAPContext reqContext,
                              SOAPContext resContext) throws Exception {
    try {
```

Get the body content from the envelope, and from the body entries get the first body block. This will be the XML node created by the clients that will contain the information about the new employee:

```
      Body reqBody = reqEnvelope.getBody();
      Vector reqBodyEntries = reqBody.getBodyEntries();
      Node bodyNode = (Node)reqBodyEntries.elementAt(0);
      Node employeeNode = bodyNode.getFirstChild();

      synchronized(this) {
```

Change the owner document of the `employee` node:

```
Node importedNode = employeeDOM.importNode(employeeNode, true);
```

Add the new `employee` node to the document element of the employee DOM:

```
employeeDOM.getDocumentElement().appendChild(importedNode);
```

Serialize the DOM and store it to the persistent backup:

```
        FileWriter fw = new FileWriter(DATA_LOCATION);
        DOMWriter.serializeAsXML(employeeDOM, fw);
        fw.close();
      }
```

Call the service to return the new list of employees:

```
        getEmployeeList(reqEnvelope, reqContext, resContext);

      } catch(Exception e) {
        e.printStackTrace();
        throw e;
      }
    }
  }
```

Employee DOM

This is some sample data that we will store as `C:/employee.xml`:

```
<?xml version="1.0"?>
<employees>
  <employee>
    <id>1</id>
    <name>Luca Vialli</name>
    <gender>Male</gender>
    <marital-status>Single</marital-status>
    <department>Sales</department>
    <comments/>
  </employee>
  <employee>
    <id>2</id>
    <name>Franco Zola</name>
    <gender>Male</gender>
    <marital-status>Single</marital-status>
    <department>Sales</department>
    <comments/>
  </employee>
</employees>
```

SOAP Envelope

Now we will have a look at the sample request and response envelope for the above services. The snippet below shows the request envelope for the `getEmployeeList` service. The XML for the SOAP envelopes is generated by the Apache-SOAP implementation. Apache SOAP also provides a utility tool for viewing the envelopes that are exchanged between the parties participating in the data interchange.

```
<env:envelope xmlns:env="http://www.w3.org/2001/06/soap-envelope">
  <env:body>
    <getEmployeeList xmlns="urn:employee-service">
    </getEmployeeList>
  </env:body>
</env:envelope>
```

The snippet below shows the request envelope for the `addEmployee` service:

```
<env:envelope xmlns:env="http://www.w3.org/2001/06/soap-envelope">
  <env:body>
    <addEmployee xmlns="urn:employee-service">
      <employee>
        <id>1</id>
        <name>Luca Vialli</name>
        <gender>Male</gender>
        <marital-status>Single</marital-status>
        <department>Sales</department>
        <comments/>
      </employee>
    </addEmployee>
  </env:body>
</env:envelope>
```

The document below shows the response envelope for both the services:

```
<env:envelope xmlns:env="http://www.w3.org/2001/06/soap-envelope">
  <env:body>
    <employees>
      <employee>
        <id>1</id>
        <name>Luca Vialli</name>
        <gender>Male</gender>
        <marital-status>Single</marital-status>
        <department>Sales</department>
        <comments/>
      </employee>
      <employee>
        <id>2</id>
        <name>Franco Zola</name>
        <gender>Male</gender>
        <marital-status>Single</marital-status>
        <department>Sales</department>
        <comments/>
      </employee>
    </employees>
  </env:body>
</env:envelope>
```

The DepartmentService Class

The `DepartmentService` class will define the methods for the services to get the current list of departments. The instance of this class is defined to live for the entire lifecycle of the application in the deployment descriptor. Then, when the instance is constructed, the class reads an XML file that contains the department data, parses it to an XML DOM, and stores it in an instance variable. When a request comes for the current list of departments, the class returns the document element of the employee DOM wrapped in a SOAP envelope:

```
package services;

import org.apache.soap.*;
import org.apache.soap.rpc.SOAPContext;
import org.apache.soap.util.xml.*;
import org.w3c.dom.*;
import org.xml.sax.InputSource;
import java.io.*;
import java.util.Vector;
import javax.xml.parsers.DocumentBuilder;

public class DepartmentService {
```

The location of the file that contains the department data (again, change this as required for your system):

```
  public static final String DATA_LOCATION = "c:/department.xml";
```

This is the in-memory copy of the department DOM:

```
  public Document departmentDOM;
```

The department XML is read, parsed, and stored as an in-memory DOM in the constructor:

```
  public DepartmentService() throws Exception {
    try {
      FileReader fr = new FileReader(DATA_LOCATION);
      DocumentBuilder xdb = XMLParserUtils.getXMLDocBuilder();
      departmentDOM = xdb.parse(new InputSource(fr));
      fr.close();
      System.out.println("Department service: Started");

    } catch(Exception e) {
        e.printStackTrace();
        throw e;
    }
  }
```

We declare a method that gets a list of employees:

```
  public void getDepartmentList(Envelope reqEnvelope,
      SOAPContext reqContext, SOAPContext resContext) throws Exception {
    try {
```

Create a new envelope:

```
        Envelope resEnvelope = new Envelope();
```

Create a new vector that holds body blocks:

```
        Vector resBodyEntries = new Vector();
```

Create a new body:

```
        Body resBody = new Body();
```

Add the department DOM document element to the vector:

```
        resBodyEntries.addElement(departmentDOM.getDocumentElement());
```

Set the body entries and the body:

```
        resBody.setBodyEntries(resBodyEntries);
        resEnvelope.setBody(resBody);
```

Marshall the envelope and return it to the client using the response context:

```
        StringWriter sw = new StringWriter();
        XMLJavaMappingRegistry reg = new XMLJavaMappingRegistry();
        resEnvelope.marshall(sw, reg, resContext);
        resContext.setRootPart(sw.toString(), "text/xml");

      } catch(Exception e) {
        e.printStackTrace();
        throw e;
      }
    }
  }
```

Department DOM

This is some sample data that we will store as `C:/department.xml`:

```
<?xml version="1.0"?>
<departments>
  <department>Sale</department>
  <department>Production</department>
</departments>
```

SOAP Envelope

Now we will have a look at the sample request and response envelope for the above services. The snippet below shows the request envelope for the `getDepartmentList` service.

```
<env:envelope xmlns:env="http://www.w3.org/2001/06/soap-envelope">
  <env:body>
    <getDepartmentList xmlns="urn:department-service">
    </getDepartmentist>
  </env:body>
</env:envelope>
```

The snippet below shows the response envelope for the `getDepartmentList` service:

```
<env:envelope xmlns:env="http://www.w3.org/2001/06/soap-envelope">
  <env:body>
    <departments>
      <department>Sales</department>
      <department>Production</department>
    </departments>
  </env:body>
</env:envelope>
```

Deploying the Services

Next, we'll deploy our two web services using the Administration tool that comes as part of the Apache SOAP Implementation. Make sure that you have installed the SOAP web application, start up Tomcat, and then navigate to http://localhost:8080/soap/admin:

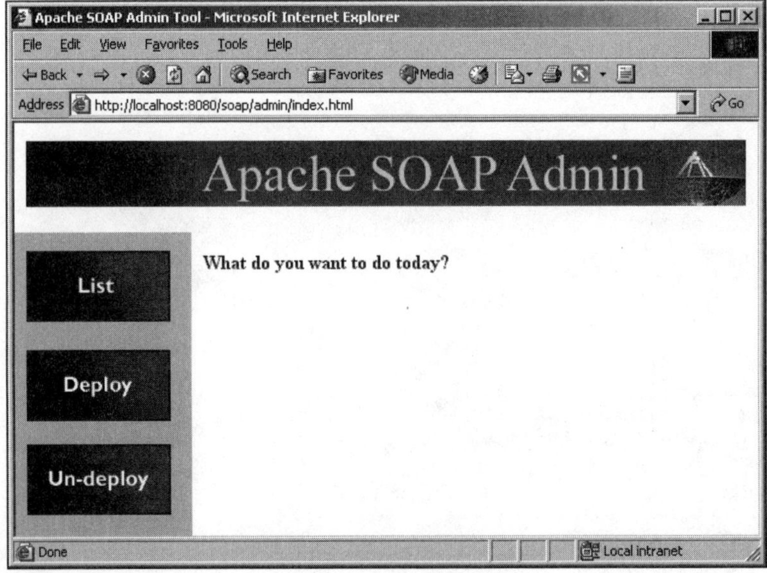

We have three options. We can list all the services currently deployed, deploy a new service, or un-deploy an existing service. We need to deploy two new services, so click the Deploy link:

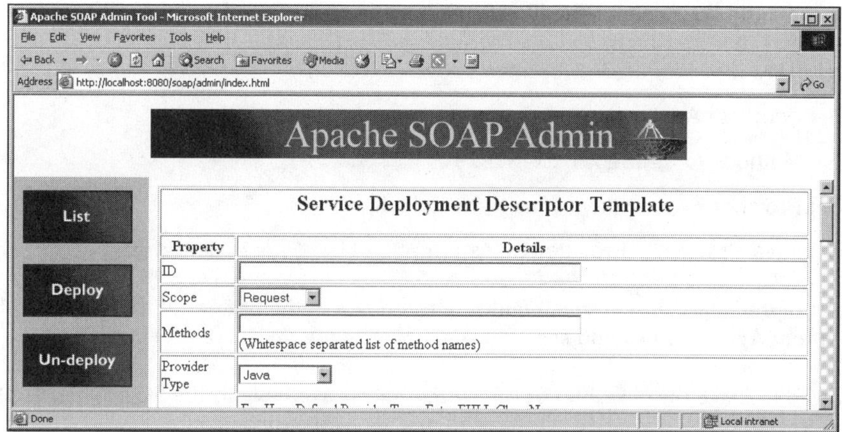

We need to set a few of these options. For the employee service we need to:

- Set **ID** to `urn:employee-service`
- Set **Scope** to **Application**
- Set **Methods** to `getEmployeeList addEmployee`
- Set **Provider Type** to **Java** (this is the default)
- Set **Java Provider – Provider Class** to `services.EmployeeService`

For the rest of the fields, accept the defaults. Scroll down to the bottom of the screen and click on the **Deploy** button. If the deployment is successful, the following message is displayed:

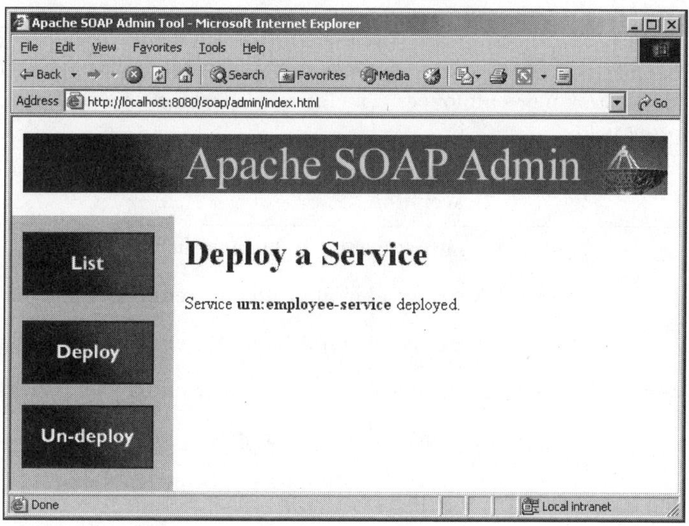

Now we need to do the same for the Department service. Click on Deploy, and enter the following:

- Set ID to `urn:department-service`
- Set Scope to Application
- Set Methods to `getDepartmentList`
- Set Provider Type to Java (this is the default)
- Set Java Provider – Provider Class to `services.DepartmentService`

For the rest of the fields, accept the defaults. Scroll down to the bottom of the screen and click on the Deploy button. Again, you should see a message confirming the successful deployment of the service.

Now we need to make the class files of the target objects available to the SOAP web application:

- Create a directory called `services` under the `WEB-INF\classes\` directory of the SOAP web application
- Compile the classes `EmployeeService` and `DepartmentService`
- Make sure that all the JAR files mentioned above are in the classpath
- Copy the class files to the `WEB-INF\classes\services\` directory
- Ensure that you have the employee and department XML files that contain the relevant data in the locations specified by the instance variables

Now our web services are ready to serve client requests and we are in a position to create the web tier using the XML-JSP framework from Chapters 15 and 16 to access these services.

DOM Generation

In the section on application configuration we have said that XML DOM generation is switched on only for the requests for creating new employees. The form for entering new employee information will provide the following fields:

Field	Description
`id`	A numeric value indicating the employee id
`name`	A string value indicating the employee's name
`gender`	A string value indicating the employee's gender
`marital-status`	A string value indicating the employee's marital status
`department`	A string value indicating the employee's department
`comment`	A string value representing any comment

The DOM generator will create a. XML node as shown below that can be sent as a part of the body block to the SOAP service for creating new employees:

```
<employee
      xmlns:xsi="http://www.w3.org/2001/XMLSchema-instance"
      xsi:noNamespaceSchemaLocation=
          "http://localhost:8080/employee/schema/employee.xsd">
  <id>1</id>
  <name>Luca Vialli</name>
  <gender>Male</gender>
  <marital-status>Single</marital-status>
  <department>Sales</department>
  <comments/>
</employee>
```

The DOM generator will also set up the schema location that can be used later by the validation module for validating the data entered by the end users.

The EmployeeDOMGenerator Class

Let's look at the source code for the DOM generator associated with the request URI `EmployeeCreate.do`:

```
package application.xml;

import javax.xml.parsers.*;
import javax.servlet.http.HttpServletRequest;
import org.w3c.dom.*;
import framework.system.*;
import framework.xml.DOMGenerator;

public class EmployeeDOMGenerator implements DOMGenerator {
```

Define the expected request parameter names:

```
  private static final String[] elements =
          {"id","name","gender","marital-status","department","comments"};

  public Node generateDOM(HttpServletRequest request,
                      RequestMapping mapping) throws FrameworkException {
    try {
```

Get the `Schema` object associated with the mapping:

```
      Schema schema = mapping.getSchema();
```

Create an empty XML document using the standard JAXP API:

```
DocumentBuilderFactory factory = DocumentBuilderFactory.newInstance();
factory.setNamespaceAware(true);

DocumentBuilder builder =  factory.newDocumentBuilder();
Document document = builder.newDocument();

DOMInfo domInfo = mapping.getDOMInfo();
Element root = document.createElement("employee");
```

If the `Schema` object is not null, set the `noNamespaceSchemaLocation` attribute for the document element:

```
if(schema != null) {
  Attr schemaNS = document.createAttribute("xmlns:xsi");
  schemaNS.setValue("http://www.w3.org/2001/XMLSchema-instance");
  root.setAttributeNode(schemaNS);

  Attr schemaLoc = document.createAttribute(
                                  "xsi:noNamespaceSchemaLocation");
  schemaLoc.setValue(schema.getLocation());
  root.setAttributeNode(schemaLoc);

}
```

Iterate through the array of expected request parameter names and if it is present in the current request, and the value is not an empty string, create an element with name as the request parameter name and content as the request parameter value. Then append this element to the document element:

```
for(int i = 0;i < elements.length;i++) {
  Element child = document.createElement(elements[i]);
  String value = request.getParameter(elements[i]);

  if(value != null && !value.trim().equals("")) {
    Text text = document.createTextNode(value);
    child.appendChild(text);
    root.appendChild(child);
  }
}
```

Return the document element:

```
        return root;

      } catch(ParserConfigurationException e) {
        throw new FrameworkException(e, Severity.UNEXPECTED);
      }
    }
  }
```

The Schema Document

Now we will have a look at the schema document that will be used to validate the employee information entered by the end users. The schema will enforce the following validation constraints:

- Users must enter values for id, name, gender, marital status, department and location
- The value entered for id must be an integer

The example below shows the content of the schema document `employee.xsd`:

```
<xsd:schema xmlns:xsd="http://www.w3.org/2001/XMLSchema">
```

Declare the document element:

```
  <xsd:element name="employee" type="Employee"/>
```

Define the type for the document element:

```
  <xsd:complexType name="Employee">
    <xsd:sequence>
```

Declare the element `id` as of type `int`. The element is expected to appear exactly once in the parent elements content:

```
      <xsd:element name="id" minOccurs="1" type="xsd:int"/>
```

All the other elements are declared as type `string`. These elements are expected to appear exactly once in the parent elements content:

```
      <xsd:element name="name" minOccurs="1" type="xsd:string"/>
      <xsd:element name="gender" minOccurs="1" type="xsd:string"/>
      <xsd:element name="marital-status" type="xsd:string"/>
      <xsd:element name="department" minOccurs="1" type="xsd:string"/>
      <xsd:element name="comments" minOccurs="1" type="xsd:string"/>
    </xsd:sequence>
  </xsd:complexType>
</xsd:schema>
```

Request Handlers

In this section, we will cover the request handler implementations used in the system. We have already seen that the system will be using three request handlers (one each for `EmployeeList.do`, `EmployeeCreate.do`, and `EmployeeNew.do`). All the request handlers will access the SOAP message services for retrieving/updating information.

The request handler for listing the employees will create a body block with the root element name and namespace URI mapping to the employee list web service. The body block returned from the web service - is a list of employees as an XML node - will be stored as a request scope bean and the response will be forwarded to the resource `EmployeeList.jsp`. This JSP page will then use the tags from XML tag library to iterate over the list of employees and render the details.

The request handler for displaying the form to enter new employees will create a body block with the root element name and namespace URI mapping to the department list web service. The body block returned from the web service is a list of departments as an XML node, and will be stored as a request scope bean and the response will be forwarded to the resource `EmployeeNew.jsp`. This JSP page will use the tags from our HTML tag library to render the employee form as well as the XML tag library to iterate over the list of departments and display it as a dropdown list box.

The request handler for creating new employees will create a body block with the root element name and namespace URI mapping to the employee create web service. It will also add the employee node that contains the details of the new employee to be created generated by the DOM generator as an immediate child of the body block. The body block returned from the web service is the new list of employees as an XML node, which will be stored as a request scope bean and the response will be forwarded to the resource `EmployeeList.jsp`. This JSP page will use the tags from our XML tag library to iterate over the list of employees and render the details.

From this discussion, it is evident that all the three request handlers share common functionality that can be abstracted to a delegate or a superclass. The only things the handlers need to do are to provide:

- The immediate child node of the body block
- The method name of the service
- The id of the target object

The abstraction can create a body block with the root element name as the name of the web service and namespace URI as the target object id. The body block child provided by the handlers may be inserted into the body block root and the envelope may be sent to the service. The body block of the response envelope may be extracted and returned to the handlers.

We will create a common superclass that will provide the functionality of handling SOAP envelopes for all our handlers.

The AbstractSOAPHandler Class

This class serves as the ancestor for all the handlers that send and receive SOAP envelopes:

```
package application.handlers;

import java.util.Vector;
import java.net.*;
import javax.xml.parsers.*;
import javax.xml.transform.TransformerException;
import org.w3c.dom.*;
import org.xml.sax.SAXException;
import org.apache.soap.*;
```

```
import org.apache.soap.messaging.Message;
import framework.system.*;
import framework.controller.RequestHandler;

public abstract class AbstractSOAPHandler implements RequestHandler {
```

Define the URL to the SOAP message router:

```
  private static final String ROUTER =
                      "http://localhost:8080/soap/servlet/messagerouter";
```

This method is called from the subclasses, takes the child element of the body block, method name of the web service and the id of the target object that implements the web service, and returns a body block node:

```
  protected Node getSOAPRequestNode(String method,
                                    String URN,
                                    Node dataNode)
                throws FrameworkException {
    try {
```

Create an empty document using the standard JAXP API:

```
      DocumentBuilderFactory factory = DocumentBuilderFactory.newInstance();
      DocumentBuilder builder = factory.newDocumentBuilder();
      Document document = builder.newDocument();
```

Create the body block root node and set the namespace URI as the target object id:

```
      Element soapRequestNode = document.createElement(method);
      soapRequestNode.setAttribute("xmlns", URN);
```

If the child element of the body block is not null, add it to the body block:

```
      if(dataNode != null) {
        Node importedNode = document.importNode(dataNode, true);
        soapRequestNode.appendChild(importedNode);
      }
```

Return the body block:

```
      return soapRequestNode;

    } catch(ParserConfigurationException e) {
      throw new FrameworkException(e, Severity.UNEXPECTED);
    } catch(Exception e) {
      throw new FrameworkException(e, Severity.UNEXPECTED);
    }
  }
```

This method accepts a body block, sends it as a SOAP envelope, accepts the response envelope, extracts the response body block and returns it to the subclass:

```
  protected Node getSOAPResponseNode(Node soapRequestNode)
                                              throws FrameworkException {
    try {
```

Create a new envelope and body. Create a vector that represents the body blocks and add the body block node. Add the body entries to the body and the body to the envelope:

```
      Envelope msgEnv = new Envelope();
      Body body = new Body();
      Vector bodyEntries = new Vector();
      bodyEntries.addElement(soapRequestNode);
      body.setBodyEntries(bodyEntries);
      msgEnv.setBody(body);
```

Send the message to the SOAP message router:

```
      Message msg = new Message();
      msg.send(new URL(ROUTER), "something", msgEnv);
```

Receive the envelope, extract the body block and return it to the subclass:

```
      Envelope resEnvelope = msg.receiveEnvelope();
      Vector resBodyEntries = resEnvelope.getBody().getBodyEntries();

      return (Node)resBodyEntries.elementAt(0);

    } catch(MalformedURLException e) {
      throw new FrameworkException(e, Severity.UNEXPECTED);
    } catch(SOAPException e) {
      throw new FrameworkException(e, Severity.UNEXPECTED);
    } catch(Exception e) {
      throw new FrameworkException(e, Severity.UNEXPECTED);
    }
  }
}
```

The sequence of events that occurs within the handler classes used in the system may be generalized as follows.

- The dispatcher servlet calls the `processRequest` method on the handler class.
- The handler class calls the super class method `getSOAPRequestNode` to get the SOAP body block that represents the request by passing the remote method name, remote object URI and the XML node containing the data entered by the end user.
- The XML node representing the SOAP request node is passed to the super class method `getSOAPResponseNode` to get the response from the web service an XML node.
- This XML node is stored as a request scope bean and a reference to the `Forward` object defined in the configuration file by the name `SUCCESS` is returned

The EmployeeListHandler Class

In this section, we will have a look at the source code for the handler that will produce the list of employees:

```
package application.handlers;

import javax.servlet.http.*;
import framework.system.*;
import framework.controller.RequestHandler;
import org.w3c.dom.*;

public class EmployeeListHandler extends AbstractSOAPHandler {
```

Define the service method name and the target object id:

```
  private static final String URN = "urn:employee-service";
  private static final String METHOD = "getEmployeeList";
```

Please note that for the `processRequest()` method of this handler a null value is passed for `inputDOM` because there is no DOM generator associated with this URI:

```
  public Forward processRequest(HttpServletRequest request,
                                HttpServletResponse response,
                                RequestMapping mapping,
                                Node inputDOM)
                 throws FrameworkException {
```

Call the super class method to create the body block:

```
    Node soapRequestNode = getSOAPRequestNode(METHOD, URN, null);
```

Call the super class method to send the request envelope and get the body block of the response envelope:

```
    Node employeeListNode = getSOAPResponseNode(soapRequestNode);
```

Store the XML node returned from the web service as a request scope bean. This node contains the list of employees:

```
    request.setAttribute("employeeList", employeeListNode);
```

Return the Forward object corresponding to the logical name `SUCCESS` to the dispatcher servlet. This Forward object maps to `EmployeeList.jsp` in the configuration file:

```
     return mapping.getForward("SUCCESS");
  }
}
```

The EmployeeNewHandler Class

In this section, we will have a look at the source code for the handler that will generate the new form for creating an employee with a dropdown list box pre-populated with the list of departments:

```
package application.handlers;

import javax.servlet.http.*;
import framework.system.*;
import framework.controller.RequestHandler;
import org.w3c.dom.*;

public class EmployeeNewHandler extends AbstractSOAPHandler {
```

Define the service method name and the target object id:

```
  private static final String URN = "urn:department-service";
  private static final String METHOD = "getDepartmentList";
```

For the `processRequest()` method of this handler a null value is passed for `inputDOM` because there is no DOM generator associated with this URI:

```
  public Forward processRequest(HttpServletRequest request,
                               HttpServletResponse response,
                               RequestMapping mapping,
                               Node inputDOM)
                 throws FrameworkException {
```

Call the super class method to create the body block:

```
    Node soapRequestNode = getSOAPRequestNode(METHOD, URN, null);
```

Call the super class method to send the request envelope and get the body block of the response envelope:

```
    Node employeeListNode = getSOAPResponseNode(soapRequestNode);
```

Store the XML node returned from the web service as a request scope bean. This node contains the list of departments:

```
    request.setAttribute("departmentList", employeeListNode);
```

Return the `Forward` object corresponding to the logical name `SUCCESS` to the dispatcher servlet. This Forward object maps to `EmployeeNew.jsp` in the configuration file:

```
    return mapping.getForward("SUCCESS");
  }
}
```

The EmployeeCreateHandler Class

In this section, we will have a look at the source code for the handler that will create the new employee and return the new list of employees:

```
package application.handlers;

import javax.servlet.http.HttpServletRequest;
import javax.servlet.http.HttpServletResponse;

import framework.system.FrameworkException;
import framework.system.RequestMapping;
import framework.system.Forward;

import framework.controller.RequestHandler;

import org.w3c.dom.Document;
import org.w3c.dom.Node;

public class EmployeeCreateHandler extends AbstractSOAPHandler {
```

Define the service method name and the target object id:

```
  private static final String URN = "urn:employee-service";
  private static final String METHOD = "addEmployee";
```

Please note that for the `processRequest()` method of this handler the employee node generated by the DOM generator is passed for `inputDOM`. This will be passed to the web service as a child of the body block:

```
  public Forward processRequest(HttpServletRequest request,
                                HttpServletResponse response,
                                RequestMapping mapping,
                                Node inputDOM) throws FrameworkException {
```

Call the super class method to create the body block:

```
    Node soapRequestNode = getSOAPRequestNode(METHOD, URN, inputDOM);
```

Call the super class method to send the request envelope and get the body block of the response envelope:

```
    Node employeeListNode = getSOAPResponseNode(soapRequestNode);
```

Store the XML node returned from the web service as a request scope bean. This node contains the list of employees:

```
      request.setAttribute("employeeList", employeeListNode);
```

Return the `Forward` object corresponding to the logical name `SUCCESS` to the dispatcher servlet. This `Forward` object maps to `EmployeeList.jsp` in the configuration file:

```
      return mapping.getForward("SUCCESS");
    }
  }
```

The JavaServer Pages

In this section, we will have a look at the JSP pages used in the application:

- `EmployeeList.jsp`
  This JSP page displays the list of existing employees.
- `EmployeeNew.jsp`
  This JSP page displays the form for adding a new employee.

The EmployeeList JSP

This is the source code for `EmployeeList.jsp`:

```
<%@ taglib uri="/WEB-INF/xml.tld" prefix="xml" %>

<html>
  <head>
    <title></title>
  </head>
  <body>
    <table border="1">
      <tr>
        <td><b>ID</b></td>
        <td><b>Name</b></td>
        <td><b>Gender</b></td>
        <td><b>Marital Status</b></td>
        <td><b>Department</b></td>
        <td><b>Comments</b></td>
      </tr>
```

Use the XML `forEach` tag to iterate through the employees node stored as a request attribute under the name `employeeList`. The current node from the list selected by the XPath expression is exposed as a page scope bean by the name `employee`:

```
      <xml:forEach name="employeeList" path="employee" id="employee">
        <tr>
```

Use the XML valueOf tag to print the sub elements of the employee node:

```
            <td><xml:valueOf node="employee" path="id/text()"/></td>
            <td><xml:valueOf node="employee" path="name/text()"/></td>
            <td><xml:valueOf node="employee" path="gender/text()"/></td>
            <td><xml:valueOf node="employee"
                             path="marital-status/text()"/></td>
            <td><xml:valueOf node="employee" path="department/text()"/></td>
            <td><xml:valueOf node="employee" path="comments/text()"/></td>
          <tr>
        </xml:forEach>
      </table>
      <br/>
```

Write the link to the resource that displays the form for adding new employees:

```
      <a href="EmployeeNew.do">Add Employee</a>
    </body>
  </html>
```

The EmployeeNew JSP

In this section, we will have a look at the source code for EmployeeNew.jsp:

```
  <%@ taglib uri="/WEB-INF/html.tld" prefix="html" %>
  <%@ taglib uri="/WEB-INF/xml.tld" prefix="xml" %>
```

This bean is used for displaying error messages. If the JSP is sent back due to validation errors, there will be a bean of type String by the name ERROR_MESSAGE already present in the request scope. Otherwise, a new String object will be created and it will be an empty string. Hence, no error message will be displayed:

```
  <jsp:useBean id="ERROR_MESSAGE" class="java.lang.String" scope="request"/>

  <html>
    <head>
      <title></title>
    </head>
    <body>
```

Display the error message:

```
      <%= ERROR_MESSAGE %>
```

Use the HTML `form` tag to render the form. This form will be linked to the DOM generated for the request mapping with the URI attribute as `EmployeeCreate.do`:

```
<html:form name="EmployeeForm" action="EmployeeCreate.do">
  <table>
    <tr>
      <td align="right">
        ID:
      </td>
      <td>
```

Render the id field using the HTML `text` tag:

```
        <html:text name="id" path="id/text()"/>
      </td>
    </tr>
    <tr>
      <td align="right">
        Name:
      </td>
      <td>
```

Render the name field using the HTML `text` tag:

```
        <html:text name="name" path="name/text()"/>
      </td>
    </tr>
    <tr>
      <td align="right">
        Sex:
      </td>
      <td>
```

Render the gender field as radio buttons using the HTML `radio` tag:

```
        <html:radio name="gender" value="Male" path="gender/text()"/>
        Male
        </br>
        <html:radio name="gender" value="Female" path="gender/text()"/>
        Female
      </td>
    </tr>
    <tr>
      <td align="right">
```

Render the marital status field as a checkbox using the HTML `checkbox` tag:

```
        Married:
      </td>
      <td>
        <html:checkbox name="marital-status" value="Y"
```

```
                                path="marital-status/text()"/>
          </td>
        </tr>
        <tr>
          <td align="right">
            Department:
          </td>
          <td>
```

Render the department field as a dropdown list box using the HTML `select` tag. The options for the select element are extracted from the department DOM using the XML `forEach` tag and rendered using the HTML `option` tag:

```
            <html:select name="department" path="department/text()">
              <xml:forEach name="departmentList" id="currDepartment"
                                path="department">
                <html:option name="currDepartment" labelPath="text()"/>
              </xml:forEach>
            </html:select>
          </td>
        </tr>
        <tr>
          <td align="right">
            Comments:
          </td>
          <td>
```

Render the comment field as a textarea using the HTML `textarea` tag:

```
            <html:textarea name="comments" rows="3" cols="20"
                                path="comments/text()"/>
          </td>
        </tr>
        <tr>
          <td colspan="2" align="center">
```

Render the submit button using the HTML `submit` tag:

```
            <html:submit value="Add"/>
          </td>
        </tr>
      </table>
    </html:form>
  </body>
</html>
```

Deploying the Application

Deploying our sample application is much the same as deploying any other web application. First though, we need to build and package our framework classes into a JAR named `framework.jar`. You will need to have the following classes in your classpath when compiling the framework classes:

- `xalan.jar`
- `xerces.jar`

The code download for Chapters 15, 16, and 17 includes a pre-built copy of the framework. As usual this is available from http://www.wrox.com/

The next step is to compile, and make available, the classes used by the web services. You will need the following JAR files in your classpath to compile `EmployeeService` and `DepartmentService`:

- `mail.jar`
- `activation.jar`
- `soap.jar`
- `xerces.jar`

These classes, `EmployeeService` and `DepartmentService` must be made available to the SOAP web application we installed earlier. We can do this in two ways:

- Package `EmployeeService` and `DepartmentService` into a JAR, which is then placed in the `WEB-INF/lib` folder of the SOAP web application
- Place `EmployeeService` and `DepartmentService` under the `WEB-INF/classes` directory of the SOAP web application

Once these classes are in place we're ready to build our sample application. Create a new web application named `employee`. You will need to have the following JAR files in the `WEB-INF/lib` folder of `employee`:

- `mail.jar`
- `activation.jar`
- `soap.jar`
- `xalan.jar`
- `xerces.jar`
- `framework.jar`

Next, you need to compile the classes used by the `employee` web application, and place them in the `WEB-INF/classes` folder. The `WEB-INF` folder will also need to contain `html.tld` and `xml.tld` – the tag library descriptor files for our custom tag libraries, as well as `web.xml`

You should add the JSP pages, `EmployeeList.jsp` and `EmployeeNew.jsp` to the root directory of the web application.

The next stage is to create two folders in the root directory of the web application, `config` and `schema`. The `config.xml` file must be stored in `config` and the schema `employee.xsd` must be stored in `schema`.

The completed web application should contain the following files and directories:

```
EmployeeList.jsp
EmployeeNew.jsp
config/
       config.xml
schema/
       employee.xsd
WEB-INF/
        html.tld
        xml.tld
        app.tld
        web.xml
        classes/application/
                            handlers/
                                     AbstractSOAPHandler.class
                                     EmployeeCreateHandler.class
                                     EmployeeListHandler.class
                                     EmployeeNewHandler.class
                            xml/
                                EmployeeDOMGenerator.class
        lib/
            activation.jar
            mail.jar
            framework.jar
            xerces.jar
            xalan.jar
            soap.jar
```

Running the Application

To run the application, start Tomcat and navigate to http://localhost:8080/employee/EmployeeList.do:

Click on the Add Employee link:

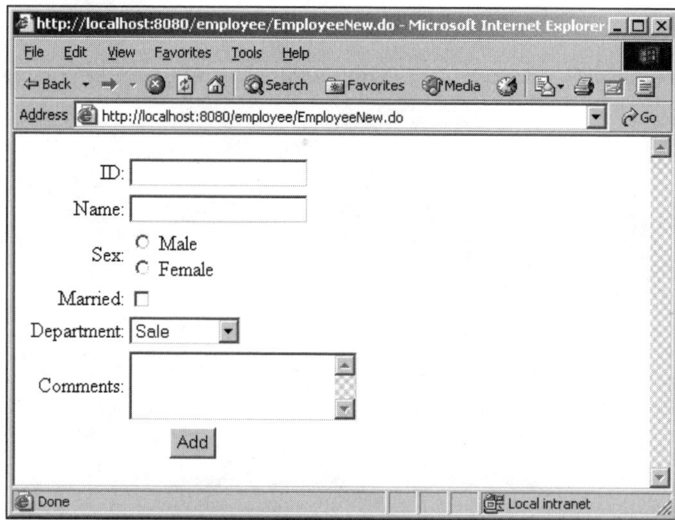

Add data for all the fields with a non-numeric value for the ID field and submit the form:

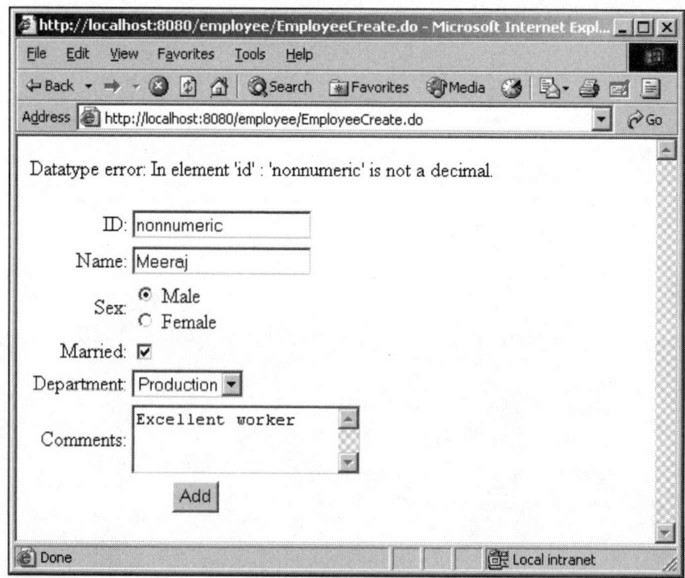

Add a numeric value for the id field and submit the form. The new employee that we added is now shown:

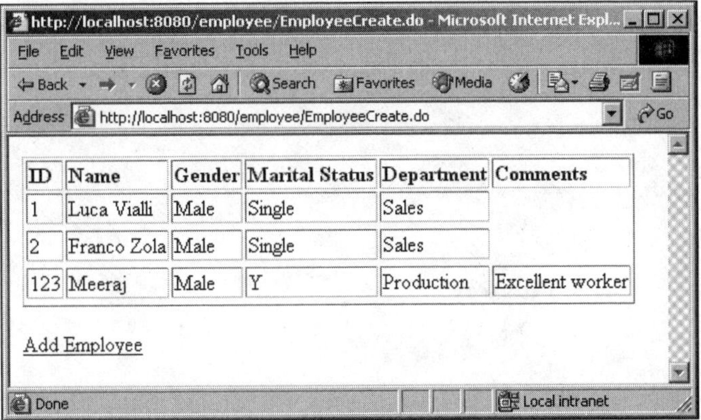

Summary

We've covered a lot in the last three chapters. We've designed and implemented a framework from scratch that allows us to build web applications that can easily function as a front end for enterprise systems that generate and consume XML.

In this chapter we set our framework to work. We designed a web application that uses many of the features of the framework, including:

- XML generation
- Schema validation
- Request delegation
- Error handling
- Custom tags for rendering XML data in both editable and read only forms

In order to demonstrate the ease with which a web application built using our framework could communicate with an enterprise that generates and consumes XML we needed to create some web services. This necessitated a quick introduction to SOAP, and we saw how to deploy our custom web services using the Apache implementation of SOAP.

We've finished our treatment of the XML-JSP Framework and hopefully we'll have given you plenty to think about – you can use this framework to build web applications that can interact with all sorts of web services.

In the next chapter we're going to look at some of the important issues that surround the performance and scalability of web applications, including how to create web applications that run across more than one machine.

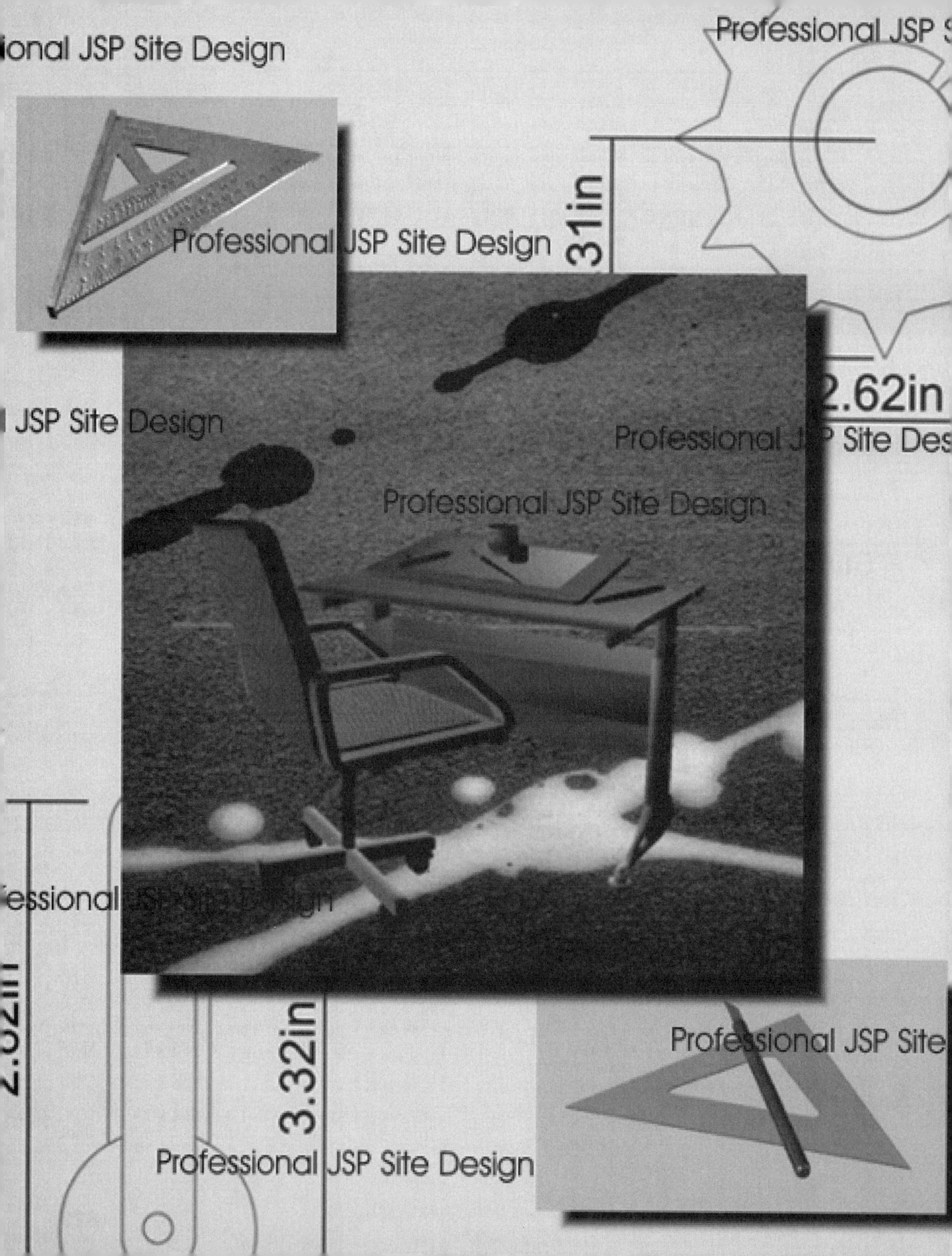
Professional JSP Site Design
31in
Professional JSP Site Design
3.32in
Professional JSP Site Design

18

Web Application Scalability and Deployment

Most web applications start out with little thought for the potential number of clients they may have to handle. The ability to provide a means for handling more clients is called **scalability**, and the process of providing scalability involves both hardware and software solutions to achieve the primary goal: providing a site that can handle any reasonable growth of traffic. In this chapter we will examine both solutions focusing primarily on the development of a simple but scalable web application. In particular we will examine:

- The architecture of a scalable web site.
- Web tier development to achieve scalability in the web tier.
- Project strategy (development, testing, staging and deployment): optimal configuration for testing an application before deployment; tools during and after development; hardware requirements for a scalable application including load balancers and servers; and a configuration for a fault-tolerant solution that could be hosted at a co-location facility.
- Further considerations when choosing and configuring your production enviroment.

As you learn about scalability you will come to realize that scalability and performance are two sides of the same coin. If we achieve one, the other follows. For example if we are taking appropriate care with the connections we make to the database pooling and freeing them as soon as their work is over, not only do we improve the performance, but more users can use the same pool. So the solution automatically becomes scalable as well. As you develop software for scalability you are indirectly adding better performance for your site. As you write code for better performance you are often providing a more scalable implementation as well. The next section will start you off with what goes into building a scalable web site.

Architecture

Have you ever thought about scalability during the initial phase of a project, or for that matter, at all? For most developers, it is not often though about when implementing a project. Along the path to completion amongst hurried schedules, developers often have to overlook important aspects of good design like profiling code, testing for scalability, unit and stub testing, and so on.

The architecture of a scalable web application consists of the right hardware and server software, and an application written to take advantage of these. The right hardware consists of servers configured in such a way as to support clustering of a web application. In a more robust solution, the application may be broken up into tiers, separating business logic into its own tier (or group) of servers, and the web specific code into its own tier. The web tier would most likely run a web server and servlet container; the middle tier would run an application server, most likely conforming to the J2EE specification; and the persistence tier is where the database server resides. Several J2EE application servers contain an all in one solution, like WebLogic and Orion; others offer just the web and servlet/JSP serving, such as Resin and Jetty. In some cases you may see the use of Apache or IIS web servers, configured to pass on any Java specific requests (such as JSP) to a servlet container like Resin, or even servers capable of more than just servlet container capabilities.

When setting up a scalable site, each server may run one or more instances of the application server software; each instance would run in a separate JVM on the same server. It is important to understand the license agreement of your application server software. Some application servers require one license per server, no matter how many instances of it you run. Others will require one license per CPU. In the latter case, if you have a server with four CPUs, even if you run only a single instance of your application server software, you may be required to pay for four licenses, or you may only have to pay for one license per instance running.

Because of the way J2EE is based on open APIs, it is possible to develop using one vendor application server, test on another, then deploy to yet another. You can even do this across various platforms. For example, Windows machines are generally easiest to set up, but because of instability issues, Windows machines are not often the preferred choice for production environments. Not to worry, you can use the Windows machines for development, then deploy into a Unix/Solaris server, quite possibly on a different vendor's J2EE application server.

But keep one important issue in mind should you develop and deploy in this manner: you must abide by all J2EE standard APIs and not utilize any vendor specific APIs. Some vendor implementations not only support the J2EE specification, but additionally offer APIs to aid the developer in many areas such as usage statistic APIs to generate charts on site usage, logging APIs for more detailed information of users actions, click stream APIs, and many other proprietary features that save you time (and money) from re-inventing the wheel. It is possible that the application server you choose runs on many platforms. In fact, most J2EE application servers are completely written in Java and should have little problem running on any platform, although each vendor will list what platforms they do offer support for. As an example, the Jetty open-source servlet engine and web server can run on any platform that supports the Java 2 runtime. Orion is another that has this capability.

Web Tier Development

In this section we will look at some of the idiosyncrasies to look out for when developing an application for scalability. We'll take a look at the MVC development pattern and how it relates to the web tier, proper use of user sessions, session fail-over (what it is and how to develop for it), and clustering of the web tier for maximum scalability and fault tolerance.

MVC

By now you should have an understanding of MVC; it has been thoroughly explained and demonstrated in this and other Wrox books. The source code for the example application that goes with this chapter uses an MVC framework called **Theseus**. Theseus is similar to Struts in functionality and terminology, but is not quite as feature rich, lacking add ons such as internationalization and custom tag-library support. What it lacks in features it tries to make up for in simplicity. You can learn more about Theseus and how to use it at http://www theseus.org/.

Having worked with the many flavors of web tier development (Model 1, Model 1.5, Model 2) I can faithfully say that despite the little bit of extra work required, the Model 2 MVC architecture offers the best path to web application scalability as well as maintenance:

- The Model 1 approach, where JSP pages call directly upon other JSP pages, is great for small sites and simple prototypes.
- Model 1.5 adds a bit more separation by using JavaBeans to split out business logic, but both approaches can easily become difficult to manage and ever more difficult to scale.
- The Model 2 approach (when adhered to) offers better management of the web application as well as providing a better means of scalability. Apart from any other reason, the ability to break code out of the JSP pages by using tag-libraries for display logic makes it much easier (and more productive) for web page developers to create pages. Meanwhile, the server-side developer can focus on the JavaBeans for storing the state of a user session, and the action classes to perform the business logic and save the results in the JavaBean used on the JSP view.

Sessions

Sessions are used to maintain a user's state across requests. A website needs more than this, though, to be scalable as well as fault tolerant. There must be assurances that, should a server fail, any sessions in existence on that server are saved in such a way that another server can step in, and the users that had sessions on the now failed server do not see any disruption in their use of the site. This can be done in a couple of ways:

- In-memory replication of sessions across two (or more) servers
- Centralized persistence of sessions that two (or more) servers have access to

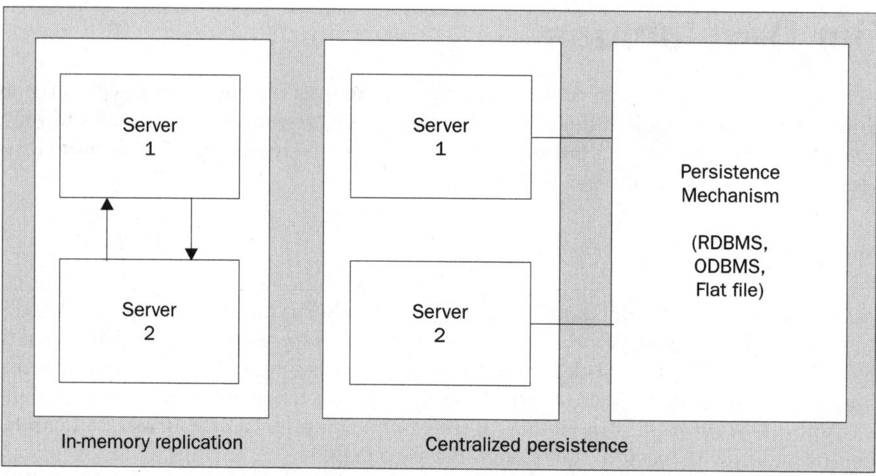

The servlet container almost always implements sessions by way of a map of maps; it may choose to use a `HashMap` or `Hashtable` for either or both maps. Ideally each session should be stored in a `Hashtable`, because more than one thread can store objects into a session. However, a container may choose to use a `HashMap` and synchronize portions of the session implementation methods rather than the entire session object. Developers do need to be aware that nothing prevents two or more threads from getting a reference to the same object, and modifying one or more of that objects' instance fields or references, which would most likely result in a concurrency exception.

To understand how this is possible you have to consider that a user can open up a new window from within the window that created the session. While this may be undesirable, you cannot prevent a user from doing this, as it is a feature of the browser. This may not happen too often, but it is possible on sites that take a long time to return a response (perhaps from a search); the user may get tired of waiting and do one of three things:

- Hit the Stop button and resubmit the form
- Right-click on a link and open it up in a new window
- Click on another link on the page

All three would submit a new request using the same session id to the server, thus providing the means for a potential concurrency exception.

Before we move on to serialization, it is important to note that all objects stored in the `HttpSession` must implement the `java.io.Serializable` interface. This interface is nothing more than a tagging interface that just denotes that a class can be serialized. Serialization is used because of the way in which a servlet container saves the state of a session, and replicates sessions when being clustered as we'll see in the next two sections.

Serialization

Serialization is the process of turning an object into a stream of bytes, so that it may be streamed to a destination such as a disk for storage, or across the network to be used remotely (RMI) or reconstructed as a new object (replication). This is the mechanism used by web containers for features like session fail-over and hot-deploy. Another use for serialization is saving the session state across server restarts during development. This is basically what hot deploy is, but it is important for us developers because quite simply, it saves the time of having to redo any steps taken to test a modification. All too often you make a simple fix and you have to restart the server to test it.

Some application servers, like Orion (http://www.ironflare.com/) allow a "development mode" where it will reload individual classes for you as you change them. If your servlet container does not support this feature, it may support reloading a web application if the `web.xml` file is modified, or perhaps a specific server configuration file will force web applications to be reloaded. In this case, you can use a tool like ant, from the Jakarta project (http://jakarta.apache.org/ant/), to do your builds and then automatically "touch" a specific file to force the reloading of your web application.

The Importance of SUID

Developers should add SUIDs (`serialVersionUID`) to every class that implements `Serializable`. During development, you often make many changes to various classes. As explained above, you can speed up development if a servlet container supports the ability to preserve sessions across a server restart. However, if you happen to modify a class that is part of the session object hierarchy saved during the restart, and do not include SUIDs in your classes, you will destroy your session and thus lose the ability to more rapidly test changes.

This is due to the way Java serialization works, rather than the way the servlet container implements this feature. The container serializes to disk the object the container uses to implement sessions. When restarting the server, it will first load your web app classes, then try to deserialize the session back into memory. The problem is that if you do not include the SUID in a given class, the serialization assumes that any class could have changed (and there is no way of knowing without the SUID), so the entire serialized object becomes invalid, and thus all sessions are lost.

By adding the SUID to every class stored in the session, the serialization mechanism can compare the classes in the JVM to the objects in the serialized container session object. Should they all match, then the session is reloaded, but if you changed any signature of any method of any class, the entire session will no longer be valid.

The reason for this is not immediately apparent, but imagine that in the serialized container session object you have two objects, A and B, where object A references object B. Now what happens if object B's class has changed? The reference that object A has is possibly no longer valid, and could cause a constraint violation on object A. Therefore the safest bet is to discard the entire serialized object. Adding the SUID also allows you to change the implementation of a method without destroying the session. So long as you don't change the return types and arguments of any methods – just the implementation of one or more methods – the SUID does *not* change and therefore the newly modified class will match the serialized version of the old class. If you did not include the SUID the session would be discarded immediately, as we have seen.

Adding a SUID

To create a SUID, simply run the serialver utility (provided with your JDK) on the class. Running the serialver utility can be difficult to figure out; I suggest opening a command window (in Windows) or starting a new terminal (in Linux/Unix), and navigating to your compiler output directory. You will need the reference that the class you are attempting to get a SUID for may rely on, either in the CLASSPATH or using the `-classpath` parameter with specific locations of classes and JAR files.

Lastly, I suggest using the `-show` option, which pops up a GUI panel allowing you to type in the class, and displaying the SUID for that class or any error message. This is not necessary, and may not even be possible if you're not in a GUI environment. You also, obviously, need to make sure your installed JDK `bin` directory is in the path so that the `serialver` utility is found.

```
serialver -show -classpath /mypath/myfile.jar
```

This will pop up a window like so:

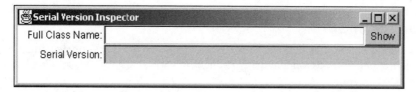

Next, you need to type in the fully qualified class name (including the package name, in other words) in the Full Class Name field. When done, click the Show button, and in the Serial Version box you should see a serial version string similar to the one shown below. You simply copy and paste this into your class, preferably at the start of the class, right after the opening brace:

```
static final long serialVersionUID = 1332247911804731234L;
```

It is possible that you may see an error message in the lower left corner, or a stack trace output in the command window (if visible). This could be because your class does not implement `Serializable`, or the class may not be found. The error message displayed should be sufficient to figure out what went wrong.

Session Fail-Over

Session fail-over is the process of guaranteeing that user sessions will not be terminated arbitrarily should the server that a session was created on fail. Another term for this is **fault tolerance**. In order to facilitate this level of guarantee, special managing of sessions must be done at the Servlet container level to replicate all user sessions to at least one other server. How a Servlet container replicates sessions is not defined in the Servlet or J2EE specifications, nor is it required to meet J2EE standards. However, in order for a Servlet container to provide high availability and fault tolerance the container must provide some means for the replication of sessions to at least one other JVM instance or server, in case the server should fail.

You need to ensure a few requirements are met for session replication to work properly. As explained in the preceding two sections, sessions are maintained in `Hashtable` objects and all objects in each `Hashtable` session must implement `Serializable` and should contain a valid SUID. For the most part this is all that is required on your part.

As already said, vendors can choose to implement session fail over in their own way. Because of this it is important that you understand in which way the servlet container *you* use implements this feature. As we saw earlier, there are two primary implementations commonly used: in memory session replication and persistent session replication. We'll have a look at both and what you will need to do to use either one.

In-Memory Replication

In-memory replication replicates sessions by serializing the entire map associated with a session into a raw byte stream, and sending it to one or more JVMs that are in the same cluster. Those JVMs deserialize the stream, overwriting or merging with the existing session with the same id. This can be relatively fast because all objects are in memory throughout the process (except during the transfer to the other JVM, which requires the use of the network).

This replication usually occurs after each and every request. Some servlet containers prefer to replicate an object only when it is inserted into the session. The advantage to this approach is that it requires less time to serialize and deserialize a single object, and it takes less network bandwidth to send that object. The disadvantage is that it requires you to do some extra coding. This method will rely on the `setAttribute()` or (deprecated) `putValue()` methods of the `HttpSession` interface to signal to the container that it should replicate the object being inserted. As an example, look at the following snippet of code:

```
HttpSession session = request.getSession(true);
MyObject myObject = (MyObject) session.getAttribute("MyObject");
if (myObject != null) {
  myObject.getAddress().setCity("San Francisco");
  myObject.getAddress().setState("California");
}
```

There is nothing wrong with the above code. It works fine... or does it? The problem with this code is that you have taken an object from the session and modified two fields of an object to which it holds a reference. When running in a single JVM, this code works fine. But when building a scalable application that will use single object replication, other JVMs in the same cluster have no way of knowing that this code modified a reference of an object.

The only way for other JVMs to know is if your application lets them know by replicating the object to them; you do this by setting the object back into the session. The proper "scalable" solution to the above example is listed next:

```
HttpSession session = request.getSession(true);
MyObject myObject = (MyObject) session.getAttribute("MyObject");
if (myObject != null) {
  myObject.getAddress().setCity("San Francisco");
  myObject.getAddress().setState("California");
  session.setAttribute("MyObject", myObject);
}
```

The last line of code puts the object back into the session. Because it is the same object reference it does not overwrite the existing object reference held under the name `"MyObject"`, but it does trigger the replication of the `myObject` instance to any other JVM in the same cluster. It is important to keep in mind that this above syntax only applies to servlet containers that implement session fail-over in this manner, such as the Orion Application Server (http://www.ironflare.com/). You may need to contact your servlet container vendor and ask what kind of session fail-over support is implemented and if any extra work is required by you for the servlet container you use to properly handle session fail-over.

In the Theseus framework, the JavaBean used for an action is automatically inserted into the session by the framework (when using the `FastServlet` controller). This ensures that the JavaBean, if modified in any way, is always properly replicated on servers that implement session management this way. On those that don't, the time taken up for each object to be "re-inserted" into the session is minimal.

In memory session replication requires all servers in the cluster to contain enough memory to hold not only its own sessions, but also those sessions from other servers in the same cluster. I recommend using just two servers in a single cluster, to cut down on memory requirements and ensure maximum scalability. We'll look at clustering in more detail later.

Persistent Replication

Persistent replication requires the use of a database to store the serialized session, instead of memory. If a container implements this method of session fail-over you should not have to apply any extra coding for session fail-over to work properly. You may, however, have to instruct the container about the whereabouts of the database it is to use for persistence. This may be as simple as specifying JDBC settings (user/password, IP, etc.), or could be more complex; each vendor implementing this form of session fail-over will have specific setup information.

By using a database, each server only consumes the memory used by its own sessions, and not of other servers as with in-memory session fail-over. It does, however, take up space in a database. Once again, the actual implementation details are specific to each vendor, but in general the process is to replicate the entire user session at the end of a request to the database.

When using persistent fail-over, it is without a doubt important to make sure the same level of fault tolerance is implemented for the database storing the sessions as for other tiers. If a group of servers are all accessing the same central persistent mechanism (which could be a database, a flat file or some other method of storing data), it is possible the database server itself could fail; in such a case, with fault tolerance in place, all requests for data would then kick over to another database server. This is in principle the same thing in-memory fail-over does, only without using memory (most likely hard drives).

Be aware, however, that persistent storage of sessions can result in a lot of database activity. It is highly recommended to use a separate database for storing sessions, which should reside on its own server. One step better would be to keep the database for web-tier session fail-over in the same vicinity as that of the web servers themselves. By this I mean that often, in a multi-tier production environment, you will have a router and possibly a firewall in front of each of the three tiers (web, business/EJB, and persistence/database). Whenever you introduce the need to kick over to another server should one fail, you need a device that can be alerted to a failure and properly reroute requests to another server. Also, when you have two (or more) servers accessing the next tier (as is the case when a web-tier servlet accesses an EJB in the business logic tier), they all will need to access a single point of entry to that tier so as not to be bothered about the details of how many servers are in that tier.

Imagine you had a servlet getting an EJB reference from the middle tier. If you only had one EJB server, you could simply do the lookup on that one computer. But if you have two (or more should you add more servers when scaling is needed), how does that servlet know what middle-tier server to ask for the EJB reference? Each time you added a new server to the middle-tier, you would need to add in the new IP address for that server, so that the servlet could choose that IP when it asks for an EJB reference. While this could work, you would now need to implement on the web tier some way to "balance" the calls to the various servers in the middle tier.

This is the job of a load balancer. Hardware is much faster at this than implementing this into your application, and in the long run is most likely much cheaper given the hours involved in writing a good load balancing algorithm. The load balancer is situated in front of a group of servers and will properly deliver requests to one or more servers, evenly distributing the load. Some load balancers can even determine how much load each server is capable of handling, thus giving more load to faster computers.

If you follow the suggestion of using a separate database cluster for session persistence, you may ask if the database servers used for this task go in the same tier as the database servers used for your application. This question isn't always easy to answer; it really depends on the architecture of your production environment. If the only way to gain access to your main application database were through the middle-tier (perhaps for security reasons), then storing sessions would require the use of middle-tier logic. This would introduce yet another layer, possibly hampering performance. Ideally, a separate database cluster for session persistence should be accessible only to the web tier and therefore doesn't need to be behind any extra firewalls. Each web-tier cluster accesses the load balancer IP, which is used to distribute load, and properly fail over should one of the database servers fail.

Forms of Session Replication

Before we leave this section, let's examine what the benefits are of a few ways session replication can occur and why they are important to your decision in the servlet container you choose. The two most common forms of replication are:

- **Object replication**
  Every time an object is set into the user session, the servlet container immediately replicates just that one object to all other servers in the same cluster.
- **User session replication**
  At the end of each request, the entire user session is replicated to all servers in the cluster.

As we have seen, there are no doubt other ways to implement session replication. Both of these methods can be implemented to use in memory replication or persistent storage of sessions. Looking at the two most common ways, it is apparent that the easiest way for the developer is to replicate a user session at the end of each request. This allows the developer to focus on the application and not have to force updates of objects back into the session. The problem with this approach is that it does not provide linear scalability. Each session may have one or more objects in it, and each object could have any number of nested objects in its hierarchy. The more objects in each session, the more memory used on each server, thus the longer it takes to replicate the session.

In contrast, single object replication replicates only one object when it is inserted into the session via the `setAttribute()` call. This method is much faster, with less resources being used, and thus provides a much more linear curve of scalability. In the application accompanying this chapter, it is assumed that the servlet container used is capable of object replication. The good news is that even if you code your application in this manner, if your servlet container doesn't support object replication it most likely uses session replication and your user sessions will still get replicated. Because of this, we recommend you develop applications for both scenarios.

Clustering

Clustering is nothing more than a group of servers acting as a unit to help increase performance of a web site (although clustering can be used in many other areas as well, such as the middle-tier, persistence tier and so on). Generally you will want to set up a cluster of servers in a few circumstances:

- Your site can no longer handle the number of users accessing it.
- Your site is resource intensive and a single server cannot provide enough resources to accommodate the site's requirements.
- You want to ensure fault tolerance and 24/7 up time in case of a server failure.

There are no doubt other reasons for clustering, but these are the more common ones. The good news is that clustering isn't all that difficult to do. You will need a load balancer, which distributes the load between two (or more) servers as well as require at least two servers, although you can cluster two (or more) JVM instances (each running an application server instance set up for clustering) on a single server. Setting up the cluster generally involves connecting the load balancer and the two servers to the same network, then accessing the cluster through the load balancer IP address. The load balancer will then use any one of many different possible algorithms to load balance between the two servers. The most common algorithm is often called **round robin**; it alternates between the two servers for subsequent requests, not taking heed of the fact that the servers may be of varying performance. Advanced load balancers can keep track of the amount of traffic each server has hitting it, as well as keeping track of session ids to send the user to the same server their session was created on, using cookies.

If your site is running up against peak load problems, you may be able to get away with upgrading your hardware, for example by providing more powerful servers, a faster load balancer, and gigabit networks. If the CPU utilization of your servers is low, but you're seeing a dramatic slow down in performance, look at the memory being used and check to see if so much memory is in use that the OS swap file system is the culprit. In this case, you may want to run a profiling tool and look into the possible reasons so much memory is being used. You may need to rewrite portions of your application to use memory more efficiently.

We have already looked at fault tolerance and how to obtain this through your application. Clustering at the hardware level is essential to a good fault tolerance implementation. At a bare minimum we recommend using a load balancer to distribute the load between two servers, each configured to replicate sessions to one another using in-memory replication. Should one server fail, the load balancer will redirect all requests to the other server. In-memory replication ensures that all sessions on the failed server also exist on the second server.

The reason for having only two servers in a single cluster is to conserve the amount of memory used to maintain session state across the servers. While we want fault tolerance, we also would like to avoid degrading site performance and resource usage as much as possible. Each server in a cluster must have enough memory to handle its own sessions as well as the sessions of every other server in the same cluster. For this reason it is recommended to use at least two servers, but ideally no more than three servers per cluster. Two servers is the minimum in a cluster to guarantee fault tolerance. If one server fails for any reason, the second server picks up the load the failed server was handling. Because of session replication, users that have sessions in this particular cluster would not see any interruption or loss of data. Better, however, is the use of three servers for optimum fail-over per cluster. We say optimum because should one server fail, there are still two servers maintaining the contract of a minimum fail-over setup, although not without consequences. Adding a third server to the equation means each require more memory to maintain three servers worth of sessions.

A powerful feature of setting up each cluster in the above mentioned manner is the ease of scaling a site should load exceed the existing capabilities. You add another cluster of three servers to instantly upgrade your load capability. In the *Project Strategy* section we will explain how you can get an idea of how much each cluster can handle so you can gauge how many clusters you may require initially, and how many you may need to add should you need to scale.

Before we move on to hot deploy, we would like to mention that when building a site that may potentially grow to many clusters, you will need to keep in mind the limits of a load balancer. Load balancers will often have a fixed number of ports that it can distribute the load between. More robust load balancers are programmable and handle more. But at some point, you may run out of ports and will require one or more additional load balancers. The details of how multiple load balancers are used are beyond the scope of this chapter, but it is important to keep in mind when developing a site that will potentially grow beyond the use of a single load balancer.

Hot Deploy

Servlet containers like Orion, Web Logic, Jetty, and Resin support a feature called **hot deploy**. Hot deploy is the ability to reload a web application with potentially modified classes without losing the state of any active sessions. Users on the site are not affected by the web application being reloaded; anybody logged in stays logged in, and anybody filling out a wizard of forms does not lose information during the re-deploy. Hot deploy is often used to add fixes, enhancements and maybe even new features at any time of the day. A few years ago it was unthinkable to upload fixes in the middle of the day while users were using your site. Today deployment can be done at any time of the day so long as the container implements hot deploy.

Hot deploy works in one of two ways:

- A servlet container can load a new web application into memory while the old one is still in memory. It then routes all new requests to this new web application while it lets any existing requests executing within the old web application finish out their activity and send back their responses. Once all threads from the old web application are extinguished, the servlet container then unloads the old web application completely.
- The second way is to save the state of all sessions, unload the existing web application and reload the new web application, then deserialize all the sessions to restore the session state. Some containers may even save the entire web application context including application-scoped objects.

As with everything, both processes have pros and cons associated with them. The objective of hot deploy is to keep existing sessions alive *and* load new classes over old ones so that any modifications of code can take place once deployed. All of this has to be transparent to the users of your site. The first method requires more memory, because both web applications are in memory at the same time. It does however make sure that there is no interruption to incoming requests.

The second approach leaves a door open to potential issues with incoming requests while it unloads the old web application and reloads the new one. Hopefully, if your servlet container implements this feature it properly queues incoming requests while the new application is loading, then unloads them onto the new application once it's running. The advantage of the second approach is that it requires less memory.

Both approaches can run into problems when attempting to save the session state. Recall from earlier that the Java serialization process will scrap the entire serialized object if any changes occur to any of the newly loaded classes as compared to the same class in the serialized object. Because of this you must be careful when hot deploying a web application into a production environment. You do run the risk of losing user sessions if the web application is not written properly; we looked earlier at using SUIDs for all objects stored in the `HttpSession`.

Project Strategy

At some point your web application will need to be deployed into a production environment. All too often the production environment is quite different from that used for development. These differences and some others may determine part of how a web application must be written. We will examine a good development to production strategy, as well as considering why it is important to understand these differences and how they affect the development of a web application.

There are far too many possible scenarios between development and deployment to production to examine in this one section. However, what we will see is an ideal strategy for your organization to follow through the course of developing a web application. This strategy will also work for emergency fixes after deployment, and will allow multiple projects to be developed and tested at the same time in a manner that is efficient and productive. We will examine four stages:

- Development
- Quality Assurance (QA)
- Staging
- Production

If you are wondering what all this has to do with developing a scalable application, read on and you will learn that each stage will play an important role in reaching this goal.

Development

The first stage is development. (We will not get into all that goes into a project before the developers start their work.) However, web applications often change during the course of development, so it may be necessary for the development and design stages to continue for a period of time before a final "locked" design is committed and developers can focus on the implementation without further changes. During the development stage, developers often work on local boxes, writing code and unit testing their progress making sure it properly implements the design.

One important aspect of this stage is profiling. We are after all looking at building a scalable application. A profiler like OptimizeIt or JProbe can greatly help a developer locate inefficient code that may cause bottlenecks or memory issues. Keep in mind that when developing locally, you will see only a small inkling of the load you will find in a production site. Therefore, a profile that shows a small but potential problem could be exponentially worse on a high-traffic production site.

Today computers are very fast, memory is cheap, and business needs often outweigh the time required to profile and fix potential problems. What appears to be a couple of milliseconds by a single request thread could be seconds when hundreds of threads hit that same application on a production server. Let's not forget the cardinal rule of web sites: anything longer than 5 seconds and you may lose a visitor. Of course this doesn't always apply. B2B sites may be used as tools for clients, and therefore the wait can be longer. I do suggest that any time you're aware of a page that takes more than five to ten seconds to load, you should try to implement some sort of transition page, like an animated gif or some text to read. This makes the perceived wait less than it really is.

Quality Assurance

The second stage is that of quality assurance. Believe it or not, QA and developing play an equal role in producing a quality project. QA is not a glory job; it is often repetitive and boring. It also requires some ingenuity in finding different ways to break various parts of an application. When you add to the mix the various internet browsers, vendors of those browsers, and platforms those browsers run on, the job of a QA engineer can be more overwhelming than any other job in the project. In small companies the QA engineer may also be responsible for doing builds, deploying, having the final say if a project is good enough to deploy, taking blame for any problems found after deployment, and quite possibly handling the task of load testing the site as well. And you thought it was rough being a developer!

There are two divisions to QA:

- First, you have the QA team, consisting of one or more engineers whose job it is to test every aspect of a web application on as many browsers, platforms and operating systems as possible.
- The second part is the QA environment. Every organization will run their QA department as they see fit, so I won't get into that. What I will recommend, however, is a good overall QA environment.

A QA environment consists of one or more servers to run the web application on, and a QA lab full of computers with different operating systems and web browsers. You can usually get away with a single QA server running the web application, even if you are using multiple tiers. For example, the use of a web server, servlet engine, and EJB application server can all run on one machine at the same time. Apache is the most popular web server and works well with servlet engines. The latest breed of J2EE compatible servlet engines also include built-in web server capabilities which have proven in some cases to return dynamic pages faster than those that plug in a servlet engine into a web server. Orion application server is one such example, integrating a web server, servlet engine, and EJB container in one complete package. Another solution is the open-source Jetty servlet engine and web server packaged with jBoss application server. Both projects utilize the java JMX API to allow seamless integration.

I recommend two QA servers. One would be for immediate projects, while the other QA server is used for such things as emergency fixes to an existing code base in production. This may seem a bit odd at first, but let me give two scenarios where this is an effective approach:

- First, you just deployed a project that was tested on one of the QA servers. A new project is started and the second QA server is now used in conjunction with that project to start testing it. Meanwhile, an emergency arises on the production site. A quick fix is done and needs to be tested. But currently the QA server has a new project being tested.

  You can always reconfigure to test the new fix of the old project, then reconfigure again for the new project, carrying on like this until all is well. However, having two QA servers allows you to quickly apply a fix to the first QA server that was used for the deployed project. The advantage is, you don't have to spend time reconfiguring a server (if needed) for two (or more) different projects. You simply start testing the first QA server for the emergency fix, and then deploy it when it's ready. Meanwhile, the other server still has the new project on it and it can still be tested while the emergency fix is being tested.

- The second scenario is not unlike the first, the difference being that it is quite possible you will have two (or more) projects going on at the same time. While we still hold fast to keeping one of the QA servers open for emergency fixes, it is potentially efficient to allow two projects to be deployed on two different machines for more productive testing to get two projects out the door faster.

A lot of this depends on the size of your organization, the money allotted to getting hardware if required, and the project cycle your organization puts in place. You could run many applications on a single server if you're tight for money. The two-server approach is what I consider a bare minimum QA server environment.

Lastly, we will touch on the subject of a QA lab. When testing web applications there are a lot of pitfalls to worry about. Without even getting into all the nuances that can cause a web application to break, the most apparent issues are the number of platforms, browsers and browser vendors, and operating systems to contend with. It is doubtful that the same version browser runs identically on all platforms. If your clients use MS Windows, Unix, Linux, and Mac operating systems, you really have to buckle down on a solid QA lab to handle testing all these different choices. E-commerce sites probably have it hardest, because they want to allow clients all over the globe access to their site to rake in the profits. But some features may not work on earlier versions of browsers, and worse, may function differently on the same version of browsers on different platforms!

There are a couple of ways to tackle this problem. First, you can go out and buy hardware, software, and probably hire QA staff to test on all these different choices. Manually testing is, to say the least, a slow, boring, and inefficient testing process. But it is done by human operators who most likely try to learn the web application and use it not only as the developers who write it think it should be used (which is never how it is really used), but also how clients will use it. After all, a QA engineer needs to think like a normal user, and normal users run from not-so-computer-savvy users to techno-know-it-alls.

A much more robust approach to testing is software like E-Suite, which allows the QA engineer to record scripts, then play them back, and choose the browser vendor and version to emulate. This type of software is not cheap, but it is certainly much cheaper than hiring a number of QA engineers, as well as the variety of hardware and software required. E-Suite allows the same recorded script to be used in one of their products, E-Load, to simulate hundreds of virtual users for load testing a site, as we'll get to in the next section.

Staging

The last two sections may seem like they don't fit in this chapter, but there is a method to our madness. You see, this next stage, called **Staging**, is often not found in most companies. In fact, small companies often skip the QA stage as well, relying on their developers to test then deploy an application. Before we get into staging, let's backtrack and see what we have learned about the last two sections that relate to building scalable web applications.

Developers should use a code profiler to locate potential bottlenecks in their code, and fix them before releasing to QA. They should also unit test their code making sure it works as it was designed to before QA tries to break it. QA will (hopefully) utilize a tool that will allow automation of testing, writing scripts that will save valuable time. These scripts can then be applied at this stage, as we'll discuss in a minute. So developers write code, but they also attempt to remove any bottlenecks and badly written code, thus producing a more scalable site. This is so because as we noted earlier, a few milliseconds on a single machine via a single thread of testing could result in seconds of time on a server loaded with hundreds of users. The scripts that QA write will be used for regression testing on the QA server(s), and will be used for load testing your site on the staging server(s). So what is this staging stage (no pun intended)?

Staging is nothing more than an identical setup of your production environment, minus perhaps a few servers. Why would you want this? Simple! You need a way to gauge how much traffic your site can handle, and you sure don't want to do this on a production site because you would restrict your real client usage to the site in order to do this type of testing. Since we are talking about building a scalable web application, lets take a simple but real-world example of a scalable architecture that you would want your staging environment to mimic.

As we have discussed, the web tier should have at least a single cluster with two servers in it. This gives us the bare minimum of session level fail-over, and achieves fault tolerance to some degree. We would go one step further by separating the business logic into its own tier. Thus we now add two more servers for the EJB business logic tier. The reason for having two is to have fault tolerance on the middle tier as well. Should one EJB server go down, we don't want our business to stop because the web tier can't access any business logic. Finally, we add in the database servers again in some sort of fault tolerant configuration to make sure data is being duplicated just in case one server goes down. Once we have this set up, we can start running load tests against this set up and the software will yield some important information. It should be able to tell us how many pages per second we can handle. It should also allow us to adjust various parameters, such as how often request threads are generated, how many threads at one time, whether they are to use cookies for sessions, and so on. Referring again to the E-Suite software, E-Load does allow this level of configuration. It can take any script created in the E-Test module, and run it against a server creating hundreds of virtual users. We use E-Suite as an example, but other software such as QAPartner may provide similar capabilities.

So what the staging environment provides for your organization is a way to figure out exactly how much a given setup can handle, and then anticipate what sort of hardware you may need for production. It is also a good place to run final tests on a project before deploying to production. But there is perhaps one other usefulness to a staging environment. Most companies will most likely use a co-location facility for their production servers. If you were to run cheap Wintel servers in your office for QA, then move your project to a set of Unix boxes running on Solaris, you would introduce some uncertainty over whether your project is really ready for production. It is best to always test a project on the identical setup of hardware, software, and even backbone to the Internet to make sure there is nothing different between what you see on QA and what may occur in production.

Finally, while you can get away with a cheap setup for staging using a bare minimum fault-tolerant setup that mimics production, you can also use it to add more servers and see how well your site scales. Don't be fooled into thinking that adding another set of servers will double your site capabilities. Staging is the perfect environment to allow you to gather this information, which could be crucial to business planning as well.

Production

The last stage is **production**. Not much needs to be said about what this stage is for. However, what should be noted is that if you do not use a staging environment to figure out how scalable your site is, you may have to find out in this stage. I don't recommend this, primarily because you could experience some growing pains if your application is not implemented for scalability as has been shown throughout this chapter. A production environment is not the time to find out your site is not going to scale well.

We can't reiterate enough how important these four stages are in an overall web site architecture and project strategy.

Further Deployment Considerations

You need to do some research to find the right application server solution for your project, depending on your needs and budget.

Choosing the Right Application Server

Several considerations impact the choice of your application server. However, provided it implements the J2EE specification (not all application servers are J2EE certified, though). it should meet the basic requirements of your Servlet/JSP project. It is possible to move your application across application servers from different vendors and expect your application to be consistent in behavior. Therefore, you should test your application with different vendors while in development, using the trial versions of each vendor's software, and when you move into production buy the application server that best meets your requirements.

Not all application servers are created equal, though. All will implement the basic EJB specification, but will differ in performance, ease of use, and ability to handle the volume of traffic. There can be endless discussions on the merits of one application server over another, but what it comes down to is how well does a particular server handle the needs of your project.

Let's look at a checklist for choosing the right application server:

- **Which JDK?**
  This affects the performance of your application. Some JDK's are faster then others. The choice of JDK is important, as your application server's performance will be impacted by the performance of your JDK.

- **Scalability and Clustering**
  These have already been considered in detail earlier in the chapter. One important issue to consider when selecting an application server is how well it scales to the demands of increasing traffic, and whether instances can be clustered to replicate its state across different physical machines.

- **Cost and Licensing**
  Your budget is of course a criterion. The cost of application servers is normally calculated as cost per server or cost per CPU. Add to this the cost for technical support and for the developer licenses, and you can have substantial costs. Choosing the one that fits your budget while still meeting your application's needs would mean researching and contacting the sales offices of various vendors.

- **Compatibility**
  Compliance with the latest J2EE specification is a must. Some products are licensed, some are certified, and some are neither. The sales staff will let you know the status of compliance of their product. The final Servlet 2.3 and JSP 1.2 specifications (along with the rest of J2EE 1.3) are now out, and if your application needs them make sure that the application server you choose supports these specifications.

- **Performance**
  Performance is something that can depend on a lot of things. Before making a commitment to a particular application server it is important to load test your application against different application servers. Also, research through newsgroups and bulletin boards to see the general feedback from other experienced people about a particular application server.

Popular commercial application servers include BEA System WebLogic Server and IBM's Websphere. There are a variety of open source application servers as well, such as jBoss. Commercial quality application servers have the advantage of ease of installation, support, and enhancements over the open source servers; the open source servers on the other hand are free, and the source code is freely available.

Choosing the Right Servlet Engine

There are three types of servlet engines.

- **Standalone**
  A web server that supports servlets right out of the box, with the servlet engine as an integral part of the web server. Examples include Apache Tomcat, and Caucho's Resin server.
- **Add-on**
  In this case, the servlet engine is an external entity to the web server, and is composed of a web server plug-in and a servlet container. This is further divided into two types:
  - **In-Process**
    The plug-in invokes a JVM inside the web server's address space and uses JNI to pass the control to the servlet container. The advantage of this kind of configuration is better performance.
  - **Out-of-Process**
    The JVM runs outside the address space of the web server and the plug-in passes servlet requests to the servlet container using some inter-process communication mechanism. The advantage of this configuration is scalability.

  Examples of add-on servlet engines are Apache Tomcat (again) and Atlanta's ServletExec. Both Tomcat and ServletExec can be added to a variety of web servers including, but not limited to, Microsoft IIS and Apache.
- **Embeddable servlet engine**
  Embeddable servlet engines are used more often within larger applications than they are deployed on the web. The engine is embedded within another application, which may not necessarily be used on the web, but is part of an application. This application can then be used as part of an intranet wide deployment agent and may or may not serve web content. Tomcat is an example of a servlet engine that can be embedded in other applications.

Tuning the Server

You should also make sure you understand the configuration of your servlet container, and tune its settings to ensure the best possible performance for your applications:

- Modify the startup file (such as `catalina.bat` or `catalina.sh` for Tomcat 4.0) to tune the JVM parameters, for example by setting the maximum and minimum heap sizes using the `-Xms` and `-Xmx` parameters to the JVM.
- Make sure that servlet auto-reloading is disabled; in Tomcat 4.0 this means that the application's context should have the parameter for reloading set to False in `server.xml`. Servlet reloading is a useful feature during development life cycles, but a performance problem during development.

- Similarly, you should disable JSP recompilation; this can improve performance as the server is not looking for the JSP source file. An external tool to pre compile the JSP pages (JSPC for Tomcat) is usually provided.
- Disable unwanted server features. For example, on Tomcat you should disable any unused connectors in the `server.xml` file. There may well be example web applications installed by default, which should be removed in production.
- Depending on the load on the server, it may be advisable to modify the settings for the server's thread pool. You should load test your application to find the best values.

Connection Pooling and Database Access

Hopefully this is not the first time in your project lifecycle that you are considering connection pooling. Connection pooling has to be implemented programmatically. At the deployment stage, it is necessary to get the right parameters into your application, so that the database access is not a bottleneck. It has been found that in a majority of web applications database access was the main culprit for slow performance.

Application servers manage connection pools independently of any particular application. You can tune the parameters for a particular application to give a performance boost to your application. Not all servlet engines provide their own connection pooling mechanism – though Tomcat 4.0 does, as we saw when configuring the application in Chapter 8.

Choosing the Right JDBC Driver

There are several choices of JDBC drivers that are available in the market. Application servers normally provide JDBC drivers for the more popular database systems. Even Database vendors supply drivers for their own databases, mostly free of cost. Some considerations while choosing a JDBC driver are:

- **Price**
  In most cases you will not need to buy a JDBC driver; there are open source implementations available for most of the popular databases. These however lack support, and are not necessarily going to get upgraded. If you choose to buy an application server, you will receive JDBC drivers with it. Another thing to consider in the price category is whether the driver can be distributed with your application, if need be, and the number of clients that the drivers can support under your license.
- **Performance**
  While application server specific drivers are faster, as they use proprietary techniques and native layers, you pay the price by not being able to migrate the driver when either you change application servers or the operating systems.
- **Adherence to standards**
  Make sure that the driver supports the latest JDBC specifications.
- **Scaling**
  Make sure that the JDBC driver is scalable for your future needs.
- **Threading**
  The JDBC drivers should be using threads to increase performance, which allows multiple transactions to take place on the database data in a thread safe manner.

Summary

In this chapter we looked at a number of aspects to develop a scalable web application with Java technology:

- We briefly examined the architecture of a scalable application, such as hardware, software, and other requirements.
- We then delved into what this book is about, the web tier. Here we explained in some detail the various components involved in a scalable application including serialization, sessions, session fail-over, clustering, and hot-deploy of web applications. We also touched on the use of MVC as the preferred development method for scalable web applications.
- Next we looked at a project strategy and the ideal way to develop, test, load test, and deploy any web project using Java technology.
- Lastly, we considered some of the other decisions that need to be made when selecting and configuring an application server or servlet engine.

The art of developing scalable software in general, and web applications specifically could easily spread across an entire book. There are without a doubt many solutions to the vast topic of developing scalable, robust, and even manageable web applications.

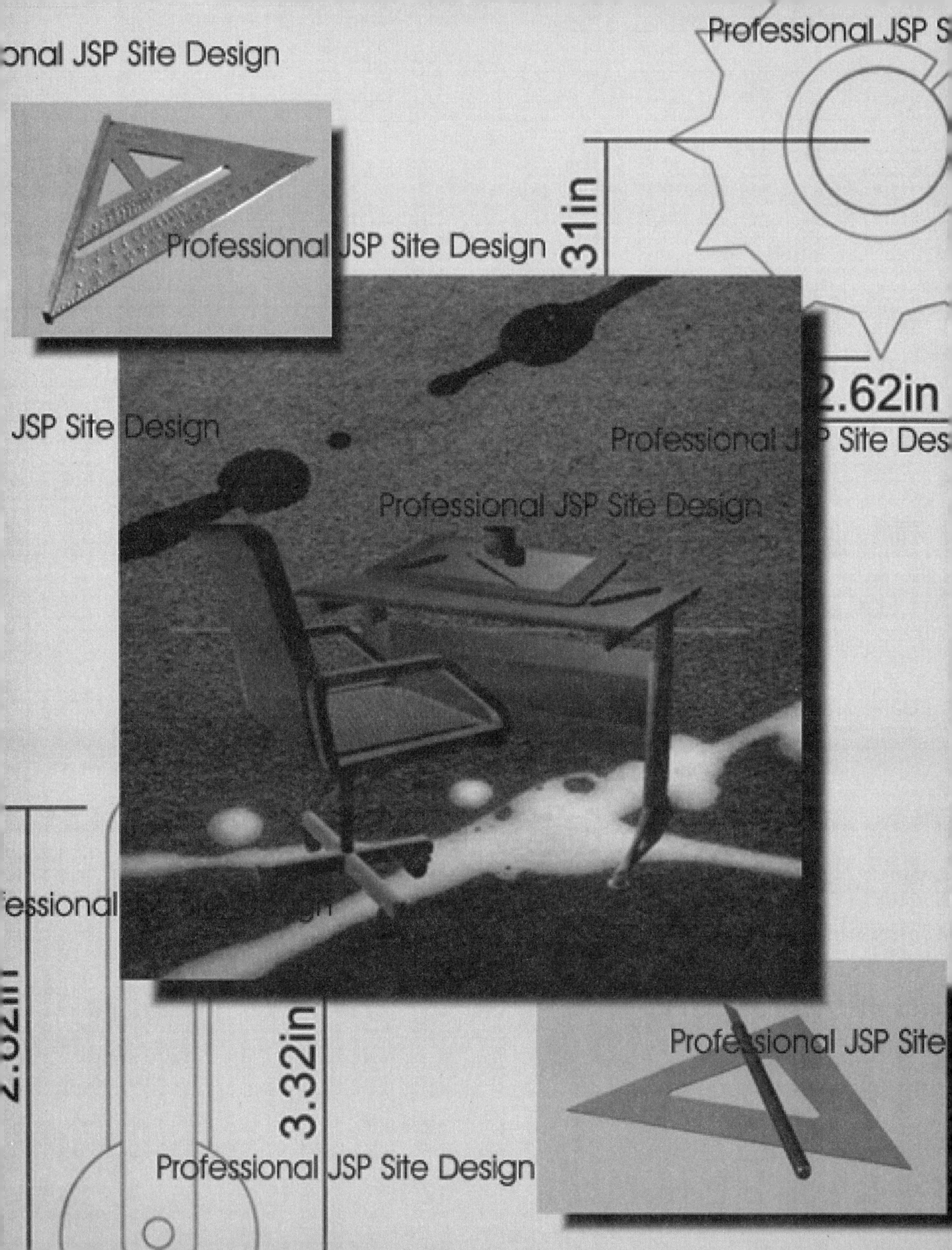
Professional JSP Site Design
31in
Professional JSP Site Design
3.32in
Professional JSP Site Design

Installing Tomcat 4.0

In this appendix we'll discuss the basics of how to install and configure Tomcat 4.0, the latest version of the open source JSP and Servlet Reference Implementation.

Installing Tomcat 4.0

While there are many servlet and JSP engines available (as of this writing, Sun's "Industry Momentum" page at http://java.sun.com/products/jsp/industry.html lists nearly 40), we have chosen to focus our attention on Tomcat 4.0. Tomcat is produced by the Apache Software Foundation's Jakarta project, and is freely available at http://jakarta.apache.org/tomcat/.

As Tomcat is primarily used by programmers, its open source development model is of particular benefit as it brings the developers and users closer together. If you find a bug, you can fix it and submit a patch. If you need a new feature, you can write it yourself, or suggest it to the development team.

Tomcat is also the reference implementation of the JSP and Servlet specifications, version 4.0 supporting the latest Servlet 2.3 and JSP 1.2 versions. Many of the principal developers are employed by Sun Microsystems, who are investing considerable manpower into ensuring that Tomcat 4.0 provides a high-quality, robust web container with excellent performance.

A Word on Naming

The naming of Tomcat 4.0 components can be a little confusing, with the names **Tomcat**, **Catalina**, and **Jasper** all flying around. So, to avoid any problems with terminology:

- **Catalina** is a servlet container – that is, an environment within which Java servlets can be hosted.
- **Jasper** is the JSP component of Tomcat – in fact, it's just a servlet that understands how to process requests for JSP pages.

- **Tomcat** comprises Catalina, plus Jasper, plus various extra bits and pieces including batch files for starting and stopping the server, some example web applications, and `mod_webapp`.

- **mod_webapp** is the component that will allow you to connect Tomcat to the Apache web server. Catalina includes a web server of its own, but you may also wish to connect it to an external web server to take advantage of Apache's extra speed when serving static content, or to allow you to run JSP or servlet-based applications alongside applications using other server-side technologies such as PHP. As of this writing `mod_webapp` is in beta testing, but expect it to become stable soon. In time, connectors for other major web servers should also appear.

Basic Tomcat Installation

These steps describe installing Tomcat 4.0 on a Windows 2000 system, but the steps are pretty generic; the main differences between platforms will be the way in which environment variables are set:

- You will need to install the Java 2 Standard Edition software development kit, if you have not already done so. JDK 1.3 can be downloaded from http://java.sun.com/j2se/1.3/.

- Download a suitable Tomcat 4.0 binary distribution for example, `jakarta-tomcat-4.0.1.zip` from http://jakarta.apache.org/builds/jakarta-tomcat-4.0/release/v4.0.1/bin/, and unzip it into a suitable directory.

- On Windows 2000 you have the alternative of downloading a Windows installer, `jakarta-tomcat-4.0.1.exe`, and simply double-clicking its icon. Note that installing Tomcat 4 as a Windows service is as easy as ticking a box.

- Create `CATALINA_HOME` and `JAVA_HOME` environment variables pointing to the directories where you installed the Tomcat and Java 2 SDK files. Typical values are `C:\jakarta-tomcat-4.0.1` for `CATALINA_HOME` and `C:\jdk1.3 for JAVA_HOME`.

Under Windows 2000, environment variables are set using the System control panel. On the Advanced tab, click on the Environment Variables... button. In the resulting dialog box, add `CATALINA_HOME` and `JAVA_HOME` as system variables:

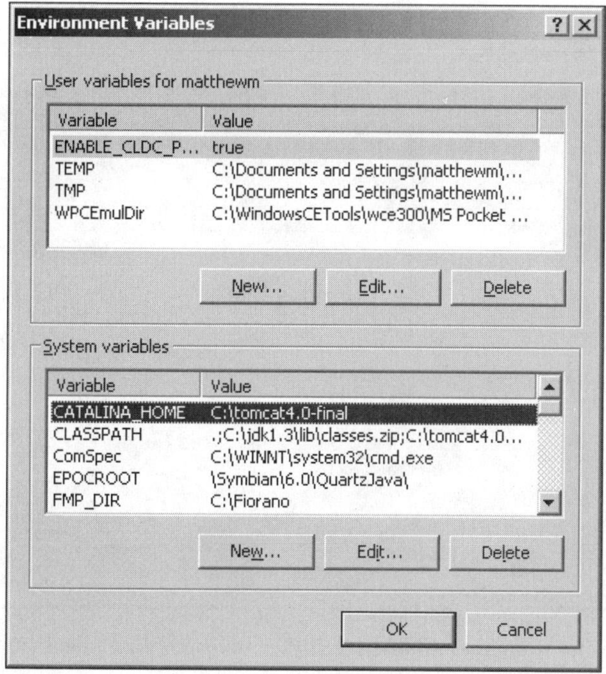

These environment variables allow Tomcat to locate both its own files (using `CATALINA_HOME`), and the Java 2 SDK components it needs, notably the Java compiler, (using `JAVA_HOME`).

If you are using Windows 98, environment variables are set by editing the `C:\autoexec.bat` file. Add the following lines:

```
set CATALINA_HOME=C:\jakarta-tomcat-4.0.1
set JAVA_HOME=C:\jdk1.3
```

Under Windows 98 you will also need to increase the environment space available, by right-clicking on your DOS prompt window, selecting **Properties**, going to the **Memory** tab, and setting the initial environment to 4096 bytes.

Editing the `autoexec.bat` file doesn't work the same on Windows Me as it does on Windows 95/98. First, you need to start Microsoft System Information. You can use either of the following methods:

- Click **Start | Programs | Accessories | System Tools | System Information**.
- Click **Start | Run**, and type `msinfo32.exe` in the **Open** box, and then click **OK**

To create a new entry:

- Select **Tools | System Configuration Utility**
- Click the **Environment** tab, and click **New**
- Enter the appropriate information in the **Variable Name** and **Variable Value** boxes, and then click **OK**

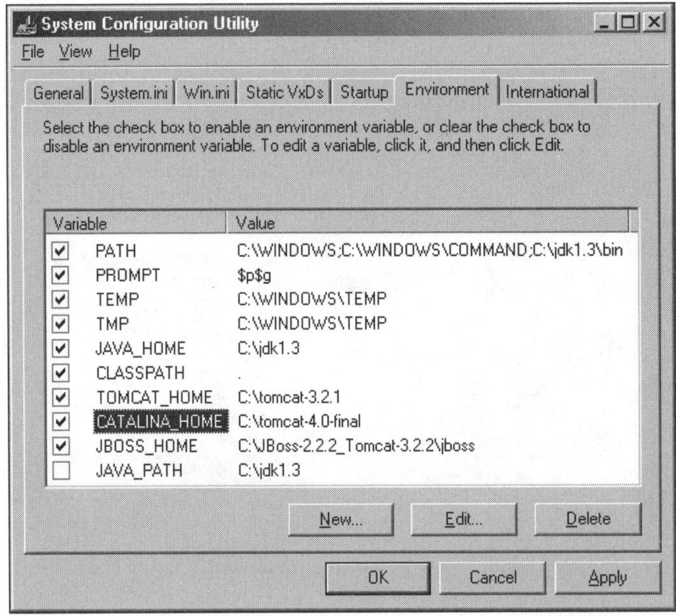

To activate the new environment variable select the corresponding check box for this entry, and restart your computer.

Running Tomcat

Start Tomcat by running the `startup.bat` batch file (`startup.sh` on Unix-type systems), which can be found in the `<CATALINA_HOME>\bin\` directory (in other words, the `bin` directory inside the directory where Tomcat is installed). Alternatively, Windows users can run Tomcat from the Start menu. Choose Start | Programs | Apache Tomcat 4 | Start Tomcat.

Tomcat will start up and print some status messages:

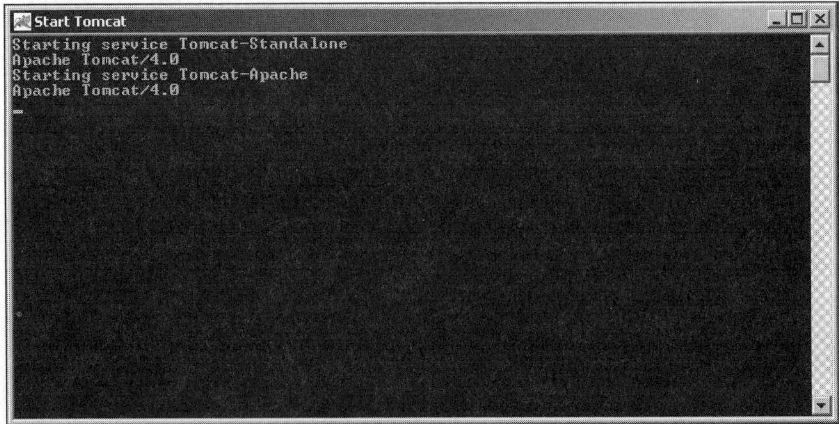

If you have installed Tomcat 4.0 as a service on Windows 2000, it is controlled instead by the Services *utility within* Administrative Tools.

We now have Tomcat 4.0 up and running, using its internal web server (on port 8080). Point your web browser at http://localhost:8080/. You should see the default Tomcat home page:

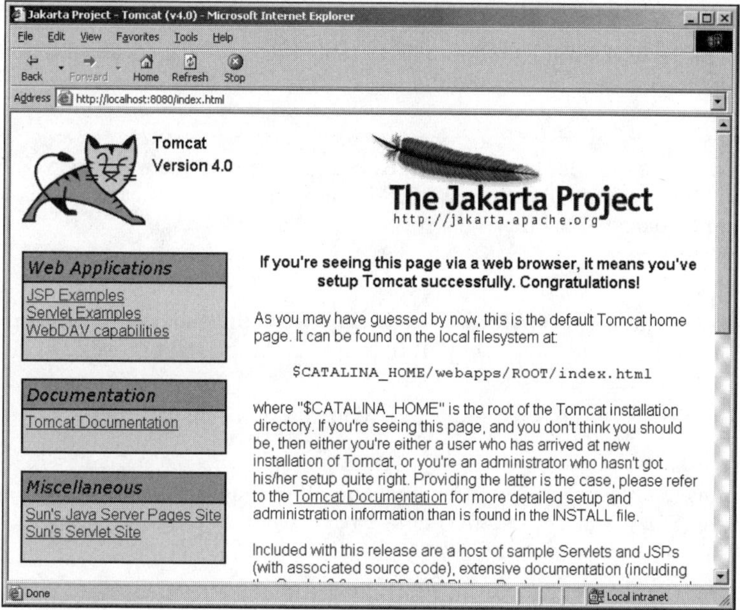

Spend some time exploring the examples and documentation provided with Tomcat.

To shut down Tomcat, run the `shutdown.bat` batch file (`shutdown.sh` on Unix-type systems), again from the `<CATALINA_HOME>\bin\` directory. Again, Windows users can accomplish the same task from the Start menu. Choose Start | Programs | Apache Tomcat 4 | Stop Tomcat.

The Tomcat 4.0 Directory Structure

Looking inside our Tomcat installation directory we find a few text files, and various directories:

- `bin`
  Contains Windows batch files and Unix shell scripts for starting and stopping Tomcat, and for other purposes, together with the `bootstrap.jar` JAR file needed for the first stage of starting Tomcat.

- `classes`
  Not created by default, but if it exists any `.class` files it contains will be visible to all web applications.

- `common`
  Contains Java code needed by all parts of Tomcat: JAR files in the `common\lib\` directory, and `.class` files in `common\classes\`. Notable among the JAR files is `servlet.jar`, which contains the classes defined by the Servlet 2.3 and JSP 1.2 specifications. You will need to have `servlet.jar` listed in your `CLASSPATH` environment variable when compiling classes (for example, servlets) that use these APIs.

- `conf`
  Contains Tomcat's configuration files, notably `server.xml` (dealt with in the *Tomcat 4.0 Configuration* section below) and the server-wide `web.xml`.

> **Note that settings in the server-wide `web.xml` file apply to the whole server, but that this behavior is not mandated by the Servlet specification. Applications making use of it will not be portable to other servlet containers.**

- `lib`
  Populated with various JAR files required by web applications, including parts of the JSP engine. You can add your own JAR files here and they will be visible to all web applications.

- `logs`
  Contains Tomcat's log files. Logging is configured in `server.xml`.

- `server`
  Contains the files comprising Catalina, and other required libraries: JAR files in `server\lib\`, and `.class` files in `server\classes\`.

- `src`
  Contains the source code for Tomcat, along with the documentation (interspersed with the source code).

- `webapps`
  The location where Tomcat looks for web applications to deploy. Any WAR file placed here, or any expanded web application directory structure stored within the directory, will automatically be deployed when Tomcat starts up.

  The URL path under which the application is deployed will correspond to the name of the WAR file or directory; for example, if you place a `myapplication.war` file or a `myapplication` directory within `webapps`, Tomcat will automatically deploy it as http://localhost:8080/myapplication/.

  The automatic deployment settings may not suit your application, in which case you may prefer to store the application outside the `webapps\` directory and configure it as desired using `server.xml`.

- `work`
  Used by Tomcat to store temporary files, notably the `.java` source files and compiled `.class` files created when processing JSP pages.

Tomcat 4.0 Configuration

The Tomcat documentation has improved vastly compared to early versions and should be your first stop if you need to configure Tomcat in any way. However, there are a few steps that are sufficiently common that we cover them here.

Deploying a Web Application

There are two ways to tell Tomcat to deploy a web application:

- As mentioned above, you can deploy an application simply by placing a WAR file or an expanded web application directory structure in the webapps directory.
- However, the default settings may not be suitable for your application, in which case it will be necessary to edit <CATALINA_HOME>\conf\server.xml and add a <Context> element for your application.

The default server.xml file is well commented, and you should read these comments to familiarize yourself with the contents of this file. Various additional elements, not shown or described here but included in the default server.xml, provide for logging and other similar functionality, and define authentication realms. The default server.xml also includes commented-out sections illustrating how to set up a secure (HTTPS) connector, and to set up database-driven authentication realms. It also includes elements that work together with the mod_webapp Apache module.

The outline structure of server.xml is as follows:

```
<Server>
  <Service>
    <Connector/>
    <Engine>
      <Host>
        <Context/>
      </Host>
    </Engine>
  </Service>
</Server>
```

At the top level is a <Server> element, representing the entire Java Virtual Machine:

```
<Server port="8005" shutdown="SHUTDOWN" debug="0">
```

The <Server> element may contain one or more <Service> elements. A <Service> element represents a collection of one or more <Connector> elements that share a single 'container' (and therefore the web applications visible within that container). Normally, that container is an <Engine> element:

```
  <Service name="Tomcat-Standalone">
```

A <Connector> represents an endpoint by which requests are received and responses are returned, passing them on to the associated <Container> (normally an <Engine>) for processing. This <Connector> element creates a non-secure HTTP/1.1 connector, listening on port 8080:

```
    <Connector className="org.apache.catalina.connector.http.HttpConnector"
               port="8080" minProcessors="5" maxProcessors="75"
               acceptCount="10" debug="0"/>
```

An <Engine> element represents the Catalina object that processes every request, passing them on to the appropriate <Host>:

```
    <Engine name="Standalone" defaultHost="localhost" debug="0">
```

The <Host> element is used to define the default virtual host:

```
      <Host name="localhost" debug="0" appBase="webapps">
```

A <Context> element is used to define an individual web application:

```
        <Context path="/examples" docBase="examples" debug="0"
                 reloadable="true">
        </Context>
```

The attributes of the <Context> element are:

- `path`
  Determines the URL prefix where the application will be deployed. In the example above, the application will be found at http://localhost:8080/examples/.
- `docBase`
  Specifies the whereabouts of the WAR file or expanded web application directory structure for the application. Since a relative file path is specified here, Tomcat will look in its `webapps` directory (this was configured in the <Host> element, above) but an absolute file path can also be used.
- `debug`
  Specifies the level of debugging information that will be produced for this application.
- `reloadable`
  Intimates whether the container should check for changes to files that would require it to reload the application. When deploying your application in a production environment, setting its value to `false` will improve performance, as Tomcat will not have to perform these checks.

```
      </Host>
    </Engine>
  </Service>
  <!-- Snip details of service for the mod_webapp connector -->
</Server>
```

The Manager Application

Tomcat 4.0's default configuration includes a web application that allows web applications to be deployed, undeployed, and reloaded while Tomcat is running. This application is installed by default in the `manager` web application, and contains four commands:

- http://localhost:8080/manager/list
  List all web applications currently deployed in this virtual host.

- http://localhost:8080/manager/deploy?path=/myapp&war=mywar
  Deploy the web application specified by the `war` request parameter, at the context path given by the `path` parameter.
- http://localhost:8080/manager/reload?path=/myapp
  Reloads all the Java classes in the specified web application. This works even if automatic class reloading is disabled.
- http://localhost:8080/manager/undeploy?path=/myapp
  Shuts down and undeploys the specified web application.

When specifying a web application to the `deploy` command, the value of the `war` request path must have one of these forms:

- file:/absolute/directory/path
  The absolute path to the directory containing the unpacked web application
- jar:file:/absolute/path/to/mywar.war!/
  A URL specifying the absolute path to the WAR file
- jar:http://host:port/path/to/mywar.war!/
  A URL specifying the location of the HTTP-accessible WAR file

Before you can use the manager application you need to set up a user in `tomcat-users.xml` with the role `manager`:

```
<tomcat-users>
  <user name="tomcat" password="tomcat" roles="tomcat" />
  <user name="role1"  password="tomcat" roles="role1"  />
  <user name="both"   password="tomcat" roles="tomcat,role1" />
  <user name="admin"  password="adminpassword" roles="manager" />
</tomcat-users>
```

With this addition, the manager application works just fine:

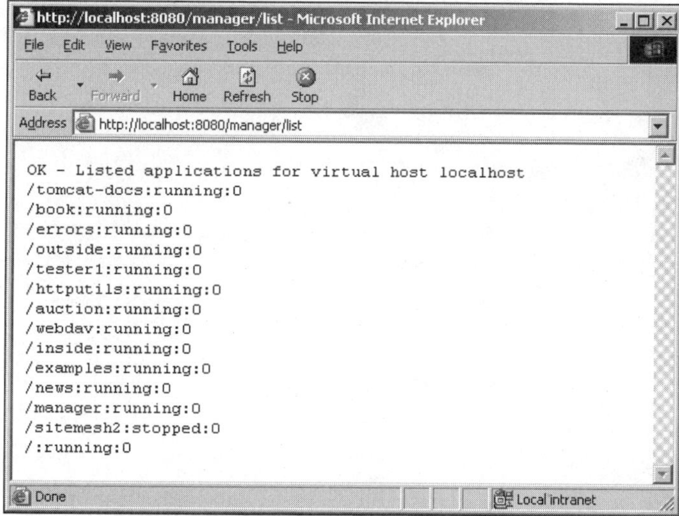

Getting Help

If you need help with Tomcat 4.0, and this appendix and the documentation just haven't helped, your first port of call should be the Tomcat web site, http://jakarta.apache.org/tomcat/. There are two mailing lists dedicated to Tomcat issues:

- tomcat-user
  This is where you can ask questions on configuring and using Tomcat. The Tomcat developers should be on hand to help out as necessary.
- tomcat-dev
  This is where the developers themselves lurk. If you decide to get stuck in with contributing to improving Tomcat itself, this is where the action is.

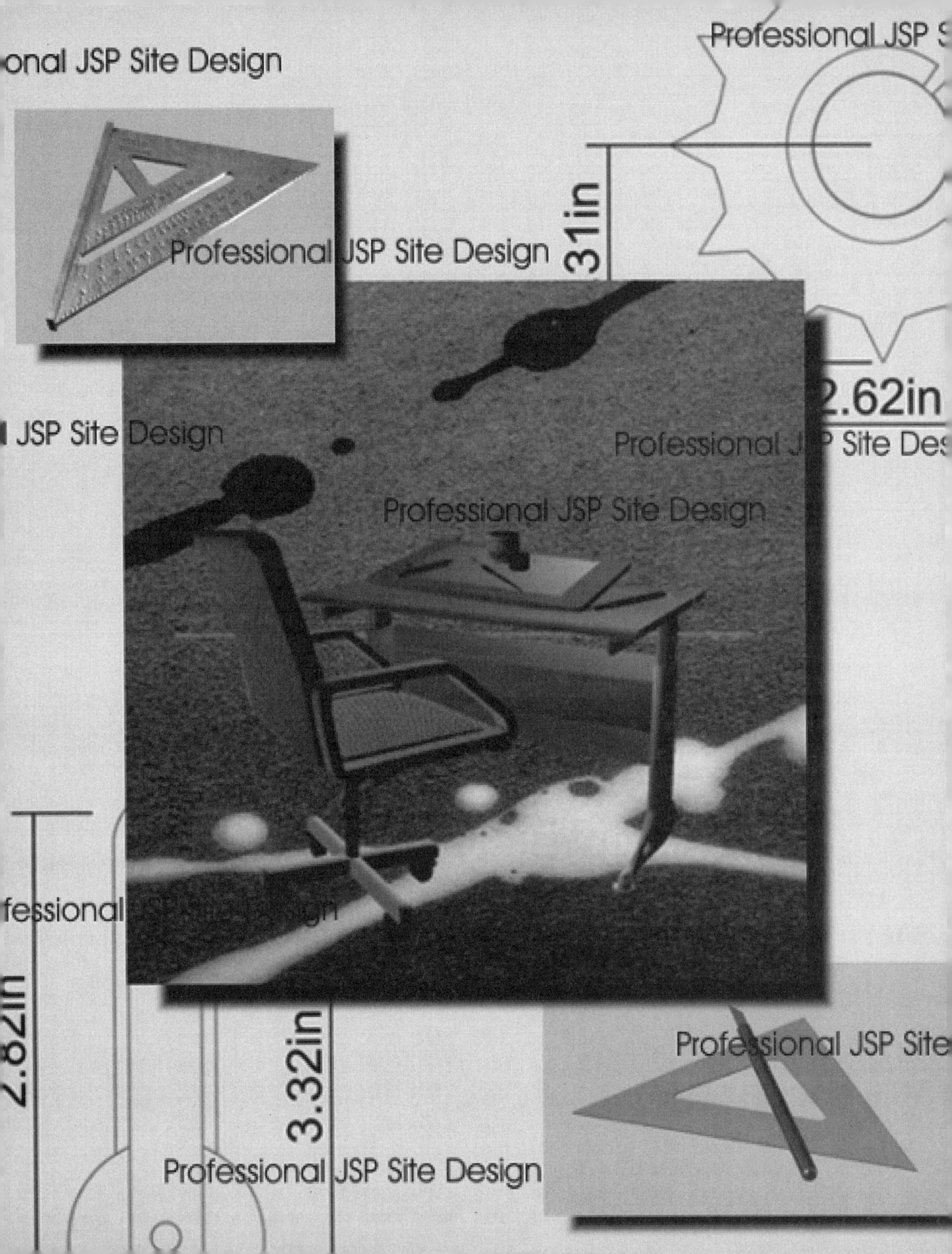

Professional JSP Site Design
31in
Professional JSP Site Design
Professional JSP Site Design
3.32in
Professional JSP Site Design

B

MySQL

This appendix is designed to get you up and running with MySQL.

Installing MySQL on Windows

You can download the latest binary version of MySQL from http://www.mysql.com/. You should download version 3.23.38 or higher, because it will then have binaries for both normal MySQL and for MySQL-Max (which supports transactions).

Here's how to install MySQL on Windows 2000:

- Download MySQL.
- Unzip it in some empty directory and run the `setup.exe` program. By default, MySQL will be installed in `C:\mysql`.
- To start MySQL as a service, you will need to open a command console and move to the folder `C:\mysql\bin`, and type:

```
mysqld-nt --install
```

- You should also start up the extremely useful `winmysqladmin` tool, by double clicking on its icon in the `C:\mysql\bin` folder. This tool allows you to control the MySQL server program. You should see a traffic signal icon representing the tool on the right hand side of your Start menu. Right clicking on this icon brings up a menu that allows you to start and stop the server. Clicking on the Show me option brings up the tool's administrative window. Open this up, and select the my.ini Setup tab. You will see a set of options labeled mysqld file on the left; select the mysqld-max option.

To install MySQL on Windows 98, you will need to follow the same instructions as above, but you should note that MySQL can only be installed as a service on Windows 2000, so skip this step.

Troubleshooting

Here are some handy tips if you encounter problems during installation:

- Check the `C:\mysql\mysql.err` file for debugging information.
- Move to the `C:\mysql\bin` folder and start up MySQL by typing:

```
mysqld --standalone
```

  In this case you may get some useful information on the screen that could help solve our problem.

- Start `mysqld` with the `--standalone` and `--debug` options. In this case `mysqld` will write a log file in `C:\mysqld.trace` that should indicate why `mysqld` won't start.

You can test whether MySQL is working by moving to the `C:\mysql\bin` folder and executing the following command:

```
mysqlshow
+-----------+
| Databases |
+-----------+
| mysql     |
| test      |
+-----------+
```

This will list out the default MySQL databases. To check on your own database, execute the following command:

```
mysqlshow my_database
```

Using MySQL

Now that we have MySQL installed, let's have a little play with it. To do this, we must first invoke the `mysql` command line tool, of which there are two versions. In your command console, move to the folder `C:\MySQL\bin\`, then execute either:

```
mysql
```

Or:

```
mysqld
```

The first command invokes the `mysql` tool compiled on native Windows, which offers very limited text editing capabilities. The second invokes the tool compiled with the Cygnus GNU compiler and libraries, which offers `readline` editing (to use this you must also copy `C:\MySQL\lib\cygwinb19.dll` to `C:\windows\system\`).

Extra care should be taken when MySQL is installed on Windows, because the default privileges on Windows give all local users full privileges to all databases. To make MySQL more secure, you should set a password for all users of MySQL, and remove the default record in the `mysql.user` table that has `Host='localhost'` and `User=''`, using the following command:

```
mysql> DELETE FROM user WHERE Host='localhost' AND User='';
mysql> QUIT
```

The first command removes the appropriate record, and the second quits from the `mysql` tool.

Now, you should also add a password for the root user. To do this, make sure that you are in the `C:\MySQL\bin\` folder, where you can use another command line tool, `mysqladmin`:

```
mysqladmin reload
mysqladmin -u root password your_password
```

After you've set the password, if you want to shutdown the `mysql` server, you can do so using this command:

```
mysqladmin --user=root --password=your_password shutdown
```

Now that you can get the MySQL server up and running securely, you can experiment with some basic database administration issues.

Connecting and Disconnecting to the MySQL Server

To connect to the server, you'll usually need to provide your MySQL username when you invoke `mysql` and, most likely, a password (don't worry about creating a new user account yet – we'll come back to that in a little while). If the server runs on a machine other than the one where you log in, you'll also need to specify a hostname:

```
mysql -h hostname -u username -p
```

Pressing *Enter*, you should see:

```
Enter password:
```

When you have entered it, you should see some introductory information followed by a `mysql>` prompt. After you have connected successfully, you can disconnect at any time by typing `QUIT` at the prompt (in which case you will receive a farewell message):

```
mysql> QUIT
Bye
```

You can also disconnect by pressing *Control-C*. Most examples in the following sections assume you are connected to the server, indicated by the presence of the mysql> prompt.

Issuing SQL Commands at the Command Prompt

It is very important to know how to issue commands and understand the basic principles of entering commands. Here's a simple command that asks the server to tell you the current date:

```
mysql> SELECT CURRENT_DATE;
+--------------+
| CURRENT_DATE |
+--------------+
| 2001-06-27   |
+--------------+
```

Note how we end a SQL statement with a semicolon. This query illustrates several things about the mysql tool:

- A command normally consists of a SQL statement followed by a semicolon. But there are some exceptions where a semicolon is not needed. QUIT, mentioned earlier, is one of them.
- When you issue a command, mysql sends it to the server for execution, and displays any results and then prints another mysql prompt to indicate that it is ready for another command.
- mysql displays query output as a table (rows and columns). The first row contains labels for the columns. The rows following are the query results. Normally, column labels are the names of the columns you fetch from database tables.
- mysql shows how many rows were returned and how long the query took to execute, which gives you a rough idea of server performance.

The command we just entered is a relatively short, single-line statement. However, you can enter multiple statements on a single line, as long as each statement ends with a semicolon. When you press *Enter*, the statements will be executed one after another. You can also carriage return within a statement, as long as you don't break up a word – until you write a semicolon and then press *Enter*, the statement will not be executed. The following table shows each of the prompts you may see and summarizes what they mean about the state that mysql is in:

Prompt	Meaning
mysql>	Ready for new command
->	Waiting for next line of multiple-line command
'>	Waiting for next line, collecting a string that begins with a single quote
">	Waiting for next line, collecting a string that begins with a double quote

MySQL Driver

A number of drivers are available for MySQL, and information about this can be obtained at the MySQL homepage at http://www.mysql.com/, under JDBC. In this book we use the MM.MySQL driver. MM.MySQL is a Type-4 JDBC driver that is available under the GNU Library License.

You should download the binary for this driver, and place it somewhere appropriate (we suggest the Tomcat common\lib\ folder). A complete listing of available JDBC drivers can be found at http://industry.java.sun.com/products/jdbc/drivers/.

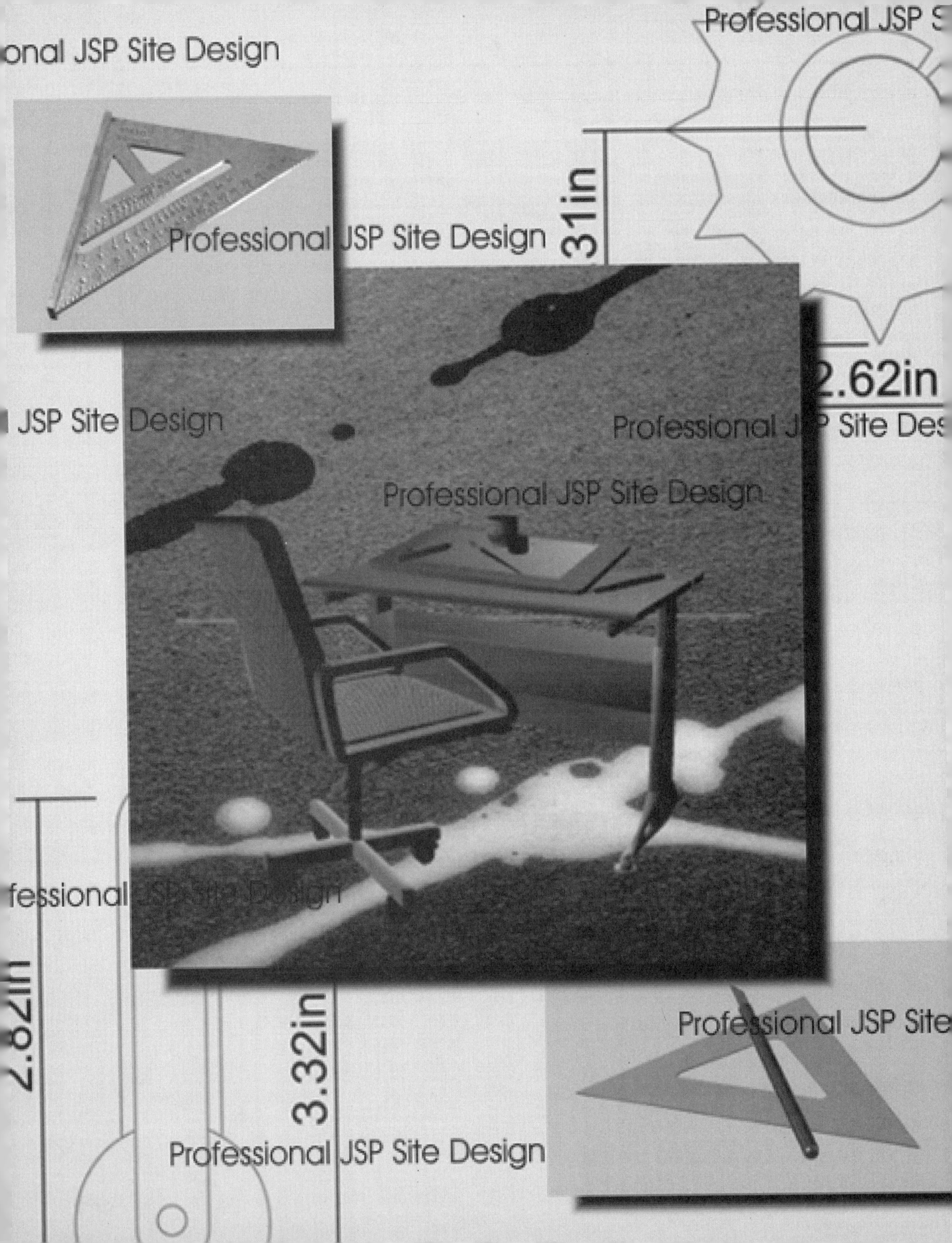
Professional JSP Site Design
Professional JSP Site Design
31in
2.62in
Professional JSP Site Design
Professional JSP Site Design
3.32in
Professional JSP Site Design
Professional JSP Site Design

The Apache Software License

This appendix contains the text of the Apache Software License, used by some of the code quoted in this book.

```
/* ====================================================================
 *
 *                  The Apache Software License, Version 1.1
 *
 *         Copyright (c) 1999, 2000 The Apache Software Foundation.
 *                           All rights reserved.
 *
 * ====================================================================
 *
 * Redistribution and use in source and binary forms, with or without modi-
 * fication, are permitted provided that the following conditions are met:
 *
 * 1. Redistributions of source code must retain the above copyright notice
 *    notice, this list of conditions and the following disclaimer.
 *
 * 2. Redistributions in binary form must reproduce the above copyright
 *    notice, this list of conditions and the following disclaimer in the
 *    documentation and/or other materials provided with the distribution.
 *
 * 3. The end-user documentation included with the redistribution, if any,
 *    must include the following acknowlegement:
 *
 *       "This product includes software developed by the Apache Software
 *        Foundation <http://www.apache.org/>."
 *
 *    Alternately, this acknowlegement may appear in the software itself, if
 *    and wherever such third-party acknowlegements normally appear.
 *
```

```
* 4. The names "The Jakarta Project", "Tomcat", and "Apache Software
 *    Foundation" must not be used to endorse or promote products derived
 *    from this software without prior written permission. For written
 *    permission, please contact <apache@apache.org>.
 *
 * 5. Products derived from this software may not be called "Apache" nor may
 *    "Apache" appear in their names without prior written permission of the
 *    Apache Software Foundation.
 *
 * THIS SOFTWARE IS PROVIDED "AS IS" AND ANY EXPRESSED OR IMPLIED WARRANTIES
 * INCLUDING, BUT NOT LIMITED TO, THE IMPLIED WARRANTIES OF MERCHANTABILITY
 * AND FITNESS FOR A PARTICULAR PURPOSE ARE DISCLAIMED. IN NO EVENT SHALL
 * THE APACHE SOFTWARE FOUNDATION OR ITS CONTRIBUTORS BE LIABLE FOR ANY
 * DIRECT, INDIRECT, INCIDENTAL, SPECIAL, EXEMPLARY, OR CONSEQUENTIAL
 * DAMAGES (INCLUDING, BUT NOT LIMITED TO, PROCUREMENT OF SUBSTITUTE GOODS
 * OR SERVICES; LOSS OF USE, DATA, OR PROFITS; OR BUSINESS INTERRUPTION)
 * HOWEVER CAUSED AND ON ANY THEORY OF LIABILITY, WHETHER IN CONTRACT,
 * STRICT LIABILITY, OR TORT (INCLUDING NEGLIGENCE OR OTHERWISE) ARISING IN
 * ANY WAY OUT OF THE USE OF THIS SOFTWARE, EVEN IF ADVISED OF THE
 * POSSIBILITY OF SUCH DAMAGE.
 *
 * ====================================================================
 *
 * This software consists of voluntary contributions made by many indivi-
 * duals on behalf of the Apache Software Foundation. For more information
 * on the Apache Software Foundation, please see <http://www.apache.org/>.
 *
 * ====================================================================
 */
```

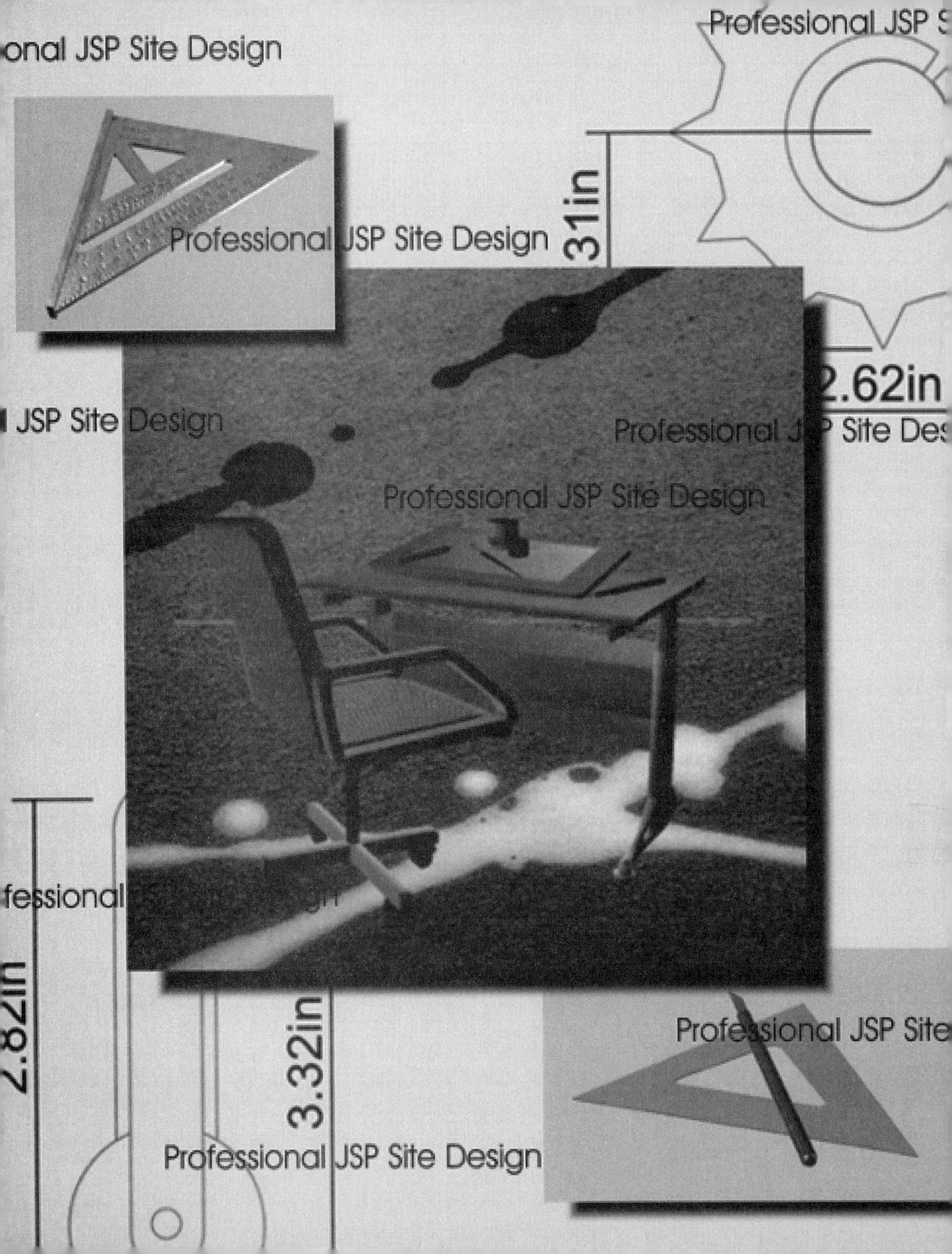
Professional JSP Site Design
31in
Professional JSP Site Design
Professional JSP Site Design
3.32in

Index

A Guide to the Index

The index is arranged hierarchically, in alphabetical order, with symbols preceding the letter A. Most second-level entries and many third-level entries also occur as first-level entries. This is to ensure that users will find the information they require however they choose to search for it.

Symbols

A

B

C

D

E

F

G

H

K

L

M

S

T

U

V

W

X

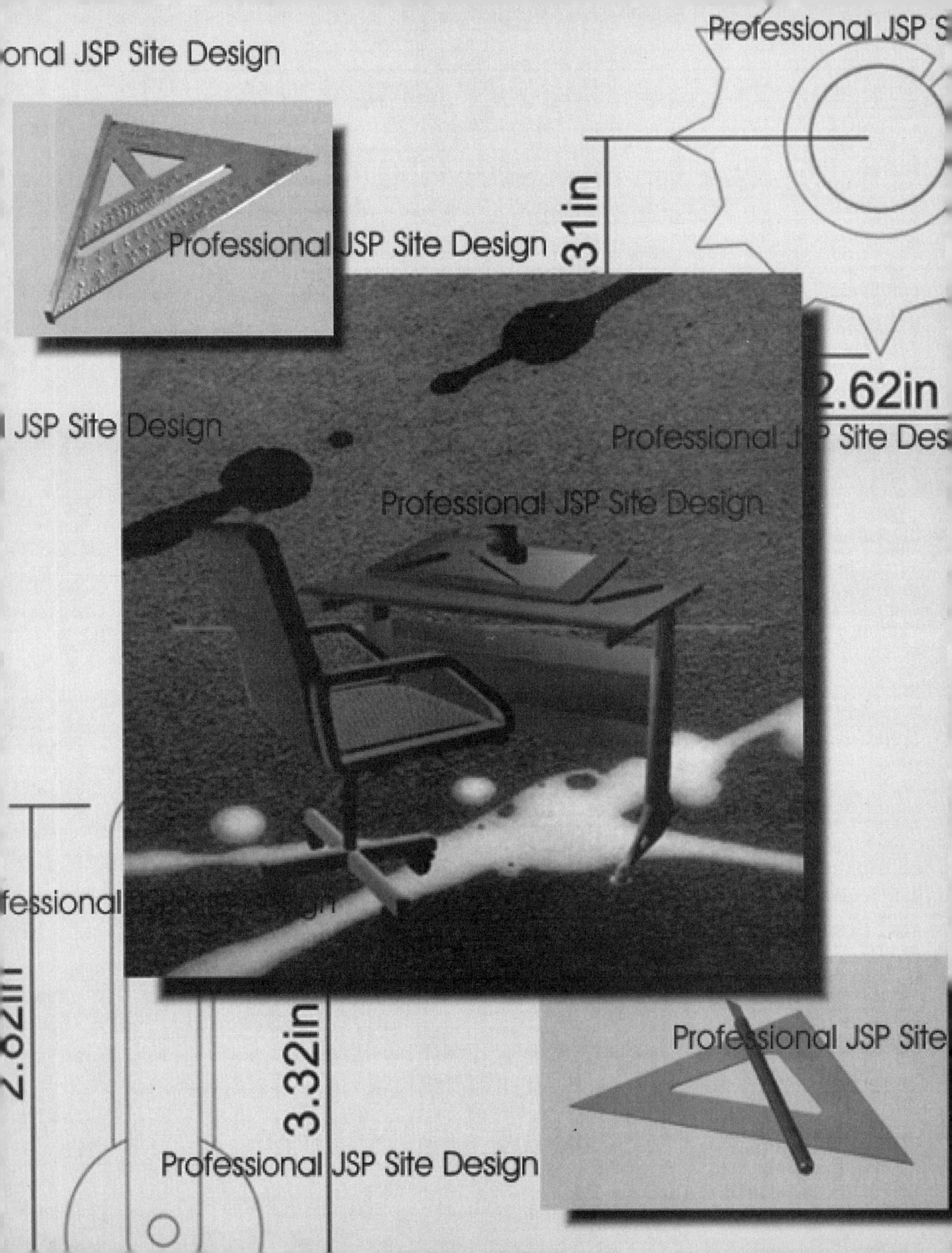
Professional JSP Site Design
31in
Professional JSP Site Design
3.32in
Professional JSP Site Design

Wrox writes books for you. Any suggestions, or ideas about how you want information given in your ideal book will be studied by our team. Your comments are always valued at Wrox.

Free phone in USA 800-USE-WROX
Fax (312) 893 8001

UK Tel.: (0121) 687 4100 Fax: (0121) 687 4101

Pro JSP Site Design – Registration Card

Name ______
Address ______

______

______

City ______ State/Region ______
Country ______ Postcode/Zip ______
E-Mail ______
Occupation ______
How did you hear about this book?
π Book review (name) ______
π Advertisement (name) ______
π Recommendation ______
π Catalog ______
π Other ______
Where did you buy this book?
π Bookstore (name) ______ City ______
π Computer store (name) ______
π Mail order ______

What influenced you in the purchase of this book?
☐ Cover Design ☐ Contents ☐ Other (please specify):

______

How did you rate the overall content of this book?
☐ Excellent ☐ Good ☐ Average ☐ Poor

What did you find most useful about this book? ______

What did you find least useful about this book? ______

Please add any additional comments. ______

What other subjects will you buy a computer book on soon?

What is the best computer book you have used this year?

Note: This information will only be used to keep you updated abo t new Wrox Press titles and will not be sed for

5512 Check here if you DO NOT want to receive support for this book ☐ 5512

Note: If you post the bounce back card below in the UK, please send it to:

Wrox Press Limited, Arden House, 1102 Warwick Road,
Acocks Green, Birmingham B27 6HB. UK.

Computer Book Publishers

NO POSTAGE
NECESSARY
IF MAILED
IN THE
UNITED STATES

BUSINESS REPLY MAIL

FIRST CLASS MAIL PERMIT#64 CHICAGO, IL

POSTAGE WILL BE PAID BY ADDRESSEE

WROX PRESS INC.
29 S. LA SALLE ST.
SUITE 520
CHICAGO IL 60603-USA